Mohammed Ali Jinnah

'If we want to make this great State of Pakistan happy and prosperous we should wholly and solely concentrate on the well-being of the people, and especially of the masses and the poor. ---- Where everyone would work together in a spirit that every one of you, no matter to what community he belongs ---- no matter what his colour, caste or creed, is first, second and last a citizen of this State with equal rights, privileges and obligations.

'You are free; you are free to go to your temples, you are free to go to your mosques or to any other place of worship ---- You may belong to any religion or creed ---- My guiding principle will be justice and complete impartiality and I am sure with your support and cooperation I can look forward to Pakistan becoming one of the greatest nations of the world'.

Quaid-e-Azam Mohammed Ali Jinnah
11th August 1947.

PAKISTAN

ROOTS, PERSPECTIVE AND GENESIS

KHAN HUSSAN ZIA

Order this book online at www.trafford.com
or email orders@trafford.com

Most Trafford titles are also available at major online book retailers.

Printed in the United States of America.

ISBN: 978-1-4269-5586-0 (sc)

Trafford rev. 01/26/2011

Trafford PUBLISHING www.trafford.com

North America & International
toll-free: 1 888 232 4444 (USA & Canada)
phone: 250 383 6864 • fax: 812 355 4082

To Mohammed Ali Jinnah

The people of Pakistan and Bangladesh owe him a profound debt of gratitude that could never be surpassed or repaid.

And

In memory of more than one million innocent men, women and children who lost their lives in the struggle for Pakistan.

Voh azaadion kay thay khursheed Jalib
Unhi kay lahoo say khilay hein gulistaan

They gave us the true light of freedom, Jalib
Their blood nourishes the gardens that now bloom.

Front cover: A *Kaflah* (caravan) of refugees on its way to Pakistan in 1947 ---- weary men, women and children of all ages with their livestock and meager belongings. These often stretched for twenty-five miles or more along the roads and remained subject to depredation by marauding bands of killers, disease, floods and vagaries of the elements for weeks before reaching safety in Pakistan. An estimated nine million Muslims were evicted from India and moved to both wings of Pakistan, mostly over a period of three months from August to November 1947. At the same time between five and six million Hindus and Sikhs migrated to India from Pakistan.

CONTENTS

PREFACE

Most of the books on the creation of Pakistan have been written before the British Government made bulk of the documents dealing with the transfer of power in India available to the public. Even though there is still some information relating to Kashmir and the division of Punjab to which access is denied, publication of the twelve volumes of *Transfer of Power* documents and the breaking of silence by some of the key players in the game has made it possible to look at the subject in new light.

Not all of the existing publications meet the desired standards in terms of reality and objectivity. Many of these have been tendentious. Historians in India generally like to blame partition of the sub-continent on some vested Muslim interests or the vanity and personal ambition of Mohammad Ali Jinnah, the founder of Pakistan. The rise in religious sentiment in Pakistan, on the other hand, has led to attempts that confuse the demand for a separate homeland for Muslims in India with the quest for an Islamic theocratic state. None of this has a basis in fact.

Some excellent books have been published in Britain in recent years. As is only natural, these have mostly viewed events from an essentially British perspective. It is not easy for outsiders to fully comprehend the deeper cultural issues that form the attitudes and ethos of people who are different and alien. The earlier books on Partition in particular suffered because of the limitation and dubious quality of some of the sources available at the time. Some of the versions of events as presented by the last Viceroy Lord Louis Mountbatten in particular have now been found to be questionable.

There is a strong tendency to view historical events from a geo-political and not so much from a human perspective. This is true for politicians as much as it is for the historians. Most of the problems found in the post-colonial world especially can be traced to this propensity. Another common error that westerners make in particular is their failure to understand and appreciate the part religion plays in the lives of both the Hindus and Muslims. It is very different to attitudes found in the West. Any understanding of India remains incomplete unless one accepts and comes to grips with this basic fact.

It is gross over-simplification and a serious misreading of history to attribute division of the country to the egotism of one man or the selfish interests of some land-owning individuals. The seeds of Pakistan lie deep in history, in the exclusive and intolerant nature that is inherent in Hinduism. The book is intended as an exploration both into India's past as well as its cultural, religious and social make-up. It is only through acquaintance with all these factors that we can begin to understand not only the country but also the inevitability of its division.

There has been much discussion of the so-called two-nation theory as the justification or basis for Pakistan. It is only relevant as an expression of the fact that Hindus and Muslims are different not simply in terms of religion and culture but their entire ethos. They were only made part of the same administrative edifice through the application of external force. Beyond this the concept of nationhood and nation-state is not strictly relevant. These institutions evolved in Europe under a very different set of circumstances. It is confusing to discuss these in the context of the situation in India.

A nation must be by-and-large homogenous by definition. Hindu society's caste structure is the very antithesis of homogeneity. Outside of the main cities, Pakistan basically remains a collection of hundreds of tribes. They may not be separated in the same way as the Hindu castes and sub-castes nor socially and culturally divided to the same extent but it still does not make them a cohesive nation. Perhaps, the people that come closest to complying with the concept in the sub-continent may only be the Bangladeshis or possibly the Sikhs.

Having said this, the people in Pakistan have a lot more in common with each other when compared with the inhabitants of most of the other countries in the area. The country is unified and rendered indivisible economically by the River Indus and its tributaries that help sustain its life. There is a common history extending back more than five thousand years to the days of the Indus Valley Civilisation. With the exception of one or two small groups, like the Brohis and Makranis, almost all of the people are descended from the same Aryan stock. They are culturally very similar, have the same religion and a common language they all understand. There are few social taboos and they readily intermarry. These are the primary attributes that form the basis of a nation. The rest is only a matter of time.

There is much propaganda these days that Pakistan may not be a viable state. The state of Israel was created at about the same time as Pakistan. The people who occupied it had never even lived in it. For two thousand years they had inhabited different parts of the world and countries with different cultures, speaking different languages and only had religion as the common bond. Despite this, no one talks of Israel as a non-viable country but there is no shortage of the detractors of Pakistan which is so much more cohesive, integrated and relevant.

Much is also made of religious extremism and incidents of terrorism in the country. These are not peculiar to Pakistan or the Muslims. According to the list compiled by FBI, Muslims were involved only in six per cent of all the terrorist acts committed in the US between 1980 and 2005, as against the Jews in seven per cent and Latinos in forty-two per cent. The European Union's *Terrorism Situation and Trend Report* for 2010 indicates that out of a total of 294 'failed, foiled or successfully executed' terrorist attacks in Europe in 2009 only one was by Muslim extremists (article by Dan Gardener in *The Ottawa Citizen* of 5th January 2011). Extremists can be found in any religion be it Christianity, Judaism or Hinduism. The same is true for acts of terrorism. Britain was subjected to these for twenty years. It is the same with Spain but no one reads anything more into these situations. Arguably, the vast majority of acts of terrorism in the Muslim countries have their basis in the excesses committed against them through economic exploitation, political interference and military occupation by the western powers.

Western civilization and culture have dominated the world for more than two centuries. Their influence on India has been profound. The reaction of the Muslims to this development has been interesting. In many ways it is an on-going saga. History appears to be repeating itself if we take a closer look at the Islamic movements that arose after the passing of the Mughal Empire and the advent of British colonialism. This is a different subject and does not form part of the present discussion. The reader may like to refer to the author's book *Muslims and the West: A Muslim Perspective* for a better understanding of developments in the Muslim world.

I was fortunate in having had the opportunity to personally discuss events related to the partition of India with some of the individuals who had been in key positions at the time. Among others, these included Christopher Beaumont, Secretary to the Radcliffe Commission; Lord Listowel, the last Secretary of State for India and Sir Ian Scott, Deputy Private Secretary to the Viceroy Lord Louis Mountbatten. It helped in clarifying some of the issues that would have remained in doubt otherwise. The copies of letters, in particular those of Christopher Beaumont, are being made available in a separate publication. His deposition and letters from Sir Ian Scott confirming Mountbatten's manipulation of the findings of the Radcliffe Commission are attached in the Annex.

It only remains for me to acknowledge my debt to scores of publishers and authors whose writings have made it possible to complete this book. It is impossible to name all of them individually. But there are a few names that must be mentioned if only because they have been quoted much more extensively. These include Annemarie Schimmel, Saad R. Khairi, Lawrence James, Sir Stanley Lane-poole, Richard Hall, Patrick French, Andrew Roberts, William Dalrymple, Beverley Nichols, Katherine Mayo, Will Durant, Nicholas Mansergh, and late Professor E.W.R. Lumby who helped compile some of the twelve volumes of *The Transfer of Power 1942-7* and whose lectures at the Royal Naval College, Greenwich did so much to develop my interest in history. To them and so many others I owe an immense debt of gratitude.

K. Hussan Zia
147 Ahmed Block
New Garden Town
Lahore.

January 2011

CHAPTER 1

HISTORY, HINDUS AND HINDUISM

The name 'India' is a western expression that originated with the Greeks. The Persians and Arabs called the inhabitants of this vast land 'Hindu', a somewhat derogatory term implying a dark-skinned person and the land itself as *Hind.* The western part of the land next to Persia was called *Sir-Hind* meaning the 'start of Hind'. The word later became Sindh and was used for the province and the river that flowed through it. The Europeans called the sub-continent Hindia or India as a derivative of Hind and the Turkic people called it Hindustan.

Ancient Hindu texts refer to the land between the rivers Sarasvati and Jumna generally as '*Bharat',* without defining any precise geographic location or boundaries. The Sarasvati flowed westward between Jumna and Sutlej rivers and may have joined up with the Indus. It dried up probably around 2,000 BC for reasons as yet undetermined. Bharat is the official name given to the present day Republic of India. It is not entirely clear what connection, if any, this name might have to the legendary figure, *Bharata,* in the seventh century BC Hindu epic, *Mahabharata.* India's western neighbours have always called it '*Hind'* or *'Hindustan',* implying land of the Hindus.

The ancient Hindus never had a name of their own for the whole of the sub-continent, only for its different regions. Their religious texts, the *Puranas*, had divided the region into nine different areas. The Chinese explorer, Hiuen Tsiang, who visited the land in seventh century AD, speaks of it as five different countries consisting of a total of eighty kingdoms. Whatever the name, India was never a unified country as such, except for relatively short periods of time, nor were its inhabitants ever a nation in the conventional sense.

As far as the inhabitants of this region are concerned, they have been more varied than perhaps in any other comparable corner of the world. They differ from each other in almost every imaginable respect, from race and colour to language, culture and religion. Kashmiris in the north are tall and have fair skins, often brown hair and Caucasoid features. Tamils in the south are black while Bengalis and Assamese in the east have dark brown skins and slightly flat features that may be indicative of admixture with East Asians. The differences in their languages, religions and cultures are equally stark. Even today, there are over two hundred distinct languages, more than fifty scripts and in excess of five hundred different dialects spoken in India. Apart from other things it indicates how disconnected and disparate various regions have remained, over long periods of time in the past, to have evolved so differently.

Politically, the region was composed of numerous small and large independent or vassal principalities that exercised varying degrees of control over thousands of fortified towns and villages, each under the thumb of the local landlord (*zamindar*). In the early nineteenth century AD, India was made up of more than six hundred and seventy five large and small independent princely states. Tropical jungle or scrub forests, infested with wild beasts and equally wild bandits (*dakoos* or *dakaits*), separated and isolated these communities from each other. In the absence of adequate year-round communication, inter-action between settlements was limited, which has been the main cause for the existence of a bewildering number of cultures and sub-cultures.

The boundaries of the states seldom had any basis in ethnicity or racial and cultural affinity. Their ownership and borders changed constantly, depending upon the relative military strength and ambitions of their rulers at any given time. It is true that for the past one thousand years or so, there was a form of central government continuously based at or near Delhi. The limits and effectiveness of its influence remained fluid and fluctuated constantly in relation to the vigour and inclination of each king. Apart from collecting taxes and dispensing favours to a chosen few, these kings did not have many other interests and the states were left to the mercy of their own individual rulers. Power has always flowed downwards in India. There was never any tradition of public participation, sharing or even consultation. Basically, this is how India remained in essence until 1859, when the British Crown formally took over the country.

MISTS OF HISTORY

The early history of India is very murky. Precious little is known about its aboriginal people and their culture. This is particularly true of those that inhabited the Gangetic plain and the Deccan plateau that constitute the territory of present day India and where most of the Hindus are concentrated. In his *Histories*, a dizzily digressive and often fanciful nine-volume account of the Persian Wars of 490 to 479 B.C, among other things, the Greek historian Herodotus speaks of India being inhabited by cannibalistic people. They left few monuments and do not appear to have mastered any form of writing. All that we know about pre-historic times, with any degree of certainty, is limited to the areas that more or less now comprise Pakistan.

The evidence so far excavated in these parts indicates the existence of an advanced civilisation all along the length of the Indus Valley at about the time when Egyptian and Sumerian civilisations flourished ---- circa 3000 BC. From all accounts, the level of sophistication, as evidenced by the relics found there, was very high by contemporary standards. There are many indications of the existence of contacts and inter-action with the civilizations in Egypt and Sumer. So far, no evidence of any kind has been unearthed that might indicate any relationship or link with people to the east in the areas that now constitute India.

Unfortunately, it has not been possible to-date to decipher the language which makes it difficult to ascertain many of the details and nature of the Indus Valley Civilisation. What is highly baffling as well as tantalising is that the pictographic script found there bears a striking and uncanny resemblance to the mysterious ancient *Rongo-Rongo* writings found half way around the world in Easter Island in the Pacific (*Mysteries From Forgotten Worlds*, by Charles Berlitz, Dell Publishing Co. Inc. New York, 1973, p.128). The Indus Valley Civilisation became extinct around 1500 BC, possibly, as a consequence of the Aryan invasions.

There is growing evidence of the existence of an equally advanced civilization, at about the same time in the Potohar Plateau to the north, centred on Taxila (Taksha Sila). Excavations carried out in the 1960s have revealed signs of an advanced stone-age human settlement at Serai Kala, close to Taxila, dating back to 3100 BC. In due course, the inhabitants of these parts developed cultural and commercial links that extended as far as Persia and Greece.

A Greek admiral, Skylax, is reported to have reconnoitered the Indus for Darius Histaspes, the Archaemenian ruler of Persia, in 512 BC. In its wake, Darius invaded and occupied the northern reaches of the territories drained by the river. Herodotus has recorded these events. Recent excavations at Mehrgarh in Baluchistan, have pushed back the history of civilised human settlement in the area to beyond 8000 BC but there is much work to be done before a more tangible picture can be pieced together.

It was some time after 3000 BC that waves of Aryan migration from Central Asia or the Caspian region started to push into northern India and eastward down the Gangetic plain, displacing the aboriginal Bheel, Gond, Santhal, Dravid, Naga and other (*Adivasi*) people in the process. The Aryans were primarily herdsmen and had no written language. The Indus Valley culture that collapsed around 1500 BC had no apparent connection to these people. It pre-dated their arrival in India and was neither the progenitor of the Aryans nor connected in any way with what was taking place in the territory of present-day India.

In purely historical terms, the time between 1500 BC and 500 BC, the so-called Vedic Age, remains a blank period in India's past. There is no evidence of any writings or written records for one thousand years. All we have are some oral traditions such as the *Vedas* and a few mythical stories like the Hindu epics *Mahabharata* and *Ramayana* to go by, none of which seem to indicate any specific knowledge, reference or connection to the earlier Indus Valley Civilisation.

These oral traditions, almost certainly, have not been preserved in their original form. Even Will Durant, who waxes lyrical about every thing Hindu, is forced to admit in his '*The Story of Civilisation: Part 1, Our Oriental Heritage*', Simon and Schuster, New York, 1954, (p.537) that the Hindu tradition has a 'school boy's scorn for dates'. It is not dates alone that are treated with scorn. Facts, figures and reality also receive the same treatment. In the face of this, it is impossible to write a credible and meaningful history based on such fanciful and rather dubious and questionable data.

In the absence of verifiable corroborative evidence of times, facts, figures and events, anyone is free to claim almost anything and flights of imagination of individuals tend to have often been labeled as history. Most of what has been written about conditions in India prior to 500 BC is little more than romantic and fanciful conjecture and guess work that should be treated with extreme caution. Even after this period, especially from about the 7th to 10th century AD, the sources need to be examined with a wary and watchful eye, if one is to avoid being misled and arrive at the wrong conclusions.

BASIS OF RELIGION

As stated earlier, the origins of Aryan culture were distinctly nomadic. After settling in the plains and cohabiting with indigenous people, a set of rules gradually evolved. These were predicated on Shamanistic beliefs adapted to local needs that incorporated Aryan exclusivity and superiority. The rules and practices eventually coalesced to form the basis of Hindu religion and its caste system. The inclusion of elements such as cow worship is clearly reflective of the nomadic herdsmen's past when life depended on the well-being of the animals they possessed.

A clear indication of the Aryan origin of Hinduism in India is evident from the prevalence and use of the swastika as a religious symbol. It is a sign like the Greek cross, with arms bent at right-angles that appears in all the cultures derived from the Aryans. The best known example, perhaps, was its depiction on the arm bands of Nazi Germans, including Hitler.

Western observers have been particularly harsh in their descriptions of Hinduism as a religion. With the apology that it is 'an attack on a system and not on a people,' the British author, columnist and Member of Parliament, Beverley Nichols, typifies these prejudices when he portrays Hinduism to be 'a mass of purely human superstitions, deifying instinct, sanctifying convenience, and giving divine authority to human passion, till it found itself saddled with thousands of gods, some of them of the most disreputable character, "gods" of greed and "gods" of lust' (*Verdict on India*, by Beverley Nichols, Jonathan Cape, London, 1944, p.77). He also quotes the late eighteenth century Frenchman, Abbe Dubois as stating:

'*The Hindus originally possessed a conception, imperfect though it was, of the true God; but this knowledge grew more and more dim, until at last it became extinguished in the darkness of error, of ignorance and of corruption. Confounding the Creator with His creatures, they set up gods who were merely myths and monstrosities, and to them they addressed their prayers and directed their worship, both of which were as false as the attributes they assigned to these divinities. And as a matter of course, the taint of corruption which characterizes all the religious institutions of the Hindus has duly left its mark on their social morality. How, indeed, could virtue prevail in a country where all the vices of mankind are justified by those of their gods?'*

The basic concepts of Hinduism are very different to those of the more commonly known religions that originated in the Middle East. Divine authority of a single central Supreme Being is diluted and diffused amongst a plethora of lesser deities. There is no book like the Bible or the Koran, no Prophet and no historical basis like that of Moses, Jesus or Mohammed. There is no church nor is there a central religious authority like the Vatican.

The nearest approach to the Bible or the Koran in Hinduism is the Bhagwat Geeta, a work of great spiritual beauty in the eyes of many. According to legend it was spoken by Lord Krishna on the battlefield of Kurukshetra. Its main teaching is that knowledge is bound up with one's inner self. Hinduism also embodies the concepts of *Karma*, re-incarnation and the caste system that are not easily explained or understood by non-Hindus in particular.

All this makes it extremely difficult to define exactly what constitutes Hinduism. There are as many different explanations and answers as there are people to explain it. To outside observers, the religion may appear more like a loose collection of local myths and nebulous notions but, as is only natural, these are very real as far as the believers are concerned. There are many forms of Hinduism that have differed from time to time and from region to region. Not all of the factions are vegetarian and some, like the devotees of Goddess *Kali*, still engage in gruesome ritualistic animal sacrifices. Whereas killing of animals is generally regarded as sin in Hinduism, killing these as sacrifice to the gods is permissible, at least, according to Mr. Gandhi ('*Mother India'*, by Katherine Mayo, Jonathan Cape, London, pp. 15, 225).

It needs to be mentioned that Katherine Mayo and the publication of her book generated a huge outcry among the Hindus. It seemed to have touched a raw nerve. All kinds of motives were attributed to Miss Mayo, including that she had been subsidized to write the book in order to degrade India in the eyes of the world and to prejudice her case for self-government. Mr. Gandhi himself became a part of the controversy (see chapter *Muslim Re-awakening*). Nonetheless, as the *Manchester Guardian* noted on 25th March 1929, '----- (the book) *had done more to help the cause of India's women than all that has been written by Indian social reformers in this century*'.

Will Durant, quoting Sir Charles Eliot ('*Buddhist India*') and H. Kohn ('*History of Nationalism in the East*'), states that at least until the last century (1854 AD) these bloody rituals involved human sacrifice as well, '*Kali particularly had an appetite for men, but the Brahmins explained that she would eat only men of the lower castes'* (pp. 509 and 520, and '*Hindu Manners, Customs and Ceremonies*, by Abbe J. A. Dubois, Clarendon Press, Oxford, 1924, p. 597 and '*The Oxford History of India*', by Vincent Smith, p.690).

It is often claimed that all this was in the distant past. That is not necessarily the case. Ritual sacrifice of infants by throwing them into the Ganges was commonly practiced by the Hindus until banned by the British in 1832. The BBC TV, in its news on 11th April 2006, aired gruesome video footage that depicted child sacrifice to Goddess *Kali* being offered in parts of India to this day. In April 2009 an Indian farmer ritually sacrificed his grand-daughter believing that it will give him a bountiful crop. Child marriage was not made illegal until 1932, against fierce resistance by most Hindus. It was never accepted and the law was found to be virtually impossible to enforce. Even the Hindu Nobel Laureate, Rabindranath Tagore defended the institution in his writings.

An English eye witness recorded in 1944, '*I have myself stood in the Monkey Temple at Benares while streams of little girls, who could not have been more than twelve years old, were dragged towards the idols to implore the blessings of fertility. Their faces were stamped with the memory of terrible things, and their bodies cringed, as though in shame, because they had not yet fulfilled the divine duty of maternity. I have seen those same little girls in the Kali Temple at Calcutta, cutting off locks of their long hair and tying them round the branches of a sacred cactus, while the Brahmin priest mumbled a string of prayers to hasten the advent of pregnancy*' (Verdict on India, p.74).

More than in any other religion, it is the priests (*Brahmins*) who decide what is permissible and acceptable and what is not. In the absence of a common standard text, their views and practices are bound to vary widely, from individual to individual and from one place to the next, which makes it all the more difficult for outsiders to comprehend the true nature of Hinduism. Whatever religious texts there were, like the *Rig Vedas,* remained in the exclusive custody of the *Brahmins* who were required to commit them to memory, as there was a ban on writing them down. The oldest known manuscript of the V*edas* dates from fifteenth century AD ---- about three thousand years after their assumed time of composition.

It is speculated that there might have been many more *Vedas* (collections of verses of knowledge) than the four that have survived. What are left are *Rig Veda* (hymns of praise), *Sama Veda* (music), *Yajur Veda* (formulas for sacrifices) and *Atharva Veda,* (magic formulas). Each of the Vedas is divided into four parts; *Mantaras* (hymns), *Brahmanas* (rituals and incantations), *Aranyaka* (texts for hermits) and *Upnishads* (philosophic discourse). Even though their origins are unknown and they have been altered and added to from time to time, the Vedas are considered by the Hindus to have been divinely inspired. Occasionally, *Sutras* (short commentaries) that are not considered Divine are added to the mass of Vedic poetry, myth, magic, ritual and philosophy.

More than any thing else, it is the philosophic thought contained in the *Upnishads* that has governed the lives of practicing Hindus to this day. According to Will Durant, '*They* (Upnishads) *represent not a consistent system of philosophy, but the opinions, apercus, and lessons of many men, in whom philosophy and religion were still fused in the attempt to understand --- and reverently unite with --- the simple and essential reality underlying the superficial multiplicity of things. They are full of absurdities and contradictions, and occasionally they anticipate all the wind of Hegelian verbiage; sometimes they present formulas as weird as that of Tom Sawyer for curing warts; sometimes they impress us as the profoundest thinking in the history of philosophy*' (p. 410).

While the Vedas remained the exclusive preserve of the Brahmins, another set of stories, superstitions and myths, known as the '*Puranas*' (old things) were compiled, reportedly over a period of a thousand years, from 500 BC to 500 AD. While the uninitiated may find these to be incomprehensible and bewildering, the believers can see great wisdom and knowledge in them. For instance, Durant writes that in the Puranas and kindred writings of medieval India, '*we find a very modern theory of the universe*'. Then he goes on to explain, '*We don't know how the universe began, if it did; perhaps, say the Puranas, Brahma* (the Creator) *laid it as an egg and then hatched it by sitting on it; perhaps, it is a passing error of the Maker, or a little joke*' (P. 513). There are many similarly incongruous statements in Durant's '*Story of Civilisation*' to raise the suspicion that the account about India's past was not written by him but for him, at least in part, by some Hindu more concerned about preserving the image of his religion and community than meeting the exacting demands of literary and historical truth and accuracy.

In addition to the numerous divine and not so divine religious texts and epics, the Hindus believe in an indeterminate number of gods. There is no clear explanation or agreement on their functions. A great majority of Hindus have an amorphous concept of one Supreme Being (*Eshvar, Bhagwan*). Then there is *Brahma,* the Creator, who is represented with four faces but not worshipped very often. He is joined by *Vishnu,* the Preserver and *Shiva,* the Destroyer as the other members of the highest triad of gods. The names of neither *Brahma* nor *Shiva* appear in the *Rig Vedas* (*The Story of Civilisation*, p.508).

The two deities, *Vishnu* and *Shiva,* are worshipped by the vast majority of Hindus. Sometimes, they are incarnated in human forms or *avatars*. *Vishnu,* for instance, has ten *avatars*. Included among these is *Krishna* in the epics *Mahabharat* and *Bhagwat-Geeta;* as well as *Rama* and the tenth *avatar* Buddha. The cult of *Shiva* worships his phallus (*lingum*) ---- a fusion of the force of destruction with the symbol of generation. In the same vein, Shiva's wife *Kali* (other names: *Parvati, Uma, Durga*) is portrayed as a grotesque figure, with a gaping mouth and tongue hanging out, adorned with snakes and dancing upon a corpse; her earrings are dead men, her necklace is a string of skulls, her face and breasts are smeared with blood; two of her four hands carry a sword and a severed head while the other two are extended, ostensibly, in blessing and protection because, apart from death and destruction, she is also the goddess of motherhood.

Shiva's son is the elephant god *Ganesha* who is supposed to represent man's animal nature as well as provide protection against evil. Monkeys, snakes, crocodiles, tigers, peacocks, parrots, even rats are considered divine in some ways and worshipped as such. Most sacred of all is the cow and no Hindu may kill or eat its meat (the killing of a cow is a criminal offence in almost all of India). Its dung is used to purify houses and places of worship and even used as an ointment. Cows' urine is drunk as a sacred wine to wash away all inner and outer uncleanness (*Hindu Manners, Customs and Ceremonies*, pp. 43, 182, 638 -9). A BBC documentary, '*Sadhus of India*' filmed in 1992, showed some of these holy men rummaging through the remains of a funeral pyre and eating pieces of charred human flesh. One of them commented when asked, '*It tastes just like chicken*'. The significance of the act was not made clear in the documentary.

The Ganges River is sacred to all Hindus. Situated along its eastern reaches is Benares, the most sacred of all the cities in the Hindu world. According to their belief, 'whoever bathes in the Ganges and drinks its water at Benares, will be cured of all diseases, provided he does not neglect the needs of the priests. Whoever dies at Benares goes straight to heaven'. Scores of thousands of Hindu sick and dying visit the city to bathe in the river every day; many of them suffering from highly infectious diseases.

There are burning platforms (*ghats*), for cremation of dead bodies, located on the river. Parts of bodies that are not completely burnt fall into the river. The bodies of dead children are not cremated but thrown directly into river. There are no latrines along the water front and people use sandy places along the water's edge. In addition, all of the city's untreated sewerage is emptied directly into the river. Yet, such is the power of faith that devout Hindus not only drink but take water from the river home for their families. They shrug off any warnings with, 'It lies not in the power of man to pollute the Ganges'. Filtered or treated water is not an acceptable substitute because, '*filtering Ganges water takes the holiness out of it'* (*Mother India*, by Katherine Mayo, pp. 317 - 8).

In reality, Hinduism is more a collection of belief systems than a monolithic religion. These different belief systems, whilst varying greatly in content and ritual, have three basic elements that are common. First and foremost among these is the acceptance of the caste system and the supremacy of the Brahmins. Secondly, they all recognise the cow as representative of divinity and, thirdly, they believe in '*Karma*' (the law of causality) along with the concept of transmigration of souls.

According to this belief, all living beings are re-incarnated after death. Their new existence reflects the penalty or the fruits of vice or virtue in some antecedent life. *Karma* is not fate but the cumulative effect of man's conduct in previous lives that determines his or her future. There is also a vague concept of heaven and hell. These are regarded as transitory stops for the soul, in between incarnations.

Though perhaps not strictly a part of religion, *Yoga* is a system of ascetic meditation, traditional among the Hindus, that has found worldwide popularity. '*Through it, a Hindu seeks to free the soul* (atman) *from all sense phenomena and bodily attachment to attain supreme enlightenment and salvation by atoning in one existence for all the sins of the soul's past incarnations'* ('*The Story of Civilisation'*, p. 543).

There are more than a billion Hindus in the world today with the vast majority of them living in India. Despite these numbers, Hinduism remains one of the least understood and discussed religions. There could be a number of reasons for the lack of interest by the outside world. One of the main factors may have something to do with the complexity of the religion itself. The world is dominated by the monotheistic creeds whose followers have a hard time comprehending the intricacies of a belief system that involves mythical dogmas, countless gods, sacred animals and no Prophet or book of Revelation.

The other reason could be that, unlike Christianity or Islam, conventional Hinduism is not too much interested in expanding its membership. Like the Jews, one has to be born a Hindu and into a specific caste. It complicates the issue of conversion to Hinduism which is rare indeed. One does not come across many Hindu missionaries trying to spread its gospel. Strictly speaking, Hinduism is not a universal creed in the sense that most of its tenets are India-centric. It is specifically and intricately linked to the history, culture as well as geography of India. The significance and holiness of the cow or River Ganges would be completely lost on an Eskimo or a North African nomad.

CASTE SYSTEM

At the core of Hindu religious and social order lies its caste (*Varna,* meaning colour) system ordained in the religious text *Bhagwat-Gita.* The name itself provides its basis and dates back to the time of the Aryan invasion when lighter skinned herdsmen from Central Asia poured into the country and subjugated its dark-skinned Dravidian population. It is a complex system aimed at horizontal division of the society into different classes in which lighter-skinned people formed the upper rungs. The caste is determined by birth, with no possibility of a change in the individual's lifetime. Social intercourse between the various castes is strictly limited and inter-marriage is forbidden. Each caste has its own local organisation to oversee observance of religious codes and look after common interests. Any one failing to observe the set rules 'loses his caste' (becomes an outcast).

At the top of the pyramid are the *Brahmins* who are the priests and teachers rather like the shamans. The next in line, *Kashatris*, are the warrior and ruler class. *Vaishyas* are the tradesmen and land owners and, last of all, *Shudras*, work as farmers and labourers. These castes are further subdivided into myriad sub-castes, each exclusive, with its own order and standing. No one knows the exact number. Some estimate it at three thousand; others think it could be as high as five thousand.

Apart from these caste Hindus, a vast section of the society remains casteless, often referred to as the 'Untouchables' or *Dalits*. There are about three hundred million of them, about twenty-five per cent of India's population, living a most wretched life even to this day. Non-caste Hindus are not considered even men and women. They are relegated to a status lower than that of the lowest animals. They are untouchable. To drink from the same cup would be spiritual poison; their very shadow is pollution. In places they are rendered 'unseeable,' meaning they can only come out at night when clouds cover the moon. The opportunities afforded to them are extremely limited. In 1944, the total number of Untouchables with a university degree in India did not exceed five hundred.

According to the publication '*Broken People: Caste Violence Against India's Untouchables*' issued by the American based Human Rights Watch in 1999, *Dalits* are not permitted to use the same wells, visit the same schools, temples or cross from their part of the village to the one occupied by higher caste Hindus. Hindu barbers will not cut their hair nor do the washer men wash their clothes. The vast majority of them can only find work as scavengers, cleaning toilets and hauling away human excrement and animal carcasses with their bare hands. The discrimination and indignities suffered by India's *Dalits* are far worse than what the black Africans had to endure under Apartheid in South Africa. If questioned, the Hindus say it is their own fault; they are paying for the sins of a previous incarnation; it does not call for any pity.

A fact that is often not appreciated outside of India is that Hindus also classify people of other races and religions as casteless or *maleech* (unclean, repulsive) and hence polluting in the same way as the Untouchables. A practicing Hindu will not eat or drink on the same table or even in the same room as a non-Hindu. If a non-Hindu were to as much as caste his shadow on the food, kitchen or eating place it becomes *bharisht* (sullied) and unusable until it is ritually cleansed. When, perforce, a good Hindu has to shake hands or come in contact with a non-Hindu, he too undergoes the same process afterwards. The Hindu greeting with folded hands (*namastay* or *namaskar*) as against the customary handshake is designed to avoid the touch of a stranger. The drinking water, eating places and washrooms on India's railway stations are segregated for Hindus and non-Hindus. An irate Hindu, Hardas Gurudas, once sued the G. I. P. Railway in British India for damages because it allocated the seat next to him to a Muslim. There were numerous other cases filed in courts throughout the country to prevent Muslims from using the same wells for drawing water as the Hindus.

The well known Muslim scholar and anthropologist, Al Beiruni, who spent considerable time doing research on the people of India in the early eleventh century notes: '*First, they differ from us in everything which other nations have in common. And here we must mention the language ------. Secondly, they totally differ from us in religion ----- all their fanaticism is directed against those who do not belong to them, against all foreigners. They call them 'mleccha', i.e. impure, and forbid having any connection with them, be it by intermarriage or by any other kind of relationship, or by sitting, eating, and drinking with them, because thereby, they think, they would be polluted. They consider as impure anything that touches the fire and water of any foreigner; and no household is without these two elements.----- They are not allowed to receive anybody who does not belong to them, even if he wished it, or was inclined to their religion -----'* (*Alberuni's India*, by Edward C. Sachau, Low Price Publications, Delhi, pp. 17-20).

Mahatama Gandhi himself said, '*The Untouchables are treated as if less than beasts. Their very shadow defiles the name of God'* (*Mother India*, p.155). The orthodox among the caste Hindus do not accept the Untouchables as Hindu. This passage explains their attitude and feelings towards these unfortunate human beings, '*Untouchability is a necessity for man's growth. Man has magnetic powers about him. This power* (*shakti*) *is like milk. It will be damaged by improper contacts. If one can keep musk and onion together, one may mix Brahmins and Untouchables. It should be enough that Untouchables are not denied the privileges of the other world,*' ('*Mother India,'* p. 154).

Beverley Nichols, the well-known British novelist and prolific writer on subjects ranging from religion to politics and travel, spent a year in India as a correspondent of Allied Papers in the 1940s. During that time, he visited almost every corner of the country and spent time with politicians of all shades, administrators, religious leaders, technocrats, military men, as well as the common people. His impressions are contained in his frank and revealing book *Verdict on India* mentioned earlier. Like all other outsiders, he experiences great difficulty in coming to terms with the incongruity and excesses of the caste system. This is an excerpt from an interview he had with Dr. Ambedkar, leader of India's Untouchables at the time:

'*Dr. Ambedkar, ------ A person to bring pollution if his Mayfair dinner-jacket should happen to brush against their dhotis. A creature from whose touch the extreme orthodox must fly as though he were a leper, a monster whose slightest contact compels them to precipitate themselves into the nearest bath-tub, to soap and pray, and pray and soap, and soap and pray so that the filth of Dr. Ambedkar (M.A. London, the shame of Dr. Ambedkar (high honours at Columbia University), the plague and scourge of Dr. Ambedkar (special distinction at Heidelberg), should be washed for ever from their immaculate and immortal souls.*

'*We are not talking of the past, but of the year 1944. These are not legends, fairy-tales, gipsy songs; they are news paragraphs, stop-press.*

'*Untouchability --- history's most flagrant example of man's inhumanity to man --- is still deeply rooted in the Hindu social system; nearly all attempts to abolish it have met with failure. If a ten per cent improvement has occurred in the last fifty years, that is an optimistic estimate. A large number of people in England and America, deluded by Gandhi's propaganda, imagine that this disease --- for what else can one call it? --- is on the wane. They have read with approval the Mahatama's denunciations of it, they have seen photographs of him with his arm round the shoulders of outcasts, and they know that he gave the title "Harijan"* (Child of God) *to his newspaper, which circulated among the high and mighty of the land. "Surely," they say to themselves, "it must be having some effect?" It is not.*

'*As for Gandhi being the Untouchables friend, let us listen to Dr. Ambedkar, who is their indisputed leader. He said to me: "Gandhi is the greatest enemy the Untouchables have ever had in India."* When the Untouchables demanded a separate electorate, Gandhi went on one of his famous 'fasts unto death' and effectively killed the proposal. He did not want the Hindu vote bank to be reduced in India. Ambedkar characterized the oppressive caste system as the tyranny and inequality as the soul of Hinduism and gave up the religion to become a Buddhist instead.

Nichols was by no means alone in his inability to comprehend Hinduism. The well-known American icon, Mark Twain, expressed exasperation in his book, *More Tramps Abroad*, in far more cynical and caustic terms: '*In Benares they tell you that if a pilgrim should ever cross to the other side of the Ganges and get caught out and die there he would at once come to life again in the form of an ass. Think of that, after all this trouble and expense. You see, the Hindu has a childish and unreasoning aversion to being turned into an ass. It is hard to tell why. One could properly expect an ass to have an aversion to being turned into a Hindu. He would lose dignity by it, self-respect, and nine-tenths of its intelligence. But the Hindu who changed into an ass would not lose anything at all ---- unless, of course, you count his religion. And he would gain much. He would gain release from his slavery to two million gods and twenty million priests, fakirs, holy mendicants and other sacred bacilli; he would escape the Hindu hell; he would also escape the Hindu heaven. These are the advantages which the Hindu ought to consider; and then ---- he'd go over and die on the other side.*'

The rules of the caste system are laid down and administered by the Brahmins as keepers of the faith. For this, they are rewarded most handsomely. When a child is born, the Brahmin is paid; sixteen days later, when the 'birth pollution' is cleansed, he is paid again. It continues when the child is named a little later, when its hair are clipped after three months, when it starts to eat solids after six months, when it starts to walk, on its first and subsequent birth days ---- the process is never unending. The really big payments become due when the child commences its education, is betrothed, marries or dies. The last of these are accompanied by feasts for the Brahmins, at first, every month after death and then yearly during his or her son's life. In between, Hindus are expected to pay the Brahmins on such occasions as lunar and solar eclipses, to ward off evil. After the Brahmin has performed any religious rite, the person concerned has to wash his feet and drink some of the used water as an act of purification. These are called the 'vested rights' of Brahmins. Any one guilty of disregarding these risks eternal damnation ('*Mother India,*' pp. 137 - 8).

Some writers have mistakenly compared Indian diversity to the conditions in the United States. The two situations are entirely different and bear no resemblance to each other even in the most rudimentary terms. Unlike in the United States, the existence of the caste system in India makes any kind of assimilation or integration impossible for outsiders or new comers. They can only live separately and will always be considered outcast 'Untouchables'. There is no historical evidence of any voluntary large-scale conversions to Hinduism since the advent of the caste system some three thousand years ago. Any apostates may, however, be re-admitted to the faith through a cleansing process known as *Shudhi*.

All non-Hindu communities like the Muslims, Christians, Parsis, Sikhs and others have always existed in separate social pockets in India. This leaves us with a region full of different ethnic and religious communities, the largest of which is itself divided into myriad mutually exclusive castes and sub-castes. Apart from the ethnic and religious divisions, each of these communities restricts marriages as well as most other social intercourse to within its own circle. They might meet at the functional level but, aside from that, there is no other meaningful social bond, affinity or cohesion that could form the basis for a nation. In the presence of the caste system, the Indians can never hope to be one. The idea of an Indian nation in the accepted sense of the word is, and will always be, an unrealistic notion and a myth residing in the minds of unrealistic and romantic politicians and scholars.

In addition to all the other ills, the caste system is responsible for creating serious obstacles in the way of economic uplift of the society. Its pervasive nature affects almost every thing including helping to mould the attitudes of people towards jobs and employment. Any work that involves reading and writing is considered status elevating because of its association with high caste Brahmins. Manual work of any kind is regarded as degrading because it is connected with people of the lower castes. Education is seen, primarily as a means of not only providing better job opportunities but also, in the process, as a vehicle for improving the social standing of the individual. This can only happen if, at the end of the day, it can help place the individual in a status enhancing employment i.e. an office job that does not involve manual work. Very few educated men and women like to work with their hands. It is one of the main causes of so much unemployment and the resulting frustration and disillusionment among the educated ranks of Indian youth. The performance and quality of the manual jobs suffer equally because of the inadequacies and limitations of the uneducated incumbents. (See also *Asian Drama: An Inquiry into the Poverty of Nations* by Karl Gunnar Myrdal).

Contrary to claims by many and despite the efforts of some reformers like Mahatama Gandhi, the caste system in India is just as alive and well today as it ever was in the past. Even though laws have been enacted against discrimination based on caste or religion, these have little meaning. After the disastrous earthquake that struck the Indian state of Gujarat in January 2001, the government felt obliged to set up six separate relief camps ---- one for each of the four castes, one for the Untouchables and the last for the Muslims (Joseph Coleman writing for the *Associated Press*, 8th February 2001). Without the caste structure Hindu society is inconceivable. It forms the core of Hindu religion and plays a determining role in the attitudes of Hindus, not only towards each other, but also towards those who are not Hindu.

Other religions like Islam, Christianity or Sikhism that preach equality among human beings are perceived as threats to Hindu faith. Most conservative Hindus, in particular members of RSS, the parent organisation of BJP, feel that Muslims and Christians living in India do not belong there because their holy lands (*punyabhoomi*) lie elsewhere (K. S. Sudarshan, President of RSS, speaking in Agra, October 2000. Also please see '*Harvesting Our Souls*', by Arun Shouri, Minister for Privatisation in the BJP cabinet). Sikhism, on the other hand, is dismissed as a heretical off-shoot of Hinduism gone astray.

Since it is the first and foremost responsibility of each caste to look after its own, the system has caused deep and permanent divisions in the Hindu society that affect every day life. Every man considers it natural, even incumbent upon him, not only to associate with but also to give preference to persons of his own caste. The roots of much of the nepotism and, to a lesser extent, corruption that is found in India can be traced to this deeply entrenched belief. Any hope for change any time soon is unrealistic and impracticable. A person's birth is determined by *Karma*, a basic tenet of Hinduism, which in turn determines his caste. Any attempt to end or change the system would amount to undermining the very basis of Hindu religion and must be considered doomed from the start.

The caste system is pervasive as well as resilient and enduring. An example of this can be found among the Sikhs. Their religion came into being primarily as a revolt against the stifling and oppressive caste divisions among the Hindus and the maltreatment of Outcastes. Five hundred years later, we find that the system has re-asserted itself and reclaimed its previous hold among the Sikhs who are now just as much divided and stratified into castes and sub-castes as their Hindu ancestors.

In the case of St. Thomas' Christians living in Kerala State, the caste has always remained a part of their society. They believe that St. Thomas, the doubting disciple of Jesus Christ, came to South India and spread the faith. The Hindus that converted to Christianity did not give up their castes and to this day their descendants worship in churches separated by caste. *Dalits* (Untouchables) may not go near a church belonging to the one of upper castes. According to tradition, St. Thomas was executed, upon his refusal to worship Hindu gods, on the orders of a raja in present-day Tamil Nadu. Subsequently, when the Portuguese landed in South India, armed with their Inquisition zeal, they persecuted these Christians and burnt many of them alive at the stake as heretics and for crimes such as reading the St. James' Bible in Aramaic, the mother tongue of both St. Thomas and Jesus Christ.

LAWS OF MANU

There was no uniform code of civil and criminal laws to govern the society in India until the establishment of Muslim rule in twelfth century AD. Before this, the law was what the local ruler wished or ordered at any time. The ordinary day-to-day personal lives of the people were governed by *Dharma Shastras* (religious codes) prepared and interpreted by the Brahmins. The best known among these is the *Code of Manu*, most likely, dating back to the early centuries of the Christian era. It was a barbaric set of rules administered by the Brahmins, primarily for their own benefit, having first exempted themselves from its application. To accuse a Brahmin of any crime is sinful even if the Brahmin happens to be guilty.

These laws required the accused to be tried by ordeal. One of these involved forcing a person charged to push his arm into a boiling mixture of oil and cow dung or in a basket full of poisonous snakes. If he was not scalded or bitten by a snake, he was pronounced innocent (*'Hindu Manners, Customs and Ceremonies'* by Abbe J.A. Dubois, Clarendon Press, Oxford, 1924, pp. 661, 717, 722). Among other things, it ordained *'all that exists in this universe is the Brahmin's property'* (*'Indian Wisdom'* by Sir Monier-Williams, p. 227). In certain areas the Brahmins also had the right to first intercourse with all brides in their territory (*'The Story of Civilisation'* by Will Durant, p. 486). In every illness, lawsuit, bad omen, unpleasant dream or new enterprise the advice of a Brahmin was mandated at a worthy fee (*'Hindu Manners, Customs and Ceremonies'*, pp. 590 - 92).

The code was not uniform in its application. Much depended on the caste of the accused and the victim. If a *Shudra* listened to the Scriptures his ears were to be filled with molten lead and if he were to recite these, his tongue was to be split in two (*'Dialogues of the Budha, ii'*, by T. W. Rhys Davis, p.97). If he messed with a Brahmin's wife, his genitals were to be cut off. If he killed another *Shudra* he could atone for it by giving ten cows to the Brahmins, or a hundred cows for a *Vaisya* and a thousand cows for a *Kashatriya* but if he killed a Brahmin then he must die (*'The Story of Civilisation'*, p. 486).

The Brahmin has to bathe every day and again after being shaved by a barber of lower caste. The place where he slept has to be purified with cow dung. He is to abstain from all animal food, including eggs, and also from onions, garlic, mushrooms and leeks. He is to drink nothing but water, that only drawn and carried by a Brahmin. He is not to use any unguents or perfumes, nor indulge in any sensual pleasure, covetousness and wrath. If he touches any unclean thing or the person of a foreigner no matter of what rank, he is to purify himself by ceremonial ablutions (*'The Story of Civilisation'*, p. 487). A Hindu can become 'unclean' in a hundred different ways ---- by improper food, by offal, by the touch of a *Shudra,* an Outcaste, a corpse, a menstruating woman or one in labour and even by leaving the country. After any such pollution, he cleansed himself by drinking the 'five substances' (*Panchagavia*) from the sacred cow, namely, milk, ghee (clarified butter), yogurt, urine and dung (*'Hindu Manners, Customs and Ceremonies,'* p. 43). At every ritual and religious ceremony, all Hindus are required to make a healthy donation to the consulting Brahmin and the local temple.

SEX AND MARRIAGE

Sex has an entirely different place and meaning in Hindu religion when compared with the monotheistic faiths that originated in the Middle East. Shiva, one of the greatest of the Hindu deities is represented in temples, homes or in personal amulets, by the image of the male generative organ. There are sculptures and paintings on temple walls and temple chariots, on palace gates and street wall frescoes, realistically demonstrating every conceivable aspect and humour of sex. An entire religious text, the Kamasutra, deals with the issues and techniques involved in it. Yet, this does not mean that all Hindus are lascivious and lewd in any way. Far from it.

Generally, there is a much greater observance of sexual morality and propriety found in India than any where in the West. It would appear that Hinduism acknowledged and revered sex as a powerful force for re-generation and pro-creation and dealt with it as such. A famous Hindu mystic confided to Mayo, 'No question of right or wrong can be involved in any aspect of such matters. I forget the act the moment I have finished it. I merely do it not to be unkind to my wife, who is less illumined than I. To do it or not to do it, signifies nothing. Such things belong only to the world of illusion' (*Mother India*, p. 34). The statement may be baffling to a westerner but different societies have evolved differently and because of it, tend to have different attitudes towards specific issues. It would be manifestly unfair to judge one by the norms and standards evolved by another.

Marriage was mandated and it could only take place within each caste. An unwed person had no social status ('*Hindu Manners, Customs and Ceremonies*,' p. 205 and *The Ideals of Indian Art*, by E. B. Havell, p. 93). The selection of spouses was the parents' responsibility. Any marriage contracted through mutual attraction (*Gandharva*) was stigmatised and not considered respectable. Child marriages were the norm and ordained by the *Dharma* (religion). Even though these had been made illegal by the British, the institution survives to this day (*The Story of Civilisation*, pp. 489 - 90 and *Mother India* pp. 48 - 65). Marriages of children between five and ten years of age are not unknown even today.

The famous Indian Nobel Laureate, Rabindranath Tagore, in an essay on 'The Indian Ideal of Marriage', explains child marriage as a flower of the sublimated spirit, a conquest over sexuality and materialism won by exalted intellect for the eugenic uplift of the race: 'The "desire"---- against which India's solution of the marriage problem declared war, is one of Nature's most powerful fighters; consequently, the question of how to overcome it was not an easy one. There is a particular age ---- at which this attraction between the sexes reaches its height; so if marriage is to be regulated according to social will, as distinguished from the choice of the individual concerned, it must be finished with before such age. Hence the Indian custom of early marriage' (*The Book of Marriage*, by Keyserling, Jonathan Cape Ltd. London, 1926).

The rules for conduct after marriage are clearly laid out in the *Padmapurana* Hindu religious text. For the woman it ordains that there is no other god on earth than her husband. Her highest achievement in life is to please him through perfect obedience. Even if he happens to be '*deformed, aged, infirm, offensive, in his manners, let him also be choleric, debauched, immoral, a drunkard, a gambler; let him frequent houses of ill repute, live in open sin with other women, have no affection whatsoever for his home; let him rave like a lunatic; let him live without honour; let him be blind, deaf, dumb or crippled, in a word, let his defects be what they may, a wife should always look upon him as her god, should lavish upon him all her attention and care, paying no heed whatsoever to his character and give him no cause whatsoever for displeasure. ---- A wife must eat after her husband has had his fill. If he does not eat she too must remain hungry. ---- She must, on the death of her husband, allow herself to be burnt alive on the same funeral pyre*'---- a practice known as '*Sattee*' or '*sati*'.

In a rough survey carried out in Bengal in the closing years of the eighteenth century, Bernier had estimated that more than 300 woman were burnt alive under this edict every year within a radius of 30 miles from Calcutta. Although outlawed by the British, the practice never ceased. There was a well-publicised case in Rajasthan of an eighteen-year-old bride burnt alive on the funeral pyre of her husband on 4th September 1987. It is by no means an isolated instance. (See *Death by Fire. Sati, Dowry Death and Female Infanticide in Modern India*, by Mala Sen, Weidenfeld & Nicholson, 2001, London and *The Age of Kali*, by William Dalrymple.)

Manu specifies that a wife who disobeyed her husband would become a jackal in her next incarnation ('*The Story of Civilisation*', p.493). Abbe Dubois found marriages among the Hindus to be governed by these same rules during the nineteenth century. He observes, 'A *real union with sincere and mutual affection, or even peace, is very rare in Hindu households. The moral gulf which exists in this country between the sexes is so great that in the eyes of a native the woman is simply a passive object who must be abjectly submissive to her husband's will and fancy. She is never looked upon as a companion who can share her husband's thoughts and be the first object of his care and affection. The Hindu wife finds in her husband only a proud and overbearing master who regards her as a fortunate woman to be allowed the honour of sharing his bed and board.'* (*Hindu Manners, Customs and Ceremonies*, p. 231 and pp. 344 - 9).

The fate of a widow in Hindu culture is most unenviable. Because of the system of child marriages, many of them became widows while they were still children. Even if they remain untouched virgins, they are not permitted to remarry. It is often contended that the reason so many Hindu women allowed themselves to be burnt alive with the bodies of their dead husbands was to escape the miserable fate of widowhood that awaited them. '*The widow becomes the menial of every other person in the house of her late husband* (Hindus customarily live in joint-family households). *All the hardest and ugliest tasks are hers, no comforts, no ease. She may take but one meal a day and that of the meanest. She must perform strict fasts. Her hair must be shaven off. She must take care to absent herself from any scene of ceremony or rejoicing, from a marriage, from a religious celebration, from the sight of an expectant mother or of any person whom the curse of her glance might harm. Those who speak to her may speak in terms of contempt and reproach; and she herself is the priestess of her own misery, for its due continuance is her one remaining merit*' (*Mother India*, p. 82).

WOMEN IN HINDUISM

There are few societies in history where the lot of women has been as unenviable as among the Hindus. According to the Code of Manu, '*The source of dishonour is woman; the source of strife is woman; the source of earthly existence is woman; therefore avoid woman. ---- A female is able to draw away from the right path in this life not only a fool but even a sage and can lead him in subjection to desire or to wrath.*' Reading and writing were considered inappropriate for women. It is recorded in the *Mahabharta* that *'for a woman to study the Vedas is a sign of confusion in the realm'* (*The Story of Civilisation*, p.493).

Manu allowed eight different forms of marriage that included purchasing or 'capturing' a wife (*Indian Wisdom*, p. 244). Polygamy was permissible and widely prevalent in Hindu India. The *Vedas* consider it 'an act of merit to support several wives and to transmit ability' (*The Story of Civilisation,* p.401). A man could take another wife if his existing spouse 'drank liquor, was diseased, rebellious, wasteful or quarrelsome'. He could divorce her for immorality but the wife could not get a divorce for any reason.

A woman becomes 'unclean' at the time of menstruation or giving birth, when she is isolated and not permitted to come in touch with the rest of the household ('*Hindu Manners, Customs and Ceremonies*', p. 180 - 81). It is because of this belief that the midwives (*da'ees*) traditionally belong to the 'Untouchable' caste who, under any other circumstances, would not be allowed to go anywhere near a caste Hindu woman. The terribly unhygienic practices associated with child-birth have been the main cause of the very high infant and female mortality rates in India (for grim and graphic details of midwifery conditions, even during more recent times, please see *Mother India,* pp. 89 - 107).

Because custom requires the parents to pay marriage dowry, a girl child is regarded as a heavy and unwelcome liability. Her birth elicits the formal condolences of family and friends. Infanticide of female children has always been more common than any one cares to admit ('*The Punjab Peasant in Prosperity and Debt*' by M. L. Darling, Oxford, 1925, pp. 58 - 9; and '*Census of India, vol. I, Part I, 1921, Appendix VI*). Katherine Mayo recalls in *Mother India* her conversation with an ingenuous Hindu landowner who told her, '*I have had twelve children. Ten girls, which, naturally, did not live. Who indeed could have borne that burden! The two boys, of course, I preserved*' (p.70).

According to an article '*Lambs to the Slaughter*' by Soma Wadhwa published recently (1999) in the respected Indian journal '*The Outlook*', more than 160,000 female infants are murdered at birth every year in the Indian state of Behar alone. It read in part, '*The rates are fixed. A local dai (midwife) in Katihar is paid Rs. 100 for the delivery of a son and Rs. 25 for a daughter. If the daughter is killed, the fee goes up to Rs. 50. ---- The methods of killing are as simple as they are varied. The baby girls are usually strangled with a piece of rope. Sometimes the dai snaps the spine by bending it backwards. A handful of fertilizer pushed down the baby's throat also does the job. A lump of black salt placed in the newborn's mouth, experienced midwifes say, takes an hour to kill the infant. ----- The less experienced midwifes choose to suffocate the baby by stuffing her into a clay pot and sealing the lid with fresh dough. The baby dies within two hours ------*' (*Death by Fire. Sati, Dowry Death and Female Infanticide in Modern India*, p.80).

Women are there to serve their husbands and bring up their children. It is only as a mother that a Hindu woman comes into her own, ruling indoors with an iron hand and stoutly maintaining the ancient traditions. Forgetting her own former misery, she controls and runs the lives of her daughters-in-law very severely indeed. Hundreds, if not thousands, of young brides die in suspicious circumstances each year in India, a phenomenon that has come to be known as 'bride burning'.

All property and wealth is inherited by the sons. Hindu tradition demands that a man must have a legitimate son to perform the proper religious ceremonies at and after the death of the father, and to crack open the father's skull on the funeral pyre, whereby the spirit is released. Salvation without a son is inconceivable and, for this reason, a Hindu will go to any lengths to get one. In case of continued failure of the wife to give him a child, the husband may send his wife on a pilgrimage to a temple, bearing gifts. At the temple by day, the woman must beseech the god for a son, and at night she must sleep within the sacred precincts. Morning come, she has a tale to tell the priest of what befell her under the veil of darkness. 'Give praise, O' daughter of honour!' he replies. 'It was the god!' And so she returns to her home. If a child comes and it lives, a year later she revisits the temple, carrying with her other gifts and hair from the child's head (*Hindu Manners, Customs and Ceremonies,* pp. 593 - 4).

There is another institution known as *Devdassis* (servants of the gods) which, although a part of Hindu religious culture, might be abhorrent to outside observers. Among the Hindus some parents, to placate and seek favours from the gods, vowed their next born to them, if it happened to be a girl. Sometimes, a particularly lovely child that was held superfluous, for some reason or another, is presented to the temple. She is taught dancing and singing by her predecessor temple women. Often by the age of five, when she is considered most desirable, she becomes the priest's own prostitute ('*Mother India*', p.52). If she survives to later years, she becomes a dancer and a singer and is held always ready, at a price, for the use of men pilgrims during their devotional sojourns in the temple precincts. When her charms fade, she is turned out upon the public, with a small allowance and the acknowledged right to a beggar's livelihood. Her parents, who may be well-to-do persons of good rank and caste, suffer little remorse or loss of face in the society by the manner in which they treated their child ('*The Golden Bough,*' by J.G. Frazer, Macmillan & Co. London, 1914).

In many parts, the parents of attractive young boys feel proud to attach them to temples as prostitutes ('*Mother India*', p. 32). According to Dubois, the institution was so common in 19th century India that the temples in some cases 'converted into mere brothels' ('*Hindu Manners, Customs and Ceremonies*', p. 585). It is still alive and well. Thousands of young girls are sold into prostitution each year in the name of pleasing the gods. It is a pitiable existence and most of them die young, primarily due to AIDS (*Serving the Goddess*, by William Dalrymple, *The New Yorker*, August 2008).

There are definite signs of change in attitude towards women, basically, among the western-educated urban Hindu elite. More and more women, forsaking their traditional roles in Hindu households, are getting educated and entering professional fields. Unfortunately, this is not true for all of them. Things are vastly different where conservatism and orthodoxy hold sway, which is true for more than half the population. The feelings there are summed up as, 'It is strictly enjoined in the religious books of the Hindus that females should not be allowed to come under any influence other than that of the family. For this reason, no system of school and college education can be made to suit their requirements. ---- Women get sufficient moral and practical training in the household and that is far more important than the type of education schools can give' (*Mother India*, p. 120).

With the help of an American producer, a brave and talented Indian film-maker, Digvijay Singh, has drawn attention to one of the distressful Hindu ceremonies related to young girls first starting to menstruate. The families celebrate their entry into puberty with a feast outside the local temple while the girls are inside being ritually raped by the priests. The practice is apparently still widespread in large parts of East and South India in the states of Orissa, Andhra Pradesh and Tamil Nadu.

It is hard to tell how widespread these practices are in India today. Understandably, the Indians themselves are reluctant to discuss the issue openly. In their time, the British had strenuously tried to eradicate many of the more inhuman and troubling customs like *sattee* and child marriages. The spread of western education has helped to change many of the attitudes particularly in the cities. That they continue to persist in at least some areas even today, is evident from the reports that surface in the world media from to time about abhorrent incidents of child sacrifice, female infanticide and sattee (see *The Age of Kali* by William Dalrymple, pp. 130 – 32).

LEGENDS AND LEGACY

Aside from the undeciphered Indus Valley script, the earliest known written language in northern India is believed to have been Sansikrit. How it came to be developed is not known with certainty. The general consensus is that it was brought to India by the Aryans as a spoken language only. The script was a later addition and appears to have been imported from the Middle East. Its use remained confined to the scholastic elite until it more or less faded away to be replaced primarily by Prakrit and Pali ---- the languages of Buddhist culture in India.

Pali was the language of the common people and its use was much more widespread than Sanskrit. When and how Pali disappeared from the scene remains a mystery, like so much else about India's distant past. A good guess would be that it had something to do with the end of Buddhism in India, around seventh and eighth centuries AD, when Hinduism re-asserted itself. Side by side with Pali and fading Sanskrit there existed a whole host of other languages and dialects, perhaps, most common among these was Prakit. Lacking any script, many of these are now lost to history and have been either replaced by or evolved into many others.

Muslims who invaded and settled in India from the north-west in 997 AD spoke Turkish but their court language for the next eight hundred years was *Farsi* (Persian). As is wont to happen, over the course of hundreds of years of co-existence and inter-action between the two cultures, a new language evolved that is a mixture of Prakit or Pali, Turkish, Persian and a smattering of Arabic. Because it developed and was spoken around the military camps at first, it was called *Urdu* ----- the Turkish word for 'army'. Statements such as, '*the invading Moslems filled Hindustani with Persian words, thereby creating a new dialect, Urdu*' ('*The Story of Civilisation*', p. 555) seem to imply mistakenly that the evolution of Urdu was an act of imposition. Apart from all else, it is historically incorrect and misleading.

Urdu was a fully developed language long before Hindi or Hindustani literature made its first appearance. '*When the British dominion extended over northern India, Urdu was the lingua franca, employed by the polite society, Muslim and Hindu, as the medium of culture and social intercourse*' (*History of the Freedom Movement in India*, by Dr. Tara Chand, Ministry of Information and Broadcasting, Government of India, New Delhi, 1983, vol. I, p. 192). Hindi was created as a literary language at Fort William College, Calcutta, the oriental institute established by the British. '*A literary language for Hindi-speaking people which could commend itself more to Hindus was very desirable, and the result was produced by taking Urdu and expelling from it words of Persian or Arabic origin, and substituting for them words of Sanskrit or Hindi origin*' (*A History of Hindi Literature*, by F. E Keay, Oxford University Press, Calcutta, 1920, p. 88). The first Hindi prose, *Prem Sagar*, by Lalluji Lal, was not published until 1809. There was no Hindi poetry until decades later.

Subject nations throughout history have, of their own volition, tried to emulate and adopt the ways of their conquerors. Hindus were no exception to this rule and needed no encouragement to change and to conform. They took to Persian and Urdu in the past for the same reasons that determined their adoption of English as one of the two official languages of India after independence. In the same way, it may have been after coming into contact with the Muslims that upper caste Hindus put their women under veil. The veil came to be regarded as a sign of respectability in India as it had been in the Middle East since the days of the Romans. The turban is another legacy of the Muslims of Central Asian origin that the Hindus have adopted as a badge of honour.

What has survived of Sanskrit is in the *Vedas* and the Hindu epics. Of the latter, *Mahabharata* and *Ramayana* are the best known and have a definite religious significance for the believers. *Mahabharta* is the tale of a great tribal battle. Originally said to have been written by Vyasa but, as Durant puts it, '*a hundred poets wrote it, a thousand singers moulded it ----*' and this happened over a period of a thousand years or so (p. 560). The tale proper begins with a lady named *Shakuntala* who had a mighty son called *Bharata*. (Kalidas, a well-known poet and courtier of King Vikramadatya, circa 400 AD has written a drama based on her story and named it after her).

Bharata sired two tribes, *Kuru* and *Pandu.* The king of the Pandus gambled away all his wealth, his kingdom, his brothers and even his wife, Darupadi, in a game in which his Kuru opponent played with loaded dice. By agreement, the Pandus were to be given back their kingdom after twelve years but the Kurus reneged on the deal and a battle ensued. It raged for eighteen days. Gods, like Krishna and others, joined the battle in human form, extolling the virtues of killing, '*it is meet and just to kill one's relatives in war*' ('*The Story of Civilisation*', p.565). There were great acts of bravery as well as sorrow. One man, Bhishma, alone managed to slay one hundred thousand men in a span of ten days. By the time the carnage was over, *several hundred million men* had been killed ----- a hyperbole considering that the entire known human population of the world at the time was perhaps no more than twenty or thirty million. It was estimated to be only three hundred million in Shakespeare's time and one billion in 1804 AD).

Mahabharta also embodies the religious text *Bhagwat Geeta* and parts of the other epic, *Ramayana.* It is said to be seven times longer than Homer's *Ilyad* and *Oddessey* put together. Although there is no historical evidence to prove if the Kurus and Pandus or any of the other characters or events mentioned in the epic ever existed or happened, Durant blandly insists in a footnote, '*References in the Vedas to certain characters of the Mahabharta indicate that the story of a great intertribal war in the second millennium B.C. is fundamentally historical*' (p. 562) ---- a curious statement coming as it does from an eminent historian. There are other instances as well in his otherwise great work that make one wonder if he had himself composed the chapter about Hinduism.

Ramayana, by comparison, is much shorter, composed only in a thousand or so pages. It is of the same general vintage as *Mahabharta*. Its authorship is attributed to Valmiki, who is also a character in the tale but, almost certainly, a large number of people contributed to it over a very long period of time. The account narrates, King Janak of Videha liked to till his own land. One day, at the touch of his plough, a lovely daughter, Sita, sprang up from a furrow of the soil. When it was time to marry Sita, a contest (*swimber*) was held in which a prince from a nearby kingdom, by the name of Rama, won her hand after successfully bending a mighty bow.

When Rama returned with Sita to his father's palace at Ayodhya, it opened a Pandora's Box of jealousy and intrigue that culminated in the couple's banishment. They found refuge in the woods where Rama met the princess, Surpa-nakha, who fell in love with him. To facilitate matters, Surpa-nakha's brother, Ravan, kidnapped Sita and took her south to Sri Lanka. Rama then raised a great army, defeated Ravan and with the assistance of the monkey god, *Hanuman*, brought Sita back to Ayodhya ---- ostensibly, in some airplane-like contraption that flew through the air ('*The Story of Civilisation*', p. 569).

Soon, Rama was consumed by doubts about Sita's relationship with Ravan during her captivity. Overcome, he banished her to the woods where she met Valmiki and bore two sons to Rama. The sons ended up in Rama's court as traveling minstrels where the father recognised them as his own. While Rama ruled for many years after that, poor Sita never made it back to him and was consumed by the mother earth from whence she had come.

The pious Hindus consider Krishna and Rama as incarnations of Divinity and pray to them as such. They also believe as a matter of faith that by studying the *Ramayana* and *Mahabharta* a Hindu will not only be cleansed of all past sins but will also beget a son. '*If a man reads the Mahabharta and has faith in its doctrines, he becomes free of all sin and ascends to heaven after his death ----. As butter is to all other food, as Brahmins are to all other men, ---- as the ocean is to a pool of water, as the cow is to all other quadrupeds, so is Mahabharta to all other histories* (*Indian Literature*, by Gowen, p. 203, 219, as quoted by Durant).

There is little doubt in the Hindu mind the epics are authentic history. As an example of how such faith can sometimes lead to tragedy; even though there is no tangible historical evidence of Rama ever having existed, a large section of Hindus from all walks of life decided that he had been born at the exact place where the Muslims had built a mosque in Ayodhya in the first half of sixteenth century AD ---- three thousand years after the god's assumed existence. In December 1992, a mob of Hindus led by among others, Mr. L.K. Advani, Murli Manohar Joshi and Uma Bhararati, all of them ministers in the BJP-led government in Delhi, demolished this Muslim place of worship that was also an irreplaceable heritage of India. All the political and law enforcement agencies of the Indian central and provincial governments silently watched the destruction by the frenzied maniacal mob, without making any attempt to stop it.

This is not by any means an isolated incident. There is a growing wave of virulent Hindu revivalism taking hold in India. Its main objective is to resurrect the glory of Hinduism's distant and imagined past. A number of fundamentalist groups like the Rashtarya Sevak Sungh that was modeled along the lines of Nazi Brown Shirts in the thirties, Shiv Sena, Bajrang Dal, Ranbir Sena and Vishwa Hindu Parishad, to name a few, have sprung up all over the country. Prime Minister Bajpai himself belonged to the extremist Rashtarya Sevak Sungh, as did Mr. Gandhi' murderer, Nathuram Godse.

In January 1999, a mob organised by one of the groups that supported the BJP Government surrounded and set fire to the car of Australian missionary, Graham Stewart, and watched him burn to death along with his two young sons who were with him in the car. ('*The Hindu*', Delhi, 24th January 1999). Scores of churches have been burnt and nuns and priests molested and murdered, in a frenzy of religious intolerance, as protest against the voluntary conversions of Hindus to Christianity ('*The Pioneer*' New Delhi, 26th Sept. 1998). According to the Catholic Bishops Conference of India, there were 67 such attacks in 1999 and close to 100 a year later ('*The Financial Times*', London, 23 / 24 December 2000). There are constant allegations of involvement by the right wing Indian BJP government itself in the brutalities against religious minorities to the extent that recently (June 2000) groups of US Congressmen led by Rep. Edolphus Townes of New York felt obliged to write and call upon President Clinton to declare India a 'terrorist state' on the basis of her abysmal human rights record.

The issues of intolerance, bigotry and violence aside, there is a noticeable yearning among sections of Hindu society to recede into the past in search of glory, in the same way as one finds among people of other faiths including Islam. Sometimes it is carried to the extent where it starts to not only appear unrealistic but also quite bizarre, as evident from the following report by the Associated Press:

'LUCKNOW, June 7, 2008: He's a monkey, he's a god, and now he's a business school chairman.

'Hanuman, the popular Hindu monkey god revered for his strength and valour, has been named official chairman of the recently opened Sardar Bhagat Singh College of Technology and Management in northern India, a school official said on Saturday.

'The position comes with an incense-filled office, a desk and a laptop computer. Four chairs will be placed facing the empty seat reserved for the 'holy chairman', but all visitors must enter the office barefoot, said Vivek Kangdi, the school's vice chairman.

"It is our belief that any job that has blessings of Lord Hanuman is bound to be a success," said Kangdi.

'All Hindus know that Hanuman can lift mountains and leap oceans, but ancient texts make no mention of his business acumen. "Never mind that," says Kangdi.—AP'

Generalisations are always dangerous. However, it is the business of historians to formulate and crystallise impressions and opinions. Like every one else, historians too are subject to their own in-built limitations, biases and prejudices. In the circumstances, it is generally wise not to rely too heavily on the views expressed by a single source. However, when a number of eminent historians arrive at the same conclusion on any particular issue, there are fewer grounds to question the objectivity or motives.

The case in point relates to the assessment of the Hindu character. *'I think we may take as their greatest vice'*, says Abbe Dubois, *'the untrustworthiness, deceit and double dealing ---- which are common to all Hindus. ---- Certain it is that there is no nation in the world which thinks so lightly of an oath or of perjury* (*Hindu Manners, Customs and Ceremonies*, p. 662). *'Lying'*, says Westermarck, *'has been called the national vice of the Hindus' (Moral Ideas, i, p.89).* According to Lord Macaulay, *'Hindus are wily and deceitful'* (*Essays,* p. 562). Katherine Mayo advises, *'In taking information from an Indian, at home or abroad, a vital preliminary step is to appreciate and keep always in mind the definition and value that he assigns to truth. ---- It is no shame to a Hindu to be caught in a lie. You do not embarrass or annoy him by so catching him. His morality is no more involved in the matter than in a move in a game of chess.'* (*Mother India,* pp. 272 - 4).

The Laws of Manu state, *'a lie told for good reasons is forgivable'* (*The story of Civilisation',* p.499). As for Mahatama (great spirit) Gandhi himself, *'Truth, to Gandhi was the ultimate reality. Gandhi's truth, however, had two facets, the absolute and the relative. ---- Gandhi's relative truth was by no means rigid. It could vary as his perceptions of a problem changed. That made him a flexible man, but it also made him appear two-faced -----* (*Freedom at Midnight*, by Collins and Lapierre, Simon and Schuster, New York, p. 106).

More recently, we have some relevant extracts from the Nixon Papers. These were released in 2005 and relate to discussions between the US President and his National Security Adviser, Henry Kissinger in July 1971. In these, Nixon has described the Indians as a 'slippery, treacherous people.' Kissinger not only agreed with this assessment but also added that they were 'insufferably arrogant.' After his meeting with the Indian Prime Minister, Mrs. Indira Gandhi on 4th November 1971, Nixon referred to her as 'an old witch' and more viciously as a 'bitch'. Kissinger again concurred, adding that 'the Indians are bastards anyway.' These are just a few examples of the assessment of the Hindu character by some prominent western scholars and personalities who have come in touch with them.

A restricted US Defence Department document released in July 2005 entitled, '*Expectations and Perceptions*,' noted the impressions held by more than forty US officials of senior Indian military and government officials with whom they had been dealing. It read in part: *'Indian bureaucrats, Generals, Admirals and Air Marshals could be "easily slighted or insulted", are "difficult to work with", harbour "deep-seated distrust" of Americans, are mostly "obsessed" with history than future and "see the world through their perennial distrust of Pakistan". ---- "For the Indians, the act is much more important than the substance; the theory is more important than execution; and the tactic is more important than strategy"* (*Of Insults, Obsessions and Distrust*, by Josy Joseph, chief correspondent of *Rediff.com*).

It is true most Hindus display a marked reluctance to be direct and to the point. In discussions they tend to be non-specific, refusing to be pinned down and indulge in vague generalisations. What are not clear are the reasons underlying these traits? It is possible that it may have something to do with their understanding and interpretation of the Hindu moral and religious edicts. Not only the religion but the approach to it is also different in Hinduism as compared with religions of the Middle East origin ---- the belief, for instance, that a sin no longer counts after you have given money to the Brahmins for its atonement. It cannot be attributed to insufficient education since the authorities mentioned in the previous paragraphs had dealings mostly with the more educated among the population. It may also have some thing to do with long centuries of slavery and subjugation. The degradation suffered under such conditions can lead to impaired morality, loss of self-respect and heightened sensitivity. Some have also alleged that Hindus suffer from a palpable sense of inferiority vis-à-vis the other races, the Europeans in particular (see comment on Jawaharlal Nehru's attitude in the chapter '*Road to Freedom*').

Another trait that stands out, especially among the Brahmins, is their inordinate pride, no doubt, as a reflection of their position in the Hindu society. It is noticeable to the extent that it makes most of them quite insufferable to the unaccustomed and uninitiated. Bertrand Russell expressed the opinion in an interview on BBC with David Frost (published in '*Life*' magazine in 1968) that he knows of no people in the world, including Nazi Germans, who could match the Hindu Brahmin when it came to matters of arrogance and conceit.

In their writings and discussions one also gets the impression that Hindus have a logic of their own which is different and often vexatious and exasperating. As a typical example of this, Gayatari Devi, the maharani of Jaipur and a member of *Lok Sabha*, the Indian Parliament, once stated to the effect that India believed in secularism and then added, '*every one knows that Hinduism is the best form of secularism*' ('*Time*' *Magazine*). Hindus frequently engage in hyperbole and indulge in what to the outsiders must appear as confused and convoluted reasoning. Their brand of logic, coupled with the sense of exclusivity and inordinate pride, makes it particularly difficult to deal with high caste Hindus, especially those in positions of authority, which they often are in India.

BUDDHIST INTERLUDE

About 2500 years ago, a prince by the name of Sidatha Gautama lived in the north of present day Behar State who founded Buddhism. He did not claim to be a Prophet in the Biblical or spiritual sense of the word. He was more a teacher, intent on alleviating the suffering of mankind, through individual endeavour, to achieve self-fulfillment and inner peace

(Nirvana). This is how H.G. Wells describes Buddhism in his *'Outline of History, vol. I '*, p. 398). *'It was primarily a religion of conduct, not a religion of observances and sacrifices. It had no temples; and, since it had no sacrifices, it had no sacred order of priests. Nor had it any theology. It neither asserted nor denied the reality of the innumerable and often grotesque gods who were worshipped in India at that time. It passed them by.'* Free of the Hindu caste system and unburdened by a plethora of gods and priest-ridden rituals, with the passage of time, Buddhism was accepted far and wide. Local influences altered its form. By the time Alexander the Great came to India, circa 328 BC, Buddhism had already made considerable inroads into the Hindu domain, particularly in the parts that now constitute Pakistan.

Alexander conquered a number of princely states in the northwest but never reached the Gangetic plain. The vestiges of Greek influence can only be found in Afghanistan and Pakistan. Thanks to Greek historians like Ptolemy, Megasthenes, Arrian and Herodotus we have the first accurately recorded accounts of these parts of the world and their inhabitants. However, there are serious gaps in information about the bulk of India that lay to the east right up to tenth century AD. It is true that the Hindus may have mastered sciences like arithmetic, astronomy and philosophy in ancient times but they had very little sense of history and kept no useful records. India produced not a single historian, worthy of the name, until the arrival of the Muslims.

After the departure of the Greeks down the Indus and back along the coast of Baluchistan, a remarkable Hindu adventurer called Chandara Gupta Maurya, counseled by a Machiavellian adviser named Kautilya Chanakya, occupied much of the north Indian plain with the help of tribesmen from the north-west in 321 BC. The devious pragmatism of Chanakya is recorded in the oldest known Sanskrit book *'Arthashastra'*. His prescription for capturing a fort, for instance, seems to come straight out of *'The Prince'* when he advises steps leading to it as *'Intrigue, spies, winning over the enemy's people, siege and assault'*.

Chandara Gupta's grandson, Ashoka (264 - 227 BC) extended the kingdom from Afghanistan to the coast of present day Orissa. He became profoundly affected by the senseless massacres of aboriginal Indians by the Hindus during his many campaigns and, forsaking violence, decided to convert to Buddhism. Ashoka is renowned for his compassion and humanitarian acts that he undertook for the benefit of his subjects. The capital, Patliputra (present day Patna) was a large and well-organised city. A twelve hundred-mile long road connected it to regions in the far northwest. Poignant reminders of this Buddhist age of enlightenment can still be seen in the scattered ruins of the Potohar Plateau, around Taxila, in the north of Pakistan and at Nalanda in Behar.

After Ashoka's death, India's history becomes patchy. There are few inscriptions or documents to reconstruct an account of that period (*Buddhist India,* p. 308; '*Oxford History of India'*, p. 126). These were very unsettled and turbulent times. We know that a Greek satrapy survived in Bactria (Balkh) long after Alexander. Greek culture and mythology profoundly permeated the psyche of the inhabitants of present-day Punjab. Its vestiges can still be discerned by a perceptive mind in the peasant folklore.

It was only when the Scythians (Sakas) from south of the Caspian Sea moved in that the last surviving vestiges of Hellenic rule in the sub-continent were finally eliminated around 120 BC. They set up the Kushan dynasty and one of its rulers, Kanishka, extended his rule all the way into present day Xinjiang. Its evidence can be found in the writings of Hiuen Tsiang and the more recent discovery of inscripted wooden plaques unearthed by Sir Aurel Stein at Khotan.

There followed a prolonged period of turmoil, interspersed with years of calm and prosperity. Many times the Persians (Sassanians) invaded and occupied areas as far as River Jhelum and beyond, only to be evicted again by the Kushans. In the beginning of fifth century AD, a Chinese traveler by the name of Fa-Hien spent six years in northern India. According to him, by this time, the Brahmins had already started to re-assert themselves, seriously weakening the influence of Buddhism. A Hindu, Gupta Dynasty ruled the Gangetic plain at this time.

Legend has it that in 40 AD Saint Thomas, one of the disciples of Jesus Christ, came to Taxila to spread the Gospel. This is based on the discovery of an undated stone cross at the site. Considering that sign of the cross was adopted as the symbol of Christianity by the Romans not until fourth century AD, the story seems highly improbable. The signs of swastika and cross are ancient symbols that pre-date the Christian era by a long margin. Another legend places Saint Thomas in South India where he was executed for refusing to worship Hindu deities.

It was around 460 AD that the White Huns from Central Asia stormed in. By all accounts, these were barbaric savages, hardly touched by civilization. It is not clear how deeply they penetrated but they ruthlessly wiped out a whole vibrant and thriving civilisation in the north of what is now Pakistan. A Chinese pilgrim, Sung Yun, who visited Punjab in 520-21 AD, noted that it was then being ruled by a cruel and vindictive despot who perpetrated the 'most barbarous atrocities.' A rare account of Kashmir compiled by a Brahmin, Kalhana, in 1149 AD recorded that the Hun King, Mehr Gul, killed thirty million men, women and children, regardless of age and that the progress of his army was marked by a cloud of vultures and crows looking to feed on the human corpses.

There is another phenomenon less known in human history that dates back to these times ---- that of the gypsies in Europe. These wanderers claim to have originated in Punjab and gradually migrated westward until they reached Europe. The timing of the migration makes it probable that it may have been precipitated by the invasion of the White Huns and the devastation that followed.

By the end of sixth century AD, the rising power of Turks had displaced the White Huns in Central Asia. Once the connection with the homeland was severed, chances are, the Hun remnants in India were gradually absorbed into the native population. The destruction visited upon Buddhism's holy sites and the savagery perpetrated on its people by these barbarians proved to be the harbinger of the virtual demise of the religion in India.

In the middle of seventh century AD, another Chinese scholar, Yuan Chwang (Hieun-Tsiang) visited India and recorded that a king named Harsha was ruling over large but undefined parts of northern India, from Kanauj. The records of all such travelers need to be treated with some caution as sources of history. In the first place, of necessity, their knowledge and understanding of the local systems and their workings tends to be superficial and largely based on hearsay. Secondly, their accounts are prone to considerable embellishment in order to help exaggerate their own importance and accomplishments.

Some records of the time also mention a Hindu revivalist, named Shankar or Shankarachariya, who roamed India in a chariot shortly after Harsha, destroying everyone and everything that did not conform to Hindu ideals. In the absence of corroborative evidence, the details are hard to reconcile with any degree of veracity or reliability.

Whatever the case, it appears that darkness descended after Hersha. India, once again, disintegrated into its mosaic of small constantly warring princely states with indeterminate borders. This is how she remained for the next three centuries. When the dust cleared at the end of tenth century AD, we find that Hinduism was firmly back in the saddle and Buddhism had been virtually wiped out from the face of the country where it had originated. There is no record of how this came about and what happened to the Buddhists themselves. Their fate is a matter for pure conjecture. They might have been forced to reconvert, killed off or banished to the neighbouring countries of Tibet, Sri Lanka and Burma. Who knows? All we know for certain is that very few of them were to be found in India and these too only in the remotest corners of the land ---- none in the Hindu heartland of the Jamuna-Gangetic plain.

There has been much re-writing of history in recent years, especially in India. Most of it reflects Hindu prejudices. There is a concerted effort to glorify all that is Hindu and assign the blame for India's past and present ills on Muslim and Christian influences, without providing any credible historical proof. Unfortunately, many western sources have, unwittingly, fallen prey to this falsification and accepted the revised and corrupted versions of events without due scrutiny and verification expected of the historian. Just to quote one or two examples, Will Durant writes in his '*The Story of Civilization: Part 1, Our Oriental Heritage*' (p.524), published in 1954, '*------ no blood has been shed for religion in India except by its invaders. Intolerance came with Islam and Christianity; the Moslems proposed to buy Paradise with the blood of the "infidels" and the Portuguese, when they captured Goa, introduced the Inquisition to India.*'

This was written just seven short years after one of worst genocides in human history was perperated in the province of East Punjab in India in 1947, where more than one million Muslims were massacred and the rest permanently driven out to live in another country by Hindus and Sikhs. The unimaginably brutal carnage continued for four long months, during which time the government of India did little to stop it. Incredibly, the much-touted apostle of non-violence, Mr. Gandhi, never bothered to visit the province even once during the entire period when the brutal savagery was being committed against innocent unarmed men, women and children whose only crime was that they professed a different faith (for some eye witness accounts of the atrocities in East Punjab please see chapter 8 '*The Road to Freedom*' and chapter 9 '*The End*', of '*The Pathans of Jullunder*' by K. Hussan Zia, Maktaba-tul-Ilmiya, Lahore, 1996). Since then, hundreds of anti-Muslim pogroms involving looting, burning, destruction of places of worship and killing of hapless people have taken place and continue to take place in India.

In the summer of 2002 Hindu mobs went on a rampage of pre-planned murder, rapes and looting of Muslims in India's Gujarat State that left thousands dead. A report released by Amnesty International reveals the extent of the horror. 'Hundreds of girls and women were dragged out of their homes, stripped naked before their own families and raped, often gang-raped, had swords thrust into their bodies and were thrown onto fires while often still alive. The pregnant women and children were particular targets. ---- There is evidence of connivance of authorities in the organisation and execution of some of the attacks. ---- At least 33,000 children, many orphans, who reached relief camps, had seen their close family members deliberately killed before their eyes'. (Also see the award-winning documentary '*The Final Solution*' at:

http://video.google.ca/videoplay?docid=3829364588351777769&q=finalsolution

In another instance after recording, '*Buddhism disappeared from India having been replaced by Hinduism by ninth century AD* (p.506) and without giving any source or supporting evidence, Durant writes, '*The Mohammedans destroyed nearly all the monasteries, Buddhist or Brahmin, in northern India. Nalanda was burned to the ground in 1197, and all its monks were slaughtered; we can never estimate the abundant life of ancient India from what these fanatics spared'*. (*Story of Civilization* p. 558).

There is no credible contemporary account to support that Nalanda or its monastries were evident in 1197 AD, four hundred years after the disappearance of Buddhism from India, let aside its destruction by the Muslims. Al Beiruni, the anthropologist who did extensive research and recorded his findings in the book, *Kitab-al-Hind*, two hundred years earlier in early eleventh century, found little trace of Bhuddhists or Buddhism in the country '*India, as far as known to Alberuni was Brahmanic and not Buddhistic. In the first half of the eleventh century all traces of Buddhism in Central Asia, Khurasan, Afghanistan and North-West India seem to have disappeared; and it is a remarkable fact that a man of the inquisitive mind of Alberuni knew anything at all about Buddhism nor had any means for procuring information on the subject*' (*Alberuni's India*, p. xiv). If there were no Buddhists left in India, it defies credulity that Nalanda or any other Buddhist monasteries should continue to operate, in complete vacuum for four long centuries, in the midst of intolerant and hostile Hindu population.

In a similar vein, some western historians have also been guilty of spreading the myth that the fabled library at Alexandria in Egypt was burnt to the ground by the Muslim conquerors in seventh century AD. The library was said to be located in the Roman temple at 'Serapeum'. Some ancient accounts attribute burning of the books to an accident when Julius Caesar invaded the city during the Alexandrian War in 48 BC. The temple was known to exist until 391 AD, when it was destroyed by a Christian mob. There were no signs of the library when the Muslims came to Egypt in the seventh century.

The accusation that the '*Muslims destroyed nearly all the monasteries of Brahmins in northern India*' is plain non-sense and a gross exaggeration. If there had been any truth to the statement, we would have been hard put to find any Hindu place of worship in northern India that was built earlier than the nineteenth century. This is hardly the case. Thousands of them can be found in-tact all over India dating back to pre-Muslim era, many of them supported with grants from Muslim kings. It only takes a visit to Anant Nag, Benares, Hardvar, Mathra, Elora, Elephanta, Ajenta or any of the other hundreds of religious sites to appreciate the falsification and baseless nature of such accusations. Religious bias, prejudice and bigotry have done more injustice and harm to truth and objectivity in the recording of human history than perhaps all the other factors combined.

REFORMS AND THE FUTURE

There have been many attempts at reform of the Hindu religion. The first of these was the advent of Buddhism. It co-existed with Hinduism for better part of a millennium without replacing the latter as it had done with the other creeds in the Far East. The main reason for the resilience of Hinduism lies in the fact that it is much more than conventional religion. It permeates the society not simply in the spiritual but every other aspect of life as well. It defines social structure, lays down rules for its management and even details of how the individual is to conduct his everyday life, within a prescribed society. It is a self-contained system, jealously controlled and administered by a priesthood that has a deeply vested interest in its preservation. No other religion could succeed among India's Hindus unless it offered an alternative on the same scale and depth. No known religion, not even Orthodox Judaism, offers such a prescription.

A Hindu convert feels quite exposed and lost without the support of his all pervasive *Dharma* and is only comfortable if he can take some of his old beliefs and practices with him into the new faith. These are the reasons why Islam and Christianity could only find converts predominantly among India's Untouchables. What makes Hindus impervious to conversion is equally effective in keeping people of other faiths from becoming Hindus. No outsider can hope to fit comfortably into the exclusive and tightly knit caste-ridden Hindu social structure.

Since Buddha, there have been many attempts at reform from within, particularly, after coming into contact with the much less complicated monotheistic creeds of Islam and Christianity. None of these attempts had any permanent and lasting effect. The greatest Hindi poet of all time, Tulsi

Das, rewrote the Ramayana in sixteenth century AD in which he has presented Rama as 'one-God, creator of heaven and earth and redeemer of mankind who became incarnate as a king and lived the life of an ordinary mortal for our sanctification'. Hindus remember Tulsi Das with great pride but his message of one God they never really accepted.

Around the same period, Bhagat Kabir tried to synthesise Hinduism and Islam in the Sufi vein. Like Tulsi Das, he too cast Rama in the one-God mould but mainstream Hindus never took to the idea. Some think, his philosophy gave rise to Sikh religion. Emperor Akbar introduced his *Deen-e-Ilahi,* with notable lack of success, in late sixteenth century. It had little meaningful to offer and died with Akbar.

In 1828, a Bengali philanthropist, Raja Ram Mohan Roy, founded a new religion called *Brahma Samaj.* It specified abolition of polytheism, polygamy, caste system, child marriage, *sattee* and idolatry and advocated the worship of only one God --- *Brahman.* No trace of it can be found today.

In more recent times, another movement, *Arya Samaj,* founded by Swami Dayananda Saraswati and subsequently led by the nationalist Lala Lajpat Rai, denounced the caste system, polytheism, superstition, idolatry and Christianity and called for a return to Vedic practices. It met with limited success, for a time, before it too faded into oblivion.

Mahatama Gandhi, an ardent Hindu himself, also tried his hand at reformation. The effort might have given him some mileage politically but it made little impression on the religious beliefs of devout Hindus. They revered him but not to the extent of accepting his ideas on religion.

All the injustices, difficulties and hardships that these movements tried to address, within the religion, still remain unresolved. The divisions and disenchantment engendered by them have, if anything increased. These are producing reactions at two different levels. There is now an increasingly open acceptance of western norms and values among the educated elite and a correspondingly greater disillusionment with traditional Hindu practices.

More ominously, the split between the caste Hindus and the Untouchables has become far more confrontational and hostility prone. The society has become deeply polarised and religious differences have been carried into politics with a vengeance. There are increasing and widespread incidents of armed clashes between rival gangs of caste Hindus and the Untouchables (*Dalits*) particularly in the populous Behar and Uttar Pradesh states.

In 1925, Madhav Sadashiv Golwalkar, an admirer of Nazis, founded the RSS (Rashtaria Sevak Sungh ---- parent body of India's ruling Bharatia

Janata Party). It has a Fascist agenda based on ethnic and religious purification that states in unequivocal terms non-Hindus may stay in the India only if wholly subordinated to the Hindu nation, claiming nothing ---- not even citizens' rights. Pundit Jawaharlal Nehru, India's first Prime minister, had described it as 'an Indian version of fascism'. RSS appears on the US list of terrorist outfits (www.terrorism.com).

Minorities have been coming under increasing attacks by extremist Hindu organizations like RSS in recent years. In addition to the Muslims, increasing numbers of Sikhs and Christians have been targeted by extremist Hindus. As stated earlier, in 2000, Congressman Edolphus Townes of New York, along with a number of others, called on President Clinton to declare India a terrorist state, based on reports by various Indian human rights organizations. These held the Indian government agencies responsible, among other things, for systematically killing nearly eighty thousand Kashmiri Muslims and two hundred and forty thousand Sikhs over a course of ten years (*The Dawn'*, 6th June 2000). A motion along the same lines was only narrowly defeated in the US Congress in 1995.

There is no solution in sight and given the attitudes it is difficult to imagine how a peaceful and permanent solution to the minority issues will be found. Add to this widespread abject poverty among large sections of the people (according to a 2007 government study, 320 million workers in the 'unorganized' sector earn less than twenty rupees {40 cents} a day), over-population and joblessness and we have an explosive mixture of monumental proportions.

Tragically, the full implications of the situation are yet to be appreciated. Even if they were, it is difficult to imagine how the hurtling juggernaut that has been set in motion could be stopped at this stage. Worst of all, the strident calls for the revival of Hindu nationalism have drowned out the voices of reason. Many institutions, like The Voice of India in Delhi, are pushing out streams of publications that would be banned, as hate literature, in the more civilised world. Most of these misrepresent, distort and falsify history to draw misleading conclusions.

Other faiths are maligned to whip up religious passions and excite emotions and chauvinism among the Hindus. There is much falsification and demonisation of the roles played by Buddhism, Islam and Christianity in the making of India as she is today. It is a trend that does not bode well for the future of India and one that carries grave implications for her neighbours as well as for the minorities that reside within the country.

CHAPTER 2

MUSLIM PERIOD

THE ARABS

Within twenty years of the death of the Prophet, Muslim Arabs had become masters of Syria, Palestine and Egypt. They invaded Iran in 642 AD and defeated the Sassanian king Yazdgard at Nihawand, south of Hamadan. After this, the Arabs set about the reduction of the provinces of the Persian Empire to the east. Contingents under Abdullah Bin Amr struck out from Kirman and Neshapur and crossing Dasht-e-Lut, captured Herat, Merv and Balkh (Bactria). By 651 AD, most of Khurasan and Mawarrunahr (Transoxania) was under Arab control.

Shortly afterwards the third caliph, Usman, was murdered and divisions appeared among the Arabs. Inevitably these troubles influenced events in Central Asia bringing to a halt all further progress. It was not until the Ummayad caliph, Abdul Malik (685 - 705 AD) assumed power in Damascus that the rest of Transoxania, as far as Khwarzem in the west, Samarkand in the north and Seestan in the south came under Muslim rule. There were a few halfhearted and desultory raids in the direction of Kabul but Afghanistan was not completely subdued until well into the ninth century.

The Arabs were already familiar with the western parts of India. Taking advantage of the seasonal winds over the Arabian Sea, they had traded along her west coast from the Persian Gulf since times immemorial. After the advent of Islam, one or two expeditions from Bahrein had raided settlements north of Bombay during the reign of the second caliph in 637 AD but these had not amounted to much.

According to the geographer–historian, Ahmed Biladuri, as quoted by Elliot and Dawson in '*Historians of Sind*', Susil Gupta Ltd. Calcutta (p.17), the third caliph despatched one Hakim bin Jaballa-al-Abdi to India to gather information about the country. He reported back, '*The water is scarce, the fruits are poor, and the robbers are bold; if few troops are sent there they will be slain, if many, they will starve'*.

A small expedition sent to India by the next caliph, Ali bin Abu Talib, in 659 AD came to nothing. Such overland raids into Baluchistan and the adjoining areas became almost a regular feature during the rule of the first Umayyed caliph, Muaviya, and Arab rule was gradually extended as far as the Mekran coast.

In 712 AD, at about the same time as Muslim armies had subdued Spain and broken into Kashghar in eastern Turkistan (now a part of China), Al-Hajjaj, governor of Iraq who was also responsible for the Arab expansion to the north and east, dispatched a punitive expedition to Sind. It consisted of a force of about fifteen thousand mostly horse and camel borne troops led by his remarkable seventeen year old cousin, Mohammed bin Kasim. This was in response to the looting of some Arab trading ships in the port of Debal and the killing of their crews by the local Hindus. Within a short period of time the city was captured.

Raja Dahir, the ruler of Sind, called for support from other neighbouring Hindu rajas but their combined armies were defeated at Rawar on the left bank of the Indus. There was a second battle at Brahmanabad, the old capital of lower Sind that opened the way for the Muslims to reach Multan. This remained the limit of Arab influence in northern India for the next two hundred years. Areas north of Multan, including much of Punjab, all of North-West Frontier Province and Afghanistan continued to be ruled by Hindu princes. The Arabs managed to establish small trading posts along the western coast of South India but used these mostly as stepping stones for trading with Sri Lanka, Indonesia, Malaysia and the Philippines. They showed no inclination to expand their political influence into eastern or southern India.

It is interesting to note from the accounts of the period (*Chhachh Nama*, by an unknown Arab contemporary of Mohammed bin Kasim, '*Futuh-ul-Baldan*', by Biladuri, '*Tarikh-e-Sind*,' by Mir Mohammed Masoom, etc.) that Baluchistan and Sind, including some western parts of Rajputana (present-day Rajesthan) and areas as far north as the borders of Kashmir, formed a loose political confederation at the time. These autonomous states, composed of more or less the same areas as the erstwhile Indus Civilisation, inter-acted almost as if they were parts of the same country. There is little historical evidence to suggest that they had any significant social, commercial or political links with the rest of the Indian sub-continent that lay across the desert wastes to the east.

Historically, the Indus Valley was never an integral part of the political map of what constituted India under the British. From time to time some parts, like Punjab and Sind, were annexed by rulers in the east, only to break away as the opportunity presented itself. Remarkably, the excavated sites of the Indus Valley Civilization barring a few exceptions are all located in areas comprising present-day Pakistan or close to its borders and nowhere east of Thar Desert, in the Jamuna-Gangetic plain or the Central and South Indian Plateau. Sind was first incorporated into the Mughal Empire in India and Delhi rule in 1592 AD when Akbar established his rule there.

The accounts by the Arab historians also confirm that Buddhism was still alive and practiced by many tribes in the beginning of the eighth century but the relationship and inter-action between them and the Hindu tribes was uneasy and hostility prone. Annemarie Schimmel notes in her '*Islam in the Subcontinent*' (reprinted by Sang-e-Meel Publications, Lahore) that the largely Buddhist population was dissatisfied with the Hindu Brahmin Raja Dahir and may have facilitated Bin Kasim's campaign. She also records, '*Muhjammad ibn al-Qasim did not attempt mass conversion; he left the people to their ancient faith, except in cases of those who wanted to become Muslims, as Beiruni rightly states. It would indeed have been difficult for the small minority, which was operating at such a distance from Damascus, the centre of government, to impose new religio-social patterns upon a country of a very different culture*' (p.4).

The fate of Mohammed bin Kasim was as tragic as that of his two other brilliant Arab contemporaries, Tarik and Moosa, who had conquered Spain only to be recalled and humiliated by their superiors. Mohammed bin Kasim had been in Sind for a little over three years when his patron and governor, Al-Hajjaj, died. The brother of the new governor, Salih bin Abdul Rahman, had been executed by Hajjaj for professing *Kharji* beliefs. He took his revenge by torturing and killing members of Hajjaj's family, including Mohammed bin Kasim. It is a familiar malaise of the autocratic systems that the purest and the best seldom receive their just recognition and very often do not survive the jealousies and intrigue that inherently abound in such courts.

Sind continued to be ruled by various Arab governors. They dealt with numerous revolts by Hindu rajas that followed Mohammed bin Kasim's premature recall. A new capital was built on the shores of the river near Brahmanabad and named Mansurah, after the reigning caliph Al Mansur

(754 – 775 AD). Elliot and Dawson are of the view that the city of Hyderabad is the site of old Mansurah, others ascribe it to Nasirpur.

The Arabs also built another city and named it Mahfoozah. As the name implies, it was meant to be a more secure place but its location is not certain beyond that it was also located on a body of water. As the central authority in Baghdad weakened, it gradually lost its grip on the outlying provinces. Sind became virtually independent (circa 879 AD) and split in two with the northern half ruled by hereditary Amirs from Multan and the south, by another Arab family, from Mansurah.

The Arabs were expanding into areas as far apart as Spain and China. At each of these places their rule is known to have been fair, just and humane. There is no reason for them to have treated Sind any differently and engaged in uncharacteristic, wanton and indiscriminate killing-for-the-sake-of-killing of Hindus, as has sometimes been alleged by some historians in India and the West. It is just one more example of a biased and jaundiced view of history, often deliberate to serve a specific political purpose. The Arabs may have been ruthless in battle but their rule was magnanimous and just throughout.

Mohammed bin Kasim retained Raja Dahir's Brahmin prime minister and most of his administrative staff in his service. This is how historian Sir Stanley Lane-Poole has recorded Mohammed Bin Kasim's treatment of Hindus in Sind based on the accounts of numerous contemporary historians, '*The fall of Multan laid the Indus valley at the feet of the conqueror. The tribes came in ringing bells and beating drums and dancing in token of welcome. The Hindu rulers had oppressed them heavily, and the Jats and the Meds and other tribes were on the side of the invaders. ---- To such suppliants Mohammad Bin Kasim gave the liberal terms that the Arabs offered to all but their inveterate foes. ---- The temples, he proclaimed, shall be inviolate, like the churches of the Christians, the synagogues of the Jews, and the altars of the Magians. ---- The citizens and the villagers were allowed to furnish the tax collectors themselves; the Brahmans were protected and entrusted with high offices, for which their education made them indispensable; and the conqueror's instructions to all his officers were wise and conciliatory :- -----* (*Mediaeval India Under Muhammedan Rule A.D. 712 - 1764,* T. Fisher Unwin Ltd. London, pp. 9 - 11).

There was no attempt at mass conversion of the local population or to replace the prevailing laws and customs with new ones. It had been the same in Syria, Iran, Egypt and all the other lands occupied by the Arabs thus far which would seem to suggest that the concept of *sharia* laws was not evident at the time and it evolved at a much later date. Had they not acted in this manner, it would have been impossible for a few thousand Arabs to maintain their uninterrupted hold on Sind for the next three centuries.

Following the conquest of Sind, a number of Arab scholars and travelers visited the area to preach, trade, study and make records of their findings. Among them the fabled Sufi, Mansur Hallaj, who made the trip in 905 AD. It was the circumstances leading to his tragic execution in 922, following a trial for heresy by a religious court in Baghdad that made his a house-hold name in Punjab and Sind and fired the imagination of countless Sufi poets and historians everywhere. Professor Louis Massignon, who spent a life-time studying Hallaj, is reported to have died reciting the same Koranic verses as Hallaj did when he was led to his execution. There is a popular misconception that Hallaj was executed for professing in ecstasy to be at one with God. According to some sources, his crime lay in his heretical insistence that it was not necessary for a believer to travel to Makkah to perform Haj. More likely, he was falsely charged by his enemies to have practised magic learnt in Sind or accused of consorting with Ismaeli (Karmatian) heretics present in Multan.

Taking advantage of the weakness of the central authority in Baghdad, a movement of heretics based at Bahrein, the Karmatians (followers of the Ismaeli Sect), plundered southern Iraq and took possession of Makkah, killing all the Hajis that had gathered there (circa 937 AD). They even carried off the sacred stone, *Hajr-al-Aswad*, from *Ka'aba*, damaging it in the process. After being driven out from Iraq they turned to Sind and took possession of both Multan and Mansurah around 985 AD. Beiruni notes in his '*Kitab al-Hind*' that they destroyed not only the famous Hindu Temple of the Sun at Multan that Bin Kasim had spared but also closed down the mosque built by Bin Kasim. According to '*Kamil-ut-Twareekh*', it was Mahmud Ghaznavi the Turk who, on his way back from the raid on the famous Hindu stronghold of Somnath, dislodged the Karmatians from Sind in 1025 AD, thus bringing the Arab rule in the province to an end.

It is strange that even though such a powerful symbol of Islam as *Hajr-al-Aswad* was missing from its holiest site for many years, there is no historical record of any calls for action against the outrage by the any of the ruling elite, clerics or even people at large for its recovery and restoration. It was the same when the crusaders occupied Jerusalem. It remained in non-Muslim hands for almost a century during which indescribable horrors were committed against its Muslim population. All the Muslim powers in the region abandoned them to their fate and took no action. When Salahuddin Ayubi finally felt compelled, his letters inviting the caliph in Baghdad and the king of Persia to join forces with him went unanswered. The manifest display of apathy and indifference remains incomprehensible unless, the prevalent religious sentiment on such matters at the time was different to what it is today.

The caliphate in Baghdad had deviated far from the Islamic ideals by the middle of ninth century AD. Unprecedented riches and opulence had corrupted the caliphs beyond belief. Disgusted with their excesses, different regions were beginning to raise their heads in revolt. In Seestan, the *Kharji* movement was strong, aided by resurgence in Iranian national spirit against Arab political and cultural domination.

The caliph turned to the local Saffarids for help and appointed their leader, Yakub, as the Amir and included Sind in his domain. He captured Kabul in 872 (H. 259), extending his rule as far as Balkh and laid the foundations of Ghazni. The local Hindushahi kings were pushed south towards Peshawar. In 875 he marched on Baghdad but was defeated. Yakub marks the beginning of non-Arab Muslim rulers who were to dominate the world of Islam in times to come.

This is also the beginning of Muslim forays deeper into India, outside of Sind. With these also came the first authentic scientific records and knowledge of conditions and events in the country. Before this, aside from what the Greeks and a couple of Chinese travelers had left behind, there is only mythology and huge yawning gaps in Indian history. The first complete and most valuable of the new accounts is by the remarkable Muslim sociologist and anthropologist, Al-Beiruni (973 - 1048) in '*Kitab-al-Hind*' (Treatise on India). He was preceded by many others like the historian Al-Baladuri (c. 840 AD), the tenth century travelers Masoodi and Ibne Haukal; the historian at the court in Ghazni, Al-Utbi, and the unknown author of a most valuable treatise, '*Hadood-al-Alam*' (Limits of the World).

THE TURKS

Ghazni was an outlying province of the Samani Empire based at Bukhara that had succeeded the Saffarids. It was ruled by '*Mamluks*' ---- slaves of Turkish descent who formed the bulk of the Muslim armies by then. In 977 AD a slave by the name of Sabuktgin, who was married to the daughter of the ruler Alaptgin, gained power in Ghazni. He gathered an army of Afghans, who had only recently converted to Islam and raided the kingdom of Hindushahi King Jaipal to the east and twice defeated him in battle.

Even though the proud Pathans may be loath to admitting it, these battles were fought between Muslim and Hindu Afghans because not all the Afghans had converted to Islam by then (*The Pathans,* by Sir Olaf Caroe, Oxford University Press, chapters VIII and IX). Sabuktgin's second son, Mahmood, came to power in 997 AD. He was one of the most outstanding military commanders in history, having never tasted defeat in scores of major campaigns stretching over a quarter of a century. By the time these were over, his domain stretched from Iran to Balkh and from Punjab to Khorasan.

Altogether, Mahmud undertook seventeen campaigns in India between 1000 and 1026 AD. The first of these was against his father's old enemy, Jaipal, in the north-west. Contrary to many assertions by mostly Hindu historians, '*Mahmood was not cruel; he seldom indulged in wanton slaughter; and when a treaty of peace had been concluded, the raja and his friends were set free,*' (*Mediaeval India,* p. 19). In subsequent years he attacked Peshawar, Waihind, Bhera, Multan, Nawasa and Nagarkot. The Hindu rulers of India were alarmed by these developments and joined forces under Jaipal's son, Anandpal. It was to no avail. Mahmud defeated the combined Rajput armies of Hindu India near Peshawar in 1008. After this the raids were extended to Lahore, Kangra, Thanesar, Mathura, Kanauj, Gwaliar and Somnath.

It is true that Mahmud was a devout Muslim but it would be wrong to say that the aim of his raids on India was exclusively in the service of Islam. Almost without exception, every Muslim invader that followed him invoked the name of Islam as a justification for his actions and intrusions. Coupled with the incidental prospects of becoming rich, it served as an excellent motivation to calm the conscience and fears of the troops. The primary and real motive was seldom much more than personal enrichment and aggrandizement. They were basically interested in confiscating the immense riches that the Hindu priests and rulers had extorted from their people and stashed in the temples and palaces. How else can one explain that while Mahmud attacked and destroyed temples in India, Hindus continued to live in peace and had complete freedom to worship in his own domain? There were many Hindus among Mahmud's troops, including one by the name of Tilak who rose to the rank of a general under his son, Masud.

It is also not true that Muslims attacked Hindu temples wantonly to destroy their idols as a religious duty. Islam prohibits idol worship for its followers but the use of force in the name of religion is strictly forbidden in the Koran, as also interference in other people's religion. The only idols that were destroyed by the Prophet were those he found in *Ka'aba*, the House of God in Makka, to cleanse it from *Shirk* (sharing with the Divine). Muslims subsequently came to rule vast areas that were littered with millions of statues of all shapes and kinds belonging to scores of different creeds and civilizations that they left unscathed. Most of these can still be found intact at the ancient sites in Egypt, Greece, the Middle East, Iran, Central Asia and India. These places have remained under Muslim control for over a thousand years. What the Taliban in Afghanistan did to Buddha's statues in Bamian was strictly against the spirit of Islam. Had it been otherwise, these could not have been left standing for the past twelve hundred years.

Temple desecration has been a common feature in Indian history which predates the arrival of Islam. The deity of each temple was rooted in the local mindset and was considered a popular symbol of political power. Any harm or insult to the temple was considered to be an insult to the kingdom. Beginning in sixth century there are several examples of Hindu victors desecrating the temples of the defeated. For instance, in 642 AD the Pallava King Narasemhavan I looted the image of Ganesha from the Chalukyan capital of Vatapi. The exploits of the Chola King Rajendra were so prolific that he decorated his capital with idols looted from a number of neighboring kingdoms. Kashmiri King Harsha reportedly raized the looting of temples to an institutionalized activity. Similarly, Hindu rulers attacked Buddhist monasteries and pillaged these mercilessly (see *Temple Desecration and Indo-Muslim States*, by Richard M. Eaton, Perigrec Books, New York, 2000).

Mahmud did not even try to establish his rule in India. He was much more interested in the west and extended his domain all the way to the Aral Sea in the north, Hamadan in the south and the mountains of Kurdistan on the Caspian in the west. If the spread and service of Islam had been his objective, history would have recorded a very different turn of events and he would have concentrated most of his energies in areas inhabited by the non-Muslims instead.

None of the Muslim invaders ever intended or attempted to turn India into an Islamic State. It is open to conjecture if conquest based on purely temporal considerations has not been deliberately misinterpreted by subsequent historians, as a form of religious crusade, on both sides of the divide for different reasons. The affect was the same, regardless of the motives. It sowed the seeds of mistrust and hatred, especially among the Hindus, and created a divide that became impossible to bridge in later years.

The inroads that Islam was beginning to make in the sub-continent were not due so much to the conquering monarchs as to the scholars and Sufis who preceded or followed them. The first known scholar to preach Islam in the north of India, Shaikh Mohammed Ismael al-Bokhari (d. 1056) was already present in Lahore when Mahmud attacked the city.

Ali ibne Usman al-Jullabi al-Hajveri (popularly known as Daata Ganj Bakhsh), the patron saint of Lahore, arrived from Ghazni shortly afterwards. His '*Kashf al-Mahjub*' is one of the very early Farsi works on Sufism. The city also hosts the shrine of Bibi Pakdamanan, attributed to seven pious Muslim ladies, whose arrival is said to date back to seventh century AD but the details are extremely vague and there is no way of confirming such a claim. Then there are the tombs of Imam Nasiruddin in Jullunder (East Punjab) and his brother in Sialkot whose arrival in India is reported to predate that of al-Bokhari in Lahore but historical details are again scanty.

In the finest Islamic tradition, Mahmud lived a simple and austere life. Much of his time was served in religious devotion and in search of knowledge and wisdom. Before he died in 1030, he had turned Ghazni into one of the great capitals and centres of learning in the world. Mahmud built one of the first universities of the Muslim world and a great library and museum in his capital along with a number of grand mosques. The professors and teachers received generous regular salaries and pensions on retirement. Two hundred thousand pounds (four hundred thousand *dirhams*) were set aside annually as grants for scholars. Poets, like Firdausi, Farrukhi and Asjudi, scientists like Al-Beiruni whose knowledge of Greek philosophy, mathematics and anthropology was masterly; philosophers like Al-Farabi, historians like Al-Utbi and Abul Fazal Baihaki and hundreds of other thinkers and academicians had flocked to make Ghazni their home.

Unfortunately, all this did not last for long. As so often happens in situations created by autocratic personal rule, the institutions seldom survive for long after the driving force behind them is removed. Mahmud's rule was very much personal. He did not create or institutionalize a system of government that could endure. His successors were men of lesser calibre. It was not within their capacity to run such a vast empire. Soon, there was dissension and decay and the empire began to shrink. Sensing weakness, Seljuks, one of the Turkish tribes from across the Oxus, established themselves at Merv, then Isphahan and, eventually, Baghdad itself in 1091.

Their leader, Alp Arsalan, operating from Herat, reduced Ghazni to a tributary status. In 1150, Ghaur tribes from central Afghanistan raided Ghazni under Ala-uddin 'Jahansoz', wreaking havoc and burning everything to the ground, including all the libraries and books. There was a struggle for ascendancy for a time with the Ghuzz tribes of Turks from the north before Ghauris could establish themselves and rebuild Ghazni in 1173 but only as a provincial town. Ibn Batuta, who passed through Ghazni in 1333, notes that the city was mostly in ruins even then.

Ala-uddin Jahansoz's nephew Muizzuddin, known to history as Mohammed Ghauri, set out to conquer India, starting with Multan in 1175. He captured Punjab from the successors of Mahmud in 1186 but failed to take Delhi in his first attempt four years later. He returned the next year to defeat the combined Hindu armies under Prithvi Raj Chauhan near Karnal. This was effectively the end of Hindu rule in Delhi until 1947. The Turks left most of the land and civil administration unchanged and intact. It was the same with the personal and social lives of the people.

The fact that the Turks managed to establish themselves in India so quickly and easily gives a strong indication that the Hindu masses were not opposed to the new rule which hardly interfered with their daily lives. It is next to impossible for a very small number of foreigners to continue to rule a vast country, uninterruptedly for over seven hundred years, without the willing acceptance and participation by the overwhelming majority of its people. Whatever resistance there was came from the privileged classes and was easily and effectively dealt with. The claim that Muslim rule in India was universally unpopular and resented is just another one of the many historical myths created in more recent times.

Much of the misinformation emanates from western sources that have a long history of antipathy towards Islam and the Muslims. This is true for India as well as in other parts of the world. At the end of nearly five centuries in Eastern Europe, Turkish Muslim rule had given rise to more than two dozen different nations with their religions, languages and cultures not only in tact but also profoundly enriched. The liberators wasted no time in expelling all the Turks and forcing the local Muslims to convert to Christianity and even change their names. It is true, the victors get to write history but when facts are deliberately misrepresented or concealed in the name of nationalism or religion, it is history that suffers.

For some strange reason, Mohammed Ghauri did not settle in Delhi but went westward to attack Khwarzem only to lose and turn back. He was assassinated on the bank of the Indus by Gakhar tribesmen (Annemarie Schimmel thinks it was the dispossessed Karmatians from Multan and

Ucch) in 1206 and, in the absence of any son, his Turkish slave, Kutab-uddin Aibak succeeded to the throne in Delhi.

Like all the rulers anywhere in the Muslim world, he obtained an investiture from the caliph in Baghdad to legitimize his rule. It was an essential formality that provided the authority to govern and have his name read in the *Khutba* during Friday prayers in every mosque in the kingdom. Kutab-uddin extended his rule over northern India all the way east as far as Bengal. The Kuwatul-Islam mosque in Delhi, with its Kutab Minar that still stands as a monument to Islamic architecture, was built during his reign. He died playing polo in 1210 and lies buried in a simple grave off Anarkali Bazar in Lahore.

His son did not prove to be a worthy ruler and the reins of the kingdom passed into the hands of another slave, Altamesh, whose successors included Razia Sultana, the first lady to ascend a throne in the history of Islam in 1236. Apart from her, Shajar-ad-dur was another Muslim lady of slave origin who ruled Egypt in 1250. She defeated the crusade of King Louis IX of France and afterwards spared his life. Coincidentally, a third Muslim lady held the reins in Faras (Iran) for a quarter of a century during the same troubled period when the Mongol hordes ravaged Iran.

It is noteworthy that at least in the case of Razia Sultana there were no objections raised to her ascending the throne, on religion grounds, by the *ulama* at the time even though she rode an elephant and appeared in public without *purdah.* Indeed, it was 400 years before some scholars in Delhi opined that the act was contrary to *Sharia*. It may be that laws of *Sharia* are not universal or immutable after all, as claimed by some, but are subject to change with time (see Maulana Maudoodi in his book '*Sood,*' p. 183 - 4).

Altamesh was a pious man with strong leanings towards Sufism. He offered to appoint Kutabuddin Bakhtyar Kaki, the well-known Sufi belonging to the Chishti *silsila*, as *Shaikh-ul-Islam*, to manage religious affairs of the state but, since Chishtis do not approve of involvement in political affairs, the offer was refused and Syed Nuruddin Mubarak Ghaznavi, a Suhrawardi disciple, was given the job instead. Chishtis have a softer approach to Islam as against a more rigid interpretation by the Suhrawardis.

It was during this period that many prominent missionaries belonging to the Suhrawardi *silsila* took up residence in Bengal, among them, Shah Jalaluddin Tabrezi, who died in Sylhet in 1244 AD and the author's progenitor, Ibrahim Danishmand. The latter was a disciple of Shaikh Mohammed Shahabuddin Suhrawardi in Baghdad at the same time as

Makhdoom Bahauddin Zakria of Multan. He died in Sonargaon, the old capital of Bengal, in 1260 AD and lies buried in a well-maintained tomb in nearby Mograpara.

The foremost Sufi missionary of India, Khwaja Hasan Moinuddin Chishti (1141 – 1236 AD) came to Delhi from Sistan in 1193, about a year after Mohammed Ghauri, and settled in Ajmer. According to him the Sufi ideal embodied that, '*The highest form of devotion is to redress the misery of those in distress, to fulfill the needs of the helpless and to feed the hungry.*' The patron saint of Sind, Lal Shahbaz Kalandar (d. 1323), originally from Sistan, was a *khalifa* (disciple) of Bahauddin Zakaria Multani. He lies buried in Sehwan in a tomb built by Sultan Feroze Shah in 1357 AD. Another revered Sufi, Shah Abdul Latif Bhittai (1689-1752) has his mausoleum near Hala, north of Hyderabad in Sind. He lived through a particularly tortured period in the sub-continent's history and recorded his message (*Risalo*) in a compendium of poems extolling virtues similar to those preached by Moinuddin Chishti.

Sufism gained rapid popularity in India, swelling the ranks of converts to Islam. Almost all of these came from the low-caste Hindus or those without any caste. It happened mostly in burgeoning cities where individuals were relatively free from the stranglehold of the caste ridden Hindu society and could experience first hand the social equality, brotherhood and justice prevalent among the Muslims. Thus it was that the growth in cities went hand in hand with the growth in the numbers of Muslims in India. The spillover into the villages was a later and different development.

In the process of spreading Islam, Sufism prompted a reaction among the Hindus, giving rise to a number of reformist movements mainly aimed at mitigating the excesses of the caste system, as mentioned earlier. The two most noteworthy Hindu reformers in sixteenth-century Punjab were Guru Nanak, whose teachings later formed the basis of Sikh religion, and Bhagat Kabir, a low-caste weaver by trade, who wanted to rid Hinduism of its oppressive castes and rituals and make it a religion more in tune with Sufi teachings of love and service to mankind.

These were also the times when most of the then known civilised world lay prostrate, having been laid waste by the Mongols. Chengez Khan, after reducing Khwarzem in 1219, turned on Ghazni. There were a series of running battles with its Afghan ruler, Jalauddin, who was pursued until he had crossed the Indus. Chengez Khan chose not to follow him and India was spared the scourge for the time being. Before returning to Mongolia, as was his custom, Chengez Khan settled a contingent of Mongols in the

Afghan uplands now known as the Hazarajat. Their descendants, called 'Hazaras', can be found there to this day as, indeed, they are found in places as far afield as parts of Russia and eastern Europe.

Chengez Khan's son, Chaghatai, inherited Central Asia when the Mongol Empire was divided up between the different hordes. It was a scorched land and there was nothing but destruction and devastation all around; no trade, no administration, no cultural activity. All Chaghatai could think of was more raids. In one of these he ransacked and destroyed Lahore in 1240.

In some ways, India benefited from the turmoil and devastation caused by the Mongol invasions. A large number of scholars as well as traders and craftsmen from Central Asia and the Middle East flocked to the Muslim kingdom in Delhi in search of peace and security. It brought prosperity as well as infusion of new thought and knowledge. An enormous amount of literature dealing with *Hadees* and *Fikah* was produced in India around this time by a large number of scholars of Islam but then stagnation seemed to have set in.

There has been little progress since then and Islam in the sub-continent and to a large extent in rest of the world as well, has remained frozen in its thirteenth century mould. Muslims seem incapable of breaking out of it to regain the dynamism inherent in Islam. There are many reasons for it, some internal others have to do with external factors but, mostly, it has been due to the inability of subsequent scholars to relate to the changed conditions and new realities that evolved. Almost all of them have sought solace in the past in the misplaced belief that by reverting to it the bygone glories will be somehow resurrected ---- a flawed piece of logic if there ever was one.

This has been by far the worst and deadliest legacy of the depredation caused by Chengez Khan and his successors. They destroyed the flourishing Islamic Civilization and its institutions so utterly and completely that it was rendered incapable of picking up the pieces again and resuming its march to progress.

Nasir-uddin, the third son of Altamesh ruled India in mid-thirteenth century ---- a pious, dervish-like character who lived simply and paid for his needs by making copies of the Koran. He was fortunate in having the services of a remarkably talented ex-slave, Ghias-uddin Balban, to manage the affairs of the state for him. Upon the king's death in 1266, Balban succeeded him in office, having risen from slave, water carrier, huntsman, general and statesman to sultan. He put down repeated revolts by various Rajput rulers and also held the Mongols at bay in the north. Amid all these campaigns he also managed to find the time and effort to build new roads and rid much of India of the scourge of organised bands of robbers and marauders that have traditionally infested its countryside. All said and done, Balban was one the ablest men ever to rule India. Although himself a Turk, he adopted the Persian style in his court and made Farsi the court language which remained in force until 1857.

Slave kings are a phenomenon peculiar to Muslim lands. In order to properly understand it, we have to understand Islam and the treatment and position of the slaves within it. These were very different to the conditions found among the Europeans who regarded slaves as sub-human and not entitled to any compassion, a blatantly racist outlook that had the support of Christian churches. Slaves had no rights and no recourse to law in the West. Crimes such as insubordination or desertion were punished by stretching alive on a torture wheel after smashing arms and legs with iron bars or impaling the victims on stakes in the ground where they might take two or three days to die. The main criticisms leveled against Islam in medieval Europe included, among other things, that the Muslims treated their women with too much respect, their slaves too kindly and they took a bath every day.

Among the Muslims, although the slave remained the property of his owner who could buy and sell him or her, for all other purposes he was treated almost the same as any other member of the family. There were no limits placed on his advancement and he remained free to rise as high within the system as his talents would take him. When someone expressed concern at the lack of a male heir to King Mohammed Ghauri, he is said to have replied, 'Have I not thousands of children in my Turkish slaves?' Four of his most important governors, Aibek in Delhi, Bakhtiyar in Bengal, Yildiz in Afghanistan and Kubacha in Multan, all originated from the slave stock.

For a slave to rise to such a high position he had to prove his worth over a long period of time. This was not necessarily the case with any son of the king who remained mostly an unknown and untested quantity. In this respect any talented and properly groomed slave held a distinct edge. Slaves formed a very significant and important component of the government. To get some measure of this, there were 180,000 slaves employed in various positions during Feroze Tughlak's rule. A whole government department, including a treasury, existed just to look after their affairs.

Balban died in 1287. His ablest son and successor, Mohammed, had died fighting the Mongols a few years earlier. An inexperienced seventeen year old grandson, Kaikobad, ascended the throne and gave himself up to lechery, debauchery and drunkenness. After much palace intrigue, Kaikobad was assassinated in 1290 and his place was taken by one of Balban's Afghan generals, Jalal-uddin Khilji. He was an aging, mild mannered and saintly individual who did not seem to fit the role assigned to him. Nonetheless, he managed to repulse a determined Mongol attack on Lahore in 1292 AD. Two years later an army led by his nephew, Alauddin, entered Deccan for the first time.

Soon, the ambitious nephew and son-in-law, Alauddin, disposed of Jalauddin and himself ascended the throne in Delhi. He was an able general and, after dealing with some extremely serious Mongol raids on Delhi, became the first Muslim ruler to subjugate the Deccan plateau. Alauddin may be regarded as ruthless and cruel for the way he dealt with the prisoners taken in the wars against the Mongols and with those who were suspected of being disloyal to him but he lived in a different era. It would be unfair to judge him by today's standards. Going by the norms of his time, Alauddin was one of the most powerful and successful kings in the history of India.

Apart from all his military successes, he developed and instituted the administrative structure and land revenue system for which Akbar was to later claim credit. It included the powerful office of *Sadr-as-Sadur* that functioned as the chief law enforcer of the kingdom as well as the administrator of religious grants and estates. Among the best known figures in Alauddin's time were the court poet, Amir Khusro, and his life-long and inseparable friend, the patron saint of Delhi Nizamuddin Aulia. The latter's *pir*, Lahore's Baba Farid Shakar Ganj (d. 1265) had belonged to the Chishti *Silsila* emanating from Moinuddin Chishti through Bakhtiar Kaki (d. 1235). He had left Delhi a little disillusioned with the affairs of the state and settled in Lahore after spending some time in Pakpattan.

The Khilji dynasty came to an end in 1321 when Aluddin's son, Mubarak Shah, was murdered by his favourite courtier, a Hindu convert called Khusrau Khan, who proclaimed himself Sultan Nasir-uddin. He was a mean and debauched man and made himself extremely unpopular with all the courtiers as well as the populace within a short period of four months through very distasteful and unsavoury acts. This prompted Ghias-uddin Tughlak Shah, one of Alauddin's very able generals, who had repulsed no less than twenty nine Mongol attacks, to take to the field and rid the country of Khusrau Khan.

Ghias-uddin quickly restored order and put the country back on its feet. He died in 1325 when the roof of a wooden pavilion collapsed over his head.

Ibn Batuta, who was in Delhi fifteen years later, quotes an eye witness to support his assertion that the accident may have been engineered by Tughlak's son, Prince Jauna (neither the historian Barani nor Farishta support the story), who then ascended the throne as Mohammed Tughlak.

Mohammed Tughlak was a talented, if erratic and impatient, monarch. He put into effect some ill fated schemes, including the introduction of token money, building of a new capital at Daulatabad in Deccan and the invasion of Tibet that came to grief. His massive failure forcefully underlines the need for a system of checks and balances if individuals in power, no matter how able and well-intended, are to be saved from going tragically and horribly wrong. Soon, the greatest empire that India had known so far started to fall apart and Deccan and Bengal broke away. It was during this time that Ibn Batuta toured and recorded his impressions of India in the years 1333 to 1347. Mohammed Tughlak died in 1351 and, in the absence of a son, was succeeded by his cousin, Feroz Shah.

Feroze was a kind, gentle and God fearing person but not much of a general. He went to great lengths to put right the wrongs done by his predecessor and it greatly increased his popularity among the people. As Afif the panegyrist who attended the court wrote after his death, '*Under Feroze all men, high and low, bonded and free, lived happily and free from care. The court was splendid. Things were plentiful and cheap. Nothing untoward happened during his reign. No village remained waste, no land uncultivated.*' He has also recorded the prevailing prices of some grains at the time. Wheat cost half a rupee per *maund* (approx 36 kilos), barley and other grains were half that price and a rupee would fetch five *seers* (4 ½ kilos) of sugar (*Mediaeval India,* p.150). Feroze Shah died in 1388, at the age of 90. A succession of rulers followed including one (Sikander Shah) who lasted only six weeks. There was also a time when there were two kings, one in Delhi and the other in Ferozabad nearby, both puppets in the hands of court officials.

The apparent weakness was an open invitation, both to the Hindu rajas to rebel and to the outsiders to try their hands at adventure in India. Taimur Shah, the Turkish ruler of Samarkand, had already over-run Iran, Mesopotamia and Afghanistan. He descended on Delhi with ninety thousand horsemen in 1398, plundering and slaughtering along the way. The city surrendered after a brief and unequal fight. Unfortunately, the terms of surrender were not met in time and it resulted in great tragedy. As Taimur has himself put it, '*All my army, no longer under control, rushed to the city and thought of nothing but killing, plundering and making prisoners. ---- Although I wished to spare them, I could not succeed, for it was the will of God that this calamity should fall upon the city*'. Only the quarter inhabited by the Syeds and *ulama* escaped the general sack. After two weeks, Taimur moved on to pillage Ferozabad, Merut and Hardwar, returning to Afghanistan via Lahore and Jammu.

He installed his own viceroy, Khizar Khan, who founded the short-lived Syed dynasty but, in reality, it was in name only and there was no effective king in Delhi. His successors' influence did not extend beyond a few score miles from the city. The country to the north lay in ruins and in the grip of famine. Elsewhere, the Hindu rajas had proclaimed their independence. The Syed dynasty was replaced in 1451 by the Lodis, a branch of Khilji Afghans.

The first of these, Bahlol Lodi, offered the Afghans attractive terms to permanently settle along India's northern borders as a means of checking tribal incursions. For a time, authority was revived in Delhi and the kingdom expanded once more but there was none of the old vigour left among the Muslims. In Lane-Poole's words, '*A race of conquerers had become a squabbling crowd, jostling each other for the luxuries of thrones, but wanting the power to hold the sceptre. The respect which belongs to a caste of foreigners, who kept themselves apart and observed strict rules of religious and social law, had been degraded when those laws were lightly esteemed, when the harems of Muslims were filled with native women, when Hindus who nominally professed Islam were promoted to high office ---- when the Mohammaden domination, in short, had become the rule of the half caste*' (*Mediaeval India,* p.189).

Sikander replaced Bahlol in 1488 and nominally ruled over a collection of nearly independent states, jagirs and provinces. His son, Ibrahim, who ascended the throne in 1518, was a tyrant and an injudicious and unwise ruler. Soon, there were revolts all over the country. This obliged some of the very people who had helped to set the Lodis on the throne to turn to the king of Afghanistan for help. That proved effectively the end of the Afghan rule in India, except for a brief interlude a few years hence.

The tribes that inhabited the areas comprising present day Pakistan had converted to Islam in the early years. This was not the case with the rest of the country. The numbers of Muslims in the rest of India remained relatively small, probably, not exceeding a few hundred thousand in the first three centuries after they captured the throne at Delhi. It raises the intriguing question as to how so few of them managed to rule over scores of millions of unwilling Hindus for so long? The answer is complex and lies mainly in the nature and make-up of the two cultures. It may not provide the complete answer and not every one may agree with all of it, but it is worth reproducing at length what a shrewd observer like Stanley Lane-Poole has to say on the subject:

' ---- *To the Indian, power is a divine gift, to be exercised absolutely by God's anointed, and obeyed unquestionably by everyone else. A king who is not absolute loses in the oriental mind the essential quality of kingship. Every eastern people, if left to itself, sets up a despot, to whose decrees of life and death it submits with the same resignation and assent that it shows towards the fiat of destiny. In the East l' etat c'est moi, the king is the state, its ministers are his instruments, its people are his slaves. His worst excesses and most savage cruelties are endured in the same way as plague and famine: all belong to the irresistible and inscrutable manifestations of the divine order of the universe. The only kind of King the East tolerates with difficulty is the faineant. Let him be strong and masterful, and he may do as he please; but the weak sovereign rarely keeps his throne long, and keeps it only by force of traditional loyalty or dread of the unknown risks of revolution.*

'In the history of Mohammedan India, then, we have to do with kings and their works. They were surrounded by a court of officers and functionaries, who are raised or displaced at royal pleasure. Beneath them toil incessantly millions of patient peasants and industrious townsfolk. These people have not changed in any essential characteristic since the dawn of history. They have witnessed the successive inroads of horde after horde of invading foreigners, and have incorporated some part of each new element into their ancient system. They have obeyed the king, whether Aryan, Hun, Greek, Persian, Rajput, Turk, Afghan, Mongol or English, with the same inveterate resignation, contented or at least not very discontented with their immemorial village system and district government, which corrected to some extent the contrasts of successive foreign innovators. Whatever king may rule, so the Indian would argue, there will be plague and famine and constant but not energetic labour, and so long as the rice and millet grow and salt is not too dear, life is much the same and the gods may be propitiated. The difference caused in the riyat's life by a good or a bad king is too slight to be worth bothering. The good and the ill are all alike things of a day; they pass away as the life passes when the king decrees a death or massacres a village; but others follow and the world goes on, and the will of God is eternal.

'The kings whose deeds are to be described were foreigners in origin, but this made little difference in the respect which their authority implied. There is of course as great a contrast between a Muslim Turk and a Hindu Rajput as between a Scottish Presbyterian and a Spanish Catholic; but the reverence paid to power overbore all distinctions of race. The caste system

had accustomed Indians to immovable barriers between classes, and though the Muslim kings had no claim of pedigree and not much distinction of ceremonial purity, they formed in a way a caste, the caste of Islam, a fellowship of equal brotherhood unsurpassed in coherence and strength in all the world. The great power of Islam as a missionary influence in India has been due to the benefits of this caste. The moment an Indian accepts Islam he enters a brotherhood which admits no distinctions of class in the sight of God, and every advancement in office and rank and marriage is open to him. To those outside Islam the yoke of the alien ruler was no worse than that of the local raja. Both represented a separate caste, and both belonged to the inscrutable workings of providence.

'The essential union of the Muslims as a conquering caste was indeed the chief cause of their successful hold of the vastly preponderating multitudes they governed. Their power in India was always that of an armed camp, but it was a camp in which all the soldiers fought shoulder to shoulder for the same cause, in which all were equal brothers; and it had the immense resource of being able to draw continuously and in unlimited numbers upon the recruiting grounds of Mohammedan countries behind it, which were always reinforcing their co-religionists by fresh bodies of hardy adventurers, free from the lethargy of self-indulgence that too often etiolates the exotic in the Indian forcing house. The very bigotry of their creed was an instrument of self-preservation; in mere self-defence they must hold together as God's elect in the face of the heathen, and they must win over proselytes from the Hindus, whether by persuasion or by the sword, to swell their isolated minority. Hence the solidarity and the zeal which, added to their greater energy and versatility, gave the Muslims their superiority over natives who were sometimes their equal in courage, though never in unity, in enthusiasm, or in persistence. The clanishness of the Hindus, their devotion to local chiefs, and their ineradicable jealousies of each other, prevented anything approaching national patriotism; and their religious system, which rested upon birth and race and class, while precluding the very idea of proselytism, deprived them of the fanatical zeal of the missionary. Moreover they were always on the defensive, and except behind ramparts the defensive position is the weaker part. The Muslims, inspired by the spirit of adventure, of militant propaganda, of spreading the kingdom of God upon earth, as well as seizing the goods of this world, had every advantage over the native Hindus, and when the invaders were led by kings who embodied these masterful qualities their triumph was assured' ('*Mediaeval India*', pp. 60 - 64).

THE MUGHALS

Babur, a charismatic military leader of rare genius and descendant of Amir Taimur, defeated Ibrahim Lodi at Panipat in 1526 to lay the foundations of the Mughal Empire in India. A year later, he delivered a resounding and comprehensive defeat to the combined Rajput armies, under Rana Sangha, at Kanwaha that broke the back of all Hindu resistance. The Afghans continued their struggle in the eastern provinces until, eventually, they too were forced to sue for peace and their rule was confined to Bengal.

Babur was not too enamoured with India. His impressions, as recorded in his diary, *Tuzk-e-Baburi*, read: 'The country and towns of Hindustan are extremely ugly. All its towns and lands have a uniform look; its gardens have no walls; the greater part of it is a level plain. ---- Hindustan is a country that has few pleasures to recommend it. The people are not good looking. They have no idea of the charms of a friendly society. They have no genius, no intellectual comprehension, no politeness, no kindness or fellow-feeling, no ingenuity or mechanical invention in planning or executing their handicrafts, no skill or knowledge in design or architecture. They have no good horses, no good meat, no grapes or musk-melons, no good fruits, no ice or cold water, no good food or bread in their bazaars, no baths, or colleges, or candles, or torches ---- never a candlestick!' The only reason he stayed was because 'the chief excellence of Hindustan is that it is a big country with plenty of gold and silver.' He died on 26th December 1530 at Agra, at the age forty eight and lies buried in a garden in Kabul that he loved.

His son, Humayun, was left with the difficult task of consolidation of the empire. It proved too much for him. A remarkable Afghan in Bengal by the name of Farid, to be known later as Sher Shah Suri, had resolved to retrieve the lost throne from the Mughals. When Humayun descended on Bengal, Sher Shah cut off his long lines of communication. Humayun called for reinforcements from Agra but his brothers hesitated. They had ambitions and designs of their own. Sher Shah delivered a surprise attack on the retreating Mughal army at Chaunsa. Humayun barely managed to escape with his life by swimming across the Ganges with the help of a water carrier. A year later, in May 1540, the two armies met again at Kanauj. There was no contest. According to the historian, Mirza Haider who was present on the occasion, '----- *the whole* (Mughal) *army was scattered and defeated by mere panic and crowding; not a gun was fired'* (*Tarikh-e-Rashidi*). Humayun fled to Sind and from there to Iran where he was not too warmly received. Eventually, he was able to wrest Kandhar and Kabul from his recalcitrant brothers and bided his time in Afghanistan.

Sher Shah Suri was not only a brilliant general but also proved to be an extremely imaginative and capable administrator. The fiscal and other reforms instituted by him in the five short years of his rule formed the basis of all the systems that were subsequently evolved for the governance of India. In the short period he not only managed to consolidate his empire but also built the fifteen hundred mile long Grand Trunk Road from Sonargaon in Bengal to Attock on the Indus. The road was dotted with 1,800 caravanserais, mosques, deep-water wells and shady banyan trees some of which survive to this day.

He was a devout Muslim and never oppressed his Hindu subjects. His historian, Abbas Khan, notes, 'From the day that Sher Shah was established on the throne no man dared to breathe in opposition to him; nor did any one raise the standard of contumacy or rebellion against him; nor was any heart-tormenting thorn grown in the garden of his kingdom; nor was there any of his nobles or soldiery, or a thief or a robber, who dared to turn the eye of dishonesty upon another's goods, nor did any robbery or stealing ever occur in his dominions. Travelers and wayfarers in Sher Shah's reign had no need to watch, nor feared to halt in the midst of a desert. They camped at night at every place, desert or inhabited, without fear; they set their goods and provisions upon the plain and turned out their mules to graze, and themselves slept with easy mind and free from care as if at home, and the *mansabdars* kept watch over them. Such a protection overshadowed the world where a cripple was not afraid of Rustam (*Tarikh-e-Sher Shahi*, pp. 427, 433). India was not to experience such peace and good government again until fairly late in the British period, at the end of the nineteenth century.

After his untimely death in a gunpowder accident in 1545 his son, Islam Shah, tried to keep the momentum going but when he died nine years later in 1554, the kingdom split into three parts as a result of factional struggles. This gave Humayun the opportunity he had been waiting for all this time. The Mughals re-established themselves in Delhi, after defeating a combined Afghan and Rajput force, under the Hindu general, Himu, in the second battle of Panipat in 1556. Humayun died the same year after tumbling down a flight of slippery stairs.

In 1501, Safawid Shah Ismail had proclaimed Shiaism as the state religion of Iran. It was his son, Tehmasp, who gave refuge to Humayun and introduced him to the sect. The experience left a profound impression on him. A number of Shia theologians, poets and artists followed Humayun to

Delhi and became a strong influence in the Mughal court. There is no evidence to suggest that Humayun became a Shia. Like the rest of the Mughal kings he continued to follow the Sufi schools prevalent in India.

He was succeeded by his fourteen-year old son, Jalaluddin Akbar, under the tutelage of one of Babur's trusted generals, Bairam Khan. It wasn't long before Bairam Khan was ousted through palace intrigue initiated by Akbar's foster mother, Maham Anaga. Historically, women have played a critical behind-the-scenes role in the royal courts and Akbar was more susceptible to it than most. However, the role popularly attributed to one of Akbar's Hindu wives called, Jodha, in present-day Indian history books is fictional. There is no historical evidence that a lady of this name ever adorned his harem, let aside, exercise the influence attributed to her.

According to Abul Fazal (author of *Akbar Nama* and *Ain-e-Akbari* who was murdered out of sheer jealousy by Akbar's son and heir, Jahangir) there were more than five thousand ladies of different rank in Akbar's harem, including Hindu, Iranian, Mughal and Armenian. After twenty years of struggle in putting down rebellions that grew like mushrooms all over India, Akbar not only recovered much of the lost territory but also managed to lay the foundations of a relatively stable Mughal rule in India. Even so, there was never a year when there was not a war that he did not have to fight somewhere or the other in the country.

Historians tend to portray Akbar's reign as a golden age for India. A closer examination would reveal that it was not very different to the rest, according to documented records of the time, at least as far as the common man was concerned. The much touted revenue and fiscal reforms with which he is credited had already been put in place by the Afghan ruler, Sher Shah Suri. If contemporary historical accounts are any guide, these were poorly administered and made little difference to the lives of the ordinary people. This would be apparent from impressions of some of the European observers at the time reproduced later in the chapter.

Even the Muslim historian, Badauni, is bitterly critical of the manner and effects of the implementation of these reforms: '*In this year* (1574) *an order was promulgated for improving the cultivation of the country and for bettering the condition of the riyats. ------ Rules were laid down but were not properly observed and much of the land was laid waste through the rapacity of the croris* (administrators); *the peasants' wives and children were sold and dispersed, and everything went into confusion. But the croris were held accountable by Raja Todar Mal* (Akbar's Revenue Minister) *and many pious men died from severe beatings and the torture of rack and pincers. Indeed so many died after long imprisonment by the revenue officers that the executioner or headsman was forestalled*' (p. 189, as quoted in *Medaeval India*).

Under the rules of Islam, all Muslims are required to pay a religiously mandated tax called *Zakat*. It is not obligatory for the non-Muslim inhabitants of the state who are also exempt from compulsory military service. The latter paid *Jazia* or poll tax in lieu, which has often been portrayed as discriminatory and coercive by Hindu and western writers. A fact that is seldom mentioned is that *jazia* collections were not credited to the king's treasury but were accounted for separately and spent exclusively on the welfare of Hindu widows and orphans.

Akbar abolished *Jazia* as well as some pilgrimage fees to various religious sites which is claimed to have made him very popular among the Hindus. If this was so, it made little difference to his relations with the Rajput and other Hindu states that continued to avail of every opportunity to raise the banner of revolt against him right to the end of his days.

It is also contended that he forbade child marriage, trial by ordeal, animal sacrifice, *sattee* (burning alive of widows) and marriage without the participants' prior consent ---- customs that are an integral part of Hindu religion (chapter 1). If indeed he did so, the effect was on paper only and there is no evidence whatsoever of any cessation or abatement in these practices, either during his rule or at any subsequent time right up to the middle of the nineteenth century. Some of these remain in vogue even to this day. It is one thing to pass an order but quite another to have it put into effect especially in the type of government system that existed at the time.

Akbar was not a very educated person but possessed a remarkably inquisitive mind. He was in the habit of arranging frequent dialogues, discussions and debates among intellectuals and religious scholars. These included Hindus, Christian missionaries, Shia and Sunni Muslims as well as persons belonging to different schools of Sufism and, sometimes, Buddhist and other monks. Some came with open minds others, like the Jesuits, had a specific agenda to convert the emperor to Christianity. It appears Akbar had doubts about Islam. In 1580, he proclaimed himself the final arbiter not only in matters of state but also in religion. He started to indulge in strange rituals involving astrology, prostrating himself before the sun and a sacred fire and making the entire court to rise and stand respectfully when the lamps were lit.

A new religion called *Deen-e-Ilahi* was proclaimed, with himself at its centre. It was a hotchpotch amalgam, put together with concepts borrowed from different creeds that not even all his courtiers chose to follow. It died on the day its prophet was laid to rest. However, there is nothing to prevent an imaginative historian from reading what he likes into any situation. While not denying the facts, Stanley Lane-Poole chose this to write about Deen-e-Ilahi, '*But the broadminded sympathy which inspired such a vision of catholicity left a lasting impress upon a land of warring creeds and tribes, and for a brief while created a nation where before there had been only factions* (*Mediaeval India,* p.282).

Unfortunately, he has not cared to elaborate on this grandiloquent and rather romantic assumption. There is little evidence in history of this 'lasting impress' of Akbar's *Deen-e-Ilahi* upon any aspect of life in India anywhere, let aside the creation of a nation. The formation of a nation is not an ephemeral affair and once formed it lasts a long time, if not forever. Like so many others, Lane-Poole has read much more into the situation than is justified by the available evidence and subsequent effects. It amounts to little more than poetic license indulged in at the expense of history.

Deen-e-Ilahi was by no means Akbar's only eccentricity. Like Mohammed Tughlak before him, he built a whole new capital at Sikri, to be henceforth known as Fatehpur. Apparently, he did this in order to be close to the Sufi saint, Salim Chishti, who lived in the village and had prophesied the birth of a son to him that would survive. Until then all of the sons born to Akbar's wives had died in their infancy. A seven-mile-long high wall with seven bastioned gates surrounded the new city. Inside there were wonderful palaces, 'peerless in all India for noble design and delicate adornment; its splendid mosque and pure marble shrine of the hermit saint; its carvings and paintings ----.'

The city was inhabited for only fourteen years and, just as with *Deen-e-Ilahi*, it was deserted after Akbar's death. Its derelict buildings, some of them five stories high, stand to this day as mute reminders of whatever lessons we may wish to draw from them. It is a curious if ironic fact that while almost all modern historians are unanimous in condemning Mohammed Tughlak's shifting of the capital to Daulatabad as an act of madness, virtually none of them has applied the same yardstick in the case of Akbar. He died in 1605, probably, due to a stroke suffered after a fit of temper to which he was prone. He was succeeded by his son, Salim Jahangir.

The main sources of history of the Muslim period had been the chronicles of courtiers and the diaries of the kings themselves. Beginning with Akbar, an increasing number of Europeans had started to arrive in India and have left most useful records of their impressions and observations of the country. These have added a valuable perspective since they were not burdened by either fear or the compulsion to be panegyric. The best known among them included the English sailor, Captain William Hawkins, whom Jahangir befriended; the first official ambassador from England, Sir Thomas Roe and a number of Portuguese and other missionaries and company officials. These were later joined by the likes of Tavernier, Thevenot, Bernier, Della Valle and Mandelso, to mention a few, from France and other continental European countries. With such a wealth of varied observations, the chances of the historian coming closer to truth and objectivity are considerably improved.

According to Stanley Lane-Poole, these Europeans *'found a novel and almost undreamt of civilisation, possessing elements of practical statesmanship and sagacity which the most philosophic of them all, the French physician Bernier, finds worthy to be commended to the serious consideration of the minister of Louis XIV. They met with a series of spectacles, ceremonies, customs, religions, systems of government, wholly unforeseen; and where they expected to find at the most rude and vacuous pomp, they encountered literature and learning, poetry and art, and a reasoned theory of government, which, in spite of their western prejudices, fairly compelled their admiration. With all this they discovered examples of superstition and degradation, and witnessed scenes of savage cruelty contrasted with barbaric splendour; yet the splendour and the degradation were such as belong not to uncivilised races, but to the exuberance of a great empire*' (*Mediaeval India*, p. 290).

There is little doubt about the economic prosperity in the land brought about in large part by the relative peace and political stability under the Mughal rule. The Portuguese Jesuit, Fr. Antonio Monserrate who was in India during Akbar's reign, noted that Lahore had grown larger and richer even than Constantinople, and with its two million inhabitants, dwarfed both London and Paris. '*The city is second to none either in Asia or in Europe, with regards either to size, population, or wealth. It is crowded with merchants, who foregather there from all over Asia. There is no art or craft useful to human life which is not practiced there. The citadel alone has a circumference of three miles.*'

Captain Hawkins landed at Surat in 1608 with a letter and some presents from King James I of England. After being subjected to some trouble and indignities by the Portuguese, who were already entrenched in India, he was conveyed to Agra where Jahangir had moved his capital. Hawkins spent three years at the court and because he could converse in Turkish, the mother tongue of the Mughals, he was to achieve a measure of intimacy with the king whom he described as a 'talented drunkard'.

He has given a lengthy account of the *mansabdari* system which, if called upon, could provide the king with an army of three hundred thousand horsemen. There were an estimated three thousand of these *mansabdars*, a kind of life-time peers, with rankings varying from '12,000 horse' down to '20 horse'. He puts the king's estimated income at the time at fifty crores of rupees (approx. fifty five million pounds) annually.

The daily expenses of the court, with its 36,000 employees, amounted to fifty thousand rupees with an additional thirty thousand for the king's household. By way of contrast, a soldier was paid two hundred rupees annually that included the upkeep of his horse. All the Mughal emperors were ceremonially weighed on their birthdays each year, once against silver, once against gold and precious stones, once against silk, gold and other cloth and, lastly, once against vittles that were later distributed among the poor, all donated by the courtiers. To get an idea of the wealth in the Mughal court, Tavernier had put the value of the peacock throne by itself at six million pounds at the time.

Contrary to the general impression, Jahangir was more feared than popular among the people. He was often cruel and liked to watch elephant fights and unarmed men being torn to pieces by lions and elephants as punishment. After early morning prayers, he went to the palace balcony to be briefly seen by the people and then slept for a couple of hours. This was followed by breakfast and a retreat to the harem. From noon until three PM he held court and then watched the elephant fights. The main meal of the day followed the afternoon prayers and then he retired to a private chamber to drink and eat opium with a few selected friends and courtiers. Soon, he would fall asleep when the guests would take leave. He was woken up and fed after a couple of hours and then slept for the rest of the night. The affairs of state were mostly handled by Queen Nur Jahan and her brother, Asif Khan, who was the prime minister and a capable administrator.

Sir Thomas Roe tried to get Jahangir to agree to Turkish style 'Capitulations' (special trading concessions and exemptions for non-Muslims that gave rise to privileged, self administering Christian communities inside Turkey) but to no avail. All he got was permission to trade like everyone else.

There were the usual insurrections in the south and in Bengal. The Rajputs revolted at Udaipur and were crushed by Prince Khurram (later Emperor Shahjahan) in 1614. Kandhar was temporarily lost to the Iranians in 1622.

Apart from this the boundaries of the empire remained largely intact. As he grew old, Jahangir's sons started to jockey for position to succeed him. The eldest, Khusro, revolted and was defeated and died in jail, apparently, of fever. It was Khurram's turn next. The ablest of them all, he too was defeated and after trying to seek refuge in Bengal and Deccan, made peace with Jahangir. In the last year of the reign, fearful of the intrigues that were afoot the able general, Mahabat Khan, took Jahangir hostage for several months until Nur Jahan manipulated to get him released. Jahangir died in 1627 and lies buried near Lahore.

When Mahabat Khan and Asif khan joined hands with Khurram, the latter's accession to the throne was assured. A third son, Parvez, who was married to Nur Jahan's daughter by her first marriage, took issue and was duly defeated and killed. Nur Jahan retired from public life and lived with admirable dignity in Lahore until she too passed away in 1646.

By this time the Europeans had already established numerous trading posts along India's coastline. These aroused little curiosity and no effort was made to learn more about where these adventurers came from, what their motives were and what effects contacts with them might have in the long term? Whatever knowledge may have become available could not be used effectively in the absence of any institution for its compilation, collation, analysis and storage.

The Mughals remained preoccupied internally with military campaigns, either expanding their territory or putting down insurgencies. If they built anything, it was glorious monuments in an attempt to immortalise themselves at the expense of the people. Little thought was given to building institutions of any kind, to research and to investigate and keep pace with modern developments in other parts of the world.

Very little changed and everything remained politically frozen in time to the period when they had first set foot in India. With hindsight it is possible to see that this was the beginning of the end, not only for the Mughals but for India as well. However, the realisation did not dawn upon them for another hundred years by which time the situation had been irretrievably lost.

After Babur, Shahjahan proved to be the ablest of the Mughal rulers. This was due in no small part to the wise counsel of men like Asif Khan, Ali Mardan, Mahabat Khan and Saad-ullah Khan, all of whom had a great deal of administrative experience and background. The Frenchman Tavernier testifies to the firm administration of justice and the universal sense of security during his reign. Even the Hindus grudgingly appreciated 'the equity of his government, the wise and generous treatment of the cultivators, the probity of the law courts and the honesty of the exchequer personally audited by this magnificent paragon of monarchs.'

Mandelslo, the representative of the Duke of Holstein who passed through India during Shahjahan's time, describes the capital Agra, a city of 600,000 people, '*as much as a horseman could do to ride around the city in a single day. Its streets are fair and spacious and there are some of them vaulted, which are above a quarter of a league in length, where the merchants and tradesmen have their shops, distinguished by their trades and the merchandises which are there sold; every trade and every merchant having a particular street and quarter assigned to him. There are eighty caravanserais for foreign merchants, most of them three stories high, with very noble lodgings, storehouses, vaults and stables. There is no nation in all the east but hath some commerce or other at the place*'. He counted seventy great mosques and over eight hundred public baths. The palaces of the rajas and nawabs were scattered all over and outside the town. The best of all was the imperial palace surrounded by a moat and drawbridge. The jealously guarded treasury's worth was estimated at over three hundred million pounds.

Mendelslo estimated the Mughal army in 1630 at 144,500 horse, besides camels and elephants. '*They have no firearms with wheels, nor yet fire-locks but their infantry are expert enough at the musket. They know nothing of the division of vanguard, main battle and rearguard and understand neither front nor file nor make any battalion but fight confusedly without any order. Their greatest strength consists of the elephants, which carry on their backs certain towers of wood, wherein there are three or four harquebouses hanging by hooks and as many men to order the artillery. The elephants serve them for a trench, to oppose the first attempt of the enemy; but it often comes to pass that the artificial fires, which are made use of to frighten these creatures, put them into such a disorder that they do much more mischief among those who brought them than they do among the enemies. They have abundance of artillery and some considerable great pieces and such as whereof it may be said the invention of them is as ancient as that of ours. They also make gunpowder but it is not so good as what is made in Europe. ---- Their armies do not march but about five kos (ten miles) a day and when they encamp they take up so great a quantity of ground that they exceed the compass of our greatest cities*' (*Mediaeval India*, p. 335 -6).

Above all Shahjahan will be most remembered for the monuments that he had built. Apart from the palaces, these include the great mosque, Moti Masjid and the incomparable Taj Mahal, tomb of his beloved wife, Mumtaz Mahal, at Agra. During the later part of his reign he built a whole new capital at New Delhi that he named Shahjanabad. This was by no means all. He even had time to build the Shalimar Gardens in Lahore. Ferguson, the historian of architecture, described the palace at Shahjahanabad as '*the most magnificent in the east, perhaps in the world.*' Bernier spent four years in New Delhi just after it had been completed. He has described the opulent splendor and magnificence of the place in great detail. '*The palace within was the most magnificent building of its kind in the east and the private rooms or mahal alone covered more than twice the space of any European palace.*' He narrates graphic details of the city, its layout, trade, industry, arts, festivals, the royal court and its proceedings, pageant, protocols and ceremonies (please see *Travels in the Mogul Empire*, by Farncois Bernier for details). By all accounts, New Delhi or Shahjahanabad must have been a fabulous and most impressive and exciting place to live in at the time.

The last of the great Mughals, Aurangzeb, came to the throne in 1658 and ruled for the next fifty years. As with Shajahan, he too was the son of a Hindu Rajput princess. He was a deeply pious, religious and ascetic man who earned his keep by making hand-written copies of the Koran. The first twenty years of his rule were, comparatively speaking; the most peaceful that India had known so far. An expedition to Assam, led by the governor of Bengal Mir Jumla, was thwarted by the rains and disease. Mir Jumla's successor, Shaista Khan, annexed Arakan in 1666 to put an end to piracy by renegade Europeans who had been operating out of Chittagong. Aurangzeb granted the British, who had been plying the Hoogly River since 1640, some land in a village called Sutanati in 1690 that eventually expanded to become the city of Calcutta.

As during the reigns of earlier kings, the Rajput states of Udaipur and Jodhpur found cause to rebel in 1681 while Jaipur remained loyal. These uprisings were swiftly squashed but not before Aurangzeb had been unpleasantly surprised and nearly deposed, in the middle of the campaign, when his son, Akbar, switched sides and joined forces with the Rajputs. In the end, Aurangzeb's personality, prestige and diplomacy prevailed with the troops and Akbar fled to Iran, never to be heard of again.

The Marhattas, a hardy race of low caste (mostly *shudra*) Hindu hill tribes, had banded together under a wily leader named Shivaji and carved out a territory for themselves out of the Deccan kingdom of Bijapur. Employing hit and run tactics, they took to raiding nearby cities. When these raids were extended to Mughal territories and the looting of and pilgims' ships at Surat as well as European settlements, Aurangzeb was obliged to take notice. After suffering heavy losses at the hands of the Mughal army, Shivaji sued for peace and agreed to become the king's vassal in 1666. He found life in the Delhi *darbar*, where he was treated with much contempt by the rest of the courtiers because of his rustic ways, not to his liking and slipped back into the Western Ghats to resume his raids into the neighbouring states. He died of illness in 1680.

Some British and Hindu historians have tried to paint Shivaji as a larger than life figure and a champion of Hindu revolt against oppressive Muslim rule. There is no basis to it in fact. He was just another crafty and opportunistic warlord who took advantage of unsettled conditions to accumulate wealth and carve out a kingdom for himself in turbulent and unsettled South India by robbing small and undefended communities, both Muslim as well as Hindu ---- just one of thousands of such unsavoury figures that litter the pages of Indian history. There are accounts of his looting Hindu temples and torturing Brahmins. The secret of his success lay in maintaining a highly mobile force that relied heavily on the element of surprise, using hit and run tactics, well-suited to the broken scrub covered hill country. His adversaries found it difficult to pin him down with their ponderous and lumbering military juggernauts.

It was never a Hindu versus Muslim issue with him. Shivaji consorted with and readily entered into constantly shifting alliances, most often with neighbouring Muslim rulers. Much of Shivaji's cavalry, and artillery when he was able to acquire it, was manned and officered by Muslims as, indeed, was that of his successors. He took meticulous care not to engage Aurangzeb in battle, knowing fully well what the outcome would be. Nor was Aurangzeb at any time conducting a holy war in the service of Islam. One of his ablest generals was a Hindu, Jai Singh, as were a large number of his troops. The creation of the modern myth of Shivaji can be traced to the prominent Hindu leader, Bal Gangadhar Tilak, himself a Marhatta, who first propagated it in 1895 at a commemoration.

Once the Rajput issue had been settled, Aurangzeb personally took command of the army to settle the affairs in Deccan. He crushed the Muslim kingdoms of Bijapur in 1686 and Golkunda a year later. The Marhattas were driven into the mountains and their leader, Shivaji's brother Sambhaji, killed in 1689. The entire peninsula, save the extreme tip south of Trichnapaly, was now a part of Aurangzeb's domain that extended northwards to the borders of Bokhara, three thousand miles away. In the east-west direction it stretched from Burma to the borders of Iran. It was a remarkable achievement that has never been equaled in Indian history, either before or since, but then Aurangzeb was an extra-ordinary man. In 1699, at the age of eighty-one, he personally led a charge on horseback against the fortress at Sattara and remained in the thick of battle when the troops around him appeared to be wavering.

There is little doubt about Aurangzeb's courage, ability and sagacity. An Italian, Dr. Gemelli Careri, spent some time at his camp in Deccan in 1695 and has carefully recorded details of his personal character as well as his style of administration and the workings of his court in *Voyage Around the World* (Churchill College iv, pp.222 –3). Apart from the Europeans' records, Aurangzeb has left a wealth of correspondence that sheds incisive light on the nature of the man and his thinking. None of this casts him in the mould of a misguided religious zealot or bigot, as he is often made out to be by some non-Muslim historians, including Lane-Poole.

These historians also classify him as a failure and hold him responsible for the decline of the Mughal Empire. According to them, Aurangzeb had alienated the Hindu population which made the decline inevitable. This is not supported by any credible evidence. Francois Bernier noted about Aurangzeb: '*Who then can wonder that the Great Mogol, though a Mahometan, and as such an enemy to the Gentiles, always keeps in his service a large retinue of Rajas, treating them with the same consideration as his other Omaras, and appointing them to important commands in his armies*?' Achlaji, son-in-law of Shivaji, and Arjuji, a first-cousin of Shivaji's father, were among the Hindus who occupied high positions (*mansabs* of five thousand and two thousand respectively) in Aurangzeb's army.

If indeed he had been a bigoted Muslim as alleged, the feelings among the Hindus should have eased and not worsened after Aurangzeb's death, making it easier and not more difficult for his successors. Aurangzeb spent much of his time subjugating rebellious states. If some of these happened to be ruled by Hindu rajas, it did not mean that he was waging a religious war against all Hindus. He took the same action against recalcitrant Muslim rulers as well.

There is little credible evidence in history of any serious Hindu-Muslim strife, at the level of the common man, during the Muslim period in India such as became increasingly common during the British rule later on. It stands to reason that if the Hindus had resented the Muslims so much, there would have been large-scale popular revolts and riots in the country, making the minority Muslim rule impossible. There is no known instance of insurgency, in the name of Hindu race or religion. Whenever there was any revolt it was always by individuals for personal gain and never by the community for the sake of religion as such.

Lane-Poole quotes some of the letters that Aurangzeb wrote just before he died, as an admission of failure. The self-deprecating tenor and tone of these letters, which is typical of Sufic tradition, is misunderstood and misconstrued because of lack of familiarity with the mind of a devout Muslim. Expressions of humility and rejection of exultation and self-aggrandisement are a part of the style and not necessarily an admission of failure. In any case, history must judge a man not by what he said but by what he did and was able to achieve.

It is true that the Mughal Empire rapidly fell apart after Aurangzeb's death in March 1707 but the same thing happened following the deaths of Babur, Sher Shah Suri as well as Ahmed Shah Abdali. If the historian can find it in him to absolve Babur, Sher Shah and Abdali of the responsibility for what happened after their deaths, why should the same yardstick not apply in the case of Aurangzeb? In each case, the primary reason for the break up and loss of the empire was the ineptitude of the rulers that succeeded the kings who proved unequal to the task of consolidating the gains of their predecessors.

In the kind of system that existed at the time, everything depended upon the character and ability of the ruler. A weak and inept king had no chance or hope of survival for any length of time. It was doubly difficult for Aurangzeb's successors because the chief source of their power, the army itself, had become disorganised, corrupt, non-professional and largely ineffective. The nature of threats that were being posed had also changed, calling for new thinking and imaginative planning and execution. There were no institutions to research and develop new devices and strategies to meet these challenges.

The downfall had become inevitable because of the cumulative effects of all these, along with a number of other factors such as the failure to evolve scientifically and technologically and not keeping pace with developments in the rest of the world. It is a serious misreading of history to blame the decline solely on Aurangzeb's allegedly flawed attitude and character. Empires are not dissolved by one single cause, much less by the religious inclination and devotion on the part of one king. They fall because of the cumulative effects of a number of political, economic, administrative and military factors that usually develop over a long period of time.

THE ADMINISTRATION

The Mughal kingdom was essentially composed of two types of territories. The states that submitted to the king's supremacy and accepted a vassal status were allowed to be ruled by their hereditary rulers under their own system of administration. Their numbers varied from time to time. Available records only refer to the larger ones among these, a majority of which were ruled by Hindu rajas.

The rest of the kingdom was divided into a number of *subas* (provinces), each under a governor (*nazim or subadar*) appointed by the king who served at his pleasure. In return, the governor reimbursed his master a fixed amount each year. The governor was free to levy taxes on all property, trade and industry within his jurisdiction, except *khalisa* lands that were directly administered by the king. This exclusion also applied to the *jageers* ---- lifetime grants of land to the king's nominees in exchange for providing a designated number of armed soldiers and horses for war when called for by the king. Each *suba* was divided into *sarkars* which in turn were divided into *mahals* or *parganas* ---- the smallest administrative units.

The governors were responsible for the administration of justice and maintaining law and order with the help of local officials like the *diwans* (ministers), *Khan-e-saman* (manager of the imperial establishment), *mansabdars* (holders of office), *kazis* (judges), *muftis* (legal advisers), *bakhshis* (administrators) *amils* (revenue officers), *kotwals* (police chiefs), *mohtasibs* (public inspectors), *faujdars* (heads of military detachments) *and karindas* (minor officials). There were a host of others at lower levels, too numerous to mention. The selection and appointment of these officials was arbitrary. There were no rules of business that controlled and regulated either the selection process or the working of the civil servants or even the military. Like much of the rest of the administration, it remained an arbitrary affair and everything, including life and property, rested on the goodwill and pleasure of the king, the governors and other high officials. In a set up of this nature, where power flows from the top, favouritism, corruption and misrule inevitably take hold and become endemic, as indeed they did in India.

The roots of this tradition of corruption are so deep-rooted and the pull of history so strong that when Benazir Bhutto became the Prime Minister of Pakistan in 1989, one of her first actions was to effectively render the selection processes for civil servants redundant. A specially created cell in her office carried out the functions of the Public Service Commission for all intents and purposes. The selections and appointments of officials in all the government departments were arbitrary and made directly by this cell.

In a short period of less than two years she placed an estimated seventy eight thousand of her cronies in government jobs ---- all but five hundred of them ethnic Sindhis from her native province who constitute about ten per cent of the total population of Pakistan (*The Dawn*). All the screening and evaluation processes were set aside and many characters with criminal past were admitted.

The interlude of a century of relatively clean and orderly administration by the British has not hindered, at least the ruling elite in Pakistan, from reverting to type in a very short space of time. It applies just as much to the masses whose apathetic and submissive attitude makes it easy for those in power to trash their rights and privileges.

The law of *Sharia* was applied only to the Muslims in Mughal India, primarily in cases involving inheritance and family affairs. The religious, personal and family affairs of non-Muslims were resolved within their own castes and communities and they only appeared before the courts for civil disputes involving property, commerce and some criminal issues. There was no universal or higher education provided by the state. This was individual responsibility and was handled within each community. It was the same with healthcare and other social services.

The common people had virtually no say in the running of the state and there was no system of checks and balances to limit the power and excesses committed by the rulers. Similarly other than the spies, no institutionalized independent system of getting any feedback from the people existed. It all boiled down to the inclination, character and ability of the ruler. Things went well when the man at the top was good and competent. When this was not so, the people suffered. More often than not, the governors were unimaginative, unscrupulous and incompetent, with the result that the Mughal Empire in India was facing one internal crisis after another throughout its three-hundred-year history.

The common people were not only excluded from having a say in the affairs of state, they also do not figure in the official records. The history of India was either not recorded at all, as during the Hindu period or, when it was written down by the later Muslim historians, the panegyric accounts remained confined primarily to the lives of kings, princes, rulers and chieftains ---- their ambitions, intrigues, fights and downfalls. It was only after the Europeans arrived in India that we get a glimpse of the conditions that prevailed outside of the royal courts.

Regardless of their origins these Europeans are unanimously agreed on the state of the people at the time. This is how they saw life during Akbar's much touted enlightened rule: '*The poor were desperately poor and the rich forever insecure in their riches. Between common robbers and levies of the throne, no man dare count on the morrow. The nobles and governing officials at high levels, though few in numbers, were almost all foreigners, whether Turks or Persians. All places and favours were bought by costly bribes and the extravagance of life was increased by the fact that whatever a rich man possessed at the time of death reverted to the royal treasury. Merchants, if prosperous, dared not live comfortably and buried their silver deep underground; for any display of wealth brought extortionists flocking to the door. The benefits of all agricultural production went to the state and the ruling class. None of it returned to the people and no communal benefits existed. Famines were a common occurrence. When the rains failed, the farmers wandered like animals in vain search of food and sold their children for less than a rupee a piece. Others sold themselves as slaves to escape starvation. Cannibalism was common in such times.*

'There were few bridges and the roads were little more than the ruts made by the plodding of bullocks' feet through dust and mud. No system of popular education or of medical relief was worked, and none of legal defence. Fine schemes were sometimes set on paper by rulers and their ministers, but practically nothing was actually done toward the economic development of the country; for if any one ruler began a work, his successor destroyed it or let it decay' (*India at the Death of Akbar*, by W. H. Moreland, Macmillan and Co., London, 1920).

The Frenchman, Francois Bernier, spent twelve years in India from 1656 to 1668. His observations with regard to land management in India at the time read in part:

'The king, as proprietor of the land, makes over a certain quantity to military men, as an equivalent of their pay ---- Similar grants are made to governors, in lieu of their salary, and also for the support of their troops, on condition that they pay a certain sum annually to the king ---- The lands not so granted are retained by the king as the peculiar domain of his house ---- and upon these domains he keeps contractors, who are also bound to pay him an annual rent.

'As the ground is seldom tilled otherwise than by compulsion, and as no person is found willing and able to repair the ditches and canals for the conveyance of water, it happens that the whole country is badly cultivated, and a great part rendered unproductive from want of irrigation ---- The peasant cannot avoid asking himself this question, "Why should I toil for a tyrant who may come tomorrow and lay rapacious hands upon all I possess and value?" ------ The governors and revenue collectors, on their part reason in this manner, "Why should the neglected state of this land create uneasiness in our minds and why should we expend our own money

and time to render it fruitful? We may be deprived of it in a single moment and our exertion would benefit neither ourselves nor our children. Let us draw from the soil all the money we can, though the peasant should starve or abscond, and we should leave it, when commanded to quit, a dreary wilderness." ----- It is owing to this miserable system of government ------ that there is no city or town which, if it be not already ruined and deserted, does not bear evident marks of approaching decay.

'The country is ruined by the necessity of defraying the enormous charges required to maintain the splendour of a numerous court, and to pay a large army maintained for the purpose of keeping the people in subjection.' (*Travels in the Mogul Empire*, by Francois Bernier, Oxford University Press, 1916, pp. 226 - 27, 230)

An employee of the Dutch East India Company, Francisco Pelsaert, having spent seven years in India, compiled a confidential report (*The Remonstrantie of Frncisco Pelsaert'*) for his principals in 1620. It contains a graphic record of life and conditions as these pertained to the common man in India at the time. An extract from it is reproduced below:

'The land would give plentiful, or even an extraordinary, yield, if the peasants were not so cruelly and pitilessly oppressed; for villages which, owing to some small shortage of produce, are unable to pay the full amount of the farm revenue, are made prize, so to speak, by their masters or governors, and wives and children sold, on pretext of a charge of rebellion. Some peasants abscond to escape their tyranny ----- and consequently the fields lie empty and unsown and grow into wilderness.

' ----- . As regards the laws, they are scarcely observed at all, for the administration is absolutely autocratic, but there are books of law which are in charge of their lawyers, the Kazis. Their laws contain such provisions as hand for hand, eye for eye, tooth for tooth; but who will excommunicate the Pope? And who would dare to ask a governor, "Why do you rule us this way or that? Our law orders thus." The facts are very different, although in every city there is a kachahri, or royal court of justice, where the Governor, the Diwan, the Bakhshi, the Kotwal, the Kazi and other officers sit together daily, or four days in the week. Here all disputes are disposed of, but not until avarice has had its share. All capital cases, such as thefts, murders or crimes are finally disposed of by the Governor, if the criminals are poor and unable to pay, and the sweepers drag them off to execution with very little ceremony. In case of other offences the criminals are seldom or never executed; their property is merely confiscated for the Governor or the Kotwal. Ordinary questions of divorce, quarrels, fights, threats and the like are in the hands of the

Kotwal and the Kazi. One must indeed be sorry for the man who has to come for judgement before these Godless "unjudges"; their eyes are bleared with greed, their mouths gape like wolves for covetousness, and their bellies hunger for the bread of the poor; everyone stands with hands open to receive, for no mercy or compassion can be had except on payment of cash. This fault shoud not be attributed to judges or officers alone, for the evil is a universal plague; from the least to the greatest, right up to the King himself, everyone is infected with insatiable greed, so that if one has any business to transact with Governors or in palaces, he must not set about it without the vision of angles, for without presents he need expect very little answer to his petitions. Our honourable employers need not deign to be surprised at this, for it is the custom of the country.

'It is important to recognize that the king is to be regarded as the king of the plains or the open roads only; for in many places you can travel only with a strong body of men, or on payment of heavy tolls to the rebels ----- and there are as many rebels as subjects. Taking the chief cities, for example, at Surat the forces of Raja Piepel come pillaging upto or inside the city, murdering the people and burning the villages, and in the same way, near Ahmedabad, Agra, Delhi, Lahore and many other cities thieves and robbers come in force by night or day like open enemies. The governors are usually bribed by the thieves to remain inactive, for avarice dominates manly honour, and, instead of maintaining troops, they fill and adorn their mahals with beautiful women, and seem to have the pleasure-house of the whole world within their walls.

'The people endure patiently, professing that they do not deserve anything better; and scarcely anyone will make an effort, for a ladder by which to climb higher is hard to find, because a workman's children can follow no occupation other than that of their father, nor can they inter-marry with other castes ---- . For workmen there are two scourges, the first of which is low wages ----- The second is the governor, the nobles, the diwan ---- and other royal officers. If any of these wants a workman, the man is not asked if he is willing to come, but is seized in the house or in the street, well beaten if he should dare to raise any objection, and in the evening paid half his wages or nothing at all.'

This state of affairs was not a passing phenomenon. It had existed for hundreds and, probably, for thousands of years. It cannot be blamed on ignorance because almost all of the Muslim rulers had been well versed in the Koran as well early history of Islam and should have known that this kind of corruption, injustice and misrule was utterly unacceptable and unforgivable. It is very likely that they might have wanted to do away with it and improve the lot of the common man but found themselves hopelessly at the mercy of a vicious system of government that would not brook any reform without jeopardising their own power and position.

Many of them simply lacked both the vision and the ability to grapple with such a vast undertaking. In the absence of appropriate institutions, they had no way of reaching the people and involving them in the affairs of the state. It was also the absence of institutions that prevented research into what ailed the country and how best to deal with each new or changed situation. It was a moribund system and the only surprise is that it lasted for so long.

Aurungzeb, for one, was certainly aware of the doomed state of affairs. It may be worth reproducing parts of a letter that he wrote, to his erstwhile tutor, outlining the limitations of his education and lack of preparation for the job (*The Story of Civilisation*, p.559 - 60):

' ------- *In the first place you have taught me that all Farangistan* (Europe) *was nothing but I know not what little island, of which the great king was he of Portugal, and next to him of Holland, and after him of England: and as to the other kings, as those of France and Andalusia, you have represented to me as our petty rajas, telling me that the kings of Hindustan were far above them altogether, the great ones, the conquerors and kings of the world; and those of Persia, and Uzbec, Kashghar, Tartary and Cathay, Pegu, China and Matchina did tremble at the name of the king of Hindustan. Admirable geography! You should rather have taught me exactly to distinguish all those states of the world, and well to understand their strength, their way of fighting, their customs, religions, governments, and interests; and by the perusal of solid history, to observe their rise, progress, decay; and whence, how and by what accidents and errors those great changes and revolutions of empires and kingdoms have happened. ------. You had a mind to teach me the Arabian tongue, to read and to write. I am much obliged, forsooth, for having made me lose so much time upon a language that requires ten or twelve years to attain its perfection; as if the son of a king should think it an honour to be a grammarian ------ he, to whom time is so precious for so many weighty things, which he ought by times to learn. ----- Should you not, instead of your flattery, have taught me somewhat of that point so important to a king, which is, what the reciprocal duties are of a sovereign to his subjects and those of subjects to their sovereigns; and ought not you to have considered that one day I should be obliged with the sword to dispute my life and my crown with my brothers? ------ Have you ever taken care to make me learn what it is to besiege a town, or set an army in array?-------*'

If this was the state of training and education for a future king, it is not difficult to imagine what it must have been like for the rest of the population. This was at a time when universities in Europe had already been imparting education and carrying out scientific research for more than five hundred years. The great revolution in liberal thought and scientific discovery was nearing maturity. The industrial revolution, that was to have such a profound effect on the course of human history, was just over the horizon. The Americas had been settled and the Muslim empires in Europe and Africa were being rolled back.

The fate of the Mughal Empire, like that of so many others, was sealed when it failed to properly appreciate the significance of these developments and made no effort to keep abreast of them. Aurangzeb may be justified in complaining but he should have appreciated that it is futile to expect something from a teacher who is himself ignorant and unable to deliver. What is worse, Aurangzeb was in a position to institute steps to remedy the situation, yet, he merely confined himself to complaining about the inadequacies of his tutor. The Mughals made the worst possible error of dwelling in the past and allowing conditions to stagnate in the country. The sub-continent continues to pay a terrible price for their mistake to this day.

There was a supercilious belief that everything about the Mughals and Muslims was superior to what the West offered at the time, be it in the field of education, culture, philosophy, administration or politics. The few Muslims from India who visited Britain and Europe in the seventeenth century observed only with a jaundiced eye and blinkered vision (Hindus did not proceed overseas because of religious compulsions). There was no logical basis to their inability to understand and assimilate which can only be attributed to ignorance and misplaced chauvinism.

The consequences brought on by such closed minds were catastrophic, not only in India but also in all the other Muslim lands. The failure to accept and learn from the developments underway in Europe led to inevitable stagnation and decline, apart from India, also in Iran, Turkey, North Africa and Central Asia. As against this, there is the example of Japan which recognized the necessity to acquire and adopt western learning and technology early on. It saved her from the ignominy and depredation that came from being subjected to the European colonization.

Curiously but not altogether surprisingly, there is no record of any census being carried out in India prior to the institution of the British Raj. It had to do both with a lack of understanding of the demands of proper and effective administration as well as the attitude where the people and their welfare only mattered to the extent of what the rulers felt appropriate. The rights belonged to the ruling class and the people could only expect what this class decided they should have. In such a system any head count had little meaning or use other than purely academic. As an educated guess, it is estimated the total population of India in 1700 AD was in the region of 175 million and hovered around this mark for the next two hundred years. Horrific rates of infant mortality, disease, famine and warfare kept an effective check on its growth. J. F. Richards, writing in *The Journal of Asia Studies* (vol. 35, 1976) under the title '*The Imperial Crisis in the Deccan*', estimates the annual revenue of the Mughal kingdom at this time to be 232 million rupees, almost all of it derived from land taxes. The bulk of the expenditure was incurred on the army campaigns and maintenance of the king and his court.

It has been alleged, especially by many of the current Hindu writers, that Muslim rulers had forcibly converted the indigenous Hindus to Islam. There is not a shred of substantive historical evidence to suggest that there was ever any such deliberate official policy. If that had indeed been the case, after eight hundred years of total domination by them, the ratio of Muslims in the Indian population would surely have been far in excess of the present thirteen per cent.

First of all, forced conversions are unacceptable in terms of the Koran. Secondly, Islam does not provide for a central directing authority nor a clerical hierarchy needed for carrying out such a systematic and sustained task as mass conversions of populations. Even if these had been carried out, there was no Inquisition type system or organisation to ensure that the proselytes did not revert to their old ways, either secretly or if an overt opportunity presented itself. Any one even mildly conversant with Hindu religion will know its highly sensitive and pivotal position in the society. Any interference, let aside, use of force in matters of *dharma* would have proved disastrous to the rule of a handful of Muslims in a sea of Hindus. The British found it out the hard way after the mutiny of 1857.

In history, whenever force was used, religious conversion never remained a half-hearted affair. There were virtually no Muslims left alive in Spain within a few short years of the overthrow of their rule in the fifteenth century. More or less the same thing happened to them in Eastern Europe, after the collapse of the Ottoman Empire. Spanish missionaries accompanying the conquistadors told the native people they encountered in Mexico and Latin America to choose between Christianity and death, giving them no more than five minutes to make up their minds. Buddhism did not disappear from the face of India in the eighth and nineth centuries through some peaceful persuasion on the part of resurgent Brahminism.

Had the Muslim rulers used any force for religious conversion, over so many centuries, it is logical to assume that as in Spain, East Europe and Latin America, the religious map of India would have been entirely different today. In all probability, British scholars may have been at least partly responsible for deliberately encouraging the spread of this myth in an attempt to sow the seeds of mistrust and disunity among the Hindus and Muslims. Playing off one against the other made it so much easier for them to rule over India.

In the July 1998 issue of the *Impact International*, London, M.H Faruqui quotes from the 1985 Khuda Bakhsh Annual Lecture delivered by the Indian historian, governor of Orissa and member of Rajya Sabha, Dr. Bhishambhar Nath Pande: '*Thus under a definite policy the Indian history textbooks were so falsified and distorted as to give an impression that the medieval* (i.e. Muslim) *period of Indian history was full of atrocities committed by Muslim rulers on their Hindu subjects and the Hindus had to suffer terrible indignities under Muslim rule. And there were no common factors* (between Hindus and Muslims) *in social, political and economic life.*'

One of Pande's revelations involved the truth concerning allegations of accesses committed against the Hindus by Tipu Sultan in eighteenth century Mysore. According to Indian textbooks, he was responsible for the suicide of 3,000 Brahmins who objected to his trying to forcibly convert them to Islam. It transpired that the story emanated from a history of Mysore, written by a Victorian Englishman, and that no such incident had ever taken place. Tipu Sultan, whose own prime minister and commander-in-chief were Brahmins, far from indulging in forcible conversions, gave annual grants to 136 Hindu temples.

The danger is that such falsification of history, if repeated often enough over a long enough period of time, has a habit of being accepted as the truth. There is all the evidence in the world to conclusively demonstrate that whatever conversions took place in India were because of the thousands of Sufi saints and scholars who had made it the mission of their lives to spread the message through amity, goodwill and personal example wherever they went. They received official support only on rare occasions and there are scores of recorded instances where they had differences with the Muslim rulers and suffered persecution as a consequence. The vast majority of Muslims who ruled India did so strictly for personal benefit and not to further the cause of Islam. Some of them, like Aurangzeb, may have been dedicated and practising Muslims but it is not the same thing as running the state for the cause of Islam.

Hindu rajas and governors were allowed to rule over most of the states and *parganas.* There were Hindu ministers and officials in the courts of all the Muslim kings. The armies of Muslim kings had Hindu generals and considerable numbers of Hindu troops, often exceeding the number of Muslims. It was the same with other state employees. This hardly paints the picture of chief instruments of the state being obsessed with fanatical proselytising zeal, crusading against hapless Hindus, murdering, pillaging and forcibly converting them to Islam. A relevant passage from '*The New Cambridge History of India',* by J.S. Grewal, Cambridge University Press, Cambridge, 1990, (p. 11), is reproduced below to illustrate the contradiction and lack of basis in any such assumption:

'*In the revenue administration of the Lodi Sultanate, particularly on the middle and lower rungs, Hindu participation was very considerable. Brahmins and Khatris in the Punjab were encouraged to learn Persian. They were associated with account keeping, some of them rising to become diwans (ministers) of the provincial governors. The local administrators often employed Hindu accountants and worked with the assistance of Hindu qanungos (revenue officials) familiar with local customs, castes and clans. Many a chaudhri (headman) of the pargana (district), or part of the pargana, who assisted the Afghan administrator in the collection of revenue was Hindu. In all the non-Muslim villages the village headmen (muqadams) were Hindu and so were many of the village accountants (patwaris) even in Muslim villages. The association of the Hindus with Afghan administration made them important collaborators at the subordinate levels'*. This is not what one would expect from some crazed fanatical regime hell-bent on forcing the local Hindu population into becoming Muslim under threat of violence. Yet, despite all the evidence to the contrary, this is precisely what is quite often suggested or implied in the present-day history books in India.

In his book, *The Discovery of India,* the first prime minister of the country, Pundit Jawaharlal Nehru, himself admits: '---- *frequent intercourse* (trade and cultural relations) *led to Indians getting to know the religion, Islam. Missionaries also came to spread the new faith and they were welcomed. Mosques were built. There was no objection raised either by the state or the people, nor were there any religious conflict ----.*

'*Mahmud's* (Gahznavi) *raids are a big event in Indian history, ----. Above all, they brought Islam, for the first time, to the accompaniment of ruthless military conquest. So far, for over 300 years, Islam had come peacefully as a religion and taken its place among the many religions of India without trouble or conflict ---- Yet when he* (Mahmud) *had established himself as a ruler ---- Hindus were appointed to high office in the army and the administration. ----*

'*It is thus wrong and misleading to think of a Moslem invasion of India or of the Moslem period in India, just as it would be wrong to refer to the coming of the British to India as a Christian invasion, or to call the British period in India a Christian period. Islam did not invade India; it had come to India some centuries earlier -----*'

Much of the criticism of Muslim rule emanates from sources in the West whose own record leaves much to be desired. Islam does not permit any killing except in war or for crimes such as murder and rebellion (*The Koran 5:32*). It also specifically forbids the Muslims to take prisoners, except during the fighting of a regular war. Prisoners must not be ill-treated and should be released after hostilities have come to an end. If no ransom is forthcoming, the prisoner must be allowed to earn money to pay the sum himself, and his captor is urged to help him out of his own pocket (*The Koran 8:68, 47:5, 24:34, 2:178*). The Prophet has specified the treatment of captives in these terms: '*You must feed them as you feed yourselves, and clothe them as you clothe yourselves, and if you should set them a hard task, you must help them in it yourselves*'.

These traditions are still followed by Muslims, even by the much-maligned Taliban. For some revealing insight, the reader may like to refer to '*In the Hands of the Taliban*' by Yvonne Ridley, Robson Books, London, 2001. She was the correspondent for the *Sunday Express* when taken prisoner in Afghanistan on spying charges, yet, she was treated with much courtesy, consideration and decorum by the regime.

As against this, at the end of the same war, thousands of Taliban troops were rounded up at Kunduz in late November 2001 and transported in sealed shipping containers to Sheberghan prison in northwestern Afghanistan, a jail under US control. Most of the prisoners suffocated to death during the journey. The drivers of the vehicles testified that upon arrival at Sheberghan they were ordered to drive the trucks to the desert of Dashte Laili where the prisoners that were still alive were shot and their bodies left to rot in hastily dug shallow mass graves.

Andrew McKntee, ex-President of Amnesty International UK and human rights lawyer, described it as '*very credible evidence and one that raises questions that will not go away*' ('*New Film Accuses US Army of War Crimes in Afghanistan*' article in '*The Guardian*' of 13th June 2002 by Kate Connolly and Rory McCarthy). In a similar action the United States

Air Force mercilessly bombed five hundred bound and blind-folded Taliban prisoners of war at Kila Jangi near Mazar-e-Sharif for three days until the last of them had been killed.

Other Taliban and al-Qaida prisoners have been kept in solitary confinement, in cages like animals, at Guantanamo Bay in Cuba by the United States military for years without recourse to law and subjected to physical and mental torture in contemptuous disregard of international conventions. Some of the men subjected to such brutalities were as old as ninety years and boys as young as eleven and twelve. It is the same in Iraq's Abu Gharaib and other prisons where US Army personnel have been subjecting Iraqis in their custody to inhuman torture and sexual depravities of the most despicable kind.

For two and a half years Serbs carried out systematic genocide of Bosnian Muslims between 1992 and 1995. The western powers not only failed to intervene but also prevented the UN or any other power from rescuing the hapless Bosnian Muslims. After fifteen years, they are still doing everything they can to ensure that the two men most responsible for executing three hundred thousand innocent and unarmed men, women and children and committing other brutally vicious crimes against the Muslims, Radovan Karadzic and Radko Mladic, were not brought to justice for more than a dozen years despite warrants for their arrest issued by the International War Crimes Tribunal in the Hague ('*A Witness to Genocide*', by Roy Gutman and '*Slaughterhouse --- Bosnia and the Failure of the West*' by David Rieff, Simon Schuster, New York). Of the two, Radko Mladic is still to be apprehended fifteen after the war ended. Yet, prejudice and bigotry continue to blind people even at the highest level in Christian hierarchy. President Bush's mentor, Franklin Graham still believes it is Islam that is '*a very evil and wicked religion*'.

END OF MUSLIM RULE

Aurangzeb died in 1707 and, according to his wishes, was buried in a simple grave near Daulatabad, north of Poona (Pune). The usual struggles for succession followed that lasted a year and a half. His son, Azam, was killed in a battle near Agra and his favourite, Kam Bakhsh, was defeated and died of his wounds near Haiderabad. This left the field clear for the eldest son, Muazzam to ascend the throne under the title of Bahadur Shah. He was seventy years old at the time. As happened at the earlier successions, the provincial rulers took advantage of the opportunity to declare their independence.

Bahadur Shah released the Marhatta chief Sahu from Mughal jail and installed him as a vassal ruler over his people. Later he made peace with the recalcitrant Rajput states that freed him to deal with the Sikhs in the north who had become increasingly bold in their raids over villages and towns in Punjab. They were pursued and driven into the mountains from where they were not heard of for many years. Just then, in 1712, Bahadur Shah died of old age.

His son, Jahandar succeeded him after the usual carnage of siblings only to be himself murdered a year later. His nephew, Farrukhsiyar, a disgraceful and cowardly individual sat on the throne for the next six years until he too was assassinated in 1719. The reins of actual power in Delhi were in the hands of two Syed brothers at this time. After a couple of young princes had tried their luck briefly, Mohammed Shah ascended the throne and remained there for the next twenty-eight years, thanks largely to his manipulative and intriguing skills.

The weakness at Delhi had encouraged the outlying provinces to break away. Bengal was already on its own. Asaf Jah had founded the Nizam dynasty in Deccan that subsisted well into the twentieth century. Avadh too was straining at the leash with the Rohilas hovering to its north. Nadir Shah from Iran was soon to relieve the empire of Kandhar, Ghazni and Kabul. The Marhattas, having captured Gujrat and Malwa in 1731, were advancing towards Delhi. All that the emperor could muster against them was a rag tag rabble force of 34,000 men. He was obliged to cede all the territories between the Narbada and the Chambal rivers in Central India to them in 1738.

The year that Aurangzeb died, Ghalji Pathans under Mir Waiz wrested Kandhar from the Safawi rulers who had ruled Iran for two hundred years. His son, Mahmood, invaded Iran to overthrow Shah Tahmasp, the last of the Safawids, and established himself at Isphahan after great brutality in 1722. He was murdered and replaced by his cousin, Ashraf, a military commander of considerable reckoning. When the Ottoman Turks, hoping to take advantage of the turmoil in Iran, sent in a powerful invading army he defeated it roundly, obliging the caliph to formally acknowledge him as the Shah of Persia in 1727.

The rough and tough Ghaljis lacked the skills and talents necessary for administering a sophisticated people like the Iranians. An Afshari Turkoman, Nadir Quli Khan, rallied the Persians to oust Ashraf from Isphahan in 1730. He expanded his domain into the territories of Abdali Afghans (now mostly known as Durranis) who lived in the vicinity of Herat and Kandhar and later captured Kabul. It was at Kandhar that Nadir

Shah met and offered an important military post to young Ahmed Shah Abdali, who was later to have a very profound effect in shaping the course of Indian history.

In 1739, Nadir Shah attacked Delhi. Mohammed Shah could only offer token resistance. The city was ravaged and ransacked for two months. '*Sleep and rest forsook the city. In every chamber and house was heard the cry of affliction. It was before a general massacre, but now the murder of individuals*' (*Siar-al-Mutakhireen*). In the end, all of the treasures, including the peacock throne alone valued by Tavernier at the time at six million pounds sterling and the famous Koh-e-Noor diamond were carted off to Iran. An estimated eight or nine million gold *mohars* (coins) were extorted from the citizens after torture. This was besides an immense treasure of gold silver plate, jewels, rich stuffs and a crowd of skilled artisans and herds of elephants, horses and camels. Only a miracle could have enabled the Mughal rule to revive after this catastrophe.

In 1747, a fellow Kizlbash Turkoman, Mohammed Khan Qajar, who founded the Qajar dynasty that ruled Iran for almost the next two centuries, murdered Nadir Shah. Ghalji and Abdali Afghans who had been loyal to Nadir Shah were obliged to leave Iran. They elected Ahmed Shah as their leader and declared their independence after capturing Kandhar, Ghazni, Kabul and Heart. This is how the country of Afghanistan came to be founded. Soon, Ahmed Shah turned his attention towards India and annexed much of Punjab to his kingdom.

While Delhi lay destitute and prostrate after Nadir Shah's raid, with its influence confined to a few districts around the capital, other players started to jockey for position. Mohammed Shah died in 1748 and was succeeded by his son Ahmed, a debauched man. Whatever was left of the actual power was in the hands of Safdar Jung, the nawab of Avadh. When the Rohillas tried to oust him, he called for help from the Marhattas. Under the leadership of Holkar and Scindia, the Marhattas ousted the Rohillas but then staked their own claims to territories that extended from Bengal to Punjab. Ahmed was succeeded by Alamgir II in 1754. Two years later, finding himself hemmed in by his vazir, Ghazi-uddin and the Rohilla chief, Najib-uddaula, the king again turned to the Marhattas for help. This time they occupied Delhi and much of Punjab. Alamgir II was murdered in a palace coup in 1759 and his successor, Shah Alam, fearing a similar fate, sought protection with the British in Bengal.

It looked as if the field was clear for the Marhattas to claim the throne and establish Hindu rule over India. There was no power in India strong enough to oppose them. Fearful of their future, the Rohillas and Avadh joined forces and asked for help from Ahmed Shah who was already alarmed by the Marhatta incursion into Punjab. Sensing that a decisive moment was at hand, the Marhattas called for all the reinforcements they could get, even asking the British for artillery support, and entrenched themselves at Panipat under their chiefs Holkar and Scindia, with Sudesheo Bhao in overall command. Their artillery was much superior and particularly effective under the command of a Muslim gunner named Ibrahim. Ahmed Shah laid siege to Panipat and waited. At one stage, the nawab of Avadh tried to negotiate with the Marhattas behind Ahmed Shah's back but his machinations were discovered and cut short before any damage could be done.

Ultimately, unable to endure shortages and deprivation any longer, Bhao decided to move out and give battle on 6th January 1761. The Marhattas had a distinct edge but Ahmed Shah's superior organisation and planning won out in the end. Bhao was killed, Holkar and Scindia saved themselves by running away, leaving their troops at the mercy of the Afghans. They found none. Ahmed Shah was determined to put an end to the menace forever and issued orders for general chase. The Marhattas were pursued, as they ran, for three hundred miles and hunted down wherever they could be found. Suddenly, with one stroke, the most powerful force in India at the time was no more. The defeat of the Marhattas was so complete that there was no possibility of their recovering from it for a very long time, if ever. It left a serious power vacuum. Ahmed Shah made a fateful decision not to fill it himself that ultimately paved the way for the British to take over India.

Ahmed Shah was content just to maintain his rule over Afghanistan, Sind, Punjab and parts of Iran and Turkistan. Unfortunately, his qualities as a military leader par excellence were not matched by his acumen for organisation and administration of a state. Conditions in Punjab were vastly different to those existing in Afghanistan that was little more than a loose confederation of self-administering tribes. Settled communities, as in Punjab, called for a 'hands on' approach and close involvement in their complex affairs. Yet, Ahmed Shah and his successors left everything to the inept and corrupt local governors. Soon, things got out of hand.

The Sikhs and other outlaws formed increasingly large marauding bands that terrorized the countryside, often with the connivance of the local governors like Adina Beg. Periodically, the Afghans sent in punitive expeditions. Ahmed Shah alone had to undertake eight such invasions. The Sikhs would simply disband or take to the hills, only to return and resume their activities after the Afghan army had returned to Kabul. If the Afghans wanted to consolidate their hold on Punjab, they needed to do the same thing as Babur had done ---- shift their capital to Lahore and maintain a permanent presence in the province. The half-measures adopted by them, in the end, resulted in total loss of control.

Ahmed Shah died when only fifty, probably, of facial skin cancer and was buried in Kandhar. He was succeeded by Taimur Shah who ruled in an undistinguished and desultory manner for the next twenty years while the kingdom stagnated and decayed. He moved the capital from Kandhar to Kabul but liked to spend the winters in Peshawar. He died in 1793 and Shah Zaman, his son from a Yusufzai wife took over. The latter led two punitive expeditions against recalcitrant Sikhs and destroyed the Sikh's Golden Temple in retaliation for desecration and burning of mosques that had become a favourite pastime with the Sikhs.

In 1799, during his second foray, he got news that his half brother, Mahmud, had raised the banner of revolt against him in Herat with help from Iran. As he rushed back, his heavy artillery pieces got stuck in the mud of Jhelum River. A wily local Sikh chief, Ranjeet Singh, had these retrieved and delivered them to Kabul. In gratitude and as a gesture of acknowledgement for this service, Shah Zaman appointed Ranjeet Singh as his representative in Lahore.

This was the beginning of the end of Muslim rule in Punjab. It also effectively isolated and cut off India from Muslim Central Asia with profoundly far reaching consequences. While palace intrigues in Kabul pitted brother against brother, Ranjeet Singh systematically proceeded to expand and consolidate his influence over the entire province of Punjab.

During the seesaw struggle for the throne in Kabul, Shah Zaman's brother, Shah Shuja, who had succeeded as king, had to flee to Lahore to save his life. He had in his possession the famous Koh-e-Noor diamond that Nadir Shah had seized in Delhi and had fallen into Ahmed Shah's hands after the death of Nadir Shah. Ranjeet Singh made a virtual prisoner out of Shah Shuja and coerced him to the point where he was obliged to part with the jewel before allowing the Afghan king to take refuge with the British at Ludhiana in 1816.

Koh-e-Noor was a large diamond whose legendary tale is woven into the history of Mughal India. It was probably mined in Deccan at some indeterminate time and was acquired by Ala-uddin Khilji at the end of the thirteenth century. Its value was placed at 'half the daily expenses of the entire world'. Somewhere along the line it came into the possession of the Hindu rajas of Gwaliar. After the first battle of Panipat in 1526 it was presented to Emperor Babur's son, Humayun, by the family of Raja Vikramjit in gratitude for the protection afforded to them. Humayun gave it to Babur and thereafter it remained a part of the Mughal crown jewels until removed by Nadir Shah to Iran in 1739. When the British defeated the Sikhs in 1846 it was surrendered to the designated Commissioner Henry Lawrence who misplaced it for a while in one of his boots before retrieving and passing it on to Queen Victoria. Since then the diamond has been cut into two parts, each forming the centrepiece of the Imperial Crowns of the British king and queen that can be seen on display at the Tower of London.

POLITICAL ETHOS AND DECLINE

There is no single cause for the decline of the Muslim rule in India but a long list of these. Many of the more specific issues are discussed in other relevant sections of the book. Here we shall only take a brief look at the broad picture and try to dispel some of the myths and misconceptions that persist. Some of these stem from lack of knowledge and misreading of history; others have been created deliberately for a purpose.

The Muslims who had conquered and ruled over India had done so basically to subjugate the local rulers and extract tribute from them for personal enrichment. Islam was there primarily to give a higher cause with which to motivate the troops. They had little interest in the local people, other than to collect tribute and taxes. Mostly, they were left to their own devices and at the mercy of the local rulers. There is no historic evidence whatsoever of any systematic and organized effort to change the religion of the inhabitants to Islam. There was no state religion as such nor any ministry or other administrative institution created for the promulgation or regulation of religious affairs along the lines that existed in Christian Europe.

The history of India as we know it today was put together by mostly British scholars. Inevitably, it reflects their perceptions and understanding of events based on their own European experiences. The books published subsequently have relied heavily on the British compilations as source material. It is only natural in the circumstances that there should be a certain amount of carry over of their influence. The other issue that somewhat distorts the picture is the tendency to view events of a different time in the context of the present and apply standards that may not be entirely appropriate and relevant.

In all, no less than eighty Muslim kings ruled India, starting with the Ghaznavids at the end of the tenth century and ending with the Mughals in 1857. These included 18 Ghaznavids including Sabuktagin, 8 Ghauris, 10 from the slave dynasty, 6 Khiljis, 11 Tughlaks, 4 from the Syed dynasty, 3 Lodis, 5 Suri Afghans and 15 Mughals. Many of them lasted only a few months. All of them ruled the land as a personal domain. The concept of public participation in government had never existed in India or the rest of Asia for that matter, barring for a few years of early Islam.

Similarly, there was little consciousness about collective political interest. India was far too large and diverse a place to develop the kind of social, cultural and economic affiliations and associations that form the basis of a single nation-state. In the absence of any institutions catering to these aspects all political power rested with individuals and loyalties had become personalised. Power was the sole criterion and the Indians gave their allegiance and served the men who held power regardless of their race, religion or origin. Born out of long experience, it is this attitude of mind and approach to life more than anything else that had made it possible for a few hundred thousand foreign invaders to conquer and rule over two hundred million Hindus for more than a thousand years.

Monarchy in India was a personal system of government in which the man at the top held absolute power and used it primarily for his own benefit. Individuals had few rights despite these being clearly stipulated in the Koran. The only rules and rights were those decreed by the king. He was not answerable and owed no allegiance or obligation to anyone else, except in name only to the caliph in Istanbul. Loyalty did not extend even as far as the immediate family. There were no established rules and the process of succession was hardly ever orderly or peaceful.

When a king died whosoever was able to seize and maintain his hold on the throne succeeded him. On each and every such occasion, there was a serious crisis. On the death of a king and sometimes even before that a number of contenders raised armies and staked their claims. Ruthless intrigues and fierce battles decided the ultimate outcome each time. The unsuccessful claimants, if they did not die on the battlefield, were invariably put to death cruelly or remained incarcerated for the rest of their lives.

Another unsettling feature that recurred at each succession was that the governors and rulers of outlying provinces and states, whose loyalties died with the king, took their chances and declared independence knowing there were no guarantees for them with the new regime. Much of the new king's time and energy was spent in dealing with palace intrigues and in chastising and bringing the recalcitrant subordinate rulers to heel. The system of government, as it existed, might have worked for a small fief. It was utterly unsuitable for running a huge country that was full of complexity and diversity in every sphere of life. The decrepit and unworkable set-up never really worked satisfactorily and repressive force had to be used repeatedly, which only led to aggravation and further alienation.

All the empires in India died with the persons who had set them up, or shortly thereafter, unless the successors happened to be men of vigour and capability. The only reason the Mughal Empire lasted for as long as it did was that each of the first five or six emperors was a competent and capable man in his own right. It fell apart the moment there was weakness at the throne. In the type of system that existed there is no real continuity. A fresh start was made each time a king died and new process of consolidation put in motion. In a system of this kind it is very difficult if not impossible for institutions to flourish and progress to be made. The only logical outcome was stagnation or worse.

The uncertainty of succession created instability that often led to rebellion. It was helped in no small measure by the system that allowed subordinate rulers to raise their own armies. A system that enabled diverse elements of administration to exercise freedom of action and control within their own spheres was needed. The arbitrary rule of a single individual was at variance with the objectives of the state. The kings were more interested in personal convenience and not so much in the continued progress and prosperity of the state as a whole. The system they created was inherently antithetical to the establishment of an institution-based government.

The British understood the problem. They had the good sense not to impose an entirely new and alien system but retained what was best suited locally and only modified that which needed change. They did away with personal patronage and replaced it with an institutionalised civil administration run by trained career professionals. The local rulers were allowed to maintain only token armies. Real power was concentrated at the centre, while the authority for dealing with routine local issues was delegated all the way down to the district level. The viceroys were sent to Delhi for a limited period to exclude the possibility of any consolidation or entrenchment based on personal ambition. It was the same with the officials at the lower levels who were transferred from one appointment to another every few years. As a result of such simple measures India was to witness a century of continuous peace and development as it had never before experienced in her history.

The kings that ruled India for the most part remained detached, even alien in some ways. As Bernier observed, '*The Great Mughal is a foreigner in Hindustan: he finds himself in a hostile country, or nearly so; a country containing hundreds of Gentiles to one Mughal, or even one Mohammedan.*' It was a very lonely and threatened position to be in and led to feelings of insecurity often bordering on paranoia. The situation constantly called for manifest demonstration of strength and resolve. Any perception of weakness would have been disastrous. The harsh and Draconian measures undertaken by almost all the kings, most of the time, can only be explained in this light. These might have been effective in the short term but, when imposed over a long period of time, they led to alienation of the people and became the major cause for instability, insecurity and rebellion.

Historians have tried to distinguish between different Mughal rulers, on the basis of their styles of government, to draw lessons. In reality, the differences were superficial and inconsequential. The basic system remained the same throughout and failed to meet the demands of changing times and needs. It was this failure to change, adjust, innovate and evolve that led to the downfall and not because Aurangzeb was more religious than Akbar.

There are those who assert that Akbar had been more accommodating towards the Hindus which led to peace and stability during the reigns of his successors and that the subsequent decline was attributable to Aurangzeb's devotion and zeal towards Islam. This assumption is not borne out by facts and amounts to misreading of history. If, whatever Akbar did could not secure peace in his time, how could it have achieved it for his successors? Throughout India's past, peace and stability have depended upon the abilities of the incumbent ruler. If Jahangir and Shahjahan were successful, it was because they were capable and effective monarchs in their own rights and not because of what Akbar had done in his time.

Aurangzeb ultimately expanded his kingdom to nearly twice the size of Akbar's domain. His successors were lesser men who lacked the qualities possessed by Jahangir and Shahjahan. They did not have it in them to govern such a vast and complex empire and allowed it to stagnate and disintegrate. Had there been any cohesive political and administrative institutions, it is possible, the decline might not have been so sudden and spectacular and the situation might have been tided over until a better person came along.

One hundred and forty years after Aurangzeb, the Sikh Empire in Punjab collapsed even more dramatically after Ranjeet Singh's death. It happened for precisely the same reasons that led to the disintegration of the Mughal Empire and had very little to do with Ranjeet Singh's treatment of the

Muslims and Hindus who had formed the vast majority of the province's population. Although the Sikh rule had been far more discriminatory, oppressive and intolerant towards the Muslims in particular, it is interesting that none of the historians in this case have attributed it as the primary cause for the Sikh collapse.

The Muslim kings of India, like Ranjeet Singh, were first and foremost there to enrich themselves. In the long term, this is best achieved by levying taxes that yield the most only when the subjects are prosperous and at peace. It did not pay to alienate, impoverish and destabilise the vast majority of the country's population. That would have been tantamount to killing the goose that laid the golden egg. No king could have succeeded by resorting to such a self-defeating and destructive policy. This was true for the Muslim rule in India as it was for any other. When a historian tries to draw lessons from history that do not fit one has to be wary and must question the motives.

To some extent the Muslims who ruled India had little option but to remain outsiders considering the nature of the closed Hindu society. Their chief instrument for the exercise of power throughout remained the army. In earlier years it had been a formidable force that was kept rejuvenated and reinvigorated through the induction of fresh recruits from Central Asia. The connection with the north was allowed to gradually decline and the army became progressively indigenized. In the absence of any serious opponents, over a period of time, it lost much of its professional edge. The love of ease and comfort led to an inordinately large 'tail to teeth' ratio and transformed the army into a slow moving, cumbersome logistical nightmare. The unprofessional lumbering behemoth that the army had become was utterly unsuitable and incapable of operations against highly mobile, lightly equipped and furtive bands like the Marahattas and the Sikhs which had begun to torment the empire.

The generalship was equally unprofessional, unimaginative and incapable of effecting adjustment, innovation and improvisation to deal with new situations. When Babur came to India he swam across every river on the way. By the time Aurangzeb ascended the throne most of the professionalism had been lost and the army chiefs were carried to war in luxuriously fitted palanquins. In stark contrast, armies in Europe were already being organised along highly professional lines in the second half of the eighteenth century.

Francois Michel Louvois had introduced a standard disciplinary code, a distinctive military uniform, marching drill, maneuvers and a merit-based system of promotions in the French army of Louis XIV. The Mughal armies had probably never even heard of these developments. With such decay and decadence in the primary instrument for the exercise of power the end could never be far away. In a sense, it was the army that had failed and with it went the empire whose base had primarily rested in its efficacy. For a nation to survive it needs to expand and diversify its power base as widely as possible, at the same time, have in-built checks and balances to ensure that all of its vital institutions remain in balance, up-to-date, purposeful, vigorous, and efficient.

It is misleading to associate religion with the decline. Groups, like the Sikhs in Punjab, did not need Islam as an excuse to rebel against Delhi. They were not defending their faiths but exploiting a favourable political and military opportunity. If religion had been at the heart of their disaffection and revolt then logically the rest of the Hindu population should have joined hands with them. This never happened. Rajputs, who are often portrayed as champions of Hindu rights and symbols of their resistance, were subjugated and oppressed by the fellow Hindu Marhattas just as much as any other people. Each insurrection, as in earlier times, was and remained local in origin and restricted in its objectives. It was never a question of Hinduism versus Islam. There is no evidence to suggest that any such thought existed at the time. If it had, the Marhattas and Rajputs would not have had Muslim allies nor there would have been so many Muslims in the Sikh and Marhatta armies, nor so many Hindus working and fighting for the Mughal kings.

As mentioned before, centrifugal tendencies and movements have been an essential and inherent component of Indian history since the earliest times. The motivations behind them were always opportunistic whether it was the Hindu states breaking away from a Hindu or a Muslim ruled centre or Muslim provinces declaring their independence from a Muslim king. It is fanciful to read more into any of these situations or events. This kind of interpretation comes from projecting present day attitudes, formed after prolonged exposure to the western political concepts and models, into the past and to people who had no such awareness.

In less than twenty years the Mughal Empire was left but in name only. The sudden and dramatic collapse makes an interesting and important point. Historically, empires are kept together by the exertion of some central force. When that pressure is weakened or removed the empire falls apart. That almost never happens in the case of true nations. They may have their ups and downs but they seldom disintegrate in the fashion that empires do. India was never a nation. It was an empire and responded to the historical rules and norms that characterize and govern the fates of such entities.

With power come riches. After a period of time these lead to moral and cultural degeneration. In the case of Muslims in India the condition was epitomized in the shape of Lucknow's *bankas* ---- effete, good-for-nothing, philandering dandies totally out of touch with the gravity of their situation, who roamed the streets in the last days before the British annexed Avadh. The pursuit of pleasure to the exclusion of what was important led to terminal weakness and destroyed the will to rule or fight.

The Muslims in India had lost sight of their purpose. There could be no revival because the institutions needed to monitor the situation and effect a change had never been put in place. When dark clouds of impending disaster threatened and there was nothing else left to turn to, Muslims retreated into religion and looked for answers there. It offered no magic wand, only a distraction that did little to overcome their difficulties. God did not come to their help because He never promised to help those who did not try to help themselves in the first place. It took a long time and immense suffering before this simple truth became apparent to them.

CHAPTER 3

EUROPEAN COLONISERS

THE INDIAN OCEAN

The history of India is generally viewed in the context of her overland connections to the north and west of the country because the determining influences that decided her political fate for a very long time emanated from there. The part played by developments in the vast ocean to the south is mostly ignored. There are many reasons for this omission. In part, it is due to the unfamiliarity of the sub-continent's historians with the significance of the sea and the part it plays in influencing life on land. They concentrated almost exclusively on events in the royal courts and seats of power that were far removed from the sea. It also made it difficult to have access to written records and other source material about the sea, whatever little that might have existed. Prior to the arrival of the Europeans the sea had relatively little direct effect on political developments. As such, there was not much reason for any one to examine and explore its potential and possibilities. It has left a void in history that needs to be filled.

India's connections with the sea stretch back into antiquity. It is now generally believed that homosapiens, ancestors of the modern man, evolved in Africa. Eighty thousand years ago, some of them crossed the Red Sea to Yemen which was a much more fertile and hospitable place in those times. From there they spread along the coastline to Iran, India and beyond. Some of them went north, along the Persian Gulf. The remains of ancient settlements of these people have been discovered in Bahrein and other places.

There were commercial and cultural exchanges between the Indian sub-continent, Indo-China and the Indonesian Islands dating back two thousand years that are evident from the architecture of the ruins in Angkor Wat in Cambodia (Kampuchia), the spread of Buddhism in the Far East and the Hindu presence in the Indonesian Island of Bali. Ports in the Indus delta and along the Gujarat coast were carrying out sea-borne trade with the Sumerian and Egyptian Empires more than four thousand years ago. Throughout history River Indus has served as an important trade route not only to northern and western parts of India but also to Afghanistan, eastern Turkistan and the rest of Central Asia. The fact that half of Alexander's Greek army returned in boats along the coast of Baluchistan in 324 BC indicates prior knowledge of well-traveled existing trade routes to the Persian Gulf and the Red Sea. Later, the Roman Empire maintained commercial and political contacts and even garrisoned some troops on the coast of South India.

Trade has flourished among the countries bordering the Indian Ocean throughout the ages. In many instances, this was followed by settlements and military occupation. A Chinese traveler by the name of Kang Tai visiting a port in Satavahana Kingdom in South India circa 300 AD reported witnessing ships from Sumatra and other places loading and unloading cargoes. In a little known fact, at about the same time, seafarers from Indonesia, known as the '*Waqwaqs*', had migrated 3,500 miles across the Indian Ocean, in fairly large sailing ships called '*kunlun*' by the Chinese, to settle the hitherto uninhabited island of Madagascar. In late seventeenth century, Dutch traders recognized a distinct ethnic link and linguistic similarities between the people living in their possessions in the East Indies and those in Madagascar, particularly in the interior mountainous region. The Chinese were also aware of the existence of Madagascar and conditions along the east coast of Africa as evident from the records of Duang Chengshi (circa 863 AD), a Tang Dynasty period scholar. Hindus had been waging wars in Indonesia in the tenth century. Sumatrans had invaded present day Sri Lanka by sea more than once.

CHINESE INCURSIONS

Seamen of Arab and Iranian origin had dominated the trade routes between East Africa, India, Sri Lanka and the East Indies in their primitive and rather flimsily built *dhows* but they were not alone by any means. The Chinese were no strangers to seafaring and had been visiting the Indian Ocean in far more advanced and superior craft. In the thirteenth century the Mongol rulers had assembled 4,400 ships of various descriptions and sizes in a failed attack on Japan. Before that, they had raided Java with over 1,000 vessels. The Ming Emperor, Yongle, had organised a series of seven expeditions by a fleet of Chinese vessels, between 1405 and 1433, that are reported to have ranged as far afield as Egypt and may even have rounded the Cape of Good Hope into the Atlantic. Chinese maps dating back to 1320 AD indicate that they had knowledge of River Nile, the lakes of Central Africa and the Cape of Good Hope on the southern tip of Africa.

These expeditions were put together and led by the towering figure of a Grand Admiral of Central Asian background named, Zheng He, who happened to be a practicing Muslim. Both his father and grandfather had performed '*Hajj*' which was quite an achievement in itself in those days. The three hundred ship fleet sailed out of the mouth of Yangtze River carrying more than thirty thousand men. Many of the ships displaced over 500 tons, had four decks, spacious cabins, twelve sails and crews of hundreds of men. There were a number of Somalis among them as indeed there were in ships of all the other nationalities that plied the Indian Ocean ---- a practice that continues to this day. Each of the larger vessels carried doctors, accountants, interpreters, scholars, priests, astrologers, traders and artisans of every description. Their cargoes consisted mainly of porcelain, silk and musk from China. No nation on earth at the time had anything even remotely comparable to these veritable floating fortresses on the high seas.

The official records and reports of Zheng He's expeditions were destroyed by the courtiers, after Emperor Yongle's death, for reasons that do not concern us here. Fortunately the official historian, Ma Huang, who had accompanied He on all his expeditions, wrote a book in 1451 and it is through this account that so much has become known about China's maritime past and her interest in the Indian Ocean or, as the Chinese called it, the 'Western Ocean'. It so happens that Ma Huang was also a practicing Muslim and may well have been chosen for the task for that reason, knowing they would be sailing into places where Islam and Arabic language were predominant.

The fleet passed through the straits of Malacca and, rounding off Sri Lanka, made its way to the port of Calicut on the west coast of the South Indian peninsular. On one of the expeditions Zheng He invaded Sri Lanka in a failed attempt to capture the sacred tooth of Buddha from Kandy and took King Vira Alakesvara, along with his queen and ministers, as hostages back to China.

Because of the flourishing trade Calicut had grown into a well-run and prosperous city-state. It was ruled over by a Hindu raja with the help of mostly Muslim ministers and administrators. Thirty thousand Muslims inhabited the city that boasted twenty mosques. Arabic was commonly spoken and understood as, indeed, it was the *lingua franca* of all the coastal regions of the Indian Ocean. An Italian merchant, Nicolo de' Conti, who visited around 1425, married and raised a family in India, described Calicut as a great 'maritime city' that had a circumference of eight miles. Among other things, he also describes the gruesome practice of '*sattee*' and prevalence of polyandry, with one woman having as many as ten husbands. The men contributed among themselves to the upkeep of the shared wife who allocated her children to the husbands as she considered appropriate (polyandry is still practised by some tribesmen in the north-eastern hill tracts of India).

ARABS AND IRANIANS

Indian Ocean in the fifteenth century was a trading arena of great wealth. No other region of the world had a comparable output of manufactured products and raw materials. Included among the goods that were traded or exchanged at its ports were slaves, gold, ivory, rhinoceros horns, ambergris and exotic animals from East Africa; glassware from Syria; dates, horses, copperware and pearls from the Persian Gulf; muslin and coloured cotton, sandal wood, cinnamon, pepper, ginger and other spices from India; bronze, coconut products, precious stones, rice, sugar and spices from Sri Lanka and Indonesia; cowry shells and turtle-shell products from Maldives and Mauritius; cloves from Mafia, Zanzibar and Pemba Islands and silk, porcelain and musk from China.

The existence of such long-standing trade routes indicates fairly advanced and early knowledge of geography, navigation, astronomy and prevailing weather patterns. While there is plenty of circumstantial evidence, the records are scanty. What little has survived is from Muslim sources. The Arabs had been making settlements along Africa's eastern seaboard at least from 700 AD onward. They were mostly Omani people who have a very long history of seafaring. There is a Muslim cemetery in Chibuene in Mozambique, south of Sofala that dates back to the eighth century.

Arab merchants regularly traded inland along the Limpopo and Sabe river valleys. Portuguese Friar Joao dos Santos recorded in early sixteenth century, '*In speaking of this kingdom of Sofala it must be known that formerly upon the shore along that coast, especially at the mouths of the rivers and on the islands, there were large settlements inhabited by Moors*

(Muslims), *full of palm groves and merchandise, and each of these cities had a king ---- and they had commerce and were at peace with the Kaffir (*African) *kings who were lords of the interior'* ('*Empires of the Monsoon*', by Richard Hall, Harper Collins, London, p. 228).

The existence of humpbacked *zebu* cattle, which is an Asiatic breed, in southern Africa points to an early and sustained connection with that continent. Monsoon winds that powered the dhows did not extend beyond the latitude of Sofala and any one venturing beyond was in danger of never being able to return. This is what determined the southern-most limits of the Arab settlements on the 3,000-mile long stretch of Africa's east coast but they were well aware of the world beyond. The Arabs also settled and established similar trading posts along the west coast of India at about the same time or, perhaps, even a little earlier. Their descendants, known as '*Maplas*' still inhabit parts of South India.

An Arab writer, Abul Hasan Ali Al Masudi compiled an encyclopaedia consisting of thirty volumes. Only one of these, '*Muranj Al Zahab'* ('Meadows of Gold') written in 916 AD, has survived. It contains an account of his travels in East Africa ---- the land of *Zanj* (Black people) as he calls it, as well as India, Iran, Armenia, Syria and Egypt. There is a detailed description of the geography as well as demography, social, religious and trading practices of the people in the areas that he visited. He estimated that the trading settlements stretched 2,500 miles from the mouth of the Red Sea south along the east coast of Africa. He also had some knowledge of the Atlantic Ocean and countries in Europe. He knew, for instance, that Britain (*Britanya*) was composed of a number of islands in the north, Paris (*Barisa*) was the 'capital of the Franks' and gives an accurate list of names of the kings of France. This was at a time when Europe lay in total darkness and had little knowledge about the rest of the world.

Masudi was by no means the only scholar with knowledge of Africa and the world beyond. Ibn Haukal and Al Idrisi were among the others as was the famous Al Beiruni mentioned earlier. He was born near the Aral Sea in Central Asia in 973 AD. A mathematician, astronomer, anthropologist par excellence, among other things, Al Beiruni's more well known works are *Chronology of Ancient Nations* and *An Enquiry Into India* (*Tahkik Al Hind*). At a time when the Europeans believed the earth to be flat, with Jerusalem at its centre, he calculated its circumference that is only seventy miles out from what we know today. He had also worked out the orbits of the planets Venus and Jupiter fairly accurately.

Al Beiruni's knowledge of Africa is remarkable. He knew that the continent extended far beyond the sources of the Nile 'into regions we do not exactly know but where it is summer when there is winter in the north'. He also asserted that there was a sea route around Africa, linking the Atlantic with the Indian Ocean ---- in his words, 'One has proof of this communication.' A Dutchman named Jan van Linschoten who worked as a clerk for the archbishop of Goa at the end of sixteenth century has recorded that 'certain Moors' were in the habit of crossing Africa overland between Angola and Sofala. They knew the geography of the continent but lacked the means to navigate round it where the winds were not as predictable or helpful as the Monsoons

Monsoon winds in the Indian Ocean are a seasonal phenomenon set in motion by the alternate warming and cooling of the very large Asian landmass. They blow from the northeast in the winter and reverse direction to southwest in the summer. Taking advantage of this unchanging cycle, sailors since times immemorial have timed their voyages to and from the coasts of East Africa, Persian Gulf and India. These winds weaken and become less predictable as you move further away from the equator and die out completely past 25 degrees latitude. The sails of ships that plied the Indian Ocean were designed to take advantage of the wind from abaft the beam and could not venture beyond the limit of the monsoon latitudes for fear of never finding a wind that will enable them to return. Ship design in Europe, on the other hand, evolved to deal with the vagaries of weather in the Atlantic, enabling them to tack upwind and provide the freedom to operate in all kinds of conditions and latitudes.

Slaves were one of the main exports from East Africa. These were highly valued not only in Arabia but also in Europe as well where a white slave or a horse sold for thirty dinars but a black slave could fetch five times as much. The Arab Empire was expanding rapidly and needed a regular supply of slaves, not only from Africa but from Central Asia and elsewhere to build their cities and irrigation works, tend to their plantations, work in their mines and man their armies. Slaves from Somalia and Abyssynia were particularly valued as crewmen aboard ships and as mercenaries all around the Indian Ocean. African slaves had been a vital part of the economies of Greece and Rome and it was more or less the same when it came to the Arabs. The main difference lay in the kinder and more humane treatment accorded by the Arabs to their slaves in compliance with the Koranic injunctions. Some of them rose to great heights as noted by Ibne Jubair, a traveler from Spain who visited Baghdad in Caliph Al Amin's time (809 AD) and expressed disappointment at seeing the caliph's army commanded by a black slave named, Khalis.

Naturally, slavery is not a condition that is appreciated or relished by the slaves. As with the Greek and Roman Empires, there were many rebellions, the first of these in 689 AD near Basra, led by an African called Riyah that was reportedly put down after the army killed thousands of slaves. A much more serious revolt occurred in 869 AD during Abbasid Caliph Al-Mutadid's rule. The famous Arab historian Al-Tabri, who was alive at the time, has recorded the event. The Shia community that had helped to put the Abbasids in power had become increasingly dismayed and disenchanted by the mismanagement and corruption of their ways. An Iranian Shia, named Ali bin Mohammed claiming to be Mehdi, led a makeshift army of Karmatian Shias and slaves and was soon joined by other dissident groups including Iranians, Jews and Christians while the Kurds waged war in the north. He was able to capture much of southern Iraq and establish a state of his own with its capital at Al-Mutkhara. As mentioned in the chapter '*Muslim Period*', a detachment of the slave army was briefly able to seize control of Makkahh in 880 AD and bring back the sacred *Hajr-e-Aswad*, the meteorite buried in the wall of *Ka'aba*, to Bahrein for a time, damaging it in the process. It was not until 883, fourteen years after it started that the uprising was finally brought under control.

The coastal reaches of Africa remained exposed to unrelenting raids and resulting insecurity because of the slave trade. It discouraged inter-tribal communication and commerce and made it impossible to create food surpluses needed for the development of large cities. Without the existence of cities it was difficult, if not impossible, to develop the institutions necessary for the nurturing of a civilization. As a result, most of Africa was reduced to being a reservoir of raw materials and slave labour for the outside world. The situation was quite the reverse in India where coastal cities owed their allegiance to powerful inland states and acted as conduits for their contact with the rest of the world.

CRUSADING PORTUGUESE

Europe in the middle Ages was steeped in ignorance and religious bigotry. Whatever knowledge that existed was in the hands of theologians whose limited vision was deeply tainted with superstition, bias, and intolerance. This was particularly evident when it came to their attitudes towards people belonging to other races and faiths. Take for instance, Osorius, a fifth century Spanish priest who wrote in his '*World Encyclopaedia*' that much of Asia and most of Africa was peopled by 'troglodytes' who lived underground and gibbered like bats in an unknown tongue. There were also half human creatures looking like hyenas, men with four eyes and others with only half a head, one arm and one leg upon which they could jump to astounding heights (*Empires of the Monsoon*, p.39). Such grotesque views remained prevalent for centuries despite the knowledge that was available in nearby Muslim Spain and North Africa and with the Jewish merchants whose trading networks stretched out to the east as far as India and Central Asia.

Among the latter was the Spanish Rabbi Tudela, who spent twelve years traveling east to India over land and back by sea via Yemen in the twelfth century. He described in detail all that he observed ---- the geography, the peoples, their customs and their rulers. He describes the caliph in Baghdad 'as an excellent man, trustworthy and kindhearted towards everyone as well as extremely friendly towards the Jews'. He was similarly full of praise for the benign ruler of the Indian port of Quilon where ships called for black pepper and other spices. According to him, there were 23,000 Jews resident in present day Sri Lanka at the time and a fewer number of 'Black Jews' in South India.

During their travels, Tudela as well as Marco Polo (1253 – 1326) and Ibne Batuta (1304 – 1377) noted many people of European origin living in various remote parts of Asia including Genoese in Persia, Hungarians, Greeks, French and Englishmen in the remote Karakurram Mountains as well as in India and China. Most of these had been purchased as slaves or captured by the Mongols and taken back with them.

This was the time when the Pope had prohibited any trade with the infidel Muslims and forbade all access to the Red Sea to Christian traders. Only the Venetians felt powerful enough to defy the papal ban and buy goods from India and China from Arab merchants in the eastern Mediterranean for payment in gold and sell these at high prices in Europe. It was in 1296 that tales of the Venetian merchant Marco Polo who had spent twenty years traveling in the east were published in *A Description of the World.* His description of fabulous wealth and prospects of profitable trade gave rise to increasing curiosity and interest in the European commercial circles.

Pope Innocent IV (1243 – 53) had already been contemplating an alliance with the Mongols, after converting them to Christianity, to avenge the humiliations inflicted by the hated Muslims during the Crusades. It was a tempting proposition for the Islamic world was at its weakest at this time, having been ravaged by the earlier Mongol invasions. In 1288, a visiting emissary of the Mongol king, Arghon, of Persia received assurances from Rome as well as King Philippe IV of France and Edward I of England, promising to join the fight to extirpate the 'Mohometan heresy' for good. In the end, the dream of coalition came to nothing as the Mongol Empire started to collapse from within.

The Crusades played a crucial role in shaping ideas and events in Europe in the centuries that followed. These have become a significant part of the European psyche and their effects are very much evident even to this day. It is difficult, if not impossible, to explain western attitudes towards Islam and the Muslims without first analysing the impact of these misadventures on western religious and political thought processes.

In 1095, Pope Urban II had called for a Crusade to liberate the Holy Land from the infidels. Three large armies of feudal knights from France and Germany met in Constantinople. After wreaking havoc on Jewish populations along the way, they proceeded to capture Jerusalem and inflict a blood bath on its non-Christian population ---- mostly Muslims and Jews. The second Crusade was inconsequential but the third, led by the English King Richard, the French King Philip Augustus and the Holy Roman Emperor Frederick Barbossa (1189-1192) managed to lose Jerusalem and most of Palestine to the Muslim ruler of Egypt, Salahuddin. The fourth Crusade, instead of fighting the infidel, in 1204, ransacked Christian Constantinople and the crusaders seized domains within the Byzantine Empire for themselves. In the cold light of history, the sum total of achievement of these Christian Crusades can only be described as two centuries of misery for Europe and an even greater tragedy for the Holy Land.

The Crusades may not have achieved anything positive and may not have been of any great significance when viewed in the context of Islamic history but they remain very relevant to the understanding of European attitudes and motives. The First Crusade was not a spur of the moment decision. Many earlier Popes, including Sylvester (c.1000) and later Gregory VII had preached waging of the holy war. Apart from religion, economic motives and considerations were very much involved. Traders in the rapidly growing Italian cities of Pisa, Genoa, Venice and Amalfi were eager to end the Muslim ascendancy in eastern Mediterranean and open markets in the Near East to West European goods.

This is how Pope Urban had exhorted the faithful to join the holy war, *'O race of Franks! Race beloved and chosen by God! --- From the confines of Jerusalem and from Constantinople a grievous report has gone forth that an accursed race, wholly alienated from God, has violently invaded the lands of these Christians, and has depopulated them by pillage and fire. They have led away a part of the captives into their own country, and a part they have killed by cruel tortures. They destroy the altars, after having defiled them with their uncleanliness. The kingdom of the Greeks is now dismembered by them, and has been deprived of territory so vast in extent that it could not be traversed in two month's time.*

'---- For this land that you now inhabit, shut in on all sides by the sea and mountain peaks, is too narrow for your large population; it scarcely furnishes good enough for its cultivators. Hence it is that you murder and devour one another, that you wage wars, and that many among you perish in civil strife.

'Let hatred, therefore, depart from among you; let your quarrels end. Enter upon the road to the Holy Sepulture; wrest that land from a wicked race ---- and be assured of the reward of imperishable glory in the Kingdom of Heaven'. (*The Story of Civilization IV. The Age of Faith* by Will Durant. Simon and Schuster, New York, 1950. P. 587).

The tales of wealth in the Orient also spurred the impoverished kings of fifteenth century Portugal to look for ways of profiting from it. Unable to compete in the Mediterranean or go across North Africa, they concentrated their efforts on finding a sea route around the continent. Portuguese ships began raiding African villages along the western shores in search of gold and to capture slaves. Since horses were prized in Africa, they traded these for slaves. One horse from Morocco fetched as many as fourteen slaves. By 1458, slaves were being brought back to Portugal at the rate of 30,000 a year and many of these were exported to Spain and Italy. The Portuguese jealously guarded the secrets of their newfound trade. Sailors having knowledge of navigation could only part with the charts and ship designs at the peril of their lives.

The Portuguese kings were the most ardent in answering the strident call of the Pope for the conquest of Saracen and pagan lands for Christianity. They offered a twelve-thousand-strong army to join a Christian force proposed for the liberation of Constantinople that had recently fallen to the Ottoman Turks. They also minted a new gold coin and named it '*cruzado*' (crusade) to mark the occasion.

In return, the Pope gave Portugal the Order of Christ jurisdiction 'all the way to the Indians' that effectively shut rival Spain out of the contest. The Order of Christ was a religious and military society created by the Pope in 1319 specifically to 'defend Christians from Muslims and to carry the war to them in their own territory'. It replaced the now discredited Order of the Knights Templars and provided justification for some of the bloodiest and most heinous deeds in the history of mankind.

The year 1471 stands out in the history of Portugal. Morocco, her nearest Muslim country, had internally weakened and degenerated considerably and now presented a tempting target. A 30,000-strong Portuguese army boarded 300 ships and captured the undefended Moroccan city of Arzila. Under the orders of the king 2,000 inhabitants, men, women and children were put to the sword and 5,000 were carried off as slaves. The same pattern was repeated at Tangiers and other cities that set the tone for later conquests elsewhere in the world. The Portuguese were particularly vicious and ruthless in plundering, raping and killing without mercy. They came to accept that the lives of Muslims, men, women and children alike, counted for nothing because they were the foes of Christendom.

By this time, ship design and the science of navigation in Europe had advanced to the extent that rendered it possible to undertake prolonged voyages, out of sight of land, in the oceans. All that was lacking now was the knowledge of geographical locations. European cartographers sifted through the accounts of travelers like Marco Polo and Nicolo de' Conti to put together some crude maps of the world. One of these by an Italian monk, Brother Mauro, fell into the hands of the Portuguese. Fortuitously for them, it showed a passage, south of Africa, from the Atlantic to the Indian Ocean. The assumption was based on the accounts of some Arab or Indian sailors who had been swept past Madagascar and the tip of Africa, into South Atlantic by storms and had managed to somehow make their way back. The coming together of all these factors and developments made it possible for the Europeans to undertake the voyages of discoveries that were about to ensue and that would set in motion monumental events for the next five centuries.

The compulsions were both economic as well as political. The Pope was constantly exhorting the faithful to 'take the Ottoman Turks in the rear'. Muslims had been a thorn in the side of the Christian church ever since the two clashed in Europe. The humiliation suffered during the Crusades and the fall of Constantinople had been particularly galling. The defeats had given rise to doubts that if the Christians had followed the true religion why had God deserted them? The situation needed to be reversed quickly if faith was to be restored. It was no easy task. Its enormity and accompanying frustration sometimes led to escapism into the world of fantasy.

Included among these fantasies in twelfth-century Europe were the existence of Holy Grail, a lost chalice containing the blood of Christ that endowed miraculous powers, and the legendary ruler Prester John. The latter was supposedly 'a priest and a king who dwelt beyond Persia and Armenia in the east with his Christian people'. Some accounts placed him as the king of Ethiopia, others of India. This brave and noble make-belief Christian leader had supposedly defeated the Persians. Even letters of support to the Pope, Emperor Fredrick of the Romans and Emperor Manuel of Constantinople, alleged to have been written by him, were circulated as proof of his existence. These spoke of a 'domain with crystal waters, great caches of precious stones and forests of pepper trees. On a mountain of fire, salamanders spun threads for the precious royal garments. In his magic mirror Prester John could discern the images of his enemies ----'. Even Marco Polo goes along with the hoax in his memoirs with the added information that the king had since died. Many books had appeared in different languages, perhaps the best known among them '*Mandeville's Travels'*, to support the story of Prester John, most virtuous of Christian monarchs.

In 1487, the Portuguese King John II dispatched spies to find out everything they could about shipping routes into the Indian Ocean, its ports, the commodities that were shipped through them and to make contact with Prester John. Some of these were disguised as Muslim merchants from Morocco but mostly it was the Jews who had freedom to travel everywhere in countries ruled by the Muslims. The best known among them, Pero da Covilham criss-crossed the Indian Ocean several times, ending up in Ethiopia from where the emperor permitted no visitor to return for fear of divulging the country's secrets. Before venturing into Ethiopia, Covilham managed to send back a very detailed account of all that he had observed, by the hand of a courier in Cairo.

Included among the reports from these spies is a description of Vijayanagara, a prosperous Hindu kingdom about 150 miles east of Goa. The city itself was seven miles across and was surrounded by seven walls that protected more than half a million inhabitants. In 1530, two visiting merchants from Europe described it '*as large as Rome ---- the best provided city in the world*'. The tales of its fabulous riches are also recorded by the Persian ambassador to the court, Abdul Razzak, in 1442. According to him, 'the walls and roofs of the rooms in the royal palace were paneled with gold as thick as the blade of a sword, embellished with jewels and fastened with golden nails'. The raja's huge throne too was of 'solid gold and enriched with precious stones of extreme value'. Tales of such fabulous wealth only helped to whet the Portuguese appetite and, together with the opportunity for service to God, became a powerful incentive for reaching the land before anyone else.

The first incursion into the Indian Ocean by the Portuguese was made when Bartolomeu Dias led two caravels past the Cape of Good Hope in 1487. Fearful of the unknown that lay beyond, he turned back. Ten years later, based on the information gleaned during the intervening period, Vasco da Gama first dog-legged south-west into the Atlantic and then turned south-east, taking advantage of the trade winds, to make landfall just north of the Cape. It was an unparalleled 4,500-mile voyage out of sight of land in the annals European navigation.

To avert any possible confrontation between the Spanish and the Portuguese, the Pope negotiated the Treaty of Tordesillas in 1494, two years after Columbus visited America that divided the world between these two powers. All lands to the east of a line running roughly in the middle of the Atlantic went to Portugal and to the west of it to Spain. By this act Portugal, the smallest of the European nations at the time with a population of less than one million, was awarded divine over-lordship over some 300 million people of different races and cultures about which they had virtually no knowledge whatsoever.

The last of the Muslims had been expelled from Spain, along with the Jews, in 1492. Many of them had taken refuge in Portugal, swelling the numbers of non-Christians in the country. In 1496 it was decreed that every Jew and Muslim who had not been baptized into the Christian faith must leave the country. All Jewish and Muslim children under the age of fourteen were to be forcibly baptized; many were dragged screaming into the churches for the ceremony. Faced with the prospect of never seeing their children again if they escaped to some other country, scores of thousands of adult Jews and Muslims chose to be baptized themselves and become second class Christians in their own country. The businesses and properties of all non-Christians were expropriated by the Order of Christ. These were then sold to provide funds for the overseas expeditions.

The flotilla that Vasco da Gama led into the Indian Ocean in the *San Gabriel* consisted of four well-equipped ships, each less than 300 tons, with a total complement of 180 men. It took them five months to round the Cape. Sailing along the east African coast, they stopped at small African villages along the way until they dropped anchor in one of inlets of Zambezi River delta, missing Sofala altogether. The local people spoke Arabic and provided da Gama with information for his trip to the north. In the small port of Mozambique, a week's journey up the coast they posed as Turks to obtain provisions and the services of a pilot. Vasco da Gama made earnest enquiries about the kingdom of Prester John but found no clue.

Some disagreement with the local shaikh led to bombardment of the town and the news spread to the other ports. The expedition missed Kilwa as well and arrived at the prosperous and bustling port of Mombasa in April

1498, to a less than enthusiastic welcome. After beating a hurried retreat the ships set course for Malindi and arrived there to an uneasy standoff. There were ships from India present in the port and contrary to Portuguese expectations, these were not Christians nor did they belong to the kingdom of Prester John.

Religious belief played a fundamental role in the lives of the Europeans to an extent that is hard to imagine in the present day. It sustained the morale of the sailors who regarded their voyages as serving the purpose of God. They were convinced of the absolute superiority of the Christian message and held the Muslims to be 'damned souls in the devil's grip'. They had to be destroyed to please God. Holy war was the relentless theme of sermons that also proclaimed that the world's conversion to Christianity was ordained by the Scriptures. Sadly, similar beliefs are still prevalent among influential Christian circles in Europe as well as North America, though no longer expressed so openly. As recently as August 2001 the adviser to the US congressional panel on faith-based issues, Bishop J. Delano Ellis, proclaimed Islam as '*at best false and at worst bloody and dangerous*'.

Without overwhelmingly blind religious conviction, it would have been impossible to sustain and bear the rigours of such grueling maritime undertakings. A Frenchman of the time, Jean Mocquet, who travelled to India a few years later, has painted a picture of what it had been like to be at sea in those days. '*Amongst us was the greatest confusion and disorder imaginable, because of the people vomiting up and down, and making dung upon one another; there was nothing to be heard but lamentations and groans ---- the passengers were cursing the time of their embarkation, their fathers, mothers and themselves*'. The sailors lay dying between decks, suffering from mal-nutrition and disease, awaiting death '*having their eyes and the soles of their feet eaten up by rats*'. Like so many others, he fell victim to scurvy that he tried to treat by cutting away the dead flesh from his gums then washing his mouth with wine and applying clove oil to the wound. Most sailors leaving Lisbon expected never to return. It was rare indeed for a ship to come back with more than a third of her original crew.

When the Portuguese first set foot in East Africa, contrary to the general impression, what they found was a civilization that was in no way inferior to that in Europe. '*They found towns with tall, many-storied houses built of stone or coral, white and sparkling in the sun; harbours full of ships from other countries of the East, some of them larger and grander than their own, manned by sailors who knew their way across oceans unknown to the Portuguese, and had charts and instruments as good as theirs; a flourishing trade which gave these towns a settled air of prosperity and wealth, even luxury; and as the visitors looked about them and learned more of the land to which they had come, they realised they had reached a world with wider, possibly wealthier, contacts in trade than their own. They were not treated as rare and distinguished guests, nor was their visit regarded as a particularly noteworthy event ----- the people of the coast were used to travellers by sea and were surprised only that the visitors had come from the south'* (*Ancient African Kingdoms*, by Margaret Shinnie, St. Martin's Press, New York, 1965, p. 130).

A Portuguese named Duarte Barbosa, writing in the beginning of the sixteenth century, has given this description of Mombasa at the time. '*There is a city of the Moors called Mombasa, very large and beautiful, and built of high and handsome houses of stone and whitewash, and with very good streets ----. It has its own king, himself a Moor. The people are of dusky white and brown complexions, likewise the women who are bravely attired in silk and gold in abundance. It is a town of great trade, and has a good harbour, where there are always many ships, both those that sail for Sofala, and others which sail to the islands of Zanzibar, Mafia, and Pemba, which will be spoken further on. This Mombasa is a country well supplied with plenty of food. Here are found very fine sheep, which have round tails, and many cows, chicken, and very large goats, much rice, and millet, and plenty of oranges, sweet and bitter, and lemons, limes, pomegranates, Indian figs and all sorts of vegetables, and very good water'* (*Ancient African Kingdoms*, p. 138).

INDIA MEETS EUROPE

Vasco da Gama had tried to bribe and even tortured many of the local Arab pilots, by pouring boiling pork fat on their bodies, in an effort to get them to show the way to India but had met with little success. At Malindi, however, he struck pay dirt when an elderly 'Moor of Gujarat' named Ahmed Ibne Majid offered his services for the task. They sighted the coast of India after twenty-three days sailing and dropped anchor off Calicut on 14th May 1498. The Portuguese noted that Arab traders and ship owners played a dominant part, some of them owning more than fifty ships plying the trade routes to the Persian Gulf and Africa. They also noted that the two communities, Hindus and Muslims, lived in peace and harmony and many Hindus had converted to Islam to escape the rigours of the caste system.

The local Hindu ruler was referred to as the '*Zamorin*' ---- lord of the sea and lived in great opulence in a palace that was a mile square. Vasco da Gama called on him with gifts so meagre that these became objects of ridicule. Some misunderstanding led to his being detained by the king for four days but it was cleared and he was sent back to his ship accompanied by lavish presents. Vasco da Gama was not a forgiving man. He loaded his ships with spices and fired a broadside as a reminder to the Zamorin before setting out to sea ---- this time without the pilot Ahmed Ibne Majid. The Zamorin, like many other rajas in South India, owed nominal allegiance to the maharaja of Vijayanagara but the protection afforded by the latter was in name only.

On the way back, Vasco da Gama put in at Laccadive Islands where he met a Polish Jew, whom he converted to Christianity under torture and then proceeded to plunder the boats in the vicinity. The rest of the journey back was little short of calamitous. He lost one ship after leaving Malindi, another had been abandoned earlier. The remaining two ships limped back to Lisbon with only a third of the original crew. King Manuel was immensely pleased and showered Vasco da Gama with great honour and wealth for a feat that was unprecedented in the annals of maritime history. The voyage had covered 24,000 miles ---- four times longer than the distance covered by Columbus in discovering America.

In other ways too the 'discovery' of India was infinitely more significant than what Columbus had found in the impoverished lands of the West Indies. King Manuel ordered religious processions to celebrate this triumph and victory for Christendom. In a letter to the king of Spain he expressed the belief, 'there will be an opportunity for destroying the Moors of these parts'. Even though Vasco da Gama had found no evidence of the existence of Prester John's kingdom, hope still persisted of one day linking up European Christian forces with him for a combined assault to destroy Makkah, the 'citadel of the infidels'.

Manuel lost no time in mounting the next expedition that sailed under Pedro Alvares Cabral in March 1500, this time, with thirteen ships and 1,200 men. Like Vasco da Gama he went west until he touched the coast of Brazil before tacking for the Cape. Four ships were lost on the way and one turned back but he arrived with the rest at Kilwa, by-passing Sofala. Cabral met the sultan and told him he desired Sofala's gold and set up a trading post at Kilwa. He also demanded that the sultan and his subjects should convert to Christianity. When these demands were not met he moved on to Malindi, this time by-passing Mombasa. Here the sultan asked for Cabral's help as, according to him, the sultan of Mombasa was threatening war because of the earlier assistance that he had provided to Vasco da Gama.

Cabral merely put two of his crew ashore to look for Prester John and after looting some dhows, moved on towards India. Manuel had issued express orders that he should capture any ships of the 'Moors of Makkah' that he came across and sink them.

Until now, unhindered free trade had been the *sine qua non* of life around the Indian Ocean. Henceforward, this was going to change drastically simply because the weak have no rights in the game of nations. More specifically, the historian Joao de Barros declared, '*It is true there does exist a common right to all to navigate the seas, and in Europe we acknowledge the right which others hold against us, but that right does not extend beyond Europe ----. The Moors and Gentiles are outside the law of Jesus Christ, which is the true law ----*' (*Empires of the Monsoon,* p.190).

At Calicut Cabral demanded, on behalf of King Manuel that the Zamorin should do his duty as a good 'Christian' and expel all Muslims from his kingdom for the Portuguese intended to make war on these enemies. He had been given the impression that the Zamorin was indeed a Christian belonging to a heretic sect. Cabral then proceeded to seize a large Arab ship that was loading spices for the Red Sea. There are no Indian accounts available of the events that followed but, according to the Portuguese, riots broke out in Calicut killing fifty-three Portuguese. Cabral bombarded the city for two days and captured ten ships in the harbour killing some of their crews and burning the rest alive in sight of the inhabitants.

He then set sail for Cochin whose raja was not on good terms with the Zamorin. The ships loaded up with as many spices as they could and taking advantage of the northeast monsoon speeded home. These were sold in Europe at prices sixty times higher than what the Portuguese had paid to purchase them. The proceeds filled Manuel's coffers to the envy of rest. Apart from other things, the opening of the Cape sea route dealt a fatal blow to the great city states of Venice and Genoa for they could no longer compete in the market with goods brought overland from Asia.

Spurred on by the prospects of hitherto undreamed of riches Manuel built and sent out as many ships as he could into the Indian Ocean. These intimidated local traders into selling their goods at low prices and also engaged in plundering other vessels, killing and burning their crews alive. A Portuguese scholar, Duarte Pacheo, has described the actions of Manuel and his ships '*With these he conquered, and daily conquers, the Indian seas and the shores of Asia, killing, destroying, and burning the Moors of Cairo, of Arabia and of Mecca, and other inhabitants of the same India, together with their fleets, by which for over 800 years they have controlled their trade in precious stones, pearls and spices'*.

The reason for the total Portuguese success was the ship-borne gun, first used by the English in the battle of Sluys in 1340. None of the ships in the Indian Ocean had a comparable weapon and their bows and arrows were no match for it. The Asians were about to pay a very heavy price for neglecting to keep abreast of technological developments taking place elsewhere in the world. Worse still, in their complacency, they had also not created or developed institutions that could help them to acquire and assimilate such technology.

In 1502 Vasco da Gama made his second incursion into the Indian Ocean, this time with a fleet of twenty-five ships. On his way he encountered a large ship filled with seven hundred men, women and children returning from pilgrimage in Makkah. He confiscated its goods and then set fire to the ship. As the pilgrims jumped overboard to escape the fire Portuguese sailors in boats lanced all but twenty children who were rescued for the Franciscan fathers to be turned into Christians.

When da Gama arrived at Calicut the Zamorin sent a Brahmin to sue for peace with an offer to hand over twelve leading Arab merchants for sacrifice, in atonement for the disrespect shown to him during his previous visit, along with a vast sum of money if he would spare the city. All to no avail; da Gama imprisoned the envoy and commenced bombarding the city that lasted for three days. He rounded up a score of vessels anchored off Calicut, plundered their cargoes and made prisoners of their 800 or so crews. What followed is reproduced from '*Empires of the Monsoon*', p.198, quoting Portuguese contemporary sources:

'He told his men to parade the prisoners, then to hack off their hands, ears and noses. As the work progressed, all the amputated pieces were piled up in a small boat. The Brahmin who had been sent out by the Zamorin as an emissary was put into the boat amid its new gruesome cargo. He had also been mutilated in the ordained manner.

'When all the Indians had been thus executed, he ordered their feet tied together, as they had no hands with which to untie them and in order that they should not untie them with their teeth, he ordered them to strike upon their teeth with staves and they knocked them down their throats; and were put onboard, heaped on top of each other, mixed up with the blood which streamed from them; and he ordered mats and dry leaves to be spread over them, and the sails to be set for the shore, and the vessel set on fire -------- . A message from da Gama was sent to the Zamorin. Written on a palm leaf, it told him to make curry with the human pieces in the boat.

'The bigger ship, engulfed in flames, drifted towards the shore. The families of the men came crying to the beach, trying to put out the fire and

rescue any of those still alive, but da Gama had not quite done. He drove off the families, and had the survivors dragged from the boat. Then they were hung up from the masts, and the Portuguese crossbowmen were ordered to shoot their arrows into them that the people on shore might see. The transfixing of men hung in mid-air was the admiral's favourite forms of execution, since it gave his soldiers good practice ------------.

'When yet another Brahmin was sent from Calicut to plead for peace, he had his lips cut off and his ears cut off; the ears of a dog were sewn on instead, and the Brahmin was sent back to the Zamorin in that state. He had brought with him three boys, two of them his sons and a nephew. They were hanged from the yardarm and their bodies sent ashore.

'Keen to win approval, da Gama's captains did their best to match his deeds. One of them, Vincent Sodre, decided to make a special example of an Arab merchant whom he had been lucky enough to capture. This important prisoner, Coja Mehmed Markar, traded throughout the Red Sea and down the east African coast. His home was in Cairo.

'The account tells how Sodre had him lashed to the mast by two black sailors, then beaten with tarred ropes that he remained like dead, for he swooned from the sight of blood that flowed from him. When the prisoner was revived his mouth was held open and stuffed with dirt (excrement), despite the pleas from other Arab prisoners forced to look on. Then bacon was fastened over his mouth, which was gagged with short sticks; he was paraded with arms pinioned, then finally set free'.

Having thus finished with Calicut, da Gama set sail for Cochin where the raja received him with much pomp and fabulous gifts for Manuel, knowing perfectly well what havoc had been wrought a few days earlier. A body of Portuguese soldiers and craftsmen was landed ashore to build the first European settlement in India at Cochin in 1503. Five ships were also left behind for its protection before da Gama loaded up the rest with spices and turned back for Lisbon. It was not a very auspicious beginning of the process of the so called 'emancipation' of Indians by the Europeans that was to last for the next four hundred and fifty years.

Success of the voyages and the riches that these brought emboldened Manuel to the extent where he fancied himself as the ruler of an empire that he called 'Estado da India' (the State of India). He included in it not only India but also all the territories bordering the Indian Ocean, including Arabia, Persia, Africa and others as yet unexplored that lay further east. When the sultan of Egypt threatened to expel all the Christians if Portuguese ships did not stop interrupting trade between India and the Red Sea, he replied, 'Let the sultan be warned that Portugal intends to do its

Christian duty by entering the Red Sea, laying waste to Mecca, destroying the tomb of the false prophet Muhammad and carrying away his remains'.

He outfitted a new armada of twenty-two ships with 1,500 hand-picked soldiers and sailors and sailed it into the Indian Ocean under the command of the ruthless nobleman, Dom Francisco de Almeida, as his viceroy. His orders were to seize and plunder all ships on the high seas, close the mouth of the Red Sea to prevent any spices entering into Europe from that route and to demand that trade should be conducted with Portugal to the exclusion of every other nation.

Da Gama had already forced the sultan of Kilwa to sign a treaty declaring himself a vassal of Portugal and pay tribute to her in gold. When Almeida arrived at the port he did not see the Portuguese flag flying. It seemed treachery was in the air. He landed his troops who ransacked the city, killing many inhabitants but the sultan escaped inland. He was replaced by a more compliant shaikh and, leaving a contingent of men behind to build a fort, he sailed on to Mombasa capturing many ships along the way. At Mombasa also the same pattern of killing and looting was repeated as at Kilwa and when it ended the city was torched.

Organised warfare at sea was an unknown phenomenon in the Indian Ocean. All that threatened the ships sailing in these parts were the odd pirates wielding little more than spears and cutlasses and the occasional storm. There was real need for the merchant ships to carry guns that were not available. The technology related to warfare at sea had been developed mostly in the Atlantic during the struggles for supremacy between England, France, Holland and Spain. The experience of the Muslim powers had been confined to the Mediterranean where battles were fought with galleys powered by oars and not sails. These were quite irrelevant in the context of the Indian Ocean and no match for the powerfully armed Portuguese *naus*. If the Muslim powers were to deal with the Portuguese threat they required not only the appropriate technology but also raw materials for shipbuilding and weapons manufacture that were not found in the area.

Nonetheless, the suzerain Mamluke rulers in Cairo could not ignore cries for help from Kilwa and Mombasa. Lacking the means themselves, they enlisted the help of Venice to import ship designs, timber and foundries for forging naval cannon. A dozen ships built in the Red Sea sailed for the island of Diu on the Kathiawar coast where they destroyed a squadron of Almeida's ships in 1508, killing his son in the process. Almeida returned with a force of eighteen bigger and more heavily armed vessels. Before attacking the Egyptian ships anchored off the coast he arranged so that the governor of Diu, Russian-born Malik Ayaz, withheld support of the Muslim fleet by his own ships and shore batteries. Predictably, the Egyptians suffered heavy losses and retreated. As was his custom, Almeida lowered his boats and speared enemy survivors struggling in the water. Those taken prisoner were taken to different ports along the coast, a few of them murdered at each place and their body parts fired from the guns into the centre of the town.

A fleet cannot remain at sea forever. It needs shore bases where the men can rest, recuperate and repair their ships. The Portuguese decided upon Goa on the western coast of India for this purpose. A nobleman named Alfonso de Albuquerque was assigned the task and sailed from Lisbon with a powerful force. One of the first things he did on arriving in the Indian Ocean was to send emissaries to 'King Prester John' in Ethiopia with an invitation to join him to destroy Makkah and help divert River Nile so that instead of flowing through Egypt it would empty into the Red Sea thus starving Muslim Egypt into submission. He was utterly convinced of the existence of the mythical Christian king who ruled virtually all of Africa.

Like Almeida he too was a very ruthless man. During his stops at the small Muslim town of Hoja he attacked the defenceless community looting, torturing, killing and burning any one and everything. Rings, bracelets and earrings were taken from Muslim women by cutting off their fingers, arms and ears. Thousands of innocent men, women and children were slaughtered and the entire town burnt to the ground. The same pattern was repeated at Lamu and Brava in East Africa, the island of Socotra and at places along the coast of Arabia. About Muscat he complained that '*the town burnt very slowly because all the houses were made of stone and mortar.*' There was an orgy of killing at Hormuz, a busy port at the entrance to the Persian Gulf. One sailor alone claimed to have dispatched eighty Muslim survivors in the water in one day.

SEEDS OF COLONIZATION

Finally arriving in India, de Albuquerque confronted Almeida who promptly put him under arrest not believing that it was the king's desire that he should be relieved. It took some time for the misunderstanding to be cleared and Almeida departed for home. Near the Cape of Good Hope he tried to forcibly take some African children onboard. It enraged the natives who killed him along with many of his men. Alfonso de Albuquerque landed at Calicut with a strong force but the attack was repulsed with heavy losses. Just then he received news that Goa was undefended because the Muslim ruler of Bijapur, Sultan Ismail Aadil Shah, had withdrawn the troops for war in another part of the country. It was an easy victory and he was able to write to the king:

'Then I burnt the city and put everyone to the sword and for four days your men shed blood continuously. No matter where we found them, we did not spare the life of a single Muslim; we filled the mosques with them and set them on fire ----. We found that 6,000 Muslim souls, male and female, were dead, and many of their foot soldiers and archers had died. It was a very great deed, Sire, well fought and well accomplished. Apart from Goa being so great and important a place, until then no revenge had been taken for the treachery and wickedness of the Muslims towards Your Highness and your people' (*Empires of the Monsoon*, p. 221).

Albuquerque swore that only Christians and Hindus would be allowed to live in the new Goa that he would build. Since there were very few Christian families present, Goa was to be populated by the children of Indian women fathered by the Portuguese. Each man who volunteered for the task was given a house, a horse and some land and farm animals. As for the potential brides, he rejected South Indians as they were of dark complexion and 'dissolute'. The women had to be 'good-looking and of white colour'. After this Albuquerque went east to take control of Malacca and the approaches into the Indian Ocean. Having accomplished it, he sailed with a powerful force for the Red Sea, still hoping to link up with the illusive Prester John now firmly believed to be ruling in Ethiopia. Upon arriving in Aden in 1513 he set fire to all the merchant ships that were present in the harbour and then stormed the fort. The attack failed with heavy losses and he left to anchor further up the coast.

Not finding any signs of Prester John and his untold riches, he turned back towards Hormuz in the Persian Gulf. A young boy named Saif-uddin ruled the city under the guidance of his *vazir*, Raees Ahmed, who would not accede to the extravagant and unjust demands made by Portuguese. Albuquerque waylaid the vazir under false pretences and stabbed him to death. The frightened young ruler surrendered the city where the Portuguese built a fort to control the trade in the Persian Gulf. Earlier, he had done a similar thing in Calicut when he had failed to take the city. He arranged for the heir to the throne, Nampiadiri, to poison the Zamorin, Mana Vikrama, before signing a favourable peace treaty with him.

If there is one factor that can be singled out for the European successes in the colonization process, it is that they invariably acted for the collective national interest whereas personal gain remained of paramount concern to the Asians and Africans. The wife of one African chief betrayed her husband and the tribe to the Portuguese for just a few strings of beads, a wash basin and one piss-pot.

It was not long before the Portuguese drove out the nearly blind shaikh of Sofala and established a fort there. When some African tribesmen resisted, they were mowed down by cannon fire. In 1520, a party led by Rodrigo de Lima set out from the port of Massava in the Red Sea to again look for Prester John. It was a bizarre mission that lasted six years. The myth was held as a religious truth and could only be refuted or denied at the peril of a horrible death. De Lima eventually succeeded in meeting the legendary figure that he decided to believe was Prester John. This was the twenty three-year-old Negus of Ethiopia, Lebna Dengel. Like most such legends, this too did not measure up to expectations and de Lima declared him to be 'fickle, devious and arrogant'.

Ethiopia was a land-locked country continuously at war with its Muslim neighbours. The negus was keen to forge an alliance with Christian Europe and, with its help, capture neighbouring territories in the vicinity of the port of Zeila that would give him access to the Red Sea. In the end, common faith did not prove to be a sufficiently strong bond and the Ethiopians remained suspicious of the Europeans' intentions. There are serious religious issues that divide Ethiopia's Coptic Christians and the European Roman Catholics. De Lima's account of his stay in Ethiopia makes fascinating reading. Among other things he mentions a mountain where all the likely male heirs to the throne are held virtually as prisoners. Anyone trying to escape has his eyes put out. When the king dies one of the princes is taken out and placed on the throne while the rest continue to languish in the mountain redoubt.

After years of efforts by a priest named Mendez, the Ethiopian Emperor Susenyos decided to take an oath of allegiance to the Pope in 1626. His reason for doing so had much to do with local politics but the decision did not go down well with the populace. They were appalled the patriarch sent by Rome ordered all local churches to be re-consecrated, all clergy re-ordained, all believers re-baptized and all festivals re-fixed according to the Roman calendar. Any defiance was punished by hanging or burning at the stake. Lesser offences were dealt with by cutting out the tongues. A rebellion ensued that claimed the lives of thousands of Ethiopians. Susenyos was obliged to abdicate and all Europeans ordered to leave the country. Ethiopia was closed to white men for a long time to come. A French doctor, who was allowed in as the envoy of Louis IV in 1698, noted that the Ethiopians hated white grapes because their colour reminded them of the Portuguese who had been responsible for their brush with Roman Catholicism.

As part of the Counter-Reformation, whereby the church re-asserted its authority against the heresy of Reformation, Pope Paul III had issued a bull establishing the Society of Jesus in 1540. Theirs was a particularly intolerant brand of Christianity that gained royal favour in Portugal. One of its exponents Francis Xavier, who was raised to sainthood, travelled as far as Japan in his search for converts and died in Macao in 1552. While in India he ordered the destruction of all Hindu temples and banned the calling of Muslims to prayers in Goa. He also instituted the dreaded Inquisition in the Portuguese held lands.

The incredibly unjust, inhuman and cruel institution had been established by the Pope in 1478 that embodied religious police, prosecution, judiciary and executioners, all rolled into one, in the name of God. Spain had been a very tolerant and liberal society during the eight hundred years of Arab (Moorish) rule. After its overthrow in 1492 the Church reasserted its authority and set about 'purifying' the Christian lands with unprecedented vengeance. All the Muslims and Jews were given the simple choice to either convert to Christianity or leave the kingdom. Not having a place to go many of them chose to become Christians. This was not enough. They still remained suspect and were perceived as a threat to the purity of the 'true faith.'

Nearly eighty years earlier, Pope Benedict XIII had promulgated a papal bull in May 1415 that forbade all Jews from reading, listening to or teaching the Talmud which it called a '*depraved doctrine*'. All books that contradicted the dogmas and rites of Christianity were banned. No Jew was permitted to pronounce the names of Jesus, Mary or the saints. No new synagogue could be built or old ones refurbished. No person of Jewish faith could become a judge, physician, midwife, trader, tailor, butcher, carpenter, watchmaker or moneylender. They were forbidden from renting property, employing Christian servants and living in Christian neighbourhoods. All contracts with Jews were declared null and void and they were forbidden to eat, drink, bathe or even talk with Christians. Each of them was obliged to wear nothing but coarse clothes with a distinguishing red or yellow badge and attend at least three sermons a year that stressed the coming of Christ, the Messiah, and the errors of the Talmud (*Historia de los Judios* by J. Amador de los Rios and *The Spanish Inquisition*, by Henry Kamen, The New American Library, New York, 1968, p. 27).

There was no specified list of crimes for investigation and trial by the Inquisition. It was left to the officials themselves who were answerable 'only to God'. The more common crimes included heresy, practicing non-Christian religion, having Arabic names, showing disrespect for Christian sacraments, refusing to eat pork and drink wine and practicing circumcision. Mere suspicion was enough to arrest any man, woman or child and torture him or her with extreme cruelty until a 'confession' was obtained as proof for conviction. In most cases, the victim was eventually burnt alive at the stake in public in a ceremony known as '*auto de fe*.' The fires were deliberately kept low, as a concession to the victim, in the belief that the longer and more excruciating the suffering the better the chance for the redemption of his or her soul. The properties of the victims were confiscated and divided up between the Holy Office, the Royal Treasury and the Church. There is no record of the exact number of people that fell victim to the Inquisition worldwide but it is generally believed that millions suffered horrible injustice and indescribable cruelty before it was finally abolished in 1834. (*Histoire Critique de l'Inquisition d' Espagne,* by J. de Mariana, p 239 and '*The Spanish Inquisition*', chapter 10).

Another Jesuit priest, Goncalo da Silveira, travelled up the Zambezi to convert the powerful ruler known as Monomotapa. It backfired badly. The Africans accused him of sorcery and strangled him. Lisbon dispatched a strong expeditionary force to avenge his death. It stopped at Sena, a trading post on the Zamezi inhabited by traders from different lands. Suspecting the local Muslim community of being hostile, they ordered every one of them to be slaughtered. Father Monclaro, who was accompanying the expedition, noted, '*Strange inventions were used to kill the Muslims. Some were impaled alive, others tied to trees in the extreme branches thereof, the branches being forcibly brought together then released, the victim being thus rent asunder. Others were cut up with axes from the back, others with bombards*' ('*Empires of the Monsoon*', p. 258). The expedition met an equally dismal end. They died, almost to the last man, of disease or at the hands of the African tribesmen.

In the end, the Portuguese were obliged to restrict their activities along the coastline of Africa, displacing the Arab traders in the process. Of the latter the Dominican Friar, Joao dos Santos, at the end of the sixteenth century recorded in his treatise on Ethiopia, '*The once proud Moors of Sofala they are all poor and miserable, and generally live by serving the Portuguese in their journeys and trading and also as sailors. The Moorish women, as well as the Christians, employ themselves in cultivation, and pay tithes of all their harvests to our church.*' He also proudly mentions setting fire to a thatched mosque near Sofala. When it was reduced to ambers he notes, '*It presented a good picture of the fire in which Muhammad was burning*'.

Such visceral hatred of Islam is by no means limited to the Portuguese. It is still very much alive and virulent, albeit mostly below the surface, in all of the Christian West today. You only have to log-in to thousands of anti-

Muslim Internet sites or tune in to hundreds of private TV and radio stations to know the intensity and vicious extent of the malaise. The savagery and brutality of actions against Muslims in Bosnia, Chechniya, Kosovo, Iraq, Afghanistan and other places is only the more visible indication of the depth and pervasiveness of the hatred. This extract from the book '*The Deserter's Tale: The Story of an Ordinary American Soldier*' by Joshua Key, who served with the US Army in Iraq, reveals the attitudes and feelings towards Muslims found among the US armed services at the present time:

'(At the training camp, I) *felt myself swell with patriotism and pride when our commanders told us that Americans were the only decent people on the planet and that Muslims and terrorists all deserved to die. -------*

'One day, all 300 of us lined up on the bayonet range, each facing a life-sized dummy we were told to imagine was a Muslim man. As we stabbed the dummy with our bayonets, one of our commanders stood on a podium and shouted into a microphone: "Kill! Kill! Kill the sand niggers!" We, too, were made to shout out, "Kill the sand niggers" as we stabbed the heads, then the hearts, and then slashed the throats of our imaginary victims.

'Our commanders told us that people who were not Americans were 'terrorists' and 'slant eyes' (an obvious reference to the Chinese and other Orientals). They said that Muslims were responsible for the September 2001 attacks on our country, that the people of Afghanistan were "terrorist pieces of shit that all deserved to die." --------

*'Iraqis, I was taught to believe, were not civilians; they were not even people ---- (From our commanders we learned to call them rag-heads, Habibs, sand niggers and hajis) and they were not to be thought of with a shred of humanity. No wonder my wife and I thought ---- that all Muslims were terrorists and all terrorists were Muslims and the only solution was to kill as many Iraqis as pos*sible. --------'

Like the French in Canada and the British in Australia, the Portuguese also tried to settle the flotsam and jetsam of European society in Africa but it failed to take root because of the hostility of the natives, aided and abetted by the climate and disease. Eventually, large parcels of land were leased to private farmers. These slave plantations later became the foundation for the colony of Mozambique. Climate and diseases like malaria, cholera, dysentery, small pox and plague took a terrible toll of the Europeans in the tropics. It is estimated that only about one in five British soldiers in India were still alive after spending five years in the country.

Tired of the unending Portuguese depredations, the coastal cities appealed to the Turks for help who were now in control of Egypt. The renowned Turkish Admiral Rais Piri, who had earlier charted the coastline of South America with uncanny accuracy, was dispatched to survey the area in 1554. Alarmed at this development, a Portuguese fleet was ordered to chastise the coastal cities of East Africa that had cast their lot with the Turks. Friar Joao dos Santos, who witnessed the raid on the small port of Faza notes, '*The Portuguese would not pardon any living thing; they killed women and children, monkeys and parrots and other innocent animals, with as much rage as if they had been responsible for the sins of the city*'. After the orgy of bloodletting all the buildings were burnt and the plantations destroyed. The same scenes were repeated at the other places, including poor luck-less Mombasa.

But, by this time, Portuguese influence had started to wane. Perhaps, the greatest factor in the decline lay in their inability to make local alliances. Extreme animosity towards the Muslims, the very people in whose lands they operated, was a matter of sacred duty with them. As a Malabar Muslim, Shaikh Zia-uddin, wrote in 1570, '(Portuguese) *having made the Mohomedans to be a jest and a laughing stock; displaying towards them the greatest contempt; employing them to draw water from the wells, and in other menial employments; spitting in their faces and upon their persons; hindering them in their journeys, particularly when proceeding on pilgrimages to Mecca; destroying their property; burning their dwellings and mosques; seizing their ships; defacing and treading underfoot their archives and writings; burning their records; profaning the sanctuaries of their mosques.*' They might have formed an alliance with the Hindu states in India but by the time they realised the wisdom of such policy, the most powerful Hindu state in the area, Vijayanagara, was over-run by an alliance of neighbouring Muslim rulers in 1564 and its army of 600,000 foot soldiers, 100,000 cavalry and 500 elephants destroyed (*Further Sources of Vijayanagara History*, by K.A. Nilakanta Sastri and N. Venkataramanayya, Madras, 1946).

With a total population of no more than one million, Portugal lacked both the material and manpower resources to occupy and hold sizeable colonial real estate. The medieval form of government that rewarded position rather than talent was as ruinous as the corruption it engendered. The system was incapable of producing the leadership, discipline and morale among the men called upon to perform under extremely hard and trying conditions.

The initial spectacular successes were mostly due to the technological superiority of their ships and guns and the corresponding lack of preparedness of the local defenders. This advantage could not last forever.

There were other factors at play as well. Portugal had entered into a transient union with Spain under King Philip II in 1580. The latter undertook disastrous wars against England and Holland. The loss of the Spanish armada in 1588 in waters off England was a severe blow in which Portugal lost the cream of her navy. Even more telling was the degeneration that had set in among those in the colonies because of lax administrative and social controls. In the pursuit of pleasure and life of ease the men had lost the reason and purpose of being where they were. They had lost the will to fight.

In 1550, Sultan Saif bin Khalifa of Oman drove the Portuguese out of Muskat with ease and then started to send parties to raid their settlement in Mombasa, 2,500 miles away. After a bizarre siege that lasted nearly three years and a loss of over 6,500 men, the Portuguese surrendered Fort Jesus as well to the sultan. It broke the chain of communications between Portugal and their possessions in Asia and proved to be the beginning of the end that was to come swiftly. In a last ditch effort, they tried to capture Zanzibar in 1700 but were again beaten back by the Arabs.

OTHER INTERLOPERS

The Portuguese had tried their best to keep their discoveries in the Indian Ocean secret from rest of the Europeans but the word leaked out. Within twenty-five years of their rounding the Cape of Good Hope, the French were following in their footsteps. By 1589 the British had anchored off Zanzibar, followed by the Dutch off Java in 1597. Both these countries established trading companies with charters bestowing thinly disguised governmental status and exclusive commercial rights. In the case of the Dutch these included the building of fortified strongholds, military recruitment, negotiating treaties and waging war.

By 1607 they had raided Mozambique and were seizing Portuguese ships and cargo on the high seas. Fifteen years later they were harassing the colony of Macao on the coast of China. They drove the Portuguese out of Hormuz with the help of Shah Abbas, the ruler of Persia, obliging them to set up base in Bahrein. In 1658 Sri Lanka was lost to the Dutch and the writing was very much on the wall. At about this time the Portuguese princess, Catherine of Braganza, married King Charles II of England and brought the port of Bombay with her as dowry. Finding it of little use to himself Charles sold it to the British East India Company for the princely sum of ten pounds in 1668.

Curiously, the Europeans paid little attention to South Africa, which had vast open spaces and a much more agreeable climate from their point of view. It was mainly because they were interested only in trade and not in any permanent settlement in the century and a half following Vasco da Gama. It was the Dutch who first realised the strategic significance of the Cape and laid the foundations of the settlement at Table Bay they named Kapstaad (Cape Town) in 1652.

The local Khoikhoi people, whom they derisively called 'Hottentots' because of their strange way of speaking, had a much lighter skin colour than other Africans and were quite friendly to the settlers. Very little is known about their origins and ethnicity. These harmless herdsmen were shot on sight or captured for sale as slaves and those that survived were pushed inland as the Dutch colony expanded. There are recorded instances of white men and women organising expeditions to hunt these poor natives of South Africa for sport. The same happened with the hapless aborigines in Australia.

As far as cruelty to the local inhabitants went, the Dutch were just as vicious, if not worse, than the Portuguese. An English lady, Mrs. Jemima Kindersley, on her way to Calcutta in 1765 witnessed the torture and lynching of slaves in Cape Town that she wrote were carried out in public in a manner 'too shocking to repeat'. Any slave accused of a serious infraction, such as an attempt to escape, was stretched live on a torture wheel after smashing his arms and legs with an iron club. Others were impaled on stakes in the ground where they took two or three days to die. The Europeans viewed the slaves not as human beings but as property. There are recorded cases of slaves being beheaded to save expenses, after they had outlived their utility to the owners (*Empires of the Monsoon*, p. 362).

Perhaps, even worse in terms of cruelty to the Africans were the Belgians. In late nineteenth century, King Leopold II had staked out a huge chunk of territory, now known as the Republic of Congo, as his personal domain. His functionaries used the entire population as slaves of the king, first to get ivory out of the country and later, rubber and minerals. Until 1909, he used his mercenary army to force slaves into mines and rubber plantations, burn villages, mete out sadistic punishments, including dismemberment, and commit mass murder. The barbarous and inhuman treatment of the natives resulted in a steep decline in population. Within a short span of forty years, it was reduced by half, from twenty to ten million (see *King*

Leopold's Ghost: A Story of Greed, Terror, and Heroism in Colonial Africa, by Adam Hochschild, Mariner Books, 2006).

Before settling in Cape Town the Dutch had been concentrating on Mauritius, cultivating sugar cane introduced from Java. The island was home to a large flightless bird, known as the 'dodo' that they killed for meat. The species was rendered extinct by 1680. Not long afterwards the Dutch abandoned Mauritius to explore more profitable avenues in the east. It was the turn of the French next. By 1735 they had established a sizable colony of about 4,000 whites and 40,000 African slaves to work on sugar plantations on the island they had renamed Ile de France. There was a similar French settlement on the island of La Reunion to the south of Mauritius.

The Dutch had arrived in force off Sri Lanka and announced to the King in Kandy in 1646, 'not in the expectation of much profit that we have brought this force to this island, but only with the desire to do Your Majesty service'. Soon the Dutch East India Company (VOC) was writing to the governor-general, Antonio van Dieman, 'The time has come for driving the Portuguese from their strongholds and depriving them of their supremacy in the Indies and taking their place. The present time seems most opportune to accomplish this' (*Empires of the Monsoon*, p.296). Tired of the Portuguese excesses and believing the Dutch to be the lesser of the two evils, the king, Raja Sinha, decided to throw in his lot with the latter and the Portuguese were ousted from Sri Lanka after a series of bloody land battles.

It was a land that had been ravaged by mismanagement, sucked dry by exploitation and in a state of chaos and anarchy, largely due to religious conflict between the local Buddhists, the Portuguese Catholics and the Dutch Reformists. This is when the Dutch brought in Tamil slaves from the Coromandel Coast of South India and branded them with the insignia of the Dutch East India Company to work at their cinnamon and coconut plantations.

In time, like the Portuguese, the Dutch burghers also started to marry local Sinhalese or *mestizo* (racially mixed) women. Although the purists of the Calvinist Church frowned upon the practice, there was little choice for there were hardly any white women available on the island. To keep the races and religions apart the Dutch also passed a law under which any Christian woman found associating with a 'pagan' man was flogged in public, branded, put in chains for life and had her children enslaved. Virulent racism in its various forms has been a consistent theme in the history of European people wherever they are found, even to this day.

Fearing that France was being left out of the race for empire building, Cardinal Richelieu, chief minister of Louis XIII ordered a settlement to be built at the south tip of Madagascar that was named Fort Dauphin in 1642. Later, Louis XIV formally declared the entire island to be a part of the French Empire. This was a time when Europe was filled with dreamers and adventurers, inspired by writings such as Sir Thomas More's *Utopia* and Sir Fancis Bacon's *New Atlantis*, wishing to make fortunes and establish idealistic societies in idyllic settings to escape from the ceaseless strife and turmoil in Europe. They saw in Madagascar an earthly paradise, which in reality was a long way from the truth. Most of the settlers in Fort Dauphin died fighting the natives or succumbed to starvation and disease. The few that survived made their way to the island of Reunion or to the French settlement of Pondicherry on the east coast of India.

Madagascar became home to pirates and buccaneers. One of these, French Captain Misson, founded the Republic of Libertalia in conjunction with the renegade Dominican priest Father Caraccioli, at Diego Suarez on the northern tip. It had a parliament, a motto that read 'For God and Liberty' and a creed that proclaimed, 'It is more honourable for a man to steal from the rich with only the protection of his courage than to steal from the poor under the protection of the law'. This brave republic was over-run by the natives in due course and most of its inhabitants slaughtered. The well-known Scottish buccaneer, William Kidd, also made Madagascar his home before returning to America, only to be taken to London and being hanged after a dubious trial.

There was no gold, silver or any other exportable commodity readily available on the island but it was a great place for slaves. Apart from those captured or purchased from among the locals, large numbers of them were brought in from Mozambique and Comoro islands that had a Muslim population and were ruled by a sultan in Anjuoan Island. A bishop, sitting in a marble chair, blessed the wretched souls as they were dragged to the waiting ships and to a life of indescribable misery and early death. Conditions onboard were so wretched that on an average less than a third of the slaves survived by the time they were taken off the ships in America. Malagasy slaves were cheap as compared with those from West Africa where too much competition had driven up the prices. The slavers paid for them with guns, bangles, cloth, iron bars, beads and brandy and shipped them to plantations in the American colonies and the West Indies.

No one knows how many slaves were taken out of Africa before the trade was made illegal, first by France, after the revolution in 1789 and then by Britain through the Abolition Act of 1807. The actual owning of slaves was not abolished in England until 1833 under pressure from activists like

William Wilberforce. These were no libertarians but close-minded Evangelists. About Hinduism, for instance, Wilberforce noted, '*The Hindu divinities are absolute monsters of lust, injustice, wickedness and cruelty. In short, their religious system is one grand abomination*' (*Empires of the Monsoon*, p.378). It took another three-quarter of a century and a civil war for the United States to ban the institution.

The total number of slaves taken out of Africa must run into many millions. The Sultan of Oman alone sold more than 100,000 slaves a year from his territories in East Africa. Much of the west coast of the continent was denuded of human population by the trans-Atlantic slave trade that was conducted in ships specifically built for carrying human cargoes (for more on slavery in America please see *Rough Crossings: Britain, The Slaves and the American Revolution*, by Simon Schama, BBC Books, London).

Slavery formed a very significant part of the trade in those times. Without the assistance from this cruel and inhuman institution it is questionable if European colonisation of the Americas or the success of their commercial ventures in the east would have been possible. Because of its odious nature western historians are prone to glossing over the issue and brushing this important chapter in human history under the carpet. The powerful Jewish lobby in America has become deeply involved in this attempt in an effort to preserve the Jewish image since much of the slave trade with North America was in Jewish hands at the time. The issue does not concern us here. Anyone wishing to pursue it further may like to refer to two books by Professor Tony Martin of Wellesley College, USA, *The Secret Relationship Between Blacks and Jews*, and *The Jewish Onslaught* (The Majority Press, Dover, Massachusetts).

A BRITISH LAKE

The British were not too pleased with the Dutch influence in Sri Lanka. Their attempts to seize ports in Sri Lanka were thwarted by the arrival of a powerful French fleet under the brilliant Admiral Suffren. Not ones to give up easily, the British embarked upon an enterprise that is worth repeating for it typifies in many ways how the Europeans gained ascendancy in the East. More than half of the Dutch garrison in Sri Lanka was made up of mercenaries from Europe under the command of a Swiss colonel named Pierre de Meuron. The British Secretary of State for War, Henry Dundas, asked a professor from St. Andrews University, named Cleghorn, to approach the colonel's brother in Switzerland, Charles the Comte de Meuron, and offer him two thousand pounds if he would persuade the mercenaries to switch sides. The final deal raised the payment to five thousand pounds and included the appointment of the two brothers as generals in the British Army as well as giving employment to their men on favourable terms.

Cleghorn and the Comte then traveled together to India via Egypt from where a letter was smuggled to the colonel, concealed in a block of cheese. After reading it he marched his troops out of the fort at Colombo. The demoralised Dutch surrendered without offering any resistance when British troops invaded from Madras in 1795. Nick-named 'Switcher Troops', the mercenaries went on to fight for the British in India and were finally disbanded in Canada in 1816.

The Sinhalese still had a king, Vikrama Rajasinha, who ruled in Kandy in the central highlands. When it came time to get rid of him, the usual campaign of vilification was mounted to justify the action. He was now consistently portrayed as a sanguinary and remorseless tyrant and a monster. There was no choice but to remove him and deliver 'the hapless people from his oppression to the benign parental protection of the British rule'. In 1815 a force composed mostly of black slaves and Indian troops stormed Kandy where the king surrendered without a fight. The palaces and temples were looted and the king's throne, made of gold and studded with precious stones, was shipped off to Windsor Castle. Anyone who resisted was duly hanged. When one of them chose to commit suicide to avoid being hanged, his corpse was publicly beheaded.

With the expanding British interests it became increasingly necessary for them to control strategic points in the Indian Ocean. Fears were rampant that Napoleon might attempt a landing in India by sea. In response to these the British occupied Cape Town in 1805. Later, in 1810, they ejected the French from Mauritius, with the help of troops from India, but allowed them to remain in Reunion. They had already taken over the port of Malacca from the Dutch and now gained control of the Indian Ocean from Australia to the Persian Gulf and the Red Sea and from the Indonesian islands to South Africa, turning it into a veritable British lake that stretched over sixteen million square miles.

The British East India Company now enjoyed a monopoly over trade with China, including the export of opium from India. The Company's navy, the Bombay Marine, patrolled as far as the Red Sea and the Persian Gulf. For some obscure reasons, control over Sri Lanka, Mauritius and the coast of Africa was not handed over to the Company but was retained by the Foreign Office in London, through the Royal Navy.

It is not generally known that the sultanate of Oman was a considerable sea power in its own right at this time and ruled over much of the east African coastline and the offshore islands. In 1806, fifteen-year old Sultan Saeed gained power in Muscat after stabbing a rival cousin to death. Fearing reprisals, he threw in his lot with the British. Muscat was a rich port and trading place for merchants from all over the Indian Ocean. Apart from collecting taxes on their goods the sultan had extensive trading interests of his own mostly centered on the sale of slaves.

In return for their support, the British continually extracted more and more concessions from the sultan until there was virtually nothing left to give. In a futile attempt to develop some leverage he signed secret treaties with the Americans, French and Germans but to no avail and passed the rest of his time making groveling gestures such as making a gift of his seventy-four-gun flagship to King William IV. At least one Omani ship, the *Sultanee*, crossed the Atlantic to call at New York around this time.

Eventually, unrest and rebellion drove Sultan Saeed to settle permanently in Zanzibar in 1832, leaving Muscat in the hands of his son, Thuwain. Saeed continued to rule from there until his death in 1856. Much before this, Hilal, the eldest son and hier apparent, suspected of treachery had been banished and had died. From among the rest of his children, the epileptic Majid was put on the throne. When the youngest son, Barghash, contested the choice the British exiled him to Bombay. Later, they mediated between Majid and Thuwain in Muscat, setting up each in a separate protectorate and in the process extracting concession for themselves from both. Barghash made his way into British good books and was allowed to return to Zanzibar. Fearful, Majid moved his capital to a new city he had built on the African coast that he named Dar-as-Salam. He died there in 1870 and was replaced by Barghash but his authority was less than that of a puppet in British hands.

A number of forces had been at work in the Indian Ocean in the half century that had passed. Steam ships had gradually replaced sailing vessels at sea. These cut sailing times to a fraction of what they were before. A voyage that took six months in a ship under sail could now be performed in forty days. The opening of Suez Canal by the French reduced these times still further. Not wishing to miss out, the British Prime Minister, Benjamin Disraeli, secretly borrowed four million pounds from the Jewish bankers, Rothschilds, to buy the 43% shares in Suez owned by the bankrupt ruler of Egypt, Khadiv Ismail in 1875.

This was also a time when Europe was awash with missionary zeal to ‘civilize’ the non-white world and convert the natives to the true faith. The spirit behind it was made full use of by the explorers pushing into areas that were hitherto unknown to Europeans and by avaricious politicians wanting to acquire new colonies. They were falling over each other in their efforts to carve up territories and stake claims in non-European lands.

King Leopold of Belgium had staked his claim to the Congo basin, as mentioned earlier. The British were in possession of the Cape and Gold Coast areas; France had consolidated her hold on Madagascar and Italy, having gained control of the port of Assab in the Red Sea in 1870, was staking a claim in the Horn of Africa. The Portuguese were already firmly entrenched in Angola and Mozambique. This left Germany out of the scramble.

In 1884 a German operative named Karl Peters, pretending to be an artisan, secretly traveled inland from Zanzibar and persuaded a dozen illiterate African headmen to put their marks on pieces of paper in return for gifts of brandy and some trinkets. These 'treaties of eternal friendship' gave away all the territories of the chiefs to the Society for German Colonization for 'exclusive and universal utilisation for German colonization'. Based on these pieces of paper, German Chancellor Bismarck released a proclamation, signed by Kaiser Wilhelm, declaring a protectorate over large areas of Africa across from Zanzibar. Sultan Barghash protested as much as he could that these were and always had been parts of his sultanate but no one paid any attention to him. The British had already given tacit acceptance to the move by Germany.

A squadron of the German Navy appeared outside Zanzibar and tried to provoke the sultan into some hostile action that would give them the excuse to occupy the island. He did not oblige and surrendered quietly. The Germans forced him to cede a large section of the coastal belt, including the port of Dar-as-Salam. A joint German, French and British commission, set up at the end of 1885, carved up the territories of East Africa based on 'sound principles of law and justice', according to the British Prime Minister, Lord Salisbury. Mombasa and the other ports and more than five hundred and fifty of miles of coastline, along with its hinterland, passed into European hands. Salisbury handed over the small island of Heligoland at the head of Keil canal that had been in British hands since the Napoleonic wars, to the Germans in 1890 in exchange for recognition of Zanzibar as a British protectorate.

As far as the Africans were concerned, a terrible darkness descended on them. All trade and commerce passed out of their hands and once prosperous communities in places like Mombasa, Malindi, Kilwa, Sofala, Zanzibar and so many other towns were ruined. They were driven out of the best lands and vast herds of their cattle seized by white settlers from Europe. All they were left with was disease and famine that sent the population into a steep decline. For many of them survival lay in converting to Christianity and living on food handouts from the Missions. Any protest was met with indiscriminate and horrendous retaliation. An estimated 75,000 Africans were massacred in putting down the Maji-Maji rebellion in Tanganyika in 1905 (*A Modern History of Kenya*, by John Lonsdale and Tiyambe Zeleza, London 1989 and *Kenya Diary*, by Lieutenant Richard Meinertzhagen, London, 1983). Sir Arthur Hardinge, the first Commissioner of Kenya, summed up the attitude, '*These people must learn submission by bullets ---- it's the only school; after that you may begin more modern and humane methods of education*'.

The colonial government stole the Kenyan people's land, starved them and then blamed them for not feeding their children properly. Using the same tactics as in South Africa and Malaya, the imperial forces torched the homes of a million Kenyans then forcibly resettled them into compounds behind barbed wire when rebellion broke out against the usurpation by the settlers in the 1950s. They were branded as 'terrorists' by the government and the media ---- a term that resonates hauntingly these days. Caroline Elkins, a historian at Harvard University, has examined in detail the eight-year war waged by Britain against the Mau Mau in her book '*Imperial Reckoning: The Untold Story of Britain's Gulag in Kenya*'. It was anything but a civilizing mission as portrayed by British propagandists.

Britain engaged in an amazingly brutal campaign of ethnic cleansing that seemed to border on outright genocide. While only 32 white settlers were killed by Mau Mau insurgents, Elkins reports that tens of thousands of Kenyans were slaughtered, perhaps up to 300,000. The British interned the entire Kikuyu population the colony's largest ethnic group, an estimated one and a half million people, in barbed-wire villages. These were in effect prison camps that Elkins describes as the Kenyan 'Gulag' and served as forced-labour reserves where famine and disease ran rampant. The Kikuyu were subjected to unimaginable torture, or 'screening' as British officials called it ('rendition' in the present US lexicon), which included being whipped, beaten, sodomized, castrated, burned, and forced to eat feces and drink urine. Later, the British officials destroyed almost all official records of the campaign.

The lines drawn on maps did not take into account the existing ethnic and tribal groupings or geographical features and passed through areas that had never been visited by any Europeans. This did not concern the British foreign secretary, Lord Granville, when he remarked, 'Her Majesty's government view with favour these schemes the realisation of which will entail the civilisation of large tracts over which hitherto no European influence had been exercised'. These were simply pretentious euphemisms that concealed the real intent of economic exploitation. Any doubts about the moral propriety and justification of their actions were assuaged by mounting a propaganda campaign that de-humanized the Africans.

The shameful betrayal of the sultan of Zanzibar never bothered the conscience of Her Majesty's government. Throughout history, somehow, it is the people who have sought protection of the western powers that have suffered the most at their hands.

The industrial revolution in Europe had created surplus manufacturing capacity. There was a pressing need to find markets for their goods. Much of the rest of the world was already saturated with products from western industries. Africa had remained unexplored commercially. Its potential appeared to be vast not only for sale of goods but also as a source of raw materials. Economic exploitation lay at the heart of the scramble for colonies in Africa. It would have been difficult to sell it as such to the people of Europe. To justify their actions, powerful political and commercial interests used their influence in the press, religious and other institutions to demonize the Africans as savages in dire need of intervention by the Europeans to 'civilize' them and save their souls from eternal damnation.

The role of the church in encouraging and supporting the process of colonisation was substantial and one that is not always fully appreciated. No one ever stopped to ask what the Africans thought or wanted. Any voices of dissent were quickly and effectively silenced. It is a process that is still at work in much the same vein. Only the names of the players have changed and the techniques have become more sophisticated but the objectives and the end result remain very much the same.

There is a general misconception that the Africans acquiesced and submitted to the European occupation without any resistance. This is not true. The first signs of resistance were soon evident in the small coastal town of Pangani where the local German commander started to behave in a high-handed offensive manner, ridiculing Islam and mistreating the natives. A wealthy owner of a sugar plantation by the name of Shaikh Abushiri bin Salim led the revolt against him. He besieged the headquarters of the Germans in Pangani, giving them two days to pack up and leave. Soon, tribesmen from the interior swelled the ranks of Abushiri's supporters and with their help he cleared the Germans out of

Kilwa as well. He kept up hit and run operations until a headman, tempted by the reward placed on his head, betrayed him. The Germans hanged Abushiri and his lieutenants on 15th December 1889.

It did not end the insurrection. Africans continued to ambush and kill Germans wherever they could lay their hands on them and in turn the Germans flogged and killed anyone suspected of rebellion and set fire to crops, homes and villages indiscriminately. They had to fight for better part of ten years to pacify the country they named Tanganyika. In the end, they occupied territory in Africa that was three times the size of Germany (A Modern History of Tanganyika, by John Iliffe, Cambridge, 1979). When World War I broke out, the British and the Germans also battled it out in East Africa, each using African soldiers. Germany lost and Tanganyika became a mandated territory under the British, as did Southwest Africa under South Africa.

The weapon that made the conquests in Africa so easy was the Maxim machine gun. Invented by an American in 1884, who gave it his name, it could fire more than three hundred rounds a minute and kill people a mile away. It was deployed in battle for the first time against Muslim insurgents in Sudan and again, with equally deadly effect in East Africa, mowing down hundreds of spear-carrying tribesmen in minutes. Although it had been available earlier, it was considered 'uncivilized' to use it against other white men in war because of its deadly effectiveness. Shooting aboriginals and people of other races was a different matter (see *The Social History of the Machine Gun*, by John Ellis, The Johns Hopkins University Press, Baltimore).

It was the acquisition of superior weapons' technology that made European colonization possible. We have seen earlier the role played by the more advanced sailing vessels in the Indian Ocean. What made the difference on land in India was the artillery; it was the machine gun in Africa and electronics, aircraft and missiles now in the Middle East. It is not enough simply to possess up-to-date weapons technology. Access to it must also be denied to the potential adversaries to make subjugation easier. This was a major consideration in the decision to invade and destroy Iraq that had reached the stage of development where it could have become a serious contender for supremacy. No doubt there are other countries already in the western cross-hairs for similar reasons.

'*They were conquerors, and for that you only want brute force ---- It was just robbery with violence, aggravated murder on a grand scale, and men going at it blind ---- The conquest of the earth, which mostly means the taking it away from those who have a different complexion or slightly flatter noses than ourselves, is not a pretty thing when you look into it too much. What redeems it is the idea only* (Joseph Conrad in *Heart of Darkness*). The spirit of colonialism is not dead by any means. The process continues to live on; only the lexicon has changed. Instead of the 'white man's burden', it is now termed 'humanitarian intervention', or wars against so-called 'terrorism', and the 'axis of evil', etc.

The intense struggle for colonies and commercial advantage between Spain, Portugal, Holland, Britain and France had been mostly resolved by 1815. France had by then parted with her colonies in North America and India. Holland still held Indonesia but Portugal was left with only some small parts of her earlier possessions. The Spanish colonies in South America were shortly to gain their independence. Only Britain was left as the mistress of a vast empire on which the sun never set.

The entire continent of Africa was under occupation except for Christian-ruled Ethiopia. Russia was given the right to expand eastward and occupy all of Central Asia, Siberia and territory north of Amur River, including the port of Vladivostok, under the Treaty of Paris signed in 1856 after the Crimean War (*Russian Policy in Central Asia*, by N. A. Khalin, Moscow, 1960, p57). France occupied Indo-China and Britain extended her influence into Iran, Afghanistan and Tibet. The United States acquired the Hawaiian Islands, Puerto Rico and the Philippines and Germany was in possession of one million square miles of colonial real estate mostly in Africa, as mentioned earlier.

This period also saw the rise of Japan as a colonial power. She had mastered the technical and military skills of Europe and was looking for opportunities to exert her power. In 1895 she attacked and defeated China under the pretext of liberating Korea that had been under Chinese suzerainty for the past two centuries. As part of war reparations, China was obliged to hand over Port Arthur and opened four more ports to Japanese trade. Alarmed at the prospect of Japanese presence on the Asian mainland, Russia persuaded France and Germany to exert pressure on Japan to give up Port Arthur in return for a large cash payment from China.

The western powers loaned China the money to pay for the reparations demanded by Japan. She was now trapped with no way out of making concession after concession to the Europeans. In addition to the right to build the trans-Siberian railway through Manchuria, the Russians obtained a lease on Port Arthur. The German fleet occupied Kiaochow Bay and exacted concessions for mining and building of railroads. France was given the lease on Kwangchow Bay and Britain extended her territories into Kowloon in addition to Hong Kong that had been ceded to her after the Opium Wars of 1839 – 43 (for more on opium trade, see chapter '*British Occupation*'). Apart from cessation of territory, the concessions included unfettered access for warships to enter Chinese ports and rivers, exemption for any Europeans to be tried under the laws of China, a fixed rate of five per cent import duty on western exports and the freedom to preach Christianity throughout the country.

The rapacious political and economic exploitation led to a build-up of resentment that boiled over into widespread unrest and culminated in the Boxer Rebellion of 1900. The combined forces of Britain, France, Germany, United States and Russia ruthlessly suppressed the insurrection. Thousands of Chinese were massacred, shops pillaged and houses looted by the foreign troops. In addition to a long list of humiliating conditions, a huge indemnity was imposed to be adjusted against recoveries from customs duties and a tax on the sale of salt. Russia took the opportunity to occupy Manchuria, including Port Arthur.

It alarmed the Japanese who went to war with Russia in 1905, decimating the Russian army in Manchuria and destroying her fleet in Tsushima Straits. At a peace conference in USA, Russia agreed to return Manchuria to China and Port Arthur to Japan while Korea became independent but under Japanese influence. The ignominious defeat inflicted by Japan sent alarm bells ringing in all the capitals of Europe. A myth of European invincibility had been built up over the years that was crucial in maintaining control in the colonies. If Japan could defeat Russia in such a resounding fashion, there was nothing to stop other Asian powers from testing the waters for themselves elsewhere.

UNBRIDLED CAPITALISM

Many hypotheses have been put forward to explain the phenomenon of colonisation. These include over-population in Europe, creating the need for additional space to settle excess people. Some argued that it was the right, even the duty of Europeans to bring the blessings of Christian civilization to the natives. Lord Curzon, Viceroy in India and later Foreign Secretary, described the British Empire as '---- *under Providence, the greatest instrument for good the world has seen*'. Others believed that colonies were necessary to protect and enlarge the country's commerce. Still others looked at them as captive markets for their manufactured products' surpluses. There may be some truth in all of them but they were more in the way of justifications than underlying causes of European expansion. The Industrial Revolution had created a whole set of new economic conditions. The real compulsions at the back of the drive for expansion can only be understood by examining these conditions.

The industrial expansion had created a growing demand for raw materials. To ensure cheap and regular supply of these it was desirable to have control of their sources. A point is soon reached in the process of growth when a country is obliged to look to the outside for fresh opportunities. Take rail and road transport, for instance. Once the local needs have been met the related industries need to export to survive. The safety of investments in communications and industries abroad could either be ensured by making these in the existing colonies or by establishing a sphere of influence or protectorate over the territories subsequently.

The Industrial Revolution also generated new wealth. The surplus wealth was deposited in banks that grew as the wealth increased. The largest among these accumulated capital on hitherto unimagined scale and lent it to governments and large industrial enterprises. Investment bankers like Rothschilds and J.P. Morgan handled billions of dollars of surplus capital. Like the industrial entrepreneurs, the investment bankers also needed to look outside and were willing to underwrite loans for building railways, shipping, rubber plantations, oil wells, and extend credits to the governments of mismanaged countries such as Morocco, Egypt, Iran and Turkey.

The loans to the corrupt, inept and unwary rulers of these countries were a deadly trap. In one such deal British and French bankers floated bonds to raise a loan of 385 million dollars for Ismail, Khediv of Egypt, between 1864 and 1874. These were sold at a discount and Ismail only received 250 million dollars in his treasury. Much of what he did receive was squandered on needless luxuries but even the amount spent on useful projects was mostly wasted. For instance, he paid 15 million dollars for the construction of Alexandria harbour that should have cost only half as much. A good part of the money that was paid remained in Europe in the shape of bankers' fees, interest payments, over-payment for work done by European contractors, etc.

This could not go on forever. Ismail had been obliged to borrow more and more to pay the interest on the loans until the point was reached when there were no buyers left for the Egyptian Government bonds. This is when the governments of Britain and France obliged Ismail to abdicate in favour of his son, Tawfik, in 1879 and took over running of the administration for him, cutting down expenditure and increasing taxes. The Egyptians protested which provided the British with the pretext to invade and take over the country.

The people who benefited most from the colonial expansion were not the common men in the industrialised countries but manufacturers seeking cheap raw materials, businessmen and corporations that operated the mines, railways or plantations and bankers who lent money at high interest rates. Others included exporters of manufactured goods, especially armaments, and officers in the army, navy and the administrative services. Most of these either belonged or aspired to the upper classes that owned and controlled the machines created by the Industrial Revolution. In most cases, the push for colonies came not from the governments so much as from the classes that had the money to influence them. It was not so much a case of 'the trade following the flag' but 'the flag following the trade' ---- or the capital, more precisely.

Even though the political map of the world may look outwardly different from what it was prior to World War II, the compulsions that gave rise to the colonization phenomenon in the nineteenth century are still very much extant. What has changed is the mode of operation. The ruinous competition for the acquisition of exclusive colonial empires between the western powers has given way to an agreement for managing the world as a whole for the benefit of all of them. The impetus for this has come not so much from politics but from the giant western-owned multi-national conglomerates and corporations that now dominate the world economy.

It has become the age of 'globalization' and expanding corporate culture which now takes precedence over national interest although, for various reasons, most politicians are loathe to admitting the fact. The driving force in the West is not politics or democracy but capitalism. The survival of capitalism depends upon constantly increasing consumption and growth. Without this, economic stagnation will set in and prosperity come to an end. It needs to create greater consumption and demand that in turn calls for ever increasing numbers of consumers as well as resources and raw materials. Since there are limits to the availability of resources, a continuation of the process is bound to lead to strains and strife and put the fate of all life-forms on the planet at serious risk that may prove terminal.

Profits for the investors are the basis of capitalism. These are greater if the costs of raw materials are low and the prices of manufactures as high as possible. At the same time, control over the capital market helps to eliminate competition and establish monopolies by denying access to investment resources to others. The cost of raw materials most of which originate in the third world and Muslim countries, is controlled in the same way to ensures prosperity for the West at the expense of the erstwhile colonies.

As an example of how capitalism works, the price of cotton produced by Pakistan has remained almost constant, in real US dollar terms, for the past sixty years while the price of aircraft manufactured in the West has increased almost a thousand times. The cost of actual materials in an aircraft that sells for $100 million, like aluminum, rubber, polymers, etc. obtained from developing countries is no more than a few thousand dollars; the rest is simply added value. A western middle man pays less than $2 for a T-shirt from Bangladesh that includes the cost of materials, labour, packaging, freight and insurance and sells it for $20 in a shop in New York. A Colombian gets five cents for the coffee in the cup sold in the West for two dollars. The prices of other produce from undeveloped nations like sugar, cocoa, coffee, rice, palm oil have fallen fifty per cent in the past twenty years. Whereas before World War II the average income of a worker in the United States was sixteen times higher than that of the average worker in India, by 1970, it was forty times higher. In 2003 it was 78 times as high.

The international trade in 2006 was on average worth more than twenty billion dollars a day. Only a tiny fraction if this, 0.4 per cent, is shared with the poorest countries. American and G8 nations' capital controls 70 per cent of world markets, and because of the rules demanding the end of tariff barriers and subsidies in poor countries while ignoring protectionism in the west, the poor countries lose more than two billion dollars a day in trade.

Capital always flows into places that afford safety and security. In the old days, people could hoard gold. This has been de-linked as the currency standard. Its place has been taken by the US dollar. At the same time, movement of capital from one country to another has become very quick and easy. The net effect is an ever-increasing transfer of wealth to the so-called 'safe havens' in the West.

Much is made of the riches of the oil producing countries. It is true, they have generated trillions of dollars in revenues but the countries themselves have profited very little from it. Most of the cash has filtered back into the western coffers. Some $220 billion was literally stolen from Russia, from raw materials and icons to gold and diamonds after the collapse of the Soviet Union. All of the proceeds went to bank accounts in the West. Of the funds generated by the drug trade worldwide, it is estimated ninety-five per cent end up in the West.

In the years before 2002, the transfers of funds to the United States alone from other parts of the world averaged at over one billion dollars a day.

The rate of this flow increased every time there was political or economic instability in any country or region of the world. Turmoil in any other part of the world becomes a boon to the capital markets in the West. The same is true for the proceeds of ill gotten gains from corruption, etc. by the power elites in the more mismanaged countries.

Only a fraction of the wealth is shared with the ordinary people. Most of it is concentrated in the hands of the privileged few. The combined wealth of the world's 587 billionaires in 2005 exceeded the combined GDP of the world's 135 poorest countries. More than forty percent of the entire wealth in the world was concentrated in the hands of only 350 people ----- almost all of them, barring perhaps the Saudi Royal family and the Sultan of Brunei, were westerners and a substantial number of them Jewish. Close to half of the American billionaires are Jews. This phenomenon is by no means limited to the United States. Six of the seven Russian oligarchs happened to be Jews. It has great political implications since wealth and political power go hand in hand.

To put the corporate world in perspective, of the top one hundred biggest economies, fifty one are corporations, not countries. Only two companies dominate half the world's bananas trade and three control eighty-five per cent of the tea sold in the world. Walmart alone controls forty per cent of Mexico's retail food business. Monsanto dominates ninety-one per cent of the global genetically modified seeds market. The Swiss firm Nestle's profits are greater than Ghana's GDP and those of Unilever's a third more than the national income of Mozambique. Walmart earns more profit each year than the combined incomes of both these countries. It is the largest corporation in the world, employing one and half million people and constitutes two per cent of America's GDP.

In ten years of unbridled corporate globalization after 1995 the world's total income increased by an average of 2.5 percent a year. And yet the numbers of the poor in the world increased by 100 million. The top one percent of the world population has the same combined income as the bottom fifty-seven percent and the disparity is growing. The world spends one and half trillion dollars on the military each year. To put it in perspective, all it will take to eliminate hunger and poverty from the globe altogether and stabilize the population is a mere $ 190 billion.

NEW WORLD ORDER

Corporate interests abroad are generally short-term. These are cheaper and easier to achieve by manipulating local autocratic set-ups. All it takes is to enlist and install a suitably sympathetic candidate in position of power and make sure he or she remains secure. CIA's role and expertise in such undertakings has been legendary from Indonesia, through the Middle East to almost every country in Latin America. Since these regimes are required to sacrifice their national interest, invariably, the individuals involved are unscrupulous, avaricious, corrupt and unsavoury characters that are despised by the local masses. Because of the association this resentment and hostility gets transferred to the West (see *The Confessions of an Economic Hit Man*, by John Perkins, Random House, London, 2005 and *The Corporation: The Pathologic Pursuit of Profit and Power*, by Joel Bakan, Constable & Robinson Ltd, London, 2004).

It is also the main reason for democracy not taking root and flourishing in the less developed countries. It has simply not been given a fair chance. The surrogate puppets installed and supported to serve western corporate interests are inherently insecure and forever fearful of political dissent. They become increasingly intolerant and oppressive, driving any opposition underground and into desperate hands. In most cases, it leaves the people with only a choice between two evils.

There is an ever-increasing demand for raw materials to fuel the western economies. Unbridled growth in the West, coupled with the increasing appetite of new economic powers in East Asia and dwindling supplies, has given rise to fears of shortages in the future. It is compelling US economic interests in particular to lay exclusive claims to as many areas that produce industrial raw materials as possible. The recent US military operations in the Persian Gulf and Afghanistan have been primarily motivated by the need to ensure uninterrupted flow for its own use, at the same time, to gain control over the supplies to other rival powers.

Under overwhelming pressure from western powers, the UN organized a referendum in East Timor that resulted in the oil rich region becoming independent from Indonesia not so long ago. It remains the world's poorest country, with an unemployment rate close to ninety per cent. Most of its oil and mineral resources are exploited by Australia. The Australian Government under John Howard had no qualms in defying International Maritime Law to withhold East Timor's badly needed dues of oil and gas revenues worth eight billion US dollars ('*The Other Tsunami*' by John

Pilger in the '*New Statesman*', 10th January 2005). Altruism has no place in the scheme of corporate or national interest of the western powers.

For all the endless chatter about democracy the world today is run by three of the most secretive institutions in the world: the International Monetary Fund, the World Bank, and the World Trade Organisation, all three of which, are in turn dominated by the US. Their decisions are made in secret. The people who head them are appointed behind closed doors. Nobody really knows anything about them, their politics, their beliefs or their intentions. Nobody elected them and nobody said they could make decisions on behalf of the world. It is a frightening thought indeed ---- a world run by a handful of greedy bankers and CEOs who are not elected nor do they represent anyone except a small circle of moneyed interests.

Just as the writings of Bernard Lewis and Samuel Huntington heralded the designation of Islam and the Muslims as the new enemy of the West, fresh literature has started to appear suggesting that the concept of an American empire was both natural and necessary. Notable among this are books by the economic historian, Niall Ferguson ('*Empire*' and '*Colossus*') described, rather significantly, in the *Times* of London as 'the most brilliant British historian of his time' and advisor to John McCain in his U.S. presidential campaign. He proffers the hypothesis that since the governments in the erstwhile colonies have failed to deliver on the promises of independence, a new world-wide empire under the tutelage of (Anglo-Saxon) USA may be a natural and not such a bad idea.

Huntington too had proposed that the Anglo-Saxon world i.e. Britain and the United States, along with a few other European countries, should form an imperium against the Asian, Islamic, and African hordes. In another noteworthy political study, *The Evolution of International Society*, British analyst Adam Watson, argues that it is absurd to project balance-of-power or other procrustean systems theories onto world politics. It has been the norm for one power, whether it was the Assyrian, the Roman, or the British Empire to dominate over the rest.

Viewed in this context, British Prime Minister Tony Blair's proclamations too fall into place. In words reminiscent of Rudyard Kipling, he declared 'the need for re-ordering the world around us' in the context of the 'politics of globalization'. He also called for 'true democracy, no more excuses for dictatorship, abuses of human rights; no tolerance for bad government ---- ending the endemic corruption ---- justice to bring those same values of democracy and freedom around the world ---' (*Empire*, pp. 374-7). The expression of such noble sentiments is eerily reminiscent and rings just as hollow as the pronouncements made by his nineteenth-century colonizing predecessors to justify the rape of Asian and African continents. Whatever form this new world order may take, one thing is certain, as with its predecessors, the natives will not be its primary beneficiaries.

CHAPTER 4

SIKHISM AND THE SIKHS

Most of the people living in the southern half of what now constitutes Pakistan had converted to Islam in the eighth century. These were followed by residents in areas west of the Indus in the eleventh century. The case in Punjab was different where at the end of the fifteenth century, even after five hundred years of Afghan rule, only about half of the population was Muslim. However, the influence of Islam and the Muslims was still profound. New ideas, especially those concerning monotheism, equality among human beings and the simplicity inherent in Islam had created deep stirrings and doubts among the lower castes of the Hindu society. Even though they were too deeply involved and committed to their *dharma* to contemplate conversion, it did not stop them from looking for emancipation along the lines enjoyed by the Muslims.

Apart from the lower caste Hindus, a new class of Untouchable Outcasts had grown up that is seldom mentioned by the historians of the sub-continent on both sides of the spectrum for reasons of communal shame. During scores of raids, spanning over many centuries, Afghan soldiers had taken local Hindu wives and slave girls. These were invariably left behind for various reasons when the soldiers returned home. The laws of the Hindu society would not allow these unfortunate women to return to its fold, forcing them and their offspring to live as outcasts on the fringes of villages and towns. As their numbers increased, in the absence of a civilizing religious and societal structure, these half-castes took to concentrating in bands as wild outlaws, making a living mostly as highwaymen, robbing travelers and raiding unprotected communities. Although no figures are available, it is reasonable to assume that these Untouchable Outcasts together with low caste Hindus constituted a sizeable proportion of the non-Muslim population in Punjab.

GURU NANAK

This was the state of the society in Punjab in 1469 when the founder of Sikh religion, Guru Nanak, was born into a Hindu *Khatri* sub-caste family near the village of Talwandi. As a young man, he was employed by a Muslim landowner called Rai Bular in Nankana near Sheikhupura. It is said that his spirituality was evident even in those early days. Later, he married to raise a family and moved to Sultanpur, near Jullunder and took up service as a storekeeper with the local ruler, Daulat Khan Lodi. Around 1500 AD he left his family to travel to distant places in search of answers to some existentialist questions that had been troubling him. There is even a claim that he might also have gone to Makkah posing as a Muslim and performed *Haj* in the course of these travels.

On return more than twenty years later, he settled in Kartarpur, not far from Sultanpur, and started to preach his own understanding about the purpose of life that was not very different to what some of the other mystics and teachers like Bhagat Kabir, Farid Shakarganj and Ravidas had expostulated. His followers came to be known as '*Sikhs*' ---- pupils or disciples. He died in 1539, having appointed one of his disciples, Guru Angad, as his successor to continue his mission.

Many a historian has suggested that what Guru Nanak had preached was an amalgam of Hinduism and Islam. This is a serious misconception. Sikhism was born out of Hinduism and retains much of its form. Guru Nanak was a Hindu and remained a Hindu all his life. He never set himself up as the founder of a new religion. More accurately, he saw himself as a teacher and a reformer intent on identifying where the society had gone wrong and how best to correct it, essentially, in the context of Hinduism. The fact that he rejected polytheism and the caste system was neither new to Hinduism nor an indication of his inclination towards Islam. In fact, he rejects much of Islam and was evidently critical of the Muslims but only objected to a few of the Brahmin practices.

Sikhism embodies the Hindu reverence for the cow and includes practices and rituals associated with sacred Hindu sites along the Ganges like Benares, Mathura and Hardwar as parts of its creed. The Sikhs also believe in *karma* and transmigration of the soul, asserting that it has to go through eight million four hundred thousand different cycles to eventually take the human form. The Hindu custom of *sattee* or burning alive the widow with the body of her dead husband was also practiced among the Sikhs. It wasn't until 1860 AD that the Sikh states of Patiala and Jeend formally agreed to ban *sattee*, slavery and female infanticide under pressure from the British.

There was no commonly accepted definition of a religiously distinct Sikh until the British provided one in the Punjab Sikh Gurdwaras Act of 1925. It takes the form of an affirmation, '*I solemnly affirm that I am a Sikh, that I believe in the Guru Granth Sahib, that I believe in the Ten Gurus and that I have no other religion*'. The last part was necessary because many individuals had regarded themselves as both Hindu as well as Sikh. This definition was modified in 1945 to include '*Amrit*' (initiation) and again by the Delhi Gurdwara Act of 1971 that replaced the requirement for *Amrit* with '*kase*' (unshorn hair). Hindu purists in India, like the Arya Samaj, even today do not accept Sikhism as a separate religion but consider it an aberration of their faith.

During his prolonged wanderings Guru Nanak had come into intimate contact and spent considerable time with Sufis as well as Hindu mystics. He had lived in unstable, confused and difficult times. The message of peace and goodwill towards all (*Sulhe Kul)* and the concept of Oneness of Being (*Wahdat-al-Wajud*) contained in Sufi thought must have appealed to him as giving purpose for life and salvation for the troubled society as well as the tormented individual soul but he never approved of the Sufis as such.

His teachings are contained in the Sikh holy book, *Adi Granth*, also called *Guru Granth*. These were added to subsequently by many of his successors. The tenth Guru, Gobind Singh, wrote separately in what is called *Dasam Granth* or the tenth Granth that does not form a part of the earlier book but is meant to complement it. The present standardized texts of Guru Granth and Dasam Granth were not finalized until as recently as 1873 and 1902 respectively. Sikh revivalists only permit Adi Granth to be installed inside the *Gurdwaras* (Sikh temples) and not Dasam Granth.

Guru Nanak did not claim to be a prophet of God in Biblical terms, nor is Guru Granth the word of God unlike the Koran. In the metaphor of his fifth successor, Guru Arjun Dev, who first compiled it, 'the Book (*Guru Granth*) is the abode of God' (*Adi Granth, 1226*). It is primarily a collection of hymns composed by some of the gurus as well as extracts from the writings of a few contemporary Hindu and Muslim religious figures that have been set to music (*Later Mughal History of the Punjab*, by Hari Ram Gupta, Sang-e-Meel Publication, Lahore, 1944, p. 36). Out of a total of 5894 hymns (*shabads and shaloks)*, less than one thousand are attributed to Guru Nanak himself while eight hundred or so have been taken from the works of various Hindu and Muslim religious men. The largest contribution (2218) is by Guru Arjun Dev. The language of Guru Granth is *Gurmukhi* or the word of gurus (old Punjabi) spoken five hundred years ago and written in *Devnagri* script. Like so much else in India, origins of the latter are unknown but it has been preserved as the Sikh religious script.

As mentioned earlier, Guru Nanak's basic preaching was not very different to that of people like Bhagat Kabir, Ravidas, Gorakhnath and other Hindu reformers. While the others have faded into oblivion, Sikhism survived and prospered primarily due to the fact that Guru Nanak's message found resonance among increasing numbers of outcasts that had been rejected for centuries by the parent Hindu society in Punjab. He laid the foundations of a community which accepted these people into its fold without reservation. Although Islam had also offered the same, it had done so in an alien and unfamiliar context. Sikhism incorporated much of the old and did not constitute as much of a departure from the original. To a large extent, the acceptance and success of Sikhism was attributable more to its being an inclusive and egalitarian social order than a new religion as such.

SPREAD OF SIKHISM

After the death of Guru Nanak, Sikhism's hold on the community was consolidated by the succeeding gurus through their agents, known as *masands,* who were assigned to every locality where Sikhs were found. These were first introduced by the fourth Guru Ramdas but were later replaced by the institution of *Khalsa Sangat.* Guru Ramdas made it obligatory for every Sikh to donate ten percent of his income to a community fund. He also built a sacred water tank and named it *Amrit-sarovar* (pool of immortality) on a piece of land granted by the Mughal Emperor, Akbar. The city where it stands, Amritsar, was named after the tank.

Perhaps, the most significant factor in the rise and spread of Sikhism was the adoption of militancy as a part of its creed. Apparently, this came about in reaction to the death of Guru Arjun Dev in a Mughal jail in 1606. It changed the complextion of the society. Not only the seekers of truth but also large numbers of fugitives from justice, fortune hunters and brigands began to fill the ranks, not so much for spiritual uplift as for the opportunities for military employment, adventure and enrichment that started to become available. Conversions to Sikhism dropped dramatically and never recovered after the Sikhs lost power in Punjab in the middle of the nineteenth century. The total population of Sikhs in India at the time of independence was about six million. About four million of these had lived in British Punjab (excluding the States), less than fifteen per cent of the total population of about thirty million at the time.

It is natural that the history and development of Sikhism should be viewed in sympathetic and devotional light by Sikh writers like Grewal, Khushwant Singh and Patwant Singh. What they have written in places smacks of hagiography more than history. Grewal, in *The New Cambridge History of India - The Sikhs of the Punjab* for example, throughout refers to the deaths of Sikh gurus reverentially as 'martyrdoms.' It is not the business of the historian to assign piety and sublimation to the dead of one side in preference to another. It is distracting and leaves one with a suspicion of compromise and bias.

This is also apparent in his description of the administration as well as social, religious and economic conditions during the Sikh rule in Punjab. When compared with the observations of numerous contemporary writers and historians, the contrasts and contradictions are so great one feels inclined to classify parts of '*The Cambridge History of India*' as not much more than fanciful fiction. The affliction is not peculiar to Grewal. It is a human failing and, unfortunately, Indian historians tend to be more prone to it than some of the others. The result has been that history as a whole has suffered. In this particular case, serious shortcomings in the character and conduct of many of the Sikh leaders and rulers have been overlooked, as have been the divisions and disputes among them, to produce an account wanting in terms of factual accuracy.

In reality, many of the Sikh rulers in particular were unenlightened, rustic and often wild people, with rough and ready methods. A measure of the primitive state of their cultural development can be had from the following paragraph in '*Freedom at Midnight*', by Larry Collins and Dominique Lapierre (Simon and Schuster, New York, 1975, p. 169): '*Centerpiece of the great collection of the Sikh Maharaja of Patiala was a pearl necklace insured by Lloyds of London for one million dollars. Its most intriguing item, however, was a diamond breastplate, its luminous surface composed of 1,001 brilliantly matched blue-white diamonds. Until the turn of the century* (twentieth) *it had been the custom of the Maharaja of Patiala to appear once a year before his subjects naked except for his diamond breastplate, his organ in full and glorious erection. His performance was adjudged a kind of temporal manifestation of the Shivaling, the phallic representation of Lord Shiva's organ. As the Maharaja walked about, his subjects gleefully applauded, their cheers acknowledging both the dimension of the princely organ and the fact that it was supposed to be radiating magical powers to drive evil spirits from the land.*'

This is neither the place nor is it the intention to either raise any new controversies or to deal with existing ones in relation to Sikhism as a religious movement. Historically, many of the latter gurus found themselves on the wrong side of the law as it existed. The Sikhs believe that they had been persecuted by the Mughal kings because of their religion. The charge seems implausible if only because numerous Sikh religious leaders and institutions had been bestowed with royal favours by the Muslim rulers during the same period ('*The New Cambridge History of India'*, pp. 62, 66, 69). There is evidence that even the militant tenth Guru, Gobind Singh, had accepted and joined the service of Mughals later in his life.

Quoting various Sikh sources, as well as from the court historian Khafi Khan's '*Muntakhab-ul-Lubab*,' J. D Cunningham writes in his '*History of the Sikhs*' (p. 72), '*While engaged in his last campaign, Bahadur Shah summoned* (Guru) *Gobind to his camp. The Guru went; he was treated with respect, and he received a military command in the valley of the Godavari*'. At least on one known occasion, the same guru was saved from certain death when a seventeenth century Muslim religious leader, Mian Shaikh Darvesh, gave him sanctuary in the grand mosque in Basti Shaikh Darwesh, Jullunder.

Kings as a rule did not bestow favours nor did they gift land for the building of temples to heretical sects that they allegedly despised and persecuted. None of the Mughal Emperors, including Aurangzeb (whose own mother was a Hindu), were over-zealous Muslims and were not known for proselytizing, let aside persecuting their subjects simply on the basis of faith. Official records clearly indicate that not all the gurus had been treated unkindly and those that were, had been tried and convicted of serious infringements of the law such as refusal to pay taxes, murder, sedition and creating disorder, rebellion and waging against the state. Some of the punishments meted out were undoubtedly severe and cruel by today's standards but one has to remember that it was not specific to the Sikhs but was the same for every one regardless of religion.

The history of Sikh religion is neither happy nor peaceful. The troubles of the gurus were not with the law or the Muslim rulers alone. There were internal divisions, treachery and usurpation or worse, starting almost from the day that Guru Nanak died. There was hardly a time when there were no parallel claimants to his mantle. In 1634 Guru Hargobind, the sixth guru, had been obliged to move out of Amritsar for fear of his life, to live in Kiratpur. Pirthi Chand, the elder brother of his predecessor Guru Arjun Dev and his descendants henceforward took control of the Golden Temple.

The accession of the ninth guru, Tegh Bahadur, proved to be equally acrimonious and divisive. He was not permitted to enter and pay homage at the Golden Temple by his rivals nor was his son and successor, Guru Gobind Singh, ever allowed into Amritsar ('*Sikhism*' by Sewa Singh Kalsi, Global Books Ltd. Folkestone, UK, p. 51).

As their numbers multiplied, the Sikhs became militant and aggressive and remained continuously at war with the neighbouring Hindu hill states. The tenth and last of the traditionally recognized Sikh Gurus, Gobind Singh, died in 1708. He had purchased some horses from an Afghan. When the latter insisted on being paid, an argument ensued and the horse trader was killed. The Afghan's sons, intent on avenging their father's murder, followed the guru all over India, finally getting the opportunity to mortally wound him at Nandher (*A History of the Sikhs*, by J. D Cunningham, John Murray, 1849, p. 74 and *The Pathans*, by Sir Olaf Caroe, p.250).

He was, perhaps, the most important of Guru Nanak's successors, having made lasting changes to the ways of the Sikhs. He did away with the increasingly divisive and troublesome intermediary *masands,* replacing them with the collective *sangats,* whose decisions were binding on individual members. He also established a distinct identity for his followers by requiring them to always wear or carry on their body five distinguishing marks (*kakkas*) namely, *kachh* (boxer shorts), *kara* (steel bangle), *kanga* (comb), *kase* (unshorn hair) *and kirpan* (dagger). They were also told to add '*Singh*' (tiger) to their names to further distinguish them from the Hindus. The style of turban worn by the Sikhs is in-fact an adaptation of the Turkish head dress, denoting respect and authority.

Guru Gobind Singh also proclaimed a class of Sikhs to be known as *Khalsa* (pure) on 13th April 1699. There are various versions of the circumstances of its origin which need not be explored here. Essentially, these were Sikhs who had been initiated into the faith in a special ceremony (*pahul*) and vowed to follow a certain code that, apart from the above five *kakkas*, included abstaining from alcohol and tobacco (first introduced into India in 1617), not eating *halal* (kosher) meat and not molesting women. The Khalsa are known as *Amritdhari* (initiated) Sikhs.

According to Cunningham, Guru Gobind Singh's instructions to them in part read, '---- henceforth 'the Khalsa will rule; there will be no one else left' ('*raj karey ga Khalsa; baaki rahey na ko*'). God must be worshipped in truthfulness and sincerity, but no material presence shall degrade the Omnipotent; the Lord could only be beheld in the general body of the Khalsa. All must become one; the lowest were equal to the highest; Caste must be forgotten; ---- the Turks (Muslims) must be destroyed, and the graves of those called (Sufi) saints abandoned.

'The ways of the Hindus must be given up but their temples viewed as holy and their rivers looked upon as sacred; the Brahmin's thread (*'janeu'*) must be broken; by means of the Khalsa alone could salvation be attained' (pp. 63, 64). He also provided a long list of dos and don'ts for the *Khalsa* that cover food, dress, charity, prayers, personal conduct, hygiene, sex, etc. Some of these are quite interesting and revealing. For instance, a Khalsa proves himself 'if he mounts a warhorse; is always waging war; kills a Khan (Muslim) and slays the Turks (Muslims)' (*History of the Sikhs*, Appendix XX).

It needs to be stressed that enmity towards Muslims is an integral element of Sikh religion. The sufferings of some of their gurus at the hands of Muslim rulers are deeply etched into the Sikh psyche. Whatever the truth and reality, every Sikh deep down harbours visceral animus against all Muslims and holds them collectively and for all times responsible for what he or she believes was wrongfully done to their gurus by the Mughal rulers centuries ago. This was the main cause and justification for the wholesale slaughter of Muslim men, women and children, carried out by the Sikhs in East Punjab when India gained independence in 1947 (chapter *Road to Freedom*). If, as some may naively believe, that because of some cultural and linguistic similarities, the Sikhs can be sympathetic to the Muslims ever, they would have learnt nothing from history.

Larry Collins and Dominique Lapierre wrote in *Freedom at Midnight* (Simon and Schuster, New York, 1975, p. 230) after a visit to Amritsar '*At the Golden Temple was a museum designed to maintain alive in the memory of each succeeding generation of Sikh the details of every indignity, every horror, every atrocity their people had suffered at the hands of the Moslems. In gory profusion, huge oil paintings depicted spread-eagled Sikhs being sawed in half for refusing to embrace Islam; ground to pulp between huge stone mills; crushed between meshing wheels studded with blades like gears; Sikh women at the gates of the Mughal's palace in Lahore seeing their infants speared and beheaded by the Mughal's Praetorian Guard*'. To what extent the artists' imagination had a basis in fact is of little consequence. What matters is that it has become the truth to every Sikh and it determines for all times to come his or her feelings and attitude towards Muslims.

Guru Gobind Singh did not nominate a successor before he died, as had been the practice earlier. Henceforward, guruship devolved upon the Sikh body, *Khalsa Panth*, and the holy book, *Adi Granth*. The proposition was not accepted universally and the Sikhs became divided into *Bandai* group, the followers of his South Indian successor, Banda Beragi, who believed in a living guru, and *Tat Khalsa,* who looked to *Adi Granth* for guruship.

The temporal leadership of the Sikhs, after Guru Gobind Singh's death, was taken over by the hermit from Deccan, Banda Beragi, whose mission in life became looting and killing Muslims. Taking advantage of the confusion and paralysis in the Mughal government that followed Aurangzeb's death, he led increasingly large bands of Sikhs on plundering raids, looting whole towns and villages, indiscriminately murdering unarmed men, women and children wherever he went. In a raid on the town of Sirhind alone he claimed to have murdered ten thousand Muslims of all description, regardless of age or sex. There were similar raids on Ambala, Kunjpura, Saharanpur and a dozen other places.

Enriched and emboldened by these successes, Banda styled himself as a ruler, appointing officials and minting currency in his own name. Fortune hunters from all over East Punjab, in search of easy pickings, joined and swelled the ranks of his marauding band to over forty thousand armed men. His battle cry was simple, '*Musley da naas, Guru da parkash*' (destruction of Muslims is the will of the Guru). His activities finally attracted the attention of Emperor Farrukhsiyar who called for more resolute action against him by the governor at Lahore. Banda was eventually cornered and arrested near Gurdaspur in December 1715. He was taken to Delhi, convicted and executed, along with many of his companions, on charges of robbery, murder and insurrection against the state. Bengali Nobel laureate, Rabindranath Tagore, later eulogized Banda in his poems, along with Shivaji and Guru Gobind Singh, for having waged wars against the Muslims.

Banda's followers were pursued wherever they could be found. Most of them hid in the jungles in Malwa, south of the Sutlej and in the foothills to the east. Occasionally, they emerged to carry out minor sporadic raids but the Sikh movement had suffered a serious blow. It was leaderless and in dire straits for the next twenty-five years or so during which time Punjab heaved a sigh of relief. Nadir Shah's raid on Delhi in 1739 dealt a fatal blow to the faltering Mughal rule in Delhi and rendered the government penniless and without the necessary resources to deal with the troubles in the outlying provinces. The Sikhs were reprieved and emerged from their hiding places to resume their plundering ways against defenceless towns and villages.

RITES, RITUALS AND SECTS

Adi Granth is essentially a compilation of philosophic reflections and songs of praise (for details, please see '*History of the Sikhs*, *Appendix XVII*', by J. D Cunningham). It does not prescribe any specific rules of worship or practice of Sikh religion as such. In fact, there was not even an agreed version of Guru Granth until 1873 when the reform movement, Singh Sabha, began printing a standard text in Amritsar. Nonetheless, it has always occupied a central position in Sikh religion. The place where it is housed is called '*gurdawara*' which, apart from being a house of worship, also acts as a community centre, rather like the use of the mosques by the Muslims. The gurdawaras are marked by a distinctive saffron coloured triangular flag called '*Nishan Sahib*' that carries the Khalsa emblem, '*khanda*' ---- a double-edged dagger in a circle surrounded by two curved swords. It is regarded as a holy entity and is treated with appropriate reverence.

The holiest Sikh site is *Harminder Sahib*, commonly referred to as the Golden Temple, at Amritsar in East Punjab. It was first built by the fifth Guru Arjun Dev in 1604 on land granted by the Mughal Kings and is surrounded by a water reservoir. The well-known Muslim saint, Mian Mohammed Raza Mir, of Lahore was invited to bless its foundations. Relays of minstrels recite hymns from Guru Granth in the temple for twenty-one hours each day.

Facing Harminder Sahib is a multi-storeyed building known as *Akal Takht* (throne of God). This is where community leaders formulate policies and courses of action (*gurmatas*) in the presence of Guru Granth that are considered binding '*hukumnamas*' (orders) for the entire Sikh body. It was from the Akal Takht that Sant Jarnail Singh Bhindranwaley had launched the campaign for Khalistan, an independent Sikh state, in 1984. In a vicious attack, the Indian army destroyed Akal Takht and massacred Bhindranwaley along with all his supporters and more than twelve hundred tourists and by-standers that happened to be inside the temple at the time.

The brutal show of force and the actions that followed was a chilling reminder of the persecution suffered earlier by the Sikhs in their turbulent and violent history and will, undoubtedly, cast a long and ominous shadow on their future prospects in Hindu dominated India. Intolerance of the Sikhs is inherent in the Hindu mind. Sikhs are not alone in this. Muslims and Christians are also treated in similar fashion. The underlying cause may well have something to do with the fact that these three faiths are monotheistic and stand for equality among human beings. As such, they are perceived as a threat, particularly to the caste system that forms the basis of Hindu religion and the worship of multiple deities.

The management of gurdawaras was traditionally in the hands of priests known as '*mahants*'. Over the years, donations from devotees and official grants of land placed considerable wealth into their hands. Inevitably, it led to temptation and corruption and gurdawaras, like the Hindu temples, began to attract an unsavoury reputation. To make matters worse, inexplicably, the British granted the *mahants* title of ownership of the gurdawaras. It was not until 1925 that the situation was finally rectified, largely due to the efforts of the *Akalis* and their control handed over to Shiromani Gurdawara Parbandhak Committee, composed of 175 members that are elected by the Sikhs every five years.

Guru Granth is placed under an ornate canopy (*palki*) inside the gurdawara. The service begins with recital and singing of hymns (*shabad-kirtan*) following the tradition established by Guru Nanak. Until 1947, more often than not, Muslim minstrels (*rababis*) were employed for this service, as had the guru. Sikh families often hold services at their homes, known as *sat sang* that can last two or three hours. The service ends with *ardas* (distortion of Persian *arz dasht* ---- making a request) followed by the slogan *Wahey Guru ji da Khalsa, Wahey Guru ji di fateh* (the Khalsa belongs to God, victory belongs to God) and by reading out a random passage from the Granth that becomes the 'order of the day' (*hukumnama*). A communal feast of *karha parshad* ---- a sacred meal ritually prepared with flour, sugar and purified butter that is always received in cupped bare hands is then served to the congregation.

Amrit is the Sikh initiation ceremony first performed by Guru Gobind Singh at the festival of Baisakhi in 1699 when he anointed the '*panj piyarey*', his five dearest devotees. It involves drinking ceremonially stirred sugar water from a steel bowl and taking the Khalsa vows. All children born to devout Sikhs receive the initiation at the gurdawara and are given names chosen from Adi Granth.

Unlike Islam, marriage among the Sikhs is regarded as a pre-ordained spiritual bond rather like the Christian belief. As a rule, marriages are arranged within the same caste group. The Hindu roots of Sikhism are proving to be resilient enough to take precedence over the teachings of the gurus. The caste structure has re-asserted itself strongly in the Sikh society and recreated more or less the same social divisions and barriers among them today as are found among the Hindus. Traditionally, divorce was not an option but the Hindu Marriage Act of 1955 now provides for divorce among the Sikhs as well. Remarriage is also permitted. A widow suffers similar social stigma as found among the Hindus. The Sikhs cremate their dead like the Hindus and observe thirteen days of mourning.

They commemorate four religious days each year known as '*gurpurb*'. These comprise the birthdays of Guru Nanak and Guru Gobind Singh and death anniversaries of gurus Arjun Dev and Tegh Bahadur. The latter two had been executed. These are marked by carrying Guru Granth in a religious procession through the streets. In addition, they also celebrate the Hindu festivals of '*Divali*' that commemorates the return of Rama from exile; '*Baisakhi*' associated with harvesting the wheat crop; '*Holi*' celebrated by throwing coloured dyes on passersby (called '*Hola*' by the Sikhs) and '*Sangrand*' the first day of every month of the Hindu lunar calendar that is considered auspicious.

There are an estimated total of twenty million Sikhs scattered throughout the world today (2009). Of these, eighteen million are found in India, two thirds of them in East Punjab. Apart from this, there are sizeable numbers found in the United Kingdom, Canada and the United States --- enough for them to be able to return the odd Member of Parliament or Congressman. Generally, the Sikhs tend to be enterprising people with a strong work ethic and community spirit. It is rare indeed, if at all, to find a Sikh beggar on the streets anywhere.

The Sikhs are divided into many sects. Some of these divisions originated in history, others are caused by differences in interpretations and observances related to the scriptures. Those initiated into the Khalsa are known as *Amritdharis* and are regarded as the ideal Sikhs. *Kesdhari* is simply a term applied to a Sikh who wears unshorn hair. He may or may not be a Khalsa. On the other hand, *Sahajdharis* do not observe all of the outward signs of Sikhs and are not Khalsas.

The *Namdhari* Sect was founded by Baba Balak Singh in 1797. They believe that Guru Gobind Singh did not die at Nandher; wear white clothes and a flat turban and only marry within the community. They do not display *Nishan Sahib* and are strict vegetarians. A minor rebellion started by them in Punjab was ruthlessly put down by the British in 1872, with the culprits tied to the mouths of cannons and blown asunder in public. The *Nirankaris* came into existence as a reaction to the corruption that had crept into the Sikh society following temporal success in first half of the nineteenth century. They believe in the need for a living human guru. So do the *Radhaswamis* who are vegetarians and do not install the *Adi Granth* or any other scripture in their gurdawaras nor serve *karha parshad*.

Among the older orders are the *Ramraiyas*, found mostly in northwestern UP. Their ancestors chose to follow Ram Rai when Tegh Bahadur became the guru. The *Bandais* have been mentioned already. *Rangrhetas* are converts from among the Untouchables; and *Ramdasis* from the lower caste Hindus like *Chamars*. *Mazhabis* are generally Outcasts who first became Muslims and then joined the Sikhs, without giving up all of Islam. These are different from *Mussadis* ---- Muslims who joined the Sikhs without converting. *Gayani* is a term applied to any Sikh who is considered wise and learned. Then there are the *Akalis, Nahangs, Nirmaley, Suthra Shahis and Suchidaris* ---- all of them attributes implying pure, sinless, true, etc.

THE SIKH STATE

It has been mentioned earlier that the Mughal Empire disintegrated with astonishing rapidity after the death of Aurangzeb in 1707. There was only chaos and anarchy for the next one hundred and fifty years. Any enterprising brigand or desperado, who could muster a few hundred armed men, set himself up as the ruler of a state. Soon there were more than seven hundred such potentates in India. Almost all the administration as well as law and order had broken down and what trade and industry still existed was at the mercy of extortionist officials and bands of armed robbers.

Punjab had been annexed by Ahmed Shah Abdali, along with Kashmir, Sind and Baluchistan, in mid eighteenth century as parts of his Afghan state. In 1799, in exchange for help in retrieving some artillery pieces from the mud in Jehlum River, Ahmed Shah Abdali's grandson, Shah Zaman, appointed the wily Sikh chief of one of the armed bands, Ranjeet Singh, as governor of Lahore. This marks the beginning of half a century of Sikh rule in Punjab but to call it 'rule' will be stretching the imagination quite a bit. It is true that Ranjeet Singh, one way or another, succeeded in bringing fifty or so Sikh chieftains in different parts of Punjab under his control but this was only in the military sense. Beyond this, there was no administration and no law as such in the Sikh domain, regardless of what some Sikh historians like to claim.

Most of the time marauding bands of the Sikhs, known as *jathas* operated independently. In cases where a greater force was needed, the bands would join to form a *misel* and for still larger operations the *misels* would combine into an army or *dal khalsa*. The important decisions were made through consensus between the Sikhs and were declared as *gurmata* ---- will of the Guru that was binding. It was not long before the unchecked activities of the Sikh *misels* brought normal life in the province to a complete stop. There was no security of life or property for any individual or community and no recourse to law. Punjab was reduced to complete anarchy. Lahore, which had been a bustling and prosperous world-class city under the Mughals, became a destitute and lawless caricature of its original self.

Plunder, extortion, and chaos became the order of the day ---- a state of affairs that gave a new word to the lexicon ---- '*Sikhashahi.*' It was synonymous with arbitrariness, injustice, lawlessness and cruelty (*The Pathans*, by Sir Olaf Caroe, Oxford University Press, 1990, p. 298). Justice was a very rough and ready affair. There are numerous recorded cases of men being put to death for mercy killing a grievously injured and suffering cow, for cutting someone's hair; for using Arabic or Persian words while speaking or even for receiving or imparting education (*The Pathans of Jullunder*, p.52). Any Sikh (*Khalsa*) had the right to institute a '*dunn*' (extortion). This allowed him to block the entry to any Muslim's house or other property until his, usually monetary, demands were met. People were dispossessed of their land, shops and houses at will and left without any recourse to justice.

Muslims were forbidden to make the call for prayers (*azaan*) and were obliged to offer their prayers secretly in Sikh dominated areas. A large number of mosques and mausoleums were demolished or stripped of decorations and their marble slabs taken away to adorn *gurdwaras* and the houses of Sikh chiefs. Many mosques were converted into pig-pens. Most of the larger mosques, including the Grand Badshahi Mosque in Lahore, were used as military stables and ammunition dumps. Others like the fabulous Mahabat Khan mosque in Peshawar were completely razed to the ground. There was, probably, never a darker period in the history of Punjab. Those who lived through it have described it as an unrelenting nightmare.

Syed Mohammed Latif, in his *History of the Punjab - From the Remotest Antiquity to the Present Time* (Takhleekat, Lahore, 1994, pp. 578 - 81) writes that all the loot was divided among the leaders of the Sikh *misels.* They, in turn, distributed a part of it among their soldier volunteers. If the latter were not satisfied with the treatment or conditions, they would freely switch loyalties to a different leader. There was no code of law laid down as such. Civil and criminal cases were mostly decided by the tribal leaders. Most crimes were punished by fines. There were no limits on these and were levied taking into account not simply the gravity of the offence but also the financial situation of the accused. The fines were payable to the head of the tribe and were an important source of his enrichment. In the event of non-payment, family members of the accused were subjected to extreme cruelty and the accused thrown into dungeons where survival beyond a few weeks was unknown. The more serious crimes were punished by gauging out the eyes or cutting off the nose and ears. In cases of homicide, the accused was simply handed over to the family of the murdered person to do what they liked with him. Invariably, they lynched him after extreme and inhuman torture.

To report a theft, the victim had to deposit one quarter of the value of the stolen goods, in advance, as fee for the officials. On recovery of the stolen goods, the thief was let off if he was able to offer adequate bribe. The heads of tribes customarily gave protection to thieves and robbers in return for a share of the loot ---- a practice known as '*kundi*'. If a person died in a land dispute, his family was recompensed by paying blood money or giving a bride or 125 acres of land. Half of all the farm produce went to the local Sikh chief. In the same way, all trade goods were subjected to heavy and arbitrary taxation. The Sikhs, as a matter of right, commandeered free labour. As a result of such coercive measures, economic activity was at a stand still and life had been rendered extremely difficult for the common people. Small wonder that they greeted the British with a sigh of relief and gratitude when they finally took over the administration in Punjab in 1849.

The Sikh rule in Punjab, even though it lasted for less than half a century, did immense damage to the population in general and the Muslims in particular. The closing down of all institutions of learning and the total ban on the use of Persian and Arabic languages effectively denied them access to all knowledge. The break lasting through successive generations resulted in the creation of a largely ignorant and illiterate population. It is impossible to pick up the threads after a disruption of this kind and magnitude and the Muslim community of Punjab never fully recovered from it.

REFLECTIONS

There are a few things that stand out prominently in the history of Sikhs. There is little doubt that individually they have been brave and committed soldiers. However, their commitment was seldom to a higher motive and they had no qualms about switching sides if there were personal gains to be made in the process. Less than eight years after the British had defeated and humiliated them and deprived them of their kingdom, the Sikhs were pledging their loyalties and offering their services to the erstwhile enemies in their droves. It was in part due to the timely, enthusiastic and considerable military support provided by the likes of Sikhs that the

British were able to crush the uprising of 1857 that might have otherwise ended their rule in India.

Their readiness to accept foreigners and former enemies as their new masters and allow collaborators and traitors like Lal Singh and Tej Singh to function in their own ranks (see chapter *British Occupation*) is an indication of a basically fickle nature and indifferent standards of character and commitment. The Sikhs are known to be passionate people and can be aroused easily by invoking issues of religion. But it became repeatedly evident that these feelings too fell by the wayside in situations where personal gain became involved. As we shall see, they were badly short-changed by their own at the time of independence.

A prime example of this was witnessed in their reaction to the Indian army's invasion of the Golden Temple in 1984 and the killing of more than 20,000 Sikhs in riots all over India that followed the assassination of Prime Minister Indira Gandhi. After a short period of explosive resentment, it was business as usual for the vast majority of Sikhs in India. Possibly, this is due to a level of social consciousness that has not developed to the extent where collective interest can take precedence over personal gain in the individual mind. It is this peculiar combination of traits that renders the Sikhs highly suitable and useful in mercenary roles. The British were quick to take advantage of this and capitalized on it by inducting them in the British Indian army in large numbers.

There are other negative perceptions about the Sikhs as well. For instance, the Hindus in India tend to look upon them as belonging to a lower order of intelligence and capability. There is no logical basis or explanation for such an assumption except that the Sikh way of thinking is significantly different. Generally, they tend not to be as subtle and sophisticated as the Hindus and certainly not half as devious.

There is also a common belief in India that the Sikhs do not respond well to reason and logic and 'only understand the language of force'. It was this conviction, most likely, that led to the Indian army's attack on the Golden Temple and the subsequent brutal suppression of their ten-year struggle for some kind of autonomy within India. Ironically, the man chosen by the Indians to plan and implement these cruel repressive measures by the police was himself a Sikh by the name of K.P.S Gill. Lieutenant General Brar who commanded the troops that attacked the Golden Temple in Operation Blue Star and badly damaged the *Akal Takht* and other buildings also happened to be a Sikh.

It might have pacified the Sikhs for the time being but the underlying resentment is deep and will only add to their already troubled history. It is highly doubtful if there are many Sikhs left who deep down do not feel alienated from India as a result of the harsh and savage measures. If their past history is anything to go by, the final chapter in the Golden Temple saga is yet to be written. Already, a portrait of the chief rebel killed in the 1984 massacre, Jarnail Singh Bhindrawale, has been placed in the Golden Temple with the caption: '*The great Sikh General of the 20th century and the 14th chief of the Damdami Taksal, Sant Giani Jarnail Singh Bhindrawale, who along with numerous valiant Sikhs, attained martyrdom on Wednesday, June 6th, 1984, fighting against the Indian Armed Forces for the honour and prestige of Sri Harminder Sahib and Sri Akal Takht Sahib.*'

As mentioned elsewhere, in a joint letter addressed to President Clinton in June 2000 a number of US Congressmen, quoting data collected in India by various Human Rights organisations, alleged that more than 240,000 young Sikhs had been murdered in extra-judicial killings in cold blood and some 41,000 policemen had been awarded bounty money for carrying out the ghastly executions. They called for India to be declared a terrorist state. A resolution to the same effect was only narrowly defeated in the U S House of Representatives in 1995. The western media, for reasons of their own, have done their best to keep this gory tale out of the public eye. As against this, in a display of crass hypocrisy, they keep resurrecting the Tiananmen Square episode whenever there is a political need to embarrass or pressurize China.

For the western governments and information media to ignore such atrocities is, to some extent, understandable but the apparent passive resignation of the Sikhs to the outrage is un-natural, uncharacteristic and unlikely to last. They have not forgotten or forgiven the Muslims to this day for the alleged atrocities committed by the Mughal rulers hundreds of years earlier that pale in comparison with what was done to them in India in the 1980s and early 1990s. It may be because they lack imaginative and committed leadership. Apathy, insensitivity and indifference to atrocities more often than not is invitation to more of the same.

The Sikhs have not produced a political leader, worth the name, since Ranjeet Singh died in 1839. One explanation could be that they tend to be individualistic by nature. They are badly divided and do not find it easy to submit to the will of one of their own. A leader has to be seen to be successful, fair and above all selfless before the masses will accept and respect him as such. There have been very few among the Sikhs who can measure up to this yardstick. The crop of the past century and a half has been mostly lightweights who have not possessed the degree of vision, integrity, commitment and dedication needed for the task. There is no reason to believe that the situation will last forever. Sooner or later, someone will emerge to unite the Sikhs and give them a renewed sense of purpose and direction.

One hopes, for their sakes, that it will not be very long before they too may taste the fruits of peace, dignity and freedom enjoyed by the other major communities in the sub-continent. It will take an independent temporal authority that is free of religious constraints, inhibitions and dogma to lead them out of the quagmire. The existing set-up may be admirable for organising the religious and communal lives of the Sikhs but falls short when it comes to political matters. As will become evident from the chapter '*Road to Freedom*', they missed out badly because of this when India and Pakistan gained their independence.

CHAPTER 5

BRITISH OCCUPATION

EAST INDIA COMPANY

On 31st December 1600, a group of London traders incorporated the East India Company with the exclusive objective of trading with India. Giving her blessing to the enterprise, Queen Elizabeth directed the promoters to '*adventure after merchandise, gold, pearls, jewels and other commodities, which are to be bought, bartered, procured, exchanged or otherwise obtained'*. The expression 'otherwise obtained' covered a multitude of practices including privateering and any form of skullduggery common at the time.

In 1607, Captain Hawkins was dispatched with some cargo, in a ship called the Hector, to the Port of Surat along with letters of introduction from King James I. He tried to present these to the governor of Cambay only to be told that he should deliver these in person to the king in Agra. He experienced considerable opposition from the Portuguese already entrenched at Surat and was subjected to extortion by the local governor before he could present himself to Emperor Jahangir on 16th April 1609. Hawkins aroused Jahangir's curiosity and managed to get close to him, partly because of his knowledge of Turkish language which the Mughals spoke. He remained at the court for the next two and a half years and was able to obtain some minor trade concessions for England.

The English traders and agents were generally treated with ridicule and contempt and subjected to humiliating indignities including being forcibly driven out from public places, manhandling and arrest. Some of the ire was aroused because of the state of personal hygiene of these strangers. Europeans in those days did not believe in bathing or washing their bodies and smelt horribly which caused offence to the locals. It was only after contact with India that such luxuries as public baths, toilets and massage parlours and cotton garments came to be accepted and became more commonplace in Britain.

An enterprising Indian, by the name of Shaikh Deen Mohammed, opened a chain of restaurants and massage parlours in England in late eighteenth century. One of these, in Brighton, was granted Royal Appointment in 1783. Cotton from India made it possible to produce washable under garments and less smelly Britons. These also helped to improve hygiene and reduced the spread of communicable diseases. It is a moot point if the so-called 'Victorian values', prevalent among the British middle class in the nineteenth and early twentieth centuries, were not influenced by the cultural interaction with the Islamic civilization in India. This was particularly evident in matters of personal conduct, family life, the place and role of women in the society and attitudes towards sex, etc. These changed perceptibly from what had been the norm until then. The re-emergence of a bawdier Britain after the demise of the empire may have something to do with it, along with the changes in attitude towards class structure brought about by World War II and subsequent advent of the contraceptive pill.

The lack of initial success at the emperor's court prompted the decision by the British Government to send a man of greater substance and background as ambassador and Sir Thomas Roe arrived at Agra in January 1615. He remained there for more than three years and did his best to obtain wide-ranging concessions along the lines of the Capitulations granted in Turkey. Jahangir would have none of it and Sir Thomas Roe was obliged to report to his superiors, '*Neyther will this overgrowne Elephant descend to Article or bynde himself reciprocally to any Prince upon terms of Equality, but only by way of favour admitt our stay. You can never expect to trade here upon Capitulations that shall be permanent. Wee must serve the tyme. You shall be sure of as much privilege as any stranger*'.

Roe kept a meticulous journal of his activities and observations at Agra. These have been edited by W. H. Foster and published under the title, *The Embassy of Sir Thomas Roe to the Court of the Great Moghul*, by Hakluyt Society, London in 1899. At one point he cautioned his superiors against following an aggressive policy in India. '*A war and trafique are incompatible. By my consent, you shall no way engage yourselves but at sea, where you are like to gayne as much as to loose. It is the beggering of the Portugall, notwithstanding his many rich residences and territoryes, that hee keepes souldiers that spendes it; yet his garrisons are meane. He never profited by the Indyes since hee defended them. Observe this well. It hath beene also the error of the Dutch, who seeke Plantation heere by the sword. They have a wonderfull stocke, they proule in all Places, they Possess some of the best; yet ther dead Payes consume all the gayne. Lett this be received as a rule that if you will Profitt, seek it at Sea, and in the quiett trade; for without controversy it is an error to affect Garrisons and Land warrs in India.*'

This is basically how things remained for the East India Company for the next one hundred years. The last of the Great Mughals, Aurangzeb, died in 1707. There was no worthy successor and the empire that was based on personal rule soon fell apart like a house of cards. The reasons for the sudden collapse and what followed have been discussed earlier in the book. The resulting chaos presented tempting opportunities to ambitious adventurers who were willing to take their chances with fate.

Sensing weakness at the centre, the governors of provinces and rulers of states one after another declared their independence from Delhi and started to cast covetous eyes on their neighbours' territories. It is a process that has been a recurring feature of the history of the region since time immemorial. Soldiers of fortune gathered bands of armed men and placed their services at the disposal of any one who could promise some gain. There were no higher loyalties involved ---- national, political, ethnic, religious or any other.

There was no law or order either; only anarchy. India split up into isolated communities, as it had always done, each doing its best defend itself and subsist as best as it could. In the circumstances the trading companies, including those from Britain and the France, were also obliged to maintain their own troops to guard their interests that lay mostly in South India at the time. They soon discovered there was profit to be made also by lending the services of their levies to the local princes and rulers.

It started with hiring European troops to the contenders for the throne of Karnatak State, around 1740, in return for grants of land. The Europeans were better disciplined and better trained in relation to the local rag-tag rabble and their presence made a decisive difference in the outcome of the generally mismanaged, unprofessional and irresolute combat. Over a period of time, the successes of European troops helped to create the myth of their superiority, even invincibility, over the local soldiery. Sometimes uniquely peculiar conditions and fortuitous luck played their part in their successes, in the process re-inforcing the myth.

This myth-making soon became a part and parcel of official policy. A quotation attributed to Lord Macaulay (the first law member of the Governor-General's Council) from an address reportedly given by him to the British Parliament on 2nd February 1835 reads: '*I have travelled across the length and breadth of India and I have not seen one person who is a beggar, who is a thief, such wealth I have seen in this country, such high moral values, people of such calibre that I don't think we would ever conquer this country unless we break the very backbone of this nation which is her spiritual and cultural heritage and, therefore, I propose that we replace her old and ancient education system, her culture, for if the Indians think that all that is foreign and English is good and greater than their own, they will lose their self-esteem, their native culture and they will become what we want them, a truly dominated nation.*'

As happens so often in life, the real gainers in the turmoil that resulted from the breakup of the Mughal Empire were not the local princes or the rulers but the people who traded on their needs for war. It made little difference to the latter who won or lost; their profits generally remained secure. Like the Jewish bankers in Europe, it was the Hindu moneylenders (*sahukars*) who made their fortunes from the fighting. Waging war has always been an expensive business requiring inordinate reserves of cash. If the troops were not adequately paid and fed they deserted or mutinied. It gave *sahukars* the power to make or break almost any warlord. Marhatta Peshwa, Balaji Baji Rao once explained about his creditors, '*I am falling at their feet, till I have rubbed the skin from my forehead.*' (*A History of the Freedom Movement in India*, by T. Chand, Delhi, 1961, pp. 163- 4).

Wars created large debts and to repay these Marhattas, like all the others, were obliged to acquire more territories to gather more taxes or simply engage in indiscriminate and wanton plunder. It became an unending misery for the people, fueled by sheer mindless ambition and avarice on the part of a few, that eventually and inevitably led to the enslavement of the entire sub-continent by a foreign power.

Constant warfare creates unsettled conditions that are not good for trade. It was not enough to merely safeguard the trade goods in these circumstances. Their secure transportation and delivery needed to be ensured as well. This provided an added reason for the British and the French not only to muster larger numbers of troops but also to become actively involved in local political and administrative affairs. However, there was no hint at this stage that this political involvement had any purpose beyond the need to protect and increase their respective trading operations and profits.

The East India Company was privately owned and run for the benefit of its shareholders. From the bases (called 'factories') it had established in

Madras (1639), Bombay (1664) and Calcutta (1696), it imported spices, tea, china, cloth and other manufactured products from India and China that it sold in Britain or re-exported to other countries for considerable profit. Superior quality cloth obtained in India was sold in London at six times its purchase price. The company paid regular annual dividends of about eight per cent and by 1744 was in a position to make a loan of one million pounds to the British Government that ensured for it the monopoly of trade with India.

The profits might have been much greater but for the fact that there was no demand or market for any British goods in India. The ships returned empty and the price of imports was paid for in silver obtained from trade with other nations or piracy and looting of Spanish galleons returning from Latin America. As we shall see, this problem was soon resolved in a rather ingenious manner. The Company was able to arrange things politically so that the imports were paid for from its revenues within India itself ---- a win-win situation which cost Britain amost nothing.

FRENCH INTERVENTION

The French counter-part of the British East India Company, Compagnie des Indes, formed in 1719, was less well-organised and funded (*Myths and Realities of French Imperialism in India, 1763 – 1783*, by S. Das, New York, 1992). Pressed for funds locally and unable to communicate with their principals in reasonable time, its officials in India were obliged to exercise their initiative and acted independently on most local issues. In 1740, the French governor of Pondichery, Benoit Dumas, took a stand against the Marhatta army of Raghuji that had been looting, raping and murdering in Karnatak. Raghuji chose to back down. There were a couple of other occasions at the same time when small numbers of French troops vanquished much larger ill-disciplined Maratha detachments. It gave a welcome boost to French military reputation and the local princes began to eagerly seek their assistance and collaboration.

The first among them was Raja Chandra Singh of Karnatak who, in exchange for French assistance in war against the Raja of Tanjore, handed over possession of the port of Karaikal on the east coast. In situations like these it was but natural that the local European officials availed themselves of the opportunities to make personal gains for themselves. Robert Clive of the East India Company as well as the French Governor, Dupleix, and a host of others, made considerable personal fortunes in this way.

War broke out between France and Britain in Europe in 1744 and spilled over into the colonies and territories abroad. After some initial successes, the French in India were obliged to fall back on the defensive mostly due to the inadequacy of their sea power. However, the peace treaty signed at Aix-la-Chapelle in January 1749 restored the respective positions in India to where they had been before the war.

Both the sides had been obliged to increase their armed strength during the war. The British, in particular, had a formidable force available at sea that was placed at the Company's disposal for intimidating and coercing the local rulers. It helped restore the deposed raja of Tanjore to his seat in 1748 and, in return, obtained possession of the port city of Devikot from him. On his part, Dupleix was engaged in a similar exercise a little further to the north by helping to replace Nawab Anwar-uddin of Karnatak with his own stooge, Raja Chandra Singh, in exchange for handsome fees and grants of land. He then helped install Salabat Jung as the Nizam of Hyderabad, which gave an immeasurable boost to his standing as a power broker in south India.

The British were not amused and decided to frustrate Dupleix's designs by backing the claim of Anwar-uddin's son, Mohammed Ali Walajah, against Chandra Singh's usurpation of Karnatak. It resulted in the siege of Karnatak's capital, Arcot, in which Robert Clive was able to defeat a much larger French-led contingent. From a purely military point of view, these battles were quite insignificant, involving less than ten thousand men and bore no comparison to what had been taking place at Panipat, for instance, where the combined strengths of the belligerents had been of the order of half a million men or more. Nonetheless, historians are inclined to place Arcot on the same plane as the three battles of Panipat in terms of its political ramifications and consequences that followed. French fortunes in India went mostly downhill after this. By 1763, they had been completely neutralised and by the terms of the Treaty of Paris signed that year, were only allowed to carry on trading on the condition that they took no active part in Indian politics.

The East India Company was now in a position to freely dictate its will over the states of Tanjore and Karnatak. It used this advantage to further its trading interests by squeezing out the Indian middlemen and gaining direct access to the artisans and tradesmen. It was the Company that now determined how the weavers of southern India, for instance, organised production and what prices they could charge for their goods and services. Their situation had changed little in reality from the days of rapacious extortion by the Marhattas. The rulers of the states could provide no succour to them for they owed their position to the Company. A little war was beginning to pay big dividends to the Company.

In the years to come, with the advent of mechanized looms in Lancashire, things took a catastrophic turn for the weavers in India. English traders stifled the imports of muslins from Bengal by contriving a 75 per cent import duty on all Indian cotton goods. The next step was the duty-free admission of English cottons mass-produced on power looms, into all the territories controlled by the East India Company. In a space of thirty rears, an ancient industry on which millions of Indian handloom weavers depended was virtually wiped out.

BENGAL

Bengal was the richest and most populous province of India with about forty million people. In 1717, the British had managed to obtain the *dastaks* (rights), under a *firman* (order) from the cowardly and incompetent Emperor Farrukhsiyar (1713 – 1719) in Delhi, to transport goods within the province without having to pay any local taxes. Farrukhsiyar was an emperor in name only. His writ did not run as far as Bengal where Nawab Murshid Quli Khan, a proselyte Brahmin, was now in charge. As the Company expanded its operations in the territory, the nawab was cheated out of more and more of his revenue.

In 1756, Murshid Quli Khan's twenty three year old grandson, Siraj-uddaula, occupied the Company's bases at Kasim Bazar and Calcutta. The British garrisons failed to put up any defence. Their officers abandoned the troops and fled to the ships anchored off-shore. Leaderless men, mostly Swiss mercenaries that were left behind, broke into the wine store, got drunk and were taken prisoner. They were incarcerated in dungeons where, in the June heat, some of them succumbed to dehydration and stroke. No one knows the exact number. The incident, termed the Black Hole of Calcutta, remains controversial to this day. However, it is generally accepted that the Company exaggerated the figures to help generate sympathy and support at home for its subsequent actions.

The loss of Calcutta was an unacceptable blow to the British image and prestige. As soon as news of the disaster reached Madras, a detachment of 3,000 soldiers transported by five war ships sailed with Clive in charge. He collected some more troops when he landed and had little difficulty in expelling the garrison that Siraj-uddaula had left behind in Calcutta. A hurried truce was arranged in February 1757. After this Clive set about hatching a conspiracy to over-throw Siraj-uddaula, who could no longer be trusted, with the help of local Armenian merchants and Hindu moneylenders. No empire can function without the help of native collaborators. Here we see the beginnings of a class of people that was later to become institutionalized for making itself useful to the British in return for some personal benefits and privileges.

A Hindu merchant named Omichand struck a deal on behalf of Clive with Mir Jaffer, one of Siraj-uddaula's important generals. According to this a battle would be forced on Siraj-uddaula in which Mir Jaffer would desert taking his men with him, leaving the nawab to do what he could with what was left which could not be much. After the victory that was thus assured, Mir Jaffer would become the ruler of Bengal. In return, he agreed to cede a number of *parganas* (tax districts) to the Company; pay 550,000 pounds to the European community in Calcutta; 275,000 pounds to the Company's army; the same amount to the Royal Navy; 222,000 pounds to the Hindu merchants and 77,000 pounds to the Armenians. These payments were over and above the personal gifts that Mir Jaffer showered upon various Company and army officials. Clive, for instance, managed to squeeze a large *jageer* from the nawab that provided him with an income of 27,000 pounds annually.

Omichand had demanded five per cent of all of the nawab's wealth for his services. This was agreed but on a faked document. In the end he got nothing. Two other key players who had conspired with Clive, the nawab's *Diwan* (minister), Rai Durlabh, and his governor of Bihar, Ramnarayan, were to be allowed to continue in their positions with the new nawab for the time being. Writing to Robert Orme about the entire sordid affair, Clive himself stated, '*I am possessed of volumes of materials for the continuation of your history, in which will appear fighting, tricks, chicanery, intrigues, politics, and the Lord knows what*' ('*The Cambridge History of the British Empire, vol. IV: British India*' by H. H. Dodwell, Cambridge, 1929, p.151)

The battle that was in name only took place near the village of Plassey on 23rd June 1757. Its result was a foregone conclusion when Mir Jaffer, in accordance with the agreement, decided to stand aside. After some mismanaged and messy skirmishing, Siraj-uddaula's men bolted. He was himself caught by his own troops and stabbed to death on Mir Jaffer's orders. The total number of casualties on both sides probably numbered less than five hundred, almost all of them Indians (*Fort William – India House Correspondence,* as quoted by Lawrence James in *Raj: The Making and Unmaking of British India*, p.35). Even though no one at the time would have realised, this utterly undistinguished and insignificant military engagement, in which hardly any British blood was shed, is now credited with having laid the foundations of the British Empire in India.

There may or may not be a valid basis for the assumption but, starting with Plassey, there was a radical departure in British policy. Hitherto, they had been content to work with whosoever was in power. Now they had taken the big leap to assume the role of kingmakers in India. The second point of note in the events leading up and subsequent to Plassey is that the local Hindu merchants and officials were now willingly working for or conspiring with the British, mostly out of self interest and personal greed. It is interesting to compare the attitudes of the British with those of the Indians at the time. Both of them looked for personal gain but for the British this was subservient to the national and Company interests. Not so with the Indians who were only in it for themselves.

NO BUSINESS LIKE WAR BUSINESS

The concessions from the nawab, apart from the personal 'gifts' and awards of *jageers*, were of three kinds. The British obtained the exclusive rights to levy taxes on the movement of trade goods by the local merchants, at the same time, getting an exemption from all taxation on the trade carried out by the Company and its officials. Secondly, they were allowed to fix prices at which to purchase goods directly from the local producers and sell these to the merchants in the markets. Lastly, in increasingly large parts of the country, they started to impose and collect land revenues. They used these powers with a degree of greed and vengeance that was unknown. The burden ultimately fell on the common man who was soon squeezed out of all that he possessed. If there were any protests, the nawab was expected to put an end to these. The situation became extortionist in the extreme and soon the nawab himself was protesting. India, that had been rich, was now hemorrhaging and becoming poorer by the day as her wealth was mercilessly drained away.

There was a distinct difference between the Mughal and Company policies and methods of taxation of trade and land revenues and their effects. The Mughals had taxed the movement of goods for revenue generation whereas the Company used the mechanism to smother competition from the local traders and establish its own monopoly on trade. The proceeds of taxation and profits from trade under the Mughals remained and were recycled within India. The British took the proceeds abroad to enrich their own islands. It is a process that is still very much alive and at work, even after independence, with only a slight change in form. Now, it is done indirectly through wealthy Indians and Pakistanis who are siphoning off the country's riches into coffers abroad. There are American, British, Swiss and other bankers travelling to these countries every day to facilitate the transfer of wealth of individuals who are looking for more safe and secure havens. An estimated one billion dollars a day was being transferred to the US stock markets alone, from the rest of the world, in 2000.

Financial instability in any part of the world helps to accelerate the flight of capital to markets in the West. Writing in '*The Foreign Affairs*' (May / June 2000 issue) Mr. F. Gregory Gause III estimates that Saudi private citizens alone kept up to 800 billion dollars of their wealth abroad in the West. In 2005, British MP, George Galloway, reckoned the total investments by Muslim rulers and businessmen in the western financial institution, stock markets and real estate may amount to six trillion dollars. Mismanagement and corruption also play a significant role in this transfer of wealth. According to a report in the New York Times of 6th October 1999, out of the 18 billion dollars provided as an emergency relief to Russia by the IMF and the World Bank to save her collapsing economy, no less than 7 billion dollars had been skimmed off by corrupt officials and had found its way back into New York banks within one week.

The British victory at Plassey brought about an almost immediate and dramatic improvement in the fortunes of the Company and those of its officials. Aside from extracting all the payments agreed beforehand, Henry Vensittart, Clive's successor as governor, reserved the largest share of the province's trade for himself. Warren Hastings, who was then resident at Mir Jaffer's court in Murshidabad, was running a large and prosperous private business dealing in salt, opium, tobacco, timber and boat-building. By one estimate, these and other Company officials between them were by now netting over half a million pounds a year into their personal coffers ('*Raj*', p.38). In this free for all environment, other European entrepreneurs also accumulated great fortunes, many of them by lending money to irresponsible rulers and *zamindars* at rates of interest as high as thirty-six per cent per year.

In Britain Horace Walpole, a member of parliament was compelled to note, '*Such a scene of tyranny and plunder has been opened up as makes one shudder. ---- We are Spaniards in our lust for gold and Dutch in our delicacy of obtaining it*'. In a similar vein, Lord Chatham wrote at the same time, '*India teems with inequities so rank, as to smell to earth and heaven*' ('*The Cambridge History of the British Empire, vol. IV*, p. 187). Robert Clive himself told the court of directors of the East India Company in 1765:

'*The sudden and among many the unwarrantable acquisition of riches had introduced luxury in every shape, and its most pernicious aspect ---- everyone thought he had the right to enrich himself, at all events, with as much expedition as possible ---- The sources of tyranny and oppression, which have been opened by the European agents acting under the authority of the Company's servants, and the numberless black agents and sub-agents, acting under them, will I fear be a lasting reproach to the English name in this country; it is impossible to enumerate the complaints that have been laid before me by the unfortunate inhabitants*' ('*Empires of the Monsoon*', p. 328).

The methods employed by the Company officials were brutal, to say the least. '*They and the Hindu and Armenian merchants who were their factotums used coercion to dominate markets. The sword intruded into everyday business life, for the more ruthless commodity dealers encouraged their gumashtas* (Indian clerks and business agents) *to employ Sepoys whenever pressure was needed to secure the best bargain. Competitors were scared off and unwilling suppliers or customers who objected to inflated prices were flogged. Vansittart noted with wry amusement that gumashastas, who in Calcutta walk in rags, once inland would lord it over the country, imprisoning the ryots, and merchants, and writing and talking in the most insolent, domineering manner to the faujdars and officers. Minatory business methods were copied in southern India; in early 1770s the native factor employed by Anthony Sadler to buy cloth in Vizagapatam district was accompanied by Sepoys who beat those weavers who set what was thought to be too high a price on their goods ----.*' ('*East India Fortunes: The British in Bengal in the Eighteenth Century*', by P.J Marshal, Oxford University Press, 1976, pp. 117 – 8, 128 and others as quoted in '*Raj:* pp. 38 – 9).

Bengal was drained of most of its resources and bled white in a very short space of time through such rapacious practices. So much so that even Mir Jaffer was obliged to protest. Vensittart was not pleased with this change in attitude and promptly replaced him with Jaffer's son-in-law, Mir Kasim, as the new nawab in 1760. In return for this favour, Kasim handed over the districts of Bardwan, Midnapur and Chittagong to the Company and paid at least 200,000 pounds in brokerage fees to Vensittart and other officials. Replacement and turnover of the nawabs was proving to be a highly lucrative business all round, except for the hapless Bengali peasants who ultimately footed the bill.

It wasn't long before Mir Kasim too felt uneasy with the state of affairs. In an effort to depose him, Company troops attacked Patna but were defeated and chased across the country with heavy losses. There were more battles over the next year and a half until Mir Kasim was finally defeated at Buxar on 23rd October 1764. The causes of failure were the same as elsewhere ---- indifferent leadership, lack of proper training, poor morale and discipline, inappropriate tactics and a general absence of professionalism in the military as well as political fields. The significance of Buxar lies in that it marked the end of native rule in Bengal. Even though there would still be a nawab but in name only whose expenses were paid from a Company pension.

The Company took over collection of revenues in the province directly. A new system was introduced whereby leases of agricultural tracts (*zamindaries*) were auctioned annually and the land handed over to the highest bidder. As a result, collections increased exponentially, from eight million rupees in 1764 to twenty-five million rupees in 1790. Local *zamindars* were not in a position to bear the heavy burden of these new assessments. The only people with large reserves of cash were the Hindu money lenders (*banias, marwaris*). They soon squeezed out Muslim *zamindars* who lacked the resources to compete. Only the tenants remained Muslims and they bore the burden of all the taxes.

In 1793, the Permanent Settlement Act was passed that virtually closed the doors of *zamindari* to Muslims for the future. In more than a third of the cases, the *banias* and *marwaris* merely acted as front men for influential company officials. The coming together of these vested interests gave birth to a symbiotic relationship between the two that held profound implications for the future.

There was a curious concern for observing legal niceties and maintaining at least the appearance of legitimacy. This was true for the British just as much as it was for the Marhattas and all the rest of them. It was, perhaps, the only reason why the utterly ineffectual remnants of Mughal monarchy remained undisturbed in Delhi for so long. They served a purpose by conferring the needed legitimacy to make the interlopers acceptable to the people. This was also the reason why, despite considerable pressure, Bengal was not made into a British colony. In the latter case, technically, the king of England would have become a vassal of the Mughal Emperor in Delhi.

The British now effectively ruled the province under a charter obtained from Emperor Shah Alam II (1759 – 1806) who had fled from his murdering courtiers in Delhi and taken refuge with the Company at Allahabad. He had little choice. The defeat of Marhattas at Panipat by Ahmed Shah Abdali three years earlier had left a power vacuum in the country that the latter had chosen not to fill. All the wars and repeated sacking of Delhi by Nadir Shah and Ahmed Shah had drained the imperial purse completely. There was no way to replenish it with revenues from the ever shrinking Mughal Empire in India. Shah Alam was only too pleased to accept Clive's offer of 272,000 pounds as annual tribute in exchange for granting the right to the Company, in perpetuity, to collect taxes estimated at thirty three million pounds a year from the provinces of Bengal, Behar and Orissa. As in the past, there was something in the deal for Clive as well in the form of a substantial personal *jageer*. With one easy stroke and at little expence to themselves the British had become the largest landlord and most dominant power in the sub-continent.

One Company official later quipped, '*We acquired our Influence and Possessions by force, it is by force we must retain them*' (*Raj*, p. 42). Although the statement became the guiding principle for nearly two centuries of British rule in India, it reflects only a part of the truth. There was a whole lot more involved in the British success than mere force. First of all, the circumstances had been fortuitous for them. If Aurangzeb's successors had not been as inept, things may well have turned out quite differently. Secondly, what the British won through political skill, guile, manipulation and intrigue was far in excess of anything that they might have gained from the use of force.

Lastly, it was a contest between two peoples that differed widely in terms of orientation and motivation. Whereas the British tended to be 'mission' oriented i.e. striving for a higher common cause, the Indians were in it exclusively for their individual and personal gain. The unity of purpose made destructive and dangerous internal divisions and differences less likely and enabled the British to prevail against seemingly impossible odds time and time again. The Indian rulers, on the other hand, never seemed to comprehend what was really at stake until it was far too late. Their aims were narrow, selfish and senseless that courted nothing but disaster, which they ultimately got with a vengeance.

Success creates its own myths. So it was with the British in superstition ridden India. Their initial successes helped to create an aura of invincibility about them. They took every opportunity to meticulously preserve and propagate this myth, even going to the extent of trying to convince the Indians, by all the means at their disposal that the latter were inherently inferior and could never expect to acquire the same level of skills and competence as the British. Given the impossible odds that existed against them, it was just as necessary for the British in India to believe in the myth as it was for the Indians. Repeated often and over a long enough period human beings can be made to believe in almost any myth, especially if care is taken not to allow anyone to question or put its veracity to test. The British rule in India lasted for as long as it did primarily because of the myth of their superiority which the Indian, in particular the Hindu mind by its nature and history, was predisposed to accepting and believing. Others like the Greeks and the Romans had done the same thing before and it is interesting to note that the Israelis, taking a leaf out of the same book of Imperial domination, are trying to create a similar myth of their invincibility vis-à-vis the Arabs today.

Credit must be given where it is due. The shrewdness with which the British were able to first analyse the Indian mind and then set about capitalising on its weaknesses was remarkable. For them to appreciate the influence and significance of myths for the natives and to devise ways to promote and perpetuate these in those early days is very remarkable, indeed astonishing. For this reason, despite any personal shortcomings that he may have had, Robert Clive's name will remain foremost among a handful of men who profoundly altered the course of history in India, as had the Spaniards Cortes and Pizarro done a century and a half before him in Latin America. He was the first to identify and exploit the weaknesses in the Indian character to the advantage of his nation. What the Muslims had achieved through force of arms and shedding of precious blood, Clive was able to obtain through subtle and cunning manipulation of the Indian psyche that cost the British almost nothing. He had a vision of a British future in India and worked hard and fearlessly to achieve it. Others mostly followed in the trail blazed by him.

Success almost inevitably brings jealousies with it. The newly acquired fame and fortunes by people like Robert Clive, Warren Hastings and Vensittart did not sit too well with the establishment in Britain. Charges of mismanagement, corruption and misconduct were brought against them when they returned home. Not much came of these except that they helped to create increased level of awareness and interest among the British public in the events taking place in India.

Edmund Burke, who impeached Warren Hastings in the Parliament on 13th of February 1788, charged him with oppression, corruption, gross abuse of power, and for ruthlessly plundering India: ' ---- *cruelties unheard of and devastations almost without name ---- crimes which have their rise in the wicked dispositions of men ---- in avarice, rapacity, pride, cruelty, malignity, haughtiness, insolence, in short everything that manifests a heart blackened to the very blackest, a heart dyed in blackness, a heart gangrened to the core ----. We have brought before you the head, the captain general of iniquity, one in whom all the fraud, all the tyranny of India are embodied.*'

When Burke began to describe the violation of Bengali virgins and their mothers, by the rapacious tax collectors the British employed ---- '*they were dragged out, naked and exposed to the public view, and scourged before all the people ---- they put the nipples of the women into the sharp edges of split bamboos and tore them from their bodies ----*' one Mrs. Sheridan was so overpowered that she fainted and had to be carried from the hall. After a trial lasting nearly ten years Hastings was eventually acquitted on all charges.

Despite considerable resistance from commercial and trading quarters, the Parliament had been obliged to pass the Regulating Act of 1773 that gave the British Government the right to oversee the affairs of the Company and rein in some of the excesses of its officials. This was followed by the India Act of 1784 that placed the administration of British ruled India under a form of dual stewardship, with a new Board of Control that was headed by a cabinet minister in London, to supervise the workings of the Company's Directors.

The East India Company, in effect now became the official agent of the British Government in India. In 1833, to preclude any conflict of interest, the Company was ordered to cease all trading and commercial activities. Henceforth, it was to confine its activities solely to civil administration of the country and the control and management of it armies. The appointments to the Indian civil service were opened to public competition in 1853.

Meanwhile in India the wars continued. In 1774, the nawab of Avadh hired the services of the Company's army for a sum of forty lakh (four million) rupees, plus the expenses of the expedition, to bring Rohilkhand to the north under his control. The Rohillas constituted a confederacy of Pathan chieftains who had a dispute over a treaty signed with the nawab. They fought bravely as Col. Champion, commander of the British brigade described, '*---- great bravery and resolution ---- they gave proof of a good share of military knowledge by showing inclinations to force both our flanks at the same time and endeavouring to call off our attention by a brisk fire on our centre ---- it is impossible to describe a more obstinate firmness of resolution than the enemy displayed*', (*The Cambridge History*, p.219 – 20). Alas, all of this was of no avail against the combined strength of the Company and the nawab's army.

There was no reason or justification for the British to get involved other than simply to make money. At a subsequent parliamentary inquiry Major Marasack, a British officer who had participated in the campaign, testified that the Hindu peasantry had been benevolently treated by their Rohilla masters and as a consequence the country reached '*the greatest Height of Opulence.*' After the conquest and on arrival of the nawab's tax collectors, the region's prosperity disappeared (*House of Commons Special Papers: George III, Reports Concerning Hasting's Impeachment 58, 21 – 2*, S. Lambert, Wilmington, 1975). How else could the nawab have paid for the Company's services except by squeezing the peasants? In the end, a small piece of the territory was joined to Rampur and left in possession of Faizullah Khan, son of the Rohilla chief.

At about the same time the Mughal Emperor Shah Alam II, decided to leave Allahabad and return to Delhi to seek protection from the Marhattas. It gave the Company the excuse to stop paying him the tribute that had been agreed earlier. He had taken over the districts of Allahabad and Kora from the nawab of Avadh. The latter was allowed to re-occupy these in 1773, after paying fifty lakh rupees to the Company. There was no shortage of ways for making money in India provided there was strength on your side. Governor-General Hastings, in defending his hiring of troops to the nawab, has recorded, '*The absence of the Marathas and the weak state of the Rohillas, promised an easy conquest of them, and I own that much was my idea of the Company's distress at home, added to my knowledge of their wants abroad, that I should have been glad of any occasion to employ their forces, that saves so much of their pay and expenses*', (*Hastings and the Rohilla War*', by Sir John Strachey, 1892, p.55).

Aside from all this, there was another more potent and compulsive reason to make war. This is best explained in the words of two experienced and senior British officials of the time. The first, in 1805, by John Malcolm who served in India in various capacities for close to half a century '*It was a true saying which the great Lord Clive applied to the progress of the British Empire in India ---- To stop is dangerous; to recede ruin. And if we do recede, either from our right pretensions and claims ---- nay, if we look as if we thought of receding ---- we shall have a host of enemies, and thousands who dare not even harbour a thought of opposing the irresistible tide of our success, will hasten to attack a nation which shows by diffidence in its own power that it anticipates its downfall*' (*The Life and Correspondence of Charles, Lord Metcalfe vol. I*', by J.W Kaye p. 320 - 21).

There was an ever-present fear in the minds of Company men that unless they demonstrated a ruthless resolve to keep the Indians subjugated at all costs, by all means and at all times, the latter may rise up and over-whelm them at any moment. No occasion or excuse was missed for a show of force and strength, often without any justification. It was a psychology born out of profound fear as typified in the following quote in 1844 from Lord Hardinge, the then Governor-General, "*In India no man can say what may produce in a country of 120 millions of inhabitants governed by an army which is officered by aliens, whilst the mass of the force under these foreign officers consents to coerce their own countrymen, merely for the sake of pay and pension ---- mesmerised as it were by a handful of officers exhibiting in the working of the system the greatest phenomenon that the world ever witnessed* ('*The Letters of the First Lord Viscount Hardinge of Lahore to Lady Hardinge and Sir Walter and Lady James*', by B.S. Singh, Camden Society, 1986, p. 36

It needs to be stressed that there is no historical evidence of any grand design in the beginning for the conquest of India by the British. They just kept encroaching and expanding their control, on an ad hoc basis in a series of steps, over a period of nearly a century, taking on one adversary at a time. Neither the Company Directors nor the British Government advocated or willingly supported an aggressive expansionist policy in India. In almost each case, it was the local officials and commanders who forced their hands and left them with little choice but to approve the decisions that had already been made locally. The delays involved in communications made it extremely difficult for London to remain in close and constant touch with events in India. It could take anything up to six months to write a letter and get a reply from England. In the circumstances much was left to the discretion of the local commanders whose attitudes and objectives were not always governed by the same vision or motives as those of the Government.

The existing rules allowed for the spoils of war to be distributed proportionately among the participating troops as 'Prize Money'. This could amount to a considerable sum in the case of a senior officer. For instance, General Viscount Lake received 38,000 pounds for the capture of Agra from the Marhattas in 1803. He captured many other cities as well, including Delhi, during this campaign. The Governor-General, Marquess Hastings, was awarded 260,000 pounds by the Company Directors (*The Private Journal of the Marquess of Hastings*, ed. by Marchioness of Bute, 1858).

Aside from the Prize Money there were other benefits like fees for issuing permits to sell liquor, opium, tobacco, *ganja* (cannabis), etc. in the camp followers' bazaar that accompanied the army. The major beneficiaries of these proceeds were the field commanders. Each officer and man received a substantial field allowance (*bhatta*) whilst on campaign. Service in India was highly sought after by all young Britons because it afforded prospects of becoming rich very quickly. It is, therefore, reasonable to assume that the local officers were not exactly averse to the prospects of war and, conceivably, might have encouraged or even found excuse to start one.

We also need to remember that the British had lost America in 1783. They needed to compensate for this loss by acquiring new territories and markets for their trade. Any expansion in India was going to have a decidedly positive effect on public morale. Therefore, even if the British Government may not have been actively instigating and pursuing it, they could not have been too unhappy with the aggressive expansion that was under way in India at this time.

This expansion went far beyond the traditional norms of international trade. For instance, the British introduced tea from China to the Indians and actively promoted the use of Indian-grown opium in China. Soon British ships were carrying increasing quantities of opium from Calcutta to be consumed by the Chinese and returning with tea for sale in India and Europe. The obscene profits made in the process filled the coffers of companies in London in return for very little investment.

The story of opium trade is not very well known because it is seldom discussed in detail by the historians. The British had a huge balance of payments problem in relation to China. They were importing far more than they were exporting to the country. In order to balance this trade the first Governor-General, Warren Hastings, came up with the idea to export and aggressively promote the use of opium in China, beginning around 1780. Within a period of thirty years large numbers of Chinese had become addicted to the drug. Its production increased in proportion to the demand until its profits accounted for almost one fifth of the government revenues in India. This remained the case until 1920. Even today, the largest opium factory in the world can be found at Ghazipur in India.

When the Manchu emperors in China attempted to control the inflow of opium, in 1842, the British government declared what became known as the Opium Wars. Combined armies of Britain and France occupied and looted Peking, burning down the emperor's palace. A series of treaties were forced on China that included the ceding of Hong Kong to Britain and opening up of a dozen major cities to the Europeans where they had immunity from Chinese laws, taxes and customs duties.

SOUTH INDIA

Apart from Bengal, there were British Presidencies in Madras and Bombay that were engaged in similar interventionist and expansionist policies of their own. The Presidencies, each controlled by a separate council, cooperated and supported each other despite the occasional rivalry and petty intrigue. Their overall direction and coordination was placed in the hands of the Governor-General in Calcutta, a position first created and assigned to Warren Hastings after the Regulating Act of 1773. The organisation and its workings were far from smooth or satisfactory. They simply muddled through. Disaster was averted only because the opposition was even more fragmented, disorganised and inept. It never got to a level where it could seriously pose a threat to the British, especially, after the French had faded from the scene.

In addition to Karnatak, the other sizeable Indian powers in the areas of the Madras and Bombay Presidencies were the Marahattas and the Nizam of Hyderabad. The rather fluid situation in South India, brought about by the ouster of the French, was further complicated by the emergence of Mysore as a player of some reckoning. The state had formed part of Aurangzeb's empire but was now being run by two Brahmin brothers. Haider Ali, the chief minister of the state, sidelined the ineffectual Hindu raja and took matters into his own hands. Although unlettered, he was a man of rare vision and ability and soon made his presence felt by expanding his influence into the neighbouring territories. These included Bangalore, Seringapatum (1761 AD), Calicut and Malabar that brought him into conflict with the Marhattas.

It also alarmed the Nizam who entered into an alliance with the British in November 1766 to receive military assistance in exchange for ceding the five northern *sarkars* (districts) of his state to them. After this the two joined hands with the Marhattas and their combined armies invaded Mysore the following year. The attack failed to make headway. Soon the Marhattas lost heart and departed from the field to be followed by the Nizam shortly afterwards. This left the British to face Haider Ali by themselves. Placing too much trust on allies for waging war on an enemy is always an unsatisfactory and uncertain business at best.

After two years of isolated battles at a number of places, claimed as 'tactical successes' by the British, Haider Ali laid siege to Madras. The Company sued for peace and was obliged to accept the terms granted by Haider Ali in April 1769 that were generous by its own admission. The next year, he concluded a similar arrangement with the British in Bombay.

It vexed Haider Ali that despite all his military successes on the battlefield, he was unable to finish off the British. He was acutely aware of the facility that was afforded to his adversaries because of their command of the sea. When pressed, they could always board the ships and put themselves out of his reach as well as bring in re-enforcements safely whenever needed. In frustration, he is reported to have once remarked, 'I can defeat the British at will on land but I cannot drink the sea.'

Regardless of what face they tried to put on it in public, the British felt humiliated by the outcome of their struggle against Haider Ali. The treaties of friendship signed with him were never honoured and at one stage in 1771, they seriously considered going to the aid of the Marahatta chief Madhu Rao, in his war against Haider Ali. When reminded of the obligations under the Treaty of Madras by the council, this is what Harland, local representative of the British Government had to say, '*Should it be found expedient to enter into an alliance with any Indian power for the preservation of the Carnatick, for the security of the possessions of the East India Company in it, and to give a probability of permanency to the British interests in this country, which may be incompatible with the agreement you made with Hyder Ali, in 1769, it would be so far from a breach of national faith that even as private persons you stand exculpated*' (*The Cambridge History of the British Empire, vol. IV*', p.279).

In the ten years that followed the British increased their strength and consolidated their position in Deccan. General Munro, the victor of Buxar, had taken over command of the Madras army and there was considerable confidence about the situation when Haider Ali was provoked into what came to be called the Second Mysore War. It began with a lightening raid into Karnatak by Haider Ali in July 1980. Munro met him at Conjeeveram and after a sharp skirmish ran headlong for cover in Madras. Seeing the fate of his protectors the nawab of Karnatak he capitulated, offering only token resistance. When news of the disaster reached Calcutta, Hastings ordered the Commander-in-Chief, General Coote, to march the Bengal army overland and take command of the operations against Haider Ali. The governor of Madras, Whitehill, was sacked and replaced by Lord Macarteny.

Despite claims of what *The Cambridge History* so often euphemistically describes as British 'tactical victories' in 1781, the situation on the ground changed not a whit. Haider Ali remained firmly in control of Karnatak and showed no visible signs of being evicted. In the autumn of 1782 Coote was relieved by General Stuart who could do no better. Largely because of their own doings, the British were fighting the war without any substantial Indian allies after Karnatak's capitulation and finding themselves mired in all kinds of difficulties with no early solution in sight and their confidence severely shaken.

Desperate efforts were made to bring the Marhattas onside despite the ongoing war with them in central India. These eventually culminated in the Treaty of Salbai signed in May 1782 under which the British withdrew from all the territories taken from the Marhattas since 1776 in return for a promise of peace and friendship. It also called upon Haider Ali to withdraw from all the territories he had taken from the British as well as the nawab of Karnatak. Not all the Marhatta rulers were in agreement with signing the treaty and some, including Nana Phadnavis (Balaji Janardhan) did so with considerable reservations, still hoping for an alliance with Haider Ali. The latter was reportedly quite disconcerted by these developments. It is said that before he died of cancer on 7th December 1782, he left a note for his son, Tipu Sultan, to settle terms with the British and not continue to pursue hostilities against them in isolation and on his own (*The Cambridge History* ----, p.271).

In an attempt to distract Haider Ali, a contingent of Bombay army under Colonel Humberstone marched towards Mysore from the west towards the end of 1782. Haider Ali despatched Tipu Sultan to take care of it, which he did. Later, the ruler of Mysore's Bednur province, Ayaz Khan, was bribed to surrender to the British under Brigadier Mathews from Bombay. The victory was short-lived. Tipu routed Mathews and took him and all his surviving troops prisoner. Things were looking quite bleak and desperate for the British at this point.

As if this was not enough, a French fleet appeared on the east coast and landed a contingent of troops at Cuddalore under Bussy, a man who had previously had considerable success in keeping the Nizam in French hands. As Stuart marched to meet the French, there was every possibility that a coordinated attack by Tipu Sultan from the west would finish the British in South India. Just in the nick of time Providence intervened and news of cessation of hostilities between the British and the French in Europe reached India on 23rd June 1783. Bussy suspended all action and Tipu Sultan was left to deal with the British and their allies by himself.

It had been a long war and the British were just as much exhausted by it as Tipu Sultan, if not more. The governor of Madras, Lord Macarteny, finding his coffers drained, considered the time opportune and with the approval of the Governor-General negotiated a peace treaty at Mangalore where a British force had just surrendered to Tipu Sultan on 7th March

1784. By the terms of this treaty, both parties agreed to give up their conquests and release each other's prisoners. There was a general feeling that the agreement was humiliating for the British on the grounds that Tipu Sultan had not treated the British representatives with due decorum. There was not much truth to it but Warren Hastings, who was engaged in fierce ongoing rivalry and in-fighting with Macarteny, seized on the issue to castigate the latter, terming the treaty as '*humiliating pacification.*'

Most British historians prefer not to dwell on these reverses at the hands of the Indians. In an article in the *Guardian*, 26th Sept. 2004, Linda Colley wrote:

'*Naturally, in the years before the Raj was securely established, there were also many British captives in India. In 1780, perhaps one in five British-born soldiers in India were being held in captivity, most of them in the powerful southern Indian state of Mysore.-----*

'*When the British empire was still in existence, the more embarrassing and painful aspects of these captivity episodes were often airbrushed out of the official story. Members of the master race were not to be seen as suffering in such a disadvantaged fashion.*

'*Professional historians of the British empire now tend to focus on its elites not the sort of people who always formed the bulk of captives: common soldiers, sailors, small traders, mere womenfolk and the like.*'

The successes of the Mysore army were largely due to the genius of Haider Ali. He had realised that the British were masters of European style set piece battles. Their artillery and infantry were better equipped, more disciplined and much better trained and organised. The frontal mass assaults employed by the half-trained and ill disciplined native armies proved disastrous in battles against the British. Instead of going down the same beaten path as the rest of them, Hyder Ali looked for weaknesses and found these in the British army's lack of mobility and its dependence on ponderous lumbering logistic trains. To exploit these handicaps he developed a highly mobile cavalry that lived off the land as far as possible. With this he delivered lightening strikes against the enemy, at the same time avoiding being pinned down in any pitched battles. The British never did find an effective answer to this highly mobile form of warfare.

Although Haider Ali had shown the way, the other rulers showed no signs of learning any lessons from it. Like so many other things in the administration of India, warfare too was an ad-hoc amateurish affair. There were no organised or regular institutions for the specific study and development of warfare and valuable lessons and experiences gained on the battlefields fell by the wayside and were lost.

Tipu Sultan was now the dominant power in South India. Both the Nizam of Hyderabad and the Marhattas to his north felt exposed and threatened. It led them to form an alliance against Tipu. Cornwalis, who had replaced Hastings as Governor-General, saw the British interests in India threatened in a different perspective. In a letter to Sir Charles Malet, the British Resident at Poona, referring to the Treaty of Mangalore he wrote in March 1788, *'I look upon a rupture with Tipu as a certain and immediate consequence of a war with France and in that event a vigorous co-operation of the Marathas would certainly be of the utmost importance to our interests in this country'* (*The Cambridge History*, p.334). Two years later, the 'Triple Alliance' between the British, Marhattas and the Nizam was formed against Tipu Sultan and war began in May 1790.

Mysore was attacked from the west by the Bombay army of the British, from the north by the Marhattas and the Nizam and from the east by the British army from Madras. The war lasted two years. Things were not going too well for the Madras army that was engaged with Tipu Sultan in the first year and Cornwalis himself took over command from General Medows. He too failed to perform and was pushed back. There were a number of seesaw battles but, eventually, Tipu's resources were exhausted and he was gradually forced back. The Allies too were not unhappy when Tipu sued for peace. He was made to surrender half of his territory in the north to the Marhattas and the Nizam and all the land along the west coast to the British. The British also took Tipu's two young sons as hostages to Calcutta.

The wars with Haider Ali and Tipu Sultan had aroused a great deal of interest not only among the British in India but also with the public in England. The two were held up as the greatest villains by the British press at the time and stories were printed about them in the same vein as about Hitler and Saddam Hussein in more recent times. Every schoolboy learned to hate them viscerally. The British in India took perverse pleasure in naming their dogs 'Tipu' for the next century and a half as an expression of condemnation and insult. In retrospect, the father and son were no worse and probably treated the British better than most of the other Indian rulers. The difference was that they did so from a position of equality, and not obsequious subservience, which was unacceptable and unforgivable in British eyes.

The other equally potent causes for the extreme reaction were firstly that the two had shattered the myth of British invincibility by repeatedly inflicting decisive defeats upon them and secondly that Haider Ali and Tipu Sultan were Muslims. While writing to the Duke of Wellington on 4th October 1842, Governor General Lord Ellenborough observed, '*It seems to me most unwise, when we are sure of the hostility of one-tenth, not to secure the enthusiastic support of the nine-tenth which are faithful. ----- that race* (Muslims) *is fundamentally hostile to us and therefore true policy is to conciliate the Hindus* (*History of the Indian Administration of Lord Ellenborough*, by Lord Colchester, pp. 296, 322, as quoted by Saad R. Khairi in *Jinnah Reinterpreted*).

Anti-Muslim feelings among the British have never been much below the surface to the extent that even the more observant non-Muslim historians have noticed and commented upon it (see Khushwant Singh in *How the Sikhs Lost their Empire*, UBS Publishers, New Delhi, 1996, p. 94, etc.). A poll conducted in the early nineties indicated that among all the western nations, anti-Muslim sentiment was found to be greatest among the British (see also report by Clare Garner about the findings of the Commission on British Muslims and Islamphobia set up by the Runnymede Trust, in '*The Independent*', London, 21st February 1997).

In 1794 the Marhattas attacked the Nizam of Hyderabad. The new Governor-General, Sir John Shore, refused to fulfill the treaty obligations and go to the Nizam's support. He lost and was obliged to cede territory and pay tribute to the invaders. There had been a revolution in France and Indian rulers disillusioned with the British, including Tipu Sultan, looked to her with new hope or, at least, so the British perceived. Richard Wellesley, Earl of Mornington, who had replaced Shore, leaned heavily against Tipu Sultan asking that he give up his alleged alliance with France and then progressed to placing ever increasing demands on his territories. He had decided to finish Tipu Sultan and had already issued orders to prepare for war.

The justification given for the aggression was that France had landed troops in Egypt and was threatening India. In the end, the French could not even establish themselves in Egypt let aside march their army thousands of miles across some the most inhospitable terrain in the world through hostile Arabia, Persia and Afghanistan to join forces with Tipu Sultan, a further fifteen hundred miles away in the south of India. The Royal Navy, enjoying overwhelming superiority, had exercised uncontested control over the Indian Ocean. The French could neither hope to transport troops nor support them by sea at such long distances. The proposition made no sense and could not be taken seriously. One can understand the politicians' need to find excuses for going to war but for the historians to accept these unquestioningly and try to provide justifications for them is problematic (see H. H. Dodwell in *The Cambridge History*, pp. 338 – 43).

Aided by the Marhattas and the Nizam, whose troops were commanded by Arthur Wellesley, younger brother of the Governor-General and later to be the victor of Waterloo and British Prime Minister, the British armies marched on Mysore from Madras as well as Bombay on 3rd February 1799. There were three Wellesley brothers serving in prominent positions in India at the time, which inevitably gave rise to accusations of nepotism against the Governor-General. After a series of set backs, Tipu Sultan fell back on his capital Seringapatam. He was surrounded and on 4th of May a combined force of British and the Nizam's troops made the final assault through a breach in the battered walls. Tipu died fighting and his body lay with those of his troops where it was found.

The bulk of his domain was taken over by the British thus 'securing an uninterrupted tract of territory from the coast of Coromandal to that of Malabar, together with the entire sea-coast of the kingdom of Mysore', according to Wellesley. What remained after the Allies had taken their pick of the spoils of war was restored to the Hindu family that had been displaced by Haider Ali. A five-year-old boy was named the new raja, under the tutelage of a British resident, in return for payment of a hefty annual subsidy to the Company. Among other things, Mysore was not permitted to raise an army again, except in token form for ceremonial purposes.

Shortly after this an Indian army contingent was dispatched to Egypt to help clear out Napoleon's troops. The practice of using Indian troops to fight British wars overseas remains in vogue to this day with the employment of Nepalese Gurkhas in the British army.

William Dalrymple is an eminent historian who has done extensive research and written a number of commendable books on India's past and present, including *White Mughals* and *The Last Mughal*. In the 24th May 2005 issue of *The Guardian*, he published an article headed, *An Essay on Imperial Villain-making*, about Tipu Sultan that is worth quoting at some length:

'----- *Richard Wellesley was sent out to India in 1798 as governor general with specific instructions to effect regime change in Mysore and replace Tipu with a western-backed puppet. First, however, Wellesley and Dundas had to justify to the British public a policy whose outcome had long been decided in private.*

'Wellesley therefore began a campaign of vilification against Tipu, portraying him as an aggressive Muslim monster who divided his time between oppressing his subjects and planning to drive the British into the sea. This essay in imperial villain-making opened the way for a lucrative conquest and the installation of a more pliable regime that would, in the words of Wellesley, allow the British to give the impression they were handing the country back to its rightful owners while in reality maintaining firm control.

'According to British sources, this chief of state was an "intolerant bigot", a "furious fanatic" with a "rooted and inveterate hatred of Europeans", who had "perpetually on his tongue the projects of jihad". He was also deemed to be "oppressive and unjust ... [a] sanguinary tyrant, [and a] perfidious negotiator".

'It is a truth universally acknowledged that a politician in search of a war is not over-scrupulous with matters of fact. Until recently, the British propaganda offensive against Tipu has determined the way that we --- and many Indians --- remember him. But, as with more recent dossiers produced to justify pre-emptive military action against mineral-rich Muslim states, the evidence reveals far more about the desires of the attacker than it does about the reality of the attacked.

'Recent work by scholars has succeeded in reconstructing a very different Tipu to the one-dimensional fanatic invented by Wellesley. Tipu, it is now clear, was one of the most innovative and far-sighted rulers of the pre-colonial period. He tried to warn other Indian rulers of the dangers of an increasingly arrogant and aggressive west. "Know you not the custom of the English?" he wrote in vain to the nizam of Hyderabad in 1796. "Wherever they fix their talons they contrive little by little to work themselves into the whole management of affairs."

'What really worried the British was less that Tipu was a Muslim fanatic, something strange and alien, but that he was frighteningly familiar: a modernising technocrat who used the weapons of the west against their inventors. Indeed, in many ways, he beat them at their own game: the Mysore sepoy's flintlocks --- as the examples for sale in an auction of Tipu memorabilia at Sotheby's tomorrow demonstrate --- were based on the latest French designs, and were much superior to the company's old matchlocks.

'Tipu also tried to import industrial technology through French engineers, and experimented with harnessing water-power to drive his machinery. He

sent envoys to southern China to bring back silkworm eggs and established sericulture in Mysore --- an innovation that still enriches the region today. More remarkably, he created what amounted to a state trading company with its own ships and factories dotted across the (Persian) *Gulf. British propaganda might portray Tipu as a savage barbarian, but he was something of a connoisseur, with a library of about 2,000 volumes in several languages.*

'Moreover, contrary to the propaganda of the British, Tipu --- far from being some sort of fundamentalist --- continued the Indo-Islamic tradition of syncretism. He certainly destroyed temples in Hindu states that he conquered in war, but temples lying within his domains were viewed as protected state property and generously supported with lands and gifts of money and even padshah lingams --- a unique case of a Muslim sultan facilitating the Shaivite phallus veneration. When the great Sringeri temple was destroyed by a Maratha raiding party, Tipu sent funds for its rebuilding. "People who have sinned against such a holy place," wrote a solicitous Tipu, "are sure soon to suffer the consequences of their misdeeds."

'Tipu knew what he was risking when he took on the British, but he said, "I would rather live a day as a tiger than a lifetime as a sheep." As the objects in tomorrow's sale (at Sothebys) *show, the culture of innovation Tipu fostered in Mysore stands record to a man very different from that imagined by the Islamophobic propaganda of the British --- and the startling inaccuracy of Wellesley's "dodgy dossier" of 1799. The fanatical bigot and savage was in fact an intellectual.*

'The whole episode is a sobering reminder of the degree to which old-style imperialism has made a comeback under Bush and Blair. There is nothing new about the neocons. Not only are westerners again playing their old game of installing puppet regimes, propped up by western garrisons, for their own political and economic ends but, more alarmingly, the intellectual attitudes that buttressed and sustained such imperial adventures remain intact.'

There was much distortion of Indian history that was not simply confined to the British. All the court historians during the Muslim period, as mentioned earlier, wrote accounts that resembled hagiography and were often inaccurate. Since Independence much of the history has been re-written in India as well as Pakistan to reflect specific points of view. It came to the point where Dr. B.N Pande, the Governor of Orissa and Chancellor of the state's five universities had to completely overturn their curricula and revise all the textbooks on history (see chapter 2, *Muslim Rule*).

AVADH AND KARNATAK

The removal of Tipu Sultan ended the last serious challenge to British hegemony in India and they proceeded to seize territories from the remaining states, one after another, in rapid succession. Wellesley had less scruples than even Clive when dealing with the local rulers and it mattered not whether they were friends or otherwise. Treaties and commitments carried no meaning for him and he had no inhibitions about breaking them if there was some gain likely to accrue from it. The nawab of Avadh (present day Utter Pradesh) had been a long time ally and friend of the Company. The British had imposed an annual tribute of 7.4 million rupees to be paid by him along with bearing the cost of two British army brigades stationed in his territory. It was a heavy burden that became difficult to manage and the nawab requested for a reduction in the pecuniary demands and removal of one of the brigades. This brought forth a whole series of accusations that included moral turpitude, mismanagement, corruption, the poor state of his troops being a threat to British interests and anything else that they could think of.

At this point the old nawab died, conveniently for the Company, and was replaced by his son Wazir Ali. Shortly after recognising him as the new nawab the Company withdrew its support and nominated his uncle, Saadat Ali, to take his place. The reason given by the Governor-General was that not only Wazir Ali but all of his brothers as well were illegitimate and, hence, ineligible ('*The Cambridge History* ----- ', p.350). On 21st January 1798 Saadat Ali signed a new treaty that raised the amount of the tribute further still, increased the number of British troops stationed in Avadh at his expence to 10,000 while substantially reduced the size of his own military and made him surrender all rights for defence and foreign relations to the British. Soon afterwards Wellesley doubled the number of British troops that were paid for by the nawab and undertook to provide personal protection for the latter for an additional payment of five million rupees a year. As Dodwell puts it in *The Cambridge History* ----, p.351, '*It was a heavy burden but protection could not be had for nothing*'. Protection from whom? It was never spelt out.

Concessions are never enough in the world of international politics. They only point the way down a slippery road and whet the appetite of the oppressor to press for more. As if the burdens already imposed on the nawab were not enough, Wellesley ordered several more British regiments to be moved into Avadh and asked the nawab to pay for them. The nawab's objections that the move was contrary to the provisions of the treaty negotiated between them were rudely brushed aside. A new treaty was imposed, in November 1801 that made him cede a large chunk of his territory to the Company and left him nawab of the rest in name only. Wellesley's other brother, Henry, was put in-charge of the districts ceded by Avadh. International treaties between unequal parties are binding only for weaker party. The dominant power is seldom burdened by any such constraint. In this case the entire exercise had been pre-planned from the start to yield the results that it did i.e. gaining more territory and reducing the nawab's powers to those of a nominal figurehead.

After Lord Hastings took over as Governor-General he persuaded Nawab Haider-uddin Ghazi, the successor to Saadat Ali Khan, to renounce his allegiance to the Mughal throne and proclaim himself king. '*In the governor-general's opinion this act would benefit the British Government by causing a division between these important leaders of the Muhammadan community*' (*The Cambridge History* -----, p.575). The nawab's renunciation was not well received in most quarters.

The powers of the Nizam of Hyderabad had been curtailed earlier in similar fashion. Now it was the turn of the nawab of Karnatak, another long time ally of the Company. Nawab Mohammed Ali had borrowed heavily from private British and European moneylenders to meet the Company's demands for payment of annual tribute and military expenditure imposed upon him as the price for British friendship. The interest charged was astronomical with the result that he was unable to pay back the loan.

In a series of steps the Company took over internal and external control of the affairs of the state on the pretext that it was necessary due to the wars with Haider Ali and Tipu Sultan. The poor peasants, who bore the brunt of any financial squeeze, were left destitute. The Company owed them nothing and was not in the least concerned what happened to them as long as it got its pound of flesh.

Mohammed Ali died in October 1795 and was succeeded by his son Umdat-ul-Umara. First, Shore then Wellesley did their best to modify the existing treaty and get more out the new nawab as they had done in Bengal, Avadh and other states in similar situations but Umdat-ul-Umara would not give in willingly. At this time a dispute arose concerning succession in the neighbouring state of Tanjore. Wellesley personally solved it by assigning the state's civil and military administration to the Company and paying small stipends to the two contestants. According to '*The Cambridge History of India, vol. III* ', by Thornton, pp. 103 – 4, it was all done for the benefit of the people of Tanjore!

So far the Company Directors had resisted Wellesley's efforts to do the same in Karnatak. After the defeat and death of Tipu Sultan Wellesley claimed there was evidence of Mohammed Ali and his son having corresponded with Haider Ali and Tipu Sultan. The nature of the correspondence is not known but it was considered reason enough for the nawab to lose his claim to being an ally and friend under the treaties that he had signed with the Company.

Once again, propitiously for the British, Nawab Umdat-ul-Umara died just at this time and 'the succession was offered to the son, or presumed son, of the Nawab Ali Hussain, if he would accept the terms offered ---- a sum sufficient for his maintenance in state and dignity and the transference of the government to the Company.' When he refused, Wellesley invited Umdat-ul-Umara's nephew, Azim-uddaula, to take over which he duly did, accepting the same conditions.

This is how Wellesley justified the whole sordid affair for historic record, 'The nawabs were not independent princes but the creatures of the Company, established and maintained by their assistance. Mohammed Ali and Umdat-ul-Umara had by their treachery forfeited all claims to consideration for themselves or their line. The condition of Carnatak was a standing menace to the British position in Southern India, and a scandalous blot on the principles of peace, justice and prosperity which English rulers had endeavoured to introduce. A definite settlement was absolutely demanded. And no injustice was done to Ali Hussain, for he rejected the terms offered which his successor accepted.' Thus, from the British perspective, a stable and honest government was at last given by Wellesley to the land which had been the earliest to enter into close association with England (*The Cambridge History ---- vol. IV*, p.362). Power and success are heady wines. They change almost everything, including scruples, logic and reasoning of those who possess them.

There is little doubt that the Indian rulers had been corrupt and mistreated their subjects. The British were hardly any different in this respect. When they deposed a particular nawab or raja they did so because it was in their interest to do it. However, the reasons given were always the same that the man was cruel, unjust, inefficient, depraved, treacherous, lacked compassion for his subjects, sometimes, even illegitimate. It is interesting how all these adverse traits seem to become noteworthy only when the need arose to depose a ruler and not before.

Some things never seem to change in human history. In more recent times, the Americans supported Saddam Hussein in his war with Iran for eight years even though he was reported to have made indiscriminate use of poison gas to suppress his own people and killed thousands of innocent men, woman and children. The U.S. ambassador, April Glaspie, said of him, '*He is a man we can work with*'. When the Director of CIA, Robert Gates, was pressed for an explanation, replied to the effect, '*We know Saddam is a son-of-a-bitch but he is our son-of-a-bitch*' (John Pilger in ITV programme '*Paying the Price*', aired on ITV, 6th March 2000). Throughout history there has been a perverse kind of love affair between these 'sons of bitches' and the dominant powers. As far as they are concerned, conscience or morality does not enter into it and all kinds of excuses, justifications and media ploys are put forward to allay any misgivings and qualms on the part of the people.

MARHATTAS AND GURKHAS

Wellesley was on a roll now. His next targets were the Marhattas, the Company's allies in its war against Tipu Sultan. They occupied a vast chunk of territory in central and western India from the Sutlej to the borders of Mysore. Their combined strength was formidable but, fortunately for the British, their chiefs were divided by mutual suspicions and personal rivalries, so that the British were able to deal with them piece meal. The inner workings of the Marhatta polity were a much too complicated affair to be explained in detail in the available space. In any case, it is not very relevant for our purposes. For that reason only an over-view has been recorded.

The origins of Marhatta power in South India have been described in the chapter, '*Muslims in India*'. They were able to bounce back from the terrible defeat inflicted upon them by Ahmed Shah Abdali at Panipat in 1761 because he decided not to follow up his victory and went back to his native Afghanistan. Within twenty five years they were back in Delhi dictating terms to the decrepit Mughal Emperor Shah Alam II.

At this time, there was a confederacy of Marhatta states. The nominal head of the confederacy was the raja of Sattara, a descendant of Shiva Ji based in Poona. The real power rested in the hands of the *Peshwa*, originally, a position roughly comparable to master of the royal household. With the passage of time, the institution of the Peshwa, partly by virtue of the incumbent being a Brahmin, assumed much greater political as well as social and religious significance. It became hereditary when Balaji Vishwanath held the office early in the eighteenth century. The power of the Marhatta state was based on a host of big and small estate holders and chiefs who, in return for their fiefs, provided troops and military service when called upon to do so. They owed their position to the Peshwa which made him a very powerful and influential figure.

Under the Peshwa there were a number of hereditary generals who administered large and small states virtually as independent rulers. Raghuji Bhonsle was the raja of Berar that stretched from Nagpur in central India to Cuttack on the Bay of Bengal. Sayaji Gaekwad, an imbecile, ruled over Gujarat and Kathiawar Peninsular under the regency of his younger brother, Fateh Singh. The territories of Holkar in Southwest Malwa were in the hands of a capable woman called Ahalya Bai for thirty years, until 1795. Mahadaji Sindhia had occupied Gwaliar with his European trained and led troops and ranged north to Agra and Delhi where the powerless emperor had appointed him *Wakil-e-Mutlak* (vice regent) of his empire. There were scores of other lesser Marhatta rulers scattered throughout west and southwest India. Apart from these, there was Balaji Janardhan commonly known as Nana Phadnavis, a minister at Sattara, who played a significant role in the proceedings and intrigues that went on in the Confederacy. He had been greatly instrumental in holding it together.

Shivaji had resurrected and re-instituted the ancient Hindu system of government outlined in the *Arthashastra* by Kautilya Chanakya more than two thousand years earlier. It remained prevalent throughout the Marhatta Confederacy with occasional modifications at the discretion of the Peshwa. At best, it was arbitrary and autocratic. Details can be seen in *Administrative System of the Marathas*, by S. N. Sen, Calcutta, 1925, *Institutions of the Maratha People* ', by W. H. Tone, Calcutta, 1918, and '*The Cambridge History of the British Empire vol. IV*, pp. 384 – 399. Quoting an anonymous writer on this period, the latter publication records (pp. 376 – 7), '*Never had there been such intense and general suffering in India; the native states were disorganised, and society on the verge of dissolution; the people crushed by exactions; the country overrun by bandits and its resources wasted by enemies; armed forces existed only to plunder, torture and mutiny; government had ceased to exist; there remained only oppression and misery*'.

Nana Phadnavis died in March 1800. He had controlled much of Marahatta politics for thirty-eight years through guile and manipulation. Vicious infighting broke out almost immediately. The Peshwa and Sindhia joined hands but were defeated by Holkar at Poona in 1802. The capital was ravaged and the Peshwa, Baji Rao, fled to Bassein. There he signed a treaty with the British in which, apart from the agreement to protect each others possessions, he consented to maintain at least six British battalions on his soil; refrain from employing other Europeans in his service; relinquish all claims to Surat; accept British suzerainty over the Gaekwad as well as their arbitration in any disputes with him or the Nizam and to abstain from hostilities or negotiations with any other states without prior approval from the British. After this Arthur Wellesley marched to Poona, evicted Holkar from there and reinstalled the Peshwa in May 1803.

Other Marhatta states were alarmed by the treaty. It had virtually removed all prospects of their acting in concert in the future. Wellesley lost no time and moved against Sindhia to capture the valuable tract of land that lay between the Ganges and the Jumuna, including Agra and Delhi, in August 1803 and then moved into Bundelkhand and Orissa. In the south his brother, Arthur, defeated the combined force of Sindhia and Bhonsle at Assaye. The rest of Sindhia's army was destroyed at Laswari in Alwar state by General Lake. In two separate treaties signed at Deogaon and Surji Arjangaon in December that year, Sindhia agreed to part with most of his territory and accepted a position similar to that assigned to the Peshwa at Bassein.

That left Holkar. He was attacked from three sides with Lake from the north, Arthur Wellesley from the south and General Murray from Gujarat in the west. Each side had its share of successes and failures, with Holkar getting the worst of it, but the British failed to take Bharatpur. The protracted war against the Marhattas was proving to be costly and generating criticism at home. As a result a peace treaty was concluded that left the Rajputana states in Holkar's hands but only for the time being.

In the meantime, Gaekwad of Baroda, who had always been loyal to the British, died. The inevitable struggle for succession ensued. With by now familiar alacrity the Company sent in its army in support of one of the contenders, Anand Rao, and relieved him of a good piece of his territory for the services thus rendered. In April 1805 he was ordered to host and maintain at his expense a British force in his state and submit all control of his external relations to the Company.

A century had passed since Aurangzeb's death. During this entire period there had been no peace in any part of the late emperor's domain for more than a year or two at a stretch. Apart from the big players like the British, the French, the Marhattas, Rohillas and the Nizam, hundereds of lesser warlords had been pillaging and plundering at will. In the anarchy that prevailed, normal business became impossible. Commerce was reduced to minimum and harvesting at best a gamble. The only activity that still offered an opportunity for making a living was war. Service in one of the armies brought in prospects of more or less regular pay and occasional bounty. When service was unavailable in a regular army, young men sought adventure with one of the lesser marauding bands.

As the Company became more assertive and insisted on reducing the size of armies that the local rulers could maintain, there was a surplus of unemployed soldiers. Finding no employment opportunities, the more desperate and the less scrupulous among them engaged in private enterprise of their own, forming gangs that stalked the roads and raided isolated villages. In the absence of any government capable of protecting its citizens, the size and power of the marauding bands grew. The local rajas gave them sanctuary in return for a share in the booty.

Two of the best known among these groups were the *Thugs* and the *Pindaris.* The Company became alarmed when their activities spilled over into its territories and started to hurt its business. It was finally obliged to take action against the menace in the second decade of the nineteenth century under orders from London. There is an English translation of an interesting personal account of these operations in *From Sepoy to Subedar*, by a Company soldier named Sita Ram, published by Routledge & Kegan Paul, London.

Sensing opportunities arising out of the disruption in India, Gurkha hill tribesmen from the Himalayan range had begun raiding the border districts and occupied valuable tracts of land. In 1814 a Company army sent for their chastisement met with severe resistance. It wasn't until two years later that the Gurkhas were finally pacified. They handed over Garhwal, Kumaon and lower Tarai foothills and accepted a British Resident at Khatmandu. The British had earlier obtained ten million rupees (1.1 million pounds) from the nawab of Avadh to punish the Gurkhas but spent the amount elsewhere. He was pressed into parting with a similar amount again for the campaign (*The Cambridge History* ----- p. 575).

By this time trouble was again brewing with the Marahattas. In June 1817, after a show of force, the Peshwa was made to renounce his position as head of the Confederacy and cede the Konkan region and some other parts to the British. The Governor-General, Lord Hastings marched on Gwaliar and forced Sindhia into giving up suzerainty rights over Bhopal, Jaipur, Jodhpur, Udaipur and fifteen other states. The Peshwa showed resentment at the turn of events. He was defeated and deposed. A year later Bhonsle met a similar fate at Nagpur. In the mean time, Holkar had been made to sign a treaty at Mandasor under which he ceded all the territory south of Narbada River and gave up any claim on the Rajput states.

Then it was back to Sindhia. This time he was obliged to part with Ajmer and some more areas. Gaekwad was not spared either and for no particular reason was told to pay for the maintenance of additional British troops in his state and give up Ahmedabad. In 1820 all the remaining Marhatta chiefs along the west coast between Kolhapur and Goa were sent packing and their states taken over. That was the end of the Marhatta Confederacy.

'There can be no doubt that the English and Marhatta Governments could not co-exist in India; for the practical working of the Marhatta system, which was inspired more deeply than has hitherto been recognised by the doctrines of the ancient Hindu text-books of autocracy, was oppressive to the general mass of the people, destitute of moral ideas, and directly antagonistic to the fundamental principles of the Company rule ---------' (*The Cambridge History* --------, p.382). The victor makes all the rules, including those that govern the limits of morality, justice, fair play and sometimes, even logic.

SIND

These were the times of great empire building in Africa and Asia by the European powers. While the rest of them had crossed the seas to establish colonies, the Russians were expanding overland into the steppes of Central Asia. Their progress had been sporadic and slow at first but the technological edge acquired after the industrial revolution gave them immense superiority over the tribal herdsmen that inhabited the region. Their swords and spears were no match to the Russian cannon and later machine guns. The pace of Russian conquest quickened as the nineteenth century progressed. It alarmed the British and they began to worry about the future of Iran and India itself. The Russians had to be kept away from the borders of India at all costs and, at the same time, prevented from gaining access to the warm waters of the Arabian Sea.

The fledgling country of Afghanistan assumed pivotal significance in this game. If India was to be saved then the Russians must be prevented from gaining control of Afghanistan. To forestall such an eventuality, the British decided to back Shah Shuja, the deposed ruler of Afghanistan, who had been ousted by Amir Dost Mohammed Khan from Kabul and had taken refuge in Ludhiana in 1816. A military force was mustered to place him on the throne at Kabul. The borders of British India at the time were not contiguous with Afghanistan. The Mirs of Sind and the Khan of Kalat were bullied into allowing passage of a large force through their territory to attack Afghanistan.

The expedition turned into an unmitigated disaster. Of the entire force only one man, a doctor by the name of Brydon, was able to make it safely back from Kabul to Jalalabad. The Afghans remember the event in a song whose refrain runs, '*Az chil hazar paltan yak kas na raft London*' (Of the forty thousand strong British military force not one man got back to London).

The defeat raised a host of problems for the British. In addition to being a severe blow to their prestige and reputation in India, it was going to provide considerable comfort and encouragement to the Russians. It was also realised that launching any such undertakings through territories belonging to independent rulers in the future was not a satisfactory proposition. The answer lay in annexing all the intervening domains to British India at the earliest opportunity. Punjab was a tough nut to crack under Ranjeet Singh and his European trained and led army, therefore, attention was directed at Sind first.

Sind had remained an independent state, with its capital at Thatta, until 1592 when its Tarkhan rulers were made nominal tributaries to Akbar. A century later, the Kalhora tribe replaced Tarkhans. They had to cede territories west of the Indus to Iran's Nadir Shah. A little later, Ahmed Shah Abdali made upper Sind a part of his Afghan kingdom.

The Kalhoras set up their capital at Hyderabad, a city they founded in 1768. Five years later, they were overthrown by the Talpurs, a Baluchi tribe from southern Punjab, led by Fateh Ali Khan. When he died in 1802, for a time, his three brothers shared the sovereignty. In turn their sons, Subadar Khan, Nasir Khan, Mir Mohammed Khan and Mir Noor Mohammed Khan came to jointly rule the land, with the last named occupying the senior position.

In the north of Sind, another family had established itself at Khairpur at about the same time. In 1838 it was headed by Mir Rustam Khan. The third seat of government in Sind was at Mirpur where Sher Mohammed ruled with blessings, in part, from the Mirs at Hyderabad.

As early as 1555, Portuguese had attacked and destroyed much of Thatta. The East India Company established a 'factory' at Thatta in 1758 but abandoned it after a few years. Later, in 1809 and 1820 the British signed treaties with the Mirs at Hyderabad to exclude the French and other Europeans (including Americans) from the area. The Indus River had aroused great interest as a possible means of transporting trade goods to and from Central Asia.

Colonel Sir Alexander Burnes, along with Lieutenant Wood of the Royal Navy, sailed up the river from Thatta to Kalabagh and then on to Kabul to carry out a survey and gather intelligence. He counted upwards of ten thousand boats, some of them displacing over one thousand tons, down river from Hyderabad alone. A navigation treaty was signed with the Mirs at Hyderabad and Khairpur on condition that no warships or troops would enter the river and no Englishman would be allowed to settle in Sind. These two stipulations were removed from the treaty under duress when the British marched across Sind into Afghanistan.

Having consolidated his position in Punjab, Ranjeet Singh was casting covetous eyes on Sind. He had occupied a fort near Shikarpur and was demanding heavy tribute from the Mirs under threat of invasion. It was an opportunity not to be missed and the British offered to mediate between the two on the condition that the Mirs would agree to the stationing of British troops in Sind and pay for their upkeep. Just at this time, the fateful decision to attack Afghanistan was made in response to a crisis that mostly existed in the British imagination. The results of this misadventure had been far from sanguine as we saw above. It changed the British attitude completely. They were no longer interested in acting as mediators but had decided to annex Sind.

The Mirs were made to sign treaties, one after another, thick and fast. Burnes forced a treaty on Rustam Khan of Khairpur on Christmas Eve 1838 under which he handed over Sukkur, Bhakkar Island in the Indus and control of the state's external relations to the British. He also promised to provide troops to the latter when called upon to do so. Three months later, the Mirs of Hyderabad accepted to dissolve their confederacy and placed Sind under British protection. They also agreed to pay for the stationing of a British force and not to levy toll on any trade by the British plying the Indus. Karachi had already been handed over to them a month earlier. Mirpur's turn came in July 1841 when its Mir accepted British protection in return for payment of annual tribute. This was not a situation that the Mirs would have expected or anticipated when they had declared their independence from the Afghans only a few years earlier.

Another interesting development that took place at this time was the arrival of the Agha Khan in India. Hasan Ali Shah, who was married to the daughter of the Qajari king of Iran, Fateh Ali Shah, fell out of royal favour and settled in Sind in 1840. He is reputed to have provided valuable services to the British when the latter invaded the province shortly afterwards (*Islam in the Indian Subcontinent*, by Annemarie Schimmel, p. 171). A court in Bombay accepted his claim as the spiritual head of the Khoja Ismailis living in Gujarat, Sind, Hunza and Chitral and he then took up residence in Bombay.

In the way of background, Ismailis are a sub-sect of Shiaism. The latter splinter group of Islam formed after the confrontation between the fourth Caliph of Islam, Hazrat Ali and Muawiyyah, the governor of Syria, at Siffin in 657 AD. Hazrat Ali was later assassintated in 661 AD. As Karen Armstrong put it (*Islam: A Short History*, Phoenix Press, London, p. 31) '*The fate of Ali, a man betrayed by his friends as well as his enemies, became a symbol of the inherent injustice of life. From time to time, Muslims who protested against the behaviour of the reigning caliph would retreat from the ummah, like the Kharjiites, and summon all Muslims to join them in the struggle* (jihad) *for higher Islamic standards.*' The assassination of Hazrat Imam Husain, the Prophet's grandson, at the hands of Umayyed troops at Kerbela in 680 AD, was further evidence of inequity, arbitrariness and despotism that had taken over the world of Islam.

The Shia sect subsequently splintered along different lines. The first of these acknowledge Imam Husain's grandson, Zaid, as the fifth and last imam. Known as Zaidis, they ruled Yemen until recently. Other Shias regard Zaid's brother, Mohammed al-Baqir, as the fifth imam. The latter's son, Imam Jaffer-as-Sadik founded the school of Shia jurisprudence that became known as *Fika Jafferia.*

There was further division at the time of the seventh imam. Those that followed the line of Imam Jaffer's son, Musa al-Kazim, to the twelfth imam, Mohammed al-Mehdi, are known as *isna ashari*. It is this branch of Shiaism that has formed the state religion of Iran since 1501 AD. Mohammed al-Mehdi, also known as *imam ghaib*, is not believed to have died but simply became invisible in 874 AD. He continues to guide the *mujtahid* (religious scholars) from the Unseen.

Members of the Ismaili group follow the line of Musa al-Kazim's brother, Ismail (d. circa 765 AD) and are again sub-divided into many factions. Karamatians believe Ismail's son, Mohammed, to be the last imam. In 930 AD, they raided Kaaba and took away *Hajr-e-Aswad* to Bahrein with the result that no Haj was performed for twenty-two years. Banished from there, they formed a small state in Multan for some time. Fatimids, who established a parallel caliphate in Egypt in 969 AD, were also Ismailis as are the Druze in Lebanon.

The Fatimid line split in 1094 when the Egyptians decided to follow Caliph Mustansir's younger son, Mustali. The heir apparent, Nizar, fled to the mountain redoubt of Hasan bin Sabah, founder of the infamous Assassins, at Alamut in Iran. The followers of Mustali later ended up in Yemen. It was the tradesmen and missionaries from Yemen that brought Ismaili Islam to Sind and Gujarat. Its adherents, known as Bohras, accept *Sayyedina* (spiritual leader) as their guide. Unlike the Agha Khan, he does not claim to be the *Imam Hazir* (present imam). Among others, the first Muslim president of the Indian National Congress, Badruddin Tayyabji, and the founder of Pakistan, Mohammed Ali Jinnah, belonged to the Bohra community.

After the fall of Alamut to the Mongols in 1256 AD, the Agha Khan, leader of Nizari Ismailis, continued to live in Iran until obliged to move to Sind. Apart from Pakistan and Bombay, his followers can be found in large numbers in East Africa and Canada. It is an extremely well-organised community that lays great stress on education, particularly that of the women.

Getting back to Sind, it wasn't long before the Mirs of Sind were accused of being disloyal and plotting against the British. The charges were extremely vague and general and no specific instances or evidence was provided. It mattered little. There is no record of the Mirs' side of the story. In accepting the stationing troops at Karachi, Sukkur, Rohri, Shikarpur and approaches to the Bolan Pass the Mirs had themselves provided the means for the conquest of Sind. The British were not going to miss the opportunity. As Sir Charles Napier noted in his diary, '*We have no right to seize Sind, yet we shall do so and a very advantageous piece of rascality it will be.*'

Napier landed at Karachi in April 1842 to make the necessary preparations. He presented the Mirs with a new treaty requiring them to cede the districts of Karachi, Thatta and large chunks of territory in the north to the British and the nawab of Bahawalpur in perpetuity, as well as stamp British imprint on Sind currency. At the same time, the Mir of Khairpur was told to hand over Sukkur and Rohri to the British and all land to the north of these to the nawab of Bahawalpur. Even before sending the drafts of the new treaties to the Mirs, Napier issued a proclamation on 1st December 1842 announcing his intention to occupy the territories named in his 'just demands'.

The Mirs conveyed their acceptance of the new treaties but they were accused of doing so in bad faith. Mir Rustam Khan of Khairpur decided to abdicate in favour of his son, Mohammed Hussain, at this time. Napier had favoured his brother Ali Murad instead because the latter had offered his complete loyalty and services to the British in return. When the tribal chiefs demurred, with Ali Murad in tow, Napier decided on a show of force. Rustam Khan took to the desert with his chiefs. Napier chased after him and destroyed the undefended fort at Imam Garh in January 1843 for no apparent reason. He then invited Rustam and his chiefs to meet him. Fearing a plot, they sent their representatives instead and matters remained unresolved for the time being.

The British highhandedness was raising quite a few hackles in Sind. The Resident at Hyderabad, Major Outram, who had been opposed to Napier's aggressive policies all along, was insulted in the streets and forced out of the city. Napier, in the meantime, had moved his troops to the outskirts of Hyderabad. The Mirs had moved out to Miani where a number of Baluch tribes joined them. On 17th February Napier marched on Miani and after a sharp battle, forced the surrender of the Mirs. Mirpur was taken a month later thus completing the annexation of Lower Sind. It took some time to pacify the province that was mostly a collection of autonomous tribal territories each under its own chief (*wadera*). The system remained more or less the same under the British. Civil administration only extended as far the main towns and cities of the province. The rural areas were left to the local *sirdars* or *waderas*.

It has been suggested by a few that Napier may have experienced guilt and remorse about the capture of Sind. This is altogether fanciful and without any truth. In January 1843 he wrote to Sir James Outram, '*Now I do not agree with you in thinking the Amirs are fools. I think them cunning rascals to a man if measured by our standard of honesty; but assuredly Lord Auckland's policy was not calculated to make them form a higher estimate of us. Well, they saw our defeat and that encouraged them to break existing treaties, it gave them heart, and that they hoped to have a second Caubool affair is as clear to me as the sun now shining ------. Now what is to be done? That which is best for the advancement of good government and well being of the population; we must not sacrifice all this to a minute endeavour, utterly hopeless, I may say impossible, to give to these tyrannical, drunken, debauched, cheating, intriguing, contemptible Ameers, a due portion of the plunder they have amassed from the ruined people they conquered sixty years ago. They are fortunate robbers one and all, and though I most decidedly condemn the way we entered this country (just as honest, however, as that by which the Talpoors got it from the Kalloras) I would equally condemn any policy that allowed these rascals to go on plundering the country to supply their debaucheries after we had raised the hopes of every respectable man in the country* (*Life of Sir Charles Napier, vol. II*, p. 300).

Less than two months after writing this grandiloquent proclamation he handed over Khairpur state to Ali Murad as a reward for services rendered. Sind was made a part of Bombay Presidency in 1849. '*It is allowable to indulge feelings of satisfaction when the course of events brings the fall of barbarians and selfish rulers*,' reflected Lord Ellenbrough, the Governor-General. Britain, he said, had been morally right '*to extend ---- the benefits of a beneficent and enlightened rule*.'

PUNJAB

It may be recalled that in 1799 the Afghan ruler, Shah Zaman, had appointed the Sikh Ranjeet Singh, as his representative in Lahore as a reward for extricating some of his heavy artillery pieces from the mud in Jhelum River and dispatching these to Kabul. Punjab had been ravaged for nearly a hundred years by the marauding armies of the Marahatta, Sikh and Afghan chiefs. Through guile, bluster and intrigue Ranjeet Singh managed to free himself from the Afghan yoke and gradually extended his rule over the entire province.

His success owed much to a combination of many favourable circumstances that enabled the Sikhs, who constituted a small minority of the population, to gain control. Mostly, it was because of a power vacuum in the province. The Mughals had long since ceased to be of any significance. Marhattas had not yet recovered from the catastrophe inflicted upon them at Panipat in 1761 AD and had withdrawn to the south. Ahmed Shah's successors had bickered and fought each other in Afghanistan ever since his passing, leaving Punjab for the taking.

Ranjeet Singh skillfully knitted the Sikh chieftains together and with their help gradually extended his rule over not only the province but Kashmir as well. These were mostly unlettered and wild men, quite unfamiliar with the art of governance. Most of them had their origins among cattle rustlers and highwaymen. To administer the province's financial and revenue matters Ranjeet Singh engaged a Kashmiri Brahmin, Dina Nath and for external relations and negotiations he relied on Fakir Aziz-uddin, a Muslim, whose younger brother, Nur-uddin, acted as the court physician as well as counselor.

When the British squeezed the Marhattas out of northern India, Ranjeet Singh asserted his control over the Malwa Sikh states that lie between Sutlej and Jamuna rivers. In 1806 he captured Ludhiana and followed it up two years later by annexing Faridkot and Ambala. The British were alarmed and felt obliged to extend their protection to the threatened chiefs in Malwa and Sirhind. A treaty was signed in 1809 and Ranjeet Singh withdrew from Faridkot and Ambala but retained some territories across Sutlej. He had seen the military capabilities of the British at first hand that dissuaded him from risking a confrontation with them. To improve the state of his own army he employed forty or so European officers. With their help he turned it into a highly effective fighting force.

With any expansion to the south now denied, Ranjeet Singh turned his attention first to the Gurkhas, from whom he took Kangra in 1811, Jammu a year later and then to the Afghan possessions in the north and west. He captured Attock in 1813 but was repulsed in his first attempt on Kashmir by the Afghan governor and later King Azem Khan. Taking advantage of the interminable struggles being waged at the time for possession of the throne in Kabul that took Azem Khan and his troops out of Kashmir, Ranjeet Singh occupied it in 1819. This ended the Afghan possession of the state that had lasted for sixty-seven years and interrupted the Muslim rule that had been established since 1341.

After repeated efforts, Multan was finally annexed in 1818 when the Afghans were busy fighting the prolonged and bloody civil war between the Saddozai and the Barakzai factions for Kabul. Shah Shuja, the deposed Afghan king living in Ludhiana, ceded all the frontier territories to the west of the Indus in return for Ranjeet Singh's promise of help in regaining Kabul. He was enabled to make his way to Kandhar, via Sind, where Amir Dost Mohammed defeated him, and again he returned to the protection of the British in Ludhiana in 1821.

Ranjeet Singh attacked Peshawar in 1823. Khatak and Yusufzai Pathans gathered near Naushera in support of Azem Khan who camped on the opposite side of the river. A fierce battle raged all day in which, as Ranjeet Singh later admitted, only a disciplined stand by the Gurkhas saved him. For some unexplained reason Azem Khan failed to join the battle and, leaving the Pathans to their fate, returned to Kabul with his troops. Ranjeet Singh ransacked and ravaged Peshawar in typical Sikh fashion and then left it in the hands of Yar Mohammed, one of Azem Khan's estranged brothers, as a tributary. The devastation wreaked on Peshawar was so complete that no architectural monuments of any value were left standing that could provide a link or testify to its antiquity or past grandeur.

The Pathans did not take kindly to Sikh rule and rebellions sprang up all over. Yar Mohammed was killed in one of these uprisings and was replaced by his renegade brother Sultan Mohammed from whom the last ruling family of Afghanistan is descended. While the proud tribesmen were dying to rid themselves of the Sikh yoke, their leaders were falling over each to sell their souls to the enemy.

The Sikh rule in Peshawar was interrupted for a while by a remarkable Muslim reformer (*mujaddid*) named Syed Ahmed Barelvi. He had been in the service of the Pathan soldier of fortune, Amir Khan, who had joined the Marhattas and later the British in their operations against the Pindaris. After the campaign, Amir Khan was made the nawab of Tonk in Central India and his mercenary force was disbanded. Syed Ahmed went to Delhi and was profoundly affected by the decline and degradation of the Muslims that he witnessed. It led him to the conclusion that their salvation lay in returning to the basic message that was in the Koran, without any amalgamation with subsequent human interpretations and elaborations. In times of extreme difficulty religion has always offered hope and sustenance to people in distress. The time was right and Syed Ahmed's message fell on fertile ground, making him exceedingly popular.

He left for Haj in 1822 where he was deeply influenced by the puritanical Wahabi movement. Returning four years later, he called for a holy struggle against the non-believers who were displacing the Muslim supremacy. There was little hope left in India itself. He turned to Afghanistan but was rebuffed in Kandhar. With his one thousand followers he later founded a colony north of Swabi in Yusufzai territory. Pathan tribesmen flocked under his banner and with their help he defeated a Sikh force led by Budh Singh Sandhawalia, an associate of Ranjeet Singh, who was killed in the battle. In 1829 he attacked and briefly occupied Peshawar, killing the puppet Barakzai governor, Yar Mohammed and evicting Ranjeet Singh's French General Ventura.

There were further, mostly inconclusive, battles with the Sikhs who had been obliged to withdraw east of the Indus. In 1831 the Yusufzai's deserted him, just as they had done with another Pathan reformer, Pir Bayazeed (Pir Roshaan) in 1581. Left only with a small band of followers, Syed Ahmed was surprised and killed by the Sikhs at Balakot. The Yusufzais took care of the rest of his followers and deputies that were left among them, killing each and every one, as they slept on a winter night.

Thus ended the only large-scale resistance that was put up strictly in the name of Islam, against the non-Muslim advance in India. All the rest of the struggles had been primarily motivated by personal or individual gain. There were many Muslims in Ranjeet Singh's army and their ratio in the British armies was even higher. Ranjeet Singh's highly effective artillery was exclusively officered and manned by Muslims. It was not because the

Muslims were devoid of any religious feeling. After nearly one hundred years of incessant strife, instability and lawlessness, few opportunities for gainful employment existed, other than the profession of arms. Most able-bodied young men had little choice but to join whichever army provided the best opportunity. At times, it must have looked as if the only profitable business left in India was making war.

In 1834 Ranjeet Singh appointed his favourite General Hari Singh as governor of Peshawar, in place of Sultan Mohammed, who instituted a rule of terror in the province in the usual Sikh style. When he started to encroach further into Afghanistan and build fortifications in the approaches to Khaibar Pass, Amir Dost Mohammed Khan, who had taken over Kabul after the death of Azem Kham, sent a force from Kabul under his son Akbar Khan in April 1837. He routed the Sikh army near Jamrud but for reasons that are not clear returned to Kabul without making any attempt to retake Peshawar. Hari Singh was killed in the battle. A greatly disturbed Ranjeet Singh sent in a new army under Dhyan Singh and appointed the barbarous Italian General Avitable as governor whose favourite punishment for almost any crime was to order the convicts to be hanged from the minarets of Peshawar mosques.

The British concluded a tripartite treaty with Ranjeet Singh and Shah Shuja in June 1838. The latter was made to give up claims on Kashmir, Peshawar, Bannu, Dera Imail Khan, Dera Ghazi Khan and Multan, that had been a part of Afghanistan since Ahmed Shah's days, in favour of Ranjeet Singh. He also agreed that the question of Ranjeet Singh's claim to Shikarpur and other parts of Sind should be resolved in accordance with the wishes of the British and at their convenience. In addition, he was to pay two lakh rupees a year to Ranjeet Singh for the help that he had promised to provide in the projected invasion of Afghanistan. The British would guarantee this payment.

The shah also agreed to renounce all Afghan claims to Sind in the future. The Mirs would be permitted to keep Sind but will pay an agreed sum to Ranjeet Singh for a promise not to attack them. In return for all this, Shah Shuja would be installed on the throne of what was left of Ahmed Shah's domain that in his time had extended over all the territories that lay between the Indus and Khorasan, including Sind and Baluchistan.

It must be one of most unconscionable sell-outs of national interests in history and illustrates the depths of betrayal and treachery some men would descend to in the hope of making personal gain. As should have been evident from the start, it was an unworkable arrangement. It might have been feasible to put Shah Shuja on the throne but there was no way to ensure that he would remain there unless the British intended to maintain a substantial permanent presence in the country. The only gainer in the whole affair was Ranjeet Singh whose contribution was the least of all.

If the British were worried about the Russian advance, they could not possibly live with a strong Sikh state in India that was not subject to their will. It could only mean that at best the treaty was negotiated as a temporary expediency and the British would soon find some excuse not to honour it. The Mirs of Sind, who stood to lose the most, were not even apprised of the arrangement until a month after the treaty had been signed. Another factor involved in the equation was the treaty of Tehran signed between Iran and the British in 1814. As per its terms Iran had undertaken to come to the aid of the British and attack Afghanistan in case the latter ventured into India at any time.

The underlying consideration in the British policy is summed up in a letter that J. R. Colvin, one of the policy makers for Governor-General, Lord Auckland, wrote to Alexander Burnes on 26th July 1837, '*A consolidated and powerful Mahommedan State on our frontier might be anything rather than safe and useful to us. The existing division of strength seems far preferable, excepting as it adds to the risk of Herat's being attacked by Persia*' (*The Cambridge History* ------, p 491). In a similar vein, Sir Fredrick Currie, the chief secretary to the Company Government, wrote to the British Resident in Punjab, Major Broadfoot, on 19th January 1845, '*I imagine we shall be forced to cross the Sutlej sooner or later, and you will see we are sending troops for whatever may turn up. We must not have a Mohammedan power on this side of Attock. The Rajputs of the hills* (Dogras) *could not hold the Punjab, and if it cannot be Sikh, it must, I suppose, be British*' ('*How the Sikhs Lost their Kingdom,*' by Khushwant Singh, UBS Publishers, Delhi, 1996, p. 94).

British motives in not allowing the rise in power of a Muslim state in the region are unclear. It may be because they regarded the Muslims as intrinsically hostile and potentially a greater threat to their interests in the area. Whatever the reason, mistrust and anti-Muslim feelings among the British, though not always overtly apparent, have remained a constant in history.

A total of four different armies marched towards Afghanistan in January 1839. Since Ranjeet Singh never trusted the British, he refused to allow them passage through Punjab. The only other option was to go through Sind. The Mirs had little choice but to acquiesce. The British force from Bombay marched up the Indus from the south while the second British army assembled at Ferozepur. Shah Shuja's contingent from Ludhiana, traversing through Bahawalpur, joined up with the main body at Sukkur. The combined force then marched to Kandhar, via Quetta, after making arrangements with the Khan of Kalat. It did not experience much difficulty in installing Shah Shuja on the Kabul throne.

Amir Dost Mohammed surrendered himself after some desultory resistance and was deported to Calcutta. It was his son, Akbar Khan, who carried on the fight and eventually inflicted an ignominious defeat on the British, resulting in total destruction of their army in Afghanistan. Shah Shuja was killed and the British extricated themselves by making a deal with Amir Dost Mohammed in the summer of 1842.

In the meantime, Ranjeet Singh had died at the end of June 1839 due mainly to causes connected with excessive indulgence in drink, drugs and women. All the baseness and barbarity associated with the Sikh rule made itself evident in the events that followed. The eldest son, Kharak Singh, an imbecile of a man who was even more given to opium, drinking and debauchery than his father, succeeded him. Ranjeet Singh had a number of other sons from many different wives and concubines. Most of these were believed to be illegitimate. One of them, Sher Singh, disputed Kharak Singh's claim even before the old chief's body was cremated.

Almost at the same time, Kharak Singh's impetuous young son, Nao Nihal Singh, too jumped into the fray and announced his intentions to exercise power on behalf of his incompetent father. Each of the contenders had their backers among Ranjeet Singh's courtiers, not to mention the British who waited in the wings. A convoluted and contorted tale of vicious intrigue, betrayal and brutal murders began to unfold. Space does not permit description of all of its twisted and sordid details. Only the more significant events will be mentioned, as briefly as possible, to give an idea of the state of affairs that prevailed.

Nao Nehal Singh, impatient and jealous of his father's adviser Chet Singh Bajwa, in conspiracy with the two powerful factions led by Dogra and Sandhawalia brothers, bribed the guards to enter his father's sleeping quarters and disemboweled Chet Singh in the former's presence. All of Chet Singh's appointees and accomplices were killed or imprisoned. The message was clear. Kharak Singh abdicated in favour of Nao Nihal Singh.

Kharak Singh died shortly afterwards, in November 1840, and was cremated along with two of his widows and eleven concubines, as per the *sattee* ritual. On his way back to Lahore Fort from his father's funeral, Nao Nehal Singh also perished when the inner arch of Roshanai Darwaza fell on him. The Chief Minister, Dhyan Singh Dogra, arranged for afore-mentioned Sher Singh to take the reins of power. (The Dogras, who played a very significant part in the events subsequent to the death of Ranjeet Singh, were not Sikhs but Hindu Rajputs).

Kharak Singh's widow, Chand Kaur, refused to go along with the arrangement and installed herself as *Malika Mukadis* (Holy Empress). When Sher Singh marched on Lahore, the Sikh army that had not been paid for many months went over to him. Lahore was taken and its shops and houses looted for many days. Chand Kaur agreed to marry Sher Singh but before that could happen she was murdered in her sleep. It is suspected that Chand Kaur's accomplice, Gulab Singh Dogra (Dhyan Singh's brother and at times rival), who later purchased Kashmir from the British, had stolen the state treasure and might have arranged the murder (*How the Sikhs Lost their Kingdom*, p.49).

With the treasury empty, Sher Singh was unable to clear the arrears of pay of the army. The soldiers mutinied, murdering the officers and plundering the city again for two months. Almost all the European officers in the Sikh army had left by then and the soldiers, contemptuous and distrustful of their corrupt superiors, took it upon themselves to make all the decisions and run the army. Sher Singh, happy with his women and wine, decided to mount an expedition to attack Gilgit and Tibet to get the troublesome troops out of his front yard. It did not do him much good. He was murdered by his newfound friend and companion, Ajit Singh Sandhawalia, along with his eleven year old son, Partap Singh. The heads of the father and son were then mounted on spears and paraded through the city.

The Sandhawalias also caught up with their old foe, Dhyan Singh Dogra, who had wielded considerable influence with Ranjeet Singh as well as Sher Singh, and murdered him in cold blood. Dhyan Singh's brother, Suchet Singh and son, Hira Singh, escaped and took refuge with the army. On promise of pay rise, the soldiers stormed Lahore Fort on 15th September 1843. There was an orgy of blood-letting in which more than six hundred Sandhawalias and their supporters were butchered in revenge for the earlier killings. Those that survived crossed the Sutlej to the protection of the British.

Ranjeet Singh's youngest son, six-year old Daleep Singh, was made the new ruler with Hira Singh Dogra acting as his mentor and chief minister. Pundits at the court duly prophesied that Daleep Singh would be as illustrious a conqueror as Alexander the Great. Hira Singh's uncle, Suchet Singh, who had an on-going liaison with Daleep Singh's comely mother, Rani Jindan, felt left out. Ranjeet Singh's remaining two sons, Peshawra and Kashmira were also unhappy with the arrangement. Adding to this confusing picture were Jawahar Singh, whose influence was by virtue of being Rani Jindan's brother, and Pundit Jalla, who had been Hira Singh's tutor.

All of them constantly intrigued against each other but the real power brokers were now the *panches* (elected representatives of soldiers) who had become the final arbiters in the process. This is not altogether uncommon in situations where politicians lose sight of the collective or national aim for the sake of personal ambition. It creates room for third parties to muscle in and take over. When Suchet Singh tried to get the army on his side, Hira Singh countered by offering each soldier a piece of gold, which did the trick. Suchet Singh was duly murdered along with his supporters.

Atar Singh Sandhawalia then rejoined Kashmira and Peshawra in revolt. They were defeated and only Peshawra managed to escape with his life and seek asylum with the British. There were revolts also in Kashmir, Multan and Peshawar that were put down for the time being. Resentful of Hira Singh's growing power, Rani Jindan, who had taken a new lover in Lal Singh, pleaded with the army for help. Hira Singh tried to escape to join his uncle, Gulab Singh Dogra, in Jammu but was intercepted and killed along with his supporters that included Pundit Jalla. Their heads were impaled on spears and duly paraded through the streets of Lahore on 21st December 1844. Hira Singh's memory is preserved in the market (Hira Mandi) named after him in Lahore that became a den of prostitution.

By this time, what little government there had been in Punjab was gone. It had given way to mismanagement and anarchy of the worst order. The state appeared to exist only to support the army whose burden became unbearable by the day. To get an idea of what this meant, soldiers in the best-paid British East India Company's army at the time drew a salary of eight rupees a month, as compared with twelve and half rupees per month received by the Sikh soldiers. This was in addition to all the bonuses and prize money that were distributed periodically. The army itself was without any discipline and out of the control of its officers.

A century of lawlessness had put a virtual end to all trade and agriculture in the province. Usurpation and extortion had depleted all private savings. The entire province's wealth lay in the hands of the Sikh chieftains. As sources of revenue dried up, the state treasury too became empty. The situation could not be redeemed by invading the neighbouring states, as Ranjeet Singh had done to pay his troops, because these too were by now equally destitute. Inevitably, the Sikhs turned on each other, starting with Gulab Singh and his wealth that was stashed in Jammu.

In July 1845 Peshawra Singh, the only other surviving son of Ranjeet Singh, tricked his way into Attock Fort and staked his claim to the throne. Rani Jindan and Jawahar Singh sent a detachment of troops to bring him to Lahore for a settlement. On the way, he was strangled to death. Disgusted, the army *panches* decided to take power directly into their own hands. They ordered the Rani and her brother brought before them in Mian Mir Cantonment outside Lahore where Jawahar Singh was hacked to death on arrival. In his place they appointed Lal Singh as chief minister with Tej Singh as the army chief ---- both of them were secretly aligned with the British.

The weakness and disruption at Lahore induced the British to mass troops along the Sutlej. They waited for the weather to turn cool before starting the campaign to annex Punjab. The Governor-General, Lord Hardinge, arrived to take personal command of the operation. Only about half of the troops available to the Sikhs, led by Lal Singh and Tej Singh, were dispatched to meet the threat. Raja Gulab Singh of Jammu decided to keep out of the war altogether.

The first encounter at Murki on 21st December 1845 was bloody but indecisive. That night Lal Singh decamped, leaving his troops to their fate. The next day there was another prolonged and bloody clash at Ferozeshehr that carried well into the night. By this time the British were out of ammunition and staring defeat in the face. Inexplicably the next morning Tej Singh, instead of delivering a *coup de grace*, ordered his army to withdraw. Squabbles broke out in the Sikh camp, giving the British an easy victory.

After a short lull that gave time to the British to get reinforcements, there were further engagements at Aliwal and Sabraon. It was the same story of treachery and betrayal, with Tej Singh and Lal Singh doing their best to ensure that the British did not suffer too much inconvenience. Rani Jindan invited Gulab Singh Dogra to Lahore for help. He made sure that provisions and reinforcements destined for the army did not reach where they were needed. He also wasted no time in opening up negotiations with the British. As at Murki, Lal Singh once again left the troops to their fate at Sabraon. The leaderless army suffered terrible casualties and was comprehensively defeated.

The road to Lahore was now clear for the British. The Sikh chieftains brought young Daleep Singh to make his submission to the Governor-General camped at the village of Lalliani a few miles south of Lahore. They ceded all the territory between Sutlej and Bias Rivers, agreed to pay fifteen million rupees in war reparations, surrendered all the guns and pledged to reduce the size of the Sikh army to a total of 20,000 infantry and 12,000 cavalry. Kashmir and Hazara were separated from the Sikh kingdom and sold to Gulab Singh Dogra for one million pounds.

As explained to Queen Victoria by Henry Hardinge himself, the sale was considered to be a convenient way to recover most of the costs of the First Sikh War for which the Sikhs themselves were unable to pay ('*The Letters of Queen Victoria. A Selection of Her Majesty's Correspondence between the Years 1837 and 1861. Vol II. 1844 – 1853*' by A. C Benson & Viscount Esher, London, 1908, pp. 73 – 74). When Gulab Singh was unable to bring the Hazara inhabitants to submit, as compensation, he was awarded two million rupees from the Sikh treasury along with additional territory around Jammu and the sale price was reduced by twenty five per cent.

Later, when Shaikh Imad-uddin, the governor of Kashmir, barred Gulab Singh's entry into the valley, he again turned to the British Agent, Henry Lawrence, for help. At the behest of the latter, a Sikh army of twenty thousand secured Kashmir for the Dogra. The Treaty of Lahore was formally signed on 8th March 1846. Lal Singh and rest of the Sikh collaborators feared for their lives after signing the treaty and asked for British protection. A British army contingent was provided to them in Lahore at an annual rent of twenty-two thousand pounds.

The intrigues and machinations at the Sikh court did not end with the ignominious surrender but continued unabated. There is seldom any honour among men who sell their souls. Soon, Lal Singh managed to earn displeasure of the British. He was found guilty of intriguing against Gulab Singh and was expelled from Punjab.

Lord Hardinge returned to Lahore in December that year to lay down further conditions that gave the British Agent absolute powers over the Sikh government. He also took young Daleep Singh under British control and when Rani Jindan objected, excuses were found to have her pensioned off to Benares. The incident added to the resentment that was already building up among the Sikhs. Shortly afterwards an attempt was made to replace the governor of Multan, Moolraj, when he expressed his inability to meet the increased demand in annual payment. It backfired and rebellious troops murdered the British officers who had been sent to Multan with Gurkha troops to install the new governor.

At this point, there was a clear division among the Sikhs with regards to their attitude towards the British. Their chiefs were for the latter because it ensured preservation of their *jageers* and privileged positions. The soldiers, on the other hand, were unhappy because their lavish pay scales had been drastically curtailed after the British intervention. The British themselves were also not satisfied with the existing situation in Punjab and decided to annex the province to the rest of British India.

The mutiny in Multan provided the needed excuse for them to intervene militarily. They implicated the governor of Peshawar, Chattar Singh Atariwala, whose daughter was betrothed to Daleep Singh, in the murder of an American in Haripur. Chattar Singh's son, Sher Singh, was leading a Sikh contingent at this time to recover Multan from Moolraj. He claimed that officers from the accompanying British force had tried to arrest him through trickery. The British had also made similar moves earlier in Attock, Amritsar and Lahore arresting any one suspected of being unsympathetic to their cause.

As far as Lord Dalhousie, the new governor-general, was concerned a state of war now existed without specifying precisely with whom ---- Moolraj, Chattar Singh or the state of Punjab. The three were by no means acting in concert at this time. Lord Gough, the British commander-in-chief, crossed the Sutlej with a large force in November 1848 and occupied Lahore without meeting any resistance. In fact, they found most of the Sikh chiefs, like Lehna Singh Majithia to be supportive and loyal.

Sher Singh and his father Chattar Singh Atariwala had joined forces to the west of River Chenab. After a series of short, sharp but inconclusive battles at Ram Nagar, Sadulapur, Rasul and Chelianwala, the British finally pinned down and decisively defeated the Sikh army outside Gujarat on 21st February 1849. Gulab Singh Dogra played a significant role, in support of the British, during the campaign and was duly rewarded for his services. Chattar Singh and Sher Singh surrendered with what were left of their troops near Rawalpindi on 14th March and Punjab was formally annexed through a proclamation read out in Lahore on 29th March 1849.

SUPERIOR RACE

The British had annexed the island of Ceylon (present day Sri Lanka) in stages between 1798 and 1815 when the king of Kandy was deported to India. After the conquest of Punjab only Burma remained outside the British purview in the sub-continent. Parts of it, including the Chittagong hill tracts, Arakan, Tenesseram, Manipur and Assam had already been incorporated in 1824. The rest of Burma was taken over in 1852. This was by no means the end of British expansion. Lord Dalhousie, appointed governor-general in 1847, found an ingenious way to take over the territories of even those Indian states that had already submitted to British rule, by passing a law, sometimes referred to as the doctrine of 'lapse', under which if a ruler died without leaving a direct male heir his state would be forfeited to the Company. In this way he was able to acquire Sattara, Sambalpur, Jhansi and Nagpur during his nine-year rule. In February 1856, he ordered the largest and the richest state in India, Avadh, to be annexed and its nawab deported to Calcutta on charges of mismanagement. These measures made the rulers of the rest of the 675 states in India feel quite insecure and unhappy.

Lord Dalhousie and his successor, Lord Canning, cared little about such feelings. The British were all powerful and power has its own brand of disdain and arrogance that comes with it. They saw the Indians as uncivilised and belonging to an inferior race. The well-known nineteenth century Evangelist and anti-slavery crusader, William Wilberforce, noted about Hinduism: '*Our religion is sublime, pure and beneficent. Theirs is mean, licentious and cruel* ------' (*British Attitudes Towards India*, by G.D. Beace, Oxford University Press, 1961, p.82). Brigadier John Jacob, a celebrated cavalry officer in India, assumed that the British were masters of the country because they were 'superior beings by nature to the Asiatic'.

The mistreatment of Indians by the British was on a grand scale. The correspondent for *The Times,* Sir William Howard Russell, himself an Irishman, was 'shocked to see two native servants, covered with plasters and bandages, and bloody, who were lying on *charpais* moaning'. They were the servants of an Englishman who had just 'licked' them. Even when not beaten, 'the tones in which they were spoken to have rarely one note of kindness, often many of anger in them' (*My Diary in India in the year 1858-9*, London 1960, by W. H Russell). A British subaltern, angry with his servant for not cleaning his boots properly, kicked him until he died. The next day *The Delhi Gazette* wrote an editorial, commiserating with him and condemning the wretch for causing needless distress to the officer by dying during the beating! These were by no means some isolated cases but more often the norm.

In the campaign against Chitral in 1895, there were fears that the newly introduced .303 rifle bullets were not as effective against the charging Pathans as the earlier .457 ammunition. A series of tests were carried out to determine if this was indeed the case. In each of these, Pathan prisoners were executed at different ranges, using the two types of ammunition and their relative effects compared after post mortems (*Raj*, p. 410). Ironically, it wasn't long after this that Rudyard Kipling was writing about 'The White Man's Burden' '---- *piously sacrificing the flower of white talent*' in the effort to civilise what were, according to him, the inferior races, '*Send forth the best ye breed*' to emancipate the *'Half devil and half child*'.

The Europeans' haughty superciliousness manifested itself in different ways. Many of them, for instance, dismissed the ruins of Kanauj as 'nothing but old bricks and rubbish'. Others gave picnic breakfasts in mosques and danced quadrilles to the music of regimental bands on the marble terrace beside the mausoleum of Mumtaz Mahal in Agra. Governor General William Bentinck had even proposed. '*We should pull down the Taj Mahal at Agra and sell the blocks of marble*' (*My Diary in India*, p.77). Two million acres of lands donated to mosques, madrassas and Muslim shrines, as *waqf*, were confiscated between 1828 and 1840. Some of these were used for building new churches. Often old mosques were given to missionaries to be used as residences (*The Last Mughal*, by William Dalrymple, Bloomsbury, London, 2006, p. 69)

They were shocked if a 'nigger' tried to enter the railway carriage in which a white man was seated, just as they were at the thought of Indians being admitted to white men's clubs as members rather than as servants. Some of these institutions even had signs posted on their gates, 'Dogs and Indians not Admitted'. Surprisingly, some of these institutions continued to maintain their exclusivity long after India became independent, as the writer discovered at the Cochin Club in 1954. They preferred to live in spacious bungalows in exclusive housing estates, euphemistically called the 'civil lines', some distance removed from the areas inhabited by the natives. Any European not conforming to this code or found fraternizing with the natives was quickly put right and sometimes ostrecised ---- as the remarkable Maverick orientalist and historian H.G. Raverty was to discover to his discomfort during his time in Punjab and the the Frontier.

British soldiers with Indian wives were not permitted to take them and their children back to England and were forced to leave them behind. It was important to maintain the 'purity' of the British race. The ugly streak of racism inherent in the European culture was in full bloom, frequently in distasteful colours. Even the pages of some of the diaries kept by the British in India that contained accounts of close social contacts with the natives have been found to be torn out by their descendants to avoid the stigma attached with such association.

The disease of racism has been the bane endemic among the white people throughout the ages. Nowhere was it more apparent than in the United States. The country was built on the backs of slaves from Africa. Twelve million of them were forcibly transported in ships specially built to carry slaves under the most abominable conditions. Three million of them perished before reaching their destination. Slavery remained Britain's principal trade for over two hundred years. The barbarity had the sanction of the church. It was justified on the grounds that the slaves possessed no soul, hence, they could be treated in any inhuman way (see *Rough Crossings: Britain, the Slaves and American Revolution* by Simon Schama, BBC Books, London, 2006).

Racism did not end with the abolition of slavery in the West in the nineteenth century. Lynching of blacks was not made a crime in many states of the US for another hundred years after that. According to official record, a total of 4,872 black people were lynched legally in village and town squares and other public places across America between 1882 and 1955 ---- often for such petty crimes as cursing a white man. The actual total, including unrecorded cases was far greater, probably three times as many. The slaves were bought and sold like cattle and not treated much better on the plantations. They were not allowed to speak their own languages, practice their religion and could not have even their own names. They were forbidden to read or write and allowed to attend schools only in comparatively recent times.

It was the intense rivalry of the 'cold war' with the Soviet Union after World War II that eventually obliged the officially sanctioned segregation of the blacks in schools, colleges, buses and other public places in the United States to be brought to an end. It was done in the face of often violent local opposition, because such overt racism made America look bad, relative to the communists, in the eyes of the non-white people of the world. The persecution of Blacks is by no means over. They still face hostility, prejudice and isolation. Their churches are still burnt in USA with regular monotony.

It is not only the blacks that suffered at the hands of virulent racism intrinsic among the Europeans. Entire populations of the original inhabitants of West Indies, as also the Hottentot race in South Africa, were completely wiped out after the arrival of white settlers. The aboriginal peoples of North America and Australia were decimated in the genocide that accompanied colonization of their territories. These days, it is the Arabs and Muslims that are bearing the brunt of it, treated with intense dislike, even hatred and contemptuously dubbed as rag-heads, Habibs, sand niggers and Hajis in the popular lexicon (see *Muslims and the West: A Muslim Perspective* by the author).

Race and religion have remained inextricably intertwined in the history of both Judaism and Christianity. Based on the injunctions in the Old Testament related to the Israelites, the Jews believe themselves to be the 'chosen people of God'. The orthodox among them also claim that to be a Jew one has to be born to Jewish parents. Later, the Roman Catholic Church declared that Jews were no longer the chosen people since they had deviated from the 'true path' and the status now belonged to the Christians. With the advent of Protestantism this too became a matter of dispute since its adherents believed that they were the exclusive inheritors of this right. Now it is the Evangelists in America who think they are the 'chosen people' with the divine mission 'to deliver the world to God's Dominion' ---- the assumption being that God cannot bring this about without their help.

It would be a serious misconception that attitudes may have changed and religion may no longer play a significant part in politics in the West. To know the reality one only has to look at President Bush's numerous speeches during his two terms in office or Barack Obama's strenuous efforts to convince the voters that he was a practicing Christian and nothing else.

Chris Hedges, one time foreign correspondent for the *New York Times* and the author of *War Is a Force That Gives Us Meaning* and *Losing Moses on the Freeway*, attended the annual convention of the National Religious Broadcasters in Anaheim, California, along with some 1,600 Christian radio and television personalities who claim to reach up to 141 million listeners and viewers. He has described its proceedings in the May 2005 issue of the *Harpers Magazine*.

According to him, the disparate sects belonging to the Christian revivalism in America have joined hands in a movement for gaining political power, known as 'Dominionism'. They claim that Jesus has called them to build Christian dominion over the nation and, eventually, throughout the world. America will become an agent of God, and all political and intellectual opponents of America's Christian leaders the agents of Satan. The Ten Commandments will form the basis of its legal system, Creationism and 'Christian values' will be the basis of the educational system. Aside from its proselytizing mandate, the federal government will be reduced to the protection of property rights and 'homeland' security. A number of influential Dominionists advocate the death penalty for a host of 'moral crimes,' including apostasy, blasphemy, sodomy, and witchcraft. The only legitimate voices in this state will be Christian. All others will be silenced.

'---------- *the convention is meant to serve as a rallying cry for a new and particularly militant movement in Christian politics, one that is sometimes mistaken for another outbreak of mere revivalism. In fact, this movement is a curious hybrid of fundamentalists, Pentecostals, Southern Baptists, conservative Catholics, Charismatics, and other evangelicals, all of whom are at war doctrinally but who nonetheless share a belief that America is destined to become a Christian nation, led by Christian men who are in turn directed by God.* --------

At a Sunday morning breakfast during the convention, hosted by the Israeli Ministry of Tourism, ----- *American churchgoing people are seated at round tables* ---- *I count no more than half a dozen people who are not white. On the platform is a huge picture of the Dome of the Rock, the spot in Jerusalem where the third Temple will be rebuilt to herald, at least according to the Christians in the room, the second coming of Christ.*

'*The strange alliance in this case is premised upon the Dominionist belief that Israel must rule the biblical land in order for Christ to return, though when he does, all Jews who do not convert to Christianity supposedly will be incinerated as the believers are lifted into heaven; all this is courteously left unmentioned at the breakfast.* -------'

'Christian Right' in America is by no means a fringe group but very much mainstream and exercises an inceasingly inordinate amount of influence on her politics, particularly in the Republican Party. It is credited with putting Presidents Ronald Reagan, George Bush Senior and later his son, Bush Junior, in the Whitehouse. In 2006, no less than 130 members of the House of Representatives were avowed 'born-again' Christians.

Getting back to India, Sir William Russell observed in *My Diary in India* (p. 51), '*The fact is, I fear, that the favourites of Heaven, the civilisers of the world* ---- *are naturally the most intolerant in the world* ----' He also quotes a British army major as saying, '*By Jove! Sir, Those niggers are such a confounded lazy sensual set, cramming themselves with ghee and sweetmeats, and smoking their cursed chillums all day and all night, that you might as well think to train pigs.*'

This was a sea change from the days when Englishmen vied with each other to emulate the style, manners and customs of Muslim aristocracy in particular. It was estimated that until the end of the eighteenth century at least one in three British men in India lived with Indian women and had taken on Indian ways, even religions (see *White Mughals*, a fascinating account of the lives of the earlier British in India by William Dalrymple, Harper Collins, London). Now, Indian culture was much less respected than mocked at by British officials. Lord Macaulay, a member of the Governor General's council, ridiculed Hindu 'medical doctrines that would disgrace an English farrier. ---- Astronomy, which would be laughed at by girls at an English boarding school ---- History abounding with kings thirty feet high, and reigns thirty thousand years long ---- and Geography, made up of seas of treacle and butter.'

A long time resident in India, Frank Brown, wrote home in 1857, 'If a man who left this country thirty years ago were now to visit it he would scarcely credit the changes he would witness in the treatment of the Natives, high and low. The English were not then the masters everywhere. Now they are, restraint is cast away ---- and they display a supercilious arrogance and contempt of the people.'

More and more Britons considered it their divine obligation to set the Indians on the right path now that they had full power over them. As *The Edinburgh Review* put it at the time, '*---- it was the glorious destiny of England to govern, to civilize, to educate and to improve the innumerable tribes and races whom Providence had placed beneath her scepter.*'

Missionaries that had not been allowed in India in the eighteenth century had opened schools and were preaching in ever-increasing numbers. They looked to the day 'when all men would embrace Christianity and turn against their heathen gods.' Many of the British military officers and civil officials too considered it their duty to spread the Gospel.

The commissioner of Peshawar, Herbert Edwardes, believed that India had been given to England rather than to Portugal or France because England had made 'the greatest effort to preserve the Christian religion in its purest apostolic form.' Judge Robert Tucker set up large stone columns inscribed with the ten commandments in Urdu, Hindi, Persian and English on both sides of the road leading to Fatehpur and read Bible to large crowds of natives assembled in the courts' compound two or three times a week.

One British account of the period exulted: '*The missionary is truly the regenerator of India. The land is being leavened, and Hindooism is everywhere being undermined. Great will some day, in God's appointed time, be the fall of it. The time appears to have come when earnest consideration should be given to the question whether or not all men should embrace the same religion.*' The wife of the commissioner of Avadh, Honoria Lawrence, proclaimed, '*There is something very oppressive in being surrounded by heathen and Mohammedan darkness, in seeing idol worship all around. When you see the deep and debasing hold these principles have on the people, it is difficult to believe they can ever be freed from it.*'

In the end, despite all the efforts, conversions to Christianity were few and far between. Those that did convert were almost exclusively from among the Untouchables of the Hindu caste system and did so for mainly pecuniary and other benefits. Sometimes described as 'Rice Christians', they received incentives and preferential treatment by the British in terms of education, job opportunities and some paltry pecuniary rewards but it did not improve their position in society vis-a-vis the Hindus or the British in any way. For them they still remained Untouchable Outcastes and 'niggers'. The zealous attempts at proselytizing spread fear among both the Hindus and Muslims that the Company was about to embark upon a campaign of forced conversions. Their religion and culture now appeared under threat.

History has an uncanny way of repeating itself. After the destruction and occupation of Iraq by the United States and Britain in 2003 missionaries, mostly Evangelical and Baptist, have flocked there in their droves to spread the message despite the risk that it entails. In order not to cause alarm among the local Muslims, the missionaries dye their hair black and dress like the Arabs. Church services are held in secret. Converts are enticed with monetary rewards and job offers which are hard to come by in the devastated land. They have also been active in Afghanistan ever since it too was occupied, using humanitarian organizations as cover, but have not met with much success for various reasons. It is all done in the Biblical belief that once all the people are converted it will hasten the second coming of Christ and the 'Kingdom of God'. More likely, it will only lead to much needless strife and tragedy because Islam and the Muslims in these two countries are not nearly as tolerant as had been the case in the Indian sub-continent.

Company officials in India were increasingly riding rough-shod over local religious practices, customs and traditions in the name of reforms. Even when well-intended, these were viewed with suspicion and were not well-received. Such measures as Lord Wellesley's banning of infant sacrifice by throwing them into the Ganges by the Hindus, the abolition of *sattee* and allowing Hindu widows to re-marry by Bentinck in 1827 were perceived as threatening the Hindu *dharma* (faith). Orthodox Hindus were deeply offended by this intrusion and viewed it as part of a plan by the Company to impose Christianity on India. All kinds of rumours began to circulate, giving rise to misgivings and unease among the natives.

The practice of allowing prisoners in jails to prepare their own meals was abolished in favour of communal cooking. It was highly repugnant to Hindus who did not eat food unless it was prepared by one of their own caste or sub-caste. Muslim prisoners were ordered to shave their beards and only one tooth brush was provided that everyone must use. Under a new law any army unit could be ordered to proceed overseas. Hindu religion forbade its adherents from crossing the sea by ship or to proceed west of the Indus overland. When remnants of the Indian army returned from the campaigns in Afghanistan, the Hindu soldiers among them were treated as outcastes and were not allowed to mix or eat with their comrades (*A Matter of Honour: An Account of the Indian Army, its Officers and Men,* by Philip Mason, London, 1974, p. 243).

GATHERING STORM

Any uncalled-for external interference with religion in India, Hinduism, Islam or any other, is like playing with fire as it can give rise to uncontrolled passions. The significance of how the Indians viewed the imposition of changes and reforms was lost on the British. Their newly acquired position of absolute power and control rendered them insensitive, unmindful and out of touch with their subjects. It nearly cost them the precious empire. What followed taught them a lesson they never forgot. Sadly, one cannot say the same about their successors. The brutal treatment meted out to the Sikhs by Indira Gandhi in East Punjab and the insane military action ordered by General Musharraf against mosques and seminaries in Islamabad and other places would seem to confirm that not much has been learnt from history.

All of the seventy-two battalions in the Bengal Army had only British officers. No Indian was commissioned as an officer. Indian junior commissioned officers (JCOs) were not allowed to order any European soldier. An account of their treatment of Indian soldiers reads in part: '---- *The sepoy is an inferior creature. He is sworn at. He is treated roughly. He is spoken of as a "nigger". He is addressed as "suar" or pig an epithet most opprobrious to a respectable native, especially the Mussalman, and which cuts him to the quick. The old* (officers) *are less guilty ---- but the younger men seem to regard it as an excellent joke, as an evidence of spirit and a praiseworthy sense of superiority over the sepoy to treat him as an inferior animal*' (*Eighteen Fifty Seven,* by Surendra Nath Sen, Delhi, 1958, p. 23).

There was great disparity in the pay, allowances and living conditions afforded to the European soldiers and the sepoys. A retired British Officer explained it in his paper titled '*Mutiny in the Bengal Army*' published in 1857; '*The entire army of India amounts to 315,520 men costing 9,802,235 pounds. Out of this sum no less than 5,668,110 pounds are expended on 51,316 European officers and soldiers. Moreover the European corps takes no share in the rough ordinary duties of the service. They are lodged, fed and paid in a manner unknown to other soldiers.*'

All the discrimination, indignities, insults and interference in religion had built up resentment against the British. It manifested itself in the form of defiance and sporadic small-scale mutinies by a number of army units in different parts of the country. These had been put down with a heavy hand but the basic issues remained unresolved. In July 1806, about 1,500 sepoys of the Madras army mutinied and tried to capture Vellore Fort where Tipu Sultan's sons had been imprisoned. 350 of them were killed in the fighting. Many others were tried and sentenced to death or deportation for life.

'In 1824 General Edward Paget, a British Regular Army Officer who was then commanding the Bengal Army laid the foundation of a chain of events which contributed a significant deal to the sepoys' distrust of the British as far as the Bengal Army was concerned. Paget had taken over as Commander-in-Chief Bengal Army with no prior experience of India or the sepoy army. He mishandled the 47th Native Infantry over a minor administrative matter and used force while trying to disarm them, without any visible provocation on 47th Native Infantry's part. He then ordered European artillery to open fire on them without prior warning resulting in killing of between 60 to 100 sepoys. The next day he instituted a court martial which sentenced 41 sepoys to death. All this happened just because 47th Native Infantry had genuinely complained about their knapsacks being old and torn while under orders to march to Burma' (*Fidelity and Honour*, by Lieutenant General S.L Menezes,Viking, New Delhi,1990, pp 108).

By the middle of the nineteenth century, discontent in the Bengal army was palpable in most of its units. The British officers were aware of the situation but appeared unwilling to accept or face the reality. The Commander-in-Chief, General Sir Charles Napier, felt that the entire army was on the verge of mutiny but the Governor General, Lord Dalhousie, did not accept his assessment and Napier resigned under protest (*A Matter of Honour*, 231 – 6).

Just at this time, new Enfield rifles were inducted into the army units. Their cartridges had caps that had to be torn off manually before loading. This paper casing was greased with animal fat. It could be either beef, pig fat or both, touching which was sacrilegious to both the major religious groups of sepoys. Their objections were not only ignored but in many cases the officers abused the soldiers on parade 'in the most insulting language imaginable,' for not wanting to follow instructions. The contentious issue was poorly handled and became one more straw that eventually broke the proverbial camel's back.

In March 1857, a mysterious occurrence was noticed in which *chapatees* (unleavened tortilla-like bread) were distributed to villages at night, with instructions for each of them to make four more and send these to four other villages. The speed at which the *chapatees* traveled was astonishing; estimated at over a hundred miles a night. There was no explanation and the purpose of this exercise remains unclear to this day. Nonetheless, in an already charged environment, rumour mills went into over-drive. There were reports of *fakirs,* agents of dispossessed princes and agitators preying on the fears and suspicions of the villagers and warning them that their religion was in danger and urging them to stand firm against the *farangees* (foreigners).

A number of British officers had been informed by their servants and spies that a large-scale insurrection was imminent but they continued to disbelieve and ignore these warnings. Then, on 29th March 1857, a Hindu sepoy in the 34th Native Infantry at Barrackpore, Mangal Panday, turned up half-dressed before the quarter guard, with a loaded gun and started shouting for others to join him in the fight to save their religion. He appeared to be hallucinating under the influence of hashish or some other similar drug. When a British officer on a horse tried to run him down, he fired at him but missed and killed the horse instead. Panday then drew his sword and cut the officer across his shoulder. When a British sergeant intervened, he too was knocked down. Their lives were saved by a Muslim sepoy, Shaikh Paltu, who rushed in and grabbed Panday round the waste. Other sepoys at the scene called on Paltu to release Panday or else they would shoot him.

It took some time to restore some semblance of order among the men. When an attempt was made to arrest Panday, he turned the gun on himself and fired a shot that wounded him in the chest. He was tried, along with the commander of the quarter guard, and both of them were shot a few days later. The two native regiments involved in the incident, the 19th and the 34th, were disbanded and their sepoys dismissed from service amid calls from the European officers for all of them to be blown up from the artillery's guns.

The issue of the cartridges simmered on and there was further trouble at the musketry depot in Ambala. At about the same time General George Anson, the Commander-in-Chief in India, was visiting the depot when he was confronted with a near mutiny. Fires broke out in the bungalows of officers and the huts of sepoys who had used the cartridges, burning them to the ground. Anson was a known racist who admitted that he never saw an Indian soldier 'without turning away in disgust at his unsoldier-like appearance'.

The signs were getting from bad to worse and there were graphic reports and dire warnings from officers in the units. In one of these, Captain E. M. Martineau, commanding officer of the depot in Ambala had reported, '---- *I know that at the present moment an unusual agitation is pervading the ranks of the entire army ---- I can hear the moaning of the hurricane, but I can't say how, when or where it will break forth*' (*The Great Mutiny: India 1857*, Penguin Books, London, 1978). As with so many others, he was not believed.

Captain Fredrick Roberts (later, Field Marshal Roberts) wrote to his mother from Amritsar, '---- *you would not believe Englishmen could ever have been guilty of such imbecility as has almost invariably been displayed during this crisis; some few have shone, but they are exceptions ---- Perfectly ridiculous, an army going to pieces in this way ---- You would scarcely believe how paralysed everything is ---- We have a most dilatory, undecided Commander-in Chief* (*Forty-one Years in India*, by Field Marshal Earl Roberts, London, 1924).

Fredrick's father, General Sir Abraham Roberts KCB, had another son, John, by a Muslim lady. He was a practicing Muslim and an Urdu poet to boot with the pen-name '*Jan*'. It was strange irony that John had chosen to fight against the British at Lucknow for which he was disowned by his father. It was not an isolated case by any means. There were a few other similar instances but British historians in the past have chosen not to dwell on these for reasons of their own.

A particularly inept officer in Merut, Colonel Carmichael-Smyth, tried to force his sepoys to use the feared cartridges. They tried to explain that this would defile their religion and render them outcastes, pleading with him not to press the issue, but he would hear none of it. When ultimately they refused, he had eighty-five of them tried, convicted and sentenced to ten years hard labour. The men were assembled on the parade ground, surrounded by European troops with loaded guns and rifles, stripped of their uniforms and marched off to jail in shackles.

THE MUTINY

It was a shameful spectacle and too much to bear in an already charged atmosphere. The next day, on 10th May, rest of the native troops broke open the armoury, freed their comrades from the jail and went on rampage, looting, burning and killing the Europeans wherever they found them. Even the women and children were not spared. It was complete mayhem. Ruffians from the city had joined in the fray while policemen stood aside.

It took inordinately long for the 1,700 European troops in Merut to mobilize and even then there was confusion as to what action they should take. In the mean time, the mutineers made their way to Delhi ---- to look for some one to lead and direct their future course of action.

At this stage, all they knew was that they had acted in response to the intrusion and oppression of much-disliked Europeans into their religious and social beliefs. They had no leader, no plan and no idea of what to do next. Even the telegraph lines were left mostly intact, allowing the British to transmit warnings to the rest of country. It enabled them to disarm native units stationed in Punjab and other places before they could join the mutineers. By and large, sympathies of people in the countryside lay with the mutineers but in the absence of any central direction and control their actions remained disjointed and uncoordinated.

As the news spread, there were mutinies among the native troops at Lucknow, Cawnpore, Azamgarh, Allahabad and Bareilly and later at Gwaliar and Jhansi. All of these were located in the western Gangetic plain. The rest of India remained mostly unaffected. There was no trouble in either the Madras or Bombay armies. The vast majority of rulers of the Indian states remained loyal to the British, as did the landlords, Hindu businessmen and the hated money lenders. Even among the regiments that mutinied, not all the sepoys joined in. Many of them either went home or remained loyal to the Company.

The mutiny is some times described as the 'war of independence'. If it was a war, its military aspect was abysmally mismanaged by the mutineers. They had no clearly defined objectives, no coherent plan, virtually no organization and no leadership to speak of. The whole affair started as an expression of resentment against the degrading and contemptuous treatment of Indian soldiers by the British officers, aggravated by fears of religious interference. They were joined by some disgruntled rulers who had been dispossessed and mistreated by the British. These included, Dhondu Pant, the adopted son of Marhatta Peshwa Baji Rao II, also known as Nana Sahib, who laid siege to Cawnpore and the remarkable Lakshmi Bai, Rani of Jhansi. Both of them had been dispossessed of their states under Dalhousie's doctrine of 'lapse'.

The situation soon metamorphosed into chaos, punctuated by perfunctory and irresolute skirmishes that seemed to have no real purpose in the case of the mutineers. In the absence of effective leadership they lost both the initiative and control and sepoys mostly acted on their own. They committed horrific atrocities at a number of places, even killing innocent and unarmed women and children in the process. At the same time, there were others who went out of their way to protect the Europeans and helped them to escape to safety.

Perhaps, the worst of the atrocities in the early stages were committed by Nana Sahib's men at Cawnpore. Under an agreement reached with him, a contingent of besieged British soldiers and civilians was allowed safe passage out of the city. As they attempted to board the boats for transport down the Ganges, they were attacked. Most of the men were killed or executed and 125 women and children taken hostage. They were lodged in a building in the town, known as Bibi Ghar, and kept under the most appalling conditions. When the British later mounted a rescue effort, the hostages were all murdered by local ruffians, after the soldiers refused Nana Sahib's orders to carry out the grisly task. There were other incidents of brutality carried out against the Europeans at different places but not on the same scale.

Among the British, there was definitely a deliberate effort to falsify and exaggerate the atrocities in the most lurid terms in order to inflame public opinion and motivate the soldiers. Stories of women raped, children tortured and, in one persistent tale, roasted alive and fed to their parents were rampant in Britain. Not all of what was said and written was true by any means. Christopher Hibbert notes: '*But most of the appalling crimes rumoured to have happened, and reported as facts in letters to England, bore scant relation to the truth. Magistrates and Special Commissioners who endeavoured to discover reliable evidence of widespread torture and rape failed to do so. ---- Yet letters written by the officers to their families were full of the most lurid details of rapes and violations and of what Lieutenant Arthur Moffat called "perpetual lying reports about massacres in churches and other places"*' (*The Great Mutiny*, p. 213).

Lady Canning, wife of the Governor General, commented: '*A child who was said to have been killed slowly, bit by bit cut off, was certainly killed at once by a talwar, and so it is in each place ---- People on the spot say the stories going about are not true of that place but happened elsewhere, and so on. Those who have gone from place to place never find evidence of the horrible treatment everyone here believes. Only the massacres are really certain*' (Canning Papers).

These lurid, often baseless or grossly exaggerated accounts soon began to appear in the British press, along with plays, novels and imaginary paintings depicting gruesome atrocities. Public reaction was understandably fierce. Charles Dickens, always a racist at heart, wrote, '*I wish I were commander-in-chief in India. I should do my utmost to exterminate the Race upon whom the stain of the late cruelties rested.*'

Church leaders of all prominent denominations were equally strident in their calls for revenge, reminding their congregations of Old Testament demands delivered by Jehovah to the Israelites for mass slaughter (*Raj*, p. 287).

Within days of the outbreak the Chief Commissioner of Punjab, Sir John Lawrence, ordered all suspect native regiments to be disarmed. Any sepoy trying to abscond was rounded up and shot. In one account Major Bailie, stationed in Peshawar, wrote to his wife, ' -------- *I fancy the 51st must be pretty well disposed of ---- about 100 shot one way or another at the first start, then another 100 or so in the pursuit, then our 192, and a lot of prisoners that the villagers were bringing in all night. ------ I will say this for the wretches, they took it all in the most unconcerned way possible ---- marching steadily, halting, fronting opposite our firing parties, just as if they were only at drill.*'

Quoting from Sir John Kaye's *History of the Sepoy War in India 1857-1858*, Christopher Hibbert in his *The Great Mutiny* (p. 132) writes: '*At Ajnala near Amritsar, 282 Sepoys of the 26th Native infantry who had deserted from Lahore and subsequently surrendered in the belief* (actually, lured into believing) *that they were to be given a fair trial, were executed summarily by the Deputy Commissioner of the district, Frederic Cooper, a proud Christian of the "true English stamp and mould". They were brought out of the tehsil in batches of ten to be shot by Cooper's Sikhs. While the first two hundred or so were being killed, the remainder were kept locked up in one of the bastions of the tehsil. When the door was opened to bring out these others out, so Cooper wrote in his account of the discharge of his "tremendous responsibility, Behold! Unconsciously the tragedy of Holwell's Black Hole had been re-enacted ---- Fort-five bodies, dead from fright, exhaustion, fatigue, heat and partial suffocation, were dragged out. These bodies, together with those of the survivors who were shot, were tipped into a dry well near the police station on top of their comrades already deposited there by the village sweepers".*

'*Both Lawrence and Montgomery* (the Judicial Commissioner) *congratulated Cooper on his "energy and spirit". His action would a feather in his cap as long as he lived, Montgomery said, adding that any stragglers who might be picked up were to be sent to Lahore: "You have had slaughter enough. We want a few for the troops here and also for evidence.'*

Most of the regiments that mutinied made their way to Delhi to pledge allegiance to the octogenarian Mughal King Bahadur Shah. He was addicted to opium and king in name only, living on stipend from the

British. He had no prior knowledge or warning of the mutiny and did not welcome the development. His hands were forced when the sepoys threatened that if he did not give them his blessing they would take matters into their own and do as they pleased in the city. In the end, Bahadur Shah's acquiescence was only of symbolic significance for he was in no position to provide any meaningful leadership or help the troops in any other way.

About two-thirds of the mutineers were Hindus and the rest Muslims, united in their opposition to the British rule. They attacked the Europeans, murdered Indian and Eurasian converts and desecrated churches. The king had given protection to many European families inside Red Fort. These too were shamefully not spared. The situation was soon out of hand and beyond the control of the king. The sepoys did as they pleased, often looting and robbing the local money lenders, shopkeepers and residents.

In the mean time, the British had established a position outside Delhi on a ridge. There were not many of them and even those that were there were inadequately equipped and in poor shape. Considering the resources available to the mutineers, they could have easily wiped out this post and moved on but their heart was not in it. They had quickly become accustomed to enjoying life without discipline or restraints in the city. When pressed, some of them would venture out to engage in half-hearted desultory skirmishes and then rush back inside the city walls.

Bahadur Shah had appointed one of his sons and a grandson to lead the troops. They had little knowledge of military matters, no experience and were the first to take to their heels when action commenced. For a very short period a Rohilla Subedar, Bakht Khan, took charge of the operations and began to make a difference. He didn't last long and was soon sidelined and rendered ineffective by Bahadur Shah's courtiers.

The Hindu soldiers, in particular, soon began to lose heart. The only people who stood their ground, time after time, and showed any stomach for fighting were the *jihadi* volunteers, as evident from this account by Syed Mubarak Shah (quoted by Dalrymple in his *The Last Mughal*, p. 269 -70):

'*Several of these fanatics engaged in hand to hand combat, and great numbers were killed by the Europeans. Frequently two old withered Musalman women from Rampur would lead the rebels going far in advance with naked swords, bitterly taunting the Sepoys when they held back, calling them cowards and shouting to them to see how women went in front where they dared not follow: "we go without flinching among the showers of grape* (shot) *you flee from." The Sepoys would excuse themselves saying "We go to fetch ammunition", but the women would reply "you stop and fight, and we will get your ammunition for you." These women did frequently bring supplies of cartridges to the men in the batteries, and walked fearlessly in perfect showers of grape, but by the will of God were never hit. At length, one of the two was taken prisoner ---- When the band of ghazees moved off to the assault, the women invariably went in advance of all.'*

There have been volumes written about the heroics of Rani of Jhansi who was primarily fighting for restitution of her personal rights. It is sad commentary on Muslim historians of the sub-continent that hardly any information has been recorded about these remarkable ladies, not even their names or eventual fates are known with certainty.

In the end, there were an estimated 30,000 or more rebels holed up inside the city walls. For some inexplicable reason they made no attempt to lay siege to the ridge to cut off logistical supplies and prevent reinforcements from reaching the British. They also failed to make any arrangements for regular supply of food and other materials to meet their own needs as well as those of the city. It wasn't long before there were shortages and signs of hunger began to appear. The morale of the troops started to crumble and along with it the discipline. The number of desertions increased sharply and, perhaps, close to half of them left Delhi in disgust and disillusionment. Those that remained become an unruly mob that was out of control. Their supplies had run out and there was no money to pay the salaries. The inability of the sepoys to capitalize on the situation and act decisively in time cost them dearly. Bahadur Shah was well aware of the desperate situation and gave in to despair.

The British position, on the other hand, improved steadily with the arrival of European troops from Punjab, along with large mercenary contingents composed of Gurkhas, Sikhs and Pathans. For the Sikhs it was their religious duty to kill Muslims, as ordained by the tenth Guru Gobind Singh (see chapter '*Sikhism and Sikhs*') but the Pathans and Gurkhas were in it just for the money and the looting. There were more reinforcements on the way from places as far afield as South Africa, Malta, Burma and China. They had secure lines of communication and supplies and experienced none of the shortages that plagued people in the city. Confident of their strength, they attacked the city on 14th September and captured it after bitter hand-to-hand fighting in the streets and inside houses. The soldiers had orders not to take any prisoners which led to awful wholesale slaughter:

'Before long the ground was covered with the dead and writhing bodies of Sepoys. The piles, five feet high in places, were so densely entangled that the wounded could not extricate themselves from the squirming mass, but lay their struggling and hissing curses at the British soldiers -------' (*The Great Mutiny*, p. 343).

It also gave license to the mercenaries, in particular the Sikhs, to engage in killing for the sake of killing of Muslims. '*Sikh hatred of the Muslims mirrored that of the British soldiers towards the Sepoys. In one incident during the capture of Lucknow in March 1858, a band of Muslim fanatics, wearing green scarves, defended a bungalow to the last man, killing a British officer from a Sikh unit. The Sikhs snatched the last survivor and stabbed and burned him to death as the British officers and men stood by*' (*Raj,* p.256).

There is little doubt that the defenders fought bravely, particularly the jihadis. Unfortunately, bravery by itself is never enough to ensure victory in battle. It cannot compensate for the lack of a clear and well-defined strategy, good planning, organisation and effective tactics. Apart from these, the quality of professionalism and leadership among the British officers was far superior. It made defeat of the mutineers a foregone conclusion. Even so, the outcome remained uncertain in Delhi for some time and General Wilson seriously contemplated withdrawal. In the end, leadership failed the sepoys and their resistance collapsed.

The king fled with his family and entourage. He was captured just five miles to the south of Delhi, holed up in the tomb of Emperor Humayun. The officer in charge of the troops in pursuit, Major Hodson, made three of the king's sons strip naked in front of a crowd and then shot them in cold blood. Their bodies were brought to Delhi and left in a street for all to see. Hodson also burned twenty-three sepoys alive after they had fled to a building and was known to be a 'consummate looter' (*Raj*, p. 258).

Gallows were immediately erected all over the city, and the hangings began. Anyone suspected of complicity with the rebels was summarily tried and executed: ' ------- *hundreds of natives were shot or hanged while British officers sat by puffing contentedly on their cigars and soldiers evidently bribed the executioners to keep the condemned men "a long time hanging, as they liked to see the criminals dance a Pandee's hornpipe* (a reference to Mangal Panday) *as they termed the dying struggles of the wretches*' (*Life of Sir Henry Lawrence*, by H.B Edwardes and H. Merivale, London 1878, p. 60, *History of the Indian Mutiny*, T. Rice Holmes, London 1898, p. 398).

One of the officers, Richard Barter, recalled: '*It was simply awful. Our advance guard, consisting of cavalry and artillery, had burst and squashed the dead bodies which lay swelled to an enormous size, and the stench was awful -------*' (p. 323).

Lieutenant Fairweather agreed: 'But *at the same time it gave a feeling of gratified revenge ----- Among the corpses were several women ----- I saw the body of a woman lying with a cross-belt upon her and by her a dead baby also shot with two bullet wounds in it. The poor woman had tied the wounds round with a rag ----- McQueen told me he had seen a Highlander bayonet another woman -----*'

A soldier wrote to *The Bombay Telegraph*, decrying the orders to spare the women and children as 'hokum'. They were 'not human beings but fiends, or, at best, wild beasts deserving only the death of dogs'. '*All the city people found within the walls when our troops entered were bayoneted on the spot; and the number was considerable, as you may suppose when I tell you that some forty or fifty persons were often found hiding in one house. They were not mutineers, but residents of the city, who trusted to our well-known mild rule for pardon. I am glad to say they were to be disappointed.*' (*Indian Empire; vol. II*, by R. Montgomery Martin, London, 1860, p.449).

Mirza Ghalib, doyen of Urdu poets, who lived in Delhi during the time, noted in his *Dastanbuy* (p. 40), '*The victors killed all of whom they found on the streets. When the angry lions entered the city, they killed the helpless and weak and they burned their houses. Mass slaughter was rampant and streets were filled with horror.*'

The bloodlust was horrendous. All prisoners were slaughtered out of hand. George Blake recorded one wholesale execution: '*I proceeded to deal with the prisoners, marching them down to where my guard was stationed. I told the guard that any man who wanted to fire off his musket might come and shoot a sepoy -----. Only one prisoner, a low-caste man, fell at my feet and asked for mercy ----- All the rest died bravely and their bodies were hove into the river.*'

It was the same story all over the affected areas. Men in villages around Merut that were suspected of harbouring rebels were burnt alive as a matter of course (*Raj,* p.276). During the campaign in Malwa, Dr. Sylvester noted: '*Having seized on the native liquor shops, they* (British soldiers) *then commenced looting and killing every thing black, old men and young, women and children ----- Streete says he saw a room full of dead women with children sucking at their breasts. Other women brought out dead children supplicating for mercy*' ((*The Great Mutiny*, pp. 331, 377).

The rebellion simmered on and mopping-up operations lasted another two years before calm, more like stupefying numbness, was restored to the country. All of the surviving rebel leaders with the exception of Nana Sahib were captured, mainly through betrayal, and hanged. Nana Sahib escaped to Nepal and was never heard of again. Rani of Jhansi died fighting valiantly.

Bahadur Shah was kept on display to European visitors whilst awaiting trial, ' ----- *the dim-wandering eyed, dreamy old man, with feeble hanging nether lip and toothless gums, who sat on his haunches ----- dressed in an ordinary and rather dirty muslin tunic and small thin cambric skull cap*'. On 29th March 1858, a court found him guilty on all charges. The decrepit old man did not understand nor did he participate in any of the court proceedings. He was sentenced to be transported for life to Rangoon.

Apart from other things, the trial helped bring into the open the true extent of the intense innate hatred and hostility that the British harboured towards the Muslims, in common with the other Europeans. The prosecutor, Major Harriott, '*maintained that Zafar was the evil genius and lynchpin behind an international Muslim conspiracy stretching from Constantinople, Mecca and Iran to the walls of the Red Fort.------ Contrary to all the evidence that the Uprising broke out first among the overwhelmingly Hindu Sepoys, and that it was high-caste Hindu Sepoys who all along formed the bulk of the fighting force; and ignoring all the evident distinctions between the Sepoys, the jihadis, the Shia Muslims of Persia and the Sunni court of Delhi, Major Harriott argued that the Mutiny was the product of the convergence of all these conspiring forces around the fanatical Islamic dynastic ambitions of Zafar: " To Musalman intrigues and Mahommedan conspiracy we may mainly attribute the dreadful calamities of the year 1857. ------ The known restless spirit of Mahommedan fanaticism has been the first aggressor, the vindictive intolerance of that peculiar faith has been struggling for mastery, seditious conspiracy has been its means,------. The bitter zeal of Mahommedanism meets us everywhere ------ perfectly demonic in its actions ------.*"

Dalrymple comes to the conclusion (p. 440) that '*The Uprising in fact showed every sign of being initiated by upper-caste Hindu Sepoys reacting against specifically military grievances perceived as a threat to the faith and dharma; it then spread rapidly through the country, attracting a fractured and diffuse collection of other groups alienated by aggressively insensitive and brutal British policies. Lieutenant Edward Ommaney* (the king's jailer) *was quite clear that what the prosecution was alleging was nonsense ----- "In my opinion, the Musalman origin of the outbreak is a fallacy. ------"*

The Chief Commissioner of Punjab, John Lawrence, concurred, '*We have been almost as much to blame for what occurred as have the people. I have yet neither seen nor heard anything to make me believe any conspiracy existed beyond the army, and even in it one can scarcely say there was a conspiracy ---. The army had for a long time been in an unsatisfactory state ------*' (*Lawrence Papers*).

Yet, in his closing speech, Harriott pointed out, '*After what has been proved in regard to Mahommedan treachery ------ we shall see how exclusively Mahommedan are all the prominent points that attach to it. A Mahommedan priest, with pretended visions, and assumed miraculous powers --- a Mahommedan King, his dupe and his accomplice --- a Mahommedan clandestine embassy to the Mahommedan powers of Persia and Turkey --- Mahommedan prophecies as to the downfall of our power --- Mahommedan rule as the successor to our own --- the most cold blooded murders by Mahommedan assassins --- a religious war for Mahommedan ascendancy --- a Mahommedan press unscrupulously abetting --- and Mahommedan Sepoys initiating the mutiny. Hinduism, I may say, is nowhere either reflected or represented ------*" (*The Last Mughal,* pp. 439 – 443.)

One of the charges leveled against Bahadur Shah was that he was 'ungrateful for rising against his benefactors.' In actual fact, it was the Company that was guilty of rebellion against the king, having acknowledged for more than a century of being his vassal and agent and sworn allegiance to the king. Even the coins it issued testified to this effect. Moral considerations or points of law are irrelevant when it comes to victor's justice, which is what was meted out to Bahadur Shah. William Russell noted: '------ *but to talk of ingratitude on the part of one who saw that all the dominions of his ancestors had been gradually taken away from him until he was left with an empty title, and more empty exchequer, and a palace full of penniless princesses, is perfectly preposterous. Was he to be grateful to the Company for the condition he found himself* (in)? (*The Last Mughal,* P. 434.)

This was the pitiful end of the Mughal dynasty that had ruled India, barring a short intermission, for more than three centuries. Accompanied by his wife and two young sons Bahadur Shah spent the rest of his days in Rangoon, as a prisoner in abject poverty, misery and degradation, until his death on 7th November 1862 and was buried in an unmarked grave in a jungle clearing. In February 1991, some labourers digging a drain near the spot accidentally uncovered a brick-lined grave with the king's remains. Local Muslims, who regard Bahadur Shah as a Sufi, have built a modest shrine over it. The family sold every thing they possessed just to survive. The descendants of his son, Jawan Bakht, are reported to be still living in Rangoon, having married into local Muslims. A great-grandson of Bahadur Shah, Jamshid Bakht, runs a tea stall in Calcutta's Howrah train station.

An eminent Urdu poet in his own right with the pen-name, Zafar, he wrote his own epitaph with words that resonate with poignant pathos:

Kitna hai bud naseeb Zafar dafan kay leeyai, do guz zameen bhi nah milee kooey yaar mein.

'How unfortunate is Zafar that he was denied even two square yards of land for a grave in the beloved land.'

UNFETTERED VENGEANCE

The British were by no means finished yet. Small parties, led by magistrates, fanned out looking for fugitives from village to village and meting out vengeance. All of the king's male relatives, young and old, along with the courtiers were hunted down and hanged or shot out of hand. According to some reports, two of the princes managed to elude the dragnet, only to spend the rest of their days begging in disguise on the streets in Rajputana.

Lieutenant Kendal Coghill boasted: '*We burnt every village and hanged all the villagers who had treated our fugitives badly until every tree was covered with scoundrels hanging from every branch.*' The trials were in name only and lasted no more than a few minutes. Officers confessed they hanged all suspects whether or not they were found to be guilty. Often, they were flogged, tortured, smeared with excrement and had their mouths stuffed with beef and pig's meat before execution.

The sight of corpses hanging from the trees had become a familiar sight. After a time hardly any one took notice of them. Lieutenant John Fairweather recalled an experience at an auction of confiscated goods: '*I fancied a man behind me was pressing rather rudely against me. I dug him with my elbows but he seemed to return my dig. I then turned round rather angrily towards the man and found it was the body of a rebel that had been hanged on a tree ----- a swinging corpse forming part of a crowd at an auction seemed to affect no one.*'

Hibbert records, '*The bravery and resignation with which the prisoners died struck all who witnessed their executions. They did not struggle or attempt to grab the rope when the carts were driven away from beneath the trees. "Often and often I have seen natives executed, of all ages, of every caste, and every position in society," wrote Robert Dunlop, a Deputy Commissioner in the Punjab. "Yet never have I seen one of them misbehave. They died with a stoicism that in Europe would excite astonishment and admiration -----*

'*F. A. V. Thurburn reported that a native officer in his regiment who was hanged as a mutineer called out to him, "When you write to the adjutant remember me very kindly to him. Then springing from the platform he launched himself into eternity with the greatest nonchalance and coolness. Captain Charles Gordon, who watched scores of natives being hanged, never saw one "care twopence about it"* (*The Great Mutiny*, pp. 123 - 4).

Delhi had experienced brutality and massacres before, at the hands of foreign invaders, but never on this scale. The last time, it was Nadir Shah from Iran in 1739 whose troops murdered civilians wholesale in Delhi. It lasted only a day before he put a stop to it. The wanton killing by the British went on for years. The brutality attributed to Chengez Khan and Hilaku pales in comparison to what was perpetrated in North India after the mutiny. There are no published records of the numbers that were killed. Only some indirect indications are available that may give an idea of the magnitude of the holocaust. Postal authorities in India reported that addressees of two million letters could not be found and these lay unopened in government warehouses. According to civil servants, it showed 'the kind of vengeance our boys must have wreaked on the abject Hindoos and Mohammadens, who killed our women and children.'

British labour force records of the period after the mutiny show a drop in manpower of between a fifth and a third across vast swaths of India which, as one British official records, was 'on account of the undisputed display of British power, necessary during those terrible and wretched days ---- millions of wretches seemed to have died.' Acute labour shortages, coupled with trauma, trepidation and uncertainty, led to precipitous drops in agricultural production. In some recent estimates, Indian research scholars have put the figure of the dead due to all causes, including starvation and disease, as high as ten million (*War of Civilisations:1857 A.D* by Amaresh Misra, Rupa Publications, Delhi, 2007). Others think it may be less but it is impossible to quote a figure with any degree of certainty.

It took six days to capture Delhi. The city was soon reduced to a living hell, largely due to lack of control and discipline among the British troops as well as mercenaries. It was the direct outcome of the freedom given to them to loot, rape and kill any one they liked. Major Hodson wrote, '*The fact is, the troops are utterly demoralized by hard work and hard drink. For the first time in my life I have had to see English soldiers refusing repeatedly to follow their officers.*' Dr. Wise noted: '*We cannot advance on account of drunkenness of our men ----- They make a point of running away, and it is said the officers show them the way ----- A nice state that we cannot advance on account of our men getting drunk!*' (*Diary of a Medical Officer*, by James Wise, Cork, London, 1894)

'*The revenge was appalling. Old men were shot without a second thought; groups of younger men endeavouring to escape from the city were rounded up and executed in the ditch outside the gates. No one with a coloured skin could feel himself safe. The murders were committed without compunction or regret----.*'

'*Many who had never struck a blow against us ----- who had tried to follow their peaceful pursuits ---- and who had been plundered and buffeted by our own countrymen, were pierced by our bayonets, or cloven by our sabers, or brained by our muskets or rifles* (*The History of the Indian Mutiny*, by Sir John Kaye, Allen & Co., London, 1876, p. 635).

'*Some women came out of their houses along with their children and killed themselves by jumping into the wells. Others were killed by their husbands or fathers. "We found fourteen women with their throats cut from ear to ear by their own husbands, and laid out on shawls, for fear they should fall into our hands ---- their husbands had done the best they could afterwards and killed themselves*" (*The Narrative of the Siege of Delhi*, as quoted in *The Great Mutiny*, p. 313).

There was also revulsion and contrition at the senseless and indiscriminate slaughter among the more sensitive in the British ranks: '*Many of the citizens were shot, clasping their hands for mercy. It was known, too, that a large proportion had wished us well. Helplessness ought to be respected in either sex, especially in those who had never done us wrong. It is as unmanly for an officer to drive his sword through a trembling old man, or a soldier to blow out the brains of a wounded boy, as to strike a woman* (*A History of the Siege of Delhi by an Officer Who Served There*, by William Ireland, Edinburgh, 1861).

A British army wife living in the Fort wrote, '*Delhi was now truly a city of the dead. The death-like silence of that Delhi was truly appalling. All you could see were empty houses ----- The utter stillness was indescribably sad. It seemed as if something had gone out of our lives*' (*An Englishwoman in India, The Memoirs of Harriet Tytler 1828 – 1858*, Oxford 1986, p.165).

Perhaps the greatest Urdu poet that ever lived, Asadullah Khan Ghalib managed to hide in a basement undetected, for a month, until food and water ran out. He was duly produced before a court for sentencing. Fortuitously for him, he had in his possession a letter of thanks from the Secretary of State for a eulogy he had composed for Queen Victoria. It saved his life. After what he saw, he wrote: '*The light has gone out of India. The land is without a lamp. Hundreds of thousands are dead and hundreds of the survivors are imprisoned. People go mad from unbearable grief. Would it be surprising if I too should lose my mind ------ What grief have I not suffered; grief in death, in separation, in loss of income, and in honour? Besides the tragic events in the Red Fort, so many of my Delhi friends have been killed ------ How can I forget them? How can I ever bring them back --- relatives, friends, students, lovers. Now every one of them is gone. It is so terribly difficult to mourn for a single relative or friend. Think of me who has to mourn for so many. My God! So many of my friends and relatives have died that if now I were to die, not a single soul would be there to mourn for me. --- My sorrows are inconsolable and my wounds will never heal. I feel I am already dead*' (*Urdu Language and Literature: Critical Perspectives,* by Gopi Chand Narang, New Delhi, 1991, pp. 2, 3).

Once the killing had subsided, the entire population was driven out of Delhi. Tens of thousands of inhabitants were expelled into the country and forced to give up their possessions to the soldiers at the gates. The city appeared like a deserted charnel house. ' ----- *it is to be hoped the poor creatures were saved from starvation; but we had our doubts on the subject, and, knowing how callous with regard to human suffering the authorities had become, I fear that many perished from want and exposure*' (*The Narrative of the Siege of Delhi*, p.200). A surgeon reported, '*The wretched inhabitants have been driven out to starve* -------' Five weeks after the fall, Mrs. Saunders, wife of the Commissioner, wrote: '*every house in the city was desolate ----- The inhabitants of this huge place seven miles round are dying daily of starvation and want of shelter. The Prize Agents are digging for treasure in the houses.*'

Mirza Ghalib wrote: '*In the entire city of Delhi it is impossible to find one thousand Muslims; and I am one of them. Some have gone so far from the city it seems as if they were never residents of Delhi. Many very important residents are living outside the city, on ridges and under thatched roofs, in ditches and mud huts*' (*Dastanbuy*).

British officers did little to stop their men from raping women in Delhi, believing that sepoys had done the same to British women. A commission of enquiry instituted by the Commissioner of Delhi, Charles Saunders, verified there was no basis to this assumption and there was not a single instance of any rape by the sepoys. The same enquiry concluded that as many as three hundred begums of the royal house ---- not including former concubines in the palace ---- had been 'taken away by our troops after the fall of Delhi, and that many of those who had not been abducted were now making their living as courtesans.'

In a letter Ghalib noted: '*The female descendants of the king, if old, are bawds; if young, are prostitutes ---- you would have seen the ladies of the Fort moving about the city, their faces as fair as the moon and their clothes dirty, their pyjama legs torn, and their slippers falling to pieces. This is no exaggeration.*' (*The Last Mughal,* p. 463.)

'*The people are abject because they are starved out, banished and plundered. Thousands of Muslims are wandering houseless and homeless; the Hindus, pluming themselves on their assumed loyalty, strut about the streets giving themselves airs. Let not the public think that Delhi has not been punished. Wend through the grass-grown streets, mark the uprooted houses, and shot-riddled palaces*' (*Mufussilite*, June 1860, as quoted in *The Last Mughal*, p.461). Preferential treatment of the Hindus was part of a deliberate and carefully crafted policy to drive a wedge between the two communities. As the Viceroy, Lord Canning, wrote to the Board of Control in London, '*The men who fought us at Delhi were of both creeds. ---- As we must rule 150 million people by a handful* (*more or less*) *of Englishmen, let us do it in the manner best calculated to leave them* (Hindus and Muslims) *divided*' (*Canning Papers*).

There were strident calls among the British to obliterate the city altogether as 'a just retribution'. *The Lahore Chronicle* asked to level Delhi completely. This was echoed by people in Britain, like Prime Minister Lord Palmerston, 'Delhi should be deleted from the map. Every civil building connected with the Mohammedan tradition should be leveled to the ground without regard to antiquarian veneration or artistic predilections' (letter dated 9th October 1857, *Canning Papers*). Others called for all mosques, including the Jamia Masjid, to be razed or converted into churches. Fortuitously, the administration of the city was transferred to the Punjab Government in early 1858. Its Chief Commissioner, John Lawrence, managed to persuade the Viceroy Lord Canning that it was in Britain's long term interests to end the indiscriminate mass slaughter (in his words, 'war of extermination') and limit the destruction of the city.

Even so, there was considerable devastation as large-scale demolition operations went on for another two years, according to the *Delhi Gazette*. The king's palace was the first to go. It was a huge complex. '*The harem alone had occupied an area twice the size of any palace in Europe, measuring about 1,000 feet each way. ---- Even the fort's glorious gardens, notably Hayat Bakhsh Bagh and Mehtab Bagh, were swept away. All that was left at the end was about one fifth of the original fabric. ---- what remained of the fort became grey British barracks ---- without those who carried out this fearful piece of vandalism, thinking it even worthwhile to make a plan of what they were destroying or preserving any record of the most splendid palace in the world*' (*History of Indian and Eastern Architecture*, by James Fergusson, London, 1876, as quoted in *The Last Mughal*, p. 459).

Vast swathes of land were cleared in the vicinity of the Red Fort. Four of the most magnificent palaces were completely destroyed after the British troops had looted every thing inside. Centuries-old priceless carpets, paintings, jewelry, precious stones, decorative pieces, art work and any thing else they could find was taken away and lost forever. Some of the city's finest mosques, such as Akbarabadi and Kashmiri Katra Masjids, along with Sufi shrines, *imambaras*, beautiful buildings and exquisite *havelis* belonging to Muslim aristocrats were razed to the ground. Jamia Masjid was a heap of rubble that served as the barracks for Sikh troops. The great caravanserai of Shah Jahan's daughter, Jahanara, was demolished and replaced by the town hall. Shalimar Bagh was sold off and put to agricultural use. The only Mughal buildings left standing were those occupied by the British.

After some weeks, Hindus were permitted to return to the city and allowed to take possession of their properties, on payment of ten percent of the value to the Prize Agents. Confiscated properties of Muslims were sold to Hindu bankers and money lenders. These included the city's two most famous mosques --- Fatehpuri Masjid and Zeenat-ul-Masajid.

Muslims continued to languish and perish in the wilderness. It wasn't until 1860, more than two years later that they were re-admitted and allowed to take possession of what was left of their properties. The rate of payment to the agents in their case was fixed at twenty-five percent of the value. In addition, they were required to provide proof of their loyalty to the British. Any one unable to do so had his property confiscated. '---- *they* (Muslims) *deliberately planned and tried to carry out a war of extermination and retaliation in such a case is sanctioned by every human law. If the Musalman could by any means be entirely exterminated, it could be the greatest possible step towards civilizing and Christianizing Hindustan*' (A.C Lyall, English civil servant, in letter to his father dated 14th May 1858).

Muslims were singled out for the worst kind of retribution. It may have been in part because they represented a rival source of power to the British in India but there is more to it. In any confrontation involving Muslims, no matter where, people of the European race are invariably seen to react in the same visceral way. It is evident even now in the events that followed the crashing of four hi-jacked airliners in USA in September 2001, allegedly, by a group of young Arabs. Without waiting for a tangible proof of any kind, the religion of Islam and its followers everywhere were implicitly being held to account.

Even though none of the accused belonged to Afghanistan or Iraq, the two countries were subjected to the most horrendous bombardment the world has ever seen. In the years following their occupation by western troops, more than a million innocent civilian Muslim men, women and children in each of the two countries have met with violent deaths and the killing continues nine years later without arousing any sympathy, compassion, concern or remorse. Quite to the contrary, using remote-controlled missile-carrying drones the circle of death was extended in 2008 to include the western highlands of Pakistan with tacit approval from her rulers who remain beholden to the West for their survival (see chapter 3 - '*European Colonisation*' extract from the book, *The Deserter's Tale: the Story of an Ordinary American Soldier*).

There are striking similarities in the reactions to the mutiny in the sub-continent and the event of September 2001. We see the same disregard for cause and effect; the same contempt for due processes of law and justice; the same irresponsible and hateful rhetoric; the same exploitation and de-humanization of Muslims and the same display of ruthless and relentless power against the powerless and the have-nots.

In 1862, Ghalib wrote to a friend, '*This is not the Delhi in which you were born, not the Delhi in which you got your schooling, not the Delhi in which you used to come to your lessons with me, not the Delhi in which I have passed fifty-one years of my life. It is a camp. The only Muslims here are artisans or servants of the British authorities. All the rest are Hindus.*' Other Urdu writers like Rashid-ul-Khairi and Hasan Nizami have recorded the tragedy and plight of the Muslims in heart-rending detail. Generations of Muslims in India have shed copious tears reading these compilations of sorrow.

The destruction was not just limited to wanton demolition of buildings, looting, rape and mass murder of citizens. The madrassas were all closed, their buildings sold to Hindu traders and money lenders who either demolished or converted them to warehouses. All public and private libraries were gutted and their irreplaceable collections, amassed over hundreds of years, destroyed. Ghalib could not find any bookseller, binder or calligrapher in a city that had been the proud repository of India's literary heritage only a few months earlier.

The effects of this cultural devastation linger to this day. Zauq and Ghalib, both Muslims, were undoubtedly among the greatest Urdu poets that ever lived. Delhi was their home and they loved the city (*Kaon jaayey Zauq par Dilli ki galyan chhor kar*). The lack of respect and recognition reserved for them in present-day independent India can be gauged from the fact that a municipal urinal has been constructed over the tomb of Zauq in Delhi and Ghalib's house has been converted into a coal store (*The Last Mughal*, p. 24).

As Dalrymple so aptly put it, '*Without the Delhi college and the great madrasas, without the printing presses and Urdu newspapers, and without* (the patronage of) *the Mughal court --- the driving force behind Delhi's renaissance and artistic flourishing was gone. The beating heart of Indo-Islamic civilization had been ripped out and could not be replaced.*'

DIVIDE AND RULE

There was more involved in this wanton devastation than inherent animosity and hatred towards the Muslims or the desire to avenge past humiliations and defeats. In retrospect it would appear this was the time when the ancient Roman dictum *divide et impera* (divide and rule) was adopted as the official policy of the British rule in India. Henceforward, Hindus were to be encouraged and granted privileges and preference over the Muslims in every sphere of life be it education, government service, acquisition of property or commercial enterprise. It pleased the Hindus not only for the rewards that came with it but also because in the British they had found an ally against the Muslims who had ruled over them for so long. By embracing this divide, without realizing it, they also laid down the foundation of India's subsequent division and the creation of Pakistan.

The British had chosen to rule India as masters, distancing themselves from its people, their culture and civilization. The new-found arrogance of power led them to believe that they were superior beings and found it below their dignity to assimilate and be a part of the country. Instead, they created a class of semi-Anglicised Indians, within each community, to deal with the natives and run the day-to-day affairs for them. They could buy the loyalties of this class through patronage jobs, land grants and other such favours and through them continue to exploit the rest.

An empire created on a base of precarious foundations, such as these, carries within it the seeds of its own destruction. Probably, the same arrogance of power prevented the British from drawing the right conclusions from India's history. Any rule based on exercise of power does not last for long. For it to endure, people at large have to identify themselves, their lives and aspirations with those of their rulers.

Whereas early British writings had expressed admiration for the achievements by the Muslims in India, the mood of the later historians took an abrupt turn in mid-nineteenth century. The history books prescribed for the colleges and universities now portrayed the Muslim rule as evil and malicious, particularly towards the Hindus. This was done by misquoting sources, mistranslating, twisting facts and presenting the Muslims in adverse light in whatever way possible. There was a specific underlying motive, as evident from the introduction to Elliot and Dawson's *History of India as told by its own Historians* (Kitab Mahal, Allahabad, reprinted 1964 and as quoted by Khairi:

The authors oddly complain '---- *there is not one of this slavish crew* (Hindu writers) *who treats the history of his country subjectively, or presents us with thoughts, emotions and raptures which a long oppressed race might be supposed to give vent to, when freed from the tyranny of its former masters and allowed to express itself in the natural language of the heart without constraint and without adulation* ----. In the absence of any charges by the Hindus, he specifies these himself, '*Hindus slain for disputing with Muhammadans, of general prohibitions against processions, worship and ablutions, and of other intolerant measures, of idols mutilated, of temples razed, of forcible conversions and marriages, of proscriptions and confiscations, of murders and massacres, and of the sensuality and drunkenness of the tyrants* (p. xxi).

'(The book) *will serve to dissipate the gorgeous illusions which are commonly entertained regarding the dynasties that have passed, and show him* (the reader that) ---- *we have already, within half century of our dominion, done more for the substantial benefit of the people than our predecessors, in the country of their adoption, were able to do in more than ten times that period; drawing auguries from the past, he will derive hope for the future, that ---- we shall follow them up by continuous efforts to fulfill our high destiny as the rulers of India ---- we should be spared the rash declarations respecting Muhammadan India, which are frequently made by persons not otherwise ignorant ----*' (p. xxvii).

The books by these two authors were prescribed reading for history classes in the colleges all over India.

Of late, a great deal has been published in Britain and elsewhere about the British rule in India. Most of it is new wine in old bottles but there is much also that is refreshingly honest, based on archives that have lain unexplored in government vaults until now, especially in Delhi and Lahore. The younger generation of British writers in particular, unencumbered by the prejudices and attitudes of the Raj, has been more objective in its approach. Despite these attempts at objectivity and balance, history of India still remains very much a victor's version of events. Sadly, there have been very few who have tried to match the objectivity and absence of bias and prejudice found in the writings of William Dalrymple, Lawrence James, Andrew Roberts, perhaps Peter French but certainly the American, Stanley Wolpert.

Has this new-found objectivity among historians made a difference? It is hard to tell. Looking at the developments following September 2001, not much seems to have changed. Any lingering doubts were largely dispelled when British Prime Minister, Gordon Brown, proudly announced in the summer of 2007 that Britain had nothing to be ashamed of or apologise for her Empire. It was something to celebrate, he said. May be for him, but that was certainly never the case for those who had been at the receiving end of British colonialism.

In a recent essay, *The Empire Strikes Back*, William Dalrymple sums up the situation: '---- we British should keep our nostalgia and self-congratulation over the Raj within strict limits. For all the irrigation projects, the great engineering achievements, and the famous imperviousness to bribes of the officers of the Indian Civil Service, the Raj nevertheless presided over the destruction of Indian political, cultural and artistic self-confidence, while the economic figures speak for themselves: in 1600 when the East India Company was founded Britain was generating 1.8 per cent of the world's GDP, while India was producing 22.5 per cent. By 1870, at the peak of the Raj, Britain was generating 9.1 per cent, while

India had been reduced for the first time to the epitome of a Third World nation, a symbol across the globe of famine, poverty and deprivation'.

The inimitable British author and columnist, George Monbiot, elaborated in *The Guarian* under the heading, '*The Turks Haven't Learned the British Way of Denying Past Atrocities*':

'*In his book Late Victorian Holocausts, published in 2001, Mike Davis tells the story of famines that killed between 12 and 29 million Indians. These people were, he demonstrates, murdered by British state policy. When an El Niño drought destituted the farmers of the Deccan plateau in 1876 there was a net surplus of rice and wheat in India. But the viceroy, Lord Lytton, insisted that nothing should prevent its export to England. In 1877 and 1878, at the height of the famine, grain merchants exported a record 6.4 million hundredweight of wheat. As the peasants began to starve, officials were ordered "to discourage relief works in every possible way". The Anti-Charitable Contributions Act of 1877 prohibited "at the pain of imprisonment private relief donations that potentially interfered with the market fixing of grain prices". The only relief permitted in most districts was hard labour, from which anyone in an advanced state of starvation was turned away. In the labour camps, the workers were given less food than inmates of Buchenwald. In 1877, monthly mortality in the camps equated to an annual death rate of 94 per cent.*

'*As millions died, the imperial government launched "a militarised campaign to collect the tax arrears accumulated during the drought". The money, which ruined those who might otherwise have survived the famine, was used by Lytton to fund his war in Afghanistan. Even in places that had produced a crop surplus, the government's export policies, like Stalin's in Ukraine, manufactured hunger. In the north-western provinces, Oud and the Punjab, which had brought in record harvests in the preceding three years, at least 1.25 million died.*

'*Three recent books --- Britain's Gulag by Caroline Elkins, Histories of the Hanged by David Anderson, and Web of Deceit by Mark Curtis --- show how white settlers and British troops suppressed the Mau Mau revolt in Kenya in the 1950s. Thrown off their best land and deprived of political rights, the Kikuyu started to organise --- some of them violently --- against colonial rule. The British responded by driving up to 320,000 of them into concentration camps. Most of the remainder --- more than a million --- were held in "enclosed villages". Prisoners were questioned with the help of "slicing off ears, boring holes in eardrums, flogging until death, pouring paraffin over suspects who were then set alight, and burning eardrums with lit cigarettes". British soldiers used a "metal castrating instrument" to cut off testicles and fingers. "By the time I cut his balls off," one settler boasted," he had no ears, and his eyeball, the right one, I think, was hanging out of its socket." The soldiers were told they could shoot anyone they liked "provided they were black". Elkins's evidence suggests that more than 100,000 Kikuyu were either killed or died of disease and starvation in the camps. David Anderson documents the hanging of 1,090 suspected rebels: far more than the French executed in Algeria. Thousands more were summarily executed by soldiers, who claimed they had "failed to halt" when challenged.* U.S President Obama's grandfather, Hussein Onyango Obama, was among those tortured by British forces during Kenya's struggle for independence ('*No Special Relationship Now*', by Tristram Hunt in *The Guardian*, 13th January 2009).

'*These are just two examples of at least 20 such atrocities overseen and organised by the British government or British colonial settlers; they include, for example, the Tasmanian genocide, the use of collective punishment in Malaya, the bombing of villages in Oman, the dirty war in North Yemen, the evacuation of Diego Garcia. Some of them might trigger a vague, brainstem memory in a few thousand readers, but most people would have no idea what I'm talking about. ----*

'*There is one, rightly sacred Holocaust in European history. All the others can be denied, ignored, or belittled. As Mark Curtis points out, the dominant system of thought in Britain promotes one key concept that underpins everything else --- the idea of Britain's basic benevolence. Criticism of foreign policies is certainly possible, and normal, but within narrow limits which show 'exceptions' to, or 'mistakes' in, promoting the rule of basic benevolence". This idea, I fear, is the true "sense of British cultural identity" whose alleged loss Max laments today. No judge or censor is required to enforce it. The men who own the papers simply commission the stories they want to read.*'

Regardless of the outcome, British rule in India had been severely jolted by the mutiny. It left a legacy of paranoia and continued to cast a long and dark shadow on all subsequent policies and actions in the country, right to the end. Once public anger had subsided in Britain, the inevitable recrimination and soul-searching began. Policies of the Company, its unpopular reforms and their inept implementation, the conduct and activities of its officials and missionaries were all questioned in a

Commons select committee. Sir George Cornewall Lewis, former chancellor of the exchequer went so far as to claim, '*I do must confidently maintain that no civilized government ever existed on the face of this earth which was more corrupt, more perfidious and more capricious*' (Empires of the Monsoon, p. 329).

It was time for the Company to be wound up. The end came officially on 1st November 1858 when a proclamation by Queen Victoria was read out to the Indians, after the passage of the India Act in Parliament. India was brought under the direct rule of the British government. Executive power was bifurcated between the Secretary of State for India, who answered to the Parliament, and the Viceroy who administered the country from Calcutta. The latter presided over a legislative council composed of senior civil servants and military officers. In later years, some selected Indian princes and prominent citizens, loyal to the crown, began to be co-opted to the council. The day-to-day business of administration was done by the governors of provinces with the help of a plethora of civil servants of all ranks and description.

In societies with a tribal structure, as was the case in most of Sind, Baluchistan and NWFP, there was minimal interference and their chiefs were allowed to implement and administer their own rules and laws. It was the same for the states except that a British Resident was stationed to keep an eye on the activities of the nawab or raja.

An elitist Indian Civil Service (ICS) formed the backbone of the administration, with about a thousand members. It was an exclusive club staffed, to start with, by the scions of professional and upper-middle class British families educated at the best schools and universities. During the Company rule, the selection had been by patronage. Individuals nominated by Company directors and political figures underwent training at an academy set up in Haileybury (England) for two years before proceeding to take up appointments in India. This was changed and candidates came to be selected on merit assessed through a competitive examination. It required considerable familiarity with Latin, Greek and English literature among other subjects not familiar to Indians to qualify. Coupled with the fact that the examinations were conducted in England, it virtually ensured their exclusion. In any case, since the days of Lord Cornwallis the policy had been to restrict the Indians to the lower grades of service. This was changed later but even so their proportion in the ICS was less than six percent in 1910 ---- almost all of these were Hindus.

ICS officers were paid extremely well and, in return, were expected to maintain impeccable standards of professional and personal conduct. They more than met these expectations. It would be a fair assessment that the Indian masses never experienced better government and fairer justice as they did at the hands of this institution. It prompted Churchill to remark at one stage that under the British administration a woman could walk unmolested from one end of India to another which could not be said of England at the time. Many would go so far as to say that it was the finest civil service to have existed anywhere in the history of mankind.

It was not a civil service in the ordinary sense. The officers acted more like proconsuls, unlike their counterparts in Britain who performed mostly clerical functions. The fact that the British rule lasted peacefully for as long as it did was in large part due to the dedication, commitment, integrity and competence of these extra-ordinary men (for more details about the ICS, please see *The Men Who Ruled India* by Philip Woodward and *The Ruling Caste* by David Gilmour, Pimlico, London, 2007).

It is a fact that at no stage did the total number of Britons of all description in India exceed one half of one per cent of the total population. To rule over a veritable continent with so few numbers so successfully is a remarkable achievement by any standards. It could not have been possible through the use of force alone. The co-operation and collaboration by the Indians themselves was a major factor. These could only be harnessed though astute politics, good judgement and superb organization, not to speak of the dedication and commitment on the part of the individuals involved.

There are other aspects to the mutiny that are worth noting. It was brought on primarily because the British officers became hopelessly out of touch with feelings among the Indian sepoys that was compounded by the scorn and haughty disdain with which they were treated ---- an open invitation to calamity and disaster in the military, if there ever was one. The fact that the mutiny was put down had everything to do with the ineptitude of the sepoys. The British had crucially failed to read the signs and anticipate the gathering storm, retreating into a denial mode instead. Worse still, they had no contingency plan in place for dealing with such exigencies. Their response was disorganized and tardy. In any other circumstances, it would probably have cost them the empire.

What would have happened to India if the British had lost? Neither Bahadur Shah nor the sepoys were in any position to provide the country with an effective rule. There is every likelihood that the states would have broken away from Delhi one by one and declared their independence. Inevitably, wars would have broken out between them, leading to widespread anarchy and chaos. The doors to foreign intervention would have opened once again, possibly, providing the British with the opportunity to return. In the end, chances are, the final outcome would have been the same no matter who had won.

The people who like to think of the sepoy mutiny as India's 'war of independence' ignore the fact that most of India chose not to get engaged or involved in it. The struggle remained localised to a few areas in and around Delhi, Avadh and some eastern parts of Rajputana; the rest of India abstained and remained loyal to Britain. Even among the sepoys only the Bengal Army was affected. Both the others --- Bombay and Madras armies, did not join the fray. Gurkha, Sikh and Pathan mercenaries actively sided with the British in crushing the rebellion, as did the vast majority of the rulers of states. The rajas of the Sikh states of Patiala, Nabha, Jeend and Kapoorthala deputed their entire armies to help out the British. This marked absence of common cause and fraternal feeling among the natives calls into serious question not only the notion of a national war of independence but also the very idea of India being one nation.

There are a multitude of other reasons that contributed to British success. The chief among these must be the inability of the Indians to keep abreast of developments in rest of the world, in particular, Europe. When it first encountered the Europeans, India was culturally and technologically more advanced. There was not much it could learn from them. It gave rise to arrogance and complacency. But, it was a time of rapid change in Europe which was never appreciated by the Indians until it was far too late. This time of upsurge in Europe coincided with a period of political, economic and technological downturn in India that made her easy pickings for any adventurer.

In the past, India had suffered foreign rule of a different kind. The invaders settled down and became a part of India. Apart from a few brief exceptions, India's wealth remained in India. During the rule by the Turks and the Mughals, who also originated from outside India, the country prospered and her economy flourished to the extent that it constituted fully one quarter of the entire world economy. The eighteenth century historian Alexander Dow acknowledged: 'Bengal was one of the richest, most populous and best cultivated kingdoms in the world ---- We may date the commencement of decline from the day on which Bengal fell under the dominion of foreigners (*from Europe*).' They were primarily concerned with siphoning off India's wealth to enrich investors in England. Muslim rule had not been colonial in nature which was not the case with the Europeans. Had this difference been appreciated by the Indians earlier, their tolerance and acceptance of the Europeans would not have been the same and the story may well have unfolded quite differently.

Again, it boils down to the absence of institutions for analysis and research that could have warned Indians of the lurking danger and brought them abreast of the changing world. These engines of learning were needed to develop logic, philosophy and technology required for dealing with the European challenge. India lost not to superior weapons but to superior thought processes developed during the Renaissance in Europe. Lacking such enlightenment, the Indians failed to develop a collective sense of responsibility or esprit de corps. Their loyalties remained tied to individuals rather than the society or the country as a whole, making it easier to divide and use them against each other. It is a lesson that the Muslim world has not assimilated to this day.

There is a fundamental difference in the mental make-up of the Europeans and Asians in general. Its roots lie deep in pre-history and it may have something to do with the ecological environment in which the respective cultures evolved. In Asia, human beings settled in agricultural communities much earlier. It provided them with regular and assured supply of food, along with many other advantages, but the compulsive need for constant technological innovation was not one of them. The Europeans, on the other hand, remained hunter-gatherers for a much longer period. It involved pitting their wits against a steadily decreasing supply of animals. In order to survive, they needed to develop new weapons and techniques to outwit the game that was getting increasingly wily and difficult to hunt. Faced with the challenge over a very long period of time, technological innovation became second nature for them. It was the same when it came to organisation and coordination of effort that were so critical to the success of a hunt, as was the need to subjugate personal interest for the greater good of the community. These traits are bred into the European mind, giving it inherent innate advantage in conflict situations against people of settled farming backgrounds.

There were other, more tangible, factors as well that led to the development of superior technological skills in Europe at this time. Most important among these was the acquisition of scientific knowledge that had become readily and widely available after Renaissance. There was growing population pressure in Europe that strained the limits of indigenously available resources. It compelled the Europeans to look outwards and develop the means, not simply to trade, but to colonise and exploit lands beyond their own borders. Since they could not rely on superiority of numbers in far off lands, their only other realistic hope lay in the deployment of decisively superior weapons and concepts to manipulate and exploit divisions and cleavages among the natives. Their task was made that much easier in a country like India that was splintered into hundreds of competing states, inhabited by people divided by scores of different religions and speaking 222 different vernaculars.

Unlike India or China, Europe was not a centrally controlled polity. It consisted of a number of large and small independent states that had been more or less perpetually at war with one another. Nothing gives greater impetus to the development of technology and innovation than war. This applies just as much to weaponry as it does to tactics and methods of training and operational planning. As against the Europeans, prosecution of war by the Indians remained an amateurish affair, barring a few exceptions such as Haider Ali's development of a highly mobile force living off the land, against which the British remained powerless. Strangely but significantly, perhaps luckily for the British, no attempt was made by the Indians to study the model and draw any lessons from the latter's successes.

On the whole, the British soldier was always better trained, better disciplined and better motivated than his Indian counterpart who remained little more than a mercenary at heart. The quality of leadership provided by the British officers was far superior and made all the difference to the outcome of a battle. It bolstered confidence among the troops, giving them an aura of invincibility. This myth was assiduously cultivated and instilled, not only among the British troops, but the natives were also kept constantly reminded of it to maintain the illusion without which British rule would be hard, if not impossible to sustain. There was a conscious and deliberate effort to demoralise the Indians and impress upon them in a thousand different ways that the British were a superior race. That they could never equal their masters and it would be pointless for them to even try.

Incredibly, until the rebellion in 1857, the British continued to be treated like any other player on the local political chessboard by the Indians and not as aliens and common enemies of India. When people like Haider Ali and Tipu Sultan tried to draw attention to the menace and proposed unified action to deal with it, their calls were not only ignored but important rulers, like the Nizam of Hyderabad and the Marhattas, joined hands against them and chose to side with the British instead. There are no indications that there was ever a realization of the disastrous consequences of such actions. In the absence of a cohesive, well-directed national spirit and awareness of larger and over-riding national interest there was little chance that the outcome could have been anything but disastrous. The only thing that mattered to the Indian players in the game was personal gain and interest even at the expense of the state. In they end they lost on both counts.

The British, on the other hand, owed their allegiance to a higher entity ---- the country and the Company. Unlike those of the rajas and nawabs, the latter's interests were more long-term, focused and impersonal that did not die with the ruler. The objectives could be conceptualised and planned against a much longer-term perspective. It was much easier and simpler to identify and abide by these, without any fear or ambivalence and without any qualms of conscience. It inculcated a higher sense of purpose and feeling of righteousness that in turn fostered the all important unity of purpose in the ranks.

All this aside, the mutiny had a profound affect on the British psyche nonetheless, driving home realization of the precarious and tenuous nature of their hold on India. It was not something that could be taken for granted. Henceforward, a firm administration that responded to the feelings and reactions of Indians, but not necessarily to their needs, became the objective. Any signs of trouble perceived or otherwise were dealt with quickly and resolutely, for fears of a repeat of the events of 1857 always lurked at the back of their minds. Sometimes it led to over-zealous reaction, as happened at Jallianwala Bagh in 1919, with tragic consequences. In the end, what made the people of India reconcile to the British rule was not the use of force but experience of a government at the local level that was just, efficient, effecatious, impartial and responsive. It was a far cry from the ad-hoc dispensation they had become used to receiving at the hands of the local rulers of states in the past.

CONSEQUENCES FOR INDIA

The overall objective of the British rule remained the same as always ---- exploitation of India's resources to enrich Britain. The former was viewed essentially as a source of industrial raw materials, a consumer of value-added goods exported from Britain and as a provider of manpower for the army. Through an elaborate set of rules and regulations, the Indians were prevented from setting up manufacturing plants and taking advantage of the industrial revolution that was sweeping through Europe at the time. The net result was a continuous outflow of wealth from India to Britain. Before the arrival of the British, India's share in the world trade had amounted to almost twenty-five per cent. When they left, it had been reduced to mere one per cent. There was no increase in India's per capita income for two hundred years, from 1757 to 1947. South Indian labourers who had higher earnings than their British counterparts in the 18th century and lived lives of greater financial security, now began to starve.

As early as 1772, Horace Walpole, author and long-standing member of British Parliament, wrote: '*We have outdone the Spaniards in Peru! They were at least butchers on a religious principle, however diabolical their zeal. We have murdered, plundered, usurped ---- nay what think you of the famine in Bengal, in which three million perished, being caused by a monopoly of provisions by the servants of the East Indies* (Company)' {as quoted by Khairi in *Jinnah Reinterpreted,* p. 13}. The Company had imposed stringent conditions on local industry and trade. It dictated how the production of goods was organized, systematically squeezing out Indian investors and entrepreneurs. India's textile industry, famous throughout the world for its fine muslin and other wears, was totally wrecked and the country rendered dependent on imports of cloth from the mills in Lancashire.

There were many different ways to ensure British interests remained paramount. India's currency had been linked to the British pound and remained so until 1931 when the great worldwide economic depression obliged Britain to delink the pound from the Gold Standard. The Government of India did not feel it in her interest to follow suit. This meant delinking the Indian rupee from the pound and with it the ensuing adverse consequences for British trade. The Secretary of State for India, Sir Samuel Hoare, tried to force the Viceroy but the issue was of such significance that the entire Executive Council, including the Europeans, threatened to resign. Hoare then got in touch with one of Gandhi's financiers, Birla, to put pressure on Gandhi, who was in London at the time for the Round Table Conference. At Gandhi's urging, the Viceroy relented and persuaded the Council members not to come in the way of re-establishing the rupee-pound link (*India's Fight for Freedom*, by Kanji Dwarkadas, Popular Prakashan, Bombay, 1967, p. 398 – 9).

The replacement of indigenous inland river transport with British owned railways is another example of how India's economic interests were sacrificed. For thousands of years, the Indus and its tributaries had served as the primary means of communication for transport of goods from the west inland to all parts of Central Asia and India. Emperor Aurangzeb had built a canal that joined the Sutlej and Jamuna, via Sirhind, specifically to facilitate navigation to Delhi, Agra and beyond. Tens of thousands of large and small boats, powered by steam and sail, plied the Indus at the time of the British invasion (*Cabool: A Personal Narrative of a Journey to and*

Residence in That City in the Years 1836, 37 and 38 by Lieutenant Colonel Sir Alexander Burnes, Feroze Sons, Lahore).

As soon as they had consolidated their hold over Punjab and Sind, British companies moved in to lay down railway lines that connected all points of commercial and strategic interest. It costs ten times more to ship goods by train than by inland barges. The railways would have found it hard to compete for the shipment of bulk cargoes with water-borne transport. The problem was deftly resolved when Karachi replaced Thatta as the point of entry from and to the sea and no provision was made for inland navigation in the construction of Sukkur barrage on the Indus and its associated system of irrigation canals. An industry that had flourished for thousands of years died unlamented, soon to be forgotten. In the absence of competition, railways became increasingly profitable, making their owners in London correspondingly rich, at the expense of hapless Indians.

One of the secrets of Europe's economic success lay in the development of the concept of the 'Company'. Industrial revolution had made production of goods on a large scale possible at relatively low cost. The industrial units involved were of necessity large and required considerable investment capital that was beyond the reach of most individual entrepreneurs. The formation of a jointly owned 'Company', by pooling together financial resources of a number of investors, made it possible to engage in commercial enterprises regardless of their size and cost. The concept was alien to India and remained so until fairly recent times. Moreover, British regulatory policies were designed to ensure that capital gravitated towards London and was not so readily available to the Indian investors. It restricted the size of industrial operations to what could be managed by individuals or immediate family members from their own limited resources. The net result was that except for basic cottage industries, India was unable to compete in value-added manufactures and was reduced to the role of a consumer of imported goods and exporter of basic commodities, making her poorer by the year.

CHAPTER 6

MUSLIM RE-AWAKENING

MUSLIM RELIGIOUS MOVEMENTS

We have seen how the incompetence and ineptitude of Aurangzeb's successors had led to divisions and intrigue at the court in Delhi, weakening their hold on power. It encouraged revolts, with provinces breaking away from the centre one after another. Bengal became virtually independent in 1717, as did Avadh six year later and Deccan in 1724. Even in places like Punjab that nominally remained in the imperial fold, there was gross mismanagement and corruption that caused sharp declines in revenues. It left few resources for defence of the realm.

This created opportunity for adventurers, like Nadir Shah, to plunder the land at will. He duly obliged by ransacking Delhi in 1739 and murdering 30,000 of its inhabitants. On his way back, he carried away a huge treasure, including the fabled *Takht-e-Taoos* (the Peacock Throne) and the *Koh-e-Noor* diamond. This was followed by Ahmed Shah Abdali's raids, beginning in 1748, when he annexed Punjab to his domain. The Jats from adjacent areas looted Delhi in 1754. Three years later, Ahmed Shah returned and then again 1759.

His defeat of the Marhattas at Panipat in 1761 did not help in consolidating the Mughal rule in any way. The machinations and vicious intrigue at the court continued unabated. The king was no more than a puppet in the hands of various power players, alternating between the Rohillas, the nawab of Avadh and the Marhattas. It was the British who ultimately prevailed and took firm control of the kings of Delhi towards the closing stages of the century.

The rapid decline from the position of power and prestige that Muslims had occupied in India for eight hundred years left them unprepared for the fate that awaited them. The new reality affected not only the rulers but almost all of them in one way or another. There was lack of acceptance for a while among some. Others, though resigned, were ill-equipped to deal with the change and found it difficult to adjust.

In retrospect, the outcome should not have come as a surprise since the signs had been apparent for a long time. But, in the absence of appropriate institutions for scientific study, research and analysis, these mostly went un-noticed and un-attended. It did not end there. After the collapse, the absence of such institutions prevented appropriate lessons from being learnt and the direction set right.

The soul-searching that took place was at the individual level and led to different paths. The foremost spiritualist thinker of the time was Shah Waliullah Dehlavi (1703 – 1762). He was instrumental in inviting Ahmed Shah Abdali to the aid of Muslims in India, calling it *farz-e-ain* (irresistible over-riding duty). He belonged to a family of Islamic scholars that profoundly influenced Muslim thought in India over a long period of time. His grandfather had founded the famous Rahimiyya Madrassa in Delhi and his father was one of the compilers of *Fatawa-e-Alamgiri*, the well-known treatise on Islamic law.

Shah Waliullah performed Haj in 1730 and stayed on in Makka to study *Hadees* for two years under the same teachers who had taught Abdul Wahab, the father of the Saudi brand of Islam, notably Mohammed Hayat as-Sindi and Abul Hasan as-Sindi. A prolific writer, he authored a number of works on religious philosophy and practice. His most important work was *Hujjat Allah al-bilagha,* in which he discusses the causes of decline, theories of religion, man's spiritual development, economics, political philosophy, etc. One of his works in Arabic, *Al-fauz al-Kabir,* is prescribed reading at Al-Azhar University. He also translated the Koran into Persian as he felt it necessary to understand the text oneself rather than rely on any *tafseer* or *tashrih* (explanation, elucidation) by some one else. Later, his descendants continued with the tradition and apart from translating the Koran into Urdu, acquainted and influenced with his teachings some of the most important leaders of the early nineteenth century.

Like so many other scholars of his time, Shah Waliullah was particularly severe on the devotees of Sufi mystics: '*Every one who goes to the country of Ajmer or to the tomb of Salar Masud* (nineteen-year-old nephew of Mahmud Ghaznavi who had died in battle) *or similar places because of a need which he wants to be fulfilled is a sinner ----*'. He condemned the philosophers and students of other sciences as 'dogs because they lick bones two thousand years old while *ilm* lies in the Koran and *Hadees.*' Wayward monarchs, soldiers in fancy dresses, immoral preachers and keepers of *khanquahs* (mausoleums) come in for equally harsh treatment. In his view, Islam in India had become corrupted through needless emphasis on philosophy, pseudo-Sufism and Saint worship. The way out lay in returning to the basic and pure form of the religion (*Salafism*).

These ideas also reflected the influence of the sixteenth century theologian, Ahmed Sirhindi (1564 – 1624), a *Nakshbandi* revivalist deeply opposed to Akbar's religious innovations. He is often referred to as *Mujaddid alf-e-sani*, a figure expected to rejuvenate Islam in the second millennium, and is widely credited with saving Islam in India from possible diffusion and disintegration. Suspicious of his radically orthodox views, Emperor Jahangir put him in prison for a year in Gwaliar in 1619.

The traumatic events witnessed by Shah Waliullah in his time affected him profoundly and persuaded him to become politically active and involved, siding with the Rohilla leader, Najibuddaula, at the court in Delhi. Strange though it may seem, he failed to see the threat posed by the British to the future of Muslims in India. There were many others like him, including Khwaja Mir Dard, the poet and composer of *Naala-e-andaleeb;* theologian, Mazhar Jan-e-janan, Abdul Ali *Bahr-al-uloom* of Karnatak and Azad Bilgrami from Deccan. All of them were contemporaries, more or less, of Mir Jaffer in Bengal and witnessed the struggles of Haider Ali and his son, Tipu Sultan, against the British in the south. Yet, in their preoccupation with religion, they overlooked these significant political developments and their likely implications for the future.

Perhaps, they were conscious of all this but found the situation too overwhelming and preferred to look for sanctuary in religion. More likely, there was a misplaced belief that religion was the panacea for all ills. If only they became good and proper Muslims, the problems confronting them would somehow get resolved on their own and the looming threats would melt away.

There were others who considered that it had become a religious duty to confront the advance by the unbelievers militarily, in the name of *jihad.* In 1803, Shah Waliullah's son, Shah Abdul Aziz, issued a *fatwa* in Delhi that parts of India that were controlled by the British and where Muslims were no longer free to practice their religion, had become *Dar-ul-harb* (zone of hostility). The struggle waged by Syed Ahmed Shaheed and his companions against the Sikhs that ended in failure, has been described earlier. It is not generally realized, but the movement was much more widespread and lasted for a considerable period of time.

The early British used such terms as 'Fanatic Host' or 'Mohammedan Crescentaders' to describe the individuals involved in the insurrection, only to change it to '*Wahabis*' and later, contemptuously, to '*Jihadis*'. These people remained active for better part of the nineteenth century with their headquarters first in Swat and later at Patna in Bihar. Most noteworthy among them were the *Jamaat-e-Mujahideen*. They had support among all sections of the Muslim society and operated their own independent courts and treasury. In Bengal the scholar Haji Shariatullah set up the *Faraiziya* movement that was later fostered by his son, Dadhu Mian. There was another similar Muslim peasant revolt in 1830, led by Titu Mir.

Bengal was also the home of Maulana Karamat Ali Jaunpuri, a more enlightened Muslim reformer in the sense that along with the return to basic Islam, he advocated the acquisition of scientific and other knowledge from the Europeans. This was rejected by the traditional madrassas on the grounds that skills for earning a living must not be mixed with religious studies.

These movements gradually lost momentum, especially, after the suppression and collapse that followed the sepoy insurrection in 1857. In 1870, both the Sunni and Shia theologians in India disowned and distanced themselves from Wahabism. The decision was as much a reaction to the latter's inability to accommodate other theological points of view as it had to do with political expediency. Regardless, even the more informed among the British could not help but admire the *Mujahideen*. As W. W. Hunter, not always sympathetic to the Muslims, wrote in his report '*The Indian Musalmans: Are They Bound in Conscience to Rebel Against the Queen?*' (London 1871, pp. 68, 70): '*Indefatigable as missionaries, careless of themselves, blameless in their lives, supremely devoted to the overthrow of the English infidels, admirably skilful in organizing a permanent system for supplying money and recruits, the Patna Caliphs stand forth as the types and examples of the sect. Much of their teaching was faultless, and it has been given to them to stir up thousands of their countrymen to a purer life, and a truer conception of the Almighty ----.*

Dangerous firebrands as the local missionaries sometimes prove, I find it impossible to speak of them without respect ----.'

There is a sense of déjà vu today as we witness Muslims struggling against foreign occupation of their homelands in Chechnya, Palestine, Kashmir, Afghanistan, Iraq and other places. Once again, derogatory epithets like 'extremists', 'terrorists', 'Islamists,' 'Islamofascists,' 'jihadis', etc. are being employed to malign them in the public eye, just as it was done two centuries ago by the British in India. The only difference is that this time there is a class of westernized Muslim elite who, in their ignorance of history and inability to separate the cause from effect, not only accept but also mimic the latter's descriptions of what are manifestly genuine and legitimate struggles for independence. More significantly, they have sidelined and abandoned religion and left it at the mercy of obscurantist bigots, which can lead to potentially more dangerous consequences.

Fighting and dying for a cause one believes in is a noble act regardless of who undertakes it. When it is undertaken to help others who are weak and oppressed, the selflessness involved can only be admired as supreme to the point of being sublime. This will always be so as long as the actions remain directed against the aggressor and not against any innocent people. Looking at it in any other way would be both subjective and narrow-minded. The criterion rests in the nature of the motive and the spirit involved in the sacrifice and not on whose behalf it is undertaken. If it is laudable for Lord Byron to fight for the independence of Greece from the Turks and for George Orwell and Ernest Hemingway to join the International Brigade in Spain along with thousands of other volunteers, it should not be any different when Muslims go to the aid of their suffering brothers in Kashmir, Afghanistan, Iraq or any other place.

An off-shoot of *Tarika-e-Mohammediya*, a fundamentalist *Nakshbandi* movement founded in 1734 by Nasir Mohammed in Delhi and endorsed by Shah Waliullah that has survived to the present day is the orthodoxy of *Ahle Hadees*, as represented by the Deoband school {not to be confused with the later day syncretism of Maulana Ahmed Raza Khan Barelvi (1856 – 1921) with a party of similar name (*Ahle Sunnat-val-Hadees*)}. The two have been viscerally opposed to each other on religious as well as political issues. Deobandis hold the Koran and authentic Hadees to be the only true guide in life and reject the concepts of *Ijma* and *Ijtehad* (consensus and endeavour). Even though they accept the Sufi ideals of *Islam* (submission to God), *Imaan* (faith) *and Ihsan* (righteousness), as parts of their belief system, their attitude towards Sufism is not favourable as such.

The theological school, *Dar-al-uloom*, that was set up in Deoband has played a critical and, at the same time, controversial role in the subsequent history of Islam in India. Its founders denounced Sir Syed Ahmed's efforts to ameliorate the lot of the Muslims in the aftermath of their collapse, branding him 'a deadly poison', 'the modern Prophet of nature worshippers' and worse. They rejected his assertion that the Muslims of India constituted a separate nation and later aligned themselves with the Indian National Congress in opposition to the Muslim League. In the same vein, its scholars, led by the *Shaikh-ul-Hind* Hasan Ahmed Madani, bitterly opposed both Iqbal and Jinnah for their demand for a separate state for the Muslims. *Jamiyat-ul-ulemai-Hind*, a political organization inspired by religion, owes its origins to Deoband. Maulana Abul Ala Maudoodi, who later founded the Jamaat-e-Islami, was one of the editors of its journal.

The rejectionist nature of orthodoxy in Islam, its ill-conceived forays into the domain of politics and other matters of purely secular nature, coupled with occasional corruption and readiness among theologians to compromise on principles, has been the cause of major difficulties for Muslims throughout history. It has taken bizarre forms at various times. Mahmud Khilji ruler of Malwa (1436 – 69) obtained *fatwa* from *ulama* in 1450 to go to the assistance of the Hindu ruler of neighbouring Champaner State who was under attack from Mohammed Shah, the Muslim ruler of Gujarat. The *ulama* in Turkey banned Muslims from owning or operating the printing press. Electrical machines were declared the work of the Devil and Sultan Abdul Hameed was obliged to get special vacuum cleaners that worked on steam manufactured in Britain to clean the palace carpets. When the Russians invaded Central Asia, some mullas insisted that their attacks should be resisted using only the weapons that had been in vogue in the time of the Prophet. Their counterparts in India issued *fatwas* that teaching science and English in schools was 'un-Islamic' and to study these subjects '*haraam*'. They also objected to the printing presses and declared the loudspeakers as Devil's instruments.

The situation is no different today. In 2008, a TV channel in India ran a sting operation called, 'Cash-for-*fatwas*' (*Time Magazine*, 21st Septembr 2006). It showed several Indian Muslim clerics allegedly taking, or demanding, bribes of as little as sixty dollars for issuing a desired *fatwa*. In one instance there were two separate *fatwas* from the same source, directly opposed to each other, on whether it was permissible for Muslims to watch

TV. Others concerned the use of credit cards, double beds, camera-equipped cell phones, acting in films, donating organs and teaching English to children. The *fatwas* were 'sold' by not only marginal clerics but also by some noted and respected scholars from well-known institutions ---- one of them from the famous Darul Uloom at Deoband. It underlines the dangers inherent in some self-appointed *ulama* assuming the role of clergy that has no sanction in the Koran and only brings Islam into difficulty, even disrepute.

In a sharp reaction to the fundamentalist attitude adopted at Deoband, an eminent scholar of the time and a professor of Arabic at Aligarh, Maulana Shibli Naumani (1857 – 1914), founded *Nadva-tul-ulama* at Lucknow in 1894 and dedicated it to reform, moderation and rapprochement between the various schools of Muslim thought. Its curriculum was broad-based and included English language as well as other non-religious subjects but was by no means as modern in outlook as Aligarh. Shibli wished to reform Islam from within and viewed western values through an Islamic prism. Perhaps, his most significant contribution is his biography of the second caliph, Umar Farooq. Apart from this, he also wrote *Sheer-e-Ajam*, a book on Persian poetry and *Seerat-un-Nabi*, an unfinished biography of the Prophet.

Another literary figure and Islamic reformist of the time was Altaf Husain Hali (1837 – 1914) a pupil of the great poet, Asadullah Khan Ghalib. Perhaps, best known for his *Mussadis-e-Hali*, a lament on the sorry state to which the Muslims had reduced themselves. Annemarie Schimmel thinks, 'it was the first great Indo-Muslim poem that touched reality instead of dwelling upon metaphorical or divine love ---- neither high-soaring mystical dreams nor complicated rhetorical devices, let alone the flirtatious and immoral tone of the Lucknow ghazal, could help the Muslims face their basic duties and lead them towards a more glorious future.' It was a wake-up call to face the realities as they existed and not dwell in the past or indulge in escapism, as evident at the time in many quarters.

The plight of the Muslim women in India was particularly pitiful. Mostly confined to their homes, they received next to no education. Most of what they learnt was confined to *Bahishti Zeyvar,* a voluminous compilation of religious and social instructions by Maulana Ashraf Ali Thanvi of Deoband (1863 – 1943) which they studied at home. It was given to the brides as a part of their dowry and served as a reference book for subsequent life. It was rare indeed for a girl from among the 'respectable' Muslim families to be allowed to leave home to attend school.

Hali was moved by the sorry state of the Muslim family and the problems of women in particular which became the subject of his *Majlis-an-niswan* in 1874. Earlier in 1869, Deputy Nazir Ahmed (1831 – 1912), a civil servant and an intrepid social reformer, had painted the portrait of a model Muslim woman in his *Mirat-al-Urus* (The Bride's Mirror). He also wrote *Ibnul Waqt* (Man of the Time) in which he discusses the dilemma of a young man devoted to western ways of life. In 1892, Mirza Qalich Beg from Sind wrote about the emancipation of women in his novel *Zeenat*. Mumtaz Ali Taj published the hugely popular magazine for women *Tehzeeb-e-Niswan* from Lahore and looked forward to the day when educated Muslim women would complement the work of men.

One of the earliest schools for Muslim girls was founded by Allahbakhsh Abbujha in Karachi at the end of the nineteenth century. There was a strong, widespread and passionate opposition to the setting up of such institutions. A few men of vision, conviction and courage, on the other hand, believed that emancipation of the society, without first educating women, was next to impossible. One of them, Maulana Abdul Haq Abbas, set up the first residential school for Muslim girls, *Madrassa-tul-Banat*, in Jullunder at the turn of the last century, entirely from his own resources. Despite vehement opposition from orthodox quarters, it became hugely popular among middle class Muslim families. Within a span of forty years, it became a sprawling university for women spread over twenty-five acres, financed exclusively by private donations.

The names of two Muslim jurists of the period are also noteworthy in the context of reform. Akbar Allahabadi (1846 – 1921) a judge of the High Court wrote verses that ridiculed the eagerness on the part of some Muslims to mimic the westerners as well as those who, while outwardly observing the rituals, neglected or ignored the true spirit of Islam. Syed Ameer Ali, belonging to a Shia family in Bengal, was a barrister who rose to become a member of the Viceroy's Executive Council in 1883. His best-known work, *The Spirit of Islam*, presents the religion as a civilizing force and a modern and progressive movement. He also wrote, *A Short History of the Saracens*, in 1899 that recounts their past achievements.

Perhaps, the most controversial movement to emerge in the dying days of the nineteenth century was the *Ahmadiya* founded by Mirza Ghulam Ahmad of Qadian. After some Epiphany-like experience, he declared himself to be the Promised Messiah (*Maseeh-e-Maood*) or *Mehdi* in the reformist mode in 1891. He was an ardent admirer of Queen Victoria and the British rule in India, terming the latter as just and fair. Any struggle against it was not considered justified since it did not obstruct or interfere in the observance and practice of Islam in any way. Other Muslims, including Sir Syed and the poet, Dr. Iqbal, questioned his claims on religious as well as nationalistic grounds. In 1914, the movement split in two, Lahori and Qadiani, with the former disowning Mirza Ghulam Ahmad as the Messiah, calling him a *Mujaddid* or reformer instead.

In 1975, the Saudis declared Ahmadism a heresy and banned its members from entering the country, even for Haj. Shortly afterwards, Zulfiquar Ali Bhutto of Pakistan had a resolution passed in the National Assembly branding Ahmadis as non-Muslims. Later, during the obscurantist reign of his successor, General Zia-ul-Haq, the community was badly persecuted. Islam has always been a very tolerant and inclusive religion. Given its history of acceptance and accommodation of other creeds in the sub-continent, it is incongruous that its followers should adopt such an extreme attitude, in the modern day and age, towards one of its own sects.

A much later addition to the reform movements within Islam was the advent of *Tablighi Jamaat* that found home in Raiwind. It originated basically as a reaction to the Hindu *Shudhi* movement in the 1920s. The latter was aimed at, if necessary, forcibly re-converting Muslims whose ancestors had been Hindus at some stage. *Tablighi Jamaat* never had any political aspirations and concerned itself primarily with educating Muslims about the true values of Islam and purifying it by getting rid of the extraneous influences that had crept in from external sources and other creeds. It holds its annual gathering in the town of Raiwind in Punjab, attended by the largest number of Muslims in the world, next only to *Hajj*.

One of the greatest and most influential figures in the history of Muslims in India, Sir Syed Ahmed Khan, was born in 1817. He took up employment with the East India Company as a judge when barely in his twenties. During the mutiny of 1857, out of compassion, he helped to save the lives of many Englishmen stranded in Bijnaur. Subsequently, he wrote *Asbab-e-Baghavat-e-Hind*, a dissertation that laid the blame for the insurrection on both the parties involved.

In 1869 – 70, he spent some time in England that was to have a profound affect on his thinking. He learnt to admire the British, their achievements and their rule in India. 'If through the will of God we are subjugated by a nation which gives religious freedom, rules with justice, maintains peace in the country and respects our individuality and property as it is done by the British rule in India, we should be loyal to it.' Such views did not meet with approval among the orthodox Muslims and he was duly labeled as a *kafir* (infidel) or apostate. Even people like Akbar Allahabadi were cynical and contemptuous of his Anglophilia.

It did not shake him from his conviction that by secluding themselves from modern science and sources of knowledge, Muslims would be condemned to a very bleak and uncertain future. Muslim children attended madrassas run according to antiquated medieval syllabi whereas Hindus had no qualms about going to schools run by the government or Christian Missionaries. It created a widening gap between the two communities in terms of ability to benefit from the available economic, social and political opportunities that was to have a telling effect in the future.

In his own words, Sir Syed wanted 'to make the Muslims of India desirous of the best kind of civilisation so that it shall remove the contempt with which civilized peoples regard the Muslims, and the latter shall become reckoned among the respected and civilized people in the world.' He believed that the path to emancipation of the Muslims lay in the kind and quality of the education they received and worked tirelessly to convince others of this point of view.

His efforts bore fruit in 1877 when the foundations for the Anglo-Indian College were laid at Aligarh. It was converted into a university in 1920. However, the British turned down the request for it to open subsidiary colleges for Muslims throughout India along the lines of the London University. The so-called Aligarh Movement, born out of the Muhammadan Anglo-Oriental Educational Conference of 1886, became an instrument for propagation of Sir Syed's ideas throughout Muslim India. It led to the founding of similar institutions in other parts of the country, including the Dacca College by Ubaidullah Suhrawardi that too became a university after World War I.

All these developments made the orthodox clergy deeply suspicious of Sir Syed. They even went as far as Makkah and Medina to obtain *fatwas* that he had become 'the *khalifa* of *Shaitaan* (Devil's Deputy) himself who is intent upon leading the Muslims astray; whose perfidy is worse than that of the Jews and the Christians' (*Sayyid Ahmad Khan: Reinterpretation of Muslim Theology*, by Christian W. Troll, p.21). Mirza Ghulam Ahmad, founder of the Ahmadi sect, dubbed him as a *necharee* (a rationalist who denies the supernatural) and vehemently condemned him.

The university at Aligarh was to play a crucial role in the destiny of Muslim India. As Khairi has put it, 'The students at Aligarh came from far and wide, but by studying and playing in groups, arguing and debating with each other, and eating and living together, they developed a strong bond of mutual sympathy and a common outlook. ---- They came to the college as Bengalis, Biharis and Punjabis, Pathans and Gujaratis, and went out simply as Aligarians and Muslims ----- (with) a powerful Islamic consciousness, and a sense of mission. No educational institution ever played such a decisive role in the fortunes of any nation as Aligarh did in the case of Indian Muslims.'

Sir Syed held widely divergent views on Islam from those of the orthodox preachers. Among other things, he rejected Hadees that did not conform to reason and insisted upon a more 'practical' interpretation of the Koran. The *Hadood* punishments mentioned in Sura 5:33, for instance, are valid only if the country is too poor to maintain prisons for thieves and wrong-doers. Taking of interest was permissible; it is only usury that is condemned. Slavery was permitted only in the beginning but not after the Prophet's return to Makkah. Maulana Shibli Naumani appears to be broadly in agreement with such interpretations (*Al-Farooq*). He was acutely aware of the danger in Islam being turned into a synonym for *Fikah* (code of law) as a result of the excessive preoccupation with the latter.

In the course of time, the human opinion of the *ulama* came to be identified with the will of Allah and His word had become encrusted with layers of secondary interpretations. Nothing in the Koran was contrary to nature and *Vahee* (Divine inspiration) and natural law are identical. He also proclaimed, 'Philosophy will be in our right hand, natural science in our left, and the crown of *La ilaha il-Allah, Mohammed-ar-rasul Allah* (there is no deity but God and Mohammed is His messenger) on our head. In some ways these were not very different to the *Mutazilite* School in the ninth century.

Sir Syed was politically inclined only to the extent where it concerned the rights and emancipation of the Muslims of India whom he believed to be a separate nation. He was not enamoured of pan-Islamism and did not contribute to the idea that the Sultan of Turkey was the caliph of Muslims everywhere. 'For a thousand years, our own religion of Islam had been intimately bound up with India; and in India, Islam had won some of its greatest triumphs, for its own popular form of civilization.' It prompted the Maverick pan-Islamist, Jamaluddin Afghani, to brand him as a *Dahri*, materialist and an agent of the British. As we shall see, abolition of the caliphate in Turkey by Mustafa Kamal at the end of World War I was destined to become a serious issue in the politics of India.

When Mongols put an end to the Abbasid caliphate in Baghdad in 1258, an heir was installed in Egypt as the Fatimid caliph and various Muslim rulers used his authority to legitimize their assumption of power. The Ottoman Sultans assumed this role after Selim I annexed Egypt in 1517. The institution faded away with the decline of Ottoman rule. It was revived again in the nineteenth century in the hope that it would serve as a political centre for the Muslims. Jamaluddin Afghani had been one of its main proponents.

There is no historical basis for the assumption that a caliph wields spiritual authority over all Muslims. The Koran does not specify any system of government as such; only that the Muslims should resolve any collective issues through mutual consultation and consensus (42:38 and Maulana Maudoodi's *Khilafat-o-Malukiat*). The Prophet also did not express a preference for any particular administrative regime (*Al-Farooq*, p. 575). Leaving aside the first half-century or so following the demise of the Prophet, the caliph remained a political leader guided in varying degrees by the juridical opinion of the court *ulama*. During the Abbasid caliphate (750-1258) when Baghdad was the capital of the Islamic world, the court was ruled by an aristocratic ethos, which had little to do with Islam. The *Sharia* initially developed as a countercultural revolt against this ethos. The clerics and the ruling class thus operated according to entirely different norms.

In essence, *Sharia* is a loosely defined way of life derived from the principles and edicts laid down in the Koran and the sayings of the Prophet. It is not a Divine code of laws, as erroneously claimed in some quarters. The Arabic word *Sharia* literally means 'the way'. It appears in the Koran, only in this context. It can be confusing when the same word is used to describe a set of man-made laws. The two are not the same. One expresses a way of life based on the Koran and Sunnah and the other is simply a code of laws, enacted through subsequent human endeavour, to serve a basically legal purpose.

It is generally agreed that there are six basic principles of *Sharia* as the way of life and rights for Muslims derived from the Koran. These include the right to the protection of life, the protection of family, the protection of religion, the protection of property and the rights to education and preservation of human dignity.

The so-called Islamic law, known as *fikah*, is a code based on individual interpretations of *Sharia*. These interpretations have varied from time to time and from person to person, giving rise to a number of schools of *fikah*, the major ones being the *Hanafia, Hunmbli, Maliki, Shaafi* and *Jaafria*. Each of these differs from the rest. These differences have only widened with the passage of time as was brought to light in a stark manner when an Islamic court in Dubai sentenced a couple caught having sex on the beech to three months in prison (AFP, 16th October 2008). Had the offence been committed in any other Islamic country the punishment in all probability would have been quite different.

The position with regards to the imposition of *Sharia* or *Fikah* in the present time is spelt out by Maulana Abul Ala Maudoodi who admits in his book '*Sood*' (pp. 183-4), '*We accept, conditions in the world have changed. A great revolution has taken place in cultural and economic fields and it has completely altered the financial and commercial environment. Under these new conditions the evolutionary stipulations that were put into effect in the early days of Islam, based on the economic and cultural conditions in Hijaz, Iraq, Syria and Egypt, do not meet the present requirements of Muslims. The rules of Sharia formulated by the theologians in the past were relevant only to the conditions that existed around them at the time. Many of these conditions are no longer relevant and many new situations have arisen that did not exist in the past. Therefore, the provisions concerning commerce, finance and economics found in the old books of Fika are in need of considerable elaboration and broadening in scope. There is no disputing the fact that the Islamic laws governing economic and financial matters need to be revised. All that remain to be determined are the lines along which this should be done.*'

This naturally raises a number of questions. If it is necessary to bring in line the laws concerning economic and financial matters with the prevailing conditions, should the principle not apply equally to the rest of the body of law? Secondly, would it not be simpler and much more practical to leave the existing code of law that has been tested over a period of centuries as it is and exclude only those stipulations from it that contravene the spirit of Koranic injunctions rather than devising a whole new code of untried law *ab initio*?

Developing new laws is a highly complex issue requiring great legal skills and experience. It takes a long time to test and establish precedence for these at various levels in courts. It is also open to serious question if the theologians who are not familiar and well-versed with the complexities and requirements of modern jurisprudence are the best people to meddle in these affairs? If attempted, any such adventure will almost certainly lead to massive confusion and disruption, in the process, bringing Islam into needless disrepute.

None-the-less, there are many religious zealots today who believe that by regulating personal behaviour through the imposition of *Sharia*, it is possible to achieve the Islamic ideal. The issue has been turned into a political tool concerned with power. The aim is not the sublimation of the soul or sharing of the aspirations of the people and alleviating their sufferings but mobilizing them for decidedly political objectives. Theirs is a very limited and time-bound political agenda. It can only lead to a retrogressive and dysfunctional theocratic police state and nothing more.

An Islamic order reduced to a penal code, stripped of its humanism, aesthetics, intellectual quests, and spiritual devotion distorts religion, debases tradition, and twists the political process wherever it unfolds. We have seen this absolute assertion of one, generally de-contextualized aspect of religion, to the exclusion of the rest, bring chaos, misery and disillusionment to Algeria in the nineteenth century and more recently to Iran, Sudan and Taliban ruled Afghanistan. The ultimate effect of the exercise has been to present an inherently dynamic and humane religion in bad light and provide ammunition to its detractors to misrepresent and defame the good name of Islam.

REPRESSION WITH A VENGEANCE

The removal and humiliation inflicted on Bahadur Shah Zafar in 1858 signaled the termination of what remained of the Mughal rule and with it the end of a civilization in India. The new order that replaced the old did not accept or acknowledge the Indians as a composite society but one that was divided between many groups, the principal among them being Hindus and Muslims. They were to be approached differently, with the latter being singled out for extremely discriminatory and harsh treatment.

As stated earlier, Islamophobia runs deep in the psyche of the European race. Most historians attribute it to the defeats suffered in Spain, the Crusades and East Europe. There may be more to it. European Christians are ideologically pre-disposed to looking down upon people of other religions and races, regarding them not simply as different but also inferior in some way. It may have its roots in religion itself. Like the Jews who consider themselves a cut above the rest as 'the chosen people of God' based on a Biblical injunction, the westerners too have come to believe that if you are not of European and Christian descent, somehow, you must be inferior, sometimes even sub-human.

At the end of first century AD, Saint Paul proclaimed his 'Supersessionist Theory' that the followers of Jesus had replaced the 'true Israel' as the 'chosen people'. In 1095, when Pope Urban II declared holy war to capture Jerusalem and Palestine, he addressed the European Christians as 'the race beloved and chosen by God.' During the Second Crusade half a century later, Peter the Venerable incited his troops to liberate the Holy Sepulcher in Jerusalem as a way to confirm the rejection of the Jews and the election of the believers in Christ.

The Supersessionist Theory also motivated the expulsion of Muslims and Jews in 1492 from Spain, as their refusal to convert clashed with the Spanish claim to be replacing the Hebrews as the new 'Chosen People' who would transform Spain into 'God's Land,' and the royal family into the new 'House of David.' Even Hitler used Christian theology to justify his slaughter of Jews, writing in Mein Kampf, '*By fighting off the Jews, I am doing the Lord's work.*' For him, the choice was unequivocal: '*There cannot be two Chosen People,*' he once said. '*We are God's People.*'

This urge to discredit the merit of Judaism also explains the Christian obsession with Jews as the killers of Christ ---- an element in the religion's early attempt to vilify Jews. As characterized by the scholar David Flusser, 'Christian anti-Judaism was not a coincidental lapse' but a tool serving as 'godfather to the formation of Christianity' (*The Abraham Complex* by Avi Beker, Professor at Georgetown University and Secretary General of the World Jewish Congress in *The New Republic,* July 2008).

Like the Jews and the Gypsies, Muslims were also singled out and persecuted on the assumption that they posed a threat to Christendom. Extensive legislation was enacted to mark, isolate and quarantine Muslims to prevent 'contamination' of Christians through religious, social, sexual or similar other contact. This was in marked contrast to the situation in the Middle East where Muslims and Christians co-existed amicably, even sharing their places of worship. For a deeper insight into the attitude of the European Christians, in particular, towards Islam and the Muslims, please see *Saracens: Islam in the Medieval European Imagination* by John V. Tolan, Columbia University Press, New York, 2002.

William Dalrymple notes (pp. 477 - 79): '*For the British after 1857, the Indian Muslim became an almost subhuman creature, to be classified in unembarrassedly racist imperial literature alongside such other despised and subject specimens, such as Irish Catholics or the "Wandering Jew". The depth to which Indian Muslims had sunk in British eyes is visible in an 1868 production called* 'The People of India', *which contains photographs of the different castes and tribes of South Asia ranging from Tibetans and Aboriginals (illustrated with a picture of a naked tribal) to the Doms of Bihar. The image of "the Mahomedan" is illustrated by a picture of an Aligarh labourer who is given the following caption: "His features are peculiarly Mahomedan ----* (and) *exemplify in a strong manner the obstinacy, sensuality, ignorance and bigotry of his class. It is hardly possible, perhaps, to conceive features more essentially repulsive."*

'*The profound contempt that the British so openly expressed for the Indian Muslim and Mughal culture proved contagious, particularly to the ascendant Hindus, who quickly hardened their attitude to all things Islamic ------.*'

This was much more than a simple attempt at widening the Hindu-Muslim divide. It was confirmation, if indeed one was needed, of the pre-existence of inherent visceral hatred of Islam and the Muslims among the British that only found its full expression after the collapse of the mutiny. To a large extent, the same is true for the Hindus. Without prior adverse predisposition among the Hindus, the British would have found it hard if not impossible to sow the seeds of division between them and the Muslims. Instead, they found fertile ground in the exclusive Hinduism to sow the seeds of mistrust and misgivings. Had India been one nation, as was later claimed, three quarters of its population could not have collaborated so fully and wholeheartedly with the invaders and turned against their own so readily as the Hindus did against the Muslims after 1857.

We can see signs of exclusion, separation and animosity even today, long after the British had departed. The Indians erected statues of Shivaji, the Rani of Jhansi and other Hindu heroes everywhere after independence but none to commemorate Haider Ali, Tipu Sultan or any of the other Muslims who had resisted the British. ' ------ *for many Indians today, rightly or wrongly, the Mughals are still perceived as it suited the British to portray them in the imperial propaganda that they taught in Indian schools after 1857: as sensual, decadent, temple-destroying invaders --- something that was forcefully and depressingly demonstrated by the whole episode of the demolition of the Baburi Masjid at Ayodhya in 1992. The profoundly sophisticated, liberal and plural civilization championed by Akbar, Dara Shikoh or the later Mughal emperors has only a limited resonance for the urban middle class in modern India. Many of these are now deeply ambivalent about the achievements of the Mughals, even if they will still happily eat a Mughal meal, or flock to the cinema to watch a Bollywood Mughal epic, or indeed head to the Red Fort to hear their Prime Minister give the annual Independence Day speech from the battlements in front of the Lahore Gate*' (*The Last Mughal*, p. 479).

Since the start of their political ambitions in the country, the British had viewed the Muslims in India as their main rivals. As more and more areas came under their control, they embarked upon a deliberate policy to undermine and weaken the position of Muslims in whatever way possible. In 1772, the land revenue system was changed to one based on auctioning the receipts to highest bidders for limited time periods. Any *zamindar* (farmer) unable to pay the dues had his holding confiscated. It called for availability of large amounts of ready cash to own land which could only be mustered by Hindu money lenders or the Company officials. As a result, over the course of the next few years, the Muslim *zamindars* were practically reduced to the status of serfdom throughout the Company controlled lands. The Permanent Settlement legislation of 1793 completed the process, virtually transferring all *zamindaris* to the Hindus and, in the process, giving rise to a symbiotic relationship between them and the British, based on mutual profit at the expense of the Muslims (see Chapter5: British Occupation).

Within a very short period of time, Muslim aristocracy was wiped out and replaced by a new middle class of Hindu *zamindars* and financial and commercial entrepreneurs. British interest in India had been primarily economic and commercial, especially during the Company rule. Hindus acting as the middlemen became familiar with European methods and ideas much earlier and benefited economically and in other ways in the process. The centres of power in India also shifted from their traditional seats in places like Delhi, Agra and Lahore to the new commercial hubs like Calcutta, Bombay and Madras.

Prior to the arrival of the British in India, the education system for the Muslims was based on religion and paid for through charitable endowments, known as *waqfs*. There was a madrassa attached to almost every mosque. In addition, there were thousands of other institutions in all the larger population centres dedicated to the pursuit of knowledge which is regarded as a religious duty in Islam. The larger institutions relied on incomes from land grants specifically made to support them. Under the newly enacted Resumption Regulations, the Company confiscated more than two million acres of these *waqf* lands in its jurisdiction between 1828 and 1840. Many mosques were taken over and some of these were auctioned off to Hindus, others handed over as residences for Christian missionaries.

The effect on the Muslims was devastating. As W. W Hunter noted in his report, '*An additional revenue of 300,000 pounds a year was permanently gained by the state, representing a capital at 5 per cent of six million sterling. A large part of this sum was derived from the lands held rent free by Musalmans or Muhammadan foundations. The panic and hatred which ensued have stamped themselves for ever on the rural records. Hundreds of ancient families were ruined and the education system of the Musalmans which was almost entirely maintained by rentfree grants, received its death blow. The scholarly class of the Muhammadans emerged from the eighteen years of harrying absolutely ruined.*' Since, unlike the Hindus, the Muslims were averse to attending Company or Mission-operated educational institutions, they now lacked the skills and standards needed for gainful employment. From here on it was a long, slippery slope to deprivation and degradation for them.

The punitive measures against the Muslims were not simply confined to the confiscation of lands and forfeiture of pensions. '*Oriental departments were abolished at government colleges; Persian schools were taken over by the education department; the court of Sadar diwani adalat was set aside ---- in 1868 the centre of government in NWP* (later named UP) *was moved from Agra, scene of great Mughal glories, to Allahabad, holy city of the Hindus*' (*Separatism Among the Indian Muslims* by Francis Robinson, Cambridge University Press, London, 1974, p.101).

Apart from military and civil service, the Muslims had also been traditionally engaged in the maritime trade, manufacture of leather goods, jewellery and weaving carpets, silk, muslin and embroidered fabrics. All of these were systematically destroyed by the Company policies. As Khairi put it, '*The Company policies had been calamitous for them* (the Muslims) *as a community. Their ruling class was eliminated. Their upper classes lost their land and the higher jobs in government. Their middle class could no longer find traditional careers in the military and civil police. Their working classes were thrown out of employment because of the collapse of their industries. Their cultivator classes were driven to starvation by the tyranny of the revenue collectors. Their trading class lost their business. Their scholars lost their means of sustenance because of the Resumptions. All classes were affected. The Indian Muslims in 1856 were, in the words of Sir William Hunter, "a race ruined under British rule"* (p. 19).

Concurrently, there were efforts afoot to revive and rejuvenate Hinduism and Hindu identity. While earlier British visitors to India had expressed fawning admiration for the Mughals, their new historians danced to a very different tune. They were now describing the Muslim rule as unmitigated disaster for the Hindus in particular, who were asked to be grateful to the British for saving them from the tyranny. New books based on mistranslation of sources, fanciful editing and tangential representation of facts became prescribed reading for history classes in schools and colleges throughout India. In the main, they painted a picture of two enlightened and glorious periods in Indian history, one under the Hindus and the other under the British, intervened by eight hundred years of oppression and darkness under the Muslims.

It didn't take long for the effects of the policies of bias and discrimination to take effect. The population of Bengal was largely Muslim. According to Hunter, 'A hundred and seventy years ago it was impossible for a well-born Musalman in Bengal to become poor; at present (1871) it is almost impossible for him to continue rich ----. None of the native gentlemen in the Covenanted Civil Services or up to the bench of the High Court are Musalmans.' The situation was not much different in the lower grades. In 1850, the number of Muslim lawyers at the High Court Bar had exceeded that of Hindus and British put together but after that, of the two hundred and forty natives that were admitted, there was only one who was Muslim.

The British intended to fundamentally alter the Indian society as a matter of deliberate policy. This was enunciated by Lord Macaulay in February 1835: '*It is impossible for us, with our limited means, to attempt to educate the body of the people. We must at present do our best to form a class who may be interpreters between us and the millions whom we govern; a class of persons, Indian in blood and colour, but English in taste, in opinions, in morals, and in intellect. To that class we may leave it to refine the vernacular dialects of the country, to enrich those dialects with terms of science borrowed from the Western nomenclature, and to render them by degrees fit vehicles for conveying knowledge to the great mass of the population.*' The 'class' of people they chose to bring this about was from among the Hindus.

Hunter also noted that 'it was not because qualified Muslims were not available, for even when qualified for Government employ they are studiously kept out of it by Government notification; the Government publicity singles out Muhammadans in Gazettes for exclusion from the posts. ---- In fact, there is now scarcely a Government office in Calcutta in which a Muhammadan can hope for any post above the rank of porter, messenger, filler of inkpots and mender of pens. ---- It matters not what department or profession I turn the result is the same.' The situation in the educational institutions was particularly alarming and entailed devastating long-term consequences. According to a note recorded by the Viceroy Lord Mayo on 26th June 1871, the number of Muslim students in Bengal was only about twelve per cent of the total while they accounted for more than half the population of the province. The rest were all Hindus. (Some specific instances of bias against the Muslims have also been discussed in the chapters on *British Occupation* and *Crystallising A Deam*).

The self-imposed Muslim aversion to Government and Missionary schools and colleges only helped to widen the burgeoning economic and political gap between them and the Hindus still further. There were other impediments as well that made the situation worse in certain specific sectors like finance and banking, for instance. Religious taboos against usury, that were extended to include interest by orthodox mullas, prevented many Muslims from joining these professions. Similarly *fatwas* against the learning of science and English came in the way of more of them by not allowing them to be appropriately and adequately qualified for the new jobs market.

Persian had been the court language in India since the thirteenth century, even when the country was ruled by the Turkish-speaking Mughals. During this period, as a result of prolonged contacts between the ordinary citizens, a new language gradually evolved that was a mixture of mostly dialects indigenous to northern India and words from Persian, Turkish and Arabic. In the early stages, it was only spoken in military camps, hence its name 'Urdu', which refers to the army in Turkish. Although written in Persian script, its vocabulary consists of mostly Prakit (an indigenous Indian language) words as does its syntax and grammar. After Chinese and English, it is the third most widely spoken and understood language in the world.

Whereas Persian, Turkish and Arabic were essentially languages of the Muslims, Urdu was a product exclusive to India. By the time the British had asserted their authority over India, Urdu had become the *lingua franca* in the civilized circles of northern India, both Hindu and Muslim. In 1831, the British abolished Persian as the official language of the state. After this, in the effort to widen the gulf between the Hindus and the Muslims, they proceeded to create a separate language for the former. Sanskrit was not in common use, other than in the religious texts. Instead, they purged as many Persian and Arabic words as possible from Urdu and replaced these with Sanskrit substitutes, calling the new product Hindi or, as the British later referred to it, Hindustani. The script was changed from Persian to Devnagri. All government officials were required to develop a prescribed level of proficiency in the new language. The first Hindi book in prose, *Prem Sagar*, by Lalluji Lal was published by the British at Fort William College in 1809 (see *A History of Hindi Literature*, by F. E Keay, Oxford University Press, Calcutta, 1920). It is now the official language of India, along with English.

Its use in courts and government offices was mandated as early as 1872 in the Central Provinces, followed by Behar (then part of Bengal) and UP, the cradle of Urdu. Ten years later, the use of Persian script in official documents was completely forbidden. Even though it was a transparently divisive move, the Hindus welcomed and embraced it enthusiastically. This repudiation of the common culture by the Hindus left many a Muslim highly disillusioned, foremost among them Sir Syed Ahmad Khan. According to his biographer, Altaf Hussain Hali, he told some friends in words that became prophetic, 'Now I am convinced that the two nations will not join wholeheartedly in anything. At present, there is no open hostility between the two nations, but on account of the so-called "educated" people it will increase immensely in the future. He who will still be alive will see' (*Hayat-e-Javaid*, p. 194).

The signs of parting of the ways had been there for a long time but the Muslim leaders failed to take notice or did not wish to believe the reality that was becoming increasingly apparent. By disowning a common heritage and seeking a separate cultural and national identity for themselves, the Hindus had sown the seeds for division of the country and eventual creation of Pakistan. The exclusive and dominant position now held by the Hindus in the economic, commercial, administrative and political fields, only added to the misgivings, alienation and resentment among the Muslims.

In the past, there had been a number of Hindu reform movements that had been primarily religious in nature or concerned with internal social issues. Familiarity with British institutions and ways of working brought with it a new awareness of political rights and aspirations. As early as mid-nineteenth century, they began to form associations with a view to organizing public opinion and liaising with the British authorities on collective issues. These activities were quickly extended to London to enlist support in prominent political circles, particularly Irish and Liberal sympathisers. A Parsi businessman Dadabhai Naoroji, even got himself elected as a Liberal MP from Finsbury from 1892 - 95. The demands of these outfits became more assertive and strident in tenor and tone as they gained support and confidence with the passage of time.

Hindus also became aware of the power inherent in the press quite early on. A host of publications began to appear in the local languages but it was the English press that mattered the most. Newspapers like the *Amrit Bazar Putrica* and the *Hindu Patriot* in Bengal, the *Indian Herald* in UP, the *Hindu* in Madras, the *Marhatta* in Bombay and the *Tribune* in Lahore, all influential in their own right, came into existence at this time. These proved highly effective in moulding public opinion on the one hand, espousing Hindu causes and keeping the authorities reminded of these on the other. With the awareness of this new-found strength came restiveness and the desire for a greater share of power. The British were beginning to face resistance and opposition to their rule, albeit, of a token nature at first.

This was mostly relevant to the Hindus. Muslims had lost ground in every sphere of life. They had been squeezed economically, outclassed in education and marginalized in the affairs of government. Worse still, they had no voice and no means to express their feelings. Added to the existing resentment against the British due to events leading up and subsequent to the mutiny, it had created a potentially worrisome situation. A commission of enquiry was set up in Bengal under William Hunter, a British civil servant, to examine and report on all of its aspects. His findings were published in 1871 in the book, *The Indian Musalmans: Are They Bound in Conscience to Rebel Against the Queen?* (Reprinted by Premier Book House, Lahore, 1974). It painted a grim picture of the plight of Muslims, through discrimination, deprivation and neglect, supported by facts, figures and statistics gathered by Hunter, as quoted in parts earlier. A similar study, carried out in Madras, *Muhammadan Education and Employment of Muhammadans in Public Services*, was equally damning in its conclusions.

It became obvious that the British had gone too far in placating and pandering to the Hindu interests at the expense of the Muslims. There were growing fears of a backlash born out of desperation among the latter. The calls for a 'change of course' took a long time to be heard before the wheels of bureaucracy could start to grind slowly into action. In any case, it was a daunting task since Hindus had already gained a lead of over a century in terms of education, employment and economic advantage. It has remained a catch-up game for the Muslims ever since.

THE GREAT GAME

While this was going on, a new situation had developed beyond India's north-western border. The sustained Russian advance into Central Asia was getting ever closer and had become a source of consternation both in London and Calcutta. The assumption was that it was a prelude to the invasion and occupation of India. In order to forestall any such move, it was decided to bring Afghanistan under British control. In 1878, a mission led by General Sir Neville Chamberlain was dispatched to negotiate terms with the Amir, Sher Ali Khan, but the latter refused to entertain the general. An ultimatum was issued and when that expired without any response, a force led by General Roberts invaded Afghanistan.

It was equipped with the latest guns with rifled barrels, long-range rifles and Gattling machine guns to which the poor Afghans had no answer. Kabul was occupied with ease. Sher Ali tried to take refuge in Turkmenistan but the Russians turned him down. He died soon afterwards. The British installed his son, Yakub Khan on the throne and made him sign the treaty of Gandamak. Under its terms, the Amir was to receive an annual stipend of 60,000 pounds in return for surrendering control over Khaibar Pass and some adjoining areas. In addition, he was required to accept a British Resident who would oversee and advise the king on matters of policy.

The British had learnt nothing from the earlier disastrous Afghan campaign of 1938 (see previous chapter). No sooner had the force withdrawn, the Afghans murdered the Resident, Major Cavignari, and his detachment. Roberts was told to return to Kabul with orders for vengeance from Viceroy Lytton, '*Your objects should be to strike terror and strike it swiftly and deeply; but to avoid a reign of terror.*' Roberts carried out simultaneous public hangings of scores of men in the city and razed numerous buildings to the ground. A series of punitive expeditions were undertaken deep into outlying districts, with accompanying atrocities. He was ruthless: '*In addition to the natural hatred which every Afghan feels towards a foreign invader, there is a strong underlying current of fanaticism which, unless promptly checked, becomes at times, and especially against a Christian enemy uncontrollable*' (*Roberts in India: The Military Papers of Field Marshal Lord Roberts, 1876 - 1893*, Army Records Society).

Amir Yakub Khan was taken prisoner and deported to Calcutta and plans were made to partition the country, with Herat being handed over to Persia. Things did not quite work out in this way. Yakub Khan's younger brother, Ayub Khan, had gathered a number of tribes in western Afghanistan to resist the occupation. They decimated a British force sent to intercept them at Maiwand, north of Kandhar. Roberts took a large force out of Kabul and managed to defeat Ayub Khan. A peace deal was signed restoring status quo in Afghanistan, with Yakub Khan's nephew, Abdul Rahman Khan, as the new Amir.

After occupying Turkmenistan in 1884 - 85, the Russians advanced into western Afghanistan and captured Panjdeh. It created a tense situation and there was a danger of confrontation between the two colonial powers. The possibility of war was averted since none of them was in a position to sustain one at this time. Instead, it was agreed that the Russian-Afghan border should be settled by a joint Anglo-Russian commission.

The Great Game did not end there. The Russian advance into Central Asia continued unabated as the British kept a wary eye on its course. Much of what transpired was linked to the political developments in Europe and the dwindling Ottoman Empire in particular. Opinion in Britain was divided, with the Tories favouring a 'forward' policy while the Liberals took a less aggressive approach. At one stage (1903 – 04), Tibet was invaded and occupied on the unfounded pretext that the Russians were making inroads into the country. The Game finally came to an end after the Japanese inflicted a resounding defeat on Russia in the Far East in 1905, emasculating the latter both militarily as well as economically and leaving her in no position to pose a serious threat.

RISE OF HINDU NATIONALISM

It was inevitable that contacts with Europe and introduction to western political thought and development should give rise to similar awareness and ambition in India. Historical novels and books started to be published extolling the Hindu past in an effort to revive and regain national pride.

Perhaps, the best known among these were the history books for school children written by a Hindu judge, Romesh Chandra Dutt. The parts of India under British control soon began to exhibit signs of diffused but palpable discontent and restiveness. As early as 1868, a member of the Governor General's Council, Sir John Strachey, had noted: 'There is hardly any class of population which hates us more thoroughly than the highly educated gentlemen of lower Bengal.' There was a need to provide a release mechanism for such pent up feelings if a widespread explosion was to be avoided in India.

After much thought, deliberation and planning at the highest level, it was decided to create a forum for the educated Indians where they could vent their feeling more openly and where their activities could be monitored and channeled easily. There is evidence to suggest that the plan for All India Congress was prepared and approved at the highest level, with the active participation of Governor General Lord Dufferin and cleared by Whitehall before it was presented to the public in 1885 by the retired British civil servant A.O Hume (see *Alan Octavian Hume* by Sir William Wedderburn, Fisher and Unwin, London, 1913, pp. 59 – 60; also *The History of Indian National Congress*, by B. P Sitaramayya, 1935, pp. 23 – 24). Hume remained the General Secretary of the Congress for the first twenty one years.

The Congress was not meant to be a primarily political organization. One of its objectives was 'the fusion of various diverse elements into one national whole.' Others aimed at the 'regeneration of social, moral, spiritual and political aspects of the nation thus evolved' and, 'consolidation of the union between England and India.' It was a contradiction in terms that the British who, as a matter of policy wished to keep the Indians divided to help perpetuate their rule should now want to actively promote unity in the country. It is not possible that they were unaware of the paradox and one must assume that unity was not going to be a serious objective of the Congress Movement, at least, as far as the British were concerned,

As the name suggests, it originated as a congress and not as a political party per se but more like a talking shop. It held annual sessions in different cities that lasted for three days. Often, these were presided over by British officials, politicians and businessmen. The first session was held in Calcutta in December 1885. It included seventy two delegates, only two of which were Muslims. Subsequently, Badruddin Tayyabji, a prominent Muslim leader from Bombay was invited to chair the third Congress. By and large, Muslims were wary of the set up and remained away. Sir Syed Ahmad Khan was highly critical and remained firm in his argument that Hindus and Muslims were two separate nations with different aims and objectives. They could agree on a few common goals but these could not form the basis of a united nation.

Sir Syed also remained deeply skeptical about the prospects for democracy in its conventional form in India ---- a country deeply polarised along caste and religious lines. The interests of the larger and most powerful community would always over-ride those of the smaller ones in what Jinnah was to later describe as 'the tyranny of the majority.' Sir Syed's concern was always for the Muslims and their interest which, he felt, would be best served as long as power rested in neutral hands. It earned him bitter epithets from the Hindus, as well as orthodox Muslim mullas, who accused him of being a stooge, queer, foolish, sycophantic, etc. Hume labeled him as 'a little insane', 'a fossil' and 'senile'. Still, the response from the Muslims towards Congress remained lukewarm at best.

Their doubts and apprehensions were not without basis. A virulent form of Hindu nationalism was taking root in India, with the encouragement and support of the British. More than anything else, it was directed against the Muslims. Bankim Chandra Chatterji, author of the Bengali novel, *Anand Math*, is regarded as one its progenitors. The novel is about a young Hindu, Bhaonand, who leads a revolt against Nawab Sirajuddaula, with the help of *sanyasi* (monk) followers of the goddess Kali. They go on a rampage, massacring Muslim communities, plundering and burning Muslim villages. It ends when they are mystically made aware that the British had already destroyed the Muslim power and have ascended the throne as friends of the Hindus and there is no more cause for violence.

Bandey Matram was the hymn of the anti-Muslim warriors in the novel that was subsequently adopted as the official anthem of Indian National Congress. When the latter formed governments in eight of the eleven provinces in 1937, its recitation was made mandatory in schools, colleges and the provincial assemblies. Chatterji also wrote a number of other novels, like *Raj Sinha*, based on Muslim historical figures cast in roles that were highly disparaging and had no basis in fact.

In an article published in 1872, he explained: 'I am a Hindu ---- I must do what is good for all the Hindus, and abstain from doing what is bad for any Hindu ---- it is the duty of the Hindus to take counsel together and agree upon a definite policy and chalk out a common line of action. This conception is the first half of nationalism. But there were many other nations, and what was good for them was not necessarily good for the Hindus. In such cases we must so act as to deprive them of the good. If this involves oppression of other nations we shall not shrink from it. Similarly, something that is good to us might bring evil to them. Even so, we must not cease to work for the good of our nation; if that means causing evil to another nation, we shall do so. This is the second half of our nationalism.' '*This was not an isolated expression of views, casually formed, but rested on a deep-rooted conviction which, at first confined to a small section, was gradually imbibed, consciously or unconsciously, by a large majority of educated people*' (*History of Political Thought, vol. I*, by B. Majumdar, University of Calcutta, p.294, as quoted by Khairi).

There were others, like Nabagopal Mitra, Rajnarain Bose, Arubandu Ghosh, Bipin Chadra Pal and Ramesh Dutt who worked tirelessly to bring about awareness of a united Hindu nation based on religion. Interestingly, for them Hindu nationalism and Indian nationalism were one and the same thing, as it has been for many others that followed. The notion was born out of the conviction that India was Hindu and belonged to the Hindus. It was an exclusive concept that considered people of religions and races other than Hindu as intruders, hence, not relevant. Antagonism towards Islam and the Muslims, dismissed disparagingly as *maleech* (unclean, repulsive), was integral to this new-found sense of nationalism. Bal Gangadhar Tilak, a member of Congress, was engaged in a similar exercise in Maharashtra. He was jailed for inciting murder and is best remembered for nurturing the cult of Shivaji and promoting him as the hero who fought for the cause of Hinduism against the Mughals. No matter how fanciful, it remains a highly popular interpretation of history among the Hindus to this day.

Swami Dayanand Sarswati, founder of the *Arya Samaj* (Exalted Society) aggressively preached a return to the basic Vedas. He was particularly intolerant of Islam, Christianity as well as other religions and caused a stir among the Sikhs by classifying them as basically Hindus. The movement was directed at creating an exclusively Hindu Indian nation based on common religion and culture and doing away with the impediments of caste. He also proclaimed, 'Hindutava secularises Hinduism by sacralising the nation' (whatever that may mean). Non-Hindus were to be converted to Hinduism through a process known as *Shudhi*. Arya Samaj set up cow protection societies to stop Muslims from slaughtering the animals and organized interference at prayer times in mosques. Soon, communal riots broke out in various cities and towns of Punjab as a consequence of these aggressive confrontations.

PARTITION OF BENGAL

The province of Bengal in late Mughal and early British period was larger than any European country barring Russia. It incorporated the present territories of Bengal, Bangladesh, Behar, Orissa, Assam, Mizoram, Meghalaya, Manipur, Tripura, Nagaland and Arunachal Pradesh. With its large and varied population, scores of languages, poor communications, etc. it remained an administrative nightmare. In 1874 Assam, including Sylhet, was severed from Bengal to form a new Chief-Commissionership. Lushai Hills were incorporated into it in 1898. Even so, Bengal was still too large, varied and cumbersome to be administered properly.

Lord Curzon, according to his own description 'a superior person' became Governor General in 1899. He was a man of considerable intellect and capability. After much thought, planning and consultation, a scheme was prepared for division of the province to make it more manageable. A new province, called 'Eastern Bengal and Assam', with its capital at Dhaka, was created on 16th October 1905. Apart from Assam, it consisted of Tripura state, the divisions of Chittagong, Dhaka and Rajshahi and the district of Malda. It had an area of 106,540 sq. miles and a population of 31 million comprising of 18 million Muslims and 12 million Hindus. After giving up some non-Bengali areas to the Central Provinces, the redefined province of Bengal was left with an area of 141,580 sq. miles and a population of 54 million, of which 42 million were Hindus and 9 million Muslims.

From the very outset the partition plan was denounced by the influential educated middle-class Hindus. Various groups, including Calcutta's business community, lawyers, journalists and *zamindars* felt their interests had been put at risk. They regarded it as a veiled attempt to strangle the spirit of nationalism in Bengal. Virtually every Hindu believed that its real objective was to encourage the growth of a Muslim power in eastern Bengal to thwart the rapidly growing strength of the educated Hindu community. As Mohindra Chandra Nandi, Maharaja of Cassimbazar, put it: '*In the new province the Mahomedan population would preponderate ----. We shall be strangers in our own land. I dread the prospect and the outlook fills me with anxiety as to the future of our race*' (as quoted by Khairi). Even some British administrators and the press generally had opposed the plan for reasons of their own.

The opposition to the partition soon coalesced into an organized movement. It started as a peaceful protest but took on a communal and increasingly violent complexion, involving bomb throwing and murders of Europeans. Its demand was no longer confined to the annulment of the partition of Bengal but became centred on the wider issue of self-government (*sawaraj*) for India. People all over India were called upon to boycott official services and British goods and patronize those manufactured in India (*swadeshi*). It gained widespread support not only in the political circles but also among influential intellectuals like Rabindranath Tagore, who exhorted their readers with their Bengali nationalistic writings and songs. Educated and politically conscious Hindus throughout India responded enthusiastically to the call.

Tagore is generally regarded as a universal thinker and poet. Yet, deep down, he too was a Hindu nationalist like the rest of them, with an innate antipathy towards the Muslims that was not always overtly apparent. In many of his songs he glorified characters like Shivaji, the Sikh Guru Gobind Singh and the incredibly violent Banda Beragi who slaughtered innocent Muslim men, women and children, regardless of their age or sex in their thousands and down to the last infant (see chapter *Sikhism and Sikhs*). His heroes were always characters who fought against the Muslims. Haider Ali or Tipu Sultan, who fought to keep the British out of India, find no place in his poetry.

The demand for indigenous manufactures brought about investments in textiles, steel, glass and match factories giving rise to the dawn of industrialization in India. It also led to the establishment of new communal schools, colleges and universities, by mostly Hindu organisations. There was other fall-out as well. Boycott, *swadeshi* and *sawaraj* had proved such effective tools that these were adopted by Mr. Gandhi subsequently for his non-cooperation, *Satiagarha* and *khadi* movements. Most importantly, the Hindus were able to hone their skills at harnessing the power of the press, mobilizing public opinion and organizing sustained protest campaigns. From these angles, the movement proved to be a watershed in Indian history.

One unintended consequence was the fillip it gave to Indian National Congress. It changed its character radically from being an upper middle class pressure group to becoming a mass movement. Its leaders, led by Lajpat Rai, Bal Gangadhar Tilak and Bipin Chandra Pal took a hard line, labeling the partition as an attempt to divide and rule and vehemently denounced it in public meetings all over India while a few, like Gopal

Krishna Gokhale, Surindranath Bannerji and Dadabhai Naoroji, advised moderation.

For the Muslims too it was a watershed of a different sort. Initially, they had been sympathetic to the movement in the name of Bengali nationalism but things began to change when it took a communal and violent turn. It was abhorrent to the Muslim mind that young activists should take oath in the temple of goddess Kali, considered the patron saint of Bengal, and sing *Bandey Matram* at their meetings and rallies. They were alarmed the movement was not so much against partition of the province as it was against the prospects of there being a Muslim majority in the new province. It was also disillusioning for them to note the strength of communal feeling in Congress. When the chips were down, it revealed its true nature and acted as a Hindu and not an Indian national body. Most of all, they realized Sir Syed's policy of acquiescence to the British in the hope that it would bring about political accommodation did not work.

For the British too it was time for reflection. Their policy of nurturing Hindu nationalism, at the expense of Muslims, seemed to be back-firing. Hindus had aims and aspirations that did not always coincide with those of the British and did not extend much beyond the desire to keep the Muslims down. The depth of feeling among the Hindus against the British rule though natural was for the rulers surprisingly unexpected. They considered it ingratitude but should have known better. Gratitude is arguably the least reliable currency when it comes to international relations.

When the agitation showed no signs of abating, the British began to have second thoughts about the partition. Hard-line Tory government in Whitehall had been replaced and Liberals had come in power. Earlier, Lord Curzon had resigned when his proposal to make the Commander-in-Chief answerable to the Governor General was turned down. In the face of Hindu outcries of bias in favour of the Muslims and because of his differences with the policy in Calcutta, the Governor of East Bengal, Bampfylde Fuller, also resigned. There was growing concern the agitation may spread to the rest of the country and become unmanageable. The stirrings in Punjab, the main source of recruits for the army, were particularly worrying. Army Intelligence reports indicated that disaffection was beginning to spread to its ranks, raising the sepectre of a repeat of 1857 (*Raj*, pp.422 - 24). A change of course seemed necessary to defuse the situation. The Secretary of State, Lord Morley, indicated this by expressing willingness to grant the Indians a greater say in their affairs.

King George V, at his Coronation *Darbar* in Delhi in December 1911, announced revocation of the partition of Bengal and that the capital will be moved from Calcutta to Delhi. With effect from 1st April 1912, the five Bengali speaking divisions, Calcutta, Burdwan, Dhaka, Rajshahi and Chittagong were united into a presidency to be administered by a governor-in-council. The area of this province would be approximately 70,000 square miles, with a population of 42 million, of which a little over half would be Muslims. A lieutenant-governor-in-council with a Legislative Council was to govern the province comprising of Bihar, Chhota Nagpur and Orissa. Assam was reverted back to the rule of a Chief Commissioner.

POLITICAL STIRRING

In an effort to win the allegiance of the educated Indians, local municipal councils were set up in 1892, elected by rate-payers. Since the latter were mostly Hindus, not many Muslims got elected. According to Robinson (p.122) in the district of Muzaffarnagar, which had 41 per cent Muslim population, just one Muslim had been returned by the rate payers against twelve Hindus. In Shikarpur, with it's more than ninety per cent Muslims, only two of them found seats on the board against fifteen Hindus. The situation was the same in virtually every sphere of administrative, economic and social activity (see chapter '*Crystallizing a Dream*'). The prospects of electoral reforms based on a unified electorate deeply worried the Muslims for fear that these would result in similarly lop-sided representation at the higher levels of government.

A deputation composed of thirty-five prominent Muslims from all over India, belonging to different walks of life, led by Sir Agha Khan III, called on the Governor-General Lord Minto in October 1906 to plead the case for separate electorates for the Muslims. Neither Minto nor Lord Morley, Secretary of State for India, were in favour of the idea but with the Hindu agitation in Bengal growing in strength, it was considered unwise to alienate the Muslims at this time. The proposal was accepted in principle and was incorporated in a watered down form in the Minto-Morley reforms package of 1909.

The events of the past few years had highlighted the need for a separate organization to represent and safeguard interests of the Muslims. Experience had clearly shown that these were not the same as those of the

Hindus and Congress was pre-disposed to act primarily on behalf of the latter. By caving in to the Hindu demand for undoing the partition of Bengal, it became patently evident that the British were there to look after their own interests and not those of the Muslims. A prominent leader of the time, Nawab Salimullah, summed up the situation as, '*No bombs, no boons.*' Viqarul Mulk, Secretary of Aligarh, elaborated, '*It is now as clear as the mid-day sun that, after these happenings, the Muslims can no longer be advised to depend on the government. The time for such reliance is long past ---- After our faith in God, the next best thing is to depend on our own strength; and we have the example of our compatriots before us*' (*Hayat-e-Viqar*, by Ikramullah Nadvi, Academy of Education Research, Karachi, 1984, p.693).

In a reversal of Sir Syed Ahmad's policy of non-involvement in politics, leaders from different parts of India assembled in Dhaka for the Muslim Education Conference passed a resolution for the establishment of All India Muslim League on 30th December 1906. Its objectives included the promotion of loyal and amicable relations with the British Government, protection and promotion of the political interests of the Muslims and the advancement of communal harmony in India. Six years later, these were re-stated in less subservient and more positive and assertive terms, adding a demand for self-government to them. The first session of the League was held in Karachi in December 1907 with Sir Adamjee Peerbhoy in the chair to draft its constitution. Among other details, it appointed Agha Khan III as its permanent president.

The League and its demand for separate electorates was viewed with suspicion, even hostility, by Hindu nationalists but there were others, like Gopal Krishna Gokhale, who were much more understanding: '*Confronted by an overwhelming Hindu majority the Muslims are naturally afraid that release from the British yoke might in their case mean enslavement to the Hindus. This is not a fear to be ridiculed. Were the Hindus similarly situated in regard to numbers and other things, would they not have entertained similar misgivings? We would undoubtedly have felt the same fears and adopted the identical policy which the Muslims are adopting today*' (*Some Recent Speeches and Writings of Mr. Jinnah, vol. I*, Jamiluddin Ahmad, Lahore, 1976, p. 496).

The British thought the formation of Muslim League would make for trouble. When a delegation led by the League Secretary, Wazir Hasan and Maulana Mohammed Ali Jauhar later arrived in England to explain the Muslim perspective, none of the British ministers agreed to meet them. All the same, the educated Muslims in India welcomed the development as did almost all of their leaders. The only notable opposition came from the orthodox religious establishment ---- the Deoband School, Maulana Shibli Naumani and Sir Syed Ahmad's biographer, Altaf Husain Hali. A distinguished Muslim barrister with a large and prosperous practice in Bombay named, Mohammed Ali Jinnah, was also not too enamoured of the idea at the time. He was a committed Indian nationalist belonging to the moderate wing of Congress and opposed to any kind of communal factionalism. Even when his political mentor, Gokhale, had accepted the need for separate electorates, Jinnah remained adamant in his opposition. He did not join the delegation that met Minto in Simla nor did he agree to join the League at that time.

The main focus of attention for Jinnah at this stage was to bring about a rapprochement between the Hindus and Muslims. Instead of looking to the British for safeguarding the interests of Muslims, it would better if the League made common cause with Congress. He was working for mutual understanding and cooperation; merger was never on the cards, as wrongly alleged by some. He attended the meeting of the League Council at Bankipur in 1913 but not as a member. That would come later. The mood at the meeting was sullen and not well disposed, particularly towards the British. The trend eventually caused Sir Agha Khan to resign as the president but Jinnah persisted. His efforts led to the League and Congress holding their annual sessions at the same time in 1915 in Bombay. Apart from Jinnah, the League also invited other Congress leaders, including its President Sinha, Surindranath Bannerji, Mrs. Annie Besant, Madan Lal Malviya, Sarojini Naidu and M. K Gandhi to its session. Two of its moderate stalwarts and Jinnah's supporters, Gopal Krishna Gokhale and Dadabhai Naoroji had passed away earlier.

The parties set up committees to formulate joint proposals for reforms that were adopted by both the League and Congress in their sessions at Lucknow in 1916 and came to be known as the Lucknow Pact. Apart from other things, it constituted de facto recognition by Congress that Muslim League was the sole representative of Muslims in India. Its salient features included the agreement that a resolution affecting any of the two communities will not be passed in any Council without the support of three-fourth of the members of the community involved. There will be a fixed number of seats for the Muslims in each Council and Muslim members will be elected through separate electorates. In exchange for extra seats at the Centre and in provincial Councils where they were in minority, Muslims agreed to give up their majority claims in the Bengal and Punjab assemblies.

Jinnah was hailed as the ambassador of Hindu-Muslim unity. He had achieved it mostly by allaying the fears of the Muslims living in a Hindu dominated system and providing them with the necessary safeguards: '*A minority must, above everything else, have a complete sense of security before its broader political sense can be evoked for co-operation and united endeavours in the national tasks. To the Musalmans of India that security can only come through adequate and effective safeguards as regards their political existence as a community. ---- Co-operation in the cause of our motherland should be our guiding principle. India's real progress can only be achieved by a true understanding and harmonious relations between the two sister communities* (*Quaid-e-Azam Mohammad Ali Jinnah: Rare Speeches 1910 -18*, Al-Mahfooz Research Academy, Karachi, 1973, p. 115). A public fund was set up to build a hall in his honour in Bombay to be called 'People's Jinnah Hall. It still stands in the compound of the Congress Building, under the abbreviated name 'P. J. Hall'.

It was in this spirit that the two sides started to have regular meetings to formulate a joint plan of action and passed resolutions demanding the early establishment of full self-government. The British were none too pleased with this development and dubbed it as 'subversive' and inspired by 'German intrigue'. Not everyone in England believed it.

A remarkable British activist for women's rights, Mrs. Annie Besant, had come to India to help further the cause. The wife of a clergyman, she had renounced Christianity and joined the Secular and Fabian Societies. She was also deeply interested in theosophy and Hindu beliefs of *karma, reincarnation* and *nirvana.* As an indication of how attitudes change, when she published a work advocating birth control, *The Times* accused her of writing 'an indecent, lewd, filthy, bawdy and obscene book.' A court convicted and sentenced her along with Charles Bradlaugh, MP from Northampton to six months in prison for another similar publication. Bradlaugh was expelled from the Parliament in 1880 for refusing to take oath on the Bible.

In India, Besant set up the Home Rule League. When the movement started to gain momentum, she was jailed. A travel ban was also put on Jinnah who had become president of the Bombay chapter of the Home Rule League. Even so, he remained confident that as long as Hindus and

Muslims worked together the requisite measure of self-government could be achieved through constitutional means and without resorting to mob agitation and violence. In one of many strange twists, Mr. Gandhi, freshly out of South Africa, refused to support any struggle against the British whose rule he believed was benign and beneficent. He told Besant, '*You are distrustful of the British; I am not, and I will not help in any agitation against them during the war*' (*Mahatama Gandhi*, by B. R Nanda, New Delhi, 1989, p. 97).

The partition of Bengal had not only strengthened the cause of *sawaraj* (self rule) but also introduced violence as a means of achieving political ends. Apart from the bomb throwing incidents and assassinations in Bengal, an Indian activist shot dead the Secretary of State's political assistant, Sir William Curzon Wyllie, in London. A bomb was thrown at Viceroy Minto in a train and his successor, Hardinge, was severely wounded in another attack while riding an elephant in a procession in Chandani Chowk, Delhi. An attempt was also made to blow up the Governor of Bengal, Sir Andrew Fraser, by exploding a bomb under his train.

In 1905, a group of Indian students started to publish a magazine in London called *The Indian Sociologist* that preached rebellion. They also established contacts with the Irish nationalists and activists in Egypt. Their leader, Vinayak Savarkar, a staunch Hindu nationalist, was arrested and imprisoned in the Andemans. On his release, he founded the hard-line Hindu Mahasabha. Another activist, Lala Hardayal, who started a free newspaper called *Ghadar*, managed to escape from London to Berlin and from there made his way to the United States. He had considerable success in raising funds and support for the freedom movement in India, particularly among the Irish Americans. There were plots within India itself that were put down with a heavy hand. In one case in Punjab, eighteen accused were hanged and more than one hundred transported to the Andemans for life. The Defence of India Act passed in 1915 gave wide powers to the administration to arrest, detain and deport suspects without trial or stating cause.

It was in these conditions that Mr. Mohandas Karamchand Gandhi made his appearance on the Indian political scene. Earlier, he had enrolled at the Inner Temple Inn and passed the Bar exam. Back in India, he tried practicing law in Bombay without success. He did some clerical work for a couple of years before leaving for South Africa in response to a job offer from a law firm owned by a Gujarati Muslim. Things were not working out any better here either until he found his true vocation when the Natal Government tried to deprive the immigrants from India of their voting rights. He took up the immigrants' cause and launched a popular campaign. Later, in 1906, he campaigned against the Transvaal government's Asiatic Registration Bill and was jailed for organizing protest burnings of the registration certificates. The issue was resolved with the intervention of Governor General Hardinge in Calcutta since the fate of immigrants had become a source of concern in India. It made Gandhi a hero in the eyes of the Indians who credited him with the success.

Curiously, throughout the two decades spent in South Africa, there is no record of Gandhi providing any support for the cause of the black South Africans. On the other hand, during the Boer War and the brutal suppression of the so-called Zulu Rebellion, he organized and served in an Indian medical unit, in the rank of sergeant major, in support of government troops and urged other Indians to fight on the side of the British (*The Life and Death of Mahatama Gandhi*, by Robert Payne, 1969, as quoted in *Gandhi: Behind the Mask of Divinity* by G. B. Singh, Prometheus Books, New York, 2004, p.63).

Gandhi had been deeply influenced in the development of his thinking by John Ruskin's *Unto This Last*, Leo Tolstoy's *The Kingdom of God is Within You* and Henry Thoreau's essay *On Civil Disobedience* as well as the Biblical injunction on 'turning the other cheek' in the event of aggression and *Bhagwat Gita's* denunciation of desire and pursuit for material possessions. It led him to taking the vow of *Brahamchariya* in 1906 that involved abstinence from such things as sex and material comforts and to lead a chaste and ascetic existence. The political philosophy of non-violence and civil disobedience that he later espoused was the sum total of all these influences and experiences.

Gandhi returned to India in January 1915 and was awarded the prestigious Kaiser-e-Hind gold medal that year by the viceroy for his services to the Indian immigrants in South Africa. He claimed that he had come back at the urging of the veteran Congress leader Gokhale. This is open to question for there was a world of difference in the approach to politics by the two leaders. Gokhale was a liberal at heart who abhorred overt confrontation and agitation, favouring diplomacy and constitutional measures instead. In his book, *Jinnah Reinterpreted*, Khairi makes a detailed compelling case wherein he argues that Gandhi's return to India was engineered by the British Government and not by Gokhale. The former had hoped that Gandhi's pacifist approach would help to dampen the growing trend of extremism and violence among the Indian nationalists. He had encouraged the Indians to join the army in support of Britain's 1914 – 18 war against Germany, even inviting Jinnah, at one stage, to join the recruitment drive (*Day-to-Day With Gandhi*, by Mahadev Desai, Varanasi, 1968, vol. I, p.169).

Capitalising on his new-found popularity, he undertook an extensive tour of the country to acquaint himself first hand with the problems of the people. It was a shrewd and propitious move. The people got to know him and he the people and their conditions and needs. They liked his down-to-the-basics folksy manner and could relate to him, which was not the case with some of the other leaders devoted to western ways and paraphernalia. It was around this time that both Naoroji and Gokhale passed away. The remaining old guard looked at Gandhi with a wary eye, keeping him at bay and out of the Congress' inner circle.

He needed a cause at the national level to propel his career. There were one or two minor ones along the way, like the protests at Champaran, Ahmeḍabad and Khadda but these were localized. The real opportunity only came in 1919, after the brutal British actions in Punjab, following the imposition of the Rowlatt Act and the start of the *Khilafat Movement* by the Muslims. It was a turning point in Gandhi's career and he never looked back. Soon, he was not only a part of the inner circle of the Congress but began to control its policy and direction. All those who did not agree with him were sidelined. Over the years, the victims' list came to include such stalwarts as Jinnah, Besant, Nariman, C. R. Das, Khare, Motilal (father of Jawaharlal) Nehru, M. N. Roy, Rajgopalachari and Subhas Chandra Bose.

For the next more than three decades Gandhi dominated the Indian political scene using a mixture of guile, cunning and charm to manipulate the party, while often claiming that he was not even its card-holding member. In order to make sense of the developments that subsequently took shape, it is essential to know what he believed in and how he thought and operated. This is by no means easy for he was an immensely complicated person. His devotees believed he was a saint. His opponents, on the other hand, thought he was a highly devious, slippery and manipulative character. The British came to describe him as 'a twister, as cunning as a cartload of monkeys'. Even some Hindu Indians have lately started to look at him in very irreverent light. In April 1995, Ashok Row Kavi, a well-known Indian journalist, called him a 'bastard *bania*' on Star TV's programme *Nikki Tonight*. He said, '*People want to put him on a pedestal and call him a saint, when really he was just a crazy fanatic. Putting M. K. Gandhi in charge of India's freedom movement was ---- a big mistake* (*Liberty or Death: India's Journey to Independence and Division*, by Patrick French, Flamingo Books, London, 1997, p. 21). The programme was taken off the air after it was censured in Parliament and a court case instituted against Kavi by Gandhi's grandson, Tushar.

Outside the circle of serious historians, most people know about Gandhi from Richard Attenborough's 1982 film *Gandhi*, a factually and historically inaccurate hagiographic presentation, financed by the Indian Government that depicted him as a Christ-like figure. The reality is very different and often hard to fathom. Commenting on his biography, '*Day-to-Day With Gandhi*, by his long-time secretary Mahadev Desai, French writes, 'On one page Gandhi would be instructing a follower to add turmeric to her diet; on the next he will be promoting the need for cow protection, absolute punctuality and the use of Hindi; then he will begin attacking "the drink evil" and the smoking of cigarettes; next he will condemn inter-caste liaisons and the remarriage of widows, only to change his mind a few pages later and vigorously promote it. The logic of some of his pronouncements is hard to follow. After the massacre at Jallianwala Bagh in Amritsar in 1919, he complained that the dead *"were definitely not heroic martyrs. Were they heroes they would have unsheathed the sword, or used at least their sticks or they would have bared their breast to Dyer and died bravely when he came there in all insolence. They would never have taken to their heels*" (p. 20).

Gandhi must be one of the most written-about men in history. There are an estimated five thousand books published about him. Most of the content in the words of one Indian writer, 'is Gandhian hagiography, noted for its ornate redundancy, its petrified Victorian Indian-English, its grandiloquent claims, and its reverent lore'. The Indian Government has gathered and published all of what Gandhi is known to have written and said, some 30 million words, in ninety volumes. These, cover a bewildering range of subjects and ideas, varying from advice on diet, bowel movements, human excrement, personal hygiene, habits, efficacy of enema, sex, religion, protection of cows, social issues of Hindus and occasionally, politics.

Despite outward appearances, he was a troubled man inside, prone to fits of excessive anger. On one occasion he was so inflamed that he 'rose and struck myself hard blows and only then did I have peace'. There were many other aspects of his life that would not be construed as 'normal' by every day standards. Perhaps the most troubling among these was his practice of going to bed naked with young girls every night, including his own grand-niece, Manu (*Liberty or Death*, p.19 and *Freedom at Midnight*, by Larry Collins and Dominique Lapierre, Simon & Schuster, New York, 1975, p.193).

He nurtured profound mistrust and contempt for all things western. For instance, he regarded vaccination against diseases such as small pox evil ---- 'a filthy process ---- that is little short of eating beef.' He advised the patients to instead cure themselves by taking enemas, fresh air, sleeping on a damp sheet and a change of diet (*The Collected Works of Mahatama Gandhi, XLII,* p. 470 and *XLIII*, p. 224). In February 1944 his wife contracted acute bronchitis and died while incarcerated in the Agha Khan's palace in Poona with him. The British flew vials of at the time rare penicillin for her treatment from England. 'When Gandhi learned that the drug which could have saved his dying wife would have to be administered intravenously, he refused her doctors permission to give it to her. He believed in nature cures and he also believed administering medicine by hypodermic needle contravened his dogma of non-violence, because it performed violence upon the human body' (*Freedom at Midnight*, p. 75).

In his eyes, '*Hospitals are institutions for propagating sin. European doctors are the worst of all ---- quacks whom we know are better than the doctors who put on an air of humaneness*' (*Mother India*, pp. 387- 8). But when he developed appendicitis in jail and the British surgeon was hesitant to operate upon him for fear of the consequences in case of an unfortunate outcome, Mr. Gandhi told him, '*If you will consent to operate, I will call in my friends, now, and explain to them that you do so at my request*'. Later, Gandhi explained that he had allowed the operation as an expression of goodwill, '*I endeavoured to show that I had no distrust either in their* (doctors') *ability or good faith*' (*After Mother India*, by Harry H. Field, Harcourt Brace and Company, New York, 1929, pp. 21- 25 and *Mother India*, p.345).

He set up a model community for himself called Sevagram in 1936 where he was joined by a Japanese monk, a Pole, a leper, an academic who wandered naked with his lips sealed and an assortment of other oddball characters. One of his trusted lieutenants in Congress, Sardar Vallabbhai Patel, called the place a 'menagerie'. He travelled in the third class by train in a bogey that was specially furnished and equipped. While in Delhi, Gandhi took up residence in the *Bhangi* (Untouchables) colony. It prompted Sarojini Naidu to quip, '*If only the old man knew how much it costs us to keep him in poverty*' (*Wavell* vol. 2, p. 383). For details of some other myths and foibles please see *Gandhi and his Apostles* by Ved Mehta, Yale University Press, 1977, New Haven, USA and *Gandhi: Behind the Mask of Divinity* by G. B. Singh, Prometheus Books, New York, 2004).

His concept of truth was strange, to say the least. According to him, there were two kinds of truth ---- absolute and relative. To differentiate between the two, he liked to relate a parable, '*Put your left hand in a bowl of ice-cold water, then in a bowl of lukewarm water. The lukewarm water feels hot. Then put the right hand in a bowl of hot water and into the same bowl of lukewarm water. Now the lukewarm water feels cold; yet its temperature is constant. The absolute truth is the water's constant temperature but the relative truth perceived by the human hand varied*' (*Freedom at Midnight*, p.106). Gandhi's relative truth was by no means rigid. It could vary as his perceptions of a problem changed. That made him a flexible man but it also made him appear two-faced. Even one of his disciples once exclaimed in exasperation, 'Gandhi Ji, I don't understand you. How can you say one thing last week and something quite different this week?' Gandhi replied, 'Because I have learnt something since last week'.

It was the same when it came to his commitment to non-violence. When Mountbatten first approached Gandhi on the subject of partition of the country, Gandhi replied, '*Don't partition India, don't divide India even if refusing to do so means shedding rivers of blood*'. He told his prayer meeting shortly afterwards, '*Let the whole nation be in flames; we will not concede one inch of Pakistan*' (*Freedom at Midnight*, p. 107, 193). When Mussolini had invaded Ethiopia, he advised the Ethiopians to 'allow themselves to be slaughtered' to counter the invasion, 'after all, Mussolini didn't want a desert'. But to the British he counseled, '*Invite Hitler to take what they want of the countries you call your possessions. Let them take possession of your beautiful island with as many beautiful buildings. You will give all this but neither your mind nor souls*' (*Freedom at Midnight*, p.72). It does not end there. When Poland was invaded by Germany, he observed, '---- *for the Poles to stand bravely against the German hordes vastly superior in number and strength was almost non-violent*' (*Verdict on India*, p. 172). It was even more exasperating when he refused to see the contradictions in what he said to the same or different people at different times.

In his mind every thing was fluid and it adjusted to his personal whim. As a consequence, his own recollections of discussions rarely tallied with those of the other participants. It got him into unsavoury disputes, including one with the celebrated American researcher, Katherine Mayo, when he denied the proceedings of an interview she had with him: '*I do not remember having given the message Miss Mayo imputes to me and the only one present who took any notes at the time has no recollection of the message imputed to me*'. As it turned out, he had not only said the things, he had also confirmed these in writing in a detailed signed statement, with a covering letter addressed to Miss Mayo (*Verdict on India*, p. 159).

Even more troubling were the claims of his divinity and interventions by his 'inner voice' in crucial political negotiations. On a number of occasions he claimed, 'God has chosen me as his instrument' and also, 'I am the Hindu mind'. J. N. Sahni, long-time editor of the *Hindustan Times,* wrote in his article '*Pakistan's Quaid-e-Azam*' in the *Illustrated Weekly of India* of 26th December 1976 about Gandhi's failed negotiations with Jinnah in 1944: '*On one occasion, when Jinnah felt that Gandhi had broken a promise and the latter claimed his "inner light" had ordered his change of mind, Jinnah said: To hell with his "inner light"! Why can't he be honest and admit that he made a mistake?*' Because of such experiences almost everyone who negotiated with Gandhi found it an exasperating and next to impossible task.

One of the harshest critics of Mr. Gandhi was Dr. B. R. Ambedkar, alumnus of London, Heidelberg and Columbia universities and leader of India's Untouchables in the freedom movement. The Untouchables constitute about a quarter of India's population and are abominably treated by the caste Hindus (see chapter *History, Hindus and Hinduism*). Mr. Gandhi took up their cause, amid great publicity and fanfare, but without achieving any notable success for a variety of reasons. After the Muslims managed to obtain separate electorates to ensure adequate representation, the Untouchables also demanded similar treatment and not to be counted as a sub-section of the Hindus. The Communal Award proclaimed by the British PM Ramsay MacDonald in 1932 granted them this right, along with the Sikhs, Indian Christians and Anglo-Indians. Gandhi fiercely opposed the move on the grounds that it was an excuse to divide the Hindus. His real reason was the fear that the Untouchables might side with the Muslims, which they probably would have done. In order to press home the point, he resorted to one of his many 'fasts unto death' that he claimed was directly inspired by God (*The Collected Works of Mahatama Gandhi, LI*, p.140).

As usual, a flurry of activity in the Hindu media followed, obliging the poor Untouchables to back down and compromise. A bitterly disappointed Ambedkar told visiting Beverley Nichols, '*Gandhi is the greatest enemy the Untouchables ever had in India*' (*Verdict on India*, p. 38). He characterized the oppressive caste system as the tyranny and inequality as the soul of Hinduism. After spending a lifetime of crusading against the oppression of its caste system, Ambedkar renounced Hinduism for Buddhism and exhorted his followers to do the same.

A Pakistani columnist, Ardsher Cowasjee, has recoded an anecdote that sheds light on Gandhi's famous fasts as a tool for achieving political objectives: 'Legend has it that the astute Gandhi would give notice to the government of his intention to embark upon a fast after ascertaining that Colonel Narriman Mehta, a physician and an officer of the illustrious Indian Medical Service, was still around. The notice would be conveyed to the Viceroy through various channels, the Viceroy would notify the Secretary of State for India in London, who in turn would inform the Prime Minister, who in conference with his ministers would then discuss what it was that Gandhi wanted of them. They would decide on what could and could not be granted and when. Thereafter, Gandhi would be taken into custody, incarcerated in the Aga Khan's palace in Poona or some other such comparably comfortable quarters. And incarcerated in the room next to Gandhi would be none other than Gandhi's favourite physician, Colonel Mehta, who had been given instructions to see "that the old buzzard does not die" (*The Dawn*, 9th December 2007).

Most Pakistanis regard Gandhi as a somewhat devious character, as indeed did the British at the time, who was willing to resort to all means fair and foul to get his way. This is both harsh as well as unfair. He had a vision of India that was different. His belief that Ram Raj (*Hindu theocratic rule*) once established would cure most if not all of India's ills was genuine. It was not very different to the ideas held by many devoted Muslims about an ideal Islamic State. Some of the things he did may appear to be quirky but there can be no doubting his sincerity to his cause and beliefs. Above all, he was a Hindu and he said so himself. Hindus regard the cows as sacred for instance, even calling it 'mother' (*gow mata*); Muslims killed and ate its meat. It was not something that would endear them to any believing Hindu, including Gandhi. In fact, considering the enormity of the sacrilege from his point of view, he acted with remarkable constraint and civility towards the Muslims. To expect more from a believing Hindu would have been unrealistic and unfair.

At the end of World War I the Viceroy, Lord Chemsford, introduced the Rowlatt Act in the Central Legislative Council that extended some of the wartime provisions of the Defence of India Act indefinitely. All twenty-two elected Indian members of the Council opposed it. It was a Draconian measure, giving arbitrary powers of arrest and deportation of suspects to the government. Jinnah said there was 'no precedent or parallel in the legal history of any civilized country to the enactment of such laws' and when Chemsford passed it into law, in March 1919, with the help of the thirty-four government appointed members, he resigned from the Council. This was not what the Indians had expected for all the support and sacrifice they had made for the British in the war. Seizing the opportunity, Mr. Gandhi called for a *Satiagarha* (moral force) campaign; a concept derived mainly from Jesus Christ's Sermon on the Mount. It led to widespread strikes and agitation.

When some political leaders were arrested by the police, riots broke out in Amritsar in which three Europeans were killed. The Governor, Sir Michael O'Dwyer, a diehard colonial master, put the city under army control. Brigadier R. E. Dyer, a particularly aggressive and unwise dolt of a man, commanded the operation. A protest meeting had been organized in Jalliawala Bagh, a walled park that had only one narrow point of entry and exit. Dyer stationed a detachment of about one hundred Gurkha and Sikh troops on either side of the entrance and, without giving any warning or opportunity to the assembled gathering to disperse, ordered the troops to open fire on the unarmed and entirely peaceful people. One Gurkha was later reported to have told a British officer, 'Sahib, while it lasted it was splendid; we fired every round we had.' Thousands of people, including women and children, had nowhere to run or hide. In their panic, many jumped into a deep well to escape the enfilade and died. The total number of dead and wounded was officially declared as 1,561 but is believed to have exceeded two thousand. There was no one to tend to the wounded since a Curfew had been imposed on the city (for details, please see *The Amritsar Massacre*, by Alfred Draper, Buchan & Enright, London, 1985).

The brutal crackdown caused an outpouring of grief and anger throughout India, particularly in Punjab. Almost every one, except the Europeans, felt utterly dismayed, disillusioned and distrustful of the British. Riots broke out all over the province and O'Dwyer declared martial law. In Gujranwala, a group of rioters was strafed by an aircraft. Anyone caught was flogged in public, with British spectators shouting, 'Strike hard, strike more'. Respectable men in Kasur were whipped naked in front of local prostitutes. In Amritsar, for a long time, natives were made to crawl on their bellies in the street where a British lady had been assaulted but rescued by other Indians. Every Indian was ordered to salute any European he or she encountered. In their ignorance of actual history or due to selective amnesia, people like British Prime Minister Gordon Brown, fail to take events and acts like these into account when they declare: 'Britain had nothing to be ashamed of or apologise for her Empire. It was something to celebrate'. Really?

O'Dwyer's actions had the full support of the government in Delhi but an enquiry committee set up under Lord Hunter was highly critical. When its report became public, there was a predictable reaction in the press but some papers in Britain, like *The Spectator* and *The Morning Post*, came out strongly in defence of Dyer. When the government decided to retire him, a fund-raising campaign fetched him the extraordinarily sum, in those days, of over twenty-six thousand pounds and a jewel-studded sword. He remained unrepentant and told a reporter on his return to England, 'Every Englishman I met in India approved my act'. He also said that he would liked to have killed more and 'I would do the same thing again, if I had to'. This was reflective of the widespread belief among his race that the 'natives only understand the language of force' and that the life of a native was not the same as that of a Christian European. There was acrimonious debate in Parliament. While supporting the government action in the house, as a matter of duty, Secretary of State for War Winston Churchill endorsed Dyer's actions in private (*Raj*, p. 480). The House of Lords too came out in support of Dyer. He died six years later of natural causes but not so Michael O'Dwyer. A Sikh activist, Udham Singh, finally caught up with him and gunned him down in London in 1940.

Events in recent history seem to indicate that attitudes have not changed much. The carnage in Iraq and Afghanistan by the U.S and Britain is a clear example. The lessons of history are not only lost on these two powers but also on the people who inherited the empire from the British. In 1984, Mrs. Indira Gandhi ordered a savage military attack on the holiest shrine of the Sikhs, the *Akal Takht* in the Golden Temple at Amritsar, killing hundreds and leaving the community bitter, angry and alienated, perhaps, forever. She paid for the crime with her life when her own Sikh bodyguard killed her. The same stupidity was replicated by Pakistan's military dictator, General Musharraf, in the 2007 commando raid on the seminary, *Jamia Hafsa*, in Islamabad that killed hundreds of unarmed girl students. The country will, no doubt, continue to pay a hefty price for the sin for a long time to come.

In an important way, the Jallianwala Bagh affair was a crucial turning point in Indian history and a parting of ways. After this, it would be impossible to convince the Indians that they could live in partnership with the British or accept any solution other than complete independence. Even though six months later some political (Montegu-Chemsford) reforms were introduced and amnesty declared for the political prisoners, it was too little too late. Gandhi, who had suspended the *satiagarha* in the wake of the tragedy, sensed the mood and re-instituted it in the session of the Congress in Nagpur in December 1920, promising *sawaraj* within one year.

He called for a number of measures aimed at making the country ungovernable for the British. These included work stoppage by the government servants, boycott of official functions, renouncing titles and awards, not attending government schools and courts, withholding taxes, shunning imported goods, etc. A serious effort was also made to bring awareness in the villages and include the farming community in the struggle. Some of the steps like work stoppage by the government workers involved undue hardship and were unlikely to be followed but he was not deterred.

It is not generally appreciated that Gandhi's vision of the future was not simply an independent India but, ultimately, an independent Hindu India. He was shrewd enough not to say as much in public for fear of completely alienating the Muslims and other minorities. He walked a tight-rope, tacitly implying to the Hindus that his aim was to restore the golden age of *Ram Raj,* when mythical god Rama ruled the country, while appealing to the spirit of Indian nationalism among the Muslims. In private, he told his secretary and confidant, Mahadev Desai in 1918, '*Though we do say that Hindus and Muslims are brothers, I cannot conceive of their being brothers right today ---- Not all religious distinctions will be wiped out in future but Hinduism will captivate Muslims by the power of its compassion*'.

At his heart, he was always a diehard Hindu and he said so: '*So far as I am concerned, my heart owes allegiance to only one religion --- the Hindu Dharma*' (*Liberty or Death*, pp. 38, 39). When his son Manilal wanted to marry a Muslim lady, he left no stone unturned to make him desist. He did the same when Motilal Nehru's daughter, Sawarup (later known as Vijay Lukshmi Pundit) married a Muslim, Syed Hossain, in 1919 against her father's wishes. She was packed off to Gandhi's *ashram* and Hossain to England. The two didn't see each other again for nearly twenty years. It was one thing to claim that Hindus and Muslims were brothers belonging to one nation but quite another when the illusion came too close to becoming a reality.

The attitude was not simply confined to Gandhi. Other Congress leaders like Vallabbhai Patel and Rajendra Prasad were no different. Even Nehru admitted, '*Many a Congressman was a communalist under his national cloak*' (*Jawaharlal Nehru: A Biography*, *vol. I*, by Sarvepalli Gopal, London, 1974 – 85, p. 136). Ian Stephens, editor of *The Statesman*, said much the same about Nehru himself, '(Nehru's) *passionate animosity towards Jinnah and the Muslim League stemmed not only from his high-caste Hinduism, but also from that strange, special distaste for Islam ---- as compared with other religions ---- shown by the British secularist intelligentsia*' (*Liberty or Death*, p. 265). In a pointed barb he once went so far as to dismiss Muslim culture in India as little more than a *lota* (water can used for ablutions) and *pyjama* (common dress for Muslim men in U.P, Bihar and adjoining areas).

Indian politics until this point had been almost exclusively the preserve of the western-educated elite. By bringing the masses into it, Gandhi had fundamentally altered its character. He had succeeded by invoking Hindu religion that is deeply ingrained and shapes the life of the overwhelming majority of the country's population. In doing so, he was aware of the danger of alienating non-Hindus but hoped that by appealing to their sense of nationalism, the effect would be minimal. For the next few years, he tried hard to allay any fears or misgivings on the part of the Muslims, mostly by incorporating some of their causes in the national agenda. It was a gamble, particularly because the underlying motive was not sincere. At best, it might work in the short term but not for long.

It perturbed Jinnah who declared after the Nagpur Congress session, '*I will have nothing to do with his* (Gandhi's*) pseudo-religious approach to politics. I part company with the Congress and Gandhi. I do not believe in working up mob hysteria. Politics is a gentlemen's game*' (*From Curzon to Nehru and After*, by Durga Das, Collins, London, 1969, pp.76, 77).

Getting the masses involved was the easy part, keeping their emotions and rage under control was another matter. By mixing religious passions with politics he made it almost impossible to keep the excesses in check. As French puts it, '*He was a Gujarati Hindu to the core, who lived at a pitch of overblown idealism that came to alienate other groups in Indian society. His was not a cynical choice, yet he was taking significant risk, like a person who lights a match to inspect a firework*' (*Liberty or Death*, p.39). The horrible tragedy that befell India in 1947 was the direct result of this fateful choice.

Not all of the Congress leaders favoured the line taken by Gandhi but passions ran high in its support. The resolution proposing the resumption of *satiagarha*, introduced by him at the Nagpur session and seconded by Lala Lajpat Rai, was greeted with deafening, prolonged cheers and applause. When Jinnah tried to warn that a political campaign should not be turned into a spiritual movement, he was shouted down with cries of 'shame, shame'.

At one point he referred to the proposer as 'Mister Gandhi'. There was loud and angry protest, with the audience demanding that he should prefix the name with 'Mahatama' (Great Spirit) and not 'Mister'. Five years earlier, after the Lucknow Pact, Jinnah had been hailed as the architect and ambassador of Hindu-Muslim unity; the same man was now hounded out of the conference, thoroughly dejected and disillusioned. Gandhi had changed the complexion of Indian politics, making Congress primarily responsive to the aspirations and expectations of the majority Hindu community.

KHILAFAT MOVEMENT

These were anxious times for Muslims, not only in India but all over the globe, from Morocco to the Philippines. Many of their countries had been enslaved by the western powers. At the end of World War I, what remained of the Turkish Empire was divided up between them under the Sykes-Picot Agreement of 1916. Palestine, almost exclusively inhabited by the Arabs at the time, was turned into a 'Homeland for Jews' (euphemism for Jewish State) by the British Foreign Secretary Arthur Balfour a year later. The Sultan of Turkey, acknowledged as the symbolic political head of all Muslims (*khalifa*), was a virtual prisoner in the hands of Allied Powers who had taken control of Istanbul.

Muslims in India have always harboured strong fraternal feelings for the Turks. The word 'Turk' was practically synonymous and often used in place of 'Muslim' since the days of Sultan Mahmood Ghaznavi. When war with Turkey broke out, Muslim leaders and press tried to express their sympathy and support for her. It became a source serious concern for the government in India, particularly because Muslims constituted a large part of the Indian army. A Muslim regiment in Allenby's 1916 campaign in Palestine had refused to fight against fellow Muslims. It was disbanded and hundreds of soldiers were tried and shot for not carrying out orders. There were fears the trouble would spread if the news leaked and passions were aroused. As a precautionary measure, prominent Muslim leaders were rounded up and put in jail and a number of publications were closed down. At the same time, the government propaganda machine went into overdrive to assure Muslims that British actions were defensive in nature and not directed against Islam and that its holy sites would be protected.

It did little to allay Muslim apprehensions and suspicions. At the Muslim League conference in December 1918, the presidential address read in part, '*The Great World War, which appears to be ending so happily and triumphantly for the Allies, has unfortunately brought deep and gloomy foreboding to Muslim minds. We cannot forget that Turkey raises, for all Muslims, the question of Khilafat and protection of our holy places ---- temporal loyalty is subject to the limitations imposed by our undoubted loyalty to our faith*'. The meeting passed a resolution demanding that '---- *the fullest consideration be paid to the requirements of the Islamic law with regard to the full and independent control by the Sultan of Turkey, Khalifa of the Prophet (pbuh), over the holy places and over the Jazira-tul-Arab as delimited in the Muslim books*'. The British duly proscribed the entire proceedings of the meeting (*Jinnah Reinterpreted*, p.141). The meeting was, for the first time, attended by a number of Muslim religious leaders who liked to call themselves *ulama* (persons of knowledge).

Some Muslim leaders from Deoband had earlier tried to conspire with the Turks. The head of the institution, Mahmudul Hasan, who went under the title, *Shaikh-ul-Hind*, fled to Makkah but was betrayed and handed over to the British by Husain, Sharif of Makkah, at the end of 1916. He was incarcerated at Malta. His deputy, Obaidullah Sindhi, escaped to Kabul and helped set up the German-inspired 'Provisional Government of India' with Mahindra Pratap as its head, a Hindu revolutionary crackpot who had plans of forming a world government. There was talk of the leader of the pan-Turkish movement, Anwar Pasha, leading an army from Central Asia, through Afghanistan, to liberate India from the British. In the end, it all came to nothing.

The *ulama*, nonetheless, remained perturbed over the issue of Caliphate, even though the caliph was never a spiritual figure in Islam. The bothers Maulana Shaukat Ali and Mohammed Ali published the so-called *Khilafat*

Manifesto based on Jamaluddin Afghani's vision. Maulana Abul Kalam Azad went so far as to legitimize a 'monarchic caliphate as the spiritual centre of Islam'. Others like Hakim Ajmal Khan, Mahmudul Hasan, Dr. Ansari and Maulvi Abdul Bari were equally supportive of the movement for its preservation. There was talk of war between Christianity and Islam. On his part Jinnah had no time and little respect for the *maulanas* and regarded the movement as irrelevant and inconsequential, even harmful to Muslim interests.

But the *maulanas* were riding a wave of emotion, encouraged by the support from Gandhi and Congress. They even supported King Amanullah Khan of Afghanistan when he ordered his troops across the border into India, hoping to take advantage of the weak British military position in 1919. He hurriedly withdrew after experiencing a couple of air strikes over Jalalabad and Kabul. Muslims in India had enough problems and issues of their own to deal with at home. It made no rational sense to compromise their position in British and Hindu eyes and waste much time and energy on matters that did little to promote their real interests.

It did not end there. A religious conference was held at Larkana in June 1920 where it was decreed that India had become *Dar-al-Harb* (hostile zone) where Muslims were not free to practice their religion. Hence, it had become incumbent upon them to undertake *hijrat* (migration) from British India to other Muslim countries. Putting it bluntly, it was madness but that is what happens when political issues are left in the hands of religious zealots. Thousand of pious people sold all their worldly possessions at throw away prices and started to move to Afghanistan. Many perished on the way. Those that made it to the border found that they were not welcome in Afghanistan and were turned away. They spent the rest of their lives homeless and destitute. It was an unmitigated disaster and great tragedy for the innocent people involved.

This did not bother Gandhi who saw in the movement an opportunity for making common cause with the Muslims. He enthusiastically supported and encouraged both the Khilfat Movement and the call for *hijrat* by the Muslims, giving rise to serious questions about his motives and sincerity. In return, he got the pledge from the Muslims to join his campaign of non-cooperation, renounce their titles, resign from the legislative and municipal councils as well as from the police and military and not to pay any taxes. This they did even before Congress officially endorsed the programme which happened a while later, after the movement had been formally launched.

Durga Das, a journalist who interviewed Jinnah after the Nagpur session, records, 'Jinnah talked more in sorrow than in anger ------ He particularly deplored the Khilafat agitation which had brought the reactionary *mullah* element to the surface. He was amazed that the Hindu leaders had not realized that the movement would encourage the Pan-Islamist sentiment that the sultan of Turkey was encouraging to buttress his tottering empire and dilute the nationalism of Indian Muslims. He recalled how Tilak and he had laboured to produce the Lucknow Pact and bring the Congress and the League on a common platform. The British were playing a nefarious game in by-passing the Pact and making it appear that the Muslims could always hope for a better deal from them than from the Congress. Adding, "*Well, I shall wait and watch the developments, but as matters stand I have no place in Gandhi's Congress*" (*From Curzon to Nehru and After*, p. 77).

He was not alone in his misgivings. The movement had created a serious rift in Congress and polarized the country. Such venerable figures as Tej Bahadur Sapru, Srinivas Sastri and Surendranath Bannerji dissociated themselves from it and accepted government office instead. Jinnah, on the other hand, acted differently. He refused to stand for the election to the Imperial Legislative Council and despite his differences with Gandhi, refused to compromise himself and rebuffed all offers to side with the government in any way.

Foremost among the supporters of Gandhi's campaign was Jamiat-ul-ulama-e-Hind, the Deoband-inspired Muslim religious party. Five hundred *ulama* issued a *fatwa* in support of Gandhi's plans for *satiagarha*. Maulana Mohammed Ali declared it *haram* for the Muslims to serve in the army or facilitate the recruitment of soldiers. With the right motivation, you can get the desired *fatwa* from a maulvi on any issue (see TV 'sting' operation mentioned earlier). In this case, Maulana Ahmed Raza Khan Barelvi promptly issued one denouncing participation in the non-cooperation movement and fraternization with the Hindus. During the Kargil crisis in Kashmir in 1999, three thousand *imams* in India too declared that *jihad* against Muslim Pakistan had become the religious duty of every Muslim living in India.

There were serious doubts among Hindus on the issue of *satiagarha.* While Jinnah's objections were based on practical and constitutional grounds, Hindu hardliners saw in the Khilafat Movement the seeds of pan-Islamic domination. Lala Lajpat Rai wrote a letter to C.R Das that read in part, '*I am not afraid of the seven crores of Muslims. But I think the seven crores of Hindustan plus the armed hordes of Afghanistan, Central Asia, Mesopotamia and Turkey will be irresistible*' (*Pakistan or Partition of India*, by B. R. Ambedkar, Thacker & Co., Bombay, 1945). He was not alone. Aside from others like the president of Mahasabha Kelker, the poet Rabindranath Tagore and Annie Besant openly expressed doubts about the sincerity and loyalty of Muslims towards India. Gandhi acknowledged as much, '*Many Hindus distrust Musalmans' honestly. They believe that swaraj means Musalman Raj, for they argue that without the British, Musalmans of India will aid Musalman powers, to build a Musalman empire in India*' (*Young India*, 11th May 1921).

The movement was officially launched in August 1920 amid warnings by Jinnah that it would appeal only to the young, the ignorant and the illiterate. There was no shortage of these in India. Ali brothers, accompanied by Gandhi, toured all over India delivering fiery speeches. For a time, incorporating Muslim issues alongside the demand for self-rule in the national agenda brought Hindus and Muslims together as never before. Gandhi had become the de facto leader of the Khilafat Movement and the Muslims trusted and followed him. Reflecting the mood, Maulana Mohammed Ali Jauhar declared, '---- the best man among the Hindus to deal with was Mahatama Gandhi'. It was going to prove to be a false dawn. Hindus only looked upon the arrangement as an expedient necessity to help get rid of the British but beyond that they remained circumspect.

There was considerable unrest and disruption throughout the country. It unnerved the British. Viceroy Lord Reading offered full provincial autonomy in exchange for suspending the *satiagarha*. Gandhi turned it down. The missed opportunity did not come his way again until 1937. The British took the only course left open to them and came down hard on the protesters, throwing more than thirty thousand in jails, including Gandhi and the Ali brothers. In his *History of the Freedom Movement in India*, Majumdar writes, '*The Muslims as a general rule plunged into the movement with greater zeal and enthusiasm and consequently suffered, at the hands of the Government, a great deal more than the Hindus. It was indeed complained by the Muslims that while they formed only a small minority of the population they had to share a greater share of the brunt on their shoulders. This was true to a large extent*' (vol. III, p. 114 – 5).

There were instances of violence throughout in which many people died. The rebellion by the Maplas that took place at this time and the severity with which it was put down was particularly savage and ruthless. They are a group of Muslims of Arab stock who settled on the Malabar Coast and had been reduced to extreme poverty. They had been fighting against the Hindus as well as the British in the past also for restoration of their rights.

In February 1922, a number of policemen were burnt alive by a mob at Chauri Chaura. This is when Gandhi unilaterally called a halt to the *satiagarha*, without prior consultation or agreement with any of the other parties and leaders and without obtaining any concessions from the British in return.

The reason given for the decision was the growing violence. This seems implausible. Considering the emotive nature of the issues involved and the difficulty of enforcing strict discipline among the protesting crowds in the face of provocation, Gandhi should have known better and expected some degree of violence. There may have been other considerations that influenced his decision, importantly, his doubts about the ability of the Indians to govern themselves at this point in time.

There are many pointers to this effect. As late as 1917 he told the political conference in Gujarat that he wanted Home Rule as much as anybody, but considering the religious, racial and caste quarrels of the Indians and their inability to run civic affairs, he thought they were not ready for *sawaraj*. Much later, on 16th July 1932, he confided to his secretary, Mahadev Desai, about the *satiagarha*, '*It was all superficial. The fact is that we were not ready for sawaraj even if it is offered today as on a plate. Its establishment would be signalized by a terrible civil war ---- The temple of sawaraj is being built, brick by brick, stone by stone*' (*The Diary of Mahadev Desai*, vol. I, p. 427 – 8, as quoted by Khairi). Annie Besant, when questioned told Kanji Dwarkadas, a leader of the Home Rule League, '*My dear, Gandhi will never work with me. He does not believe in sawaraj; he does not want sawaraj*' (*India's Fight for Freedom*, by Kanji Dwarkadas, Popular Prakashan, Bombay, 1967, p. 77).

As to his attitude towards Annie Besant, Dwarkadas has reproduced a letter Gandhi had written to the Private Secretary to Lord Chemsford on 10th July 1917 when she had been arrested and put in jail, along with some other supporters of Home Rule (p.46 – 7). It was not published and the only record existed in a Government of India file: '*In my humble opinion the internments are a big blunder. Madras was absolutely calm before then, now it is badly disturbed. India as a whole had not made common cause with Mrs. Besant, but now she is in a fair way towards commanding India's identity with her methods ---- I myself do not like much in Mrs. Besant's methods. I have not liked the idea of political propaganda. And no one could deny Mrs. Besant's great sacrifice and love for India or desire to be strictly constitutional. But the whole country was against me ---- The Congress was trying to capture Mrs. Besant. The latter was trying to capture the former. Now they have almost become one ----*'. Considering the adversarial position of the British, it is strange indeed to confide in them his misgivings about Mrs. Besant whose objectives were the same as those professed by Mr. Gandhi. The fact that he was looking for sympathy and understanding from the British is incongruous and also perplexing.

If he did not believe in *sawaraj*, why did Gandhi create the storm with the 16th July 1920 promise to achieve self-rule within one year? There is no clear explanation since Gandhi alone knew the answer to this question and he never made it known. After he was released from prison in February 1924, he lost all interest in Khilafat and reverted to his basic Hindu ideology with its mythical models. Muslims found it hard to accept his very personal religious ideas as the basis for deciding the fate of the entire country and the two communities again drifted apart. Hindus no longer thought of Muslims as friends and allies and the reverse was also true.

Gandhi did little to dampen the communal feelings. In his journal *Young India* he wrote on 29th May 1924, '*There is no doubt in my mind that in the majority of quarrels the Hindu comes out second best ---- the Muslim as a rule is a bully, and the Hindu as a rule is a coward ---- where there are crowds there will always be bullies ---- I, as a Hindu, am more ashamed of Hindu cowardice than I am angry at Muslim bullying ---- Between violence and cowardly flight I can only prefer violence to cowardice*'. In the issue of 12th December 1925, he went further, '---- *If fate has decreed that we should fight a few battles among ourselves, let us* (as quoted by Khairi, p. 188).' If there was a contradiction between this and his preaching of non-violence to the rest of the world, he seems not to have noticed for that is how his mind worked

Others were much more extreme, like the revolutionary nationalist Hardial who had conspired with the Turks and the Germans during the war. According to Emily Baron in her book *Hardial* (Manohar Book Service, New Delhi, p. 233, cited by Khairi from the *Times of India* of 25th July 1925), '*I declare that the future of the Hindu race of Hindustan rests on these four pillars (i) Hindu Sanghatan* (organisation), *(ii) Hindu Raj, (iii) Shudhi* (forced conversion) *of Muslims and (iv) conquest and shudhi of Afghanistan and the Frontiers. So long as Hindu nation does not accomplish these four things, the safety of our children and great-*

grandchildren will ever be in danger, and the safety of the Hindu race will be impossible. The Hindu race has but one history, and its institutions are homogenous. But the Musalmans and Christians are far removed from the confines of Hinduism, for their religions are alien and they love Persian, Arab and European institutions. Thus, just as one removes foreign matter from the eye, shudhi must be made of these two religions'.

Most of the Hindu nationalists, including many Congress leaders, held similar views. They had formed a number of militant organizations throughout India to pursue the Hindu agenda. These were then amalgamated into a single body, Hindu Mahasabha. It held its first session at Benaras in August 1923 under Madan Mohan Malavya who had been president of Congress on two occasions. Other prominent Congress leaders, including Lala Lajpat Rai and Gandhi's close associate and friend, Swami Shardhanand were also present. In the minds of most Hindus, with rare exceptions, Indian nationalism and Hindu nationalism were one and the same and *sawaraj* was simply a euphemism for Hindu rule. A pseudo-military organization, Rashtaria Swayam Sevak Sangh (RSSS), was created at the same time that later became affiliated with parent body, Mahasabha.

Under Shardanand's guidance, Mahasabha embarked upon a campaign of forcibly converting Muslims whose ancestors they believed had been Hindu at some time in the past. The process, known as *shudhi*, involved ritual cleansing by submerging them in water tanks for prolonged periods. Many of the victims drowned as a result. Hindu writers wrote cheap books and novels about Muslim historical figures with titillating and sensual themes. It was not because they had developed interest in their lives but the object was primarily to degrade and defame Islam and cause pain to the Muslims. Communal riots broke out in Lucknow and Allahabad as tensions between the two communities worsened. Copies of the Koran were burnt in public bonfires in Sind. In 1924 Hindus distributed a number of blasphemous publications in Lahore, including *Rangeela Rasul* that was highly offensive to the Prophet of Islam and extremely provocative. Its author was murdered by a young Muslim named Ilmuddin, who was later sentenced to death. His grave has since then become a shrine of sorts.

There was growing confusion, mistrust and dismay among the Muslims. After all the sacrifices they had made, Mustafa Kamal Ataturk abolished the anachronistic institution of Khilafat on 3rd March 1924. The leadership of the Khilafat Movement splintered into different factions with only the Ali brothers still pursuing the illusion of Khilafat. Maulana Abul Kalam

Azad and Hakim Ajmal Khan went the Congress way. *Jamiat Ulama-e-Hind* decided to work for a distinct and separate identity for Muslims, within a Hindu dominated India, with their own *Amir-ul-Hind* at the head to dispense the law. A faction of the Muslim League parted company and became known as the 'Shafi League' after its leader, Sir Mohammed Shafi. This was just about the sum total of the achievement of the Khilafat Movement. Its abject failure underlined the absolute necessity for objectives to be clear, realistic and directed at achieving attainable and positive results. There is no element more important and crucial for success in any enterprise, political or any other.

SIMON COMMISSION AND NEHRU REPORT

There were splits within Congress as well. Jinnah had given up all hope of easing Gandhi's grip on the party but it did not apply to his efforts towards reconciliation between the two communities. He was once again elected un-opposed to the Central Legislative Assembly in the 1923 election by the Bombay constituency and formed a group with some of the other independent-minded members. The veteran Bengali leader, C. R. Das, along with a few of the old guard, laid the foundations of a separate Sawaraj Party. Among other issues, its agenda aimed at redressing some of the Muslim grievances in an attempt to heal the rift between the two communities. This included representation in the councils on the basis of population, a minimum of forty per cent seats for the minority community in the local bodies, appointments to government jobs on the basis of population and avoidance of interference and disruption in each others religious affairs. He recommended this so-called 'Bengal Pact' to the Congress at the end of 1923 but it made no headway. Motilal Nehru flitted between Jinnah, Besant and Das on the one hand and Gandhi on the other.

In the tense atmosphere that had been created by the Hindu-Muslim differences, the British saw an opportunity for themselves. Lord Reading tried to exploit Jinnah's disappointment and disenchantment with Gandhi and to gain Muslim support by offering knighthood to both Jinnah and Iqbal. It was a favourite British ploy for buying loyalties and it had gained them a phalanx of subservient Indian toadies. Jinnah turned down the offer with the sardonic comment that he would prefer to die as 'plain Mr. Jinnah'. While it is true the British played off one faction against another, it was carefully restricted to the leadership level. They had nothing to gain and everything to lose if it came down to the mobs squaring off against each other in the streets.

Jinnah presided over the 1924 session of the Muslim League in Lahore where he pleaded for unity among the Muslims. He deplored the bitterness that had crept in between the Hindus and Muslims, without assigning blame, and proposed steps to ameliorate the situation and restore mutual confidence by entering into negotiations with the Congress. He was optimistic, '*I have no doubt that if the Hindus and Muhammadans make a whole-hearted and earnest effort, we shall be able to find a solution as we did in 1916*'. In this he had strong support from C. R. Das. For a time there was hope but then Das passed away in 1925 and with him much of the possibility of healing the rift between the two communities.

Until now, as far as the stand against the British rule was concerned, the aims of the Muslim League and Congress had not differed significantly. Jinnah or anyone else did not think it was a contradiction of terms for him to be a member of both the parties at the same time. Both had sought self-rule that would lead to independence, as a united country at some time in the future. It was within this framework that Muslim League sought constitutional guarantees to ensure that the religious, political and economic interests of the Muslims were protected. Jinnah was focused on what he termed the 'political issue' of how to safeguard minorities in the new India and argued that the whole basis of the nation had to be renegotiated in order to safeguard the rights and interests of all minorities.

He called for a conference of all the Muslim parties to prepare specific jointly-agreed proposals and when that failed to materialize, he invited thirty important leaders to attend as individuals to meet in Delhi in March 1925. They agreed to accommodate the Hindu demand for joint electorates provided certain conditions were met. These included maintaining the existing levels of representation at the centre, separation of Sind from Bombay and institution of political reforms in NWFP and Baluchistan along the same lines as in the rest of the country and for the minorities to be treated on a uniform basis in all the provinces.

In 1927, the Secretary of State, Lord Birkenhead, dispatched a commission to India, under Sir John Simon, to review progress of the Montegu-Chemsford reforms instituted in 1919. Its members were all British, including Major Clement Attlee MP, future Prime Minister of Britain. It was a cynical Tory move primarily aimed at pre-empting anything the Labour Party may do in India if it won the forthcoming election in Britain.

The Commission was boycotted by the vast majority in India. Jinnah reacted strongly and told the League in Calcutta, '*Jallianwala Bagh was a physical butchery; the Simon Commission is a butchery of our souls. By appointing an exclusively white Commission, Lord Birkenhead has declared our unfitness for self-government ----- I welcome the hand of friendship extended to us by Hindu leaders from the platform of the Congress and the Hindu Mahasabha. For me, this offer is more valuable than any concession which the British Government can make*' (*Foundation of Pakistan: All-India Muslim League Documents, 1906 – 1947*, by Saiyid Sharifuddin Pirzada, vol. II, p. 127).

Unfortunately, not all the Muslim leaders agreed with him. Most of the important leaders from Punjab, including Sir Mohammed Shafi, Sir Fazle Husain, and Sir Feroze Khan Noon, even the revolutionary Hasrat Mohani, felt it was a mistake to give up separate electorates and that Muslims should cooperate with the Commission. There was a serious rift in the ranks of the League but Jinnah was not deterred. His Delhi proposals were endorsed by both Mahasabha and the Congress at the latter's session in Bombay in May 1927. For its part, the League agreed to participate in the all-parties conference planned to formulate the basis of a constitution for India.

Gandhi formed a committee under Motilal Nehru, with the latter's son Jawaharlal Nehru as its secretary, to make a set of proposals for consideration at the conference. All kinds of ideas were being floated, including perhaps the most interesting among them by Lala Lajpat Rai, '*My suggestion is that the Punjab should be partitioned into two provinces, the Western Punjab with a large Muslim majority to be Muslim-governed province, and the Eastern Punjab with large Hindu-Sikh majority to be non-Muslim province ---- if Bengal is prepared to accept Mr. Das' Pact, I have nothing to say ---- Under my scheme the Muslims will have four Muslim states (i) The Pathan Province or the North-West Frontier (ii) Western Punjab (iii) Sindh and (iv) Eastern Bengal*'. Why he omitted to mention Baluchistan is not clear. The statement prompted Dr. Tara Chand to observe, 'the partition of India was not the product of the fertile imagination of Muslim undergraduates of the Cambridge University, nor even poet Iqbal's fancy, but the brain-child of a hypersensitive Hindu stalwart' (*A History of the Freedom Movement in India, vol. IV*, Ministry of Information and Broadcasting, Government of India, New Delhi, 1983, p. 110).

There may be some basis to this for Iqbal had enunciated his vision of a separate state for the Muslims for the first time in his presidential address to the session of All India Muslim League in Allahabad at the end of 1930. Chaudhary Rahmat Ali, a somewhat eccentric student from Cambridge, gave the name 'Pakistan' to Iqbal's vision in pamphlets not published until 1933.

In a reversal of the assurances given at Bombay, Hindu Mahasabha refused to accept the Delhi proposals as the basis of a settlement, prompting the League to withdraw and take no further part in the proceedings. The final Nehru Committee report, as it came out, envisaged a strong centre with minimum powers for the provinces. Muslim representation was reduced from one-third to one-fourth; separate electorates were abolished as were the guarantees for the protection of minority rights. Instead, there were only some vague and wishy-washy promises. With a sleight of hand it negated all that had been achieved under the Lucknow Pact of 1916 and later the Delhi proposals. The Muslims were justifiably upset and angry.

Jinnah, who had wanted legal protection written into law and not some vague promises, balked at the proposals. Still wanting to keep the possibility of a compromise alive, he was careful in public but privately termed the report simply as the 'Hindu position'. In a last ditch effort, he made an impassioned appeal at the All-Parties Conference in Calcutta in December 1928, drawing parallels with the minority situations in Canada and Egypt where religious minorities fearful of being steam-rolled by the majorities, had been given special protection. He proposed amendments that Muslim representation at the centre should not be reduced, the form of government should be federal, with greater powers for the provinces and that the seats reserved for the Muslims in Punjab and Bengal should be in proportion to their population. The reserved seats for Muslims were necessary for even though they were in a majority in the two provinces, under the existing voting laws, the actual number of Muslim votes that could be cast did not exceed forty per cent. In the end, it was all in vain for the Congress rejected the proposal summarily. Years later, reflecting on the episode Jinnah opined it was the beginning of 'the parting of the ways'.

It effectively ended the possibility of drafting a constitution that was acceptable to both the Hindus and the Muslims. The latter saw the Nehru Report as the embodiment of what the Hindus desired. There was a need to prepare a counter-proposal that would satisfy the demands of all the different communities. These included weightage, separate electorates, powers of the provinces, etc. and were put together in a document that became known as 'Jinnah's Fourteen Points'. There was no reaction to these from the Hindus. Their sights were set in a different direction in the belief that they could go it alone.

THE ROUND TABLE AND INDIA ACT (1935)

Ramsay MacDonald had formed a Labour government in Britain in mid-1929. He was known to be sympathetic to India and much was expected of him. At his behest, the Viceroy Lord Irwin, offered Dominion status to India and called for a Round Table Conference in London to discuss the details. The announcement was welcomed by Jinnah but Congress had some reservations and wanted to lay down pre-conditions. Jinnah personally went to Gandhi's ashram at Sabarmati to persuade him not to turn down the offer. Later, a meeting was arranged by Irwin at Simla attended by Gandhi, Motilal Nehru and Jinnah among others. Gandhi demanded that the viceroy make a declaration that the conference in London will not discuss the issue of Dominion status but the constitution of the Dominion. It was not in the viceroy's powers to do so. Jinnah supported by Sapru, Speaker of the Legislative Assembly, suggested that the issue could be taken up at the conference itself but Gandhi refused to budge. He decided in favour of boycotting the Conference and resorting, yet again, to *satiagarha*. It was the second time in ten years that he had done so with the same tragic results. The worst part was that in the process he lost sympathy for India and made Ramsay MacDonald's position in the British Parliament very difficult.

The First Round Table Conference was held in November 1930. It included prominent leaders of different communities as well as the rulers of some states. In the absence of any Congress representatives there was little likelihood of a meaningful outcome. The Muslim delegation, led by the Agha Khan, was willing to accept a federal and not a united India; with joint electorates provided the Hindus accepted Jinnah's Fourteen Points. The Hindu delegation was split on the issue with Sapru, Sastri and Sitalvad in favour and Jayakar with Moonje in opposition. In the end, the session did not amount to much and the Conference was adjourned.

Congress, in the intervening years, had undergone a metamorphosis under Gandhi's influence. The western oriented, constitution-minded gentlemen, in positions of leadership, were sidelined and replaced by *khadi*-clad individuals who preferred to speak in Hindi. A new head dress, made from *khadi* cloth and labeled Gandhi cap, became a symbol of the party. Even the chairs were removed from the halls where the party held its annual sessions and participants made to sit on the floor. A tri-colour flag with saffron, white and green stripes was adopted as the national flag. Significantly, it now also claimed to represent all the people of India, including the Muslims that amounted to explicit repudiation of the Muslim League and Jinnah's position.

A whole new spirit pervaded the Congress. It had rejected the offer of full dominion status. The left-leaning revolutionary Subhas chandra Bose called for complete independence instead. Gandhi was not comfortable with his radicalism for fear of upsetting his wealthy capitalist supporters. He chose the upcoming suave and articulate Jawaharlal Nehru, who had been educated at Harrow and Cambridge, as his front man to take up the agenda instead of the firebrand Bose. At the 1929 session of Congress in Lahore, Nehru arrived riding a white horse to proclaim *pura sawaraj* (complete independence) as the goal and declared 26th January 1930 as Independence Day.

If he was doubtful or felt uncomfortable about Gandhi's notions of Hindu revivalism, commitment to *Ram Raj* or some of his other more quaint foibles, he kept any such feelings discreetly to himself. Gandhi had become a messiah in the eyes of Hindus. His image now adorned the walls of shrines in their homes and in religious festivals alongside those of the other Hindu gods. To question any of his actions or beliefs meant political suicide. The Congress party was composed of a wide assortment of people and interests. These varied from wealthy capitalists like the Tatas and Birlas to small-time Hindu money-lenders, shopkeepers, government employees as well as young nationalists, socialists and sometimes even communists. But the real power always rested in Gandhi's hands which he exercised through a group of loyalists known as 'the Old Guard'. These included Vallabbhai Patel, Rajendra Prasad, Rajgopal Achari and Acharya Kirpalani. The party and its policies were basically managed by this gang of four; the rest were only 'show boys', as Jinnah liked to call them.

Gandhi was also a consummate media manipulator with a canny talent for projecting himself and making dramatic headlines. Everything he said or did was calculated for effect ---- the way he dressed, lived, travelled and the phrases he used. All of this was in evidence when he undertook the so-called 'Salt March' in March 1930. The East India Company had levied a small tax on salt-making operations in the coastal areas of Gujarat. The amount involved was insignificant and no one took much notice until Gandhi chose to make an issue out of it. With great fanfare and as much publicity as the Congress machinery could muster, he set off for the coast on foot from Ahmadabad with eighty or so selected volunteers.

His intentions for the march had been publicized for weeks in advance and reporters from the world over were in attendance. His path was strewn with flower petals and leaves. At all the towns and villages en-route he stopped to make speeches exhorting people to shun foreign goods, renounce government posts and abstain from drinking and smoking. A frail figure dressed in a scanty loin cloth (*dhoti*), to the outside world he appeared the living symbol of the semi-starved and half-naked villagers of India. When he arrived at the destination he took a ceremonial bath in the sea and announced, 'I want world sympathy in this battle of Right against Might'.

At first the British looked at his antics with disdainful amusement and did not take serious notice but the *satiagarha* rapidly spread to other parts of the country. There were strikes, meetings and processions in all the major cities and towns. Often these turned violent as unemployed youths and petty criminals joined in to loot shops and businesses. Muslims in particular were singled out as the targets because of their lukewarm attitude to the protests. They were attacked in all the major Hindu dominated areas, especially Bombay, Benares and Cawnpore and many of them were killed.

One of the worst outbreaks of violence occurred in Peshawar where the Pathan disciple of the Mahatama, Abdul Ghaffar Khan often called the 'Frontier Gandhi', threw his *Khudaee Khidmatgars* dressed in red-brown shirts into the fray. They attacked the police and army units on the road. Thirty three of them died and thirty more were injured after the army opened fire. The atrocity provoked the Pathan tribesmen to go on the war path. At the other end of the country in Chittagong a police armoury was looted and large numbers of weapons taken away.

When police charged a violent mob with bamboo sticks anywhere, the photographs were distributed all over Europe and the United States, gaining sympathy and support for Gandhi and a bad name for the British. It was a great propaganda coup and the government could no longer afford to remain indifferent any longer. It had jailed all the important Congress leaders, along with some thirty thousand other protesters (only 1200 of these Muslim) and contemplated imposing martial law in the worst affected areas. In the end, it was not needed for the movement started to run out of steam and money. The economy was suffering which worried the men who had bank-rolled Congress.

Lord Irwin nicknamed the 'Holy Fox', played on these tycoons to bring Gandhi to the discussion table in Delhi where he agreed to end the so-called 'civil disobedience' and gave an undertaking to attend the next session of the Round Table Conference in London. After all the disturbance, destruction and deaths Gandhi landed himself precisely where he had been before it all started. No one questioned then and very few do so even today as to what his purpose was in all this? True, it brought him masses of publicity and increased his stature worldwide but was it worth the price?

The day after the meeting, on 6th March 1931, Gandhi told a press conference that he regarded the rights of minorities as a 'sacred trust' and would accept safeguards in this respect. He also said that he would resolve the issues with the Muslims before leaving for England because 'it would not be worth our while going to the Conference without solving the question' (*The History of the Indian National Congress*, by B Pattabhai Sitaramayya, Working Committee of the Congress, 1935, p. 755 – 63). Soon afterwards he started to have second thoughts and began adding conditions and qualifications, '*In private and in public he* (Gandhi) *began to say that his going to the Round Table Conference depended on his ability to solve the Hindu-Moslem question beforehand. Along with this statement he also began to say that if Moslems made a united demand on the question of representation, electorate, etc. in the new constitution, he would accept the demand ---- Soon after this, the Mahatama issued a public statement saying that he could not accept the demand made by communalist Moslem leaders, since Nationalist Moslems were opposed to them*' ('*Indian Struggle 1920 – 1942*, by Subhas Chandra Bose, Asia Publishing House, New York, 1964, pp. 214 – 15, as quoted by Khairi). In his eyes, 'Communalists' were all those Muslims who did not agree with him, including Jinnah, and 'Nationalist' meant the few Muslims still left in the Congress. This was vintage Gandhi.

Jinnah made his position very clear, '*I am an Indian first and a Muslim afterwards. But at the same time I agree that no Indian can ever serve his country if he neglects the interests of the Muslims. It was foolish to think that minorities could be held under bondage and perpetual subjugation. I have said this openly, I have no eye on any party, I have no mind for popularity. I can tell you that Hindus are foolish, utterly foolish in the attitude they have adopted today. I like straight play. Tell me that I do not want to give you a majority in the Punjab and Bengal. Hindus don't say that. They say, you can have a majority with joint electorates. Hindus know well that Muslims have got only forty per cent of voters in these provinces'* (*Foundation of Pakistan: All-India Muslim League Documents, 1906 – 1947*, by Saiyid Sharifuddin Pirzada, vol. II, p.156). In the absence of any prior agreement between the two and the shifting positions taken by Gandhi, failure of the Conference became a foregone conclusion.

The Muslim delegation to the Conference was again led by the Agha Khan and included Sir Fazle Husain and Sir Muhammed Shafi who were known for their pro-British leanings. It exasperated Jinnah. When asked for his opinion before the start of the negotiations, he replied, '*The Congress will not come to terms with me because my following is small. The Muslims do not accept my views because they take their orders from the Deputy Commissioner* (meaning the British) ---- *What can you expect from a jamboree of this kind? The British will only make an exhibition of our differences ---- They will make a fool of him* (Gandhi) *and he will make a fool of them*'. The dissentions within the ranks of Muslim delegates were painfully evident. At one stage, Sir Fazle Husain wrote to Governor Hailey who was also at the Conference, '*Frankly, I do not like the idea of Jinnah doing all the talking ---- Shafaat Ahmed* (a little known Allahabad University professor) *who I know, would be useful to Shafi and also form a somewhat effective counteraction to Jinnah*' (*Letters of Fazl-i-Husain*, by Dr. Wahid Ahmed, Research Society of Pakistan, Lahore, 1976, pp. 77, 80).

Khairi has narrated from a number of different sources to shed some light on the often bizarre goings-on at the conference. These are reproduced at some length to give an idea of the mood and measure of the personalities entrusted with determining the future of India. Quoting Sir Zafarullah Khan, then member of the Viceroy's Executive Council and H. H. the Agha Khan, he writes, '*All the members of the Muslim delegation were waiting on time anxiously for Gandhiji. The door opened and Gandhiji entered. All present stood up in his honour. On behalf of all of them His Highness Sir Aga Khan welcomed the honoured guest and offered a comfortable seat, but Gandhiji shook his head in refusal, smiled and said that he preferred to sit on the floor. In his hand was a beautiful box of teak, which he placed before him on the floor and sat down on the carpet. Some of those present also seated themselves on the carpet as a show of respect to the honoured guest; but there was not enough room for all to sit down on the floor, so the others sat down on chairs and sofas. With deliberate slow motion, Gandhiji opened his box. I was very anxious to see what comes out of the box. On opening the box out came a beautiful small brass spinning wheel* (charkha). *Gandhiji carefully put it on the floor, and quietly started to spin it. After he had spun a string or two, he looked up and smilingly indicated that he was ready for the talks*'.

'*The conversation was opened by the Aga Khan, by saying to Mahatamaji that, were he now to show himself as a real father to India's Muslims, they would respond by helping him, to the utmost of their ability, in his struggle for India's independence. Mahatamaji turned to face me* (the Agha Khan) "*I cannot in truth say that I have any feelings of paternal love towards the Muslims. But if you put the matter on the grounds of political necessity, I am ready to discuss it in a co-operative spirit. I cannot indulge in any form of sentiment.*" *This was a cold douche at the outset; and the chilly effect of it pervaded the rest of our conversation*' (p. 264 – 5).

He then goes on to quote Begum Jahanara Shahnawaz, daughter of Sir Mohammed Shafi, who was herself one of the delegates; '*Negotiations continued from day to day and went on for two months; protracted talks with Mr. Gandhi, as he sat spinning, with Father and Jinnah and sometimes the Agha Khan discussing the points raised by him, and the hours would drag on. At last the negotiations were concluded, Muslim demands were brought down to the minimum, and on the last day even Mr. Gandhi agreed that it was not possible for him to ask the Muslims for any further reduction, and that the safeguards asked by them, and as settled with him were just and reasonable. After this last talk, we all returned very happy at the prospect of a settlement in sight. Even people all round came to know that there was a chance of success, and a wave of happiness spread over Conference circles and amongst the responsible Indians in London. We of the Muslim delegation waited anxiously for four days ------ Mr. Gandhi arrived, and as usual sat down with the Agha Khan on one side and Father and Jinnah on the other. Gandhi said, "Gentlemen, I am sorry to report that I have failed in my efforts for a settlement. The Sikhs and Mahasabhites are not prepared to accept the terms decided upon by us".* She then goes on to describe how Sir Shafi begged Gandhi, with folded hands, not to miss the opportunity, having come this far, to avoid bloodshed and needless suffering in India. Gandhi was unmoved as he said, '*Shafi, I know my limitations and I cannot do it*' (p. 265 – 66).

It is impossible to figure out what was going through Gandhi's mind. In his speeches at the Conference, he constantly questioned the credentials of the Muslim delegates, almost all of whom he alleged, were not elected representatives of the people. He also claimed that Congress represented 'ninety-five per cent of the whole of India', including the states. Where he got the figure from, God only knows. Earlier, he had wanted to resolve the issue with the Muslims before arriving at the Conference; now he proposed that the Minorities Committee of the Conference should be adjourned *sine die* and the issues be resolved not immediately but after gaining *sawaraj*, '*The iceberg of communal differences will melt under the warmth of the sun of freedom*'.

If as it seems probable, he was not serious about reaching a settlement, why did he come to London and go through the charade in the first place? Also, if he believed in his claim that Congress represented virtually all the Indians, why did he feel the need to negotiate endlessly with the Muslims, especially with the leaders he had himself declared as unrepresentative? The most logical thing would have been for the Hindus and Muslims to form a common front at the Conference. Instead, Hindu attitude throughout remained non-co-operative and adversarial. Considered in the context of the larger perspective the safeguards Muslims had asked for were hardly of much consequence. By holding out against these so resolutely Gandhi stood to lose a whole lot more. Perhaps, he kept shifting his position in the hope of extracting a little more advantage each time. Looking at it through the dispassionate prism of history, the man was a total enigma whose contribution in the discussions did not go much further than causing confusion and vexation to the other participants. Not surprisingly in the end he lost it all, sowing the seeds of a holocaust the like of which India had experienced only once in 1857-58.

Undeterred, Ramsay MacDonald called into session a third Round Table Conference in November 1932 to prepare the draft of a constitution for India to be put before the Parliament. Tired of the endless wrangling on the communal issues, he asked the members of the Minority Committee, '*Will you, each and every one of you, every member of the Committee, sign a request to me to settle the community question, and pledge yourself to accept my decision?* Every one, including Gandhi, obediently signed and gave the pledge. The proposals for the constitution were assembled in the form of a White Paper. These were examined by the Parliamentary Committees whose final recommendations formed the basis of the India Bill passed into law in August 1935.

Under its provisions the provinces became self-governing and a provision was incorporated to form an Indian federation with the inclusion of the princely states. The federation provision was subject to acceptance by a substantial number of princes. Since matters never reached this stage, status quo was maintained at the centre with the viceroy continuing to exercise sweeping powers. In the provinces, it was different with the ministers selected from elected assemblies gaining wide control over the administration but still subject to discretionary powers of the Governors.

The Muslims were not treated too badly under the Act. The separate electorates were maintained, as was their one-third representation at the centre. Sind was separated from Bombay and NWFP was brought in level with the other provinces but not Baluchistan. Although they formed fifty-seven per cent of the population in Punjab and fifty-five per cent in Bengal, they were allotted only eighty-six seats in an assembly of one hundred and seventy-five in the former and one hundred and nineteen out of a total of two hundred and fifty in Bengal.

The communal award was a disappointment for Congress, Mahasabha and rest of the Hindus. The British Labour Party had close links and was sympathetic to the Congress. Ramsay MacDonald was a known proponent of Hindu interests, so much so that Mohammed Ali Jauhar had nick-named him 'Ramji Makandlal' (Hindu appellation). In appointing him as the arbitrator they felt confident he would rule in their favour. When it did not turn out entirely the way they had expected, they felt betrayed and bitter. There was no easy way out except to call upon the Muslims to jointly reject the award and re-open negotiations with the Hindus to agree on an alternative. What they offered in return was nothing more than joint electorates, without Muslim majorities and reserved seats in Punjab and Bengal, which the Muslims had been rejecting all along in the past.

If there was disappointment in the Congress ranks, the feeling was far worse among Britain's Conservatives. They formed the India Defence League in conjunction with retired army officers and civil servants, under the leadership of Winston Churchill, with Rudyard Kipling as one of the Vice Presidents. It had some support in the press, led by the *Daily Mail*, but not enough in the Parliament where Conservative Party leader Stanley Baldwin stood firmly behind Ramsay Macdonald. The sentiment among the diehard colonialists in the India Defence League was summed up by Churchill, '*It is alarming and also nauseating to see Mr. Gandhi, a seditious Middle Temple lawyer, now posing as a fakir of a type well-known in the East, striding half-naked up the steps of the Viceregal Palace, while he is still organizing and conducting a defiant campaign of civil disobedience, to parley on equal terms with the representative of the King-Emperor*'.

JINNAH'S DISILLUSIONMENT

If Churchill and his cohorts berated Gandhi so contemptuously, it did not mean that their feelings towards Jinnah and the Muslims were much different. The policy of 'divide and rule' did not mean preference for one over the other. Churchill for one, as cabinet minister in 1940, '----- *did not share the anxiety to encourage and promote unity between Hindu and Muslim communities. Such unity was, in fact, almost out of the realm of practical politics, while, if it were to be brought about, the immediate result would be that united communities would join in showing us the door. He regarded the Hindu-Muslim feud as the bulwark of British rule in India*' (*Churchill, Cripps and India*, by R. J. Moore, Oxford, 1979, p. *28*).

Jinnah was particularly disliked and considered a danger for his nationalist stance and constant efforts to reconcile and bring the two main communities in India onto a common platform: '*Whatever I have done, let me assure you, there has been no change in me, not the slightest, since the day when I joined the Indian National Congress. It may be I have been wrong on some occasions. But it has never been done in a partisan spirit. My sole and only object has been the welfare of my country. I assure you that India's interest is and will be sacred to me and nothing will make me budge an inch from that position ---- I will not and I cannot give it up. It may give me up, but I will not -----*' (*The Civil & Military Gazette*, Lahore, 3rd March 1936).

Nehru's biographer, Sarvepalli Gopal acknowledged as much (*Jawaharlal Nehru: A Biography, vol. I,* London, 1974 – 85, p. 223) '*When Jinnah took up again in 1936 the leadership of the Muslim League he was still a nationalist who had no wish to support, or rely on foreign rule. Indeed his aloofness, brittle ability and anti-imperial attitude made him as disliked by the British as any Congressman. In all his speeches in 1936 Jinnah stressed his nationalism and commitment to freedom, and his hope now was for another similar understanding* (as the Lucknow pact)'.

A senior civil servant, Sir Malcolm Hailey, reported to the Viceroy from the Round Table Conference, '*Jinnah of course is a good deal mistrusted; he did not at the opening of the Conference say what his party had agreed to, and they are a little sore in consequence. He declined to give the Conference Secretariat a copy of his speech in advance as all the others had done. But then Jinnah of course was always the perfect little bounder and as slippery as the eel which his forefathers purveyed in the Bombay market*' (letter to Lord Irwin dated 14th November 1930). The Secretary of State for India, Sir Samuel Hoare, was not even agreeable at first to invite him to the Conference, '*Of all the Indians I have met, I think I have disliked Jinnah the most. Throughout the Round Table discussions he invariably behaved like a snake, and no one seemed to trust him. I greatly hope that he is not getting a following among the Moslems*' (letter to Lord Willingdon, *Templewood Collection, vol. IV*).

Kanji Dwarkadas records a bizarre incident during the Conference that involved provision of commercial safeguards for the British (p. 385): '*Pressure was brought on Jinnah by the Conservative Party through Aga Khan but Jinnah did not budge and stood strongly for the Indian cause. Ramsay MacDonald sent for Jinnah and told him that in the new order of things that should come to India, the British Prime Minister would have to look for prominent Indians to take up the Governorships of provinces, obviously implying that Jinnah would have an excellent chance if he proved to be a good boy. Jinnah asked MacDonald if this was an attempt to bribe him to get support on the British Government's compromise suggestions, particularly commercial safeguards.*

'*The Aga Khan also tried to bring pressure on Jinnah but Jinnah remained firm. At a midnight meeting Aga Khan put it to Jinnah that if he (Jinnah) would persist in his opposition to the commercial safeguards and would continue to come to terms with Sapru, Sastri and Setalvad* (Hindu leaders) *on the Hindu-Muslim question, the Muslims of India would lose the support of the British Conservative Party for the special privileges for the Muslims of India*'.

Later, when Jinnah steered an important piece of legislation through the Central Assembly against a government motion, the Viceroy wrote to the Secretary of State, '*Jinnah and his eighteen or nineteen friends ---- are out to make things as difficult as they can for us, for they are joining up with Congress on almost every occasion ---- The leader of the Congress brought up a direct rejection amendment to our Resolution which was defeated as you know; after which Jinnah, with the guile of the serpent, put forward an amendment which the president decided to divide into three parts ----*'. (*Templewood Collection, vol. IV*, p. 240). On 6th April 1936, Viceroy Willingdon wrote to the Secretary of State, '*They wanted to down the Government* (in the Legislative Assembly) *and do something to annoy His Majesty's Government. Jinnah was the leader of the whole assault ---- He is a troublesome person and I shall warn Hopie* (the next Viceroy Lord

Linlithgow) *against him* -----'. It became much worse later on as we shall see.

The British dislike for Jinnah which permeated through all ranks of the officialdom may have had a psychological basis as well at the personal level. The kind of Indians they came across in the course of their service looked meek and humble, who bowed before their masters obsequiously with folded hands and bent over backwards to please them in any way they could. They had little self-respect and would tolerate any excesses or humiliation heaped on them, without complaining. Jinnah was altogether different. He had no such hang-ups, no fears and suffered from no complexes or feelings of inadequacy. He treated the British no differently to anyone else and looked them straight in the eye as equals. It was unusual behaviour, coming from an Indian ---- someone from an 'inferior race'. The thought of a native dealing with them on equal terms made the British of the time feel uncomfortable and also resentful. Jinnah was a native and a native should have known his place which he obviously didn't. Hence, he became 'uppity', a 'bounder' and 'faker' in their eyes ---- with one or two rare exceptions.

One of these was Beverley Nichols, author of *Verdict on India*, who simply described him as 'the most important man in Asia'. '*He can sway the battle this way or that as he chooses. His 100 million Muslims will march to the left, to the right, to the front, to the rear at his bidding, and nobody else's ---- that is the point*' (*Verdict on India*, p. 188). Another admirer was Sir Patrick Spens, the last Chief Justice of undivided India, who paid this tribute to Jinnah: '*The tallness of the man, the immaculate manner in which he turned out, the beauty of his features and the extreme courtesy with which he treated all; no one could have made a more favourable impression than he did. There is no man or woman living that imputes anything against his honour or his honesty. He was the most outright person that I know*'.

It was often alleged by the Congressites in particular and their historians to this day that the British went out of their way to support the Muslims and their interests. There is no basis to this. If anything, the reverse was true that became evident as time progressed. The British only looked after their own interests and in pursuing these they used Hindus, Muslims, Sikhs or anyone else who served their purpose at any particular time. The Hindus ought to have known this and the accusations were probably leveled as a means to gain some political mileage.

The conduct and attitudes of the Muslim leaders during the Round Table Conference had a profound effect on Jinnah. Always an Indian nationalist at heart, he was also deeply disappointed by the lack of understanding and accommodation shown by the Hindus, in particular Mr. Gandhi. Earlier, he had suffered the loss of his wife that left him with lingering remorse. There was also a sense of failure brought on by his inability to achieve the objectives he had set for himself.

About his performance at the Conference he said, '*I displeased the Muslims. I displeased my Hindu friends because of the "famous" Fourteen Points. I displeased the Princes because I was deadly against their underhand activities and I displeased the British Parliament because I had felt right from the beginning and I rebelled against it and said that it* (the India Act) *was all a fraud. Within a few weeks I did not have a friend there*' (*The Civil & Military Gazette*', Lahore, 3rd March 1936).

Reflecting some years after the Conference he confided, '*Many efforts had been made since 1924 till the Round Table Conference to settle the Muslim-Hindu question. At that time there was no pride in me and I used to beg from the Congress. I worked so incessantly to bring about a rapprochement that a newspaper remarked that Mr. Jinnah is never tired of Hindu-Muslim unity. But I received the shock of my life at the meetings of the Round Table Conference. In the face of danger, the Hindu sentiment, the Hindu mind, the Hindu attitude led me to the conclusion that there was no hope of unity. I was very pessimistic about my country. The position was most unfortunate. The Musalmans were like the No Mans Land; they were led by either the flunkies of the British Government or camp followers of the Congress. Whenever attempts were made to organize the Muslims, toadies and flunkies on one the hand, and traitors in the Congress Camp on the other frustrated the efforts. I began to feel that neither could I help India, nor change the Hindu mentality, nor could I make the Musalmans realize their precarious position. I felt so disappointed and depressed that I decided to settle down in London. Not that I did not love India: but I felt utterly helpless*' (*Glimpses of Quaid-e-Azam*, by Jamiluddin Ahmad, Educational Press Karachi, 1960, pp. 41 – 42, as quoted by Khairi). Jinnah purchased a house in Hampstead, London in 1931, where his daughter and sister joined him, and set up a lucrative law practice.

Muslim League, for all intents and purposes, existed as a political party on paper only after Jinnah's departure. There were years when it did not hold even its annual sessions. At other times, it split into different sections, each holding its session in a different location. These were dominated by people with large land holdings, very limited education and only passing awareness and interest in politics. They treated it more like a hobby than serious business. Almost all of its presidents from 1924 to 1936 were persons who were beholden to the British and recipients of British titles and awards for services rendered to the Crown.

The League had no countrywide organization or presence at the local levels. But for the dedication of an Assistant Secretary, Syed Shamsul Hasan, probably its central office in Delhi too would have ceased to function. Even members of the Council did not pay the annual fee that amounted to just one rupee. The total receipts from fees and donations for the year 1932 – 33 amounted to Rs. 1,739. The Council meetings often could not be held for lack of quorum (*Jinnah Reinterpreted*, p. 276). Worst of all, it had no press that could support and carry its message to the people. This was the state of affairs in the only national Muslim political party as it approached the elections to the provincial assemblies scheduled to be held at the end of 1936.

Congress, on the other hands, was in a much happier position. With the financial power houses like the Tatas, Oberois, Birlas and Bijajs backing it there was never any shortage of funds. Almost all the major newspapers in India were owned by the Hindus who solidly supported Gandhi and carried the Congress message to every corner of India. Most significantly, thanks to the earlier *satiagarha* and civil disobedience movements, its party apparatus was extensively established and organized at all levels throughout the country. Every Indian knew about Gandhi and his party.

The only opposition to the Congress juggernaut was expected from the regional parties like Sir Fazle Husain's Unionists in Punjab, Krishka Praja led by Fazl-ul-Haq in Bengal and National Agricultural Party in the United Provinces. Their agenda were based on local interest and enjoyed strong official support. The British were primarily interested in keeping the only two national parties Muslim League and Congress apart and their support among the voters to the minimum. There are many recorded cases where Governors of provinces used their influence to twist the arms of local politicians. Even the Agha Khan, who had been so closely associated with Muslim League, made generous donations to the election campaign of the Unionist Party.

There were other regional parties and organizations in the Muslim provinces that did not enjoy British support. These included Abdul Ghaffar

Khan's *Khudaee Khidmatgars* or Red Shirts, as they came to be called after their uniforms. It was active only in NWFP and supported Gandhi staunchly to the bitter end. The *Ahrar* in Punjab, led by the rabble rouser Ata Ullah Shah Bokhari, had confused aims at best other than claiming its basis in Islam. It was anti-British, at the same time it remained bitterly hostile to Jinnah and Muslim League, even opposing the creation of Pakistan.

Another group, the *Khaksaars* also originating in NWFP, extended their operations first into Punjab and later UP as well when its headquarters moved to Aligarh in 1941. It was a pseudo-military outfit, with grey uniforms and each member equipped with a spade in commemoration of the tradition dating back to the Battle of *Khandak* in the time of the Prophet. Its founder, Allama Mashriki, was an Islamic revivalist, bitterly critical of the *ulama* about whom he said, '*Their poverty, ignorance, vileness, destitution, helplessness, dumbness, filthiness and their tatters, all these clearly indicate that, whatever they be, they can never be leaders of this nation*' (*Modern Islam in India*, by W. C. Smith, Lahore, 1947, p. 240). It hit a nerve among the Muslim masses alarmed by the militaristic preparations of Hindu RSSS and *Arya Samaj* and they flocked to it in their droves. The party lost momentum when it was banned by the British after some clashes with the police and Allama Mashriki jailed for two years.

A Kashmiri school teacher, Shaikh Abdullah, along with Chaudhri Ghulam Abbas, Mir Waiz Mohammed Yusuf Shah, Bakhshi Ghulam Mohammed and others, founded the Muslim Conference that became highly popular among the impoverished Muslim masses in the valley suffering under the yoke of a highly oppressive Hindu Raja. The *Hurrs* in Sind are followers of Pir Pagara, a religious leader belonging to the *Kadriya* school of Sufism. They have a long tradition of supporting Muslim causes including Syed Ahmed Barelvi's *jihad* in the 1820s'. Pir Sibghatullah Shah II who, according to Annemarie Schimmel had leanings towards Congress, started an insurrection against the British in Sind. He was tried and hanged by them in 1940 and his body buried in an unmarked grave on the deserted Astola Island off the coast of Baluchistan.

There were also all kinds and shades of Muslim leaders hobnobbing with Congress in the name of Indian nationalism. These included people like Abul Kalam Azad, Dr. Ansari, Khaliquzzaman and Tassaduq Ahmad Khan Sherwani who basically served a cosmetic purpose by giving Congress the outward appearance of representing Muslims. They were hardly ever taken into confidence and had little influence on the party policies, regardless of the claims later made by Azad and perhaps others. In his presidential address at the Congress session in 1940 Azad claimed, '*I am proud of being an Indian. I am indispensable to this edifice and without me this splendid structure of India is incomplete -----*' (*India's Partition: Process, Strategy and Mobilisation* by Mushir-ul-Hasan, New Delhi, 1993, p. 67). In reality he, like all the other Congress Muslims, was no more than a puppet who did the bidding of the Old Guard.

Azad started life as a pan-Islamist and later joined Congress as a Muslim and not as a secularist, as Jinnah had done. He was an Islamic scholar of considerable repute. Included among his works is an account of the freedom struggle, *India Wins Freedom*, published after his death. A number of insiders have alleged that it is a fanciful interpretation of what actually transpired. Azad had a fondness for whiskey and champagne that he imbibed strictly in private. It prompted Nehru's secretary M. O. Mathai to rather cynically comment (*Reminiscences of the Nehru Age*, New Delhi, 1978, p. 152) that Azad might have dictated the book during moments when he was perhaps not quite sober. Be that as it may, Rajmohan Gandhi, grandson of the icon and a considerable historian in his own right, has debunked Azad's claims, line by line, in his rebuttal, '*India Wins Errors*, published in 1989.

Jinnah also had a poor opinion and his attitude towards Azad was openly contemptuous. At one stage Azad, while Congress president, queried him about some aspect of Muslim League policy. Jinnah replied in a telegram, '*I refuse to discuss with you by correspondence or otherwise, as you have completely forfeited the confidence of Muslim India. Can't you realize you are made a Muslim show-boy Congress president to give it colour that is national and to deceive foreign countries ---- the Congress is a Hindu body. If you have respect resign at once*' (*The Quaid-e-Azam on Important Issues*, by Mohammad Hanif Shahid, Lahore, 1989, p. 174). The British too acknowledged the token nature of people like Azad in Congress. In a historically crucial meeting with Gandhi and Nehru in 1946, the Viceroy Lord Wavell did not hesitate to refer to them as 'stooges' (*The Last Days of the British Raj*, by Leonard Mosley, pp. 42- 44).

The Muslims also had various reactionary religious outfits, like the Deobandis and Jamiat-ul-ulama-e-Hind that were viscerally opposed to Jinnah and Muslim League. Maulana Maudoodi declared that the Muslims in India do not constitute a national entity but rather a *jamaat* or community. He also claimed that a separate state as envisaged by Jinnah 'would be a pagan state' (*Kafiristan*), no different from the rest. The statement was disowned rather unconvincingly by Jamaat-e-Islami in Pakistan many years later. (*Muslim Modernism in the Indo-Pak Subcontinent*, by Fazlur Rahman, p. 97). Maulana Madani called the idea of a separate state for the Muslims 'a death knell for the Muslims in those areas where they were in a minority'. With Azad's conniving, Jamiat-ul-ulama-e-Hind switched their support to Congress in 1936 in return for provincial cabinet office.

This incongruous behaviour prompted Jinnah to say in Aligarh, '*What the League has done is to set you free from the reactionary elements of Muslims and to create the opinion that those who play their selfish games are traitors. It has certainly freed you from that undesirable element of maulwis and maulanas -------*' (*Deoband School and the Demand for Pakistan*, by Ziya-ul-Hasan Faruqui, Asia Publishing House, Bombay, 1963, p. 79).

The saying that you can take a man out of the country but you cannot take the country out of a man, applied just as much to Jinnah as well. In his years in England he remained in touch with all the developments in India. Muslims from all over the country and all walks of life wrote and asked him to return, as did the visitors who called on him. He helped reunite the Muslim League that had split into two factions and presided over its council meeting in Delhi in 1934. But he was still looking for national unity. '*Can we at this eleventh hour bury the hatchet and forget the past in the presence of imminent danger, and close our ranks to get sufficient strength to resist what is being hatched both at Downing Street and in Delhi? It is up to the leaders to put their heads together, and nothing will give me greater happiness than bring about complete co-operation and friendship between Hindus and Muslims*'. Congress wasn't listening and if it was, it gave no response. He tried again to reach a settlement a year later with the help of some prominent Hindu members of Congress in the Central Legislature but Gandhi and Nehru would have none of it (*India's Fight for Freedom*, p. 87).

His aim in reaching out to the Congress leadership was to get them to agree on a fundamental formula for India's future and to work together for achieving it. It was not enough for the two parties to simply oppose the British. They had to do it together, without leaving any room for misunderstanding or for the British to exploit any differences between them. It could only happen if the Muslims felt secure and had confidence that their interests would not suffer unduly under permanent Hindu majority rule. There was no reason for leaving it to the future because that could create a potentially unholy mess later on. What the Congress leadership, on the other hand, wanted was for the British to hand over power to it exclusively. They wanted the Muslims to go along and leave it to Congress to resolve the communal issues after the British had handed over power and left.

The point that Jinnah repeatedly made was simple and clear enough. If Congress was willing to accommodate the Muslims, why insist on waiting and doing so after independence? There was no obvious reason for this unless it had some reservations about keeping the promise. If the Congress hardliners were trying to drive a hard bargain, they had no idea how far they could go and if it was even worth the risk, considering the stakes that were involved. When people make blunders of this nature and magnitude it is usually when there is a predisposition or preconception at the core. One can only conjecture that Gandhi had a different vision and aim that did not include the interests of the Muslims as such. He did not come to the negotiating table with clean hands.

Other Congress leaders were cognizant of the situation but they mostly had the same or similar vision. Those that didn't, like Jawaharlal Nehru, chose not to confront Gandhi. He writes in his *Autobiography: 'Gandhiji, indeed was laying continuous stress on the religious and spiritual side of the movement. ---- the whole Non-co-operation Movement was strongly influenced by this and took on a revivalist character so far as the masses were concerned. The great majority of Congress workers naturally tried to model themselves after their leader and even repeated his language.*

'*I used to be troubled sometimes at the growth of this religious element in our politics ----Even some of Gandhiji's phrases sometimes jarred upon me ---- thus his frequent reference to Ram Raj as the golden age which was to return. But I was powerless to intervene ----*' (pp. 72, 3). It is ironic that although not once did Jinnah base his claim on Islam, it is he who should most often be blamed for bringing religion into politics by the politicians and historians and seldom Mr. Gandhi.

LIMITED SELF-GOVERNMENT

In October 1935, when the elections to the Central Legislative Assembly were held, the Muslims of Bombay once more returned Jinnah unopposed. A year later, after the India Act had been passed, he decided it was time to go back and do his duty once more. Elections for the provincial legislatures were going to be held shortly. It would be the first time the League would be taking part in these. To say that it was unprepared would be an understatement. There was no organization, no trained personnel and no funds. It woefully lacked the means to get its message across to the voters. They were familiar with the provincial parties and local issues but knew next to nothing about the League. The local Muslim leaders were primarily in it for themselves and the League had little to offer them personally ---- nothing as compared to the British, for example. When Jinnah went round the country to drum up support, he was cold shouldered by the likes of Sir Abdul Qayum in NWFP, Sir Ghulam Husain Hidayatullah and Sir Abdullah Haroon in Sind, Sir Fazle Husain and Sir Sikander Hayat in Punjab, Syed Abdul Aziz in Behar and Sir Mohammed Saadullah in Assam (*Jinnah Reinterpreted*, p. 295).

He had difficulty finding candidates even in the Muslim majority provinces. In the end, Muslim League did not contest from any seat in NWFP or Sind. It did so in Punjab from only seven out of eighty-six Muslim constituencies. The results were a foregone conclusion. Congress had absolute majorities in Bihar, Orissa, UP, CP and Madras and it was the largest single party in Bombay, Assam and NWFP legislatures. Muslim League, on the other hand, faired dismally gaining only forty out of the one hundred and nineteen reserved Muslim seats in Bengal and just two in Punjab where the Unionists dominated.

As per the figures quoted by Khairi, Congress had won 716 out of a total of 1585 seats. Out of these, 612 had been in predominantly Hindu provinces (including Assam). In Bengal, Punjab, Sind and NWFP where the majority of the population was Muslim, it had won less than twenty per cent of the seats (104 out of a total of 535 seats). Significantly, out of the 482 seats that were reserved for the Muslims in all of India, Congress had only secured 26 constituencies ---- 19 of these in NWFP, where it had joined hands and fielded its candidates under the banner of Ghaffar Khan's *Khudaee Khidmatgaars.* The rest seven seats were in the remaining ten provinces. As against this, Muslim League won 109 seats. As an indication of Congress' uncertainty about its popularity among the Muslims, it had put up candidates in only 58 of the 482 Muslim constituencies.

The rout of Muslim League in the elections was at the hands of the local parties and did not translate into a preference for Congress by the Muslims. What the elections did make clear was that both the Hindus and the Muslims regarded Congress as representative of the Hindus. This was also evident from the structure of the Congress party itself. Out of a total of 143 members of the All-India Congress Committee in 1936, there were only six Muslims ---- three of these *Khudaee Khidmatgaars* from NWFP and one ex-officio member.

The claims made by Gandhi and the others that it represented the overwhelming majority of the Indians were an illusion. Yet, it did not stop Nehru from proclaiming that there were only two parties in India ---- Congress and the Government; others must line up. He rejected any compromise with the Muslims as a group, labeling it as a 'medieval conception which has no place in the modern world' (*Towards Freedom, vol. I,* by Dr. P. N. Chopra, Council of Historical Research, New Delhi, 1985, p. 252). He also declared that he would not accept the Communal Award because it was 'not compatible with freedom', would not talk to the League because it was reactionary and would not discuss the Hindu-Muslim issue because 'it did not exist'. '(Muslim) *League's existence is seen only in a few provinces and is confined to a few Muslims belonging to the upper classes ---- There is nothing like the Hindu-Muslim question but it is just the question of doing away with the country's bondage* (*Selected Works of Jawaharlal Nehru, vol. VIII,* by S. Gopal, Orient Longman, 1976, pp. 131, 178).

This was clearly against the terms agreed at the Round Table Conference. Dr. Ambedkar who was present at the conference has noted, '*At the Round Table Conference it was agreed that the cabinets shall include members of the minority communities. The minorities insisted that a provision to the effect should be made a part of the statute. The Hindus, on the other hand, desired that the matter should be left to be regulated by convention ---- The Musalmans did not insist on making this provision a part of the statute because they depended upon the good faith of the Hindus. This agreement was broken by a party which had given the Muslims to understand that towards them its attitude would be not only correct but considerate*' (*Pakistan or Partition of India*, p. 26 – 7). After this, what trust could the Muslims place in the word of Gandhi or the Congress or in any settlement reached with them?

The Congress leadership now laid down new terms for any future co-operation with Muslim League. These required dissolution of the latter's structures in the assemblies and total submission of its members to the will and wishes of Congress. After the victory in 1937, Congress appears to have decided to go it alone and dismissed Muslim League, in Nehru's words, as representing only 'a group of Muslims functioning in the higher regions of the upper-middle classes and having no contact with the Muslim masses'. The Congress and Nehru in particular hung on to this view right to the bitter end even after Muslim League, in an incredible feat, won every single Muslim seat in the next general election. It was a fateful choice that proved to be a watershed in the history of India.

They also tried to wean away Muslims from the League through a series of underhand deals that included bribes in the form of offers for government offices, ministries, etc. One of them who fell to the temptation and was made a minister in the province of UP was Rafi Ahmed Kidwai. Similarly, Hafiz Mohammed Ibrahim, brother-in-law of the Jamiat-ul-ulama leader Maulana Hafizur Rehman, also defected from Muslim League to become a minister in the UP Congress cabinet. There was a similar high profile case in Bombay. Raja Ghazanfar Ali Khan, who was one of only two Muslim League members elected to the Punjab Assembly, defected to the Unionist Party.

The newly installed governments in the provinces began to show the shape of things to come and Congress in its true colours. They mandated the singing of '*Bandey Matram*', a Hindu pseudo-religious hymn, in schools and official functions and replaced Urdu with Hindi as the medium of instruction. The Congress party flag was flown on all the government buildings and institutions and the offices were adorned with Gandhi's portraits. The killing of cows was banned. Government functionaries in the districts were ordered to 'co-operate' with the local Congress functionaries. Perhaps worst of all, Congress ministers started to systematically weed out and replace Muslims in government offices with Hindus. Such actions were calculated to reassure and placate the Hindus and made clear that Congress was essentially a Hindu communal party. It was the beginning of *Ram Raj* as far as the Muslims were concerned. At this rate, they expected, it will be time for *shudhi* next.

This is when Iqbal wrote the Prophetic letter to Jinnah (21st June 1937) in which he stated: '*You are the only Muslim in India today to whom the community has the right to look up for safe guidance through the storm which is coming*'.

CHAPTER 7

CRYSTALLISING A DREAM

ROOTS OF ANIMUS

Hindus and Muslims were two distinct and separate communities sharing the same piece of land. The only way they could live together was by respecting the rights and accommodating each other at all levels of society. Given the structure and nature of the Hindu society at large it was a next-to-impossible proposition (see chapter *History, Hinduism and Hindus*). Any Hindu in a position of authority had a religious duty to first help and favour those belonging to his caste and after that any other Hindus. It was only after meeting these obligations that he would provide succour to people of other faiths, the last among them being Muslims. It is a fact of life that most Hindus are loathe to admitting for obvious reasons.

Sir Zafarullah Khan, a judge of the Federal and Supreme Court of India, has narrated cases in his book *The Agony of Pakistan* (pp. 10, 11) where Hindu judges of even the Lahore High Court acted inappropriately and with extreme bias against Muslim litigants in blatant disregard of their oaths of office.

In one such instance he writes, '*In January 1927 the Chief Justice* (Sir Shadi Lal) *procured the appointment to the High Court Bench, as a permanent judge, thus superseding four additional judges, of Mr. Justice Tek Chand ---- record discloses that during his period of office* (seventeen years) *this honourable judge, sitting alone or in Bench, did not decide one single case in favour of a Muslim when the other party was a non-Muslim; nor did he ever decide a case to which both parties were Muslims in favour of the party that was represented by a Muslim lawyer if the other party was represented by a non-Muslim lawyer. In the latter class of cases certain non-Muslim lawyers would charge Muslim clients enormous fees on the guarantee that the case would be allotted to the bench presided over by Mr. Justice Tek Chand and would be decided in the client's favour. The guarantee never failed to be fulfilled.*' At the time, there were only two Muslims among a total of thirteen High Court judges in Punjab where the majority of the population was Muslim.

In Bengal, despite their numerical superiority, very few Muslims found admission in professional colleges and institutions. Between 1858 and 1878, only 57 out of 3,100 graduates of Calcutta University, the premier institution for modern education in India, were Muslims. The faculty and staff in all of the universities in India, barring Aligarh and Usmania, remained mostly Hindu. Out of the 160 Fellows at Calcutta University in 1918, only seven were Muslims. The university Senate and Syndicate did not have even one Muslim member. Out of the 895 examiners, there were only nine Muslims. The situation was not much different at the Dacca University. In 1937, of the ninety students that received B.Sc. degrees only seventeen were Muslims. It was the same for the Masters programme which had eighteen Muslims out of a total of one hundred and eight.

In the Punjab University out of a total of sixty-eight professors in 1933 only nine were Muslim. In 1945, it was sixteen out of a total of eighty-two. The Boards of Studies had a total of one hundred and two members in the twenty-one university departments in 1921. Only fourteen of these were Muslims and in 1932 their number was still only nineteen (*Punjab University Calendars 1921*, pp. 479- 81; *1933*, pp. 415- 416 and *1946*, pp. 648- 9). In the first half-century of the university's existence not a single Muslim was appointed to the key Registrar's position.

In the Government College Lahore, regarded as the premier educational institution in Punjab, out of a total of 42 professors in 1928, only five were Muslim ---- three of them teaching Arabic and Persian and none in any of the science departments. King Edward Medical College, Lahore had a teaching staff of forty-two professors and demonstrators in 1917. Only three of these were Muslims. In 1930 the exclusively Hindu schools in Punjab received three times greater grants from the provincial government than did the Muslim schools.

The same sorry state for the Muslims existed in every government department and private organization, with the exception of the lower ranks in the Indian Army and police. There were a total of 957 judges and magistrates officiating in the Bengal courts in 1901 out of which only 98 were Muslims. In the five major railway companies, EBR, EIR, GIP, NWR and Burma Railways, that operated in India in 1933, out of a total of 1,048 gazetted officers there were only 45 Muslims. In the North Western Railway whose network was confined to Muslim dominated areas, of the 247 clerical staff the Muslims numbered 31 in 1927. In the Telegraph Department of the Government of India in 1910 there were a total of forty Divisional Officers. Not one of these was a Muslim. Among the lower staff, there were 12 Muslims among a total of 429.

The reason most often cited for the inadequate representation of Muslims in the services was the non-availability of suitably qualified candidates among them. In reality, the situation was manipulated so that likely Muslim candidates were excluded from the selection process. Since Hindus occupied the vast majority of administrative posts in almost every department, elaborate schemes and arrangements were devised to exclude even the most qualified Muslims. Most often Hindu clerks misdirected interview calls for Muslim candidates or posted incorrect details of dates, times and venues or simply failed to inform any Muslim that managed to get through despite all the hurdles.

The examiners, who were mostly Hindus, opted for different standards when awarding marks to Hindus and Muslims. The discrimination reached the stage where roll numbers instead of names were mandated for the examination papers. Hindu students got around the obstacle by inscribing the religious symbol '*Om*' at the top of the page to denote their religion. Any Muslim that still managed to qualify found himself discriminated against and harassed in all sorts of other ways. Qudratullah Shahab, a distinguished member of the coveted Indian Civil Service, writes about his interview for the service in his *Shahabnama* (Sang-e-meel Publications, Lahore, 1992, pp.141- 2):

'The interview board consisted of an Englishman as the president, a Muslim and a Hindu member ---- in this case Sir Radha Krishnan who later became President of India. Shahab had indicated in his application that he was interested in the study of comparative religion. It prompted Radha Krishnan to ask if he had viewed the issue as a Muslim or as a human being. After he replied that he found no cause to believe there was any difference between the two, the next questions from Radha Krishnan were: 'what is the weight of a tennis ball? How many ping-pong balls will make a combined weight of four ounces? What is the width and height of the hockey goal frame? The map of Italy is shaped like a boot. Which nearby island, if moved into position, will make it look like the shoe of a woman and not a man?' (Abbreviated and translated from Urdu.)

Admissions to professional and technical colleges and institutions were made particularly difficult for the Muslims. In an effort to reduce the imbalance, the Punjab Minister of Education, Sir Fazle Husain, introduced legislation in the mid-twenties that reserved forty per cent seats for the Muslims in the medical and engineering colleges in the province where they constituted fifty-seven per cent of the population. It brought forth a storm of protest from the Hindus, denouncing him as a 'rabid communalist', 'enemy of Hindu-Muslim unity', 'murderer of Hindus' and calling for his resignation from the Legislative Assembly (*Do Kaumi Nazria,* by Professor Ahmed Saeed, Nazria-e-Pakistan Foundation, Lahore, p. 108).

Hindus had almost exclusive control of the national press in India and they used it with great effectiveness to formulate public perceptions and opinion and project these to the authorities and the world at large. Hindu vernacular press in particular persistently used such terms as 'ruffians', 'debauched', 'cruel', and *maleech* (unclean, repulsive) to prefix the word 'Muslim' in their pages (*Do Kaumi Nazria* pp. 115– 120). The English press was hardly any better and mostly tried to portray the Muslims as genetically backward, uncouth and given to extremism by nature.

The situation was much the same in films and theatre that were also almost exclusively under Hindu control. Many of the films and plays were based on historical characters and episodes. The roles of Muslim figures were falsified and presented in derogatory terms while those of the Hindus exaggerated and glorified. In some cases things went to such extreme that it provoked country-wide protests and riots.

The printing and publishing industry was dominated by the Hindus making it difficult for Muslim writers to get their works published. Even copies of the Koran had to be printed in Hindu-owned presses because there were so few Muslims in the business. The vast majority of text books prescribed for schools and colleges were authored by Hindus. History, in particular, suffered badly as a consequence. The school books mostly glorified the Hindu period and ignored or downplayed the contributions of Muslims in the making of India.

A well-known philanthropist, Sir Ganga Ram, had established a number of charitable institutions in Lahore. The legal instruments under which these were set-up specified that their managing committees must only be composed of three non-Muslim provincial government officials and six Hindu members. Muslims were specifically not permitted to use the commercial library in the Bharat Building and the Sir Ganga Ram Abbreviation Bureau. (To the best of knowledge, the restrictions may not have applied to Sir Ganga Ram Hospital for legal and ethical reasons). The few Muslim newspapers and journals that did get published were generally excluded from libraries all over India by the mostly Hindu librarians (*Do Kaumi Nazria*, pp. 175- 78).

All India Radio, although a government controlled institution, was also dominated by the Hindus and their bias was reflected in its transmissions. Urdu programmes were systematically excluded and Hindi compositions took their place. There were constant complaints from the Muslims with little effect because most of the administrative and technical staff happened to be Hindu. The Hindu press raised much hue and cry when a Muslim (Z. A. Bukhari) was appointed its controller. In 1939, A.I. R's Bombay station invited Congress leaders Rajendra Prasad and Jawaharlal Nehru to give talks but when Bukhari, wanted to invite Jinnah on the occasion of Eid, he was turned down by the Bombay government on the plea that 'it would not have a helpful affect on the Hindus'.

Perhaps the most telling contrast in the situation of Hindus and the Muslims in India was in the economic field. The preferential treatment accorded to Hindus under the British rule eventually led to their complete domination in commerce, banking and industry. Muslims had no national bank until Habib Bank was set up in the mid-forties. Until then all sources of finance were more or less closed on them. They owned hardly any industrial units. The only shops they operated, even in towns and cities where the majority of the population was Muslim were those of the butchers and some venders of vegetables and milk products.

Any Muslim venturing into the rest of the commercial arena was denied credit and systematically squeezed out by the Hindus. In 1922, Hindu mill owners and wholesale dealers refused to supply cloth to some adventurous Muslims who tried to set-up shop outside Delhi Gate in Lahore. It was not until 1927 that a Muslim was able to open a shop for selling cloth anywhere in the city. To this day, no Hindu likes to buy merchandise from a shop owned by a Muslim. There are bizarre cases in Indian cities even now where Muslim shop vendors adopt Hindu names and attire to help them survive.

The areas that comprised Pakistan produced eighty per cent of India's jute and cotton crops but virtually all of the processing plants and facilities were sited in predominantly Hindu areas that were sliced off to become parts of India. At the time of partition, for instance, there were a total of 873 cotton mills out of which only sixteen were located in what became Pakistan. It was even worse in the case of jute mills.

Any Muslim in need of cash had to turn to a Hindu money-lender (*bania*) who charged extortionate rates of interest. Most of the time, the borrower had little understanding of the terms of the loan. Before long, he found himself deprived of the property he had pledged against it. The situation in the rural areas, where the population was that of mostly illiterate Muslim farmers, became distressingly acute. It led to the government legislating two classes of people ---- agriculturist (*kashtkar*) and non-agriculturist (*ghair kashtkar*) in Punjab whereby the latter (*bania* class) were not permitted to purchase or own agricultural land. Most of the middlemen in the rural areas were also Hindus. They mercilessly exploited ignorant Muslim farmers, paying a pittance for agricultural produce that they later sold in the market at unconscionable profit.

The end result was that virtually all of the wealth had accumulated in the hands of the Hindus. The extent of this domination became starkly evident at the time of Partition when all the Hindus and Sikhs had moved out of West Punjab. The cities appeared like ghost towns. In Lahore, for instance, all of the shops in fashionable Anarkali Bazaar and The Mall were closed down. The main roads were deserted and all of the houses in the more affluent areas empty. The number of cars that plied on the roads of this once bustling city was probably less than half a dozen. The railways ceased to operate and the road transport was reduced to a fraction of the original. It was the same with the Post and Telegraph and other service departments. All economic activity had been brought to a grinding halt. It took years to bring it to life again. The situation was, if anything worse in the other provinces from where the Hindus had also departed.

Hindus regarded and treated the Muslims in social matters as 'Untouchables' (see chapter *History, Hindus and Hinduism*). Even highly placed Hindu leaders like Bal Gangadhar Tilak and Madan Mohan Malavya refused to eat at Jinnah's house. At most official functions, the tables for Hindus were laid out separately to the rest. After any meeting with a non-Hindu, at the first opportunity, a devout Hindu cleanses himself by taking a ritual bath. Most Hindu shopkeepers would not hand over merchandise directly to a Muslim customer. It was placed at the end of a long wooden paddle and dropped into his hands or a sack to avoid any contact with the *maleech*. The Hindu form of greeting, *namastay* or *namaskar*, with the two hands joined in front as against the handshake, owes its origin to the fear of any contamination through physical contact.

The differences were not simply confined to religion. It was easy to tell a Muslim from a Hindu because they dressed differently; Hindus wore *dhotis* while the Muslims dressed in *shalwars* or pyjamas. The head dress too was different and they tied their turbans differently, even the cuts of their coats and shirts were different. They followed different calendars ---- solar for Hindus and lunar for Muslims. They lived apart in separate villages in the countryside and in segregated localities (*mohallas* and *katras*) in towns and cities. The designs of their houses were distinct and quite different. Generally, Hindus lived in congested areas in relatively expensive 'joint-family' multi-storeyed homes. Muslims, on the other hand, had more open and airy houses in treed lots. Any Muslim straying into a Hindu locality was frowned upon for even his shadow was considered 'unclean' and a source of pollution. It was rare indeed for a Hindu to rent any property to a Muslim as its occupation by the latter rendered it *bharisht* (defiled, sullied) and unusable afterwards without extensive ritual cleansing and renovation. It is still the same in India today.

The food Hindus ate was different to that of the Muslims. It was cooked in different ways and in different types of utensils. Hindus stayed in separate hotels where Muslims and Christians were not welcome. Similarly, there were separate hostels and cooking facilities for Hindu and non-Hindu students in schools and colleges. Food and water were served by separate vendors at all the railway stations. Their social customs and traditions, indeed the entire approach to life, was different. Inter-marriages were taboo. For all intents and purposes these were two solitudes that shared the same country. They did not co-exist peacefully either. Bloody riots broke out with regular monotony at the slightest provocation, mostly arising out of religious issues and events. In the face of this the claim that the Indians constituted a single unified nation can only be described as a ludicrous and delusional myth.

There is a whole gamut of facts of which the outsiders have no experience or knowledge. To them all Indians --- Hindus and Muslims --- look more or less alike. They do not have the opportunity to observe them in detail and at close quarters for any length of time. The people they come into contact with are generally the westernized elites, both Hindu and Muslim, who outwardly dress and act in ways that make them appear similar. The

Indians in particular like to stress this outward 'sameness' in an attempt to cover up the shame and embarrassment that comes with the discriminatory Hindu religious and cultural practices. It is mostly for these reasons that casual observers fail to make the distinction and comprehend the political and cultural divide and incompatibility between the two communities.

DAWN OF REALISATION

The adoption of the Nehru Report at the All Parties Conference and the summary rejection of all the amendments proposed by the Muslims at Calcutta in 1928 had given them much cause for reflection and re-consideration. The report had envisaged a unitary government and called for the abolition of separate electorates and the system of 'weightage'. There was no assurance that the Muslims will have a majority in any of the provincial legislatures, regardless of the make-up of the population. As far as they were concerned, it would simply perpetuate Hindu rule, exchanging one master with another, without affording any freedom to them.

Consciously or unconsciously, Congress was missing the point. As Jinnah explained: *It is extremely difficult to understand why our Hindu friends fail to understand the real nature of Islam and Hinduism. They are not religions in the strict sense of the word, but are in fact different and distinct social orders ---- never can a common nationality evolve ---- There is not one Indian nation ---- the Hindus and Muslims belong to two different religious philosophies, social customs, literatures. They neither inter-marry nor inter-dine together and, indeed, they belong to two different civilizations which are based mainly on conflicting ideas and conceptions. ---- They have different epics, different heroes, and different episodes. ---- To yoke together two such nations under a single state, one as a numerical minority and the other as a majority, must lead to growing discontent and final destruction of any fabric that may be so built up for the government of such a state* (*Muslim Self Statement*, by Ahmad – Grunebaum, p. 153, as quoted by Annemarie Schimmel).

The Agha Khan told *The Times* (12th &13th October 1928), '*India cannot have a unitary nor a federal government. ---- It must base its constitution on an association of free states*'. A few months later, the Muslim Conference composed of Muslims of all shades and views passed a resolution demanding complete autonomy for the provinces and the transfer of power from the British Parliament to the provinces, giving the autonomous units the right to choose the subjects to be transferred to the federal jurisdiction.

A year later, the Governor of UP told the Viceroy of his discussion with Sir Ross Masood, grandson of Sir Syed Ahmed Khan. Masood told him that the Muslims, fearing that they would be swamped by the Hindus in a self-governing India, were turning more and more to the idea of a separate federation with Afghanistan (letter by Governor Hailey dated 3rd December 1929).

The League held its annual session at Allahabad in 1930 that was presided over by Sir Mohammad Iqbal where he declared, '*The principle of European democracy cannot be applied to India without recognizing the fact of communal grouping. The Muslim demand for the creation of Muslim India within India is, therefore perfectly justified. ---- I would like to see the Punjab, the North-West Frontier Province, Sind and Baluchistan amalgamated into a single State. Self-government within the British Empire, or without the British Empire, the formation of a consolidated North-Western Indian Muslim State appears to me to be the final destiny of the Muslims, at least of North-West India.*' He subsequently proposed the same for Bengal also.

If it was a call for the partition of India and the creation of a separate Muslim state is a matter of some confusion and doubt. In his subsequent letters and statements to *The Times* and various other people Iqbal seems to disavow the idea of separation. The first time he is known to have made a reference to the idea of Pakistan was, perhaps, on 30th January 1938: '*The results of this* (Muslim) *unity will be grand. If the Muslims, somehow, could get a piece of land, it would be even better. I said, "Pakistan"? ----- call it what you may*' (*Iqbal kay Hazoor*, by Syed Nazir Niazi, Iqbal Academy, Karachi, p. 131). This may perhaps not be very significant; what matters is that more and more Muslims were beginning to think along these lines.

Among these was a group of Muslim students at Cambridge who took Iqbal's thoughts one step further, '*While he* (Iqbal) *proposed the amalgamation of these* (North-Western) *provinces into a single state forming a unit of the All-India Federation, we propose that these provinces should have a separate Federation of their own* (*Rahmat Ali, Complete Works*, by K. K. Aziz, The National Commission on Historical and Cultural Research, Islamabad, 1978, p.8). The idea of a separate, independent Muslim State named Pakistan was formally enunciated by one of these students, Chaudhary Rahmat Ali, at Cambridge in January 1933 in a pamphlet entitled, *Now or Never*. It did not seem to attract much serious attention among the Muslims at the time.

As noted in the earlier chapter, *Muslim Re-awakening*, Nehru had dismissed the Muslims and Muslim League as of little consequence and repudiated any past understanding with them after the Congress' electoral victory in 1937. It came as a severe blow to Jinnah who had striven so hard to bring about an understanding so that Hindus and Muslims could work together on the road to independence. Until then he had believed that the two communities could co-exist, not as a unified nation but as two separate entities that lived as neighbours, accommodating and adjusting to each other wherever possible, as in the pre-British past. Mutual co-operation was necessary for the concerted effort needed to drive the British out of India. But there was also going to be life after the British had departed. What shape and form it would take had to be decided before an enduring alliance could be formed that inspired confidence. Leaving it to the future, as Gandhi repeated ad nauseam, made no sense. There was real danger that it would lead to chaos and probably civil war.

Jinnah's aims had only extended as far as making a political arrangement between the two communities. He was too much of a realist to ever think that India was or could ever become a cohesive nation in the accepted sense of the word. What he had succeeded in bringing about at Lucknow in 1916 was simply a political understanding. It was reached largely because the Hindu leaders he dealt with at the time had a similarly broad vision. The edifice collapsed when new leadership took control of Congress, turning it into an essentially Hindu communal party. If Gandhi or Nehru refused to acknowledge this fundamental shift, it did not change its reality.

For Jinnah and the Muslims in general the statements by Nehru and other Hindu leaders, as well as the actions of the Congress ministries, proved to be a wake-up call. If they wanted to have their rights protected it will not be possible in a Hindu dominated united India. They will have to struggle for these on their own and in the face of opposition from both the British and Congress. Jinnah for the first time acknowledged as much in a resolution passed at the Muslim League session in Lucknow in October 1937. He said, '*The Congress masquerades under the name of nationalism, the present leadership of the Congress, especially during the past ten years, has been responsible for alienating the Musalmans of India more and more by pursuing a policy which is exclusively Hindu, and since they have formed the governments in six provinces where they are in a majority, they have by their words, deeds and programme shown more and more that Musalmans cannot expect any justice or fair play at their hand.*

'*The Muslim League stands for full national democratic self-government for India ---- it also stands certainly and definitely to safeguard the rights and interests of the Musalmans and the minorities effectively* ---- (it) *is not going to allow the Musalmans to be exploited either by the British Government or any other party.* The objective had changed. It now became '*the establishment in India of full independence in the form of a federation of free democratic States in which the rights and interests of the Musalmans and other minorities are adequately and effectively safeguarded in the constitution*'. There was still no mention of partition as such but Jinnah was coming close to it. Gandhi called his speech a 'declaration of war' and bemoaned in letters that he was 'missing the old nationalist' in Jinnah.

Jinnah received a ringing endorsement from Iqbal in a sixteen page assessment of the situation of Muslims issued on 5th February 1938: In it he wrote: *At present there is only one way ---- the Muslims should strengthen Jinnah's hand and join the League.---- Our united front is the only answer to the hostile activities of the British and Hindus. How can we get our demands accepted without it? ---- The demands are related to the protection of our national existence. ---- The united front can be established only under the leadership of the League, and the League will succeed only through Jinnah. No Musalman, except Jinnah is now qualified to lead the Muslims* (*Iqbal kay Hazoor*, p.282- 98, as quoted by Khairi).

With the new aim now clearly defined, it was time to revitalize the League. Its constitution was revised to make it more egalitarian and rules of membership made easier. There was a whole new energy infused after the Congress had shown its true colours, thanks mostly to the actions of its ministries and Jawaharlal Nehru's ill-advised and intemperate utterances. Muslims of all shades and hues began to flock to the League, most important among them, Sir Mohammed Saadullah, the chief minister of Assam, A. K. Fazl-ul-Haq, the chief minister of Bengal and Sir Sikander Hayat of Punjab. A provincial conference was held in Karachi in which the chief minister of Sind, Allah Bakhsh, was expected to announce his decision to join the League, along with members of his party but changed his mind at the last minute because of a more appealing offer from Congress.

Jinnah spent most of his time and energy from then on in turning the League into a party with grass roots, setting up branches and offices in districts all over India. A vigorous fund-raising campaign was put into effect. A Muslim vernacular press already existed in almost all the provinces. To these were added newspapers that specifically reflected the Muslim League perspective. Jinnah himself laid the foundation of the English daily *The Dawn* which still carries the inscription to this effect under its main title. It is a sign of the times and how far the Muslims in Pakistan have strayed from the heady ideal that on Jinnah's sixtieth death anniversary in September 2008, the same daily was so filled with reports and articles about issues of mostly western interest that it could not find space for even a single piece on Jinnah.

The main focus of Jinnah's attention was the educated Muslims, particularly the youth. The time was right and he struck a chord with them. Having been disillusioned, indeed betrayed, equally by the pro-British politicians and the ignorant and unscrupulous religious leaders in the past, they found in him someone they could understand, trust and identify with. He came through as a man of unparalleled honesty, integrity and honour and a leader with a vision whose only motive was to safeguard the rights, interests and the future of his people. He had given them an identity and a sense of purpose for which they had been waiting for a long time.

The illiterate masses, who could not even understand the language he spoke, too were drawn to him instinctively. They thronged to his public meetings in their hundreds of thousands and listened to him rapturously, most of them not comprehending a word of what he said. It was enough for them to just listen to the voice of their leader whom they liked and trusted implicitly. When a newspaper reporter asked a rustic Punjabi at a public meeting addressed by Jinnah in Lahore, what could he make out from the speech if he did not understand what Jinnah was saying? The man replied, 'Indeed you are right, I don't understand a word, but my heart tells me that whatever he is saying is right and the truth.'

For those who experienced the phenomenon it was little short of Epiphany. What was most remarkable was that he was not a demagogue or rabble rouser who appealed to people's emotions or passions nor did he resort to any kind of sensationalism or gimmicks. There were no cries of 'Islam being in danger' or an impending battle between good and evil nor a call for *Jihad*. All he had to offer was his sincerity, commitment, sense of purpose and a vision that resonated with the people. It profoundly altered their perceptions, the way they saw themselves and what they wanted. In the process, Jinnah too changed in some ways. He learned to speak Urdu, albeit not very well, and started to wear the *achkan* along with the lamb's wool (*karakuli*) cap that acquired his name.

Any Muslim who did not go along with Jinnah and the League found himself out on a limb. The local Muslim leaders who had played their petty little self-serving games thus far felt threatened as never before. They were shrewd enough to sense that it was hopeless to oppose the Muslim League juggernaut any longer. Every single Muslim seat that had fallen vacant in the country since 1937, bar one, had been won by the League. The only course left open for them was to join the party, not out of conviction necessarily but because it was expedient.

Unfortunately, some of the less savoury characters also managed to drift in along with the rest. Jinnah was fully conscious of the situation but considered it more important at this stage that the League should embrace as many Muslims of India as possible, regardless of their true convictions or motives. The situation was also not lost on the masses who placed their trust in Jinnah alone and not so much in any of the other leaders in the League. It was to prove to be its main strength at the time, allowing Jinnah to speak for all the Muslims, but later became a great weakness when he passed away and there were few left in Pakistan to carry on with his legacy.

The growing popularity of Muslim League and Jinnah was beginning to irk the Hindus and their leaders were resorting more and more to personal attacks with little regard for truth or accuracy. Khairi relates one such instance in which Jawaharlal Nehru, then President of Congress, issued a press statement on 30th June 1937 accusing Jinnah of issuing pamphlets invoking the name of Allah and the Holy Koran to support a candidate in a bye-election. '*To exploit the name of God and religion in an election contest is an extra-ordinary thing even for a humble canvasser. For Mr. Jinnah to do so is inexplicable ---- it means rousing religious and communal passions in political matters; it means working for the dark ages'* (*Selected Works of Jawaharlal Nehru, vol. VIII*, pp. 136- 7).

Jinnah denied issuing 'statement of any kind whatsoever'. He had not even seen the alleged pamphlet and regretted the propaganda that was being waged against him and the League. Any other reasonable politician caught out in a lie would have apologized and tried to explain the episode in some way but not the Pundit. He was unrepentant and called upon Jinnah instead 'to find out who was responsible for misuse of his name and dissociate himself from the statement in question'. He then went on to attack the League as a 'reactionary body'. The incident is not significant in itself but it does underline the unseemly atmosphere and the kind of people Jinnah was dealing with.

THE LAHORE RESOLUTION

There were intermittent exchanges of correspondence between the League and Congress on a range of issues but there was no movement as each side stuck firmly to its position. Within the League itself there was much discussion as to the course to be followed in the face of Congress' continued intransigence. In March 1939, Jinnah appointed a committee to examine the question and make recommendations. Almost all of its members rejected the idea of a federation and called for partitioning the country in the event Congress refused to accept a confederated state with a weak centre.

Liaquat Ali Khan summed up the mood in his presidential address at the Muslim League Conferencc in Merut: *If Hindus and Muslims cannot live amicably in any other way, they may be allowed to do so by dividing the country in a suitable manner ---- If this is done, a limited and specific federation would not only be easy but desirable*. Still, Jinnah did not endorse the idea in public although he did convey this as a possibility to the Viceroy, Lord Linlithgow, in his first meeting with him after the outbreak of the Second World War (Linlithgow's letter to Zetland dated 5th September 1939).

The start of the war greatly increased the level of anxiety among the politicians in Britain to keep things quiet and peaeful in India. Any outbreak of violence or uprising was the last thing Britain needed. Not only did they not have enough troops to quell any serious riots that may break out, they needed recruitment of Indians in large numbers to help fight the war with Germany. International pressure for easing Britain's hold on India, particularly from the United States, was also beginning to tell. There was now an urgency to bring Congress on side by accommodating some of its demands even if it meant sacrificing the rights and aspirations of the minorities in the country. In a letter to Lord Halifax, influential Labour Party leader with strong sympathies for the Indian National Congress, Sir Stafford Cripps wrote: *If we believe in Democracy, Congress did represent the majority of British India*. A few days later, he told the House of Commons, *'if you believe in Democracy how can you reconcile with saying that eighty million Muslims are to determine the future of India, and not the far larger number of Hindus'*? (*Hansard, Vol. XII, 1938- 39, p. 1655*). A politically significant section of the British leftist press, in particular *The Manchester Guardian* and *The New Statesman and Nation*, were also singing the same tune.

Linlithgow called a joint meeting with Gandhi, the Congress President Rajendra Prasad and Jinnah in November and asked them to formulate a joint plan for consideration by the British. Jinnah agreed and did meet with the other two, only to be told by them that the British had to concede the Congress demands first before any discussions could proceed. In a bid to put pressure on the British the provincial Congress ministries tendered their resignations. It was a Godsend for the League and it observed the declaration as a day of deliverance and thanksgiving.

The British Government was faced with a real dilemma. Congress claimed to speak for all the Indians and would not come to an arrangement with the League, while the British could not settle with either of them realistically without including the other. Instead of helping to break the impasse, Gandhi bluntly declared, '*It is an illusion created by ourselves that we must come to an agreement with all parties before we can make progress. There is only one democratic, elected political organization i.e. the Congress*' (*The Harijan*, 15th June 1940). Nehru singled out Jinnah for all the blame: *The Congress will not enter into negotiations with the Muslim League through Mr. Jinnah who is bent upon preserving British dominion in India* (*Selected Works of Jawaharlal Nehru, Vol. X*, p. 421). All Jinnah had been asking for was some guarantee for the protection of the rights of Muslims in Hindu dominated India to be built into the constitution. Why Congress chose not resolve this issue between the Indians and instead carried on endless bickering that led nowhere remains hard to explain unless one is willing to concede that it was a compulsion born out of the nature of the beast.

Jinnah's greatest fear was that the British may not wait much longer and decide to make some concessions and come to a settlement with Congress at the expense of the Muslims. Hindus had by this time realized that resignations from the ministries was a blunder and wanted a return to status quo ante badly. Using their restoration as a lever, the British might get Congress to accept the federation envisaged in the 1935 Act, with some minor face-saving modifications, and transfer power to it as the majority party at the centre. It prompted Jinnah to issue a blunt warning:

Any repetition of such a position in which the guarantees already given to the minorities are not implemented, or are not honoured in practice, will create the gravest crisis in India; and Muslim India will resist it by all means in their power and will not shrink from making any sacrifice. The British Government will be wholly responsible for the consequences if they yield or are stampeded by the threats and coercion of one party (*Glimpses of Quaid-e-Azam*, by Jamiluddin Ahmad, Educational Press, Karachi, 1960, pp. 134, 5).

Jinnah was now under intense pressure from both the British as well as from within his own party to make his position known vis-à-vis the constitution of India. He was loathe to making an irrevocable unilateral choice and hoped against hope to reach a reasonable settlement with Congress but all his attempts had been rebuffed. Since he had rejected the renewed suggestion by Linlithgow of federation with some as yet undefined modifications to the 1935 Act that would bring Congress onboard, the viceroy asked him to come up with his own proposals. There was also growing impatience within the League members that things could not be left in limbo any longer. From Mr. Gandhi's latest writings it now seemed likely that Congress would probably go along with Linlithgow. With the Congress government at the centre and its ministries back in power in the provinces, it would spell disaster for the Muslims. Jinnah had to make the League position clear sooner than later.

His original vision of the two nations living side-by-side sharing one piece of land depended on good faith and mutual accommodation. The experience under the 1937 Congress ministries had clearly shown that this was an unrealistic expectation and it was unworkable from the Muslim perspective. They had broken the trust and gone back on the agreements reached earlier. In the absence of some caste-iron guarantees built into the Constitution the only rights the minorities would have would be whatever the majority was prepared to grant them. Congress had not only rejected the notion all along but had also acted in bad faith. It was clearly a mistake to go down the same road again. The marriage had proved to be unworkable and the only sensible option left open was to look for an amicable divorce.

Jinnah announced this in the twenty-seventh session of Muslim League held in Lahore in March 1940. He spoke with great clarity that was his hallmark. He reminded the audience and regretted that Congress had broken the gentlemen's agreement once it assumed power in the provinces while the British Government in India stood idly by and did little to intervene. He was no longer willing to place his trust in either of them. '*We and we alone wish to be the final arbiter* (of our fate). ----- *The Musalmans are not a minority. The Musalmans are a nation by any definition. ----- The problem of India was not inter-communal but of an international character, and the only solution was to divide India into autonomous national States*' (*Foundation of Pakistan: All-India Muslim League Documents, 1906 – 1947, Vol. II*, p. 334, 5).

What came to be termed as the Lahore Resolution was tabled on 23rd March 1940 and was passed unanimously the next day. It demanded that '*geographically contiguous units are demarcated into regions which should be so constituted, with such territorial adjustments as may be necessary, that areas in which the Muslims are numerically in a majority as in the North-Western and Eastern zones of India, should be grouped to constitute Independent States in which the constituent units shall be autonomous and sovereign*'. It was incorporated in the constitution as the 'main aim and objective' of the League in its session at Madras the next year. Khairi has made some interesting observations on the Resolution in his *Jinnah Reinterpreted* (pp. 376, 77) that bear reproducing:

'First, it did not mention the Two Nation Theory ----- the resolution itself based the demand on the principle of numerical majority. Second, the word "Pakistan" was nowhere used. Third, the resolution concerned British India only. It did not touch the princely states. Fourth, it did not, unlike Abdul Majeed Sindhi's resolution in Karachi, envisage the possibility of any foreign country beyond the then Indian frontiers joining the Muslim Federation. Fifth, the rule of Sharia or the establishment of an Islamic State was nowhere envisaged. Sixth, there was no mention of "federations" or "confederation": areas were to be "grouped", but these terms were avoided. Two sets of words had been used freely: one was "independent", "sovereign" and "autonomous"; the other "regions", "zones" "areas", States" and "units".' He believes this was done deliberately in order to maintain flexibility and leave room for some compromise and manoeuvre.

All hell broke loose in the Hindu press the next day. India has never experienced such media frenzy before or since then. In some ways it is still continuing to this day. The press and politicians alike said the vilest things about the Resolution, often resorting to foul and highly distasteful language. Most of it is not worth repeating. Gandhi thought rather sanctimoniously it was 'an untruth' and 'a sin'. Rajgopalacharya claimed it to be the 'sign of a diseased mentality'. Nehru called it a 'mockery' and a 'mad scheme' and declared; '*there is no question of settlement or negotiations now*' (*Selected Works of Jawaharlal Nehru, vol. XI, p. 17*).

A sustained and relentless campaign was mounted to malign the idea of an independent Muslim State that did not end until after Pakistan came into being. All kinds of strange and mostly baseless inferences were drawn and misinformation spread through the Hindu press. These claimed that the state would not be viable and it would be still-born. It will soon go bankrupt and it would not be in a position to be able to defend its borders, etc.

There was gratuitous advice to the Muslims that the idea was not in their best interest. Those living in the provinces where they were in a minority were told that they were going to be abandoned and their interests sacrificed. Hindus were told that they would be made to live like slaves in the new state run by theocracy. Most often, there were hysterical cries that it was 'vivisection of Mother India (*Bharat Mata*)', like 'cutting a baby in half' or 'slaughtering the holy cow'!

As far as the Muslims were concerned, the paroxysms of hysteria had exactly the opposite effect to that intended. Hardly any one of them considered the Hindus as friends who had the best interest of Muslims at heart. It was natural for them to conclude that if the Hindus were so deeply perturbed by the idea, it could not be simply because it was bad for the Muslims. However unintended, it brought awareness and helped to galvanise opinion in support of the demand that otherwise would have taken a long time and great effort to achieve. It was not the first nor will it be the last time that Hindus shoot themselves in the foot because of uncontrolled visceral antipathy and antagonism they harbour towards Islam and the Muslims.

Neither Jinnah nor the League had made any reference to the word 'Pakistan' in the context of the Resolution. The two were rendered synonymous by the Hindu press. Jinnah acknowledged the contribution in April 1943 in a sardonic aside. '*There is new propaganda. ----- The latest argument, which I think is very wicked of all, the most wicked. ----- that Mr. Jinnah is working for the North-Western and Eastern zones as "pak"* (clean) *and the rest as "na-pak"* (unclean). *----- when we passed the Lahore Resolution, we had not used the word "Pakistan". ----- Pakistan is a word which is really foisted upon us and fathered on us by some sections of the Hindu Press and also by the British Press. Now our Resolution was known for a long time as the "Lahore Resolution, popularly known as*

Pakistan". But how long are we to have this long phrase? I now say to my Hindu and British friends: we thank you for giving us (this) *one word*' (*Foundation of Pakistan: All-India Muslim League Documents, 1906 – 1947, Vol. II*, pp. 425, 6).

Despite all the provocation, Jinnah remained conciliatory in his attitude towards Congress and the Hindus: '*I know that our reasoning and all our persuasion do not always succeed, but we must make every effort. Let us not create unnecessary bitterness against those who are at present the opponents of partition.*' He told Gandhi in November 1940, '----- *the last word in politics is never spoken. Why not you and I meet and put our heads together? If you make a practical proposition, we present a common united demand to* (Secretary of State) *Mr. Amery or for that matter to the British Parliament or the British nation if you like.* On another occasion he told him, '*If the principle was agreed to, the question of details will arise then and with goodwill, understanding and statesmanship, we shall, let us hope settle them among ourselves*' (*Glimpses of Quaid-e-Azam*, vol I, pp. 219, 281). He repeated similar offers many times. There was never any meaningful response from Congress.

The British were not certain of how they should react to the Lahore Resolution after it had been passed. It did not come as a surprise because Jinnah had earlier informed Linlithgow that if no other solution acceptable to the Muslims was forthcoming he will be obliged to call for partition of the country. In his letter to Linlithgow on 4th April 1940, the Secretary of State for India, Lord Zetland, stated that he intended '*pouring cold water on the Muslim idea of partition formally advocated in the Lahore Resolution, though not necessarily at this stage conclusively rejecting it. I should emphasise that this would be a counsel of despair and wholly at variance with the policy of a united India which British rule has achieved and which it is our aim to perpetuate after British rule ceases*'.

Linlithgow felt it advisable not to condemn the idea outright at this stage. He thought Jinnah was using it as a bargaining lever. In his response to Zetland four days later, he cautioned, ' ---- *any overemphasis on unacceptability and faults of Muslim scheme would be politically unfortunate ---- and I think you will feel with me that wise tactics would be to keep our hands free until critical moment is reached in future constitutional discussions*' (*Liberty or Death*, p. 126).

A few weeks later Zetland resigned in part because of differences with Churchill on India policy. He had been in favour of giving India dominion status after the war which was unacceptable to Churchill. The latter regarded any suggestion that entailed diminution of the empire as heresy, '*I have not become the King's First Minister to preside over the liquidation of the British Empire*'. On the eve of his appointment as viceroy, Lord Wavell noted in his diary, '*He* (Churchill) *hates India and everything to do with it ---- knows as much of the Indian problem as George III did of the American colonies*' (*Wavell: the Viceroy's journal*, Oxford University Press, 1973, p.12). Churchill also tried to exploit the situation in India in a rather cynical and unscrupulous way. As noted in the earlier chapter, '----- *he did not share the anxiety to encourage and promote unity between the Hindu and Muslim communities. ---- if it were brought about, the immediate result would be that united communities would join in showing us the door. He regarded the Hindu-Muslim feud as the bulwark of British rule in India* (*Churchill, Cripps and India*, p. 28).

Leopold Amery became the new Secretary of State for India (his son John was hanged as a traitor after the war) but the policy towards India was always dictated by Churchill until he lost the election in 1945. In his briefing Linlithgow informed Amery of the strength of Jinnah's position and told him that '*Congress is essentially a Hindu party, though it contains some Muslim elements ---- there is no justification on a broad view for regarding* (Muslims within Congress) *as of any very decisive importance ---- at present time the only organization which can speak on behalf of the Muslims of India as a whole is the Muslim League under Jinnah. There are from time to time signs of considerable internal tension in the League* (but) *Jinnah remains in complete control and is the person to be negotiated with, and the only person in a position to deliver the goods*' (Letter 30th June 1940).

Hindus, on the other hand, remained in total denial. In some ways victims of their own propaganda, they still refused to accept the League as representative of all the Muslims in India. As to the Lahore Resolution, '*The Nehru family regarded the very idea of Pakistan as a joke ---- it seemed absurd to imagine that such a thing could ever happen to India*' (Nehru's niece Nayantara Sahgal in interview with French, p.125). It seems incredible that they should be thinking along these lines at a time when more than one hundred thousand Muslims had gathered from all parts of India to attend the 1941 session of Muslim League in Madras and pledged their ecstatic support to Jinnah and his demand for a separate Muslim homeland. If Muslim League and Jinnah did not represent the Muslims of India, who else did? Why had Congress been negotiating with them in all these years and why did its leaders focus all their appeals, expectations, admonitions and opprobrium on Jinnah?

It wasn't long before the Congress propagandists started branding Pakistan as a British creation in pursuit of their policy of 'divide and rule'. Beverley Nichols addressed this question to Jinnah in a revealing interview in 1943. His response is recorded in *Verdict on India* in the chapter titled '*Dialogue With A Giant*': '*The man who makes such a suggestion must have a very poor opinion of British intelligence, apart from his opinion of my own integrity. The one thing which keeps the British in India is the false idea of a united India, as preached by Gandhi. A united India, I repeat is a British creation ---- a myth, and a very dangerous myth, which will cause endless strife. As long as that strife exists, the British have an excuse for remaining. For once in a way, 'divide and rule' does not apply*' (p. 193).

He went on to explain that the demand for Pakistan was predicated on the fact that 'the Muslims are a Nation'. This was only partly in terms of religion '*but by no means exclusively. You must remember that Islam is not merely a religious doctrine but a realistic and practical Code of Conduct. I am thinking in terms of life, of everything important in life. I am thinking in terms of our history, our heroes, our art, our architecture, our music, our laws, our jurisprudence. ---- We are different beings. There is nothing in life which links us together ----*.

'*A united India means a Hindu-dominated India. ---- Any other meaning you impose on it is mythical. India is a British creation ---- it is merely a single administrative unit governed by a bureaucracy under the sanction of the sword. That is all. It is a paper creation, it has no basis in flesh and blood*'. He then went on to quote from a speech by John Bright in the British Parliament on 4th June 1858 in which the latter had termed the proposition of a united India impractical and misguided even at that time.

To the question, 'Are the Muslims going to be richer or poorer under Pakistan', he replied, '*I'll ask you a question for a change. Supposing you were asked which would you prefer, a rich England under Germany or a poor England free, what would your answer be*'? ----- *This great ideal rises far above mere questions of personal comfort or temporary convenience. ----- What conceivable reason is there to suppose that the gift of nationality is going to be an economic liability? A sovereign nation of a hundred million Muslims ----- is hardly likely to be in a worse economic position than if its members are scattered and disorganized, under the dominance of two hundred and fifty million Hindus whose one idea is to exploit them*'.

MUSLIM DISSIDENTS

Not all the Muslims supported the idea of Pakistan. The entire phalanx of well-known *ulama* and not simply those aligned with Congress, with the exception of Maulana Shabbir Ahmad Usmani, opposed it vigorously, often in crude, unseemly and distasteful terms. The President of Jamiat-ul-ulama and premier Deoband scholar, Maulana Husain Ahmad Madani, went so far as to issue a *fatwa* in October 1945, on the eve of general elections, declaring it *haraam* (forbidden in Islam) for Muslims to become members of Muslim League. Maulana Qasim Ahmad Nanotvi, also from Jamiat, issued a *fatwa* urging Muslims to join Indian National Congress and collected similar fatwas from other *ulama* that he published under the title, *Nusrat al-Ahrar*. The Ahrar party was just as vehemently opposed to Pakistan. Mazhar Ali Azhar wrote that Jinnah was not Quaid-e-Azam but 'Kafir-e-Azam'. The *Khaksaars* even made two attempts on Jinnah's life and in one these succeeded in wounding him at his home in Bombay.

The Ameer Jamaat-e-Islami, Maulana Abul Ala Maudoodi, wrote: *As a Muslim, I have no interest in their* (Muslim) *rule in those areas of India where the Muslims are in a majority. For me the primary question is whether in this 'Pakistan' of yours the basis of government will be the sovereignty of God or, in accordance with the western idea of democracy, the sovereignty of the people. In the first case it will certainly be 'Pakistan', otherwise it will be as much of 'Na-Pakistan' as that part of the country where, according to your scheme, the rule will be that of non-Muslims: in fact, in the eyes of God it will be 'na-pak' ---- and damned. ----- Isn't that a foolish man who aims at Islamic revolution and yet endeavours for the establishment of such a democratic government which would stand in the way of that goal more than any 'kafir' government?* (*Musalman aur Maujooda Siyasi Kashmakash, vol. III*, Office of the *Tarjman-ul-Koran*, Patahankot, 1942, pp. 92, 108). In an ironic twist, Maulana Maudoodi and his cohorts moved lock stock and barrel from India to Pakistan the day the latter came into existence. If there was no difference between the two, why emigrate?

Twelve years after the *Maulana* made this stinging observation, Pakistan framed the Constitution in 1954. It was entirely based on democratic principles. According to *The Dawn* of 15th October 1954, Maulana Maudoodi issued a statement that the Constitution was, to a very large extent Islamic in character and urged its adoption. It is often hard to tell where exactly these people may stand on various political and other issues at any particular time. In a different way, it also reflects the flexibility and resilience that is inherent in Islam and should enable the Muslims to adjust to the conditions and circumstances prevailing in different places and at different times.

If Maulana Maudoodi wanted Pakistan to be an 'Islamic theocratic state', why condemn its establishment? The form of government it was going to take was not for one man to decide or impose. Jinnah never tired of repeating, '*The Constitution and the Government will be what the people will decide*'. The party that now represented the vast majority of Muslims had given no indication in the Lahore Resolution that it was in favour of theocracy. Like the rest of the *mullas*, Maudoodi had criticized Jinnah and Pakistan without offering a clearly defined alternative or paradigm for safeguarding the interests and rights of the Muslims in India. The country was going to become independent soon. It could do so either as a unified state in which case it would be forever dominated by the overwhelming Hindu majority. Muslims had already had a foretaste of what it would be like under the Congress ministries in 1937. The only other viable course open to them was that of a separate independent homeland. How would it have furthered the cause of Islam more if the Muslims had lived under Hindu rule in a united India and not in independent Muslim Pakistan?

If the *maulanas* had been sincere and true, logically, they would have welcomed the idea and worked with the rest to make it an 'Islamic state'. It appeared to be more a case of 'we are against it because it is not our idea and it does not give us the reins of power' wrapped in the cloak of Islam. They disliked and resented Jinnah partly because he was westernized in his ways but mostly because they felt sidelined and rendered ineffectual after the Muslims accepted and adopted him as their sole representative and leader. The stock of the *mullas* had never been so low in India. As an indication, the leading scholar and Congress leader, Maulana Abul Kalam Azad, had traditionally led the *Eid* congregation in Calcutta. After his opposition to Pakistan, he was no longer acceptable and Muslims refused to have him lead the prayers. There was a widespread common perception, almost certainly not true, that he had been bought over by Hindu money.

Jinnah is on record having reiterated ad infinitum that Pakistan was for protecting the freedom, rights and interests of the Muslims and nothing more. He always referred to it as a 'Muslim' State and never as an 'Islamic' State ---- a homeland for the Muslims and not a theocratic oligarchy run by a bunch of obscurantist *mullas*. This was clearly understood and accepted by everyone associated and working with him. Amir Ahmed Khan, the Raja of Mahmudabad who was personally very close to Jinnah, records that as a young man he was very keen that Pakistan should be an Islamic State. '*My advocacy of an Islamic State brought me into conflict with Jinnah. He thoroughly disapproved of my ideas and dissuaded me from expressing them publicly from the League platform lest the people might be led to believe that Jinnah shared my view and that he was asking me to convey such ideas to the public ---- Now that I look back I realize how wrong I had been*' (*Some Memories*, Raja of Mahmudabad's article in *Partition of India: Policies and Perspectives, 1935-47* by Cyril Henry Philips and M.Doreen Wainwright, pp. 388- 9, as quoted by Khairi). At the Muslim Legislators Conference in Delhi in April 1946 Jinnah said, '*What are we aiming at? It is not for theocracy, not for a theocratic state*'.

It wasn't that Jinnah had anything against Islam; far from it. He believed that religion was an issue that was between God and man. To him Islam was much more than running a state in a way conceived by a bunch of unelected *mullas*. This is not how the Koran or the Prophet envisaged Islam. It was wrong, indeed un-Islamic, to forcibly coerce the people into living under a system envisaged by one set of unrepresentative theologians who had no sanction in the Koran or a mandate from the people themselves. The Koran clearly ordains that Muslims should resolve all such issues through mutual consultation and consensus (62:38). Even Maulana Maudoodi concedes as much in his *Khilafat-o-Malookiat*.

Muslims have become divided into more than seventy sects, each with its own set of beliefs and interpretations. As already mentioned, there are many different views and schools of *fikah*, each believing that it is right. There is no single Constitution or a comprehensive and workable body of law stipulated anywhere for an Islamic State. It was morally and ethically wrong to call for the establishment of an Islamic State without first clearly defining in detail how it will function. Considering the wide divergence of views between the different sects and the depth and intensity of feelings involved, it would be next to impossible to get all of them to agree on a single model. In that event as Jinnah put it, '----- *the consequences would be a struggle of religious opinion from the very inception of the State leading to its very dissolution*.'

Unlike many a *mullah*, Jinnah believed that democracy was the Islamic way. At a press conference in Delhi on 14th July 1947, he told a correspondent, '*When you talk of democracy, I am afraid you have not studied Islam. We learnt democracy thirteen hundred years ago*'. About the constitution of Pakistan he said in 1948, '*I am sure it will be a democratic type, embodying the essential principles of Islam ----- In any case Pakistan is not going to be a theocratic state ----- to be ruled by priests with a divine mission. We have many non-Muslims, Hindus, Christians and Parsis, but all are Pakistanis. They will enjoy the same rights and privileges as any other citizens and will play their rightful part in the affairs of Pakistan*' (*Glimpses of the Quaid-e-Azam, vol. II*, p. 463). He also envisaged what he called 'Islamic socialism' for Pakistan that would avoid the pitfall of class struggle inherent in communism. He first mentioned it publicly in Chittagong on 26th March 1948. Liaquat Ali Khan reiterated it later in his address in Lahore on 3rd September 1949.

The *Maulanas* were not the only Muslims who tried to make it difficult for Jinnah. The British had carefully nurtured and extended patronage to prominent local Muslims through favours extended in exchange for their loyalty and support. These included appointments to municipal and district councils and boards, nomination of family members to the civil service, grants of titles and agricultural estates, etc. With the advent of political activity in India, they were encouraged and facilitated to enter this arena as well. In fact, they dominated the field until the early nineteen-twenties when nationalist Muslim leaders began to make their presence felt.

It was a symbiotic relationship in which one relied on the other for its survival. The rise of nationalism and the prospect of an end to the British rule carried with it the probability of termination of the perks and privileges enjoyed by this class. In the face of growing sentiment for independence any overt expression of loyalty and support for the continuation of the British rule, however much in their personal interest, had become a serious political risk. In the end, most of them drifted to the national camp not out of conviction but goaded by opportunism and expediency. Insincere in their commitment, many of them seriously harmed the cause of the Muslims by creating divisions within the League. Others resented Jinnah's authority but could do little in the face of his popularity.

Sir Sikander Hayat, the chief minister of Punjab was one of them, secretly remaining in touch and counseling the viceroy not to 'inflate Jinnah's ego or to make him more difficult to deal with'. He even considered making an alliance with Congress in 1941 and made several public statements against the Lahore Resolution, privately calling its objective *Jinnistan* (*Linlithgow Collection*, letter to Zetland dated 5th September 1939 and *Liberty or Death*, pp. 135, 169). Sir Zafarullah Khan was also keeping his options open and helping the British in ways that were not exactly conducive to the good of the League at least until 1943 (*Linlithgow letter to Amery* dated 15th May 1941 as quoted by Khairi, p. 473). We have seen earlier the role of Sir Mohammed Shafi in splitting and setting up a parallel Muslim League and later at the Round Table Conference in London.

Muslim League had expressly asked its members not to join the Viceroy's Executive Council and its chief ministers to decline the invitation to become members of the newly created National Defence Council unless certain demands had been met but the temptation proved too great for some of them. A. K. Fazl-ul-Haq, who had already joined the Defence Council, resented the decision and complied with it only reluctantly. He then left the Muslim League Parliamentary Party and, as the Chief Minister of Bengal, formed a coalition government with Congress, Hindu Mahasabha and some of the other dissident members. It was a great blow. Jinnah was left with little choice except to expel him from the party. He did the same to Nawab Chhattari and Sir Sultan Ahmed from UP who insisted on joining the Defence Council. Khizar Hayat Tiwana was expelled from the party when he would not let the League Parliamentary Party be formed in the Punjab Assembly.

There was no Muslim League Parliamentary Party in Sind at the time since the League had not fielded any candidates in the election. In 1938 Jinnah managed to persuade the badly divided Muslim assembly members to join hands but, as mentioned earlier, Allah Bakhsh balked at the last minute. He went back on a written agreement and joined hands with Congress instead to form the government as its chief minister. Soon afterwards, Sir Ghulam Husain Hidayatullah, his chief rival in the assembly followed suit and deserted the League, only to return a few years later when it became politically a more attractive proposition.

After the passing of the Lahore Resolution in 1940, Allah Bakhsh presided over what was called the Azad Muslim Conference. It was attended by all the Indian national parties, with the exception of Muslim League and the *Khaksaars*. In opposition to the Resolution it declared that, '*All the nooks and corners of the country contain the homes and hearths of the Muslims, and the cherished historic monuments of their religion and culture, which are dearer to them than their own lives*' (*Modern Islam in India*, by W. C.

Smith, Lahore, 1947, p. 280). They did not see the need for an independent homeland for the Muslims of India.

G.M. Syed was President of Sind Muslim League and member of its Council and Working Committee. At the time of elections in 1946, he felt unhappy with the allocation of some party tickets and resigned to field his own candidates in opposition to those of the League. In the event, he was routed and the League won all of the seats in the provincial assembly. It left him with a grudge that he bore against Jinnah and Pakistan till his dying day. Considering some of the unprincipled lot he had to carry with him, it is indeed a miracle that Jinnah succeeded in the end.

Some of the other detractors of Pakistan and the League among the Muslims have already been mentioned in the previous chapter. These included the *Ahrars,* the *Khaksaars* and an assortment of other smaller groups scattered in different parts of northern India. The most virulent among these were the *Khudaee Khidmatgars* in the North West Frontier Province. Their leader Abdul Ghaffar Khan, popularly known as the 'Frontier Gandhi', was affiliated with Congress and nurtured a visceral hatred towards Jinnah and Pakistan. Like Gandhi, he wanted India to become free as a united whole but when the emergence of Pakistan looked inevitable, he changed his tune and asked for the province to be also made an independent state called Pakhtunistan. In his way of thinking it was acceptable to partition Pakistan but not India. His aversion to Pakistan was such that he did not even wish to be buried in its soil. His body was interred in Jalalabad (Afghanistan) as per his wishes. His secretary, Yunas Khan, refused to stay in Pakistan, choosing to live in India instead. He was given some diplomatic assignments and later made a member of the Rajiya Sabha, the upper house of India's Parliament. To prove his loyalty and earn his keep he continued to pour vitriol against the Muslim state till the end.

CRIPPS MISSION

A new factor had emerged at this time that began to seriously impact the situation in the sub-continent. United States had entered the war after the Japanese attack on Pearl Harbour in December 1941. Shortly afterwards Singapore was lost and the Japanese were knocking on the doors of Northeast India. President Roosevelt was very keen to get India's backing and support for the Allies' war effort and was deeply concerned at the prevailing anti-British sentiment in the country. He pressurized Churchill to make concessions to the nationalists.

There was also a deeper motive aimed at gaining access to the vast Indian market that had been closed to the rest but this aspect is only indirectly relevant to the present discussion. Congress was quick to bait this potent new source of support. Nehru told a rally in Delhi, '*If today we were masters of our own destiny we would ask people to get ready and defend the country with all our might. Unfortunately obstinate worthless and incompetent Government still has its grip tight on us*' (*Transfer of Power vol. I*, p.4). He also told Roosevelt's personal envoy, Colonel Louis Johnson, that the Congress Party was ready to hitch 'India's wagon to America's star and not Britain's' (*Transfer of Power, vil. I*, p. 665). Vinayak Savarkar, president of Hindu Mahasabha, appealed directly to Roosevelt to guarantee independence for India after the war (*India Office Library, doc. 8/572A*, p. 24).

The British always had misgivings about the nationalists' commitment to the Allies and the war. Linlithgow cabled the Secretary of State, '----- *India and Burma have no natural association with the Empire, from which they are alien by race, history and religion ----- both are in the Empire because they are conquered countries which had been brought there by force, kept there by our controls, and which hitherto it has suited them to remain under our protection. I suspect that the moment they think we may lose the war or take a bad knock, their leaders would be much more concerned to make terms with the victor at our expense than to fight for ideals to which so much lip service is given*' (*Transfer of Power*, *vol. I*, pp. 48- 9).

As to the support for the war effort, the British did not need the nationalists for that. The principle requirement was for troops to serve as cannon fodder. There was no shortage of volunteers; within one year the Indian Army had nearly half a million men, about forty per cent of them Muslim and the rest Hindus, Sikhs, Gurkhas and others. By the time the war ended numbers had shot up to well over two million of which about sixty per cent were Muslims. They were joining up because there were few other jobs and not because they wanted to defend the country or the Empire nor did they hate the Germans or the Japanese. It always was and still remained a mercenary army.

Churchill had no desire and did not feel the need to make any concessions in India. Roosevelt kept prodding and pushing him nonetheless, less out of concern for the Indians and more due to the prospect of greater market share for the US after the war and the growing sympathy among the American voters. The upshot was that Labour MP Sir Stafford Cripps, Lord Privy Seal, who had close contacts and was trusted by Congress, was dispatched to Delhi. Tagging along with him was Colonel Louis Johnson, Roosevelt's personal representative, with not much knowledge or understanding of India and its politics. Roosevelt already had direct access to Churchill through his representative in London, Averell Harriman. When the latter developed illicit relations with Churchill's daughter-in-law, Pamela, Lord Beaverbrook was elated, '*To have FDR's personal representative, the man charged with keeping Britain safe, sleeping with the prime minister's daughter-in-law was a wonderful stroke of luck* (*Life of the Party*, by Christopher Ogden, London, 1994, pp. 123, 4). Apart from reflecting on the workings of the British mind and politics, it is an indication of the desperation to keep the Americans involved and committed to the war.

Cripps landed in Delhi on 23rd March 1942 to offer India dominion status after the war with a constitution to be framed by an elected assembly. If any of the provinces wished to secede they will have the freedom to do so. In the mean time, there would be a national unity government under the viceroy and his council. When Cripps showed the proposal to Jinnah, he asked for clarification of the position of Punjab and Bengal in the scheme and suggested a change to the phraseology to specify the 'possibility of a second Dominion being set up'. He did not give his reaction immediately but promised to convey it after due deliberation and consultation. Later that afternoon, Gandhi told Cripps the offer was unacceptable to Congress because it envisaged 'perpetual vivisection of India'. '*In the first instance he expressed the very definite view that Congress would not accept the document* (which he called) *an invitation to the Moslems to create a Pakistan*' (Note by Cripps "*My Interview with Mahatama Gandhi,*" *Transfer of Power, I* , p. 498). According to Gandhi, Cripps was 'offering a post-dated cheque on a failing bank'.

Although Congress had rejected the first part of the offer, negotiations went on for some time on the formation of an interim government. These too were inconclusive. Congress wanted the right to nominate the minister of defence, with full powers resting in the cabinet and the viceroy only acting as the constitutional head. Churchill found it unacceptable. He never had any intentions of parting with India and was merely going through the motions. The Mission had served its purpose; he could now tell Roosevelt that progress could not be made due to the intransigence of Congress. It did not fool the Americans but they did not wish to cause a rift with Britain for the sake of India at this stage.

It was hard to keep track of the confusing messages sent out by Congress from time to time. A week after the breakdown of talks with Cripps, Gandhi wrote in *The Harijan* (19th April) that India could only attain its independence by Hindus and Muslims working together to arrive at an amicable settlement. If most Muslims really wanted a '*separate nation no power on earth can compel them to think otherwise*'. If Hindus wanted to fight against such a division, '*That way lies suicide ---- In that case goodbye to independence*'. All of his earlier and subsequent actions had not been in conformity with this line of reasoning. Shortly afterwards, the Madras Congress Party passed a resolution recognizing Muslim League's 'right of separation' and the creation of Pakistan, if that proved to be the preference of the majority, when a constitution was framed. Nehru and Abul Kalam Azad 'disagreed entirely' forcing Rajgopalacharya who had sponsored the resolution to resign from the Working Committee. This was after the two gentlemen had themselves, in their talks with Cripps, '*---- said they were prepared to envisage the possibility of Pakistan*' (*Note by Cripps "My Interview with Jawaharlal Nehru and Maulana Azad"*, 29th March 1942, *Transfer of Power vol. I*, p. 530). Among other things it underlines Jinnah's difficulty in negotiating with this lot that kept changing its position and thought nothing of it.

Shortly after Cripps returned to England, Congress passed a resolution in Allahabad that read in part: '*---- India will attain her freedom through her own strength and will retain it likewise ---- Britain must abandon her hold on India. It is on the basis of independence alone that India can deal with Britain or other nations*'. Gandhi added his own footnote to this in *The Harijan* of 10th May 1942: '*---- I feel British cannot suddenly change their traditional nature; racial superiority is treated not as a vice but as virtue not only in India but in Africa, Burma and Ceylon. This drastic disease requires drastic remedy, complete and immediate orderly withdrawal from India ---- I must devote whole of my energy to realization of this supreme act. Presence of British in India is invitation to Japan to invade India. Their withdrawal removes that bait*'.

For the British to carry out the 'orderly withdrawal' from India, they had to hand over power to some effective body in a manner that was acceptable to all the major parties if chaos and bloodshed were to be avoided. Gandhi's solution was spelt out in a talk with a journalist of *The News Chronicle* on 14th May: '*Leave India in God's hands, but in modern parlance to anarchy, and that anarchy may lead to internecine warfare for a time or to unrestrained dacoities. ---- From these a true India will arise in the place of the false one we see*' (*The Collected Works of Mahatama Gandhi*, vol. 76, p. 133. He repeated this in *The Harijan* of 24th May 1942: (*Transfer of power II*, p.115). Clearly he wanted the British to leave, preferably after handing over power to Congress. If that was not possible for any reason, they must leave any way and let the Indians battle it out among themselves afterwards.

With the communal situation as it existed at the time, it would have led to monumental chaos accompanied by unprecedented loss of life and no way of knowing what the final outcome would be. Gandhi may have hoped that the Hindus would win to establish Ram Raj in the whole of India but there was much greater likelihood of the country breaking up into many different parts along communal lines. The only realistic solution was for Hindus and Muslims to formalise a mutually acceptable arrangement and then jointly confront the British. Yet, every time Jinnah made the suggestion, Congress and Gandhi poured cold water on it, telling him that the League and Jinnah did not speak for the Muslims of India, only Congress did.

QUIT INDIA MOVEMENT

Earlier, Nehru had been in Bombay holding private talks with Congress functionaries. In a confidential note the governor of Bombay reported to the viceroy that '*Nehru has convinced himself that the present situation is intolerable and that action is necessary. ---- that Hindus must face up to the fact that they must fight the Muslims, or any other minority which "revolts" against a Congress attempt at domination*' (*Transfer of Power II*, p. 240). Jinnah had known this all along and never entertained any misgivings about the motives of Gandhi and Congress. He made his own assessment known in a press statement issued on 22nd June: '*Gandhi never wanted to settle Hindu-Muslim question except on his own terms of Hindu domination. ---- He wants British Government to accept that Congress means India and Gandhi means Congress, and to come to terms with him as spokesman of all India with regard to transfer of power to self-styled Indian National Congress, and to keep in power by means of British bayonets, so that Hindu Congress raj can dominate Muslims and other minorities*'.

There was a strong sense among the Congress leaders that conditions were ripe to push for India's independence. British power was at low ebb after the military setbacks in Europe, the Far East and Burma. Her fate now lay in the hands of the United States where public opinion was strongly in favour of India's freedom. The insurrection by Pir Pagara's Hurrs was already underway. They had been murdering and looting passengers in trains and buses around Tando Adam in Sind. Britain was vulnerable and could be coerced into making concessions by resorting to civil disobedience and unrest in the country that will seriously undermine the war effort.

They could have carried the Muslims with them but that meant making concessions that were anathema to the Hindus. In the event they decided to go it alone. On 14th July the Congress Working Committee passed a resolution calling for the British rule to end immediately failing which Congress would have to resort to full use of its 'non-violent strength'. On 8th August it launched countrywide *Satiagarha* what came to be dubbed as the 'Quit India Movement'. Gandhi announced, '*We shall either free India or die in the attempt; we shall not live to see the perpetuation of our slavery*' ---- "*karaingay ya maraingay* (will do or die)".

The plan called for general strikes in schools, colleges, government offices, mills, public utilities, markets and other such places. It included cutting telephone and telegraph wires, uprooting railway lines, occupying government offices, police stations, withholding rents and taxes and disrupting other public services. Although the planning had been done in secret, the British were kept well-informed of its progress and details by their informers and were ready with plans of their own. The same night as Gandhi made the announcement he was arrested, along with all the members of Congress Working Committee. Gandhi and his entourage, including his wife Kastura Bai, were lodged in the Agha Khan's palace in Poona. The rest of the committee members that included Nehru, Patel, Azad and others were taken to the Mughal fort at Ahmedabad.

Violence erupted in Bombay as the news of the arrests broke and spread to different parts of the country. There were strikes in schools, mills closed down and railway traffic was disrupted. A group of policemen were doused with kerosene and burnt to death as were the wives and children of some others. All kinds of shady characters including criminals, bandits and even anti-Brahmin activists joined in. Police and railway stations and government treasuries were attacked and houses of government officials set on fire. The violence was mainly confined to predominantly Hindu areas with Behar, parts of Orissa, Bengal and Bombay witnessing the worst of it. Muslims and Sikhs took no part in the proceedings. Jinnah termed it 'Gandhi's Himalayan blunder'.

The unrest was put down by a heavy hand. When the protesters occupied Patna railway station they were strafed by air force planes. It took nearly two months to bring the situation under control but not without causing some anxious and worrisome moments to the British. In that time, more than 60,000 Indians were put in jail, 900 hundred were officially reported killed and 600 flogged. There were substantial casualties among the police and a few among the British troops but, importantly, their line held. If Congress had aimed at paralyzing the government, it had failed to do so. In the process it had also lost sympathy among the American and British public.

Starting from the first days of his incarceration Gandhi had been writing letters to the viceroy, mostly calling for a meeting with him which Linlithgow declined. At the end of the year, sensing the S*atiagarha* had failed to achieve what he had hoped it would, Gandhi wrote to the viceroy, '*The law of Satiagarha as I know prescribes a remedy in such moments of trial ---- crucify the flesh by fasting. That same law forbids its use except as a last resort. I do not want to use it if I can avoid it. ---- Convince me of my error or errors and I shall make ample amends*'. In his reply Linlithgow asked if Gandhi was 'ready to retrace his rebellious steps'. He refused adding, '*If then I can't get soothing balm for my pain, I must ---- commence after the early morning breakfast on the 9th February a fast for 21 days*' (*Transfer of Power, III*, pp. 440, 559).

On the advice of his council, Linlithgow was inclined to release Gandhi but Churchill overruled '---- this was not the time to cringe before a miserable little old man who had always been our enemy'. There was concern in various circles about Gandhi's fate for fear of the reaction among India's masses if he were to die. Roosevelt told the Secretary of State 'our biggest desire is not to see the fellow die in prison'. When the American envoy to India, William Phillips, asked Linlithgow what would happen if he did die, he was told, '*Six months unpleasantness steadily declining in volume. After it was over ---- India would be far more reliable as a base of operations. Moreover the prospect of a settlement would be greatly enhanced by the disappearance of Gandhi*'. Despite many fears and predictions from medical and other quarters Gandhi survived, apparently living only on water and some fruit juice.

In his book *Shameful Flight* (Oxford University Press, p. 57) Stanley Wolpert quotes from a 'STRICTLY SECRET' report about a Muslim League meeting in Delhi shortly after Gandhi broke his fast. '----- the League's leader now viewed the British Raj as his League's "second enemy", the Congress Party having long been the "first". As the leaders were imprisoned, Congress was no longer capable of "harming us", and Jinnah urged Muslims to focus their energies on defeating the British enemy. He rightly anticipated that the war would last another three years or so, and predicted that Allied victory would leave the British so powerful that they would easily "defy" world opinion and ignore Muslim League's demand for the creation of Pakistan. By war's end, however, the British Raj will be "in a state of exhaustion and unwilling to face a new ordeal", he predicted, adding that "her pleasure-loving people would allow no new wars to be fought." All that his followers would then have to do was to "wrest our ideal" (Pakistan) from the second enemy's 'unwilling hands" by creating enough trouble to "compel him to surrender." (*Transfer of Power, vol. III*, p. 918).

This is not how Jinnah's mind worked. His belief and approach had been to remain within the limits of constitutional constraints. The choice of words and phrases in the statement are uncharacteristic and lack the sophistication found in Jinnah's articulation which raises some doubt as to how accurately the informant was able to reproduce what Jinnah might have actually said at the meeting. The bit about 'rightly anticipating' the end of war in three years is dubious ---- it is something that could only be said after the war was over and not while it was still in progress.

Nonetheless Linlithgow and the British Government were alarmed and concerned. Their worst nightmare was if the League and Congress were to come to an agreement and started to act jointly. In his opening address at the League meeting on 24th April 1943, Jinnah had said, '*Nobody would welcome it more than myself if Mr. Gandhi is even now really willing to come to a settlement ---- on the basis of Pakistan ---- It will be the greatest day both for the Hindus and Musalmans ---- why does he not write to me direct? Who is there who can prevent him from doing so?*' Well, there was Churchill. When Gandhi read Jinnah's statement in the papers, he wrote to Jinnah, '*Dear Quaid-e-Azam, ---- I welcome your invitation. I suggest our meeting face to face*'. The letter was intercepted on Churchill's orders and never reached Jinnah.

The densely populated Bengal province had depended partly on rice imports from Burma to meet its needs. These ended after the Japanese occupation. No provision was made to make up the shortfall, mostly due to incompetence and apathy on the part of the provincial and central governments. As food shortages became evident, traders purchased the available stocks and began hoarding in the expectation of making windfall profits from rising prices. Neighbouring provinces were extremely reluctant and unwilling to help from their stocks. As food prices rose sharply the poorest suffered the most. They flocked in large numbers to cities like Calcutta, Dacca and Chittagong in the hope of finding relief. There was no organization or arrangement for dealing with the influx. The streets were filled with starving beggars. Diseases like cholera, small pox and malaria added to the misery and death. In the one year between mid-1943 and mid-1944, according to official estimates one and a half million Bengalis perished as a result of the famine. Unofficially the death toll was put at three million.

Congress leaders and press blamed not only the British but also the ineptitude of the premier, Khwaja Nazimuddin. The provincial minister of civil supplies, Huseyn Shaheed Suhrawardy and ex-premier A.K. Fazl-ul-Haq were blamed for corruption, racketeering and misuse of position. It prompted Jinnah to issue instructions that no Muslim League official should hold position in the Bengal Government. He also proclaimed in the Legislative Assembly that the British were incompetent and irresponsible to have allowed the famine to develop, pointing out that Churchill's government would not have survived twenty four hours if people had been dying of starvation in their thousands every week on the streets of London.

Wavell replaced Linlithgow as the viceroy in October 1943. He was much more concerned about the situation in Bengal and started to press hard for relief supplies. There was little sympathy or support forthcoming from London. Churchill's assistant Lord Cherwell (erstwhile Professor Lindemann) a known bigot, who said he felt physical revulsion when non-whites were in his presence, told Wavell that the famine was a figment of the Bengali imagination. He thought the problem would be solved if a certain number of wealthy Indians were to be hanged (*The Empire at Bay: The Leo Amery Diaries, 1929 - 1945*, by Barnes, etc. London, 1988, p. 976).

At the time, the British maintained a stock of six million tons of wheat in ships in the Indian Ocean for emergency use. Instead of diverting some supplies from these in response to Wavell's persistent pleading, Churchill called upon Roosevelt for help who flatly turned him down. Words and deeds seldom match in international politics. A bill to allow just one hundred Indians as immigrants to the US annually was also defeated in the US Congress in 1945.

In May 1944 the Bombay government was sending in reports of Gandhi's deteriorating physical and mental health. In view of the seriousness of consequences if he were to die in prison, on Wavell's recommendation the British government allowed his release. Gandhi made a miraculous recovery and was almost immediately receiving old friends and admirers. He even visited the victims of a munitions explosion that had rocked Bombay's dockland in April 1944. It prompted Churchill to send a telegram asking Wavell rather peevishly why had Gandhi not died yet? (*Wavell: The Viceroy's Journal, 5th July 1944*, ed. Pendrel Moon, Oxford University Press, 1973, p. 78).

By now the strains and stresses of managing the war were beginning to take their toll on Churchill. A number of his close colleagues have recorded that he had become quite irritable and irrational especially when it came to matters relating to India. Amery noted that the prime minister complains of Indians '*breeding like rabbits*' and was '*not quite normal on the subject of India. ---- He seems quite incapable of listening to or taking in even the simplest point but goes off at a tangent on a word and then rambles on inconsecutively. ---- Certainly a complete outsider coming to the meeting and knowing nothing of his reputation would have thought him a rather amusing but quite gaga old gentleman who could not understand what people were talking about*' (*The Empire at Bay*, pp. 750, 779). Field Marshal Alanbrooke and Lord Wavell have made similar observations about Churchill.

In the hope of breaking the deadlock between Congress and the League, Rajgopalacharya made a proposal that, according to Wavell, accepted the 'principle of Pakistan' provided the districts of Punjab and Bengal provinces where the Muslims were not in absolute majority were excluded from it. He also claimed that 'Gandhi was prepared to accept it' if Jinnah did. This prompted the Hindu Mahasabha to declare, '*Hindusabhaites can never tolerate breaking up of union of India their fatherland and holyland.*' Wavell thought Jinnah committed a blunder in rejecting the formula (*Transfer of Power, vol. IV*, p.558).

If it had been the case in fact, the proposal constituted a fundamental departure from the position adopted by Congress and Gandhi thus far and was worth exploring further. It was highly uncharacteristic for Jinnah, who was vacationing in Kashmir at the time, to reject the proposal out of hand without first discussing it with the League Working Committee. Jinnah's position on what was to be included in Pakistan had always been reasonable and flexible as recorded by Cripps after the discussions in March 1942 (*Transfer of Power, vol. I,* p. 481). Wavell's information was apparently based on press reports that were repudiated at the time in *The Dawn*, the League paper. Gandhi has confirmed discussing the proposal at his next meeting with Jinnah (*Gandhi's Passion: The Life and Legacy of Mahatama Gandhi*, by Stanley Wolpert, Oxford University Press, New York, 2001, p. 210). The Devil lies in the details which were not made clear. If at some stage Jinnah had rejected the proposal it must have been for good reasons.

The much anticipated meeting between Gandhi and Jinnah took place in September in Jinnah's house in Bombay amid apprehension on the part of Amery about 'some unholy alliance between Gandhi and Jinnah for the purpose of embarrassing us'. They were not alone in their fears; Nehru noted in his diary, '*I feel stifled and unable to breathe normally ---- I have a feeling of blankness and sinking of heart*' (*Nehru: A Tryst with Destiny,* by Stanley Wolpert, Oxford University Press, 1996, p.337). In the end, the meeting was fruitless. Jinnah asked for '*the right of self-determination as a nation and not as a territorial unit, and that we are entitled to exercise our inherent right as a Muslim nation*' to be recognized. Gandhi said he was '*unable to accept the proposition that the Muslims of India are a nation, distinct from the rest of the inhabitants of India. ---- Once the principle is admitted there would be no limit to claims for cutting up India*'(*Complete Works of Mahatama Gandhi*, *vol. 78*, p. 122).

Soon after Gandhi wrote in *The Harijan*, '*I find no parallel in history for a body of converts and their descendants claiming to be a nation apart from the parent stock. If India was one nation before the advent of Islam, it must remain one in spite of the change of faith of a very large body of her children*'. He also told the press that Jinnah was '*suffering from hallucination when he imagines that an un-natural division of India could bring either happiness or prosperity to the people concerned*' (*Jinnah of Pakistan*, by Stanley Wolpert, New Delhi 1985, pp. 232 – 3, 236). Gandhi could not possibly have written and said all this if he was predisposed to accepting Rajgopalacharya's proposal, as suggested by Wavell.

Quit India Movement might have failed to achieve the aim Gandhi had set for it but the ensuing violence had a profoundly unsettling effect on the British, particularly in India. They no longer felt sanguine or secure about the future. The war in Europe had ended and the Japanese had run out of steam as well. It was clear from recent developments that Britain would not be in a position to hold on to India for much longer. In Britain too there was little desire or will to hang on except among a small band of Tory diehards led by Churchill who feared that without the empire the country would cease to be a world power.

The harsh reality was that the empire was no longer a profitable proposition. It was not even paying its own way now and Britain could no longer afford to maintain it. Her trade surplus with India had been falling steadily since the twenties. A whole host of industries had sprung up in India during the war years. Their products were now competing with imports from Britain and other countries. The economist Maynard Keynes noted in a paper in 1945 that the British debt had exceeded three billion pounds. This included two billion pounds spent on policing and administering the colonies. Unless this expenditure was brought under drastic control Britain's financial position would be 'fatally impaired'. The administrative control of the colonies could be easily shed without putting the economic interests at too much risk. The latter could be secured by retaining indirect control over the markets for capital and raw materials.

The British civil servants responsible for the administration in India could see the writing on the wall. It took inevitable toll on their commitment and morale. These were made worse in no small way by their concerns for personal safety. In the event of a future crisis the loyalty of either the police or the Indian army could by no means be guaranteed. These institutions had not remained unaffected by recent developments and nurtured a measure of sympathy for the nationalist cause. The army, in particular its Muslim elements, were becoming increasing uncomfortable at being used to re-impose colonial rule in the Middle East, Indonesia, Malaya, etc. Exhausted after the war and burdened with commitments in Europe, Palestine and other places the British army was in no position to station the very large numbers of troops that would be needed in India.

In 1942 Subhas Chandra Bose, erstwhile Congress president, had escaped to Germany via Afghanistan. There he proposed to set up a 'Free India Government' but the Nazis treated his claims about a revolution waiting to happen in India with a measure of skepticism and remained cool to the idea. He did set up an 'India Legion' with the help of some Indian volunteers and prisoners of war in German camps that fought against the Allies in Italy. A year later a German submarine transported him to Japan. The large Indian community in Southeast Asia responded enthusiastically to his call to fight for India's liberation. In addition, he was able to get a substantial number of volunteers from among the prisoners of war to form Indian National Army (INA) of about thirty thousand men. Bose appointed himself as the supreme commander as well the head of state and prime minister of a 'Provisional Government of Azad Hind'. Half a dozen or so countries recognized it, among them the Republic of Ireland.

INA saw some action on the Imphal-Arakan front but performed poorly, partly due to inadequate supply of arms and equipment. It surrendered in Rangoon in May 1945 and Bose escaped to Formosa (Taiwan). A plane carrying him to Manchuria crashed on take-off and Bose was burnt to death. Some INA prisoners were put on trial for 'waging war against the king' and handed out long prison sentences. The politicians, in particular those in Congress, were quick to play up the issue. This only helped to aggravate an already charged atmosphere and Wavell was left with little choice but to commute the sentences. Given the circumstances, the incident had a profound impact on the psyche of both the British and the Indians. While adding to the existing anxiety of the former, it helped create mythical heroes for the Indians whose memories live on to this day.

The large-scale expansion of the Indian military services in wartime had of necessity involved relaxation in recruitment standards and shortcuts in training. The quality of leadership among the officers was particularly wanting which had a direct affect on the rest. Added to it was the feeling of uncertainty about the future. The British conscripts wanted to return home and be released from service while their Indian counterparts were uncertain of the future that awaited them after their disbandment. The latter were also influenced by the political uncertainty that was affecting the rest of the country. All this manifested itself in acts of insubordination, strikes and general lack of discipline. In a much more serious case, compounded by a number of other local factors, sailors of the Royal Indian Navy mutinied in February 1946.

It started in the signal school, HMIS Talwar and quickly spread to other ships and establishments in Bombay and Karachi. As the news spread, crowds in Bombay inspired by the local Communists joined in. British officers and European civilians were attacked as well as banks, post offices and shops set on fire. The police and the navy were unable to contain the situation and the army had to be called in. When it was all over a month later, according to the official figures, there were 240 dead and over a thousand injured. There were other instances of mutiny and insubordination by the Indian Air Force ground crews at a number of air bases as well as at the Indian Army Signals Centres at Jabalpur and

Allahabad and the gunners in Madras. The clerical staff at the GHQ in Delhi also went on strike. Intelligence estimates began to cast doubt on continued reliability of the army and discounted the loyalty and trustworthiness of the navy and the air force units (*Public Records Office* WO 208/761A).

The incidents only added to the despondency and despair among the British officials in India. Wavell had been trying to convey the implications to London and urging some movement on the political front. The response took its time and it wasn't until the war had ended that Churchill approved the convening of a conference of Indian leaders to discuss the composition of a more politically representative Executive Council. Wavell ordered the release of members of the Congress Executive Committee and issued invitations to selected members of various political parties and communities to meet in Simla in June 1945.

At issue was the composition of the new Executive Council. It is unclear, once in place, how it was to function and help further India's march to freedom. The idea seems to have been simply to replace the existing placemen with politicians from various parties. The Indian toadies in the council had served their purpose and there was no further need for their services. In the end, things never got that far. Gandhi told Wavell that he '*represented nobody except himself*'. According to the latter, it was '*mainly a discursive monologue by Mr. Gandhi, interspersed by numerous digressions, such as a most graphic description of the death of his Private Secretary, and a relation of his carrying down the wounded General Woodgate from Spion Kop in 1899*' (*Wavell: The Viceroy's Journal*, by Penderel Moon, London, 1973, pp. 146-7). Jinnah wanted the Muslim nominees to be only from Muslim League which was unacceptable to Congress as well as Wavell who wished to inject a member from the Unionist Party of Punjab at Sir Khizar Hayat's insistence. In the end this is what scuttled the conference.

They rejected Jinnah's claim that the League represented the vast majority of Muslims on the grounds that it had not been tested in an election. It could be argued that on the same basis there were no grounds to deny the claim either. The proper thing would have been to hold the elections before trying to resolve the issue of representation. It did not stop Wavell from telegraphing Amery after the conference '*Muslim League does not repeat does not represent all Muslims in India and considerable section of Muslims not only in Punjab but elsewhere would be outraged by admission that it does* (*Transfer of Power, V*, p. 1125). It was a personal assessment that had no basis in fact and was quite misleading as was shown later.

Wavell noted that although Simla had failed because of 'Jinnah's arrogance and intransigence about Muslim representation', the deeper cause was genuine Muslim mistrust of Hindus. '*Their fear that the Congress by parading its national character and using Muslim dummies will permeate the entire administration of any united India is real, and cannot be dismissed as an obsession of Jinnah and his immediate entourage*' (*Transfer of Power V,* pp.1262-3). The British nonetheless were by now convinced that Jinnah and his demand for Pakistan had become hurdles in the way of early transfer of power. They had a plan for India that Jinnah was convinced was harmful to Muslim interests. It made him the 'grit in the oyster' in their eyes.

The governor of Bengal, Richard Casey, came up with the suggestion to influence Bengal's leading Muslims 'away from the Pakistan idea through discreet conversations'. Wavell approved Casey's plan in a secret letter dated 1st January 1945, '*I do not believe that Pakistan will work ---- but like all other emotional ideas that have not been properly thought out, it thrives on opposition*'. The British government '*cannot openly denounce Pakistan until we have something attractive to offer in its place*'. He went on to urge Casey to emulate the model of Sir Fazle Husain and Sir Sikander Hayat Khan in 'exploiting local patriotism' of Punjab's common language to forge a bond between Hindus, Sikhs and Muslims (*Transfer of Power*, V, pp. 345-6). Wavell also persistently urged London to expose the 'crudity of Jinnah's ideas' by launching a high-level inquiry to question the prospects for Pakistan.

The British at no stage had any illusion that India was indivisible because it was a cohesive national unit. As early as 1858 John Bright had stated in the Parliament, '---- *does any man with the smallest glimmering of common sense believe that so great a country, with its twenty different nationalities and its twenty different languages, can ever be bound up and consolidated into one compact and enduring empire confine? I believe such a thing to be utterly impossible*'. Sir John Strachey, who officiated as viceroy after Lord Mayo's assassination, had noted, '---- *the differences between the countries of Europe are undoubtedly smaller than those between the countries of India*' (*India* by James Strachey, Regan Paul, Trench & Co. 1988, p. 2). Governor General, Lord Dufferin had said, '(India was) *composed of a large number of distinct nationalities, professing various religions, practicing diverse creeds, speaking different languages, while many of them are still further separated from one another by discordant prejudices, by conflicting usages, and even antagonistic interests* (and the) '*two mighty political communities* (were) *as distinct from each other as the poles asunder*' (*Report on Indian Constitutional Reforms*, Montagu and Chemsford, London, 1918, para 141: as quoted by Khairi, p.56).

The well-known Indian scholar and writer Nirad Chaudhri, himself a Hindu, wrote in his *The Continent of Circe* (Chattoo & Windus, London, 1967, p.34), '*When I hear my foreign friends speak of an Indian or Indians I sometimes interrupt them breezily: "please do not use that word. Say Bengali, Punjabi, Hindustani, Marhati, Tamil, Sikh, Muslim and so on." As to the word "Indian", it is only a geographical definition, and very loose one at that.*'

The British simply wanted to keep the country together and opposed the creation of Pakistan for strategic considerations of their own. There were growing fears about Soviet designs in the Middle East that threatened the sources of oil in the area and communications to the Far East. A strong and united India was needed, as part of the British Commonwealth, to defend these in case of aggression. If the country was divided and Pakistan became a reality, it would not be strong enough for the job. This position was even endorsed by Field Marshal Sir Claude Auchinleck, the commander-in-chief in India, who was otherwise sympathetic to the Muslims (*Transfer of Power, XII*, pp. 801-6).

It is curious that even though no agreement could be reached at Simla because both the sides stuck to their guns, it is Jinnah alone who is blamed for the breakdown. This position is held not only by the Hindus and the British but has also been reiterated by almost every present-day western historian. If Jinnah felt it impossible to shift his stance on the issue, Congress could have just as easily accommodated him by making the same concession and saved the day. It didn't, and as such became equally responsible for the breakdown. The act was the same but it is Jinnah who is blamed for his 'intransigence' and 'unreasonableness' and not the Congress leaders. The notion that it is only reasonable if one conforms to a particular point of view, even if it is antithetical to one's beliefs and interests, is flawed logic and possibly indicative of an inherent bias and ingrained prejudice but that is a separate issue.

The Labour Party in Britain trounced Churchill's Conservatives in the July 1945 elections. It was a Godsend for Congress in India for it had a long-standing tradition of cooperation and close contacts with the British Socialists. The dislike of Jinnah nurtured by the new Prime Minister Clement Attlee more than matched that of any Hindu leader ---- '(Jinnah is) *the only Indian fascist I ever met* (*Attlee* by Kenneth Harris, London, 1995, p. 552). It emboldened Congress and made it aggressively assertive in demanding immediate handing over of power without waiting for any settlement with the Muslims.

There were intelligence reports that it was soon going to embark on plans to overthrow the government through a large-scale mass movement. Wavell cabled Pethick-Lawrence, the new secretary of state that Congress leaders had been making speeches '*intended to provoke or pave the way for mass disorder ---- asserting that the British could be turned out of India within a very short time; denying the possibility of a compromise with the Muslim League; glorifying the INA; and threatening the officials who took part in the suppression of the 1942 disturbances with trial and punishment as war criminals*' (*Transfer of Power, VI,* p. 451).

He also invited Nehru who had replaced Azad as the Congress president for a meeting. Even though twelve of the party's fifteen provincial committees had voted for Patel and Nehru had not even been nominated, Gandhi chose him for the job because he '*was educated at Harrow and Cambridge and became a barrister is greatly needed to carry on the negotiations with the Englishmen*' (*The Good Boatman* by Rajmohan Gandhi, Delhi, 1995, p. 379). Wavell appealed for ending the '*incitement of violence or threats to officials*' and to compromise with the League. Nehru replied, '*Congress could make no terms whatever with the League under its present leadership and policy, that it was a reactionary body with entirely unacceptable ideas ---- Hitlerian in its leadership and policy, and tried to bully everyone*'. Wavell feared Nehru had become '*a fanatic*' and that '*his mood is dangerous to peace*' (*Transfer of Power, VI,* pp. 439-41).

Attlee had formed the India Committee in the cabinet that included Pethick-Lawrence, Stafford Cripps, Education Minister Ellen Watkins, William Wedgewood Benn and Earl Listowel as members. All of them, as indeed the Labour Party itself had a strong bias in favour of Congress. Lawrence James notes in his *Raj* (p. 587) '*Congress had deliberately and successfully cultivated an alliance with Labour since the beginning of the century. Labour MPs had been its voice in Parliament and a number of close personal friendships had been formed between British and Indian socialists. The most important was that between Cripps and Nehru. ----*

Much was owed to the efforts of Krishna Menon, a socialist based in London who was co-chair of the Labour Party and glided through its intellectual circles, acting as a lubricant between the party and Congress and, at the same time, advocating Nehru as India's future leader. ---- In its efforts to court the Labour Party, Congress had gone to considerable lengths to represent itself as a progressive, secular movement, whereas the Muslim League was portrayed as obscurantist and bent upon creating a theocratic state'.

Wavell was called to London for consultation on steps to be taken in India next. He returned with the distinct impression that the Labour Government was '*obviously bent on handing over India to their Congress friends as soon as possible*' (*Wavell: The Viceroy's Journal*, pp. 169-70). On 19th September he announced to the Indian people that after the elections a Constitution-making body would be formed in consultation with the elected representatives as a prelude to eventual independence.

The long overdue elections to the provincial and central assemblies were held at the end of 1945 amid protest by Congress that it needed more time to prepare. Nonetheless, it won overwhelmingly the non-Muslim seats and was the majority party in the Assemblies of predominantly Hindu Bombay, Madras, Orissa, Bihar, Assam, United and Central Provinces.

Muslim League had simply campaigned on the issue of Pakistan. It achieved unprecedented success by winning eighty-seven per cent of the Muslim vote and every single seat reserved for them in the central assembly. As against this, Congress polled just one per cent of the Muslim vote. The electoral success of Muslim League was owed in no small measure to the campaigning by the students from schools and colleges, in particular those from Aligarh Muslim University, who explained the significance of the vote to the illiterate masses and drummed up support in towns and villages all over the country.

It won 428 of the total 492 (87 per cent) seats in the provincial assemblies. In Sind it won all but one seat but G.M. Syed then broke away to form his own faction. In Bengal the League collared ninety per cent of the vote. In the hope of maintaining a united Bengal, League President Huseyn Shaheed Suhrawardy tried to go it alone and include Congress in the government, without prior consent by the League Working Party, but was rebuffed by the Congress leaders in Delhi. The story was different in NWFP where Muslim League had only seventeen out of thirty-six Muslim seats. Dr. Khan Sahib of the Khudaee Khidmatgars was able to form the government there with the help of Congress.

In Punjab, the League bagged 79 of the 86 seats reserved for Muslims and was the largest party in the Assembly but the Governor called on Sir Khizar Hayat Tiwana, who's Unionist Party had only ten seats, to form the government in collaboration with Congress and assorted Hindu and Sikh groups. The absence of scruples among the politicians often leads to bizarre situations for the amusement of the cynic. Nehru never tired of condemning the Unionists as 'the most reactionary of all the provincial governments' but he wasted no time in jumping into bed with them this time. It led to relentless protests by the Muslims causing Tiwana to eventually tender his resignation on 2nd March 1947. The Governor, Sir Evan Jenkins did not call upon the Muslim League to form the government on the pretext that it would lead to communal violence. Instead, the province was put under the Governor's rule.

The election results were an emphatic repudiation of Nehru's oft-repeated boast that 'there were only two parties in India ---- Congress and the government'. It would be reasonable to assume that he would now accept Muslim League as the sole representative of Muslims in India. It never happened and he, along with the rest of the Congress hierarchy, continued to harp on the mantra that Congress represented all the Indians and that Jinnah and the League did not speak for all the Muslims ---- only the 'vested landed interests'! Many a western writer has also bought into this canard without appropriate investigation and examination.

Wavell was not too enamoured of the Congress leaders, exasperated by their fickle and evasive methods. He wrote to Pethick-Lawrence on 12th August 1945, '*Nehru has continued his injudicious speeches. ---- Congress leaders are difficult people to deal with ---- outwardly very reasonable when one meets them, but in dealing with their followers they have no balance ---- I think Nehru is trustworthy ---- but he is unbalanced and unreliable ---- I am not surprised that Jinnah is apprehensive of them.* (*Transfer of Power, VI, The Post-War Phase: New Moves by the Labour Government*, London, 1976, p. 60). About Gandhi he wrote, '*I found Gandhi pleasant to talk to, with a sense of humour and good manners, but I am quite sure he is an old humbug in many ways, and I should never trust him very far* (*Transfer of Power, V*, pp. 1275-80).

A cross-party delegation of parliamentarians visited India in January 1946 to assess the situation for themselves. On their return after a month they reported that the principle of Pakistan needed to be conceded as soon as possible. If '*the Muslim League were by-passed in relation to Constitution-making, there would be widespread violence. Therefore, it is necessary to offer Jinnah Pakistan on the basis of the Muslim Majority Areas* (*Transfer of Power, VI*, p. 950). Woodrow Wyatt, who was among the delegates, stressed that Pakistan was more than a fantasy in Jinnah's mind; it was a serious proposition with support from many Indian Muslims. The reality was at last beginning to sink in at least among the British.

At about the same time, Wavell submitted his own plan for transfer of power in case Congress and the League failed to reach a settlement. The secret document that became known as the 'Reserve Plan', envisaged that if Jinnah refused to agree to attend the Constitution-making body, he would be informed that at least two divisions of Punjab and all of West Bengal would be taken out of the areas that he envisaged as constituting Pakistan. Only the areas where Muslims '*can advance a reasonable claim*' would be included. '*Modifications in boundary might be negotiated and no doubt the interests of Sikhs in particular would be carefully considered as a way of preventing immediate violence by the Sikhs*', (*Transfer of Power, VI,* p. 913).

In that case the eastern wing would include Chittagong, Dacca and Rajshahi divisions (excluding Jalpaiguri and Darjeeling), Sylhet and the eastern districts of the Bengal Presidency but not Calcutta. The western wing would be composed of Sind, Baluchistan, NWFP and the Rawalpindi, Multan and Lahore divisions of Punjab (excluding the districts of Amritsar and Gurdaspur). The latter, although a Muslim majority district, was excluded ostensibly to provide some 'geographical protection' (whatever that means) to the Sikhs in Amritsar (*Transfer of Power, VI,* p 912). A map that was drawn up in the India Office in London with the caption 'Northern India Showing "Pakistan" Confined to Muslim-Majority Districts' however rightly showed Gurdaspur as being a part of potential Pakistan because it was a Muslim-majority district.

French has attributed it to a 'probable clerical error'. The map in question was not a part of Wavell's plan. If needed, he would have attached one of his own. Muslim civil servants who had opted to serve in Pakistan had been transferred to their new locations, prior to the issue of the Radcliffe Award in August 1947, in anticipation of these becoming a part of the new country. Gurdaspur was assumed to become a part of Pakistan and Muslim civil servants had been transferred there, including the writer's father. If it had been a 'clerical error' someone along the chain from Whitehall, through Delhi, to Lahore would surely have spotted it. The Wavell plan was never approved or adopted by the cabinet. The tentative map that included Gurdaspur in Pakistan was probably prepared by the Secretary of State at a later date in some other context.

In his note to Attlee on 28th December, Secretary of State Pethick-Lawrence had observed, '*The Viceroy contemplates that if a deadlock arises ---- HMG will give a decision on the Pakistan issue and will, if necessary, define Pakistan geographically. ---- No one believes that Pakistan is in the best interest of India ---- to give a decision that there shall be a Pakistan greatly weakens any possibility of compromise on the basis of a very loose federation*' (*Transfer of Power, VI*, pp. 702-3). French believes, 'The claim that the British had secret plans all along to partition India (an allegation that is still believed by many Indians of a certain age) cannot be supported from the internal memoranda and documentation of Whitehall officialdom' (p. 222). Even as late as May 1947, after the Congress leaders had agreed to accept Partition, the last Viceroy Mountbatten was writing to the Prime Minister, '*Partition is sheer madness, no one would ever induce me to agree to it were it not for this fantastic communal madness that has seized everybody and leaves no other course open ---- The responsibility for this mad decision must be placed squarely on Indian shoulders in the eyes of the world, for one day they will bitterly regret the decision they are about to make*' (*Freedom at Midnight*, p.134).

CABINET MISSION

A Mission composed of three senior cabinet ministers was sent to India in March 1946. Apart from the Secretary of State Pethick-lawrence as the official leader, it included Stafford Cripps and the First Lord of the Admiralty, A. V. Alexander. Its objective was '*the setting up of machinery whereby the forms under which India can realize her full independent status be determined by Indians ---- with the minimum of disturbance and the maximum of speed*' (*Transfer of Power, VII,* p.3). In addition to this, Attlee had instructed that the Mission should do all it could to preserve India intact, so that it could become a self-supporting nation which could play a key role in Britain's future plans for security in Asia (*Escape From Empire*, R. J. Moore, Oxford, 1983, pp. 63, 67).

The negotiations conducted by the Mission in India were unplanned and confused that prompted an exasperated Wavell to note that Pethick-Lawrence was a '*charming old gentleman but no man to negotiate with these tough Hindu politicians*' since he began each meeting '*by giving away independence with both hands, and practically asking Congress to state their highest demands ---- he is no poker player*' (*Wavell: The Viceroy's Journal*, p. 235).

There were repeated allegations of bias on the part of Cripps in favour of Congress: '*he is sold to the Congress point of view, and I don't think he is quite straight in his methods*' (*Wavell,* p. 211). Wavell also accused him of colluding with Nehru and passing him advance information of proceedings in the Mission. Stafford Cripps and Pethick-Lawrence often attended Gandhi's morning prayer sessions that were hardly non-political and held secret meetings with Congress leaders. It naturally raised suspicions in the minds of Muslims. Based on past assurances given to Congress by their friends in the Labour Party, they were in no mood to accommodate or compromise and expected the delegation to hand over India to them.

In an apparently magnanimous gesture Gandhi told the Mission that Jinnah should be invited to form the government of his choice in India. It was a poisoned chalice given that the Central Assembly was dominated by Congress members and would not pass any legislation that was unacceptable to them. Jinnah was not buying it and stuck firmly to his demand for Pakistan. The Mission pressed him on the basis for Pakistan and how he envisaged it would work after independence. When asked to define its boundaries he merely stated that these should ensure a 'viable' and not a 'mutilated' country. He was willing to consider 'mutual adjustments' of provincial boundaries provided the state remained economically sound. His only specific demand was for the inclusion of Calcutta because without it 'would be like asking a man to live without his heart' (*Transfer of Power, VII*, p. 124). He was not willing to be more specific, which is understandable, because he wanted to see what else was there on the table.

The almost daily discussions with leaders of all descriptions dragged on without making any progress. The Mission was particularly mindful of the interests and aspirations of the Sikhs in Punjab. Sardar Baldev Singh met Cripps on their behalf. He had considerable commercial and industrial investments in and around Calcutta and was particularly close to the Congress leaders. He had been a member of the Viceroy's Executive Council but his position in the Sikh hierarchy is not clear. The two Akali leaders that really mattered were a school teacher named Master Tara Singh and the preacher Gyani Kartar Singh. A Sikh ICS officer, Sardar Kapur Singh, who had been involved in some back room negotiations with the Sikhs, has since written the book, *Sachi Sakhi*, in which he has alleged that both these gentlemen received a retainer from Baldev Singh. He also states that Baldev Singh had no clear idea of what the Sikhs wanted and when prompted by Cripps, demanded an independent Sikh state that extended from Panipat all the way to Jhelum.

On 11th April the Mission presented two suggestions to Attlee for approval as 'possible basis of agreement'. Scheme 'A' envisaged 'a unitary India with a loose federation at the centre charged primarily with control of defence and foreign affairs', and Scheme 'B' called for 'a divided India, the Pakistan element consisting of only the majority Muslim Districts ----'. Attlee replied that Scheme 'A' was preferable; Scheme 'B' would be acceptable, if it seemed to hold the only chance of reaching agreement.

Under Scheme 'A' the provinces would be divided into three groups. Group 'A' consisting of the Muslim-majority provinces of Sind, Baluchistan, Punjab and NWFP; Group 'B' all the Hindu-majority provinces and Group 'C' Bengal and Assam. The government would be structured at three different levels. The central government would be responsible for only defence, foreign affairs and communications. The real power would rest in the groups with each having its own bicameral legislature to raise taxes and administer generally, enjoying virtual autonomy of a sovereign state. The provinces would deal with education and law and order but would remain dependent upon group legislatures for most of their funding. After ten or fifteen years, any group or any of its provinces could opt out to reconsider its constitutional position.

The Congress Working Committee passed a resolution on 24th May giving its own interpretation of the Plan. It regarded the Constituent Assembly to be 'sovereign' and '*it will be open to the Constituent Assembly itself at any stage to make changes and variations*'. It also insisted '---- *the provinces will make the choice of whether or not to belong to the sections in which they were placed*' (*Transfer of Power, VII, pp. 679-82*).

This was not what the Mission had intended and it issued the statement on 25th May '*The scheme stands as a whole* and *the interpretation put by the Congress --- to the effect that the provinces can in the first instance make the choice whether or not belong to the section in which they are placed, does not accord with the Delegation's intentions. The reasons for the groupings of the provinces are well known and this is an essential feature of the scheme*' (*Wavell,* pp. 487-8).

Based on this assurance Jinnah, put the proposition before the League Council and recommended its acceptance only because nothing better could be obtained. After much opposition and debate it was agreed to accept the plan based on the understanding that there would be definite, virtually autonomous Muslim groups of provinces that would have separate constituent assemblies. This was conveyed to the viceroy on 7th June.

While the acceptance of the 16th May Plan by Congress was still languishing in limbo largely because of its insistence that there should be only one central constituent assembly, Wavell proceeded with the task of putting together a council from the recently elected politicians that would function as the interim government. This was an integral part and the Mission 'attached the greatest importance' to this short-term plan. Again there was much haggling about the composition of the council. Jinnah was concerned what would happen if one of the parties refused to join the Interim government. Wavell had anticipated this query and noted, '*I got permission* (from the Secretary of State) *to give Jinnah a verbal assurance that we would work with the Muslim League if they accepted and the Congress refused, so summoned him again for 4 p.m. After lunch I dictated a formal assurance to Jinnah. ---- We did not propose to make any discrimination in the treatment of either party; and that we should go ahead with the plan laid down in our statement ----. The Delegation approved the assurance and also produced one from Cripps, which amounted practically to the same thing*' (*Wavell*, p. 285-6 and *Transfer of Power, VIII,* p. 784-5).

On 16th June the Delegation issued a statement that invitations were being issued to fourteen people (6 from Congress, 5 from the League and three from the minorities). 'In the event of the two major parties or either of them proving unwilling to join in the setting up of a coalition Government on the above lines, it is the intention of the viceroy to proceed with the formation of an interim Government which will be as representative as possible of those willing to accept the statement of 16th May'.

In a resolution passed on 25th June the Congress Working Party rejected the proposal made on 16th June regarding the formation of an interim government, but retrospectively accepted the 16th May Plan with serious qualifications. The viceroy, instead of calling upon the League to form the government in the light of the assurance given earlier, said it would not be possible for him to appoint an interim government of political leaders, since the Congress Party had rejected the proposals of 16th June, and decided to postpone the issue.

Wavell and the delegation met Jinnah to show him the Congress resolution in which it had expressed reservations about the groups of provinces, which the League considered the heart of the 16th May Plan. Jinnah said it was unacceptable. '*He begged the Delegation to make it clear that they did not accept the Congress interpretation. He had with great difficulty made substantial concessions in these negotiations because he felt that if we succeeded in making a settlement we would be blessed by 400 million people*' (*The Transfer of Power, VII*, p. 1046). Pethick-Lawrence disagreed, insisting that the delegation viewed the Congress letter as a definite 'acceptance' of the Mission's long-term plan.

The next morning Jinnah revealed in a public speech that Cripps went to see Gandhi. '*It seems he did not cut much ice. He came back and Lord Pethick-lawrence was put on the scent of Mr. Vallabhbhai Patel, the strong man of the Congress. He waylaid Mr. Patel on the road and took him to his house and there they concocted a scheme. The Congress was persuaded to accept the long-term proposals even with their own interpretations and reservations and the Mission assured the Congress that it would abandon the Interim Government Scheme of 16th June. This is exactly what happened. Now I ask the viceroy to issue a statement giving a categorical explanation on this point. This is a grave charge against the honour, integrity and character of the members of Cabinet Delegation and the viceroy*' (*Glimpses of Quaid-e-Azam, vol. II,* p. 310, as quoted by Khairi). Grave though the charge was it was never refuted and there was never any explanation for the collusion and perfidy on the part of the Cabinet Mission.

Jinnah was not alone in feeling disgusted by the whole affair. The third member of the Mission A. V. Alexander stated, '*He had come to India quite unbiased and in the early stages had been somewhat exasperated with Mr. Jinnah's attitude. But he was bound to say that the behaviour of the Congress in the last six weeks seemed to him the most deplorable exhibition that he had ever witnessed in his political career*' (*Transfer of Power, VII,* p. 1023-5). And Wavell noted in his journal: '*Now Cripps, having assured me categorically that Congress would never accept the statement of 16th May, instigated Congress to do so by pointing out the tactical advantage they would gain as regards the Interim Government. So did the Secretary of State. When I tackled him on this, he defended it on the grounds that to get the Congress into the Constituent Assembly was such a gain that he considered it justified. It left me in an impossible position vis-à-vis Jinnah*' (*Wavell,* p. 305).

He also recorded that the Mission had been '*unable to remain really impartial*' and had been '*living in the pocket of Congress*', further concluding the Mission '*might have succeeded had Cripps and Pethick-Lawrence not been so completely in the Congress camp*' (*Wavell,* pp. 287, 324). Jinnah wrote to Attlee, with a copy to Churchill that the conduct of the Cabinet Delegation had '*impaired the honour of the British Government and shaken the confidence of Muslim India*' and '*shattered their hopes for an honourable and peaceful settlement*' (*Transfer of Power, VII,* p. 527).

There was more to come. Nehru was re-elected as the president of Congress and told a public meeting on 4th July, '*We chose the best part of it* (Mission Plan) *and rejected the worthless ones*'. Addressing the All-India Congress Committee on 7th July he declared, '*So far as I can see, it is not a question of our accepting any plan, long or short. It is only a question of our agreeing to go into the constituent assembly. That is all, and nothing more than that*'. Three days later he told a press conference, '*We agreed to go into the constituent assembly, which was to be a Sovereign body ---- we have agreed to nothing else ----. What we do there, we are entirely and absolutely free to determine. We have not committed ourselves to any single matter to anybody*'. Asked about the grouping of provinces, he replied there was a 'big probability there will be no grouping'. He also predicted that the provincial groups will fall apart with NWFP and Assam breaking away and claimed that large numbers of people in Sind, Punjab and the Frontier were not in favour of the grouping (*Transfer of Power, VIII,* pp. 25-7).

Later, he wrote to the viceroy and informed him that it 'would not be possible to pick up again the old threads' and there was 'little hope of a successful issue along the old lines of approach'. He went on to ask for assurances that the provisional government would enjoy the status and full power of an independent cabinet before Congress joined any interim government (*Selected Works of Jawaharlal Nehru, vol. XV*, pp. 234, 237, 241-4).

Wavell called his attention to what he described as the 'intemperate statements' and 'unguarded language' used by the Congress President but

Nehru brushed it aside and instead asked him what he was doing about the constituent assembly? When Wavell said it was impossible to make a Constitution without Muslim participation, Nehru replied that as soon as the British left, the League would 'be forced to come in and take part'.

In the light of this extra-ordinary performance both by the British Government and Congress, Jinnah lost whatever little hope there was in either of them. About the Congress leaders he said they only speak for the high caste Hindus: 'They certainly do not represent the Muslims and the mere fact that they have a handful of Muslim henchmen for the purpose of window-dressing cannot give the national character which they claim, nor the right to represent India'.

The League Council met in Bombay and after three days of deliberations decided to withdraw its earlier support for the Mission's proposals because '*Congress have made it clear that they do not accept any of the terms or fundamentals of the Scheme but that they have agreed only to go into the Constituent Assembly ---- This fact, taken together with the policy of the British Government of sacrificing the interests of the Muslim Nation ---- leaves no doubt that ---- participation of the Muslims in the proposed Constitution-making machinery is fraught with danger*' (*Transfer of Power, VIII,* pp. 135-9).

Jinnah who had devoted his life to the law and never before lost his faith in British justice, had now become so utterly disillusioned that he felt there was no way left open to him except to demonstrate the feelings of Muslims through what he called 'direct action'. He declared 16th August as the Direct Action Day. It was not a call to arms or exhortation to violence, as the Indian historians like to portray. He simply asked the Muslims to renounce their titles, close shops and businesses, take out processions and hold rallies to support the call for Pakistan. He specifically stressed that the demonstrations must remain peaceful. Because it happened at a time when communal tensions were running high, there was tragic loss of life in the city of Calcutta but to put the entire blame for it on Jinnah or the Muslims is farcical.

The Indian history books describe it as 'the day when perfidious Muslim League began genocidal pogroms against defenceless Hindus'. According to one writer no Indian could ever forget '*the dastardly role of these communalists and the depths to which they descended to curry favour with their British masters ---- Muslim League perpetrated the atrocity of the Direct Action Day of 16th August 1946 in which their sectarian communalism caused the deaths of tens of thousands of Hindus*' (*Asian Age*, London, 17th July 1996 as quoted by French, P. 250). The actual number of dead after six days of rioting was put at 4,000 with 10,000 wounded. Seventy-five per cent of the casualties were Muslims (*Raj*, p. 603).

The troubles started when Muslim processions were intercepted and their progress impeded violently. It was made worse because appropriate measures to prevent or contain the violence were not put in place in time. Sir Fredrick Burrows, the governor claimed the outbreak was as much about gangland warfare as it was about politics: '*It was a pogrom between two rival armies of the Calcutta underworld. The fact that over two thousand persons of the goonda type who had been confined under the Defence of India Rules during the war were released between July and December 1945 is of great significance*' (*Liberty or Death*, p. 252). The well known Bengali writer Nirad Chaudhri has observed that most of the killing was done by these *goondas* and not the mobs. Apart from this, Sikhs were seen driving around in armed jeeps looking for Muslims to kill.

Apart from the city of Calcutta, the day had passed off peacefully throughout the rest of the country. Muslim League had nothing to gain and everything to lose in case violence erupted. Secondly, if the mayhem and rioting was planned and carried out by the Muslims it is hardly likely that they would have suffered most of the casualties. It is preposterous to suggest that the League had set out with such an evil motive in mind. Murder and mayhem had marked earlier protests during the Congress' *Satiagarhas* in 1922 and 1930 as well as the Quit India Movement in 1942 when things got out of hand but no one blamed Gandhi for these in the same way as Jinnah was being held responsible for the tragic events in Calcutta.

There is reason to believe that the disturbances may have been planned and organized by the Hindus themselves in the expectation that it will lead to dismissal of the Muslim League government in Bengal and institution of Governor's rule. In a telephone conversation with Sudhir Ghosh, the Congress emissary in London, two weeks after the Direct Action Day Vallabhbhai Patel was heard saying '*Cripps had promised if there was any disturbance in Calcutta, he will order Section 93* (Governor's Rule). *What is he doing*'? (see below and *Liberty or Death, p. 254.*)

The RSS militia, the military wing of Hindu Mahasabha had intensified its training and had been stockpiling weapons throughout India for the impending showdown even before the end of the war. It is impossible to understand the past and present events in India without taking a close look at the organization that reflects the feelings of many, if not most Hindus even today.

The Rashtriya Swayamsevak Sangh (RSS) was formed by Dr. K. B. Hedgewar in 1925. He was an admirer of Italy's fascist dictator Benito Mussolini and modeled his organization on the Italian Fascist Black Shirts, also copied later by Hitler with his Brown Shirts. M. S. Golwalkar, who became head of the RSS in 1944, wrote its defining bible called, *We, or, Our Nationhood Defined.* The theme running through the book can be easily gauged from this sample:

'Ever since that evil day, when Moslems first landed in Hindustan, right up to the present moment, the Hindu Nation has been gallantly fighting on to take on these despoilers. The Race Spirit has been awakening.----

'To keep up the purity of its race and culture, Germany shocked the world by her purging the country of the Semitic races ---- the Jews. Race pride at its highest has been manifested here ---- a good lesson for us in Hindustan to learn and profit by.'

RSS is the ideological heart, the holding company of the Hindu fundamentalist Bharatiya Janata Party, BJP, and its militias. Today RSS has 45,000 branches and seven million volunteers preaching its doctrine of hate across India. They include the former Prime Minister A. B. Vajpayee, current leader of the opposition in the Indian Parliament, L. K. Advani, the Chief Minister of Gujarat, Narendra Modi and a host of other senior politicians, bureaucrats, and police, intelligence and armed services' officers.

BJP has formed the government at the centre and in many of the states in India, including Gujarat, where thousands of Muslims were murdered in 2002. Narendra Modi, the man who presided over the Gujarat genocide as chief minister, is deeply respected by India's biggest corporate houses, Reliance and Tata. He went so far as to reward and promote the policemen who supervised and sometimes even assisted the rampaging Hindu mobs. A TV impresario and corporate spokesperson, Suhel Seth, recently said, 'Modi is God.'

Babu Bajrangi of Ahmedabad, India, who is a member of the Vishwa Hindu Parishad (VHP), a militia of the RSS and also the militant Shiv

Sena and is a close associate of the twice-elected Chief Minister of Gujarat, said this on camera after the massacre:

'*We didn't spare a single Muslim shop, we set everything on fire --- we hacked, burned, set on fire --- we believe in setting them on fire because these bastards don't want to be cremated, they're afraid of it --- I have just one last wish --- let me be sentenced to death --- I don't care if I'm hanged --- just give me two days before my hanging and I will go and have a field day in Juhapura where seven or eight lakhs [seven or eight hundred thousand] of these people stay --- I will finish them off --- let a few more of them die --- at least twenty-five thousand to fifty thousand should die*' (Article '*Mumbai Was Not Our 9/11*' by Arundhati Roy in the Guardian of 13th December 2008).

The activities of the RSS prompted the setting up of Muslim League National Guards in 1946, a motley crowd of untrained volunteers, armed with bamboo sticks. It was mostly a gesture for Muslim League lacked the organization and finances to do anything better. The incidents of violence were becoming common place. Earlier in the year a district magistrate's camp was attacked and schools disrupted in the Rajasthan state of Alwar. There was communal rioting in Bombay in April and 39 people killed and 260 wounded in anti-Muslim riots in Ahmadabad a month later. Riots also broke out in Abbotabad and Dacca but as compared with the attacks on Muslim communities in Hindu-dominated areas, the troubles in the predominantly Muslim provinces had been minimal. Communal friction was becoming increasingly palpable within the Indian Army units as well.

Violence did break out with a vengeance in November, first in Noakhali (Bengal) and then in Bihar where the Hindus were in overwhelming majority. The killings were at first centred on Patna and then spread to Monghyr, Saran and Bodh Gaya. These were carried out by gangs organized by local Hindu landlords while Marwari businessmen in Calcutta provided the funds for the purchase of weapons. Muslim League believed that officials of the Congress provincial administration, including the Chief Minister Pundit Pant, were implicated in allowing preparations for the slaughter to be made. By the time it was over, more than twenty thousand Muslim men, women and children lay dead (thirty thousand according to Jinnah) and scores of thousands had fled their homes to seek shelter wherever they could find it, some as far away as Punjab. Wavell wrote to Pethick-lawrence, '*I doubt whether anyone in England quite yet realises the extent and bestiality of the attacks on Muslims in Bihar ----* (these) *have been on the scale of numbers and degree of brutality far beyond anything that I think has as yet happened in India since British rule began. And they were undoubtedly organized ---- by supporters of Congress'* (*Transfer of Power, IX,* p. 139-40).

All the signs pointed to the violence spreading to other parts of the country. Defenceless minorities were vulnerable and faced the greatest risk. The British had neither the necessary forces available nor the will to enforce peace. Provincial governments whose responsibility it was to maintain law and order were in the hands of amateur administrators and often rank communalists, like Pant. Jinnah wondered if, given the circumstances, the solution did not lie in some form of relocation of communities to safer areas. Unable or unwilling to face the reality, the British as well as Congress felt most uneasy with such thoughts. They had no solution or plan other than to pretend that somehow the problem will go away on its own. It didn't.

In the middle of all this turmoil Wavell invited Nehru to submit 'proposals for the formation of an Interim Government'. When, goaded by Wavell, Nehru asked Jinnah to join him in organizing it, the latter expressed surprise and said he had no prior knowledge of what it entailed but invited Nehru to see him any way. The two failed to reach an agreement, mainly due to the wide divergence of views on the interpretation of the 16th May Plan. Wavell nonetheless went ahead with setting up a Congress Government, hoping the League might be persuaded to join later. It was sworn in on 2nd September with Nehru as the de facto prime minister. Soon Jinnah realized it did not serve the best interests of Muslims if the reins of government were left solely in the hands of Congress and accepted Wavell's invitation to participate in it.

Five Muslim League members joined the cabinet at the end of October led by Liaquat Ali Khan. When Wavell suggested that the League should take the Home Department at the time held by Patel, Congress threatened to bring down the whole house of cards. Under advice from Chaudhry Mohammed Ali, a civil servant in the finance ministry, Liaquat agreed to become the Finance Minister. The entire set up was dysfunctional from the start. Patel used the government intelligence agencies under him to prepare grounds for a Congress take over and snoop on the League as well as his opponents in Congress. Liaquat put together a budget that squeezed the rich Hindu commercial and industrial empires like those of the Birlas and Tatas that bankrolled Congress through a twenty-five per cent tax on all profits over one hundred thousand rupees. There was no hope of the coalition government working in these circumstances.

Wavell was fearful that the situation might soon spiral out of control. He was concerned about the safety of approximately one hundred thousand British and other European personnel in India and prepared a top secret plan for their evacuation. It was given the code name Operation Ebb Tide and involved phased withdrawal to camps in the north-eastern and north-western parts of the country. From there the personnel were to be taken out of India to safety through Karachi and Calcutta. The withdrawal was scheduled to be completed by the spring of 1948. The proposal was however rejected by the British cabinet for a host of reasons.

In December, Attlee invited two representatives each from the League, Congress and the Sikh community to meet in London in a last ditch effort to come to an agreement. It came to nothing as had been anticipated by Wavell: '*Congress feel that HMG dare not break with them ---- their aim is power and to get rid of British influence as soon as possible, after which they think they can deal with both Muslims and Princes; the former by bribery ---- and if necessary by force; the latter by stirring up their people against them ---- They will continue ---- until they consider themselves strong enough to ---- revolt against British rule*' (*Transfer of Power, IX*, pp. 240-2).

According to Sardar Kapur Singh in *Sachi Sakhi* the Sikh representative, Baldev Singh, was asked to stay back in London to see if a settlement could not be reached between the Sikhs and the League on the future of Punjab. He thinks it was with Churchill's blessings but there is no tangible proof to this effect. Worried at the prospects of losing the services of the Indian army, some elements in Britain were in favour of creating an independent Sikh state that would continue to provide troops in exchange for British patronage and protection. They felt Muslim League may accept the partition of Punjab and Bengal rather than being condemned to living in a Hindu dominated India. In that case it may be possible to carve out a separate independent Sikh state. True to his salt, Baldev Singh promptly informed Nehru of the proposal who immediately arranged to return to India and made certain that Baldev Singh travelled back with him and boarded the plane before he did.

At the cabinet meeting on 10th December Attlee concluded, '*Nehru's present policy seemed to be to secure complete domination by Congress throughout the government of India ---- there would certainly be strong reactions from Muslims. Provinces with a Muslim majority might refuse to join a central government on such terms at all; and the ultimate result of Congress policy might be the establishment of that Pakistan which they so much disliked ----. The situation might so develop as to result in civil war in India, with all the bloodshed which that would entail*' (*Transfer of Power, IX,* P. 319). Almost certainly this would have been the outcome for neither the military nor the civil administrative machine in India was any longer capable of maintaining public order in case of troubles on a large scale.

There was a sense of urgency in the Congress camp that the time had come to take over the country. With the Labour Government in place in London they had great hopes that it could be persuaded to hand over power exclusively to them. Once in place, they could sort out Jinnah and the League one way or another. Wavell had all along felt the British had a moral responsibility to ensure that power was transferred in such a way that the minorities did not suffer unduly. The *Transfer of Power* record as well his own journal is littered with his pleas and exhortations on the subject while stressing the need for honesty, fair play and justice. He was no politician and obviously had not adjusted to their ways. It made him an obstacle both for Congress as well as the British Government and the time had come for him to go home.

Gandhi dispatched an emissary from his own entourage, Sudhir Ghosh, to London. While studying at Cambridge he had established durable links with Quakers and Labour politicians, including Pethick-lawrence and Cripps. Privately, the former considered him a 'vexatious embarrassment' while Wavell referred to him as 'that little rat' and a 'snake in the grass with a very swollen head'. Nonetheless, he remained Gandhi's man for making back-room deals with Labour and had to be accepted as such. His mission was to arrange for the removal of Wavell and replace him with someone more acceptable to Congress.

Sudhir Ghosh did not cut much ice with Pethick-Lawrence this time but found Attlee 'a great deal more understanding', who told him at a meeting in early September 1946 that '*there was a good case for a new viceroy but there was no sense in making a change unless he was in a position to find someone who was obviously better than the present occupant of the post*' (*The Collected Works of Mahatama Gandhi, VXXXV,* p. 518).

A telephone conversation between Vallabhbhai Patel in Delhi and Sudhir Ghosh in London on 28th August, mentioned earlier, was intercepted and reported to Wavell. In it Patel was heard saying '*Cripps had promised if there was any disturbance in Calcutta, he will order Section 93* (dissolution of the Muslim League Provincial Government and imposition of Governor's Rule). *What is he doing*'? Ghosh told him that Cripps was out of the country but he would take up the matter with another minister. Patel then told him to remain in the country and await further orders '*We are taking charge on 2nd September*' (*Liberty or Death*, p. 254).

When Patel says in his telephone call referring to the promise made by Cripps, 'if there was any disturbance in Calcutta', it can only mean that an understanding had been reached with Cripps prior to the events of 16th August. The point has been overlooked by all the historians so far and throws a whole new light on the tragedy. It is hard to say how far Patel was implicated in fomenting the troubles as a way of getting rid of the Muslim League Government in Bengal but it can't be put past him for he was known to have done similar things in the past ---- in organizing the disturbances in 1930 for one and again in July 1947 to force rulers of the princely states to accede to the Indian Union (see chapter '*Road to Freedom*').

Wavell sent transcript of the telephone conversation to Attlee, with a note of protest stating '*I cannot continue to be responsible for the affairs in India if some members of your Government are keeping in touch with the Congress through an independent agent behind my back*' (*Transfer of power, VIII,* pp. 328-9). It had become a familiar refrain. There had been frequent complaints from him and his staff about 'lack of realism and honesty' on the part of the cabinet in London (*Wavell,* pp. 397-409). Attlee did not respond for two months and then too only offered some meaningless platitudes about being 'conscious of anxieties and potential dangers of the situation' (*Transfer of Power, IX,* p. 19).

In a report to the king after the Simla Conference, Wavell had submitted his assessment of various Indian leaders that makes for rather interesting reading. About Gandhi he wrote that he is 'a shrewd malevolent old politician who never makes a pronouncement that is not so qualified and so vaguely worded that it cannot be interpreted in whatever sense best suits him at a later stage'. Jinnah according to him was 'straighter ---- more sincere than most of the Congress leaders but he is arrogant and intransigent. He is actuated mainly by fear and distrust of the Congress. Like Gandhi he is constitutionally incapable of friendly cooperation with the other party.'

Azad was 'an old fashioned scholar with pleasant manners. His main object is to get even with Jinnah and the League Muslims who despise him as a paid servant of the Congress'. Nehru was 'sincere, intelligent and personally courageous but he is unbalanced'. Abdul Ghaffar Khan, the Frontier Gandhi was dismissed as someone, 'whose intelligence and grasp of English are both limited and was regarded by Jinnah as a gratuitous and deliberate provocation'.

The rest of the Congress Working Committee were dismissed as 'poor stuff' with the exception of Sardar Patel 'who was by far the most forcible character among them ---- his nature is fascist and he is always likely to be on the side of direct action and if necessary violence ----. He is entirely communal and has no sense of compromise or generosity towards Muslims, but he is more of a man than most of these Hindu politicians. (Report to King George VI on 8th July 1946, *Transfer of Power, VIII,* pp. 1090-95).

Among the more important rulers of the states, Nizam of Hyderabad was 'an eccentric miser with a bad record of misrule'; Maharaja of Kashmir was 'little better' and that of Mysore, 'a religious recluse'. Gwaliar 'a nice lad and means well, but cares more for his horses and racing than anything else'; Baroda 'does little for his State or people'; Nawab of Kalat was 'stupid but pleasant enough'; Kolhapur 'a minor with a mad mother'; Travancore 'a non-entity'; Udaipur 'a cripple with a medieval administration'; Bhopal 'not worth mentioning' and Indore 'a poor creature, physically and morally.'

CHAPTER 8

ROAD TO FREEDOM

ENTER MOUNTBATTEN

Lord Louis Mountbatten had been the Supreme Commander, South-East Asia Command when Nehru visited Singapore in March 1946 as representative of the Congress Party, ostensibly to observe the conditions of the Indian minority in Malaya. It was not a popular move among the British civil and military hierarchy who regarded Nehru and the Congress as traitors in the fight against Germany and Japan. The Governor of Burma, Sir Reginald Dorman-Smith refused to receive him and the army command declined to provide him with official transport. Mountbatten, on the other hand, decided to treat him as the 'future prime minister of India', taking him everywhere in his own staff car and entertaining him royally. According to Mountbatten's biographer, Philip Ziegler, at the end of his visit '*Nehru left Government House in the conviction that he had met an English couple whom he could trust and who understood and sympathized with the needs of India*' (*Mountbatten*, Harper & Row, New York, 1986, p. 328).

There could have been a couple of reasons why Mountbatten went out of his way to ingratiate himself with an Indian leader who was so obviously unpopular with the rest of the British. As early as 1943, Churchill had hinted to Mountbatten that he may have him in mind when the time came to replace Wavell. That time had now come. Since the elections the Labour Government had been casting around for a suitable replacement for Wavell. It was common knowledge that there were very close links between the Labour and Congress. It is possible that Mountbatten may have been positioning himself for the job by creating a favourable impression on Nehru. The fact that he denied having such an ambition later on is neither here nor there. Even if this were true, it could not have done Mountbatten's future naval career any harm by making the right impression on the Labour Party.

In mid-December Attlee sounded out forty-six year old Mountbatten to replace Wavell as the viceroy and governor general of India. It would not be surprising, given the circumstances, if the choice was made with the prior consultation and acceptance by Congress. Krishna Menon had indeed conveyed it to Cripps in a secret meeting earlier that Mountbatten's selection would be most acceptable to Congress (*Freedom at Midnight*, foot note p.19). When Valabhbhai Patel learnt of the appointment he reportedly made the comment, '*Ah, he will be a toy for Jawaharlalji to play with ---- while we arrange the revolution*, (*The Last Days of the British Raj*, by Leonard Mosley, London, 1961, p. 81). Aside from anything else, it is an indication of the power shift that was taking place within the Congress Party, with Gandhi being sidelined and losing ground.

The timing and the manner in which Wavell was treated left a lot to be desired and was, perhaps, reflective of the growing lack of confidence in his ability to deliver what the cabinet desired. It had been customary to give six months' notice to the viceroy but Wavell was officially informed and given just one month to give up charge and leave.

On 5th March 1947 Cripps moved the House for approval to transfer the power in India by June the next year. Filled with emotion, Churchill named it 'Operation Scuttle', '*The Government by their fourteen months' time limit, have put an end to all prospect of unity ---- Will it not be a terrible disgrace to our name and record if, after our fourteen months' time limit, we allow one fifth of the population of the globe ---- to fall into chaos and carnage? ---- But, at least, let us not add by shameless flight, by our premature, hurried scuttle, at least, let us not add, to the pangs of sorrow so many of us feel, the taint and smear of shame*' (*Hansard*, 6th March 1947. cols. 671-8). The House passed the bill by a majority of 337 to 185 votes.

Mountbatten's aircraft landed in Delhi on 22nd March. Nehru was waiting at the bottom of the ladder with a bunch of red roses. Together they drove off straight to the Viceregal Lodge. Two days later he was sworn in as the viceroy. Communal riots had already intensified in Punjab with all the indications of worse to come. If there was any concern or remorse it was not apparent from what Mountbatten told Collins and Lappier later. It was the ceremony that impressed him more: '*What a ceremony. Everyone who mattered was there. All the Princes. All the leaders. All the diplomats. I put on everything. My white full dress uniform. Orders, decorations, medals, the whole lot ---- Obviously I wore the Garter. Then I wore the Star of India, I was the Grand Master of the Order. I wore the Star of the Indian Empire and then I wore the Royal Victorian Order and that made the four; that's all you are allowed to wear. And I wore the aiguillettes as personal aide-de-camp to the King-Emperor*'.

And then for good measure he added, '*Lady Wavell looked just like my wife's maid. She was very, sort of, mundane. And people out there were enormously struck by the difference ---- we went in with panache which was entirely lacking before*' (*Eminent Churchillians*, p. 81). He could be petty and often was.

Before examining the mandate given to the new viceroy and how it was put into effect, it is necessary to look into the background and personality of Mountbatten. It was to have a profound bearing on the events that followed. He was from German stock, with connections to the Russian, British and other royal families of Europe. His father, Louis Battenburg, left Germany to join the British Royal Navy. He rose to become an admiral of the fleet and the First Sea Lord in 1912. When war broke out with Germany in 1914 he was obliged to resign amid unfounded suspicions because of his German ancestry. In the meantime young Louis, nicknamed 'Dickie', too had joined the navy as a cadet at the Royal Naval College, Osborne, later progressing to the Royal Naval College, Dartmouth in 1915. His performance was not exactly stellar and he was particularly poor at sports. The family's Germanic name was changed to Mountbatten in 1917 through a royal decree.

The young man matured into a lithe handsome naval officer, brimming with infectious enthusiasm, confidence and joie de vivre. The two characteristics that defined his personality from the start were unbounded ambition and a penchant for publicity and self-promotion. He never allowed scruples or any other such consideration to come in the way and used his connections and personal charm unabashedly and with great effect to browbeat and manipulate the less wary.

After very persistent courting he married Edwina, the daughter of Wilfred Ashley, a Conservative Member of Parliament, in July 1922 in a ceremony that was dubbed as 'the event of the year' by the London press. Edwina was the only grand-child of Sir Ernest Cassel, an immensely rich Jewish banker who managed the finances of King Edward VII and was one of the most powerful and influential people in Europe. From him Edwina inherited close to ten million pounds and the massive 'Brooke House' on Park Lane. Mountbatten's total personal income at this time had amounted to just over six hundred pounds a year.

The marriage, coupled with his royal connections, was a decided asset in the smooth advancement of his career in the navy. Contrary to the unwritten but well-established code of conduct for officers in the tradition-ridden Royal Navy, he went out of his way in search of glitz and glamour. The couple made trips to Hollywood and attended parties with the likes of Charlie Chaplin, Cary Grant and Shirley Maclaine. There were other frequent and intimate companions from the arts and theatre world like Noel Coward, Cecil B. Demille, Douglas Fairbanks and the usual circle of European nobility. There was also a murkier and grubbier side to his and Edwina's personal life, not uncommon in the higher echelons of most societies. It would be an unnecessary diversion to delve into it in the present context. Andrew Roberts, among others, has explored some of it in his book *Eminent Churchillians* (Weidenfeld & Nicolson, 1994, London).

Regardless of the British wartime propaganda, Mountbatten's performance during World War II had not been as great as it was made out to be. He managed to lose two destroyers under his command in questionable circumstances. But Britain needed heroes in the dark early days of the war and Mountbatten had all the right qualifications to be turned into one. His friend Noel Coward obliged by making the film '*In Which We Serve*', based on mostly fictional information. The significance was not lost on Churchill who promoted him to the acting rank of vice admiral and appointed him Director Combined Operations against the advice of his military staff. In that capacity Mountbatten planned and executed the disastrous raid on Dieppe (Operation Jubilee) that cost the lives of three and a half thousand Canadian soldiers with little to show for it. It simply confirmed the opinion of his peers in the navy about him as 'the master of disaster'. Characteristically, he put the blame for the failure on everyone else but himself.

Churchill then made him the Supreme Commander, Allied Forces Southeast Asia. It involved working closely with the Americans who, in Churchill's opinion, were greatly impressed by Mountbatten's royal connection and his irresistible charm. The Chief of the Imperial General Staff Field Marshall Alanbrooke thought of Mountbatten as '*an over-*

promoted nuisance as Chief of Combined Operations ---- and a totally inadequate ---- and professionally unsuitable Supreme Commander Southeast Asia' (*Eminent Churchillians*, p. 72) . An entry in Alanbrooke's diary of 7th August 1945 reads, 'Seldom has a Supreme Commander been more deficient of the main attributes of a Supreme Commander than Dickie Mountbatten'. He made sure that the latter simply handled diplomacy, administration and public relations. The planning and conduct of actual military operations remained in the hands of the commanders on the ground, General Sir Oliver Leese and General Sir William Slim.

The American General 'Vinegar Joe' Stillwell noted about his conferences with Mountbatten as '*terrible, dumb, sad and zero*'. Field Marshal Montgomery had no illusions about his military talent either, '*Dickie Mountbatten is, of course, quite unfit to be a Supreme Commander. He is a delightful person, has a quick and alert brain and has many good ideas. But his knowledge of how to make war is really NIL*' (*Monty: Master of the Battlefield 142-44, vol. 2*, by Nigel Hamilton, p. 597). The fact that such derogatory assessments have mostly remained out of the public eye is a tribute to Mountbatten's masterly skills at public relations and manipulation of the media. What accounted for his rapid rise in the service was his ability to by-pass the military hierarchy and ingratiate himself with the politicians directly, in particular Churchill and later Attlee.

There was more. His personal character also left a lot to be desired. According to Ziegler, Admiral Sir Caspar John, the First Sea Lord, '*disliked Mountbatten's theatricality and found his tactics often devious if not dishonest*' (*Mountbatten*, p.568). Prime Minister Anthony Eden, who had succeeded Churchill, called Mountbatten '*a congenital liar*' at the time of the Suez crisis in 1956 when he was the First Sea Lord (*Anthony Eden*, by R. R. James, 1986, pp. 458 and 617). Another Tory Prime Minister Harold Macmillan dismissed him as 'a popinjay, all those uniforms'! At one point during his tenure as the Chief of Defence Staff, the army chief General Sir Gerald Templer in utter exasperation told him, '*Your are so crooked, Dickie, if you swallowed a nail you'd shit a corkscrew*'. According to the Permanent Secretary at the War Office, Mountbatten was '*probably the most distrusted of all senior officers in the three services*', partly because of his practice of deliberately misreporting decisions that had been taken at the various committees on which he sat (*Six Men Out of the Ordinary*, by Lord Zuckerman, 1992, p. 160). A Southampton University professor who had worked on his files deposited there said about him, '*He was an awful crook*' (*Eminent Churchillians*, p. 128).

A well-known British writer and columnist, John Keegan, has summed up, '*Mountbatten was essentially an insecure and ultimately a lonely man who craved an affection his wife would not give him. He was someone who had countless friends and a dozen "best friends", but no real intimate of his own class or age*' (The *Sunday Times,* 17th March 1995). This was the man who had been entrusted with the fate of 400 million Indians at perhaps the most critical juncture in their history.

In the light of what we know about Mountbatten's disregard for truth and accuracy in matters where he was personally involved, there is a need to exercise extreme caution in taking him at his word or using him as a primary source for recording history, without corroboration from some other more reliable sources. There were instances in which he went out of his way to cover up or hide the truth. At one stage he asked Sir Evan Jenkins, the last governor of Punjab, not to have any dealings with Leonard Mosley, who wanted to write a book on the last days of the Raj. He told Jenkins that if he went ahead Longman, the publishers, had already assured him they would not publish the book on the grounds that it was hostile (*Raj,* p. 609). It is a pity this should be so for Mountbatten was the most important character in the whole drama that was to follow. Apart from all else, history has suffered greatly and the job of historians made that much more difficult. This is something earlier historians like Collins and Lappiere or even Ziegler may not have fully realized.

On the afternoon of 22nd March Mountbatten met Nehru and asked him about Jinnah. As can be expected, Nehru's assessment of the latter was not exactly flattering. He said Jinnah was a 'mediocre lawyer' whose creed was to refuse to hold meetings or to answer questions and never to make a progressive statement (*Transfer of Power, X, The Mountbatten Viceroyalty*, pp. 11-12). Stanley Wolpert thinks 'Nehru's negative assessment of Jinnah would never be erased from Mountbatten's mind and probably did more damage to Pakistan, influencing Mountbatten's decisions on the drawing of border lines in India's favour, than has been realized. Of course, Jinnah's refusal to accept Mountbatten's repeated offer to serve as Pakistan's Governor-General, which Nehru so warmly invited him to do for India, was also important in tilting what should have been Great Britain's even-handed transfer of power balance in favour of India' (*Shameful Flight*, p. 135).

These arguments do not hold much water. If Mountbatten did not approve of Jinnah for whatever reasons, he must have known that he could not take it out on all the Muslims of India. And even if he didn't there were many in Delhi and Whitehall who could have corrected him. The British had detested Gandhi much more than Jinnah but they never penalized Hindus, Congress or India for it.

On the governor-general issue, having said and done what he did to Jinnah and Pakistan, for Mountbatten to expect to be invited for the job is to be out of touch with reality and quite ludicrous. In any case, Jinnah did not pour cold water on Mountbatten's wish to become the Governor Genral of Pakistan until July, a month before independence. By this time the deed had been virtually done. In the ultimatele analysis Mountbatten was only a servant of the British Government and the extent to which he could help Pakistan was quite limited given the over-riding proclivity on the part of the British to keep on the right side of Congress and India. In hindsight, it was another bullet that Jinnah and Pakistan dodged. With Jinnah dead in 1948 and Mountbatten still the Governor General, who knows what he might have done?

Mountbatten was not the sole or final arbiter of India's fate although he may have tried to convey the impression for effect. At a dinner on 27th March 1947 he told Lieut. General Sir Reginald Savory that he had 'practically carte blanche' to settle India's outstanding problems. At other times, he said he had been given plenipotentiary powers (*Raj.* P. 612). There is no official record of it anywhere, only Mountbatten's word for it and from what we know now, that is hardly enough. Even his own personal staff, including Vice Admiral Sir Ronald Brockman, has expressed serious reservations on the issue (*Mountbatten*, p. 355). In any case, with the availability of virtually instant communications between Delhi and London there was no need or occasion to grant plenipotentiary powers to the viceroy.

Mountbatten had no prior experience of India or the complexities of its politics. He was also known to be impetuous and not much given to reasoned introspection. His limitations were not hidden either. Churchill's Parliamentary Private Secretary Brendan Bracken thought he was 'a miserable creature, power mad, publicity mad' who had fallen under Nehru's spell. An erstwhile Information Minister, Sir John Reith had mused 'more can be done by the viceroy in the next year than in the last hundred, and they choose that fraud and counterfeit' (*Eminent Churchillians*, pp. 80, 81). It is inconceivable that the cabinet should place its fate and that of India completely in the hands of a novice with so many apparent and known character flaws. Indeed, it was because of these misgivings that General Sir Hastings ('Pug') Ismay was appointed to the specially created post of Chief of Staff to the Viceroy and Cripps had even offered to come to India with the new viceroy to hold his hand (*Transfer of Power*, *IX*, p. 667).

Having written this, in the lengthy discussion the writer had in March 1996 with Lord Listowel, who had taken over as the Secretary of State for India from Lord Pethick-Lawrence in 1947, the former insisted that Mountbatten did have plenipotentiary powers. It has to be qualified, for Listowel was not speaking from any record and he held an unusually fawning view of Mountbatten. He gave me manuscript of the chapter from his autobiography (Chapter 9: *Secretary of State For India Until Independence: 1947*) that dealt with India, for comments. It was apparent from this unpublished account that he was not really a part of the inner circle that made the crucial decisions about India. In it he had relied almost exclusively on Mountbatten's version of events. The only players in the cabinet that mattered were Attlee, Cripps and to some extent the Foreign Secretary, Ernest Bevan. Ultimately, it was they who took the final decisions but let Mountbatten be the fall-guy ---- the proverbial patsy, a victim of his own over-inflated ego.

An interesting piece of information that Lord Listowel mentioned repeatedly during the course of the discussion was that there was not a single person in the British Government who was in favour of partitioning India. He was emphatic that it only happened because Jinnah left them with no other option ---- 'if it hadn't been for Mr. Jinnah, there would be no Pakistan', he said many times. This is decidedly contrary to the hypothesis proffered by most Indian historians and mimicked by the less wary elsewhere that Pakistan was somehow a creation of the British.

HOBSON'S CHOICE

Shortly after Nehru's return from London in December 1946, Congress did a remarkable volte-face. It found the announcement by the British Government that it will hand over power by June 1948, to the 'existing provincial governments' in the event there was no agreement on a federal structure quite disconcerting. There was little hope of any agreement with Jinnah after the Cabinet Mission fiasco. If power were to be transferred to each of the provinces there were no guarantees of what they will do. Left with no other viable alternative, it decided to give tacit acceptance to Pakistan by passing a resolution on 8th March 1947 that called for the immediate division of both Punjab and Bengal provinces, separating the Muslim majority areas from the rest. It was done without the approval of Gandhi who was away 'applying balm to the wounds in Behar and Bengal' and later complained, '*No one listens to me anymore. I am crying in the wilderness*' (*Gandhi: Prisoner of Hope*, by Judith Brown, New Haven, CT, 1989, p.369).

It appears Nehru and Patel had decided to take matters in their own hands and not allow Gandhi to continue to complicate matters any further. With hind sight it seems they had made a plan of their own for the future which did not coincide exactly with Gandhi's vision. Mountbatten also disregarded much of what he had to say in the subsequent negotiations although he continued to treat him with great reverence and respect. From time to time there was speculation about rivalry within the Congress Party, especially between Nehru and Patel. If there was any, it did not seem to have been of any significance, as the Reforms Commissioner and Patel's confidant V. P. Menon told the viceroy's staff, '*Sardar Patel and Pundit Nehru were invariably in complete agreement on fundamental issues*, (*Transfer of Power, XI,* p. 134).

There is some evidence that the March resolution may have been discussed beforehand between Delhi and Whitehall. V. P. Menon has claimed that he had been in touch with Patel and forwarded details of the planned move by Congress, on latter's advice, to London (*Transfer of Power in India*, by V. P. Menon, Madras, 1957, p.p. 358-9).

Menon had an astonishing career. Having been inducted as a clerk in the viceroy's office in Simla in 1929, with very little formal education, he had risen to become the Reforms Commissioner, the highest position ever held by an Indian on the viceroy's staff, in less than seventeen years. In late 1946 Wavell had expressed fears that V. P. Menon was turning into a 'mouthpiece' for Patel. The viceroy's Private Secretary George Abell wrote a confidential note to Mountbatten in March 1947 that Menon had lately come '*under pressure from Congress ---- Mr. Menon now is genuinely convinced of the rightness of the Congress view on the general political position. Thus, although he is an old friend of mine, and one of the people I like best in Delhi, I am convinced that it is not possible to take him into confidence as fully as has been done in the past*' (*Transfer of Power, X*, p. 27).

Yet, he continued to attend all the viceroy's sensitive staff meetings in which no Muslim was allowed to be present (*India Office Library and*

Records, F200/203, 21July 1947). Chaudhri Muhammad Ali, a civil servant in the Finance Ministry at the time and later Prime Minister of Pakistan, wrote: '*It was known to Mountbatten, and indeed to all, that V. P. Menon was, to use* (Mountbatten's Press Attaché) *Alan Campbell-Johnson's phrase "the trusted confidant of Valabhbhai Patel", who was thereby not only kept informed of the inner councils of the Viceroy, but was also able to influence Viceroy's policies through this mouthpiece. If a Muslim officer had been in V. P. Menon's position and was known to maintain a liaison with Jinnah, no Viceroy would have tolerated it without laying himself open to charges of partisanship*' (*Emergence of Pakistan*, by Chaudhri Muhammad Ali, Columbia University Press, New York, 1967, p. 125). Mountbatten had an entirely different perspective. He probably felt Menon's inclusion in the viceroy's inner circle would be reassuring to Congress and useful in dealing with it. By this time he was convinced that the key to finding a solution lay in keeping on the right side of Congress.

As to Patel himself, his early discussions with Mountbatten are quite revealing. At one time he told Mountbatten that his opposition to Jinnah was partly based on the assumption that eighty per cent of India's Muslims were 'forcible converts' from Hinduism. When asked to elaborate on the purpose of these forced religious conversions, Patel said, he could not discuss the matter 'because *he had no idea of the Muslim mentality*'. Alan Campbell Johnson thought the Home Minister was at least straightforward in his opinions: '*His approach to the whole problem was clear and decisive. India must get rid of the Moslem League*' (*Liberty or Death,* p. 292, *Transfer of Power, X*, p. 425, and *Mission with Mountbatten*, p. 46).

The timing and manner in which Congress had agreed to accept partition would strongly suggest that it could not have been done without first receiving assurances from the British Government on some key issues. There had been some discussions between the Congress representative Krishna Menon and the Labour in February on the future of Kashmir and Calcutta but the nature of any understanding or agreement reached is not clear as yet. The British were particularly mindful of the strategic importance of Kashmir with respect to the Soviet threat and wished that in the event of partition India being the stronger entity should have its control. The Congress' interest in Calcutta was primarily economic. It was India's largest city and its industrial and commercial hub. Both of these went to India in the end in circumstances that were dubious and even perfidious.

There is evidence to suggest that the Congress leaders accepted Pakistan only as a stopgap measure. It was predicated on the assumption that if Pakistan were to be handed over in a severely truncated form it would not survive for long and will sooner than later revert to becoming a part of India. Nehru, in a letter to India's representative in China, K. P. S. Menon, wrote on 29th April 1947 that he was in no doubt eventually India would have to become one country, and it could well be that Partition was but a stepping stone on the path towards that goal (*Nehru: The Making of India*, by M. J. Akbar, London, 1989, p. 405).

He had good reason to believe this because NWFP was firmly in the hands of the 'Frontier Gandhi' and his brother, Dr. Khan Sahib, at the time. Both of them nurtured a visceral dislike, indeed hatred, of Jinnah, Muslim League and Pakistan. With the partition of Punjab and Bengal there would be hardly anything left worth having. The British were not averse to the idea either, given their proclivity for keeping the country and its army undivided and under strong central control. For the time being though there was no escaping from Pakistan if a civil war was to be averted but it could be arranged that the country did not survive for long after its inception. The offer of a truncated Pakistan would confront Jinnah with the Hobson's choice of accepting an un-workable country or not having one at all.

How far the British were complicit in the scheme is clear from the minutes of the meeting Mountbatten had with the Provincial Governors on 15th April. In it he told them '------ *partition of India would be a most serious potential source of war.* ----- *A quick decision would also give Pakistan a greater chance to fail on its demerits. The great problem was to reveal the limits of Pakistan so that the Muslim League could revert to an unified India with honour*'. When the Acting Governor of Bengal informed him that in the event of partition, '*Eastern Bengal alone was not a going concern and never would be. It could not feed itself* ---- *It would become a rural slum* ---- *Muslims knew it as well as Hindus, so they felt that the object of the cry* (by the Hindus) *to partition Bengal was to torpedo Pakistan*', Mountbatten replied, *Anything that resulted in torpedoing Pakistan was of advantage in that it led the way back to a more common-sense solution*' (*Transfer of Power*, *X*, pp. 242 -244, 250 and *Shameful Flight*, p. 142). On 25th April he mused with his staff 'whether there were likely to be sufficiently intelligent Muslim officials to administer Pakistan'? (*Eminent Churchillians*, p. 85). This is when Mountbatten had been in India for just about one month. It was not time enough for him to form such drastic opinions on his own and discuss these so openly with the governors unless he had some prior indication or briefing on the issue from His Majesty's Government in London.

It is interesting that in his above statement Mountbatten anticipates outbreak of violence as a consequence of Partition. He had been telling the cabinet on numerous occasions earlier that he expects civil war to break out if the country was not partitioned. It seems he liked to use both sides of an argument depending upon what was demanded by the situation at any particular time. Dealing with such people can be exasperating and one cannot but sympathise with Jinnah for having to bear the worst of it.

Jinnah had come to the conclusion that the only way to forestall the partitioning of Punjab was to somehow get the Sikhs on his side. If Punjab was not divided, there would be less justification to divide Bengal as well. The attempt for talks with Baldev Singh in London had not worked out. After some indirect discussions, Jinnah was ready to make a detailed proposal that involved the creation of an autonomous Sikh state within Pakistan provided Punjab was not divided. It would be composed of roughly the same areas as East Punjab. The Sikhs will have one third seats reserved for them in the provincial assembly and one fifth in the central legislature and a similar proportion in the provincial High Court and the Supreme Court. A Sikh will always be either the Chief Minister or the Governor of Punjab. Forty per cent of the Pakistan Army will be composed of Sikhs. No law shall be passed that will be adjudged by the courts to be contrary to the interests of the Sikh community. It was an incredibly generous offer considering that the Sikhs would have formed about five per cent of the total population of Pakistan, including undivided Punjab and Bengal.

A meeting was arranged between Jinnah and Master Tara Singh of the Akali Dal, a third- grade school teacher, to discuss the proposal in Lahore in May. Tara Singh arrived early and after some discussion with other Sikh leaders, quietly slipped away through a back door. When Jinnah turned up at the appointed time, there was no one there to negotiate with. Later when Sardar Kapur Singh, the Sikh ICS officer who had been acting as the go-between, questioned Tara Singh, he replied that a settlement with the Muslims was out of the question for a Mughal king had the two sons of Guru Gobind Singh murdered in the seventeenth century. He was also upset by the earlier Sikh-Muslim riots near Rawalpindi. If that was the case, why did he agree to meet with Jinnah and turn up in the first place?

The Sikh leaders generally and Master Tara Singh in particular were given to making highly intemperate and provocative statements like 'the Sikhs will only permit the creation of Pakistan over their dead bodies'. It vitiated the atmosphere and was largely responsible for creating the conditions that led to the massacres later on in East Punjab. It was unfortunate that at such a critical juncture the Sikhs should have been saddled with a leadership that was so whimsical and below par.

Finding the door closed with the Akali Dal, Jinnah approached the Maharaja of Patiala, the largest of the Sikh states. At a secret meeting in Patiala he suggested that the Sikh states of Punjab, along with some additional areas, should join together and agree to form a super-state as a part of Pakistan. In return they would enjoy the same privileges as were offered earlier to Master Tara Singh. The Maharaja agreed to consider the proposition and in due course inform Jinnah of his reaction. That same night he got in touch with the Congress leaders in Delhi and conveyed the details of the offer to them. When Jinnah became aware of it he broke off the negotiations. Later the maharaja issued a statement to the press that the Sikhs would '*under no circumstances accept Pakistan*' (*Liberty or Death*, p. 333).

It was not that Master Tara Singh or the Maharaja of Patiala spurned Jinnah's offers for something better in return from the Congress. The latter had offered them nothing nor did the British for that matter. Simply put, they sacrificed the best deal they could ever make and with it the future of the Sikhs in India at the altar of religious hatred towards the Muslims. It was pathetic in many ways. According to Sardar Kapur Singh, when Mountbatten raised the Sikh question with Sardar Patel, he replied, '*These imbecilic people have slit their own throats. They have missed the boat and not much can be done about it*' (*Sachi Sakhi*). Jinnah was more diplomatic when he told the British High Commissioner in Delhi, Sir Terrence Shone, '*Sikhs were in many ways admirable people,* (but) *they lacked leadership of a high order*' (*Transfer of Power, X*, p. 280).

Some years later after independence the Sikhs, frustrated with their situation in Hindu-dominated India, started an agitation and Master Tara Singh undertook a Gandhi-style 'fast-unto-death' in support of their claims. He was no Gandhi and the government in Delhi took no notice. When some Sikh leaders called on Pundit Nehru and beseeched him to intercede he told them, 'I have not asked or ordered Tara Singh to fast. If he wants to die, so be it.' They went back a few days later to tell him that his condition was deteriorating rapidly and begged for some symbolic gesture from him but Nehru was unmoved. Shortly afterwards a disillusioned Master Tara Singh abandoned his 'fast-unto-death' and a photograph appeared in the Indian press of a group of Sikhs offering an orange to Tara Singh. The caption underneath stated that a basket of oranges had been delivered to the Sikh leader with the compliments of Pundit Nehru (Ardesher Cowasji in *The Dawn*, 9th December, 2007).

In the end it was just as well that Punjab was divided and the Sikhs chose to remain in India. Had they accepted Jinnah's proposals, the enormous tragedy that was soon to engulf the province perhaps might have been mitigated but there would have been no guarantees for the future. Given the nature of the Sikh belief system and their attitude towards the Muslims, it would have been an extremely difficult marriage and would almost certainly have led to great unrest and instability with an unpredictable outcome. Jinnah failed to see it because his experience and understanding of Sikhs and Sikhism was limited. This was the second time he dodged the bullet ---- the first was when he accepted the Cabinet Mission proposal and Nehru bungled it. He was basically interested in keeping a united Punjab inside Pakistan for economic reasons. In his vision it would not have posed a serious problem as he expected the two countries would co-exist side by side after independence in a spirit of friendship and cooperation and not confrontation.

Mountbatten continued with his meetings with leaders from different political parties and walks of life to elicit information that would help him formulate a plan for the transfer of power. Gandhi again came up with the proposal for inviting Jinnah to form a new government at the centre. Mountbatten did not think much of it but swore Gandhi to 'complete secrecy particularly as far as the press were concerned' (*Transfer of Power, X*, p. 84). He then proceeded to discuss it with Nehru and Azad but did not mention it to Jinnah. Nehru was both surprised and angry that Gandhi had not discussed the idea with him or any of the other Hindu leaders beforehand. In the end it came to nothing except that it diminished the trust that had existed between Gandhi and Nehru. It wasn't long before the shrewd Gandhi was warning both Nehru and Patel to beware of Mountbatten, '*an unknown friend*', more '*dangerous to us*' than such '*known enemies*' as the earlier Viceroys *Linlithgow and Wavell'* (*Gandhi's Passion*: *The Life and Legacy of Mahatma Gandhi*, by Staley Wolpert, Oxford University Press, New York, 2001, p. 237).

Jinnah was one of the last to be called for a meeting. Mountbatten thought he was 'most frigid, haughty and disdainful'. He said, I have '*the most enormous conceit in my ability to persuade people to do the right thing, not because I am persuasive so much as because I have the knack of being able to present the facts in their most favourable light'. ---- I tried every trick I could play, used every appeal I could imagine'* to shake Jinnah's determination to have partition: Nothing would. There was no trick, no argument that could move him from his consuming determination to realize the impossible dream of Pakistan (*Freedom at Midnight*, p. 118). The discussion between the two was almost exclusively confined to the issues related to partition, with Mountbatten suggesting that it was not a viable proposition especially, as it seemed appropriate, both Punjab and Bengal would also have to be partitioned.

Along the line he told Jinnah that Suhrawardy was asking for British help for an independent united Bengal and asked for his views. Jinnah replied 'I should be delighted'. What is the use of Bengal without Calcutta; they had much better remain united and independent; I am sure they would be on friendly terms with us (*Transfer of Power, X*, p. 452). Mountbatten then added that Suhrawardy would wish to remain within the British Commonwealth. Jinnah said, '*Of course, just as I indicated to you that Pakistan would wish to remain within the Commonwealth*'. The possibility of Bengal remaining united failed to materialise not because of Jinnah but because Congress wanted Calcutta and the prosperous western districts to become a part of India.

Patel wrote to a political associate in Calcutta on 23rd May, '*Talk of the idea of a sovereign republic of independent Bengal is a trap to induce the unwary and unwise to enter into the parlour of the Muslim League ---- Bengal must be partitioned, if the non-Muslim population is to survive*' (*Sardar Patel's Correspondence 1945 – 50*, by Durga Das, Ahmedabad, 1971-74). An army of Hindu volunteers, led by the Mahasabha leader Shyama Parshad Mookerji and supported by Congress mounted a campaign, taking out processions and demanding a 'Hindu Homeland' in Bengal (*Shameless Flight*, p. 141). The very parties that had fought so hard to keep Bengal united four decades earlier were now clamouring for it to be divided. A unified province was only acceptable if it was not going to be ruled by the Muslim majority.

The British, in particular Mountbatten, disliked Jinnah intensely. He was rich, elitist, enjoyed a western style of living and suffered from no hang-ups or complexes. He dealt with the British on an equal footing and expected the same from them. It made them feel ill-at-ease for after nearly two hundred years of colonial rule and domination, it was not a customary situation for them. Contrary to the Congress propaganda, he was never an insider in British governing circles. There was hardly an Englishman who felt comfortable in Jinnah's company and it had nothing to do with his personal conduct or moral character which was always impeccable. In many ways it was the same with Gandhi. To the British he looked like a 'naked fakir', as Churchill called him, and was expected to behave like one but didn't.

It was very different with Nehru who seemed to suffer from a crisis of identity. French thinks 'there was a side of Nehru that sought the approbation of the British Establishment, and the reverence of Dickie and Edwina came as more than a political boon: it was an affirmation of his own identity' (P. 294). His own secretary and biographer, M. O. Mathai wrote: '*One thing I could not fail to notice was that whenever Nehru stood by the side of Lady Mountbatten, he had a sense of triumph*' (*Reminiscences of the Nehru Age*, New Delhi, 1978, p. 209).

As the time passed, Mountbatten's dislike for Jinnah started to border on the pathological. He wrote to London that Jinnah '*was a psychopathic case, hell bent on his Pakistan*' and told Collins and Lappiere, 'He was completely impossible. I don't think ---- we could have waited for him to die because I don't think we could have afforded the time, nor could we have felt certain of it.' The other epithets he reserved for Jinnah included 'evil genius', 'clot', 'lunatic' and 'bastard'. Jinnah had done Mountbatten no personal harm nor could he be faulted if he believed in what was good for his people and strived for it. He was not alone in this; the entire nation was behind him. His real crime was that he was a Muslim and was fighting for a Muslim cause that did not sit well with the British designs.

The Congress leaders took advantage of Mountbatten's growing mistrust of Jinnah. One of these was Krishna Menon who had access to the highest levels in the British Government largely due to his position in the Labour Party. He was in regular communication with Mountbatten providing briefing papers as necessary. These indicate a considerable measure of informality and trust between the two. In one letter to Mountbatten after meeting with Attlee, he wrote: '*no lack of desire on the part of the P.M to be of assistance. I found there and everywhere else that the Fuhrer* (Jinnah) *had overplayed his hand'* (*Transfer of Power, XII*, p.255).

Mountbatten's claim that his antipathy towards Jinnah was due to his inflexible attitude on Pakistan is belied by his own words and record. In fact, he had himself come to the same conclusion as Jinnah that the only solution to India's problems lay in the creation of Pakistan. He admitted to a TOP SECRET meeting of his staff on 1st May ---- although he made sure the words were deleted from the minutes ---- '*If he* (Mountbatten) *fell foul of the Congress it would be impossible to continue to run the country ---- it was evident ---- that anything but a clean partition would produce enmity on the part of Congress*' (*Transfer of power, X,* p. 511 and *Liberty or Death*, p. 296). If Jinnah asked for partition and Congress had agreed to it, why continue to despise and deride Jinnah in such visceral terms?

It may not be politically correct to suggest, but the sad truth is that beneath the surface it is hard to find many westerners who do not nurture a measure of abhorrence and malevolence towards Islam and the Muslims and Mountbatten was no exception. There may have been an added factor; Jinnah was a very astute and experienced lawyer. It could not have taken him long to get a measure of Mountbatten's strengths as well as personal inadequacies. The realization was likely to be particularly galling as well as disconcerting for an excessively egotistical man like Mountbatten. He could never reconcile with Jinnah's integrity and commitment to principles that contrasted so sharply with his own lack of character nor forgive him for seeing through his posturing and petty games. The fact that Jinnah was an 'inferior' Indian and a Muslim at that could not have helped either. Jinnah was an Indian and he was expected to behave like an Indian ---- just like Nehru. He paid the price for nothing more than being self-respecting and loyal to his people.

After his consultations with various leaders Mountbatten put together his plan for the transfer of power. What became known as the Balkan Plan was essentially a rehash of the Cabinet Mission proposal. It envisaged devolution of powers to the provinces, with the option to split Punjab and Bengal in two. The states were left to decide their own future. Subsequently, these units could unite to form groupings of their choice. General Ismay took it to London where the plan was fine-tuned and approved. The cabinet had been given the impression that it would be acceptable to all the parties which, as it turned out, was not the case. None of the leaders had even seen the draft let aside indicated acceptance.

In the meantime, Mountbatten and his wife drove to Simla for some rest and recreation, taking Nehru and Krishna Menon along as their guests. Whether through design or on impulse (Mountbatten called it 'a hunch') he gave a copy of the plan to Nehru, before any of the other leaders was made aware of it. Nehru 'reacted strongly', in his own words and dropped what Mountbatten called the 'Nehru bombshell' by rejecting it out of hand. This is when the Reforms Commissioner and Patel's confidant, V.P. Menon, was summoned and told to produce a fresh plan that would meet with the approval of Congress.

In Collins and Lappier's words, 'The man who had begun his career as a two-finger typist had culminated it by redrafting, in barely six hours ---- a plan that was going to encompass the future of one fifth of humanity, reorder the subcontinent, and alter the map of the world' (p. 163). This was not all that he was doing, as V. P. Menon himself recorded, '*I was keeping Vallabhbhai Patel informed of the developments in Simla and he was delighted by the turn of events*' (*The Transfer of Power in India*, p. 365). So was Mountbatten, even more so, with V. P. Menon whom he called 'my brilliant Indian Staff Officer'. He also admitted, '*I was very greatly influenced in my own negotiation and development by his ideas*' (*Mountbatten and the Partition of India*, by Larry Collins and Louis Lapierre, New Delhi, 1982, p. 31). When he went to London next and called on the king emperor he took Menon along with him.

The new plan envisaged setting up two separate dominions and the division of Punjab and Bengal provinces. Interestingly, by this time Suhrawardy and the Bengal Congress Party leader K. S. Roy had reached agreement that called for a united 'Free State of Bengal'. They pleaded with Congress leaders in Delhi to support the plan only to be rebuffed. When asked on 27th May, Nehru reacted strongly, saying there was no chance of the Hindus there agreeing to put themselves under permanent Muslim domination but he would have no objection if a united Bengal were to become part of Hindustan. Muslims may live under Hindu rule permanently but it was not acceptable the other way round to Congress, the party that claimed to represent all of the people in India. Mountbatten echoed Nehru's views including that East Bengal was 'likely to be a great embarrassment to Pakistan and bound to sooner or later rejoin India' (*Transfer of Power, XI*, p. 3). Based on this he brushed the agreement aside as a needless complication that would involve wasting too much time setting up a third Dominion.

To save time it was left to each of the dominions to make its own constitution and in the interim use the India Act of 1935, modified as necessary. An essential element stressed in the settlement was 'the early transfer of power to India on a Dominion status basis'. Cripps was not too happy with this and some of the other aspects, particularly in relation to the Sikhs and Punjab, and offered to fly out to India to help resolve these. This was the last thing Mountbatten wanted. The rest of the cabinet was equally confused by the new development and it was decided to call Mountbatten to London to explain. Before leaving with V. P. Menon in tow on 18th May, he 'tried to persuade Jinnah and Liaquat to sign a copy of his proposed final plan, indicating their agreement to it, but both adamantly refused' (*Shameful Flight*, p. 146).

At his staff meeting on 16th May, Mountbatten had said 'that he had already cautiously tried out threatening Mr. Jinnah'. He warned that he might pass on power to an all-India interim Government with Dominion status. Jinnah had taken this threat calmly and said that he could not in any event prevent such a step. 'This abnormal reaction, which was typical of Mr. Jinnah, was rather disturbing'. He suspected 'Jinnah would derive great satisfaction by going down to history as a martyr for his cause, butchered by the British on the Congress altar'. He never used such language to describe any Congress leader. Jinnah was merely demanding a constitutional outcome in which the sub-continent's 92 million Muslims would not be forced into a single state inevitably dominated by 255 million Hindus and was perfectly within his rights in doing so (*Eminent Churchillians*, p. 86).

Objecting to the new plan, Jinnah made his final attempt to prevent the partition of Punjab and Bengal and on 17th May he wrote to the British Cabinet: '*The Muslim League cannot agree to the partition of Bengal and the Punjab. ---- It cannot be justified historically, economically, geographically, politically or morally. ---- The principle underlying the demand for establishment of Pakistan and Hindustan is totally different. ---- In the name of justice and fair play, do not submit ---- to this clamour. For it will be sowing the seeds of future serious trouble and the results will be disastrous for the life of these two provinces*' (*Transfer of Power, X*, p. 852). The warning was peremptorily ignored both in Delhi and London.

The Congress position was summed up by Mountbatten in his briefing to the British Cabinet two days later in London: '*it had become clear that the Muslim League would resort to arms if Pakistan in some form were not conceded. In the face of this threat, the Congress leaders had modified their former attitude; indeed, they were now inclined to feel that it would be to their advantage to be relieved of responsibility for the provinces that would form Pakistan, while at the same time they were confident that those provinces would ultimately have to seek re-union with the remainder of India*' (*Transfer of Power, X,* p. 896).

Earlier, Jinnah had proposed holding a referendum in Calcutta that he was certain Muslim League would win. Mountbatten told him there was 'not time for a plebiscite anywhere'. Later he revealed to his staff, '*it would be most undesirable to lay down a procedure for self-determination which would give the wrong answer*' (*Eminent Churchillians*, p. 85). There had also been a suggestion to hold referenda in the disputed provinces including Bengal, Assam and Punjab to ascertain the will of the people. This too was found unacceptable since, apart from the Muslims, there was every likelihood that the Untouchables (Scheduled Castes) and Christians would have voted to join Pakistan ('*The Partition of India and the Prospects of Pakistan*' by Professor O. H. K. Spate in the *Geographic Review, vol. 38, Issue 1, Jan. 1948*, p. 10).

One of the reasons for speeding up the transfer process may well have been to forestall the option of ascertaining the wishes of the people in Punjab and Bengal in particular. Democracy may be good for the West but when it comes to western interests and non-Europeans its principles are flexible and adjustable as required, depending upon the place and the situation. Jinnah then proposed that the work of dividing Punjab and Bengal should be entrusted to the United Nations. This too was unacceptable to Congress (*Transfer of Power, XI,* p. 324). It left the drawing of borders completely at Britain's discretion.

When it became clear in May that there was to be a referendum in NWFP, Nehru started to allege that the highly popular and respected governor of the province Sir Olaf Caroe was not impartial. Later when Gandhi called on Mountbatten on 2nd June, he too asked for the governor to be removed (*Transfer of Power, XI*, p. 48). The viceroy said that although 'he was personally convinced that Sir Olaf Caroe was completely honest' nevertheless 'circumstances might lead to his having to call for his resignation'. He then wrote to the Secretary of State, '*I like him immensely and in my opinion he is a very competent, loyal and honest official but if he had lost confidence of the Congress Party and by his presence was impeding a settlement, it was for the greater good that he should go*' (*Transfer of Power, X*, p.530).

The British cabinet had many other things to take care of in war ravaged Britain. There was neither the inclination nor the means to do anything other than hand over power in India as early as possible and leave. All the ministers wished for was a safe and dignified withdrawal that had the appearance of liberation bestowed with grace and magnanimity. They approved Mountbatten's new plan without too much investigation or questioning and left him to get on with it.

On return from London Mountbatten convened a meeting of the Indian leaders on 2nd June to seek their consent to the plan before it was announced in Parliament. He explained its salient features, including the appointment of a Commission to divide the two major provinces. A referendum was to be held in NWFP and Sylhet to decide if they were to join India or Pakistan and the fate of Baluchistan would be determined by its tribal chiefs. Calcutta would become part of India. He also wanted the immediate acceptance in principle of the plan by the leaders. Jinnah wanted time to consult the Muslim League Council but when Mountbatten insisted on a reply that day he accepted, subject to final approval by the Council.

At the Muslim League Council session a group of Khaksaars, wielding knives and intent on killing Jinnah, tried to storm the hall but were stopped in time by the police. The meeting passed a resolution accepting the Plan. Both Nehru and Patel complained to Mountbatten about the language used in it and the speeches by some of the delegates (*Transfer of Power, XI, docs 129, 130, 150*). Maulana Azad, seconded the acceptance resolution passed by the All India Congress Committee saying, '*The division is only of the map of the country and not in the hearts of the people, and I am sure it is going to be a short-lived partition*', (*Transfer of Power in India*, p.385). The Legislative Assemblies in Punjab and Bengal voted along communal lines with the majority against dividing the province and in favour of making it a part of Pakistan as a whole. It is worth mentioning that all the Christian members of the Punjab Legislative Assembly voted in favour of Pakistan while some of the Muslim members with large land holdings did not. There was a clear majority in Sind for Pakistan and later in Baluchistan as well.

In NWFP the Governor Sir Olaf Caroe was told by Mountbatten to proceed on 'extended leave' before voting could take place in the proposed referendum. Congress had alleged that he was biased in favour of the League. Nehru then undertook to canvas among the Pathans on behalf of Abdul Ghaffar Khan and his brother Dr. Khan Sahib's campaign to make the province a part of India. He was met with jeers and insults wherever he went and had to cut short the visit fearing for his life. In the end the vote on 15th – 17th July was a foregone conclusion with 289,000 opting for Pakistan and 2,900 for India. To save face, Abdul Ghaffar Khan and Congress decided to boycott the referendum. It was interesting that during the campaign the Fakir of Ipi, an influential mullah in Waziristan, had been providing funds and support to Congress (*Transfer of Power, XII*, pp. 295, 297).

The Menon Plan, as it was referred to for a while, was announced in the Parliament and in New Delhi on 3rd June. After Mountbatten, the leaders of the three communities briefly addressed their audiences over All-India Radio. Jinnah asked every one, in particular the Muslims, for calm and peace and ended by calling out *Pakistan Zindabad* (long live Pakistan). Patel set the tone for what followed between the two countries in the coming months and years by protesting to the viceroy that the Muslim leader had abused the hospitality extended to him by All-India Radio and '*committed sacrilege by making a political, partisan and propagandist speech*' (*Sardar Patel's Correspondence*, vol. 4, p. 125).

As a parting kick, Mountbatten announced that the plan will come into effect on 15th August 1947 instead of 30th June 1948. It came as a great shock as there had not been any indication of this earlier and Jinnah had all along pleaded for more time, quoting the example of Ireland where the British had taken more than two years just to agree on the modalities of the transfer of power. He was being asked to set up a new country from scratch in less than two and half months. It was just another link in the chain of events designed to set-up Pakistan for failure. There was not much that he or anyone else could do and no one he could turn to for help. Worse still, there was more of the same to come.

On 4th June a press conference was called. It was an immense public relations exercise and by far the greatest media circus India had ever experienced. Mountbatten was in his elements when he addressed correspondents from all over the world to explain his triumphal achievement and explain and justify the actions he took. '*I did my best ---- the people of India should now take it upon themselves to make up their own minds what they wanted to do for the future of their country. ---- the adult franchise plebiscite* (was the) *democratic* (way but) *such a process was utterly impracticable ---- when we wanted a very quick answer and speed was the one thing which everybody desired*'. The fact that Jinnah had been asking for slowing down the speed of transfer and in later stages even Gandhi had done the same was completely ignored. He also got carried away and said something quite revealing. '---- *all leaders wanted speed in the actual transfer of power ---- Why should we wait? Waiting would only mean that I should be responsible ultimately for law and order*' (*Transfer of Power, XI*, p. 113).

He went to some length to explain why Punjab had to be divided, '*I found it was mainly at the request of the Sikh community that Congress had put forward the Resolution on the partition of the Punjab ---- I was not aware of all the details ---- but when I sent for a map and studied the distribution of the Sikh population under this proposal, I must say I was astounded ---- I am not a miracle worker and I have not found that solution*' to keep the Sikh community more together (*Transfer of Power, XI, p.112*). The total number of Sikhs in all of British Punjab in 1947, excluding the states, was less than four million out of a total population of about thirty two million. The figure of six million quoted by some historians is for all of India, including the states. The British concern and effort on their behalf was totally out of proportion if we consider that there were one hundred million Untouchables, the 'children of a lesser god', as the gumptious Indian writer Arundhati Roy was to aptly name them many years later, whose fate was hardly discussed throughout the proceedings. It was claimed this was in appreciation of the Sikh contribution to the Indian Army. Considering that the number of Muslims who enrolled in the army in the two Great Wars was much greater than the number of Sikhs, it would seem a rather weak argument for justifying the division of the province in the way that it was done.

One of the more serious implications of the devolution process was that in the interim period the existing Congress-controlled government would hold power. As early as April, the Viceroy's Private Secretary George Abell and the Governor of Punjab Evan Jenkins had prepared a document entitled, '*The Administrative Consequences of Partition*'. Why would they do that before there was a decision to partition the country, is a mystery. But it listed procedures for the demarcation of boundaries, re-allocation of government personnel, division of monetary reserves, departments, armed forces, railways and all the other divisible assets including and down to animals in veterinary hospitals. The rules may have been all there but their implementation was under the control of the interim government that was committed to making it as difficult for Pakistan as possible.

Soon after his arrival Mountbatten had transferred all the ministries in the interim government to Congress, allowing Muslim League to maintain a liaison person in each of them. There were disagreements on almost everything starting with if the power had devolved from the Crown to the two countries simultaneously. Nehru insisted that it was not so and that Pakistan was in fact seceding from India. Mountbatten went with Nehru.

At one point Liaquat and Nehru almost came to blows in the council chamber over Nehru's insistence to appoint his sister, Mrs. Vijay Lakshmi Pundit as India's ambassador to Moscow. Liaquat refused to agree which caused Nehru to shout he would not tolerate interference by the League. Then 'pandemonium broke loose and everyone talked at once' (*Shameful Flight*, p. 158). Governor Jenkins reported from Lahore on 15th June, '*Congressmen think it a master stroke by Patel, who having pushed Muslims into a corner will be able to destroy them before very long ----* (A) *Minister in the Coalition Government told me he had heard him* (Patel) *say that Hindustan could quickly make an end of its Muslim inhabitants if Pakistan did not behave*' (*Transfer of Power, XI,* p. 402-3).

A Partition Council consisting of Patel and Rajendra Prasad for Congress and Liaquat Ali Khan and Sirdar Abdul Rab Nishtar for the League was set up to deal with the issue of division of assets between the two countries. The division applied to personnel as well who were asked to choose to remain in India or go to Pakistan. Those that had opted for Pakistan were unceremoniously turfed out of their offices without waiting for Independence, under pressure from Patel. They were not allowed to take any files or office equipment with them. Many of them ended up working in the open under trees or make-shift tents. Although it had been agreed that Pakistan would receive seventeen and a half per cent of the cash reserves, none were transferred. To tide over the difficulty the Nizam of Hyderabad loaned two hundred million rupees to the fledgling state. India refused to share the currency printing press and until such time that the new notes could be printed elsewhere, Indian notes with 'Pakistan Government' stamped across the face became Pakistan's first official currency.

The entire thrust of the Indians was aimed at ensuring that Pakistan did not survive. As Field Marshal Sir Claude Auchinleck, who became Supreme Commander of both India and Pakistan after Partition reported to Whitehall on 28th September 1947: '*I have no hesitation whatever in affirming that the present India Cabinet are implacably determined to do all in their power to prevent the establishment of the Dominion of Pakistan on a firm basis. In this I am supported by the unanimous opinion of my senior officers, and indeed by all British officers cognizant of the situation,* (*Auchinleck*, London, 1959, p. 1379).

Mountbatten had been pressing hard to be made the first governor general of both Pakistan and India. Congress had accepted the proposition early on but Jinnah avoided giving an answer for as long as he could. On 3rd July Mountbatten insisted Jinnah must give a definite reply. When the latter told him that the job was not open, he had great difficulty in accepting the decision. By his own account he argued with Jinnah for four hours '*trying to make him realize the advantages that Pakistan would gain from having the same Governor General as India*'. This same person who was now offering himself as a well-wisher and friend of Pakistan had told the Provincial Governors a mere six weeks earlier that '*Anything that resulted in torpedoing Pakistan was of advantage in that it led the way back to a more common-sense solution*'. Unable to shake Jinnah's resolve he got up and left the room angrily threatening, '*It may cost you the whole of your assets and the future of Pakistan*' (*Transfer of Power, XI,* p. 898-900).

He then wrote a TOP SECRET report giving details of the meeting in which he said Jinnah ' ---- *was suffering from megalomania in its worst form*' and gave it to Ismay to take it to London personally the next day to show to the cabinet and the king. The reaction was excessive and abnormal to say the least considering that Jinnah's doubts about Mountbatten's sincerity and impartiality were perfectly justified and understandable given the latter's overweening support of Congress. Every historian so far has made much of Mountbatten's hurt ego but could it be that there was more than just the ego involved? Did the news of Jinnah's refusal warrant a TOP SECRET classification which is reserved only for matters involving the gravest threat to national security? Why did the Chief of Staff have to carry the letter personally when it could have been easily transmitted through an encrypted cable? Was the cabinet really that much concerned about an issue that on the face of it was essentially personal to Mountbatten? These and a host of other questions still await satisfactory and convincing answers.

RADCLIFFE COMMISSION

Sir Cyril Radcliff, a prominent London barrister from the Inner Temple was appointed to demarcate the boundaries between East and West Punjab as well as between East and West Bengal, on strictly impartial grounds. During the war he had served as the Director General in the Ministry of Information. French has described him as 'the ultimate Establishment figure who could be trusted to put the interests of the state before any other consideration. ---- His loyalty was to the nation rather than any political party, and after the war he was quickly absorbed into the ruling Labour Party power nexus'.

'Another myth' he adds, 'to compliment the image of the disinterested barrister is that during Radcliffe's six weeks in India from 8th July 1947 he was closeted in hot purdah, isolated entirely from any social contact and far removed from political machinations of the closing days of British rule. This is untrue: during his brief stay he dined with Auchinleck, Mountbatten, the Chief Justice Sir Patrick Spens, Sir Walter Monckton, the Governor of Punjab Sir Evan Jenkins, and several other figures of influence within British Indian society'. Jinnah may or may not have been aware of Radcliffe's situation but he did not have sufficient grounds to object to his appointment.

The image that Radcliffe and Mountbatten were '*mutually most careful never to have any discussions about the boundaries*' was false. Mountbatten's Deputy Private Secretary Sir Ian Scott has recorded (*Transfer of Power, XII,* pp. 290-1) that the viceroy attended a meeting of the Boundary Commission in Lahore on 22nd July, and '*there is thus no question, as people like Ronnie Brockman and Campbell-Johnson* (Mountbatten's personal staff) *maintain, that he kept aloof*'. French also quotes Alastair Lamb, historian and author of *Kashmir: A Disputed Legacy, 1846 – 1990*, as saying '*There is simply no way that the Government of India would have allowed somebody with so little experience of India to make the key decisions. Radcliffe was a barrister following a brief*' (p. 322).

The brief given to Radcliffe was to 'demarcate the boundaries of the parts of provinces on the basis of ascertaining the contiguous majority areas of Muslims and non-Muslims. In doing so he was to also take into account other factors'. These 'other factors' were never specified or defined but it was agreed between Mountbatten and Nehru that it would give the Commissions the flexibility to disregard the majority principle wherever necessary (*Transfer of Power, XI,* p.292-3). The real purpose for introducing the provision soon became clear and much of the tragedy that followed the partition and continues to bedevil the relations between the two countries can be traced to it.

For statistical purposes the total population of India, according to the last census held in 1941, was 386.7 million including 94.4 million Muslims. Total population in Punjab was 28.4 million in a total area of almost one hundred thousand square miles. Out of this 16.2 million were Muslims and the rest Hindus, Sikhs, Scheduled Castes, Christians, etc. The total area of Punjab included in Pakistan was 62,000 square miles with a population of 15.8 million out of which 11.85 million were Muslims. East Punjab had a population of 12.6 million and a total area of 37,000 square miles, with 4.375 million Muslims. The distribution of population in districts and *tehsils* is shown in the attached maps. The population of all the communities had increased by about fifteen per cent by August 1947. The population figures do not reflect those in the princely states. Radcliffe used the 1931 census figures in his deliberations as specifically demanded by the Sikhs because it favoured their position slightly. It was of little consequence in the end.

The Boundary Commissions for each of the provinces included two Muslim and two Hindu or Sikh Commissioners. Radcliffe also had a British ICS officer, Christopher Beaumont, assigned to him as Private Secretary and a Hindu named V. D. Iyer as Assistant Secretary. About the latter, Beaumont wrote, '*I have not the slightest doubt that Iyer kept Nehru and V. P. Menon informed of progress*' (see Beaumont's affidavit at the Annex). He thought it was a mistake to have an Indian as one of only three people who knew how the Commission's frontier-drawing was progressing. The two public sessions of the Punjab Commission that were held on 21st and 31st July in Lahore were not attended by Radcliffe. The Commission then assembled in Simla to write its report but there was no agreement and it was left to Radcliffe to make the Award. Mountbatten had wanted it done before 10th August and the decision was handed over to him by Radcliffe a day earlier on 9th August.

We do not know the reasons that formed the basis of Radcliffe's Award. He never gave any and later apparently destroyed all of the relevant record (*Eminent Churchillians*, p. 97 and *Liberty or Death*, p.324). This was just one of many bizarre events that formed part of this sordid affair.

All of the districts in Punjab west of the Bias-Sutlej line had Muslim majorities, except Amritsar where they constituted 46.5 per cent of the population. The main issue had centred on the four central districts of Punjab namely, Ferozepur, Jullunder, Amritsar and Gurdaspur, three of them with a Muslim majority. Radcliffe did not draw the line along the district but along *tehsil* (sub-district) boundaries. In eight of the fifteen *tehsils* in these four districts that were contiguous with Pakistan, Muslims made up the majority of population ---- Shakargarh, Gurdaspur and Batala in Gurdaspur Disrict; Ajnala in Amritsar Disrict; Ferozepur and Zira in

Ferozepur District and Jullunder and Nakodar in Jullunder District. As per the terms of the Commission these should have been included in Pakistan but Radcliffe awarded all fifteen of the *telsils* to India, except a part of Shakargarh Tehsil. In addition, a part of Lahore District with Muslim majority was also given to India for unknown reasons. Not a single *tehsil* with any kind of non-Muslim majority was included in Pakistan. The division was neither impartial nor did it conform to the spirit of the Commission's terms of reference. It was manifestly arbitrary, unjust and dishonest.

It cannot be that all this was done to accommodate the Sikhs who did not constitute an absolute majority in any of the fifteen *tehsils* in question, not even in Amritsar. If the intention was to link Amritsar with India, it could have been done by providing a connection through Ferozepur or even via Hoshiarpur and a part of Batala (see map). In any case Gurdaspur was to the north of Amritsar and its inclusion could not be justified on these grounds either. Clearly, the intention all along had been to provide an all-weather land route from India to Kashmir that was only possible through Gurdaspur.

Further proof can be seen in the way Shakargarh *tehsil* was further partitioned and its eastern boundary shifted westward from its original position to make more room for the connection to Kashmir. Some miles downstream from the Jammu border it left the mainstream of River Ravi and followed a northerly course along a small creek, giving a part of the *tehsil* on Pakistan's side of the river to India. If it had been decided to award Shakargarh *Tehsil* to Pakistan, why slice off its north-east corner and give it to India for no apparent reason? It can only make sense in the context of providing a land route between India and Kashmir.

Under the 3rd June Plan a provisional boundary had been drawn between the two parts of Punjab and made known to the provincial officials for administrative planning purposes. It had included all the four *tehsils* of Gurdaspur District in Pakistan. In his Award, Radcliffe gave away three of these to India without assigning any reason or justification. It was not done by altering the Award after it had been finalized, as generally suspected. Radcliffe had started with the premise that the three *tehsils* had to be allocated to India. The Private Secretary to Radcliffe, Christopher Beaumont told the writer personally as well as conveyed to me in his letter dated 22nd February 1995 that although Gurdaspur District had a Muslim majority, Radcliffe had decided from the start that it had to go to India. It was never an issue with him. Considering that three of the *tehsils* in

Gurdaspur had a Muslim majority and the fourth was not contiguous with India, why would Radcliffe start with the premise that these had to go to India and not even consider any other option unless he had a prior brief to this effect? It was a done deal from the very beginning the details about which will only become known after all the documents relating to Kashmir and the partition of Punjab are made available to the public.

Mountbatten had been taking considerable interest in the affairs of Kashmir since his arrival. In 1935 the Government of India had leased the strategic Gilgit Agency in the north of Kashmir from the Maharaja to keep a closer eye on any Soviet moves in the area. Although it was not due to expire until 1995, Mountbatten wrote to the Secretary of State on 29th April 1947 to terminate the lease and return the area to the state. At his meeting with Jawaharlal Nehru on 22nd April Mountbatten told him that the Princely States 'would have complete freedom of choice' as to which successor entity to the British they could join 'independent of geographical considerations'. Nehru remarked that 'the future of Kashmir might produce a difficult problem' (*Transfer of Power, X*, p. 194). At a meeting with the Nawab of Bhopal and the Maharaja of Indore on 4th August Mountbatten said the State of Jammu and Kashmir was '*so placed geographically that it could join either Dominion, provided part of Gurdaspur were put into East Punjab by the Boundary Commission*' (*Transfer of Power, XII*, p. 335).

At his press conference on 4th June Mountbatten was asked why he had specifically stated in his broadcast the previous day that the boundaries will be settled by the Boundary Commission and will almost certainly not be identical with those which have been previously adopted? Mountbatten replied, 'I put that in for the simple reason that in the district of Gurdaspur the population is 50. 4 per cent Muslim (actually 51. 14), I think and 49.6 per cent non-Muslims. With a difference of 0.8 per cent you will see at once that it is unlikely that the Boundary Commission will throw the whole of the district into the Muslim majority areas'. Apart from the fact that given his position, he should not have been expressing an opinion on a matter that was sub-judice, it goes to show that Gurdaspur had already been on his mind and receiving considerable attention. He could easily have given the example of Jullunder which also had small Muslim majority but didn't because it had already been included in India. If a community had a relatively small majority how does it justify awarding the district to the minority community instead?

After the announcement on 3rd June there were indications that both Hyderabad and Kashmir may wish to become independent. On learning this Mountbatten told the British Residents in both states to ask the rulers to stay their decision until after he had an opportunity to visit and discuss the matter with them in person (*Transfer of Power, XI*, p. 108). On 14th June Krishna Menon wrote a letter telling Mountbatten that if Kashmir were to go Pakistan, such a development would not be at all popular in the newly independent India and it might put at risk the extensive British interests in the country. It was essential in his view that the state be brought within the Indian fold (*Transfer of Power, XI*, p. 201). Menon had asked for his letter to be destroyed after reading but it has somehow survived in Mountbatten's papers. Three days later Mountbatten, accompanied by General Ismay and Lady Mountbatten arrived in Srinagar, ostensibly for a holiday but carrying a written brief on Kashmir that had been given to him by Nehru. Lamb is of the opinion (*Kashmir:* pp. 114-17) that the Maharaja may have been assured at some point that an all-weather land link between India and Kashmir was going to be provided and he need have no fear on that score when making his decision.

At a lunch at the United Services Club in Simla with his Commissioners in early August, Radcliffe told them that he would award a portion of Ferozepur District with a nominal Muslim majority to Pakistan, '*In return for giving Gurdaspur and part of Lahore District*' to India (*Transfer of Power, XII*, p. 619). Justice Munir who had been one of the four judges on the Commission narrated in an article entitled '*Days to Remember*' many years later, '*I was told by Radcliffe in the most unequivocal terms that three tehsils Ferozepur, Zira and Fazilka, were coming to Pakistan and that it was unnecessary for me to discuss this part of the case with him. I still remember the description of the terrain of these tehsils he gave me and the main reason for their transfer*' (see also *Transfer of Power, XII*, p.395).

On the basis of the Award made by Radcliffe and given to the viceroy, Mountbatten's Private Secretary Sir George Abell wrote a letter giving advance warning to the Governor of Punjab Sir Evan Jenkins that read: '*I enclose a map showing roughly the boundary, which Sir Cyril Radcliffe proposes to demarcate and a note by Christopher Beaumont describing it ---- There will not be any great changes from this boundary ----*' (*File V-I, Vol. II, Part II*, The National Documentation Centre). The line in the letter and the map followed the present day border from Kashmir southwest along Ravi to a point where it meets Lahore District and then cut across Kasur *tehsil* to cross the Sutlej River and included both Zira and Ferozepur *tehsils* in Pakistan. Jenkins passed this information to the Deputy Commissioners on 8th August for making the necessary adjustments.

When the Deputy Commissioner Ferozepur informed the Chief Engineer Irrigation Mr. Sarup Singh that he will have to re-locate his headquarters, the latter immediately got in touch with the Chief Engineer in-charge of irrigation in Bekaner State, Dr. Kunwar Sain. On learning that the headworks of the canal supplying water to the state would be located in Pakistan the Maharaja sent a cable to Mountbatten and also sent his Prime Minister Sirdar Pannikar and the chief engineer to call on him. The next morning on 9th August Nehru wrote a letter to Mountbatten and enclosed a note from Mr. Khosa, Chairman Central Waterways, Irrigation and Navigation Commission stating that both from the strategic as well as irrigation aspect no area east of the Sutlej must on any account go to Pakistan.

The minutes of the Viceroy's 69th Staff Meeting held on the same day (9th August) make an interesting point. '*It was stated that Sir Cyril Radcliffe would be ready by that evening to announce the award of the Punjab Boundary Commission ---- the Viceroy emphasized the necessity to maintain secrecy not only on the terms of the award but also of the fact that it would be ready that day*'. The Secretary to the Viceroy, Sir John Christie's diary entry for 9th August read, '*Staff meeting today concerned with Boundary Commission timing of announcement and precautions. George* (Abell) *tells me His Excellency is in a tired flap and is having to be strenuously dissuaded from asking Radcliffe to alter his award*' (*Transfer of Power*, *XII*, p. 611).

Jinnah, perturbed at the rumours of Gurdaspur being awarded to India, sent a message to the Chief of Staff General Ismay through Chaudhri Muhammad Ali that such a step would have very serious repercussions. When he conveyed the message on 10th August, '*Ismay professed complete ignorance of Radcliffe's ideas about the boundary and stated categorically that neither Mountbatten nor he himself had ever discussed the question with him. It was entirely for Radcliffe to decide; no suggestion of any kind had been or would ever be made to him. When I plied Ismay with details of what had been reported to us, he said he could not follow me. There was a map hanging in the room and I beckoned him to the map so that I could explain the position to him with its help. There was a pencil line drawn across the map of the Punjab. The line followed the boundary that had been reported to the Quaid-e-Azam. I said that it was necessary for me to explain further since the line already drawn on the map indicated the boundary I had been talking about. Ismay turned pale and asked in confusion who had been fooling with his map? This line differed from the final boundary in only one respect, the Muslim majority tehsils of Ferozepur and Zira in the Ferozepur district were still on the side of Pakistan as in the sketch map*' (*Emergence of Pakistan*, p. 218-9).

In the meantime, the Prime Minister of Bekaner State Sirdar Pannikar along with Dr. Kunwar Sain met Mountbatten and told him, '*The Maharaja has asked us to convey that if the Ferozepur Headworks and Ganga Canal go to Pakistan, His Highness, in the interest of his subjects, would have no option but to opt for Pakistan. As I said this I could see a change in the colour of the face of Lord Mountbatten*' (*Reminiscences of an Engineer*, by Dr. Kunwar Sain, Young Asia Publication, 1978, p.122).

On the evening of 11th August the announcement of the award which was scheduled for 13th August was postponed and Sir Evan Jenkins received a coded telegram from the viceroy's office that read '*Eliminate salient*', ---- in other words take away Zira and Ferozepur from Pakistan. The change had nothing to do with accommodating the Sikhs, as suggested by some of the British apologists. Maharaja of Bikaner, Sadul Singh, wrote a personal confidential letter to Mountbatten to '*convey my most grateful thanks*' for '*the action which you so kindly and promptly took after your talk with Mr. Pannikar in regard to the protection of interests ---- of my state*' (*Transfer of Power, XII*, p. 645).

Close to midnight on 11th August, V.P. Menon on orders from Mountbatten went to see Radcliffe but was turned away by Beaumont. The next day General Ismay invited Radcliffe for lunch and specifically asked him not the bring Beaumont with him. As Beaumont puts it, '*This was the first time, however, that Radcliffe and I had been separated on any sort of function. That evening, the Punjab line was changed ---- Ferozepur going to India. No change, as was subsequently rumoured, was made in the northern (Gurdaspur) part of the line; nor in the Bengal line. So Mountbatten cheated and Radcliffe allowed himself to be overborne*' (see Beaumont's Affidavit at Annex).

Jinnah's reaction to the chicanery, injustice and betrayal involved in the gerrymandering was characteristic: '*The division of India is now finally and irrevocably effected. No doubt, we feel that the carving out of this great independent sovereign Muslim state has suffered injustices. We have been squeezed in as much as it was possible and the latest blow that we have received was the Award of the Boundary Commission. It is an unjust, incomprehensible and even perverse Award. It may be wrong, unjust and perverse and it may not be judicial but political Award, but we had agreed to abide by it and is binding on us. As honourable people we must abide by it*'. It is not hard to imagine how petty little men like Mountbatten must have felt, knowing that Jinnah was what they were not ---- an honourable man. There may be some justice in that the names of these conniving and manipulating humbugs have long since been consigned to the dustbin of history wrapped in ignominy whereas that of Jinnah lives on untarnished and cherished and revered by millions

There were furtive efforts to keep under wraps the whole disgraceful affair that cast a very dark shadow on the integrity, honesty and impartiality of the highest in the British system. The British Government denied any wrong-doing when Pakistan denounced the alteration to the UN Security Council. Insiders like Lord Ismay, Sir George Abell, Sir Ian Scott and Christopher Beaumont considered it best not to discuss the issue: '*We all agreed it was better for relations between the two countries for us not to spill the beans*' (*Eminent Churchillians*, p. 98). The historian Sir Penderel Moon was prevailed upon to 'skirt around the issue' in his book *The British Conquest and Dominion of India* (*Ismay Papers, III / 7 / 13a, 12th February 1948*). This is after he found certain documents pertaining to Ferozepur missing from the official record that had been quoted by Dr. Kunwar Sain in his book. Mountbatten wrote letters to Ismay, Jenkins and others, in effect asking them to remember things differently to what had actually transpired.

On return to England Beaumont went to see Radcliffe to ask what had made him change the Award. In his words, '*He was very sheepish and never denied it. He didn't welcome my visit, said he was busy and shuffled me off*'. But he did admit to the Secretary of State for Commonwealth Relations Philip Noel-Baker that 'he showed the first draft of the proposed Award to the authorities in Delhi and that, on further consideration, he made the award in terms which departed from the first draft' (*The Partition of India and Mountbatten*, by Latif Ahmed Sherwani, The Council of Pakistan Studies, 1986).

Be that as it may, it is wrong to single out Mountbatten and Radcliffe for the blame, as most historians seem to have done. They were not independent agents acting on their own but were chosen by the British Government to represent and look after its interests in India in line with the briefs provided to them. The responsibility for the way in which the events were handled rests squarely with the British Government one way or the other.

It is reasonable to assume that whatever actions Mountbatten had taken in India were with the knowledge and approval of the British Government. It is impossible that the viceroy should be unaware of the rules, regulations and conventions pertaining to Commissions and Awards and the implications of breaching these. Mountbatten not only did this but did it with the active involvement and participation of the Commission itself. Radcliffe was not ignorant of the law and could not have become an accessory in its breach unless his brief from the British Government had allowed him this freedom.

Even if we were to assume that Mountbatten was a rogue Maverick who acted on his own against the wishes of Whitehall, some action that conveyed the displeasure of His Majesty's Government would have been taken, if not immediately then some time after his return to Britain. There was never any evidence of it. He returned to a hero's welcome instead and continued to be promoted until he reached the very top of his profession. It was the same with Radcliffe. It could only happen if in the eyes of the British Government the two men had done no wrong and had acted fully in accordance with its wishes.

KASHMIR AND OTHER STATES

There were a total of 565 large and small Princely states in India. Their population and size varied greatly. Some, like Hyderabad and Kashmir were larger than many European countries. On the other hand, more than four hundred of them were less than twenty square miles in area. Together these covered approximately one third of India's total land and one quarter of her population. The legal and penal codes of British India did not apply inside the states nor did the political reforms that were introduced from time to time. The larger states even maintained armies, some equipped with tanks and aircraft of their own.

Each state was ruled by a *raja* (Hindu or Sikh) or *nawab* (Muslim). They were an anachronistic lot who regarded the state as their personal fiefdom. The stories of their degeneration and profligacy are a legion. Almost without exception they were incredibly vain and licentious, utterly incompetent and ignorant. Having little else to do, most of them whiled away their time in sports, debauchery, deviant sex and crass display of personal wealth. None of this worried the British as long as the princes remained loyal to the Crown. To ensure this, they maintained a British Resident in each of the states who kept a close watch on the proceedings at all times. It was a much sought after appointment as the princes went out of their way to keep the Resident's pleased and routinely showered them with lavish gifts.

Space does not permit nor is it necessary to go into the sordid details of the interests and activities of these rulers. Just to give an idea, a few examples mostly from *Freedom at Midnight* (pp. 165 – 181) are quoted. Some of the princes actually believed they were descended from the heavens. The Maharaja of Mysore for instance, who traced his ancestry to the moon, lived in a 600-room palace and ate ground diamonds, believing these to be aphrodisiac. His concubines rode on elephants that wore diamond earrings and whose trunks were studded with rubies. His throne, made of solid gold, weighed more than one ton.

The maharajas of Udaipur whose ancestors had ruled the state for more than two thousand years believed they were descended from the sun. The Maharaja of Bharatpur, drove a silver-plated Rolls-Royce convertible and killed more than fourteen hundred tigers. In a duck shoot he arranged for Viceroy Lord Hardinge, 4,482 birds were shot in three hours. Not to be out-done, the Maharaja of Alwar had his Rolls-Royce gold-plated inside and out, its body shaped as the replica of the coronation coach of British monarchs. The maharaja of Kapoorthala had no less than twenty seven Rolls-Royces tethered in his stable.

The Maharaja of Baroda periodically arranged fights unto death between bull elephants. The Nawab of Junagarh's dogs lived in apartments fitted with all the amenities, including telephones. When they died they were carried in ceremonial procession to be buried in marble mausoleums. He married his favourite bitch *Roshana* to the Labrador *Bobby* in an ostentatious public ceremony that cost sixty thousand pounds.

The Maharaja of Kapoorthala imported French architects and decorators to build a replica of Versailles Palace for him. He dressed his Sikh retainers in powdered wigs, silk waistcoats, knickers and silver-buckled slippers, just like the Louis XIV courtiers. He even proclaimed French as the language of his court.

The diminutive Nizam of Hyderabad, reputed to be the richest man in the world and a devout Muslim, had donated one hundred million dollars to Britain during the First World War and footed the bill for three squadrons of warplanes in World War II (*The Princes in India in the End Game of the Empire, 1917 – 1947*, by I. Copland, 1997, p. 185). There were endless stories about his miserly ways. Although he had a gold dinner service for one hundred persons, he ate from a tin plate squatting in his bedroom. His collection of jewels was enormous, 'the pearls alone would cover all the sidewalks of Piccadilly Circus'. There were truckloads of gold ingots, precious stones and currency notes stashed in the palace.

None of them was perhaps as colourful as Sir Bhupinder Singh, the seventh Maharaja of Patiala. 'During the torrid Punjab summers, the harem moved outdoors in the evening to Bhupinder's pool. The prince stationed a score of bare-breasted girls like nymphs at intervals around its rim. Chunks of ice bobbing in the water gave the hot air a delicious chill while the maharaja floated idly about, coming to port from time to time to caress a breast or have a sip of whiskey' (*Freedom at Midnight*, p. 174). The covey of young females in his harem was more than 350 strong. (for another tale about Patiala, see chapter '*Sikhism and Sikhs*).

Not all of them were as debauched or decadent. Baroda had banned polygamy and made education free and universal in the state in the nineteenth century. The Nawab of Bhopal legislated equality of status for women that was not enjoyed anywhere else in India. Mysore had an excellent science faculty, the best in Asia. Jaipur hosted one of the best astronomical observatories in the world.

Each of the states had signed a separate treaty with the Crown, acknowledging Britain as the paramount power and ceding the control of its foreign affairs and defence to her. In return they received a guarantee of continuing autonomy in the internal affairs of the state. The terms were not the same and varied from state to state. In June 1947 the Secretary of State decided that the paramountcy agreements would lapse on 15th August when India became independent. The princes would then become free to decide their own fate as they considered best.

This was not what Congress had wanted. It had hoped the states would be assimilated into India without too much fuss. Nehru threw an apoplectic fit and badgered the viceroy to dismiss Sir Conrad Corfield, who was responsible for the policy as head of the Political Department, as 'an enemy of India' (*The Last Days of the British Raj*, p. 164-5 and

Disastrous Twilight: A Personal Record of the Partition of India, by Shahid Hamid, Barnsley, 1986, p. 196). Mountbatten buckled under, putting all the blame on Corfield and even calling him a 'son-of-a-bitch'. He then took away control of the states from the Political Department and handed it over to a new States Department under Patel with V. P. Menon as the Secretary. Corfield left India in disgust, '*I boarded the plane with a feeling of nausea, as though my own honour had been smirched and I had deserted my friends*' (*The Princely India I knew*, p. 159). The Nawab of Bhopal, President of the Chamber of the Princes too had earlier resigned in protest.

Menon drew up an accession agreement asking each prince to attach his state to either India or Pakistan before 15th August. The Chamber of the Princes was called to assemble on 25th July with the Maharaja of Patiala in the chair. Mountbatten told them in effect, though not in so many words, that they had no choice but to sign the accession document. This was clearly against the commitment made by the British Government giving them the freedom to make their own choices. He made promises that he had no way of fulfilling, including that the Princes' recourse to the Crown will be protected. Some of the things he said were patently false and knowingly deceitful '*hammering home with all his might that this was an opportunity that would never be repeated, that their internal autonomy would be protected, that the bargain was so advantageous to the States that even now he was not certain he could persuade the Indian Government to accept it*' (*Mountbatten*, p. 410). Congress weighed in with its own threats to incite unrest and insurgency in any state that refused to join. Nehru openly declared '*I will encourage rebellion in all states that go against us*' (*Transfer of Power, XI*, p. 232).

The extraordinary length to which Mountbatten went not simply to tolerate but accept and accommodate Nehru is only partly explained by the desire on the part of the British Government to keep on the right side of Congress and India. There was a considerable measure of personal rapport, closeness and cordiality between the two that lasted a long time after Mountbatten had ceased to be the Governor General of India. In Delhi eyebrows had constantly been raised and tongues wagged at the relationship between Mountbatten's wife Edwina and Pundit Nehru. It was common knowledge and Mountbatten could not possibly have remained unaware of it. Every biographer and historian has remarked on it. It is an enigma how someone could remain so pleasantly disposed and on such friendly terms with a man who was suspected of having an affair with his wife? Perhaps, honour and shame carried different meanings for Mountbatten or, as the Old Bard had said, you can't shame the shameless.

It was like a blitzkrieg after Mountbatten put his weight behind the drive to get the states to accede to India. Patel and Menon traveled all over the country badgering, even blackmailing the rulers into signing the accession deed. Ironically, they were being made to accede to the 'Indian Union' when in fact it did not even exist at the time. When the Maharaja of Orissa wavered, Patel had his palace surrounded by a mob until he succumbed. Travancore's recalcitrant Prime Minister was stabbed in the face by a Congress activist. Mountbatten wrote personal letters to all the rulers beseeching them to accede to India. The letter he wrote to the Maharaja of Dholpur is just another example of his unconscionable nature and conduct. It read in part:

'*If you accede now you will be joining a Dominion with the King as Head. If they change the Constitution to a republic and leave the Commonwealth, the Instrument of Accession does not bind you in any way to remain with the republic. It would appear to me that that would be the moment for Your Highness to decide if you wish to remain with India or reclaim your sovereign independence.*

'*I know that His Majesty would personally be grieved if you elected to sever your connection with him whilst he was still the King of India now that it has been made clear that this would not involve you in accepting to remain within a republic if this was unacceptable to you when the time came. -----*' (*The Princely India I Knew*, pp. 183-5).

He invited the undecided rulers to lunches and dinners and paid visits or sent members of his personal staff to get them to accede to India. Perhaps the most bizarre case was that of Jodhpur. Its maharaja, along with that of Jaisalmer, had secretly met Jinnah in Delhi to explore the possibility of their joining Pakistan. When he got back to his hotel he found Menon waiting, having been tipped off by an operative. He told the Maharaja that the viceroy wished to see him urgently. Once at the Viceregal Lodge, Menon went looking for Mountbatten and having located him in his bath begged him to come and reason with the unwilling prince. The viceroy then proceeded to tell the young ruler that his recently deceased father would be most unhappy if he took his Hindu subjects into Pakistan and promised to prevail upon Patel to accommodate all his reasonable demands.

After Mountbatten had left, the maharaja took out a pen from his pocket and unscrewed its cap to reveal a .22 pistol that he pointed at Menon's head shouting 'I am not giving in to your threats'. Hearing the noise, Mountbatten came back and managed to calm the prince down. It took three more days before Jodhpur was finally made to accede to India. The prince then arranged a reception where he forced drinks down Menon's throat and then took him back to Delhi on a wild drunken ride in his personal plane that frightened the daylights out of Mountbatten's favourite Indian staff officer (*Freedom at Midnight*, pp. 244).

By 15th August, between Patel and Mountbatten they had managed to get the agreement of all the states to accede to India except those few that lay within Pakistan and three others that were still holding out. The latter included Junagarh, Hyderabad and Kashmir. Junagarh signed the instrument of accession to Pakistan on 15th August. The Indian Army encircled the state enforcing a complete blockade while its nawab fled to Karachi. Mountbatten arranged for an agreement under which the fate of Junagarh was to be determined by a UN supervised referendum. Without waiting for it, the Indian Army invaded and occupied the state. A plebiscite was organized under purely Indian auspices instead and the state annexed.

The Nizam of Hyderabad was determined to remain independent of both India and Pakistan. He had signed a standstill agreement while Mountbatten negotiated with him the terms of an agreement. While this was still in progress India laid an economic blockade of the state. This was in breach of the terms of the standstill agreement. When Sir Walter Monckton, who was negotiating on behalf of the state protested Mountbatten, Nehru and Patel denied any knowledge. The terms of an agreement drafted by Mountbatten shortly before he left India were unacceptable to the Nizam. The Indian Army had earlier made all the necessary preparations for Operation Polo, the invasion of Hyderabad. It moved in and occupied it without meeting much resistance in what was euphemistically termed a 'police action'.

According to the Maharwal of Dungarpur, a large number of the rulers had come close to forming a union of their own that would have spread over three hundred thousand square miles with thirty million people. He told the Political Agent, Charles Chenevix-Trench, '*But it was not to be. It was an end brought about by one man and his wife. By making them sign the Instrument of Accession, the Viceroy perpetrated the rape of the States. Had the princes been left alone, Congress could never have got them to sign away their powers and heritage within a fortnight. No, never. Being a member of the Royal Family, many Princes took Mountbatten as a friend. Nothing could be further from the truth ---- the Princes expected justice and fair play, not lies and half-truths to beguile them into a snare*' (*Viceroy's Agent*, by Charles Chenevix Trench, 1987, p. 347).

After the conquest of Punjab the British had sold the State of Kashmir to the Hindu raja of Jammu, Gulab Singh, for a sum of seven and a half million rupees (about 500,000 pounds) under the Treaty of Amritsar signed on 16th March 1846. It was the start of a century long highly oppressive rule, mismanagement and lawlessness. In 1877 - 78 the state was ravaged by famine causing large numbers of Kashmiris to migrate south into Punjab. There were periodic revolts all over the state that were put down with extreme cruelty. Partly because of this but also with an eye on strategic developments to the north the Secretary of State suggested in 1884: '*It may, indeed, be a question of whether, having regard to the circumstances under which the sovereignty of the country was entrusted to the present Hindoo family, the intervention of the British Government on behalf of the Mohammedan population has not already been too long delayed*'. The maharaja was excluded from interference in public affairs and a Council of State consisting of some nominated individuals took his place. The arrangement lasted until 1922 when the maharaja was again allowed to assume full autocratic control.

Sir Albion Bannerji, a British civil servant who had been the senior member of the Council of State, resigned in protest against misgovernment by the maharaja in 1929 stating; '*Jammu and Kashmir State is labouring under many disadvantages, with a large Mohammadan population absolutely illiterate, labouring under poverty and very low economic conditions of living in the villages and practically governed like dumb driven cattle. There is no touch between the Government and the people, no suitable opportunity for representing grievances and the administrative machinery itself requires overhauling from top to bottom to bring it up to modern conditions of efficiency. It has at present no sympathy with the people's wants and grievances*' (*Kashmiris Fight For Freedom, vol. I*, Lahore, 1977, p. 349).

In 1947 the population of the Kashmir Valley was about ninety-five per cent Muslim and there was a Muslim majority in Jammu and its outlying areas. The administration was in the firm hands of the Prime Minister of the state Pundit Kak who suffered from no illusions about Congress, Nehru or any of the other Hindu leaders. The latter were in sympathy with the National Conference, supposedly a secularist political party headed by another pretentious school teacher named Sheikh Abdullah. He was opposed by Mir Waiz Mohammed Yusuf Shah a quasi-political religious leader affiliated with the Muslim Conference. The latter held most of the seats in the State Legislative Assembly and supported Muslim League. Sheikh Abdullah had boycotted the elections in 1946.

In the note handed over to Mountbatten as he was leaving for Srinagar on 17th June Nehru had stated that although 77 per cent of the population overall was Muslim they would like to join India because the leader of the National Conference Party, Sheikh Abdullah, was a popular figure and he was not in favour of Pakistan. The Muslim Conference that wished to join Pakistan 'had little influence in the State'. '*What happens in Kashmir is of course of the first importance to India as a whole ---- because of the great strategic importance of that frontier state*'. He also alleged that the Prime Minister of Kashmir, Pundit Kak had told the Maharaja that Mountbatten would like him to join Pakistan and asked that he should be removed from his post. (There is no evidence that the viceroy had expressed any such opinion). In conclusion he wrote, '*If any attempt is made to push Kashmir into the Pakistan Constituent Assembly there is likely to be much trouble because the National Conference is not in favour of it and the Maharaja's position would also become very difficult. The normal and obvious course appears to be for Kashmir to join the Constituent Assembly of India. This will satisfy both the popular demand and the Maharaja's wishes. It is absurd to think that Pakistan would create trouble if this happens*' (*Transfer of Power*, *XI*, p. 229).

Mountbatten was unable to get any commitment from either the maharaja or Pundit Kak. When Nehru was informed of the outcome he was greatly disappointed and upset and wanted to go to Kashmir himself but Mountbatten dissuaded him, proposing that Gandhi should visit instead. Gandhi's attempts with the prime minister and the maharaja did not bear much fruit either. He was followed by the Congress President Acharya Kirpalani and the rulers of the Punjab Sikh States of Patiala, Faridkot and also Kapoorthala whose majority of population also happened to be Muslim. Sardar Patel, who was about to become the Deputy Prime Minister of India, had been writing to the maharaja privately urging him to join India 'without delay'.

It is not clear what caused the maharaja to eventually sack the Prime Minister of Kashmir, Pundit Kak and place him under house arrest. He was replaced by the maharaja's relative from the state army, Major

General Janak Singh. This is when Mountbatten wrote in his personal report, the Maharaja '*now talks of holding a referendum to decide whether to join Pakistan or India, provided that the Boundary Commission give him land communication between Kashmir and India ---- it appears, as if this great problem of the States has been satisfactorily solved within the last three weeks of British rule*' (*Tansfer of Power, XII*, pp. 456, 489). Even so, the maharaja had not signed the accession document by 15th August. Along with India and Pakistan, the state was now technically independent and entered into a standstill agreement with Pakistan but India found excuses not to sign one.

An insurgency provoked by the maharaja's excesses had been simmering in the predominantly Muslim district of Poonch in the south of Kashmir since June 1947. A great celebration of 'Pakistan Day' was observed on 14th August to mark the birth of the country. The maharaja declared martial law and clamped down hard on any demonstrations, killing a large number of people. In the meantime, the people of Gilgit Agency whose lease had been terminated by Mountbatten on 1st August refused to accept the decision that would put them back under the maharaja's rule. They declared independence from the state and decided to become a part of Pakistan.

A remarkable British army officer, Major William Brown, was commandant of the paramilitary Gilgit Scouts at the time. His sympathies lay with his men. When the maharaja ordered the 6th Kashmir Infantry, composed mostly of Sikhs to take over Gilgit, he led the Scouts to rout and destroy the invaders. The Sikhs never forgot and caught up with him ten years later in Calcutta where he was serving as the Sales Executive for the British company ICI at the time. He barely survived the murderous attack on his life. The fascinating account of the almost forgotten Gilgit episode is contained in his book *The Gilgit Rebellion 1947*, Ibex, 1998).

Bands of marauding Sikhs and Hindus, armed with guns supplied by the State, attacked Muslim villages in Jammu. An estimated 200,000 Muslims were killed and more than half a million driven out to seek shelter in Pakistan (*Kashmir*, p. 123). The refugees formed small bands of resistance in Pakistan, strengthened by ex-servicemen volunteers from the neighbouring districts in Punjab. Armed with weapons acquired from the gun factories in NWFP, they infiltrated back into the state. On 22nd October the Muslims in the 4th Jammu and Kashmir Infantry battalion stationed at Domel, the road crossing over Jhelum River mutinied, killing most of the Hindu Dogra soldiers and the colonel in-charge and joined up with the Poonch rebels.

Initially, there was very little, if any, official interference from Pakistan. Jinnah was careful not to get involved for fear of escalating the already worrisome developments. Nehru had claimed that more than one hundred thousand Pathan tribesmen from Pakistan had invaded Kashmir. This is preposterous considering the scale of logistical support needed and the difficulty in mustering, transporting and deploying this huge number of undisciplined men. Pakistan simply did not posess the financial, military and any other means to put such an operation into effect. The actual number of Pathans that did volunteer to fight in Kashmir was not more than three thousand and there is reason to believe that it happened without Jinnah's prior knowledge or approval. Their contribution to the cause has remained questionable. Nonetheless, it was termed as a 'foreign invasion' and used as the excuse for Indian intervention that followed. In fact, detachments of the Maharaja of Patiala's army that became a part of the Indian Army after 15th August had already been deployed in Srinagar much before 22nd October and prior to the accession of the state to India (*Kashmir*, pp.134, 154, 162).

It is not the intention to go into the details of all the developments related to Kashmir for that is a separate subject in itself. In any case, it is impossible to tell the entire story because the British Government still refuses to make all the Mountbatten and Secretary of State files related to Kashmir available for historical research. There are also reports that Mountbatten has subsequently tampered with his papers (*Eminent Churchillians*. P. 128). After the rebellion broke out the maharaja fled to Jammu. He now had a new Prime Minister in Mehr Chand Mahajan, a judge of the Lahore High Court who had acted as a Commissioner on behalf of Congress on the Boundary Commission. After some furtive negotiations between Mahajan, Patel and V. P. Menon, the maharaja was allegedly made to sign the accession document on 26th October and ask for military assistance from India.

Mountbatten accepted the document the next day. That same morning more than one hundred Dakota transport planes started to airlift Indian troops from different airfields in India to Srinagar. It is impossible to plan and put into effect an operation of this magnitude at the drop of a hat. The preparations must have started weeks if not months earlier when British officers were still in command. The British commanders-in chief of India's army, navy and air force issued a joint declaration that they had not been involved in any planning but they did not deny prior knowledge of the planning. Neither Mountbatten nor Field Marshal Auchinleck did anything to prevent or discourage the preparations. On the contrary, the Commander-in-Chief Pakistan Army Lieutenant General Sir Frank Messervy was '*surprised to find Mountbatten directing the military operations in Kashmir*' (*Eminent Churchillians*, p. 105).

Alarmed by the developments, Jinnah asked for Pakistani troops to be inducted into the state to restore order but the Acting Commander-in-Chief Lieutenant General Sir Douglas Gracey, unlike his British counterpart in India, declined to carry out the orders. The move became unavoidable next spring when the Poonch rebels and tribesmen began to be pushed back close to the Pakistan border by the Indian Army. The introduction of a limited number of lightly armed Pakistani troops, without any armour or air support stabilized the front, bringing about a stalemate.

On 1st January 1948, India complained to the United Nations Security Council asking it to instruct Pakistan to desist from meddling in the affairs of Kashmir. In response Pakistan called for arranging a cease-fire followed by withdrawal of all foreign troops by both the sides. The state was asked to be administered by the UN until a plebiscite was held to ascertain the wishes of the people, without any external interference. The cease-fire eventually came into effect on 1st January 1949 and has been supervised by a United Nations military presence ever since.

The UN resolution calling for a plebiscite to determine the wishes of the people was never implemented. Having accepted it, Nehru sent a three member Parliamentary team led by the Minister of Finance, Gadgil to Kashmir to get a feel of how the Kashmiris might vote. Its findings poured cold water over any notions that Kashmiris were for Sheikh Abdullah, his National Conference or India. Thereafter Nehru lost all interest in any UN supervised plebiscite and started to back-pedal furiously on the issue. All the subsequent attempts to find a solution were stonewalled by Indian intransigence, backed by the Soviet veto in the Security Council.

Pakistan's position on Kashmir, until the advent of General Musharraf, had always been that the people of the state should be allowed to decide their own future through a free and fair plebiscite. This was also the stance of the vast majority of the UN members. At the turn of the twenty-first century there was a change in the attitude of the United States. A re-evaluation of her geo-political imperatives in the area now called for much closer collaboration with India. In order to help cement these ties it prevailed upon Musharraf to abandon the principle of self-determination and settle with India on some other undefined terms. Musharraf had no mandate or authorization to deny the Kashmiris' right to self-determination. His successor, Zardari has gone a step further and labeled the Kashmiris fighting for restoration of their rights as 'terrorists'.

The principle, or lack thereof, involved in the attitude can have potentially very serious consequences. It has happened all too often in human history that politicians looked at maps and carved up territories between themselves as if these were uninhabited open spaces, forgetting that there were people involved who have views and aspirations of their own and who may find it unacceptable to live with impositions by unwanted outsiders. Ignoring the wishes of the people may seem expedient but it is also an invitation to disaster and tragedy in the future. The Balkans, Belgium, Poland and Palestine are some of the other recent examples. India's decision to take possession of the state may have had its roots in avarice, hubris and the desire to prevent it from joining Pakistan but it has been at great cost and carries within it the seeds that will ultimately weaken and divide the country. It may well turn out in the end that Mountbatten, Nehru, Patel and V. P. Menon among others did India no favour by trying to get Kashmir included in the Union against the wishes of her people.

It is unrealistic to think that she will try to reach a settlement on the issue any time soon for a number of reasons. Kashmir is economically, strategically and culturally important to Pakistan. Given the vitiated atmosphere and relations between the two countries, it will be hard to find an Indian politician willing to risk the possibility of the state joining hands with Pakistan. India has never been nor is it today a united and homogenous nation. Rightly or wrongly, they fear that if they were to let Kashmir go, it may give rise to unwelcome fissiparous tendencies in other parts of the country. They have left themselves with hardly any option other than to continue down the same old beaten path, hoping that both the people of Kashmir and Pakistan will acquiesce to the status quo and learn to somehow live with it. The notion is dangerously misplaced and does not take into account the lessons of history. It is an invitation to perpetual instability and worse.

There is a compelling political need for India to keep the bogey of hostile Muslim Pakistan alive as a threat to rally and unite the myriad diverse elements that constitute India. Without the existence of a manifest external threat there is every possibility of history taking its course and the country breaking apart. The rise of virulent Hindu nationalist *Hindutava* in the country that thrives on hate has added a new dimension to the problem. It is useful to provide an external focal point for these elements to divert and expend their energies rather than letting them create disturbance and disruption internally.

India and Pakistan are not the only interested parties in the dispute. The western powers, in particular the United States is deeply involved for reasons of its own. The prospect of success by the Muslim Kashmiris in the on-going insurgency will send the wrong signal to the oppressed Muslims in other parts of the world. The West would very much like India to maintain her hold on the state. Any resolution of the dispute that is acceptable to all the parties carries within it the risk of losing the leverage USA presently enjoys in the region by playing one country against the other. The two countries would no longer be falling over each other to keep her on their side. It will make situations like the interference in Afghanistan, for example, much more difficult for them to manage.

IS THERE NO GOD?

The idea of a Muslim homeland had provoked a strong reaction among the Sikhs from the very beginning. In August 1942, the Akali leader Gayani Kartar Singh had proclaimed in Amritsar, '*If Pakistan is foisted upon the Sikhs with the help of British bayonets, we shall tear it into shreds as Guru Gobind Singh tore up the Mughal Empire*' ('*A History of the Sikhs, vol. 2*, by Khushwant Singh, New Delhi, 1991, p. 252). The Sikhs had started collecting funds to buy arms and train large numbers of volunteers in the use of explosives to sabotage buildings, railways, water works, bridges, etc. The frightening extent of these preparations was revealed in June 1947 with the arrest of an ex-INA saboteur, Pritam Singh who had been landed by the Japanese in South India during the war (*Raj*, p. 633).

Gayani Kartar Singh openly told Governor Jenkins in July 1947 that Sikhs '*will fight on revolutionary lines ---- by murdering official, cutting railway lines and telegraph lines, destroying canal head works and so on*'. When Jenkins said it would be '*a very foolish policy ---- the Gayani retorted that if Britain were invaded, he had no doubt my feelings would be much the same as his. ---- This is the nearest thing to an ultimatum yet given on behalf of the Sikhs*' (*Transfer of Power, XII*, pp. 73-4, 429). Incredibly, the governor took no action. Had the same words been uttered by a Muslim leader the reaction by the governor, viceroy, Congress leaders and the press would have been very different indeed. Their howls would have reverberated around the globe.

The Hindus were not far behind the Sikhs in making what were little short of preparations for war. There was no shortage of funds in their case. As an RSS activist in Lahore told Ved Mehta, author of *The Ledge Between the Streams* (London 1984, p. 313), '*We Hindus have to change if we are to survive and rule India ---- the only language a Muslim understands is that of a knife and a grenade*'. In the evenings all Hindu schools in Punjab were turned into arenas for military and weapons' training for the RSS cadres, without any let or hindrance by the authorities.

There had been riots all over Punjab in February 1947. The Unionist-Congress coalition government banned the Muslim League National Guards although their alleged link to the riots was never established. Contrary to the impression generally created and unlike the RSS, it was not a militarized or armed outfit as Jinnah had specifically forbidden any such move.

Master Tara Singh threatened a Sikh uprising and declared an 'Anti-Pakistan Day' on 11th March. In a fiery speech from the steps of the Provincial Legislature he denounced Muslims, Jinnah and Pakistan '*Our motherland is calling for blood and we shall satiate the thirst of our motherland with blood ---- I have sounded the bugle. Finish the Muslim League*'. He then proclaimed the Sikh slogan '*Raj karay ga Khalsa baki rahay na* ko' (the pure Sikh will rule; no one else will survive) and proceeded to hack down the pole bearing the Muslim League flag and tore the banner to shreds with his *kirpan* (dagger) to the shouts of *Pakistan Murdabad* ---- death to Pakistan (*The Punjab Boundary Force and the Problem of Order, August 1947, vol.8*, by Robin Jeffrey, as quoted by French).

Later, there were reports that Sikhs had raped Muslim women in villages near Rawalpindi. In the already highly charged atmosphere it was like throwing a lighted matchstick in a tinderbox. Enraged Muslims attacked the Sikh villages causing mayhem and death. The exact number of casualties is not known but the Sikhs claimed three thousand may have died (*Freedom at Midnight*, pp. 226, 231). The actual number was less than two thousand according to official estimates at the time.

Tara Singh, a convert from Hinduism, was an unbalanced fanatical man prone to violence. In his report on 17th May, the Governor of Punjab Sir Evan Jenkins had said of him, '*It is lamentable that at this juncture the affairs of Punjab should be so largely in the hands of this eccentric old man*' (*Transfer of Power, X*, p. 894). Lord Wavell had described him as 'stupid and emotional' (*Liberty or Death*, p. 331).

Early in June the Sikh leaders held a secret meeting in Nedou's Hotel in Lahore to decide their strategy in case partition was accepted. There Master Tara Singh delivered another of his fiery speeches '*Oh, Sikhs, be ready for self-destruction like the Japanese and the Nazis. Our lands are about to be overrun, our women dishonoured. Arise once more destroy the Mughal invader. Our motherland is calling for blood! We shall slake her thirst with the blood of our enemies*' (*Freedom at Midnight*, p. 231).

In early August the Punjab Criminal Investigation Department (C.I.D) unearthed a plot to blow up special trains bound for Pakistan carrying her share of officials and stores to set up its government. In a separate action an attempt was going to be made on Jinnah's life on 14th August as he drove from the Constituent Assembly to the Governor General's House in Karachi (*Raj*, p.633). L. K. Advani, who later led the mob that destroyed the sixteenth century Babri Mosque in Ayodhya in 1992 and became India's Deputy Prime Minister shortly afterwards, was one of those charged in the plot to assassinate Jinnah.

Mountbatten made much of the fact that he chose to ride in the same car with Jinnah in Karachi on 14th August to allay the latter's fears. In reality, this part of the plot could not have materialized because the RSS men involved had already been arrested and charged by the police in Sind.

The plot was a collaborative effort between the Sikh extremists and the Hindu Fascist RSS. There has always been a measure of affinity between the Sikhs and the Hindus and they were united in their hostility towards the Muslims and Pakistan. When Mountbatten was apprised of the situation, he decided not to order any action against the Sikh leaders on the grounds that it may precipitate a civil war. He left it to the governor who had known for months how the situation had been steadily deteriorating and taken no steps to intervene. Tara Singh's Sikhs were left free to successfully initiate the plan on the night of 11th / 12th August by blowing up the first Pakistan bound train from Delhi near Ferozepur and killing many onboard.

In the absence of any meaningful action by the government the situation had grown out of hand in all the central districts of Punjab by this time. It is evident from this excerpt from a personal account entitled *Becoming a Pakistani*, by Maruf Khwaja whose Muslim family had lived in Ludhiana in East Punjab.

'The Hindu militants (Jan Sangh), trained in all kinds of combat, went into action when the movement for Pakistan began to look like succeeding. I'd seen them in the compound on evenings and Sundays. Their parades weren't very impressive; they made frightful noises with their *gatka* (combat) drills. All local units played a key part in organising and leading the slaughter of Muslims in Hindu-majority areas. ------------

'Meanwhile, back in Ludhiana (in the latter half of July), *Dada* (grandfather) and *Chacha* (uncle) struggled to reach the ancestral home in Gulchaman Gali hoping, praying they'd find the family still there. Instead they came upon a scene of bloody devastation.

'A Hindu-Sikh mob had taken over most of the *gali* (street). Bodies with heads or limbs cut off lay at doorsteps. Congealed blood filled the gutters. Chacha, young, well-built, and a good wrestler, leapt forward when a gun-toting stranger appeared at the doorstep of our old home. The gunshot went off as Chacha grabbed hold of the barrel. Slugs pierced his arm but he succeeded in yanking the weapon out of the intruder's hand. In minutes he and others in the party had beaten the man to a pulp.

'By now other intruders had come out of the houses. Towards the end of the *gali*, Dada's party could see friends and relative desperately waving and shouting at them to join them behind the barricades in the compound of the Naulakhas' *haveli* (large house). Five of them ran the gauntlet of *gandassa* (hatchet) and sword-waving raiders. Three, including Dada and Chacha, made it to the top. The others were hacked to pieces. The raiders couldn't follow the survivors to the gate, for it was well guarded by rifle-bearing retainers of the Naulakha clan. ------------

'Our family lost its ancestral home and, within it, four family members. Of the three women one was blind and couldn't leave the house without a guide. Two were nieces of my grandmother's sister who had stopped off in Ludhiana on their way back to their village.

'We never found out what became of them. They were almost certainly abducted and forced into marriage with their abductors or, worse still, sold off to brothels. *Dadi* (*grandmother*) mourned their loss for years and wept bitterly whenever her sister came visiting. The old man was a distant cousin of my Dada, and a veteran from the days of the First World War. He was deaf in both ears, a legacy of his time at the front with an artillery regiment, which was probably why he never heard the alarm raised when the Jan Sangh marauders came. --------------

'In the end we managed it. The train to Pakistan, guarded by a detachment of the 14th Punjab Regiment, made it to the border past many dramas, seen and unseen, mute and audible. A passenger train from Lyallpur headed the other way bearing Sikh refugees and tell-tale signs of many a gauntlet passed: battle-weary *sardars* ("chief", another name for a Sikh male) hanging on from handrails, the boldest riding the bumpers of the steam-engine itself; swords out of scabbards, polishing cloths, sharpening stones and cutlasses to cut-throat razor sharpness.

'Was it all shown for our benefit? Was it a train or the ghosts of Gulchaman Gali trundling past? Our own train slowed almost to walking pace. We looked for reassurance at the Punjab regiment escort. They smiled nervously, itchy fingers on rifle triggers. The train would move a foot forward then a foot back. What was going on? What were the drivers up to? Were the signalmen in on it? The signals were blood-red, crimson as the gutters of Gulchaman Gali.

'I could read my mother's lips reciting the *Ayat al-Qursi*, the Qu'ranic verse that guarantees delivery from evil. I too began mumbling the prayer. Father and my brother were doing it too. Would there be, any second, an onslaught by survivors of one disaster upon those of another? We won't go to the India we don't know, you won't go to the Pakistan you don't know. Let us fight and die here.

'We did not. The trains passed each other. At midnight on 10 August we crossed the border at Bahawalnagar where the whole town had turned up to greet the first official train to Pakistan. Father leaned out of the window to accept a clay pot of *pulao* and *zarda* (rice dishes), one of *aloo gosht* (meat dish), a cool *surahi* of Rooh Afza (sweet drink) and a garland of the sweetest *motia* (jasmin flowers) I had ever smelled in my life.'

By the end of July serious disturbances involving arson, bombings and stabbings had broken out in Amritsar and Lahore and Sikh *jathas* (warrior bands) had started attacking unsuspecting Muslim villages in the outlying areas. In reporting these to Mountbatten the governor wrote, '*It would be difficult enough to partition within six weeks a country of thirty million people which had been governed as a unit for ninety-three years, even if all concerned were friendly'.*

After this it was Mountbatten's turn to state the incredulous. He wrote to Attlee on 1st August, '*The country as a whole is quiet, with the exception of Punjab, where there have been continued disturbances ----* (because) *the Sikhs have 'ratted' on the undertaking they gave me*' (*Transfer of Power, XII*, pp. 444-46).

Mountbatten had delayed announcement of the Radcliffe Award until after the Independence celebrations were over. He got back to Delhi after participating in Pakistan's Independence Day ceremony at Karachi on 14th August. Rajendra Prasad and Nehru came to see him shortly after midnight and invited him to become the first Governor General of India. He wrote in his report to the Cabinet and the king:

'*The 15th August has certainly turned out to be the most remarkable and inspiring day of my life. ---- some 500 Ambassadors, Princes and the Cabinet then drove in procession ---- Never have such crowds been seen within living memory of anyone ---- Nehru and I decided that the only thing to do was to hoist the flag and fire the salute. ---- This was done amid scenes of the most fantastic rejoicing ---- Close to 3,000 people came to our evening party at Government House and stayed till after two o'clock in the morning*' (*Transfer of Power, XII*, pp. 773- 74).

It was anything but inspiring or a day of rejoicing for the people in Punjab. As Lieutenant General Savory described to his wife, Sikhs were '*going around in organized groups of about 500 strong, burning massacring and looting. Practically no trains are running into Pakistan from Delhi, as too many of them have been held up and looted and the Muslim passengers hacked to pieces ----*'. The Sikh bands or *jathas* were often armed with light machine-guns, hand grenades, Sten guns and mortars. Occasionally they combined to form a force five or six thousand strong (*Eminent Churchillians*, p.116).

'*On 15 August the day of liberation was strangely celebrated in* (Indian) *Punjab. During the afternoon a Sikh mob paraded a number of Muslim women naked through the streets of Amritsar, raped them and then hacked some of them into pieces with kirpans* (daggers) *and burned the others alive' (Autchinleck, by John Connell, London, 1959, p. 906).*

Ian Morrison, correspondent of *The Times,* London, reported from Jullunder on 24th August '*More horrible than anything we saw during the Second World War is the universal comment of experienced officers, British and Indian, on the present slaughter in East Punjab.*

'*The Sikhs are clearing East Punjab of Muslims, butchering hundreds daily, forcing thousands to flee westward, burning Muslim villages and homesteads. This violence has been organised from the highest levels of Sikh leadership, and is being done systematically, sector by sector.*'

The commanding officer of the Second Battalion of the First Gurkhas on the way from Peshawar to Allahabad saw a train that had arrived at Lala Musa in West Punjab from India. It had been ambushed by the Sikhs in Patiala and was filled with two hundred dead Muslims. '*The majority of their wounds had been caused by swords and spear thrusts*'. The victims included '*a small girl aged four or five with both legs hacked off above the knees but still alive; a pregnant woman with her baby ripped out of her womb ---- she died; an old man ---- with six spear wounds and still alive*' (*While Memory Serves*, by Sir Francis Tucker, 1949, p. 437). Inevitably, there was a reaction and thirty-five Sikhs were killed at the Lahore railway station and many others in the city. This was senseless violence that was allowed to go on unchecked because the administration was too cowardly or unconcerned to act.

The Punjab Boundary Force had been set up and became operational on 1st August. Never more than twenty-three thousand strong, it was a neutral body under the command of a British general not answerable to the Indian or Pakistani governments. There were no British troops and only a handful of British senior officers. Its mandate was to intervene in cases of violence, apprehend the culprits and hand these over to the civilian authorities. In the case of East Punjab, where the vast majority of the killings took place, there was virtually no police. Traditionally, Muslims had formed the bulk of the force. These had been disarmed and disbanded even before the country became independent. Despite low morale and insufficient numbers coupled with virtual absence of civil administration in East Punjab, the Boundary Force did make a difference.

This is clear from the diary maintained by Brigadier (then Captain) Namazi of the 2nd Behar Regiment that formed a part of the Force and was stationed at Jullunder in East Punjab. It was composed of mostly low-caste Hindus from Behar Province. Namazi had broken up his men into small teams each with a jeep and positioned each of them in a cluster of villages. He noted that the attitude of the Hindu District Magistrate was obstructionist and uncooperative from the start. Worse still, the army units had split along communal lines and the British officers abstained from taking part in any proceedings.

In one instance, which is typical of what was happening all over East Punjab on a daily basis, a Sikh *jatha* attacked the village of Chak Zinda near Maqsoodpur, close to the Grand Trunk Road, on the morning of 24th August. The local police did not intervene nor did they inform the army authorities in time. By the time Namazi arrived four hours later, there were no Muslims to be found. At the first sight of the Sikhs they had tried to run away and hide. There were bloodied corpses lying all over the nearby fields. The Sikhs were still busy rummaging through the houses collecting whatever they could find. On seeing the armed soldiers they took flight. The few survivors that could be found were taken to Maqsoodpur.

The same pattern of murder, mayhem and looting was repeated unchecked and with impunity in all the villages in the province where Muslims had lived. There were more than five thousand such undefended villages. The hellish nightmare lasted for three months and only came to an end after the last Muslim had either been killed or expelled from Indian Punjab. What was reported in the the press at the time was only a very small part of it. The countryside was not safe for anyone to walk about unless escorted by a contingent of the army. What was published was mostly what could be gleaned from the safety of hotel lobbies and that too only in the major cities. The enormity and full extent of the crime became apparent much later.

Other passages from Captain Namazi's diary read: '*On the morning of 21st August we flew over the city and saw its wretched plight. It was deserted, desolate and lifeless. There were at least thirty fires raging. A number of surrounding villages were also burning. Some people were seen collecting the dead; others were fleeing to the army cantonment to seek refuge. A marauding band of Sikhs was sighted with drawn swords shining against the morning sun. The memory of such sights continues to haunt me.*

'*Later that day I was ordered to take my platoon to the spots where troubles had been sighted. The Sikh pilot, Captain Bhatia, was reluctant to give the locations accurately. Even so I managed to reach some of these. It was awful. There were corpses strewn all over, including a man in his eighties with his neck almost completely severed. There was a small band of frightened survivors, mostly women and children who came out of some hiding places. One of them asked, "Is God dead? Why are we being massacred so mercilessly? In the name of humanity will no one protect us"?*

'On the 22nd the railway station was attacked. Captain Ray had been assigned to protect it with his platoon. He had not been present at the time of the attack and his JCO failed to take action. I was ordered to take over. It was terrible. Nearly four hours had passed and the victims were still lying there in pools of blood and covered with flies. Three of them were still alive but only barely. No one tended to them. Two Sikh magistrates were there along with a police officer. When I asked them why the wounded had not been evacuated, they said there was no transport. I put them in my truck and had the place cleaned up. There were no people, not even the railway staff. The railway station of this leading city of Punjab had been turned into a human slaughterhouse.

'The next day, in my absence, the station was again attacked killing more Muslims who had tried to take refuge there. The Hindu Risaldar belonging to the 18th Cavalry did not permit his troops to intervene. I saw a woman with sword wounds and her eight-year old daughter bleeding from a deep cut in her skull. It was a miracle that she was still alive. It is at times like these that one wonders if civilization or humanity has any meaning left? What kind of a man would attack a defenceless child in such a cruel fashion?

'It did not stop at that. At Ludhiana railway station they dragged a Muslim army officer and his wife from the train, stripped the wife naked and raped her repeatedly on the platform and then butchered her in front of a watching crowd. Later, they killed the army officer as well.

'A few days later (24th August), *Pundit Jawaharlal Nehru, India's Prime Minister was in Jullunder. A small crowd gathered at Empress Gardens to see him. He made an impromptu speech. I happened to be there and heard him myself. Mostly, he counseled peace and restoration of law and order. There were references to Punjab's glorious past, examples of troubles in other countries like China and promises of a glorious future for India. It was out of place and beyond the scope of understanding of the crowd. They started to interrupt and heckle which made him very angry and he threatened the use of force. Someone said bad things were happening in Pakistan also. He replied that he will ask them to stop it and*

if they did not, he will order the army to march into Pakistan. This drew applause from the crowd after which he sat in his latest model Packard car and drove away'.

If Nehru could send the army to restore order in Pakistan, why could he not do the same in India itself? The killing, burning and looting continued unabated. A group of local Muslim elders called on him to explain their plight and seek some protection from the marauding Sikhs. He told them that their safety only lay in migrating to Pakistan. At about the same time, India's Minister for the Interior, Vallabhbhai Patel had also visited Jullunder which had now become the capital of East Punjab. He bluntly told the same delegation that he could do very little to help and advised them to move out and make room for the refugees expected from Pakistan (personal information). This was not even a week into independence and he had already decided on an exchange of population. In their heart of hearts they were all communalists, some more bigoted than others. While hundreds of thousands of Muslims, who were now Indian citizens, were being mercilessly slaughtered in East Punjab, Gandhi announced his intentions to go and park himself in Lahore because he had learnt that some Hindus had been killed there. Words are cheap but when it came to the crunch, the only lives that mattered were those of the Hindus.

It was easy for Patel and Nehru to tell the Muslims to go to Pakistan. There were no trains or buses running. The roads were completely unsafe. There was no escort to protect them from the armed Sikh *jathas*. In the end, all they could do was to take refuge with other Muslim communities that had not been attacked and devastated thus far. Soon these places were over-run with refugees. There were some villages inhabited by Pathans to the west of Jullunder City called *Bastis*. While some Muslims took shelter in the military cantonment, others escaped to the *Bastis*. The Sikhs, knowing there would a price to pay if they attacked the Pathans, had left them alone. Almost overnight the population in the *Bastis* swelled to two or three times its original size. While there was some protection, there was not much food to go around and no facilities or medicines to treat the wounded. People who lived in villages where there were no similar safe havens nearby were doomed.

The refugees had witnessed horrible barbarity and carnage and were deeply traumatized. They could not sleep at night and would wake up from nightmares with terrifying screams. It kept everyone awake most of the night. Suddenly, someone would start shouting hysterically '*Aa Gaye, voh aa gaye*' (they are coming, they are coming) and people would get up and rush to pick up whatever they could to defend themselves.

Soon the *Bastis* too were no longer safe. The Boundary Force was disbanded on 1st September amid accusations from the Hindus and Sikhs that it was partial to the Muslims. If providing a modicum of protection against wholesale slaughter can be classified as being partial then there was perhaps some truth to it. The decision was utterly incomprehensible. However ineffective it might have been, the Force had made a difference. This became evident when compared with the situation in the Sikh States of East Punjab that were outside the jurisdiction of the Force. The scale and ferocity of the massacres in Patiala, Faridkot and Kapoorthala was infinitely greater than what had taken place in the rest of Punjab so far. It became all the same after the Boundary Force was disbanded. The Sikh *jathas*, now joined by soldiers with rifles and machineguns from the Sikh States, were given a completely free run of the province.

The makeshift refugee camp in the Cantonment was soon overflowing. There was hardly any food and no shelter, sanitation or medical care. All the local authorities were interested in was to somehow get the refugees out of the camp and out of India any way and as fast as they could. They started packing them into any trains they could lay their hands on and sending them to Lahore. The main road and rail routes passed through Amritsar, the holy city of the Sikhs that had been turned into a horrible killing ground. Any train or bus without police or army escort was stopped and all Muslim passengers systematically butchered. The same happened with escorted transports if the troops happened to be Hindus or Sikhs who simply stepped aside.

What happened to these trains at Amritsar is described by D. F. Karaka, a well-known Parsi journalist from Bombay who had the distinction of being the first Indian to become President of Oxford Union. He had visited Amritsar in mid-September at the invitation of a British general serving in the Indian Army and recorded what he had witnessed there in his autobiography, '*Then Came Hazrat Ali*'. An excerpt from the book is reproduced (pp. 259- 60):

The railway tracks were tampered with and the train was forcibly re-routed to a siding near Khalsa (Sikh) *College. Here a large mob of Sikhs lying in hiding in some broken-down railway quarters, rushed out to ambush and butcher the people in the train. The attack lasted three quarters of an hour.*

I asked, 'But who was in the train'?

'Refugees', the colonel replied, 'just refugees ---- men, women, children. Three thousand refugees. The mob attacking the train was five thousand strong. And the mob was armed'

'Armed'? I looked surprised.' Only the army had the right to be armed'.

'They carried bhalas (short spears) *and kirpans* (swords)'. *These were primitive weapons common in this area.*

'But is no license required for carrying lethal weapons'? The colonel explained that Sikhs were allowed to carry kirpans on religious grounds. Bhalas are short spears, tied to a long pole.

'By now we had reached the railway station where the train was being guarded by the army. A horrible smell exuded from the platform. The sentries on duty were wearing gauze pads as masks for the nose and mouth.

'We walked along the platform with the colonel leading the way. Two armed guards flanked us on either side, their steel bayonets glistening in the morning sun. A bit unnecessary I thought when I could see no one except three solitary individuals huddled together in the middle of the platform.

'We walked in slow step as at a funeral so that I could look into each compartment. The train was still full, but everyone in it was a corpse. Corpses were sitting close each other. Men and women were resting their heads on the shoulders of the person next to them, not because they were tired or sleeping; they were dead.

'I went closer to the compartments to look. The dead sat in different poses, their mouths invariably open. The lobes of the ears of the women and the tips of their noses had been sharply sliced off. This was in order to get more easily to the nose and ear rings.

'It was a horrible sight. Blood dripped from the carriages on to the platform. In the train, as the men and women sat huddled, their garments were soaked with blood. Some had their heads cracked open exposing the insides of their skulls. Children were not spared. One male child had its

stomach ripped open; the intestines showing. There was no distinction made between man, woman and child. Out of three thousand passengers only the three whom I saw sitting on the platform, had escaped death. It was a trio of a man, a woman and a child, the three they forgot to kill.

'All this happened the day I arrived in Amritsar. I would not have believed the story of trainful of erect corpses if I had not seen the sight myself. The general had not exaggerated.'

The attack must have taken some planning and coordination. It takes time to collect five thousand men and provide them with weapons. The train could not have been re-routed and positioned without prior arrangement with the railway authorities. Apart from time, all this must have taken considerable effort and cooperation on the part of many individuals and officials. The attack lasted for forty-five minutes. What were the Indian Army and the civil administration of Amritsar doing in all this time? The refugee trains were supposed to carry troops for protection. What were they doing when the killing started? It was not the only attack of its kind. The same thing happened to train after train, not only in Amritsar but at a dozen other railway stations all over East Punjab over a period of three months. The fact is that the atrocities were planned and carried out with the full knowledge and cooperation of the local authorities.

What happened to people in the buses and trucks will be apparent from the personal experience of Dr. Bashir M. Ulvi, an eminent plastic surgeon now living in the United States. He was eight years old at the time of Partition living in Mohalla Saidan in Jullunder City. When the troubles started the family escaped to the refugee camp in the Cantonment. In October his uncle, a Police Inspector in Lahore, hired a bus to bring all of them to Lahore. They joined other trucks and buses to form a convoy. As it entered Amritsar, the Hindu driver pulled over to the side of the road and disappeared into the streets. Soon, a large group of Sikhs surrounded the bus and started dragging people out one by one and stabbing them with their *kirpans* regardless of their age or sex.

Ulvi, along with four other children, hid under the seats until the Sikhs had finished killing and looting the bus. It was dark when they crawled out and made their way to a nearby house. When they told the Hindu woman who opened the door what had happened, she hid them under a pile of firewood and some old clothing. When her husband came to know, they could hear him arguing that she should not have done this and it was best to hand the children over to the Sikhs but fortunately for them the wife remained firm. The next day, they were returned to the refugee camp disguised as Hindus and eventually made their way to Pakistan. Ulvi knows that all the remaining members of his family members were killed, except for his mother Sultan Bibi and sister Fatima who had been five at the time. The two remain unaccounted for. All his efforts to find them have met with little success so far but he still keeps looking. It is by no means an isolated or rare case. An estimated seventy thousand women that were abducted in the holocaust have not been re-united with their families.

East Punjab had been turned into a picture of Dante's Hell. Village after Muslim village had been burnt to the ground and inhabitants struck down in the cruelest ways imaginable. Pregnant women had their bellies ripped open; others had their breasts sliced off. Many jumped into wells and killed themselves rather than fall into the hands of the murdering Sikhs. Babies were cut in half or had their skulls smashed before throwing them back to their dying mothers. Children were burnt alive in pits. The victims may have belonged to a different religion but like the rest they too had become citizens of free and professedly secular India. Yet, the State not only failed to protect them but in many cases actively facilitated the bloodlust. There were numerous cases all over the province in which local officials accompanied the bands of killers to facilitate their grisly work.

Pakistan called for an emergency Commonwealth Conference to be held to discuss the situation created by the upheaval. Mountbatten claimed that 'Pakistan's Prime Minister Liaquat Ali Khan wanted to establish the culpability of the Sikhs before the world'. On his advice the British Cabinet turned down the request with Attlee commenting that 'it was futile' (*Eminent Churchillians*, p. 124).

Almost all of the British and Indian historians with few exceptions have treated the situation in Punjab as a whole in blanket fashion and not differentiated between events on each side of the border. This is highly misleading. There is no doubt that atrocities were perpetrated on both the sides but the intent and scale involved in the two was vastly different. What was taking place in East Punjab was a deliberate and ferocious campaign of mass extermination and expulsion with official connivance and patronage. There were large bodies of organized and armed men that systematically murdered, pillaged and burnt with impunity wherever Muslims could be found. There was no attempt at intervention by the police or the army. In many cases these agencies were directly or indirectly complicit in the crimes. It was the same all over the province, in rural areas as well as in the towns and cities. It lasted unchecked for months until there were no Muslims left in the province.

The situation in West Punjab was very different. Mostly, what happened there was a reaction to the atrocities committed in East Punjab. Apart from one or two places like Lahore and Sheikhupura, there were no cases of organized attacks on communities. The killings, abductions and other acts of violence were by and large sporadic and carried out either by solitary individuals or very small groups. There were no large organized marauding bands like the Sikh *jathas* operating in West Punjab. The province had an effective police force and a working administration. Unlike in East Punjab, it had brought the situation almost completely under control within a couple of weeks after independence. The Hindus and Sikhs were fearful of reprisals especially with the arrival of the highly traumatized refugees and felt unsafe because of events across the border. Since they owned almost all of the trucks, buses and cars in the province, it was relatively easy for them to make the journey to India through any route and time of their choosing. Those who were obliged to travel on foot were seldom molested, except in instances when their path happened to cross that of the incoming traumatized and angry Muslim refugees.

As someone who had witnessed the carnage on both the sides first hand, the writer can testify that there was no comparison between the two. The total number of Muslims killed in East Punjab and Jammu was at least thirty times more than the number of Hindu and Sikh casualties in West Punjab. It is a fact that no records were kept in East Punjab, largely because the police had ceased to function there but this was not the case in Pakistan. It was easy to verify the actual number of casualties from the police diaries and district records. Even if these might not have been always totally accurate and reliable, the errors and omissions would not be significant in the context as a whole.

There is no record and no agreement on the total number that perished in the holocaust. Mountbatten said in London in a speech in November 1947 that 'only' one hundred thousand had been killed. Early historians like Moon and Ziegler similarly deluded, put the figure at two hundred thousand. It was revised drastically as the facts gradually became apparent. The Governor of West Punjab, Sir Francis Mudie thought half a million may have died in East Punjab. The British High Commissioner in Karachi Sir Graffy-Smith put the figure at eight hundred thousand. Lieutenant Colonel Philip Mitchison of the Punjab Boundary Force was convinced that the total was more like one million (*End of Empire*, by

Brian Lapping, pp. 135- 6). This was also the figure given by General Ismay to Churchill's Private Secretary, Anthony Montague Browne. Conservative elder statesman Rab Butler agreed (*Eminent Churchillians*, p. 131). Most authorities in Pakistan estimated that more than a million had perished.

The vast majority of refugees came to Pakistan on foot or by ox-carts in large groups known as *kafilas*, sometimes with military escort that was both inadequate and ineffective. The lines of carts and people on the move were endless, often stretching twenty-five miles or more. They travelled day and night, constantly harassed by the Sikh *jathas* as long as they were in India. To add to their misery, there were devastating floods in both the Ravi and Beas Rivers in late September and early October. Parts of the Grand Trunk Road were under ten feet of rushing water that swept away many refugees, their animals and carts. Others survived by climbing into trees. What little food they had was gone and they ate leaves and grass until they got to Pakistan.

People took the nearest and quickest route to Pakistan. All the refugees from Jammu and Gurdaspur made their way to Sialkot and Gujarat. Those from south of the Sutlej crossed into Kasur or Bahawalnagar. The bulk of them (including the author's family) from the central districts of Hoshiarpur, Ludhiana, Jullunder, Amritsar and the surrounding areas had to run the gauntlet along the Grand Trunk Road, past the main killing fields in Amritsar.

Given the vicious nature and extent of the calamity, it is incredible that the Congress leaders should have all along insisted that Hindus, Sikhs and Muslims were all one nation. The hatred witnessed was visceral and deep rooted. It was not a clash resulting from some localized conflict of interest or momentary aberration but a planned systematic campaign of mass extermination and expulsion that lasted until there was no Muslim left and that spared no one, regardless of age or sex. Members of a cohesive nation do not go on rampages and orgies of slaughter and mayhem against their own. It is not possible that Gandhi, Nehru, Patel and the others could not have known the feelings of the various communities towards each other. They kept up the pretence simply as a ploy to keep the Muslims from having a separate homeland of their own. Had they succeeded, the situation could well have been much worse in the long run.

A NEW BEGINNING

A huge refugee camp had been set up at the Walton Airfield east of Lahore. The material and administrative resources of the province were totally inadequate to provide for the huge numbers. All that could be done for the refugees in the early stages was to somehow keep them fed. The citizens of Lahore, as indeed in the other places, were incredibly generous. They donated food, clothing, medicines and shelter to an extent much greater than most of them could afford. All day and night there were lines of horse-drawn carts (*rehras*) laden with supplies, mostly baked *rotis* and rice rushing to the camp.

All the educational institutions in Punjab were closed in July and August for the summer holidays. To make up for the shortage of qualified personnel for dealing with the influx of refugees young men from colleges in Pakistan were invited to join the effort. They volunteered in their droves. One of these, Abdul Waheed Rathore, has recounted his experience as paraphrased below:

'I was vacationing in Murree when I received the call from the office of Punjab University Students Federation to return to Lahore for work with the refugees. About seven hundred of us were mustered there and divided into groups for work at different places. I was paired with my friend Zulfiqar Ali Khan who later became a police officer, to the work at Wagah receiving and providing first aid to the refugees as they came across the border. There was a quick course by a health officer named Musa in how to administer cholera and typhoid injections and tend to the wounded.

'Wagah is eighteen or nineteen miles from Lahore. Each time a *kafilah* (caravan) of refugees passed Amritsar in India, on average twice a week, we would be notified. It gave us about six or seven hours to get to the border. There was no public transport of any kind, only an old bicycle between the two of us. One of us sat on the steel bar in front while the other pedalled. It was hard going and we would switch roles every few miles when it became too painful. There was just a small police and army check post at the border. As the refugees came in we would administer the two injections, put a mark on the shirt and move them on to a holding area. There they would be given some food and clothing and directed to the refugee camp at the Walton Airfield if they had no specific destination of their own with relatives or friends. This went on non-stop sometime for days on end. Then there would be a lull before another *kafilah* arrived.

'The *kafilas* were generally composed of families from the same area. They came mostly on foot, some in ox-carts and a few on the backs of water buffalos. Every effort was made to keep them together and move them to the same place. From Wagah most of them trekked past Shalimar Gardens and across the River Ravi to Shaikhupura, Gujranawala and Lyallpur (now Faisalabad). Others went south on Ferozepur Road to Kasur, Montgomery (now Sahiwal), Multan and places in between.

'I can't even begin to describe the condition most of them were in, having suffered so much. They had been through hell, looking disoriented and there was constant fear in their eyes. Some of them had horrible festering wounds on the hands, arms and other parts of the body, cuts from swords and spears. Many succumbed to these and we had to bury them. A long time has passed since then and I am eighty-two years old but the picture is still just as fresh and vivid in my mind. They had seen so many of their loved ones butchered and women gang-raped by the Sikhs before their very eyes.

It happened to the two daughters of a man that I only remember as Boota. Overcome, he tried to kill himself along with the daughters by standing in front of an on-coming train. At the last minute he changed his mind and pushed the daughters away from the railway track and died alone. The two girls were cared for and brought up by the well-known politician, Raja Ghazanfar Ali Khan and Rabia Qari, Secretary of the Lahore High Court Bar Association. If you want to learn more about such things you should read books by Nasim Hijazi and Sa'adat Hasan Minto.

'More than one hundred thousand Muslim women had been abducted by mostly the Sikhs in East Punjab. A Pakistan army team under Major Tahir Husain was responsible for following up reported cases of abductions and made frequent trips to remote villages in India under armed escort. Ultimately only about half of these unfortunate ladies could be recovered; the fate of the rest remains unknown.

'After a few weeks the student groups rotated duties and I joined up with people bringing food to the refugees. It was a miracle that we didn't run short of supplies. The people of Lahore were extremely generous and gave away whatever they could spare and then some. They donated flour, rice, quilts, clothing as well as money. Mian Amir-uddin, the mayor worked tirelessly. Then there was Mian Saeed and his saintly wife Khaalaq Noor and so many others who had made it their life's mission to help the refugees. It seemed everyone in Lahore had the same mission. We delivered tons of cooked *chapattis* and rice with chickpeas to the refugees every day for four months.

'They kept coming, ten million of them by train, army trucks and on foot until December when the flow finally stopped. Some of the last to arrive were the tough Mayo (*Raangar*) tribesmen from Karnal and Ruhtak districts. With their shot guns and antiquated hunting rifles they had been fighting running battles with the Indian army that had been trying to evict them for more than two months. All of the men had long beards, having had no time to shave, but they had suffered relatively few casualties. Their fierce reputation and weapons had kept the marauding Sikhs at a distance. The last *kafila* to arrive was from Gurgaon (south of Delhi) in late November.'

In fact, this was almost all you saw on the roads in Lahore. Hindus and Sikhs, who had owned all the cars, trucks and buses, had taken these with them to India. Apart from the *tongas* (horse-drawn carriages) and a few government operated 'Omnibuses' there was no other transport. The total number of cars in the entire city at the time was probably less than half a dozen. All the main shops, banks, commercial offices, printing presses, restaurants, cinemas, clubs, even most of the schools, colleges and other public places were closed, their non-Muslim owners and operators having departed for India. The usually bustling Anarakali and The Mall wore a deserted look.

It was a very depressing picture and a stark reminder of the economic depth and deprivation to which Muslims who had ruled Punjab for nearly a thousand years, had descended in a very short period of time. It also painted the picture of what it would have been like for the Muslims of Punjab had there been no Pakistan. Yet, almost inexplicably, the people had not lost hope. There was a sense that it was a new beginning, they were going to make it and better days would be here soon.

The camp at Walton was soon overflowing with the refugees. No one knew the exact number and more arrived every day. In the unhygienic and unsanitary conditions that prevailed, inevitably, diseases like cholera and dysentery broke out, adding to all the other misery. It was urgent that people should move out as soon as possible. Anyone who had a relative or friend in any village, town or city of the province went there. Invariably they were welcomed with open arms and looked after until they could stand on their own feet. The generosity, compassion and hospitality shown by the common people have left an indelible mark on all those who experienced it. The bulk of the refugees were told to move to areas vacated by Hindus and Sikhs mainly in and around Lahore, Sheikhupura, Gujranwala, Lyallpur (Faisalabad), Montgomery (Sahiwal), Multan and Sialkot.

All the camps were emptied and closed down within a few months and resettlement of refugees was well under way. It was an incredible feat considering there were upwards of seven million refugees processed into West Punjab alone. There were a number of factors that made it possible. Most of it had to do with the indomitable spirit of the people, local as well as the refugees. The latter were determined to make it on their own as quickly as possible and the former were always willing to accommodate and lend a helping hand wherever they could. They were also fortunate in finding opportunities in the places vacated by the migrating Hindus and Sikhs. Not all the officials charged with the custody of the evacuee properties were scrupulously diligent and honest. Some took undue advantage to enrich themselves and their own in the process. Despite this, the end result was satisfactory beyond most expectations.

The worst part of the tragedy for the survivors was the memory of the horrors and atrocities and of the loved ones who had been lost. It haunted them for the rest of their lives. The pain was dulled with time but it never left them completely. The physical wounds healed but the emotional and psychological trauma they had endured scarred them forever. Many suffered recurring nightmares that would not go away; others went into deep depression and never recovered. They almost never laughed or smiled and had lost the ability to be happy ever again. Those who had experienced or witnessed this hell first hand refused to talk, even less write about it. It took the writer fifty years before he could bring himself to put down his recollections, as an act of catharsis, in *The Pathans of Jullunder* (1996).

There are memories that still continue to haunt ---- of dead bodies lying around in blood, mouths open and flies buzzing all over, mutilated women driven insane, screaming ---- men, women and children of all ages with untreated festering wounds; infants dying in your arms who had no one left alive to claim them. Some of the things, sixty years on, are still too difficult to unburden. Each night when the alarm went up I, only thirteen at the time, would pick up the shotgun and rush to the roof to take up position next to my father. As we lay there in the stillness of the dark night waiting for the attack to materialize, he would remind me that if he died first not to use up all of the cartridges but save at least one each for my mother and sisters to make sure they would not fall into the hands of the Sikhs alive. Try as one might, it is impossible to get rid of the image from the mind of what might have happened had we been overrun. Only Providence saved us from the tragic fate that befell a million others whose luck had run out.

There were refugees from other parts of India as well. Those from Behar, Assam and adjoining areas went to East Pakistan. The rest from Delhi, UP, Kathiawar, Bombay, Hyderabad, etc. made their way to Sind and Karachi by train and ship. Most of them had not been persecuted and pushed out in the same way as in East Punjab. They chose to come to Pakistan because they wanted to make a new beginning in a free country they could call their own. The process lasted for a few years after 1947 until the Indian Government fearing loss of educated and trained manpower put an end to it.

The process of resettling these latter refugees was not as organized as that in Punjab. Many of them remained housed in old army barracks and shanty towns in Karachi for ten years, until General Ayub Khan took over power in 1958. One of his first actions was to order the construction of a new town at Korangi. It was completed on an emergency basis, incredibly, within about three months and all the refugees from India were able to move into their new homes. It only goes to show what can be done when the will is there.

The rest of the refugees were mostly settled on lands and in houses vacated by the departing Hindus and Sikhs on a temporary custodial basis. It took more than ten years to finalise an agreement with India on the exchange of evacuee properties. Probably, the Indians had lingering hopes in all this time that Pakistan would collapse and rejoin them before long, making the exercise unnecessary. The agreement was restricted to areas where people had no option but to leave for reasons of safety and security, primarily in Punjab. In these cases, the respective governments provided copies of the Revenue and Municipal Records to verify the claims of refugees. Based on these, they were awarded ownership rights to comparable properties abandoned by the Hindus and Sikhs in Pakistan.

The agreement did not apply to people who were not obliged to migrate to Pakistan but did so voluntarily from other parts of India such as Behar,

U.P, Hyderabad, etc. The Indian government did not accept them as bona fide refugees and as such declined to provide the relevant records for verification of their claims. In their cases, the applicants were asked to provide any other proof of ownership of property they had abandoned in India. In the absence of any documentary corroboration, even evidence from two or more reliable witnesses was deemed as proof. The facility was abused by unscrupulous elements in some cases and became a source of fraud and corruption. There were allegations that false claims had been made and in other cases the individuals concerned had not abandoned the properties they held in India while claiming compensation in lieu in Pakistan.

The country faced enormous difficulties in those early days. A quarter of West Pakistan's population was composed of displaced and dispossessed people. Resettling some nine million refugees in all can be a daunting task even for the most prosperous of nations. This was only one of the scores of such problems that the country faced ---- a country that had no functioning government, only a handful of trained bureaucrats and no money in its coffers. There were no offices, furniture, telephones, not even paper and ink for the government in Karachi. The first make-shift offices started functioning under tents. Wooden crates and empty soap boxes served as furniture and thorns of acacia trees were used to pin together papers.

Only an insignificant portion of the agreed share of government assets was ever delivered to Pakistan. Her agreed share of the government of India funds was withheld for no reason. Government officials had to go without pay for the first few months and later took a twenty per cent pay cut to tide over the difficulties.

It was very difficult to get the economy going. There was hardly any industry. The industrialized districts had been sliced off and given to India both in Punjab and Bengal. The total number of workers employed in industry in Pakistan, a country of 70 million people, did not exceed twenty-six thousand according to the cover story published in *Life Magazine* on 5th January 1948. The total length of railways in an area of 370,000 square miles was only 7,260 miles and that of paved roads only 9,575 miles.

All the commerce had been in the hands of Hindus. When they left, all the know-how and capital went with them. They also took away all the gold bullion, jewels and liquid assets. Initially, the only trade had been with

India, mostly exports of raw materials in exchange for manufactured goods. The Indians would not return the train bogeys or would exchange these with old and decrepit rolling stock. The coal for railway engines and power generation had to be imported from India and the latter charged three times the going price for it. In 1949 the Indian rupee was devalued along with the pound sterling. Pakistan decided not to follow suit. India refused to accept the value of the Pakistan rupee and trade between the two countries came to a virtual stop.

Whatever the motives that lay at the back of India's actions, these only helped to strengthen the resolve in Pakistan to succeed. Every new obstacle was viewed as a challenge to be overcome. It was by no means easy nor was it a smooth road to success. There were mistakes, hardships, difficulties even disappointments but remarkably never any second thoughts. The determination to make things work was contagious. There was pride at every small or big achievement. It was this indomitable spirit that helped the country pull through and make a go of it in those dark and difficult days.

HISTORY'S VERDICT

What remains to be examined is if the monumental and tragic loss of life and disruption might have been avoided or at least minimized. There was a general consensus even among the British at the time, even if only admitted in private that the whole affair had been grossly mismanaged. Churchill warned of it in Parliament: '*Let us not add --- by shameful flight, by a premature hurried scuttle --- to the pangs of sorrow so many of us feel, the taint and smear of shame*'. At a meeting of the Imperial General Staff on 3rd October 1947, Field Marshal Montgomery recorded about Mountbatten's performance, '*He's made a mess of things. I'll write and tell him*' (*Eminent Churchillians*, p. 109-10). His own Chief of Staff General Ismay noted that 'Mountbatten had failed to show that quintessential viceregal quality ---- impartiality' (*Raj*, p. 637). Rab Butler a senior Conservative Party leader noted Mountbatten's '*conduct in India not good. Took sides. Anti-Muslim / pro-Hindu. Ten million displaced and one million killed: his fault. Didn't foresee and take precautions, but in history books his winding up of India looks O.K.*' (*Dixon Papers*, as quoted by Roberts, p. 110). When Mountbatten offered to nominate him for an award, the Commander-in-Chief Field Marshal Auchinleck turned him down saying that he would take nothing for what had been '*the most painful and disgraceful episode of my career*'. He also added the viceroy had made '*a mess of things*' (*Raj*, p. 638).

Nonetheless, Mountbatten returned to a hero's welcome in Britain in 1948. Anthony Eden threw a grand party in his honour. '*When Mountbatten saw Winston* (Churchill) *he headed toward him with open arms and a warm smile on his face. "Dickie stand there!" Churchill shouted, pointing a paralyzing finger at the admiral's jacket, instantly bringing the taller man to a halt. "What you did in India was like whipping your riding crop across my face". The noisy room had fallen so silent that Churchill's stentorian voice could be clearly heard by every ear in Westminster. The older man turned on his heel and strode out of the room never speaking again to Mountbatten for seven years* (*Shameful Flight*, p. 147).

While Mountbatten had been manifestly inept and guilty, the entire blame cannot be put on his shoulders. He had appeared on the scene when most of the damage had already been done. The one thing that had become clear after the Congress' Quit India Movement was that the British will not be able to hold on to India for much longer. Yet, Churchill refused to face up to the reality and valuable time was lost. Later, when Labour came to power, they too wasted precious time pursuing fruitless negotiations whose outcome was a foregone conclusion. All the warnings of impending disaster by Wavell went unheeded. Suddenly, when the reality hit home with the mutiny in the Indian Navy and growing discontent among the army units, the Cabinet got cold feet and decided to cut and run, in complete disregard of the consequences to the people of India.

It need never have happened in this way. After the decision had been made to leave India and the parties involved had failed to agree on a solution, the British Government ought to have taken matters in its own hands and devolved power according to a plan that it considered most workable. This is precisely what Ramsay MacDonald had done after the parties had failed to reach an agreement at the Round Table Conference. The scheme should have been implemented and made to work for a suitable period of time under British supervision and control. Once it was up and running only then they should have made a phased withdrawal. The excuse often made is that there were not enough British troops available to keep the peace. This was not true. According to Churchill himself there were three or four times more British troops stationed in tiny Palestine at the time than in the whole of the sub-continent.

What prevented the British from implementing a solution of this kind at first was their over-riding wish that somehow India would remain united. Later when partition had been rendered inevitable, they made things far worse than they need have been by pandering to the Indian National Congress in the expectation that in so doing it will help to protect Britain's residual interests in the sub-continent. It led to the exacerbation of the Sikh problem in Punjab and created immense difficulties for the Muslims in both the wings of Pakistan. Lastly, the wholesale slaughter in Punjab could have been minimized to a very great extent by taking resolute action against the Sikh activists in time. There was a compelling need to maintain a larger military presence in the area much earlier. Not only was it ignored but the token Boundary Force that was put in place was also disbanded at a time when it was needed the most, for entirely the wrong reasons.

The British Cabinet, having decided to get out of India, left it all in the hands of Mountbatten, a shallow publicity hungry man without too many scruples and having very questionable administrative capability and even less political experience. There was no close scrutiny or oversight of his actions. What happened in India was no longer of much concern to either the Cabinet or the Parliament. They had virtually washed their hands of all responsibility and later tried to pass it off to the British public and the world as a grand and munificent achievement.

The British are by no means the only ones to be blamed. The Government of India bears full responsibility for the unconscionable atrocities. For all intents and purposes Congress had direct control over all the ministries in Delhi long before the official transfer of power. The communal situation as it developed was fully within its knowledge. There is no evidence that it took any meaningful steps to avert the disaster. The disarming and disbanding of the police forces in East Punjab simply because these had been staffed mostly by Muslims, was a senseless act that left the government with a much weakened instrument for collecting information and enforcing the law. The policemen might have been Muslim but they had become Indian citizens and should not have been treated as enemies by the government.

The genocide in the Sikh States in particular was planned and executed by the states' armies that had come under India's operational control on 15th August. As such she bore full legal and moral responsibility for all their actions after this date. Even after killing and mayhem had engulfed the entire province the Government in Delhi remained inactive and made no visible effort to try and put an end to the atrocities. The army was there but it made no attempt to intervene or protect the people. This would certainly not have been the case if it had been Hindus at the receiving end. The systematic butchery was ignored and treated with little concern simply because the victims were Muslims. These people had become citizens of India and as such had the right to expect protection of their lives and property. When it failed to make the effort, in effect, the Indian Government indirectly became an accomplice in perpetrating the genocide.

Some writers have tried to deflect the criticism by claiming that atrocities were being committed on both sides. This is untenable; one does not justify the other. The plain fact is that Indian citizens within India were being systematically killed, mutilated and driven out of their homes in huge numbers. It went on unchecked for more than three months. The British may have been short of troops but this was certainly not the case with the Indian Army. Given the number of Indian troops in the cantonments in East Punjab, the situation could and should have been brought under control in less than ten days provided there had been the will to take some resolute action. If the situation was brought more or less under control in Pakistan within a fortnight, despite infinitely greater difficulties, it should have been possible to do it sooner in India.

It may or may not have been possible to stop the movement of refugees but that is not the point. It is that an effort was not made to stop the butchery. One can only conclude that it was deliberate policy to burden the fledgling State of Pakistan with the huge number of refugees before it had time to stand on its feet. The loss of capital, skilled manpower, administrative and managerial talent resulting from the exodus of Hindus and Sikhs further added to her difficulties and made the situation much worse. It was a calculated move to bring about an early collapse of the Muslim State. The British may not have been complicit in it but the manner in which the partition and transfer of power had been managed certainly made it look as if this was the case.

This passage from the unpublished memoirs of Arthur Williams, a British civil servant who was the District Magistrate in Lahore at the time of Partition, seems an appropriate epitaph to mark the end of British rule in India:

'*The Labour Government no doubt regarded the quitting of India as an act of great statesmanship. Others may have shared this view; it all depends upon one's standpoint and perspective. To one Punjab officer at least it appeared as an act of betrayal and even cowardice; one does not leave in the lurch and to bloody slaughter people who had trusted in one's ability to protect them. Much fine talk is made of the recognition of rights of self-determination and of the evils of autocratic and alien rule, but when responsibility for life and welfare have been assumed and exercised over a long period of years it is futile and irrelevant to harp on the rights and wrongs of that assumption and the responsibilities become a trust not to be discarded unless there is a successor at least as well able to maintain it. In India there was a gross abdication of trust and duties; a wholly arbitrary date had been set for the transfer of power ---- an act in itself inviting for violence for its seizure; much deference was paid to the wishes and behests of the Hindu Congress; and the Muslims were left to feel that they were regarded at best as a nuisance, and should fend for themselves ----*' (unpublished, personal information).

Pakistan was confronted with a huge challenge from the very day it became independent. The resettlement of refugees was only a part of the problem. There was no central government and no infrastructure with which to create one. There were very few banks operating in the country and no Central Reserve Bank to regulate the currency and rest of the financial affairs. All imports and exports had come to a halt because the institutions dealing with these had folded. Whatever industries there had been were not functioning as their owners had migrated. There was acute shortage of skilled technical labour. The armed forces had not received the equipments and supplies due to them from India. The operation of rail and road transport was unreliable and sporadic at best due to equipment and skilled manpower shortages. It was the same story in every other field. What sustained the country in those dark and difficult days was the abundant agricultural production that kept the population fed, and the refusal by the people to entertain any thoughts of failure. A few months later when the Indians shut off water supplies to the irrigation canals that had originated in East Punjab, it still didn't dampen their spirits. There were no second thoughts and no going back.

One year after realizing his dream, Jinnah passed away. It was a terrible shock. Throughout the length and breadth of the country, in cities, towns and villages, in streets, offices and homes, among both the young and the old, men and women, there was not a dry eye to be seen. They all cried unabashedly, wailing, '*Haaey, Baba mar gaya*'. They were inconsolable, people who had never even seen Jinnah. It was a phenomenon unique in the annals of human history, rarely witnessed and unlikely to be repeated

---- tens of millions shedding copious tears on the passing away of a man most of them had never seen. There could be no greater tribute to the greatness of Jinnah who had devoted his entire life and worked so tirelessly and unselfishly for his people. Unlike many others who have made grandiose claims without much substance since then, he alone among the sub-continent's politicians gave all that he could to his people and took nothing in return for himself. His Will bears testimony to it.

With the exception of some ignorant 'House Pakistanis' and other perennial detractors and malcontents, the rest of the people knew this; they trusted him and gave him their unflinching loyalty and support and he never disappointed them. Jinnah lives on, his memory warm, vibrant and fresh in the hearts of his people. All the unseemly attempts made since the day he decided to champion the cause of Muslims to tarnish his image have gone unrewarded. He still stands tall as ever ---- a giant among men who left an indelible imprint on history.

Three years later his deputy, Liaquat Ali Khan, was shot dead in Rawalpindi by an Afghan assassin, for motives that are not clear to this day. Despite these setbacks the country kept moving forward. Slowly the economy began to pick up, helped by the boom in commodity prices due to the war in Korea. The government at the centre became functional and public services were gradually restored. In twenty years the pace of growth had picked up to the extent that Pakistan came to be presented as the model of success among the third-world nations. As evidence of this the two largest banks in Asia at the time in terms of numbers of branches were the National and Habib Banks, both Pakistani. Time Magazine presented PIA as a model for other small airlines in the world. A United Nations study published in 1967 predicted that if the country maintained its existing rate of economic growth, its economy would surpass that of Italy by 1981. Why it failed to happen is another story, for another day.

ANNEXURE

DEPOSITION BY CHRISTOPHER BEAUMONT

With the death of Sir George Abell earlier this year (1989) I remain the only one who knows the truth about the 1947 partition of India and the consequent creation of Pakistan. For the sake of historical truth the facts should be recorded, but certainly not yet published.

My request is, and it can be no more than a request, that the contents of this document are not divulged to any person until:

a. After my death, and to selected persons.

b. Only by agreement between the Warden of All Souls and a Permanent Under-Secretary of the Foreign Office.

On July 6th 1947, Sir Cyril Radcliffe (later Lord Radcliffe) was appointed Joint Chairman of the Boundary Commission.

The next day I was appointed his Private Secretary and on 8th July Rao Sahib V. D. Iyer was appointed Assistant Secretary, a post involving purely clerical duties. The notification of these duties appeared in the Gazette of India dated 28th July and is attached to this document. Also attached to this document are three letters written to me in 1988 by Sir Ian Scott, (Deputy Secretary to the Viceroy). He suspected the truth. I did not enlighten him.

It was agreed between Mountbatten, Nehru and Jinnah that Radcliffe should be told that his report, both for the Punjab and Bengal, should be ready by August 15th.

Radcliffe objected since it was clearly impossible properly to complete the task in one month and nine days. His objection was overruled. Mountbatten, Nehru and Jinnah must share the blame for this irresponsible decision.

It was a serious mistake to appoint a Hindu (the same would have been true for a Moslem) to the confidential post of Assistant Secretary to the Boundary Commission. Enmity between the two communities was rising fast. There had already been too much bloodshed in the Punjab and Bengal. Iyer had doubtless been a loyal servant of the Raj, but the Raj was disappearing. An Assistant Secretary to the Commission should have been brought from the U.K.

Once the Hindu and Moslem High Court judges, who were supposed to help Radcliffe to draw his lines, had been discarded as useless, the only three persons who knew of the progress of the lines were Radcliffe, myself and Iyer. I have not the slightest doubt that Iyer kept Nehru and V. P. Menon informed of the progress. Evidence of this is to be found at the Viceregal meeting on August 12th when Nehru voiced alarm at the prospect of Chittagong Hill Tracts going to Pakistan ---- which they were. This was the day before I handed in the Reports at Viceregal Lodge. The only way in which Nehru could have known of the projected allotment of the Chittagong Hill Tracts to Pakistan was that Iyer had told him. Also in his diary for August 11th, John Christie, one of the Assistant Secretaries to the Viceroy, wrote as follows: '*H. E. is having to be strenuously dissuaded from trying to persuade Radcliffe to alter his Punjab line*'. This was on a date when H. E ought not to have known where the line was drawn. Unfortunately, I kept no diary, so I cannot be entirely sure of the dates.

The true facts are these: Radcliffe had completed the Punjab line. Ferozepur was allotted to Pakistan. Sir Evan Jenkins, the Governor of the Punjab, had asked Sir George Abell to let him know the course of the partition line so that troops could be deployed to those areas which were most under threat of violence from the inevitable dislocation which partition involved. Sir George asked me where the line would be. I told him, and a map showing the line was sent to Sir Evan by Sir George. Sir Evan unfortunately never destroyed this map which, on his departure in mid-August, came into the hands of the new Pakistan Government. Hence the suspicion by Pakistan (justified) that the line had been altered by Radcliffe under pressure from Mountbatten, in turn under pressure from

Nehru and, almost certainly from Bekaner, whose state could have been very adversely affected if the canal headworks at Ferozepore had been wholly in the hands of Pakistan.

Radcliffe and I were living alone on the Viceregal Estate. After the map with the line had been sent to Sir Evan, probably the night of August 11th, towards midnight, while Radcliffe was working, V. P. Menon ---- the key figure after Nehru in Indian politics at the time ---- appeared at the outside door, was let in by the chaprassie, or police guard on duty, and asked me if he could see Radcliffe. I told him politely that he could not. He said that Mountbatten had sent him. I told him, less politely, that it made no difference. He departed, with good grace. I think he anticipated the rebuff. He was a very able and perceptive person.

The next morning, at breakfast, I told Radcliffe what had happened. He made no comment. Later that morning, Radcliffe told me that he had been invited to lunch by Lord Ismay (Mountbatten's Private Secretary, imported from England for the purpose of Mountbatten's Vice-Royalty) but he had been asked by Ismay not to bring me with him ---- the pretext being that there would not be enough room at the table for the extra guest. Having lived for six months in the house occupied by Ismay, I knew this to be untrue. But my suspicions were not aroused, as they should have been. I was leaving India the next week, had many preoccupations and welcomed the chance to get on with my own affairs. This was the first time, however, that Radcliffe and I had been separated at any sort of function. That evening, the Punjab line was changed ---- Ferozepore going to India. No change, as has been subsequently rumoured, was made in the northern (Gurdaspur) part of the line; nor in the Bengal line.

So Mountbatten cheated and Radcliffe allowed himself to be overborne. Grave discredit to both. But there are, in both cases, mitigating circumstances, if not excuses.

Mountbatten was overworked and overtired and was doubtless told by Nehru and V. P. Menon that to give Ferozepur to Pakistan would result in war between India and Pakistan. Bekaner, I think, but do not know, played a part. He had been a personal friend of Mountbatten's and the canal headworks at Ferozepore were of great importance to his state, and Mountbatten liked Nehru and (for good reason) disliked Jinnah.

As to Radcliffe he was without doubt persuaded by Ismay and Mountbatten at the lunch from which I was so deftly excluded, that

Ferozepore was so important that to give it to Pakistan (although there was a Moslem majority in the city) would lead to civil war, or at least something like it.

Radcliffe had only been in India six weeks. He had never previously been east of Gibraltar. He probably did not know that Nehru and Menon were putting pressure on Mountbatten. He yielded, I think to what he thought was overwhelming political expediency. If Sir Evan had destroyed the map, the alteration of the award would probably never have been suspected by the new Pakistan Government.

The episode reflects discredit on Mountbatten and Nehru and less on Radcliffe.

Christopher Beaumont
20th Sept. 1989.

Letter dated 2nd February 1988 from Sir Ian Scott, Deputy Private Secretary to the Viceroy, to Mr. Christopher Beaumont.

Ash House,
Alde Lane,
Aldeburgh,
Suffolk IP1 5DZ
(072-885) 2160

2nd Feb 1988

Dear Christopher,

Thank you for your letter --- I realised those many years ago (? at Patricia Laumarque's) that you were being elusive about partition, though I couldn't think why --- except for what seemed to me a certain misplaced loyalty to Radcliffe; I pursued the matter otherwise.

I am interested to know that Philip Zeigler is "making arrangements" as you put it, to do something. I wonder if he has the material I have --- I'll write and ask him. I know him slightly from Mountbatten's book. I wonder if he's proposing an article or what. That is what I have long been meditating but would gladly hand over to him what I have.

Hope to see you both at our annual do --- this time I hope will get the Prince of Wales, but they don't make this programme for the second half of the year till the end of June.

All good wishes to you both

Yours,
Ian.

Letter dated 11th Feb. 1988 from Sir Ian Scott, Deputy Private Secretary to the Viceroy, to Mr. Christopher Beaumont.

Ash House,
Alde Lane,
Aldeburgh,
Suffolk IP1 5DZ
(072-885) 2160
11th Feb 1988

Dear Christopher,

I am trying to do some research on the Radcliffe report and keep coming across things that puzzle me --- for example that Mountbatten made derogatory remarks (in a telegram to Ismay in April 1948) about George Abell for sending on a copy of the boundary map to Jenkins; when a week before he sent it Mountbatten said in a staff meeting that George should send a copy to Jenkins as soon as it was received. There was no need for George to ask Mountbatten about sending it on --- yet Mountbatten tells Ismay that it was sent without his knowledge.

I'd be most grateful if you could tell me what date the award was actually sent to Viceroy's house --- George Abell's letter to Stuart Abbot is dated 8th August, sending on the map. Did that map come separately, do you remember, to Viceroy's House before the Report proper?

Radcliffe unfortunately destroyed his own notes and drafts, as he himself said --------.

(Rest of the letter is missing)

Letter dated 21 February 1988 from Sir Ian Scott, Deputy Private Viceroy, to Mr. Christopher Beaumont.

Ash House,
Alde Lane,
Aldeburgh,
Suffolk IP1 5DZ
(072 885) 2160

21st Feb 1988

Dear Christopher,

Many thanks for your letter. The more I read about all this, the more curious I become.

Yes, indeed, it was the 8th August that George sent the map to Jenkins together with a note by you describing in detail the proposed boundary --- George added that the Award was expected "within the next 48 hours"; and although Mountbatten frequently denied any contact with Radcliff, he (M.) attended a meeting of the Punjab Boundary Commission on the 21 July. He wrote afterwards to Radcliffe to ask for the earliest possible publication --- 10th August if possible. Radcliffe replied on the 22nd that he didn't think he could manage publication on the 10th but might manage the 12th. And George Abell wrote on the 10th that Radcliffe had dictated the Award --- why it only appeared on the 17th is not clear. Nor where the phrase "eliminate salient" came from --- which Jenkins was instructed to apply to the copy of the provisional award which George Abell had sent him. Nor what passed at a drink session of Radcliffe, Mountbatten and Ismay on the evening of 8th August. Nor why M. himself proposed postponement of seeing the award (officially) till 13th. Any-------- .

(Letter incomplete).

Letter dated 29th February 1992 from Sir Ian Scott, Deputy Secretary to the Viceroy, to Mr. Christopher Beaumont.

Ash House,
Alde Lane,
Aldeburgh,
Suffolk IP1 5DZ
(072 885) 2160

29th February 1992

Dear Christopher,

Thank you for sending me your note on the Radcliffe award. There is more corroborative evidence too; eg. the pilot who was to fly an aborted flight for Radcliffe, soon after arrival, to see the probable Punjab boundary, had a map of the final boundary (not the one you sent to George Abell) to guide him. Mountbatten attended a meeting of the commissioners in Lahore on July 22nd; there is thus no question, as people like Ronnie Brockman and Campbell Johnson maintain, that he kept aloof. And the sending by George to Stewart Abbot of the map of August 8th was in compliance with a decision made at two separate staff conferences (at which I was present) that Jenkins should have the earliest possible notice of the line, so that he could make police and military disposition. He told the 5 Deputy Commissioners involved; one was a Hindu who told his - Hindu - engineer that he would have to transfer his headquarters out of Ferozepore. This man told Bikaner's head engineer (it was obviously a matter of great importance to him as Bikaner depended for most of its irrigation on the Ferozepore barrage). He in turn told the Ruler, and next day the telegrams and the visitors arrived in Delhi.

Another interesting twist of the story is that up to August 9 Mountbatten had been pressing Radcliffe (time and again) to hurry up with his report so as to get it out of the way before August 15. From then on he back-pedalled furiously to put it off till after Aug 15 (the announcement of the award, that is), on the specious and false ground that it would cause too much trouble if announced before Independence. In a staff meeting, ably backed up at once by Ismay (this also unusual) as Ismay usually spoke late in a meeting) Mountbatten overbore his previous decision for early publication. He followed this up incidentally in April 1945 (1948) by virtually accusing George Abell, to ministers in London, of disloyalty in sending the map of August 8 to Lahore. A monstrous accusation as George was carrying out previously agreed decisions to tell Jenkins at once.

All best wishes,

Yours ever,
Ian.

SELECT BIBLIOGRAPHY

A History of Hindi Literature, by F. E Keay.

A History of the Freedom Movement in India, by T. Chand.

A History of the Siege of Delhi by an Officer Who Served There, by William Ireland.

A History of the Sikhs, by Khushwant Singh.

A Matter of Honour: An Account of the Indian Army, its Officers and Men, by Philip Mason.

A Modern History of Tanganyika, by John Iliffe.

A Short History of the Saracens by Syed Ameer Ali.

A Witness to Genocide, by Roy Gutman

Administrative System of the Marathas, by S. N. Sen.

After Mother India, by Harry H. Field.

Ain-e-Akbari, by Abul Fazal.

Akbar Nama by Abul Fazal.

Alberuni's India, by Edward C. Sachau.

Al-Farooq, by Maulana Shibli Naumani.

An Enquiry Into India (*Tahkik Al Hind*), by Al-Beiruni.

Ancient African Kingdoms, by Margaret Shinnie.

Asbab-e-Baghavat-e-Hind (Urdu), by Sir Syed Ahmad Khan.

Asian Drama: An Inquiry into the Poverty of Nations by Karl Gunnar Myrdal

Attlee, by Kenneth Harris.

Auchinleck, by John Connell.

Bahishti Zeyvar (Urdu), by Maulana Ashraf Ali Thanvi.

British Attitudes Towards India, by G.D. Beace.

Buddhist India, by Sir Charles Eliot

Bush at War, by Bob Woodward,

Cabool: A Personal Narrative of a Journey to and Residence in That City in the Years 1836, 37 and 38 by Lieutenant Colonel Sir Alexander Burnes.

Chhachh Nama (author unknown).

Chronology of Ancient Nations, by Al Beiruni.

Churchill, Cripps and India, by R. J. Moore.

Complete Works of Mahatama Gandhi, Government of India

Day-to-Day With Gandhi, by Mahadev Desai.

Death by Fire: Sati, Dowry Death and Female Infanticide in Modern India, by Mala Sen.

Deoband School and the Demand for Pakistan, by Ziya-ul-Hasan Faruqui.

Dialogues of the Buddha, by T. W. Rhys Davis

Diary of a Medical Officer, by James Wise.

Disastrous Twilight: A Personal Record of the Partition of India, By Shahid Hamid.

Do Kaumi Nazria (Urdu), by Professor Ahmed Saeed.

Eighteen Fifty Seven, by Surendra Nath Sen.

Emergence of Pakistan, by Chaudhri Muhammad Ali.

Eminent Churchillians, by Andrew Roberts.

Empire, by Niall Ferguson.

Empires of the Monsoon', by Richard Hall.

End of Empire, by Brian Lapping.

Essays, by Lord Macaulay.

Fidelity and Honour, by Lieutenant General S.L Menezes.

Forty-one Years in India, by Field Marshal Earl Roberts.

Foundation of Pakistan: All-India Muslim League Documents, 1906 – 1947, by Saiyid Sharifuddin Pirzada.

Freedom at Midnight, by Larry Collins and Dominique Lapierre.

From Curzon to Nehru and After, by Durga Das.

From Sepoy to Subedar, by Sita Ram.

Further Sources of Vijayanagara History, by K.A. Nilakanta Sastri and N. Venkataramanayya.

Futuh-ul-Baldan, by Biladuri.

Gandhi and his Apostles, by Ved Mehta.

Gandhi: Behind the Mask of Divinity, by G. B. Singh.

Gandhi: Prisoner of Hope, by Judith Brown.

Gandhi's Passion: The Life and Leagacy of Mahatama Gandhi, by Stanley Wolpert.

Glimpses of Quaid-e-Azam, by Jamiluddin Ahmad.

Hardial, by Emily Baron.

Harvesting Our Souls, by Arun Shouri.

Hastings and the Rohilla War, by Sir John Strachey.

Hayat-e-Javaid (Urdu), by Altaf Hussain Hali.

Hayat-e-Viqar (Urdu), by Ikramullah Nadvi.

Heart of Darkness by Joseph Conrad.

Hindu Manners, Customs and Ceremonies, by Abbe J. A. Dubois

Historians of Sind, by Elliot and Dawson.

History of India as told by its own Historians, by Elliot and Dawson.

History of Indian and Eastern Architecture, by James Fergusson.

History of Nationalism in the East, by and H. Kohn

History of Political Thought, by B. Majumdar.

History of the Freedom Movement in India, by Dr. Tara Chand.

History of the Indian Mutiny, by T. Rice Holmes.

History of the Punjab - From the Remotest Antiquity to the Present Time, by Syed Mohammed Latif.

History of the Sikhs, by J. D Cunningham.

How the Sikhs Lost their Kingdom, by Khushwant Singh.

Imperial Reckoning: The Untold Story of Britain's Gulag in Kenya, by Carolyn Elkins.

In the Hands of the Taliban, by Yvonne Ridley.

India at the Death of Akbar, by W. H. Moreland.

India, by James Strachey.

India's Fight for Freedom, by Kanji Dwarkadas.

India's Partition: Process, Strategy and Mobilisation by Mushir-ul-Hasan.

Indian Empire, by R. Montgomery Martin.

Indian Literature, by Gowen.

Indian Struggle 1920 – 1942, by Subhas Chandra Bose.

Indian Wisdom, by Sir Monier-Williams

Institutions of the Maratha People', by W. H. Tone.

Iqbal kay Hazoor, by Syed Nazir Niazi.

Islam in the Subcontinent, by Annemarie Schimmel.

Islam: A Short History. by Karen Armstrong.

Jawaharlal Nehru: A Biography, by Sarvepalli Gopal.

Jinnah of Pakistan, by Stanley Wolpert

Jinnah Reinterpreted, by Saad R. Khairi.

Kashmir: A Disputed Legacy, 1846 – 1990, by Alastaire Lamb.

Khilafat-o-Malookiat (Urdu), by Maulana Abul A'la Maudoodi.

King Leopold's Ghost: A Story of Greed, Terror, and Heroism in Colonial Africa, by Adam Hochschild.

Later Mughal History of the Punjab, by Hari Ram Gupta.

Letters of Fazl-i-Husain, by Dr. Wahid Ahmed.

Liberty or Death: India's Journey to Independence and Division, by Patrick French.

Life of Sir Henry Lawrence, by H.B Edwardes and H. Merivale.

Life of the Party, by Christopher Ogden.

Mahatama Gandhi, by B. R Nanda.

Mediaeval India Under Muhammedan Rule A.D. 712 - 1764, by Sir Stanley Lane-Poole.

Mediaeval India, Modern Islam in India, by W. C. Smith.

Monty: Master of the Battlefield, by Nigel Hamilton.

Moral Ideas, by Westermarck.

Mother India, by Katherine Mayo

Mountbatten and the Partition of India, by Larry Collins and Louis Lapierre.

Mountbatten, by Philip Ziegler.

Muntakhab-ul-Lubab, by Khafi Khan.

Muslim Self Statement, by Ahmad – Grunebaum.

Muslims and the West: A Muslim Perspective, by Khan Hussan Zia.

My Diary in India, by Sir William Russell.

Mysteries From Forgotten Worlds, by Charles Berlitz

Myths and Realities of French Imperialism in India, 1763 – 1783, by S. Das.

Nehru: A Tryst with Destiny, by Stanley Wolpert

Nehru: The Making of India, by M. J. Akbar.

Now or Never, by Chaudhary Rahmat Ali.

Outline of History, by H. G. Wells.

Pakistan or Partition of India, by Dr. Ambedkar.

Partition of India – Legend and Reality, by H. M. Seervai.

Partition of India: Policies and Perspectives, 1935-47, by Cyril Henry Philips and M. Doreen Wainwright.

Punjab University Calendars 1921

Quaid-e-Azam Mohammad Ali Jinnah: Rare Speeches 1910 -18, Al-Mahfooz Research Academy.

Rahmat Ali, Complete Works, by K. K. Aziz.

Raj: The Making and Unmaking of British India, by Lawrence James.

Reminiscences of an Engineer, by Dr. Kunwar Sain.

Reminiscences of the Nehru Age, by M. O. Mathai.

Roberts in India: The Military Papers of Field Marshal Lord Roberts, 1876 - 1893, Army Records Society.

Rough Crossings: Britain, The Slaves and the American Revolution, by Simon Schama.

Russian Policy in Central Asia, by N. A. Khalin.

Sachar Commission Report, Government of India publication.

Sachi Sakhi, by Sardar Kapur Singh.

Saracens: Islam in the Medieval European Imagination by John V. Tolan.

Sardar Patel's Correspondence 1945 – 50, by Durga Das.

Sayyid Ahmad Khan: Reinterpretation of Muslim Theology, by Christian W. Troll.

Selected Works of Jawaharlal Nehru, by S. Gopal.

Separatism Among the Indian Muslims by Francis Robinson.

Shahabnama (Urdu), by Qudratullah Shahab.

Shameful Flight, by Stanley Wolpert.

Sikhism, by Sewa Singh Kalsi.

Six Men Out of the Ordinary, by Lord Zuckerman.

Slaughterhouse --- Bosnia and the Failure of the West, by David Rieff.

Some Recent Speeches and Writings of Mr. Jinnah, Jamiluddin Ahmad.

Sood (Urdu), by Maulana Abul A'la Maudoodi.

Tareekh-e-Sher Shahi.

Tarikh-e-Sind, by Mir Mohammed Masoom.

Temple Desecration and Indo-Muslim States, by Richard M. Eaton.

The Age of Kali, by William Dalrymple.

The Agony of Pakistan, by Zafarullah Khan.

The Amritsar Massacre, by Alfred Draper.

The Book of Marriage, by Keyserling

The British Conquest and Dominion of India, by Penderel Moon.

The British in Bengal in the Eighteenth Century, by P.J Marshal.

The Cambridge History of India, vol. III, by Thornton.

The Cambridge History of the British Empire, vol. IV: British India, by H. H. Dodwell.

The Collected Works of Mahatama Gandhi.

The Confessions of an Economic Hit Man, by John Perkins.

The Continent of Circe, by Nirad Chaudhri.

The Corporation: The Pathologic Pursuit of Profit and Power, by Joel Bakan.

The Deserter's Tale: The Story of an Ordinary American Soldier' by Joshua Key.

The Discovery of India, by Jawaharlal Nehru.

The Embassy of Sir Thomas Roe to the Court of the Great Moghul, W.H. Foster.

The Empire at Bay: The Leo Amery Diaries, 1929 - 1945, by Barnes, etc.

The Evolution of International Society, by Adam Watson.

The Gilgit Rebellion 1947, Major William Brown.

The Golden Bough,' by J.G. Frazer

The Good Boatman, by Rajmohan Gandhi.

The Great Mutiny: India 1857, by Christopher Hibbert.

The History of Indian National Congress, by B. P Sitaramayya.

The History of the Indian Mutiny, by Sir John Kaye.

The Ideals of Indian Art, by E. B. Havell

The Indian Musalmans: *Are They Bound in Conscience to Rebel Against the Queen?* By W. W. Hunter.

The Jewish Onslaught, by Tony Martin.

The Last Days of the British Raj, by Leonard Mosley.

The Last Mughal, by William Dalrymple.

The Ledge Between the Streams, by Ved Mehta.

The Life and Correspondence of Charles, Lord Metcalfe, by J.W Kaye.

The Life and Death of Mahatama Gandhi, by Robert Payne.

The Men Who Ruled India, by Philip Woodward.

The New Cambridge History of India - The Sikhs of the Punjab, by J.S. Grewal.

The Oxford History of India, by Vincent Smith

The Partition of India and Mountbatten, by Latif Ahmed Sherwani.

The Pathans of Jullunder, by K. Hussan Zia.

The Pathans, by Sir Olaf Caroe.

The Princely India I knew, by Sir Conrad Corfield.

The Princes in India in the End Game of the Empire, 1917 – 1947, by I. Copland.

The Private Journal of the Marquess of Hastings ed. by Marchioness of Bute.

The Punjab Boundary Force and the Problem of Order, August 1947, by Robin Jeffrey.

The Punjab Peasant in Prosperity and Debt, by M. L. Darling.

The Quaid-e-Azam on Important Issues, by Mohammad Hanif Shahid.

The Remonstrantie of Frncisco Pelsaert, by Francisco Pelsaert.

The Ruling Caste, by David Gilmour.

The Secret Relationship Between Blacks and Jews, by Tony Martin.

The Social History of the Machine Gun, by John Ellis.

The Spanish Inquisition, by Henry Kamen.

The Spirit of Islam, by Syed Ameer Ali.

The Story of Civilisation, by Will Durant

The Transfer of Power 1942-7, by Nicholas Mansergh, E.W.R. Lumby and others.

Then Came Hazrat Ali, by D. F. Karaka.

Travels in the Mogul Empire, by Francois Bernier.

Urdu Language and Literature: Critical Perspectives, by Gopi Chand Narang.

Verdict on India, by Beverley Nichols.

Viceroy's Agent, by Charles Chenevix Trench.

Voyage Around the World, Churchill College.

War of Civilisations:1857 A.D, by Amaresh Misra.

Wavell: The Viceroy's Journal, ed., by Penderel Moon.

We, or, Our Nationhood Defined, by M. S. Golwalkar.

While Memory Serves, by Sir Francis Tucker.

INDEX

1

3

A

B

C

D

E

F

G

H

I

J

K

L

M

N

O

P

Q

R

S

T

U

V

W

X

Y

Z

A. V Alexander, Jinnah and Cripps

Jinnah and Gandhi

Muslim League Leaders in Lahore

Liaquat Ali Khan and Jinnah

Jinnah and Iqbal with students from Cambridge University

Mountbatten, Nehru and Edwina

Nehru, Ismay, Mountbatten and Jinnah

Jinnah with Pashtoon Maliks

Jinnah with Baluch Sardars

Lord Wavell and Pethic-Lawrence

INDIA AND PAKISTAN - AREA AND POPULATION – 1941

AREA AND POPULATION OF INDIA AND PAKISTAN, 1941*

(Population in thousands; area in square miles)

	Area	Popn.	Density	Muslim	%	Non-Muslim	%
WESTERN PAKISTAN							
West Punjab (approx.)	62,046	15,802	255	11,843	74.7	3,959	25.3
Sind	48,136	4,535	94	3,208	72.8	1,327	27.2
North-West Frontier	14,263	3,038	213	2,788	91.8	250	8.2
Baluchistan	54,456	502	9	438	87.4	63	12.6
Total Provinces	178,901	23,877	133	18,279	76.6	5,599	23.4
Bahawalpur	17,494	1,341	77	1,099	82.0	242	18.0
Khairpur	6,050	306	51	254	83.0	52	17.0
N-W Frontier Agencies	24,986	2,378†	95	2,350	98.7	28	1.3
Baluchistan States	79,546	356	4	346	97.0	10	3.0
Total States & Agencies	128,076	4,381	34	4,049	92.5	332	7.5
TOTAL WESTERN PAKISTAN	306,977	28,258	92	22,328	79.5	5,930	20.5
EASTERN PAKISTAN							
East Bengal	49,409	39,112	792	27,691	70.8	11,421	29.2
Sylhet (Assam)	4,621	2,733	594	1,690	61.8	1,043	38.2
TOTAL EASTERN PAKISTAN	54,030	41,845	775	29,381	67.8	12,464	32.2
GRAND TOTAL PAKISTAN	361,007	70,103	194	51,709	72.7	18,395	27.3
INDIAN UNION							
Provinces	632,718	230,381	364	33,428	14.5	196,953	85.5
States (excl. Kashmir & Hyderabad)§	423,317	68,438	162	3,440	5.0	64,998	95.0
TOTAL INDIAN UNION	1,056,035	298,819	283	36,868	12.3	261,951	87.7
HYDERABAD	82,313	16,338	198	2,097	12.8	14,241	87.2
KASHMIR	82,258	4,022	48	3,074	77.1	948	22.9
PORTUGUESE INDIA	1,537	624	406	no data			
FRENCH INDIA	203	323	1592	no data			

* Itemized details for India are readily available in reference books.

† This includes an estimated population of 1,624,338; 19,721 of the enumerated population were non-Muslims, and the allowance of 28,000 probably overestimates them. (See notes to Tables I and XIII of 1941 Census, Vol. I.)

§ Including Junagadh: area, 3337 square miles; population, 670,719 of which 634,321 were non-Muslims.

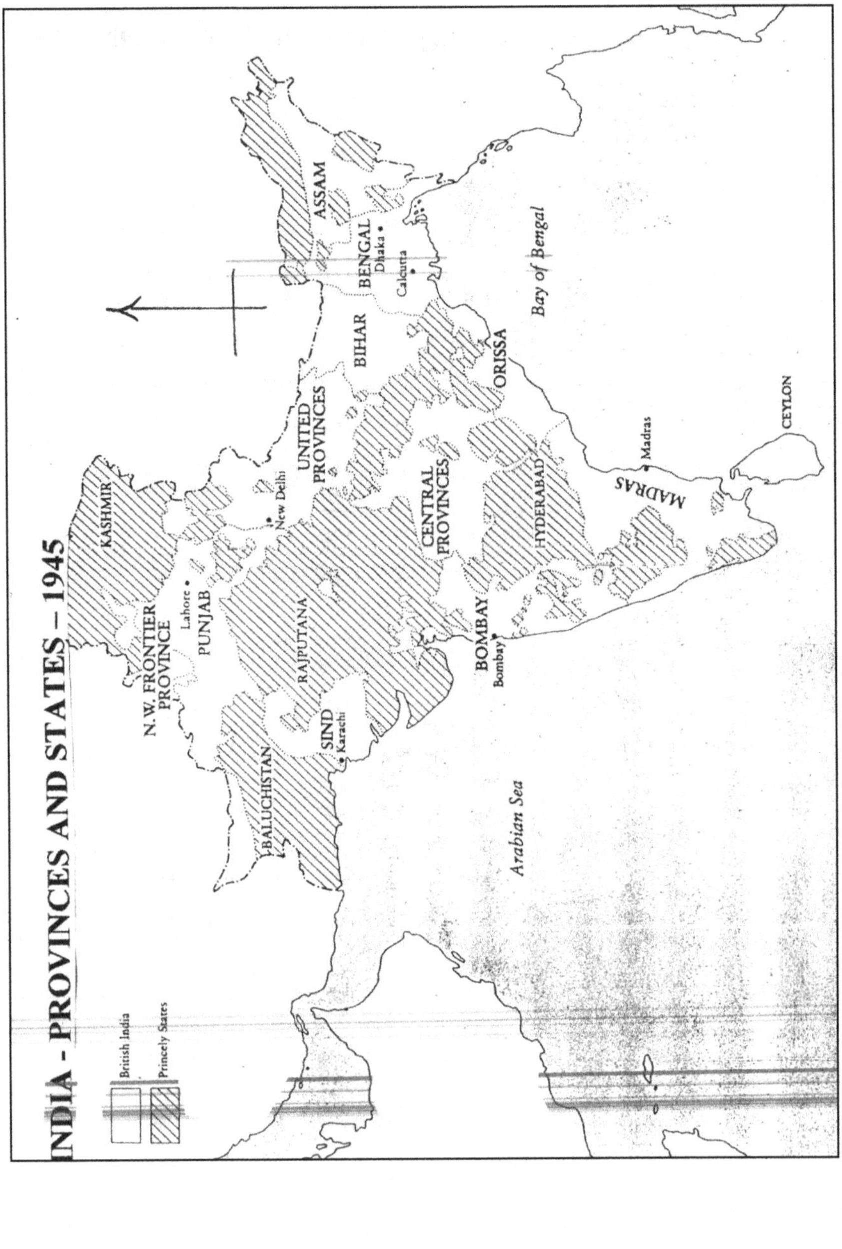
INDIA - PROVINCES AND STATES – 1945
British India
Princely States
KASHMIR
N.W. FRONTIER PROVINCE
Lahore
PUNJAB
New Delhi
UNITED PROVINCES
BIHAR
BENGAL
Dhaka
Calcutta
ASSAM
ORISSA
CENTRAL PROVINCES
RAJPUTANA
SIND
Karachi
BALUCHISTAN
BOMBAY
Bombay
HYDERABAD
MADRAS
Madras
CEYLON
Bay of Bengal
Arabian Sea

PUNJAB - DISTRIBUTION OF MUSLIMS AND SIKHS

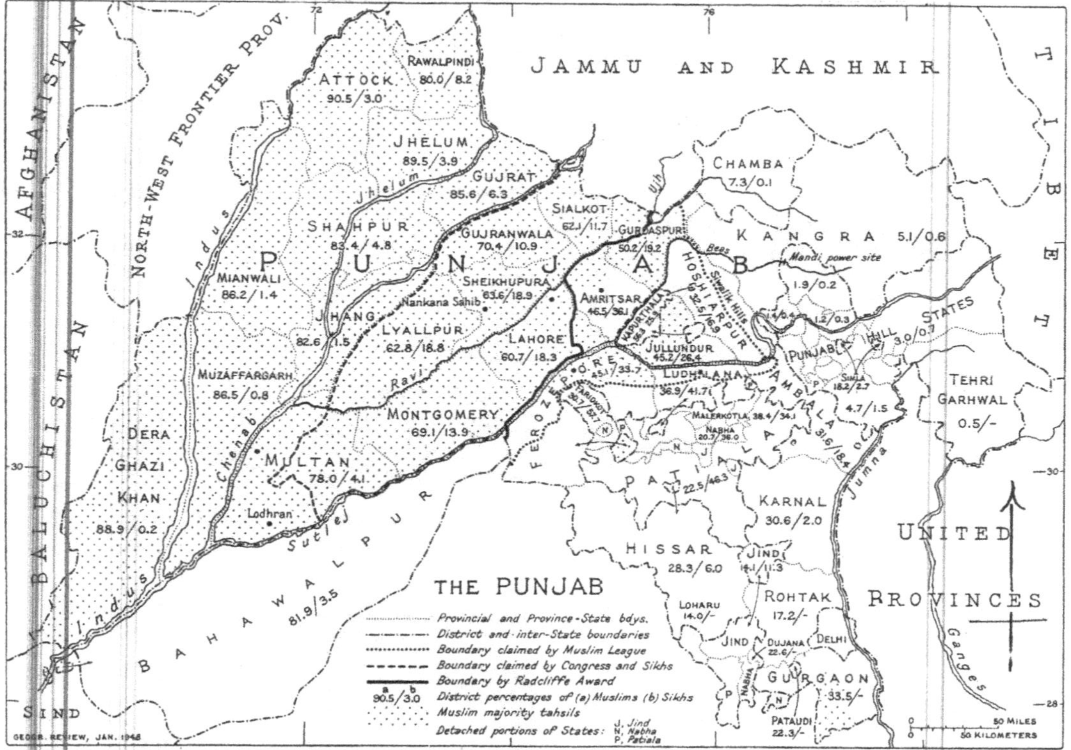

Partition of the Punjab. Detached portions of States: J, Jind; N, Nabha; P, Patiala. The claims came within the author's direct knowledge and the Boundary Award has been checked with Survey of India maps (1 : 63,360).

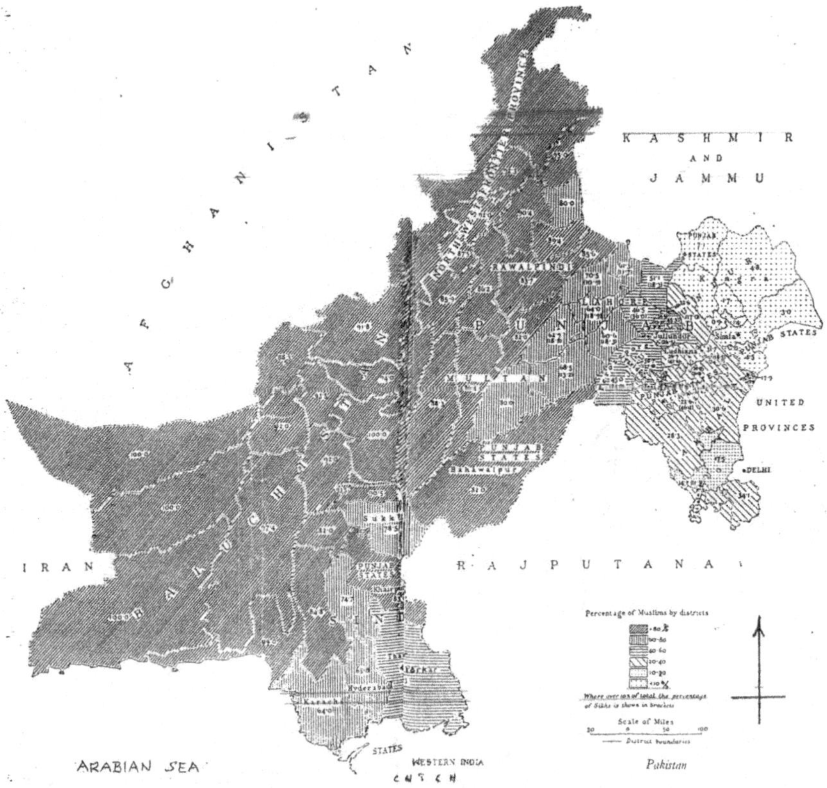

WESTERN PROVINCES - MUSLIM POPULATION

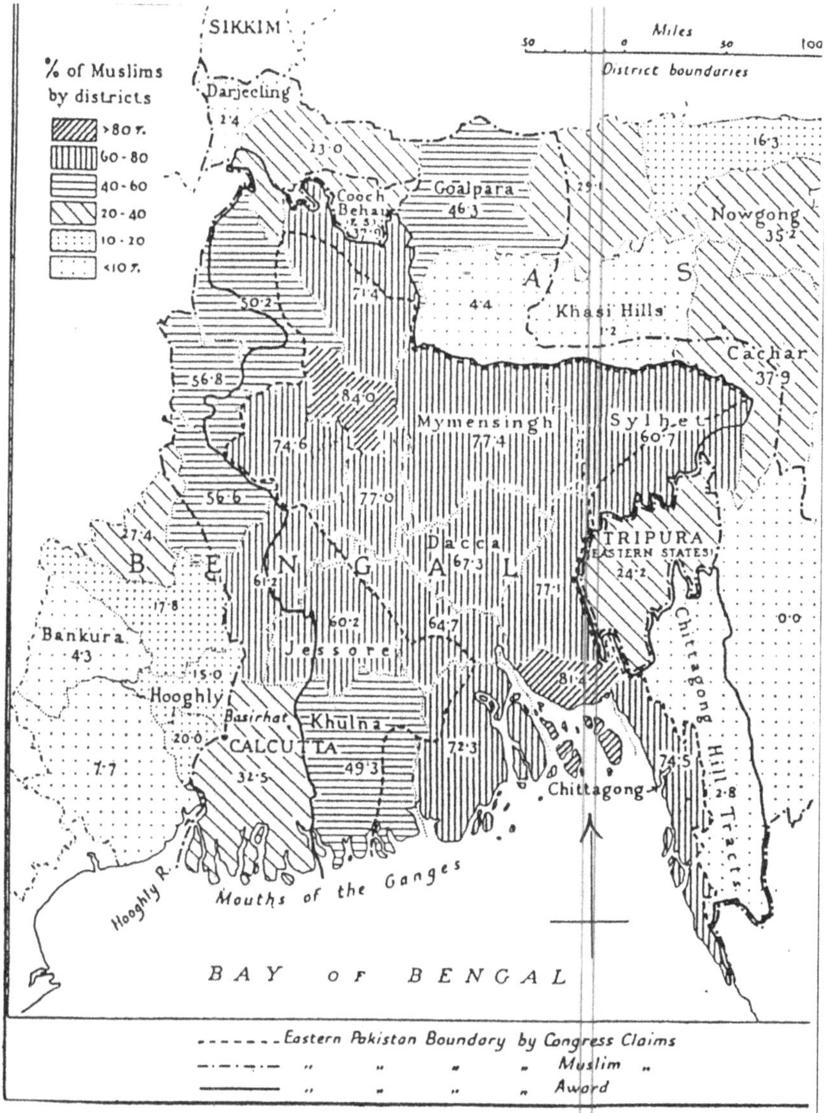

BENGAL AND ASSAM - MUSLIM POPULATION